Tolley's Tax Computations 2013/14

by
Kevin Walton MA
David Smailes FCA
Rhianon Davies BSc (Maths) CTA

Tolley®

336.2
S63
00122018RL

Members of the LexisNexis Group worldwide

United Kingdom	LexisNexis, a Division of Reed Elsevier (UK) Ltd, Lexis House, 30 Farringdon Street, London, EC4A 4HH, and London House, 20–22 East London Street, Edinburgh EH7 4BQ
Australia	LexisNexis Butterworths, Chatswood, New South Wales
Austria	LexisNexis Verlag ARD Orac GmbH & Co KG, Vienna
Canada	LexisNexis Butterworths, Markham, Ontario
Czech Republic	Nakladatelství Orac sro, Prague
France	LexisNexis SA, Paris
Germany	LexisNexis Deutschland GmbH, Munster
Hong Kong	LexisNexis Hong Kong, Hong Kong
India	LexisNexis India, New Delhi
Italy	Giuffrè Editore, Milan
Malaysia	Malayan Law Journal Sdn Bhd, Kuala Lumpur
New Zealand	LexisNexis NZ Ltd, Wellington
Poland	Wydawnictwo Prawnicze LexisNexis Sp, Warsaw
Singapore	LexisNexis Singapore, Singapore
South Africa	LexisNexis Butterworths, Durban
Switzerland	Stämpfli Verlag AG, Berne, Durban
USA	LexisNexis, Dayton, Ohio

First Published in 1987

© Reed Elsevier (UK) Ltd 2013

Published by LexisNexis

All rights reserved. No part of this publication may be reproduced in any material form (including photocopying or storing it in any medium by electronic means and whether or not transiently or incidentally to some other use of this publication) without the written permission of the copyright owner except in accordance with the provisions of the Copyright, Designs and Patents Act 1988 or under the terms of a licence issued by the Copyright Licensing Agency Ltd, Saffron House, 6–10 Kirby Street, London EC1N 8TS. Applications for the copyright owner's written permission to reproduce any part of this publication should be addressed to the publisher.
Warning: The doing of an unauthorised act in relation to a copyright work may result in both a civil claim for damages and criminal prosecution.

Crown copyright material is reproduced with the permission of the Controller of HMSO and the Queen's Printer for Scotland. Parliamentary copyright material is reproduced with the permission of the Controller of Her Majesty's Stationery Office on behalf of Parliament. Any European material in this work which has been reproduced from EUR-lex, the official European Communities legislation website, is European Communities copyright.
A CIP Catalogue record for this book is available from the British Library.

ISBN for this volume: 9780754546610

Printed and bound by Hobbs the Printers Ltd, Totton, Hampshire

Visit LexisNexis at www.lexisnexis.co.uk

About This Book

Tolley's Tax Computations is an established annual publication, having been first published in the early 1980s in response to interest shown by Tolley tax subscribers in worked examples, both to assist in understanding UK tax legislation and to provide guidance as to layout. The book is divided into six parts covering income tax, corporation tax, capital gains tax, inheritance tax, value added tax and national insurance contributions. In each part, chapters are arranged in alphabetical order by subject to assist reference. Most of the computations have explanatory notes, and statutory references are given wherever appropriate. The book also includes a table of statutes and an index.

This 2013/14 edition has been fully updated to take account of the provisions of the Finance Act 2013 and other relevant information up to 17 July 2013.

Comments on this annual publication and suggestions for improvements and additional computations are always welcome.

Contents

About This Book	iii
Abbreviations and References	ix
Table of Statutes	xi
Table of Statutory Instruments	xxiii

INCOME TAX

1	Allowances and Tax Rates
2	Accrued Income Scheme
3	Capital Allowances
4	Capital Allowances on Plant and Machinery
5	Charities
6	Deceased Estates
7	Double Tax Relief
8	Employment Income
9	Enterprise Investment Scheme
10	Herd Basis
11	Intellectual Property
12	Late Payment Interest and Penalties
13	Life Assurance Policies
14	Losses
15	Married Persons and Civil Partners
16	Non-Residents
17	Partnerships
18	Pension Provision
19	Personal Service Companies etc
20	Post-Cessation Receipts and Expenditure
21	Property Income
22	Remittance Basis
23	Savings and Investment Income
24	Seed Enterprise Investment Scheme
25	Self-Assessment
26	Settlements

27	Share-Related Employment Income and Exemptions
28	Social Security Income
29	Trading Income
30	Trading Income — Cash Basis for Small Businesses
31	Venture Capital Trusts

CORPORATION TAX

101	Accounting Periods
102	Capital Allowances
103	Capital Gains
104	Close Companies
105	Double Tax Relief
106	Group Relief
107	Income Tax in relation to a Company
108	Intangible Assets
109	Interest on Overpaid Tax
110	Interest on Unpaid Tax
111	Investment Companies and Investment Business
112	Liquidation
113	Loan Relationships
114	Losses
115	Payment of Tax
116	Profit Computations
117	Research and Development
118	Returns
119	Small Profits — Reduced Rates
120	Transfer Pricing

CAPITAL GAINS TAX

201	Annual Rates and Exemptions
202	Anti-Avoidance
203	Assets
204	Assets held on 6 April 1965
205	Assets held on 31 March 1982
206	Capital Sums Derived from Assets
207	Companies
208	Computation of Gains and Losses
209	Double Tax Relief
210	Enterprise Investment Scheme

211	Entrepreneurs' Relief
212	Exemptions and Reliefs
213	Hold-Over Reliefs
214	Indexation
215	Land
216	Losses
217	Married Persons and Civil Partners
218	Mineral Royalties
219	Offshore Settlements
220	Overseas Matters
221	Partnerships
222	Payment of Tax
223	Private Residences
224	Qualifying Corporate Bonds
225	Remittance Basis
226	Rollover Relief — Replacement of Business Assets
227	Seed Enterprise Investment Scheme
228	Settlements
229	Shares and Securities
230	Shares and Securities — Identification Rules
231	Wasting Assets

INHERITANCE TAX

301	Accumulation and Maintenance Trusts
302	Agricultural Property
303	Anti-Avoidance
304	Business Property
305	Calculation of Tax
306	Charities
307	Close Companies
308	Deeds of Variation and Disclaimers
309	Double Taxation Relief
310	Exempt Transfers
311	Gifts with Reservation
312	Interest on Tax
313	Liability for Tax
314	Life Assurance Policies
315	Mutual Transfers

Contents

316	National Heritage
317	Payment of Tax
318	Protective Trusts
319	Quick Succession Relief
320	Settlements with Interests in Possession
321	Settlements without Interests in Possession
322	Transfers on Death
323	Trusts for Bereaved Minors
324	Trusts for Disabled Persons
325	Trusts for Employees
326	Valuation
327	Woodlands

VALUE ADDED TAX

401	Bad Debt Relief
402	Capital Goods
403	Catering
404	Hotels and Holiday Accommodation
405	Input Tax
406	Motor Cars
407	Output Tax
408	Partial Exemption
409	Records
410	Reduced Rate Supplies
411	Retail Schemes
412	Second-Hand Goods

NATIONAL INSURANCE CONTRIBUTIONS

501	Age Exception
502	Aggregation of Earnings
503	Annual Maximum
504	Class 1 Contributions: Employed Earners
505	Class 1A Contributions: Benefits in Kind
506	Class 1B Contributions: PAYE Settlement Agreements
507	Class 4 Contributions: On Profits of a Trade etc.
508	Company Directors
509	Contracted-Out Employment
510	Deferment of Payment
511	Earnings from Self-Employment

512	Earnings Periods
513	Intermediaries
514	Partners
515	Repayment and Reallocation
Index	

Abbreviations and References

Abbreviations

ACT	Advance Corporation Tax
Art	Article
BPR	Business Property Relief
b/f	brought forward
C & E	Customs and Excise
CA	Court of Appeal
CAA	Capital Allowances Act
CCAB	Consultative Committee of Accountancy Bodies
Ch D	Chancery Division
c/f	carried forward
CFC	Controlled Foreign Company
CGT	Capital Gains Tax
CGTA	Capitals Gains Tax Act
CRCA	Commissioners for Revenue and Customs Act
CT	Corporation Tax
CTA	Corporation Tax Act
CTT	Capital Transfer Tax
CVS	Corporate Venturing Scheme
CY	Current Year
DTR	Double Tax Relief
EIS	Enterprise Investment Scheme
ESC	Extra-Statutory Concession
ESP	Expected Selling Price
FA	Finance Act
F(No 2)A	Finance (No 2) Act

Abbreviations and References

FIFO	First In, First Out
FII	Franked Investment Income
FY	Financial Year
FYA	First-Year Allowance
HL	House of Lords
HMIT	Her Majesty's Inspector of Taxes
IBA	Industrial Buildings Allowance
ICTA	Income and Corporation Taxes Act
IRPR	Inland Revenue Press Release
IHT	Inheritance Tax
IHTA	Inheritance Tax Act
IT	Income Tax
ITA	Income Tax Act
ITEPA	Income Tax (Earnings and Pensions) Act
ITTOIA	Income Tax (Trading and Other Income) Act
LEL	Lower Earnings Limit
LIFO	Last In, First Out
LLPA	Limited Liability Partnerships Act
NBV	Net Book Value
NIC	National Insurance Contributions
para	paragraph
PAYE	Pay As You Earn
P/e	Period ended
PET	Potentially Exempt Transfer
PR	Personal Representative
PY	Previous Year
Reg	Regulation
s	section
SC/S	Scottish Court of Session
Sch	Schedule
SI	Statutory Instrument
SSAP	Statement of Standard Accounting Practice

TCGA	Taxation of Chargeable Gains Act
TIOPA	Taxation (International and Other Provisions) Act
TMA	Taxes Management Act
UAP	Upper Accrual Point
UEL	Upper Earnings Limit
VAT	Value Added Tax
VATA	Value Added Tax Act
VCT	Venture Capital Trust
WDA	Writing-down Allowance
WDV	Written-down Value
Y/e	Year ended

References

STC	Simon's Tax Cases (LexisNexis, Halsbury House, 35 Chancery Lane, London, WC2A 1EL)
TC	Official Tax Cases (H.M. Stationery Office, P.O. Box 276, SW8 5DT)

Table of Statutes

1970 Taxes Management Act
s 42(11A) .... IT 25.2
s 59A .... IT 25.1; 25.2(A)(B)(C)
s 59B .... IT 12.1(A)
    (4) 15.1
s 59D .... CT 101.2; 115.1
s 59E .... CT 115.1
s 59FA .... CGT 220.1
s 86 .... IT 26.1
    (1)(2) .... IT 12.1(A)
s 87A .... CT 110.1
s 91 .... CT 110.2(B)
s 94(3) .... CT 118.2
ss 109B–109F .... CGT 220.1
s 118(2) .... CT 118.2
Sch 1B .... IT 25.2
    para 5 .... IT 20.1
Sch 3ZB .... CGT 220.1

1980 Finance Act
s 79 .... CGT 205.2; 213.1(C)

1984 Inheritance Tax Act
s 3 .... IHT 305.1; 305.2
    (3) .... IHT 307.3
s 3A .... IHT 305.1; 305.2
s 5 .... IHT 305.2
s 7 .... IHT 305.1; 305.2
s 8A .. IHT 308.1; 310.3; 310.3(A)–(C)
s 8B .... IHT 310.3; 310.3(A)(B)
s 8C .... IHT 310.3; 310.3(B)(C)
s 16 .... IHT 302.1(B)
s 17 .... IHT 308
s 18 .... IHT 303.1(C); 310.4; 320.3
s 19 .... IHT 310.1
    (1)(2) .... IHT 310.1(A)
    (3A) .... IHT 310.1(B)
s 21 .... IHT 310.2; 314
ss 30–32 .... IHT 316
s 31 .... IHT 316.3(B)
    (1)(5) .... IHT 316.1
ss 32, 32A .... IHT 310.3(C)
s 33 .... IHT 316
    (2ZA) .... IHT 316.2(B)
    (5) .... IHT 316.2(C); 316.5(A)
    (7) .... IHT 316.4
s 34 .... IHT 316; 316.5(A)
s 34(1) .... IHT 316.2(C)
s 35 .... IHT 316
ss 36–39 .... IHT 305.3; 305.3(C)
s 39A .... IHT 305.3; 305.3(B)(C)
s 40 .... IHT 305.3; 305.3(C)
ss 41, 42 .... IHT 305.3
s 49 .... IHT 318.2; 320
    (1A) ..... IHT 320.1; 320.2; 320.3
s 49A .... CGT 228.5; IHT 318.2; 320;
                             320.1; 320.2; 320.3
s 49B ... IHT 318.2; 320; 320.2; 320.3

1984 Inheritance Tax Act – *cont.*
s 49C .... CGT 228.5; IHT 318.2; 320;
                               320.2; 320.3
ss 49D, 49E ... IHT 318.2; 320; 320.2;
                                     320.3
s 51(1)–(1B) .... IHT 320
s 52(1)(2A) .... IHT 320
s 54A .... IHT 320
s 54B .... IHT 320
s 57 .... IHT 320
s 57A .... IHT 316
s 59(1)(2) .... IHT 320.1; 320.2; 320.3
s 64 .... IHT 321.1(A)(B)
s 65 .... IHT 321.2(A); 321.3
s 66 .... IHT 321.1(A)(B)
s 68 .... IHT 321.2(A)
s 69 .... IHT 321.3
s 70 .... IHT 306
s 71 .... IHT 301
    (1)(1A) .... IHT 301.1
    (1B) .... IHT 323.1(A)
s 71A . CGT 228.5; IHT 323; 323.1(A)
ss 71B, 71C .... IHT 323; 323.1(A)
s 71D . CGT 228.5; IHT 301.2(A); 323;
                                  323.1(B)
s 71E .. IHT 301.2(A)(B); 323; 323.1(B)
    (2) .... IHT 301.2(A)(B)
ss 71F, 71G ..... IHT 301.2(A)(B); 323;
                                    323.1(B)
s 71H .... IHT 323
s 72 .... IHT 325
s 73 .... IHT 318.1
s 74 .... IHT 324
s 77 .... IHT 316
s 78 .... IHT 316
    (3) .... IHT 316.2(C); 316.5(A)
s 78(4)(6) .... IHT 316.5(A)
s 79 .... IHT 316; 316.5(B)
s 88 .... IHT 318.2
s 89 .... IHT 324
s 89A .... IHT 324; 324.4
s 89B(1) ...... CGT 228.5; IHT 318.2;
                         320.1; 320.2; 320.3
s 94 .... IHT 307
    (1) .... IHT 307.2
    (2)(*b*) .... IHT 307.1
ss 95–97 .... IHT 307
s 98 .... IHT 307
    (3) .... IHT 307.3
s 102 .... IHT 307
s 103 .... IHT 304
s 104 .... IHT 304
s 105 .... IHT 304
ss 106–110 .... IHT 304
s 111 .... IHT 304; 304.1(A)
ss 112, 113 .... IHT 304
s 113A(3) .... IHT 304.1(D)

1984 Inheritance Tax Act – *cont.*
- s 113B .... IHT 304.1(D)
- s 114 .... IHT 302.2; 304
  - (2) .... IHT 327
- s 115 .... IHT 302
- s 116 .... IHT 302
  - (1) .... IHT 302.1(A)(B)
  - (2) .... IHT 302.1(A)(B)
  - (7) .... IHT 302.1(A)(B)
- ss 117–121 .... IHT 302
- ss 122, 123 .... IHT 302; 302.2
- s 124A .... IHT 302
  - (1)(3) .... IHT 302.1(A)
- s 124B .... IHT 302
- s 125 .... IHT 327
- s 126 .... IHT 310.3(C); 327
- s 127 .... IHT 327
  - (2) .... IHT 327.1(B)
- ss 128–130 .... IHT 327
- s 131 .... IHT 313.3
- s 141 .... IHT 315.1; 319
- s 142 .... IHT 308
  - (2) .... IHT 308.1
  - (3A)(3B) .... IHT 308.1
- s 159 .... IHT 309
- s 161 .... IHT 303.1(B); 326.2
- s 167 .... IHT 314
- ss 178–189 .... IHT 326.3
- s 190 .... IHT 326.1
- s 191 .... IHT 326.1; 326.1(A)
- s 192 .... IHT 326.1
- s 192(1) .... IHT 326.1(B)
- ss 193–197 .... IHT 326.1
- s 197A .... IHT 326.1; 326.1(A)
- s 197A(3) .... IHT 326.1(B)
- s 198 .... IHT 326.1
- s 199 .... IHT 305.1; 313.4
  - (1) .... IHT 313.1
  - (2) .... IHT 313.3
- s 200(1) .... IHT 313.2
  - (3) .... IHT 313.2
- s 201 .... IHT 313.4
  - (2) .... IHT 313.3
- s 204 .... IHT 305.1; 313.4
  - (1) .... IHT 313.2
  - (2)(3) .... IHT 313.1; 313.2
  - (5) .... IHT 313.1; 313.2
  - (6) .... IHT 313.1
- s 207 .... IHT 316
  - (1) .... IHT 316.2(C)
- s 208 .... IHT 327
- s 211 .... IHT 313.2
- s 218A .... IHT 308; 308.1
- s 226(4) .... IHT 327
- ss 227, 228 .... IHT 317
- s 233 .... IHT 312
- s 234 .... IHT 317
- s 267 .... IHT 310.4
- ss 267ZA, 267ZB .... IHT 310.4
- s 268 .... IHT 303.1(C)
- s 269 .... IHT 304

1984 Inheritance Tax Act – *cont.*
- Sch 1A paras 1–3 .... IHT 322.2(A)
  - para 5 .... IHT 322.2(A)
  - para 7 .... IHT 322.2(B)
  - para 8 .... IHT 322.2(A)
  - para 9 .... IHT 322.2(A)(B)
- Sch 2 para 3 .... IHT 320.3
  - 4 .... IHT 327
  - 5 ..... IHT 316; 316.2(C)
  - 6 .... IHT 316; 316.6
- Sch 4 .... IHT 316
  - paras 8, 12–14
  - .... IHT 316.6
- Sch 5 .... IHT 316
- Sch 6 para 4 .... IHT 316.3(B)
- Pt VI, Chapter IV .... IHT 326.1(A)

1985 Companies Act
- s 249AA(4)–(7) .... CT 120.1(A)

1986 Finance Act
- s 81 .... IHT 311
- ss 102–102C .... IHT 311
- s 103 .... IHT 322.1
- s 104 .... IHT 315; 322.1
- Sch 19 paras 26,27
  - .... IHT 313.4
  - 28 .... IHT 313.4
- Sch 20 .... IHT 311

1988 Income and Corporation Taxes Act
- s 9(1) .... CT 101.2
- s 87 .... IT 21.4(B); CGT 215.3(G)
- s 122 .... CGT 218.1
- s 155(6) .... IT 8.6(B)
- s 198 .... IT 8.3(A)
- s 200A .... IT 8.6(A)
- s 203I .... IT 8.6(A)
- s 247 .... CT 104.2(B); 118.2(A)
- s 249 .... CGT 229.7
- s 251 (2)–(4) .... CGT 229.7
- ss 266, 274 .... IT 13.4
- s 282A .... IT 15.1(B)
- s 338(1) .... CT 101.2
  - (4) .... CT 101.2
- s 380 .... IT 1.1(B); 14.5; 15.1(A)
  - (1) .... IT 14.2
  - (2) .... IT 26.2(B)
- s 381 .... IT 14.5
- s 383 .... IT 14.2
- s 385 .... IT 14.3(A)(B)
- s 385(1) .... IT 29.2(A)(B)
- s 401 .... IT 14.3(A); 31.4
- s 416(1) .... IT 16.2
  - (2) .... IT 16.2
- s 504A .... IT 21.2
  - (1)(2) .... IT 18.1(B)
- s 617(5) .... IT 1.1(A)
- s 677 .... IT 26.5
- s 825 .... CT 109
- s 826 .... CT 109
  - (7A) .... CT 109.2
- s 832 .... IT 27.2

Table of Statutes

1988 Income and Corporation Taxes Act – cont.
Sch 4 .... CT 116.1
    para 1(1) .... IT 23.1(A)
Sch 18 para 1(5) .... CGT 228.6

1988 Finance Act
s 34 .... CGT 217.2

1989 Finance Act
s 43 .... CT 116.1
s 178 .... CT 109; IHT 312

1991 Finance Act
              22, 23
.... CT 109

1992 Taxation of Chargeable Gains Act
s 2(2) .... CGT 201.2; 219.1(A)
  (4)–(8) .... CGT 201.2; 216.2
s 2A .... CGT 226.1(A)
s 3 .... CGT 201.2; 225.1; 228.1
s 4 .... CGT 201.1; 217.1
  (3) .... CGT 228.1
s 4A .... CGT 201.1
s 4B .... CGT 211.1(B)(C)
s 8(1) .... CT 101.2; 103.1
  (2) .... CGT 207.1
s 10 .... CGT 220.3
ss 10A, 10AA .... CGT 220.4
s 12 .... IT 22.1
s 13(2) .... CT 103.3(E)
ss 16ZA–16ZD .... CGT 225.1
s 16A .... CGT 207.1
s 17 .... CT 103.2(A)
ss 19, 20 .... CGT 202.3
s 22 .... CGT 206.3
  (1) .... CGT 206.1
s 23 .... CGT 206.3; 206.3(B)(C)
  (2) .... CGT 206.3(D)
s 24 .... CGT 216.1(B)
  (1) .... CGT 208.1(C)
s 25 .... CGT 220.1; 220.3
  (1)(3)(8) .... CGT 220.3
s 29 .... CGT 202.1
s 30 .... CGT 202.2
s 35 ...... CGT 205.2; 215.3(E); 221.5; 231.3(B)
  (1) .... CGT 205.1; 205.2(A)
  (2) .... CGT 205.2(A); 204.3(B); 205.2(A); 215.3(E)
  (3) ...... CGT 204.3(C); 205.2(A); 208.2(A)
    (a) .... CGT 204.3(A)(B)(C); 215.3(E)
    (b) .... CGT 204.1(B); 204.3(D)
    (c) ..... CGT 204.1(B); 205.2(B)
    (d) ..... CGT 205.3; 214.2(A)
  (4) .... CGT 204.3(B); 205.2(A)
  (5) .... CGT 204.1(A); 205.1(A)(B)
  (9) .... CGT 204
s 35A .... CGT 214.2(A)
s 38 .... CGT 208.1(A)(C)
s 39 .... CGT 208.1(A); 215.3(G)

1992 Taxation of Chargeable Gains Act – cont.
s 41 .... CGT 208.1(B); 220.2
s 42 ... CGT 204.3(E); 208.2; 215.3(B); 217.2; 229.3
  (4) .... CGT 208.2(A)
s 44 .... CGT 203.1; 231.1; 231.2
  (1)(d) .... CGT 231.3
s 45 .... CGT 231.1; 231.1(A)
s 46 .... CGT 203.1; 231.1; 231.2
s 47 .... CGT 231.1
s 52A .... CGT 214.2(A)
s 53 ...... CGT 210.1(B); 214.1; 215.4
  (1)(b) .... CGT 214.1(C)
  (2A) .... CGT 214.1(C)
  (3) .... CT 103.2(A)
s 54 .... CGT 214.1
  (1A) .... CGT 213.1(C)
  (4)(b) .... CGT 215.3(F)
s 55 .... CGT 214.1
  (1)(2) . CGT 204.1(A); 204.3(A)(C); 205.2(A); 208.2(A); 214.1(C); 215.3(E); 230.2
  (5)(6) .... CGT 214.2(A)(C)
  (7)–(9) .... CGT 214.2(C)
s 56 .... CGT 214.1
  (2) .... CT 103.3(B); CGT 214.2(A)–(D)
  (3) ... CT 103.3(B); CGT 214.2(D)
  (4) .... CGT 214.2(D)
s 58 ... CGT 214.2(A); 217.1; 217.1(B)
s 59 .... CGT 221.1
s 62 .... CGT 214.1(B)
  (2)(2A) .... CGT 216.1(C)
s 67 .... CGT 213.1(B)
s 70 .... CGT 228.3
s 71 .... CGT 228.4
  (1) .... CGT 222.1(B)
  (2)–(2D) .... CGT 228.4(B)
s 72 .... CGT 228.5
  (1) .... CGT 222.1(B)
s 76 .... CGT 228.5(B)
s 77 .... CGT 216.2
s 86 .... CGT 216.2; 219.1(A)
s 87 .... CGT 216.1(C); 216.2; 219
s 87A .... CGT 219.1(A)(B)
s 89(2) ... CGT 201.2; 216.1(C); 216.2; 219.1(A)
s 91 .... CGT 219.1(B)
s 104 .... CGT 230.1; 230.2
s 105 .... CGT 230.1; 230.2
s 106A .... CGT 224.1; 230.1
s 107 .... CGT 230.2
s 108 .... CGT 230.2
  (1) .... CGT 224.1
s 109 .... CGT 230.2
  (4) .... CGT 204.1; 204.1(A)
  (5) .... CGT 204.1
s 110 .... CGT 230.2
s 115 .... IT 2.1; CGT 224
s 116 .... CGT 224; 224.2

xvii

Table of Statutes

1992 Taxation of Chargeable Gains Act – cont.

s 116(10)	CGT 211.5; 224.2
s 117	CGT 216.3; 224; 224.1
(1)	CGT 224.1; 229.6
(7)(b)(8)	CGT 224.1
s 119	IT 2.1; CGT 214.3
s 119A	IT 27.1; 27.5
s 122	CGT 229.4(A); 229.8(A); 229.8(B)
(2)	CGT 229.8(B)
s 123	CGT 229.8(B)
(1)	CGT 229.3
s 125	CT 103.2
(1)(5)	CT 103.2(A)
s 125A	CGT 216.3
s 126	CGT 211.4; 229.1; 229.2
s 127	CGT 211.4; 224.2; 229.1; 229.1(A); 229.2; 229.3(C); 229.4(A)
s 128	CGT 224.2; 229.1; 229.2; 229.3(C); 229.7
(4)	CGT 229.3
s 129	CGT 224.2; 229.1; 229.1(A)
s 130	CGT 224.2; 229.1; 229.1(B); 229.2
s 131	CGT 229.1
s 132	CGT 229.4(E); 229.6
s 135	CGT 211.4; 229.4; 229.4(A)
s 136	CGT 211.4; 229.5
s 137	CGT 229.4
s 138	CGT 229.4; 229.5
s 138A	CGT 229.4(C)
s 140	CGT 220.4
s 141	CGT 229.7
s 142	CGT 229.7
s 144	CGT 203.1
(3)	IT 27.1
ss 144ZA–144ZD	CGT 203.1
s 145	CGT 203.1
s 146	CGT 231.2; 231.2(B)
s 150A	IT 9
(1)	IT 9.2(B); CGT 210.2; 210.3; 210.3(B)
(2)(2A)(3)	IT 9.2(C); CGT 210.1; 210.2
s 150B	IT 9; 9.2(C)
s 150D	CGT 210.3(B)
s 150E	IT 24.2(B); CGT 227.1; 227.2
s 150G	CGT 227.3
s 151A	IT 31; 31.3
s 151B	IT 31
(1)	IT 31.3
s 152	CT 103.3(D); CGT 207.2; 226; 226.1
(7)(9)	CGT 226.2(B)
s 153	CT 103.3(D); CGT 226; 226.2(A)
s 154	CGT 226; 226.3
s 155	CT 103.3(D); CGT 226
ss 156–158	CGT 226
s 161	CT 103.3(B)(C)

1992 Taxation of Chargeable Gains Act – cont.

s 161(2)	CT 103.3(C)
(3)	CT 103.3(B)
s 162	CGT 213.3(A)(B)
s 162A	CGT 213.3(B)
s 162B	CGT 213.4
s 162C	CGT 213.4; 213.4(B)
s 164A	CGT 213.3
s 165	CGT 213.1(C); 213.2; 222.1(B)
(10)	CGT 213.1(C)
ss 169B–169G	CGT 213.1(A); 223.3; 228.3(A)
s 169C(7)	CGT 222.1(B)
s 169H	CGT 211.1(A)
s 169I	IT 27.5; CGT 211.1(A)(C)
(8)	CGT 211.2
s 169J	CGT 211.1(A)
s 169K	CGT 211.1(A); 211.3
s 169L	CGT 211.1
s 169M	CGT 211.1
(1)–(3)	CGT 211.1(A)
s 169N	CGT 211.1(B)
s 169P	CGT 211.3
s 169Q	CGT 211.4
s 169S(2)–(4)	CGT 211.1(C)
(5)	CGT 211.1(C); 211.3
s 171	CT 103.3(A)(E); CGT 214.2(C)(D); 220.2
(1)	CT 103.3(B)(C)
ss 171A–171C	CT 103.3(A)
s 173(1)	CT 103.3(B)
(2)	CT 103.3(C)
s 175	CT 103.3(D)
s 176	CGT 202.4
s 177A	CT 103.3(F)
s 179	CT 103.3(E)
s 179ZA	CT 103.3(E)
ss 185, 187	CGT 220.1
ss 201–203	CGT 218.1
s 222	CGT 223.1; 223.1(B)
(5)	CGT 223.2
s 223	CGT 223.1; 223.3
(1)	CGT 223.1(A)(B); 223.3
(2)	CGT 223.3
(3)(a)(b)	CGT 223.1(B)
(4)(7)	CGT 223.1(A)(B)
s 225	CGT 228.4(A)
ss 226A, 226B	CGT 223.3
ss 241, 241A	IT 21.2
s 242	CGT 208.2(D); 215.1
(2)	CGT 215.1
s 243	CGT 215.2; 215.2(B)
ss 244–246	CGT 215.2
s 247	CGT 215.2; 215.2(A)
s 248	CGT 215.2
s 258(8)	IHT 316.3
s 260	CGT 213.1; 222.1(B); 223.3; 228.3(A)(B)
(5)	CGT 213.1(B); 213.4(B)
(7)	CGT 213.1(C); IHT 302.1(C)

Table of Statutes

1992 Taxation of Chargeable Gains Act – cont.
s 261B .... IT 14.2
s 261C .... IT 14.2
ss 261D, 261E .... IT 20.2
s 262 .... CGT 202.3
   (2) .... CGT 212.1(A)
   (3) .... CGT 212.1(B)
   (4) .... CGT 212.1(C)
ss 279A–279D .... CGT 216.4
s 280 .... CGT 222; 222.1(A)
s 281 .... CGT 222; 222.1(B)
s 288(7B) .... CGT 220.4; 230.1
Sch 1 para 2 .... CGT 228.1
Sch 2 para 1 .... CGT 204.1
    2 .... CGT 204.1
     (1) .... CGT 204.1(B)
     3 .... CGT 204.1
Sch 2 para 4 ..... CGT 204.1; 204.1(A)
    5 .... CGT 204.1
    6 .... CGT 204.1
   paras 7, 8 .... CGT 204.1
    9–15 .... CGT 204.2
   para 16 ... CGT 204.3; 204.3(D)
    (3)–(5)
   .... CGT 204.3(E)
    (8) .... CGT 204.3(E)
   paras 17, 18
   .... CGT 204.3
   para 19 .... CGT 204.3
    (1) .... CGT 204.3(C)
    (2) .... CGT 204.3(D)
    (3) .... CGT 204.3(C)(D)
Sch 3 para 1 .... CT 103.3(D); CGT 213.2(A)
    4(1) .... CGT 204.3(E); 208.2(B); 229.4(A)
    (2) .... CGT 206.3(D)
    6 .... CGT 204.3(B)
    7 .... CGT 205.2(A)
   paras 8, 9 .... CGT 205.2(A)
Sch 4 .... CGT 205.3; 213.3(A)
   para A1 .... CGT 205.3
    1 .... CGT 205.3
    9 .... CGT 205.3
Sch 5B .... CGT 210.3
   para 1(5A)
   .... CGT 211.1(A)
Sch 5BB .... CGT 227.3
Sch 5C .... IT 31
Sch 7 .... CGT 213.2
Sch 7A .... CT 103.3(F)
    10 .... CT 103.3(B)
Sch 7AC .... CT 103.4
Sch 7D para 5 .... IT 27.4
Sch 8 para 1 .... CGT 215.3 (A)(D)(E)(F)(G)
    (2) .... CGT 215.3(A)
    (4)(*b*) ...... CGT 215.3(F)
    2 .... CGT 215.3(B)(C)
    4 .... CGT 215.3(H)(J)

1992 Taxation of Chargeable Gains Act – cont.
Sch 8 para 5 ...... CGT 215.3(C)(H)(J)
    (2) ...... CGT 215.3(H)(J)
Sch 11 para 10(1) .... CGT 202.2

1992 Social Security Administration Act
s 13A .... IT 28.1

1992 Social Security Contributions and Benefits Act
s 6(3) .... NIC 501.1; 501.1(A)
   (4) .... NIC 502.3
ss 8, 9 .... NIC 504.1
s 10 .... IT 8.3(A); NIC 505.1
ss 10ZA, 10ZB .... NIC 505.1
s 10A .... NIC 506.1
s 11(4) .... NIC 502.7
s 15 .... NIC 502.8
s 19(1)(2) .... NIC 510.1; 510.2
s 122(1) .... NIC 501.1(B)
Sch 1 para 1 . NIC 502.1; 502.2; 502.3; 502.4;
Sch 2 para 3 .... NIC 511.2
    4 .... NIC 514.1

1992 Finance (No 2) Act
Sch 14 para 8 .... IHT 304
    9 .... IHT 304

1993 Pension Schemes Act
s 41 .... NIC 509.1

1994 Finance Act
s 93(1)(2) .... CGT 206.1(B); 206.2(D); 207.1(B); 212.1(D)
   (3) .... CGT 210.1(B)
Sch 12 .... CGT 216.4

1994 Value Added Tax Act
s 24(5) .... VAT 405.2
s 26A .... VAT 405.1
s 36 .... VAT 401
ss 56, 57 .... VAT 406.1
Sch A1 .... VAT 410.1
Sch 6 para 9 .... VAT 404.1
Sch 11 para 2(6) .... VAT 410

1995 Finance Act
s 155 .... IHT 302.1(B)

1995 Pensions Act
Sch 4 .... NIC 501.1(B)

1996 Finance Act
s 185 .... IHT 302.1
Sch 13 para 1 .... IT 21.1(A)

1997 Finance Act
s 90 .... CGT 210.3

1998 Finance Act
s 117 .... CT 102.2
s 121(1) .... CGT 224.1(A)
   (2) .... CGT 224.2
s 122(1) .... CGT 221.1
   (2) .... CGT 213.1(C)
   (3) .... CGT 213.1(C)
   (4) .... CGT 208.4(E); 221.1

Table of Statutes

1998 Finance Act – *cont.*
s 144 .... CGT 203.1
Sch 18 paras 3–7 .... CT 118.1
          5(1) ... CT 118.1(A)(B)(C)
        para 5(2) ...... CT 118.1(A)(B)
           (3) .... CT 118.1(C)
        14 .... CT 101.2
      paras 78–83
    .... CT 102.2
Sch 20 .... CGT 226.4
Sch 27 Part III(31)
    .... CGT 226

2000 Finance Act
s 101 .... CT 103.3(A)

2000 Limited Liability Partnerships Act
s 10(1) .... IT 17.4

2001 Capital Allowances Act
s 6 .... IT 4.1
  (6) .... IT 4.1(B)
s 18 .... CT 111.1
s 33A .... IT 4.5
s 36(1) .... IT 8.2(A)
s 38ZA .... IT 30.1
s 38A .... IT 4.6; 4.7
s 38B .... IT 4.2; 4.6; 4.7
s 45A .... CT 102.1
s 45D .... IT 4.3
s 45H .... CT 102.1
s 46(2) .... IT 4.2
s 47 .... CT 102.1
s 51A .... IT 4.6; 4.7; CT 101.2
s 51C .... CT 102.1
s 52(4) .... CT 102.2
s 55 .... CT 102.1
s 56 .... CT 102.1
  (1) .... IT 4.1(B); 4.5
  (3) .... IT 4.1(A); CT 101.2; 102.1
  (5) .... CT 102.2
s 56A .... IT 4.5
s 58 .... CT 102.2
s 61(2) .... IT 4.3
  (4) .... IT 4.3
ss 83–89 .... IT 4.4
ss 90–104E .... IT 4.5
ss 104A, 104AA .... IT 4.3
s 206 .... IT 4.3
s 213 .... IT 4.3
s 214 .... IT 4.2; 4.3
s 217 .... IT 4.2; 4.3
s 218 .... IT 4.3
ss 217, 218 .... IT 4.3
ss 234–246 .... IT 4.8
ss 247–252 .... IT 4.1(A)
s 253 .... IT 4.1(A); CT 111.1
ss 254–262 .... IT 4.1(A)
ss 265–268 .... IT 4.2
s 281 .... IT 3.3
s 295 .... IT 3.3(A)
ss 298–301 .... IT 3.3
s 302 .... IT 3.3; 3.3(B)

2001 Capital Allowances Act – *cont.*
ss 303–309 .... IT 3.3
ss 310–313 .... CT 102.1
ss 352–355 .... IT 4.1(A)
s 353 .... IT 3.3(A)
ss 360A–360Z4 .... IT 3.1
s 360Z .... IT 4.1(A)
s 391 .... IT 4.1(A)
s 392 .... IT 4.1(A)
s 393T .... IT 4.1(A)
s 396(2)(3) .... IT 3.4
s 404 .... IT 3.4
s 418(1) .... IT 3.4
s 424 .... IT 3.4
ss 437–451 .... IT 3.6
s 450 .... IT 4.1(A)
s 463 .... IT 4.1(A)
ss 464–483 .... IT 3.5
ss 478–480 .... IT 4.1(A)
ss 484–487 .... IT 3.2
s 488(4)(5) .... IT 3.2
s 489 .... IT 3.2; 4.1(A)
s 529 .... IT 4.1(A)
ss 546–551 .... IT 4.8
s 559 .... IT 4.2
s 569 .... IT 4.2
s 575 .... IT 4.3

2001 Finance Act
s 77 .... CT 103.3(A)
s 78 .... CGT 231; 231.2(B)
Sch 15 para 10 .... CGT 210.3

2002 Finance Act
s 49 .... CGT 213.3(B)
s 51 .... CGT 215.7
s 84 .... CGT 225.1(A)
s 120 .... IHT 308; 308.1
Sch 29 .... CGT 213.2(B)
    para 95 .... CGT 213.3(A)
    paras 117, 118
    .... CGT 213.3(A)
    para 121 .... CGT 213.3(A)
        132 .... CGT 213.1(A)
        137 .... CGT 226.1(A)
Sch 30 para 1 .... CT 101.2

2003 Income Tax (Earnings and Pensions) Act
s 18 .... CT 116.1
s 22 .... IT 22.1
ss 48–55 .... IT 18
s 56 .... IT 19; 19.1
ss 57–61 .... IT 19
s 75 .... IT 8.6(A)
ss 87, 88 .... IT 8.6(A)
ss 97, 98 .... IT 8.4
s 99 .... IT 8.4
  (1)(2) .... IT 8.4(A)
s 100 .... IT 8.4; 8.4(A)
ss 101–104 .... IT 8.4
ss 105, 106 .... IT 8.4; 8.5
s 107 .... IT 8.4; 8.4(B)

2003 Income Tax (Earnings and Pensions) Act – *cont.*
ss 108–113	IT 8.4
ss 114–121	IT 8.3(A)
ss 122–124	IT 8.3(A); CT 104.3
ss 125–153	IT 8.3(A)
ss 154–164	IT 8.3(B)
s 170(1A)(2)(5)	IT 8.3(B)
ss 173–180	IT 8.3(D)
s 181	IT 8.3(D); 8.5
ss 182–191	IT 8.3(D)
s 201	IT 8.6(A); NIC 505.1(A)
ss 202, 203	NIC 505.1(A)
s 204	IT 8.3(A)
ss 203–208	IT 8.3(C)
s 216	IT 8.6(A)
s 218	IT 8.6(B)
ss 229–236	IT 8.2(A)
s 239(4)(5)	IT 8.3(A)
ss 240, 241	IT 8.6(A)
ss 271–289	IT 8.5
s 313	IT 8.4; 8.4(A)
s 314	IT 8.4; 8.4(A)
s 315	IT 8.4
(5)	IT 8.4(A)
s 325	IT 8.6(B)
s 336	IT 8.2(B); 8.3(A)
ss 337–340	IT 8.2(B); 19.1
ss 346–350	IT 8.3(A)
ss 370, 371	IT 8.1
ss 410–416	IT 1.1(C)
s 420(8)	IT 27.1
ss 422–432	IT 27.2
ss 435–444	IT 27.3
ss 471–474	IT 27.1
s 475	IT 27.1; 27.4
s 476	IT 27.1; 27.5
ss 477–484	IT 27.1
ss 488–515	IT 27.4
ss 527–541	IT 27.5
ss 681B–681H	IT 28.1
s 693	IT 8.6(A)
Sch 2	IT 27.4
Sch 5	IT 27.5

2004 Finance Act
s 117	CGT 222.4
ss 188–195A	IT 18.1
ss 214–226	IT 18.2
ss 227–238A	IT 18.3
Sch 19 paras 4–7	CGT 229.5
Sch 22 paras 6–8	CGT 223.3
Sch 36 paras 7–11D	IT 18.2
para 39	IT 18.1
40	IT 18.1

2005 Income Tax (Trading and Other Income) Act
ss 13, 14	IT 16.1
s 25	IT 29.8
s 25A	IT 30.1

2005 Income Tax (Trading and Other Income) Act – *cont.*
ss 31A–31F	IT 30.1
s 33A	IT 30.1
ss 36, 37	IT 29.4
ss 45–47	IT 29.4
s 51A	IT 30.1
s 55	IT 29.4
s 57	IT 29.4
s 57B	IT 30.1
s 58	IT 30.4
ss 60–63	IT 21.4(B); CGT 215.3(G)
s 64	IT 21.4(B)(C); CGT 215.3(G)
ss 65–67	IT 21.4(B); CGT 215.3(G)
ss 94B–94I	IT 30.1
ss 111–129	IT 10
ss 148A–148J	IT 28.7
s 157	CGT 218.1
s 160	IT 29.8
ss 163, 164	IT 19; 19.1
ss 169–172	IT 29.10
s 172B	IT 29.4
s 198	NIC 507.1
s 200	NIC 507.1
ss 198–200	IT 29.1
s 201	NIC 507.1
s 202	IT 29.3
s 203	IT 17.1(B)
s 204	IT 29.1
s 205	IT 29.3
s 214	IT 29.2
(1)	IT 29.2(C)
s 215	IT 29.2
s 216	IT 4.1(B); 29.2; 29.2(A)(B)
s 217	IT 4.1(B); 29.2; 29.2(A)(B)(C)
s 218	IT 29.2
s 219	IT 29.2; 29.2(C)
s 220	IT 29.2; 29.2(B)
ss 221–225	IT 29.5; 29.6
s 226	IT 29.8
s 227A	IT 30.1
ss 228–240	IT 29.8; 29.9
ss 240A–240D	IT 30.1
ss 241–247	IT 20
s 248	IT 20
(3)(4)	IT 20.2
s 249	IT 20
s 250	IT 20; 20.2
ss 251–254	IT 201
s 255	IT 20
(4)	IT 20.2
s 256	IT 20
s 257	IT 20; 20.2
ss 263–275	IT 21.1
s 276	IT 21.4
s 277	IT 21.4; 21.4(A); CGT 215.3(C)
ss 278–281	IT 21.4; CGT 215.3(C)
ss 282–286	IT 21.4
ss 287, 288	IT 21.4; 21.4(C)
ss 289–307	IT 21.4
ss 308A–308C	IT 21.1

Table of Statutes

2005 Income Tax (Trading and Other Income) Act – *cont.*

ss 312–314	IT 21.1
s 319	CGT 218.1
ss 322–328B	IT 21.2
ss 340–343	CGT 218.1
s 397	IT 1.1
(1)	IT 1.1(C); 16.1
(2)(3)	IT 1.1(C)
(4)	IT 16.1
s 397A	IT 27.4
s 399(4)–(6)	IT 26.2
s 400(4)(5)	IT 26.2
ss 427–429	IT 23.1
ss 430–436	IT 23.1; 23.1(A)
ss 437–452	IT 23.1
s 453	IT 23.1; 23.1(A)(B)
s 454	IT 23.1; 23.1(B)
s 455	IT 23.1; 23.1(A)
ss 456–460	IT 13.1; 23.1
ss 461–490	IT 13.1
s 491	IT 13.2
ss 192–498	IT 13.1
s 499	IT 13.2
ss 500–506	IT 13.1
s 507	IT 13.2
ss 508–527	IT 13.1
s 528	IT 13.1; 13.3
s 529	IT 13.1
s 530	IT 13.1(A)(B)
s 531	IT 13.1(A)
ss 532–535	IT 13.1
s 536	IT 13.1(A)(B)
s 537	IT 13.1(B)
ss 538–541	IT 13.1
s 542	IT 13.1(A)
ss 543–546	IT 13.1
s 629	IT 26.4
ss 631, 632	IT 26.4
ss 633–638	IT 26.5
ss 649–651	IT 6
s 652	IT 6.1
s 653	IT 6
s 654(3)	IT 6.2
s 655	IT 6
s 656	IT 6.1
ss 657–660	IT 6
s 661	IT 6.2
ss 662–664	IT 6
s 665	IT 6.1
ss 666–678	IT 6
s 679	IT 6.1; 6.2
ss 680–682	IT 6
ss 784–802	IT 21.3
ss 803–828	IT 29.9
s 832	IT 22.1
ss 846–849	IT 17.1
s 850(1)	IT 17.1(A)
(2)–(5)	IT 17.2
s 851	IT 17.1(B)
ss 852, 853	IT 17.1(A)

2005 Income Tax (Trading and Other Income) Act – *cont.*

ss 854–856	IT 17.1(B)
s 863(2)	IT 17.3
Sch 1 para 106	CGT 218.1
346	IT 29.1(B)
Sch 2 para 133	IT 26.4

2005 Finance Act

ss 23–45	CGT 228.2
Sch 1	CGT 228.2
Sch 1A	CGT 228.2

2005 Finance (No 2) Act

s 38	CT 114.3(A)

2006 Finance Act

s 32	CGT 220.4
s 69	CGT 207.1
s 70(3)	CT 103.3(F)
Sch 8 Pt 4	IT 3.4(A)
Sch 9 para 13	IT 3.4(A)
Sch 12 paras 34, 36	CGT 219.1(A)
41	CGT 219.1(A)
Sch 15 Pt 1	IT 26.9
Sch 20 para 1	IHT 301.2(A)(B)
2	IHT 301; 301.1
3	IHT 301; 301.1
4	IHT 320
5	IHT 320; 320.2; 320.3
paras 12, 13	IHT 320
para 16	IHT 320
17	IHT 316
20	IHT 320.1; 320.2; 320.3
21	IHT 325

2007 Income Tax Act

ss 6–8	IT 1.1
s 9	IT 26.2
ss 10–14	IT 1.1
s 16	IT 1.1
s 18	IT 1.1
s 19	IT 1.1
s 23	IT 1.1; 11.1
s 24	IT 1.1
s 25	IT 1.1
(2)	IT 1.1(B)(C)
ss 26, 27, 29	IT 9.1(A)
s 35	IT 1.2; 5.1(C); 18.1(B); 31.2
ss 36, 37	IT 1.3
s 42	IT 1.3
s 43	IT 1.3; 1.3(C)
s 44	IT 1.3; 1.3(D); 15.1(A)(B)
s 45	IT 1.3; 15.1(A)(B)
(4)	IT 1.3(C)
s 46	IT 1.3; 1.3(D)
s 47	IT 1.3; 1.3(C)(D); 15.1(A)
ss 48–50	IT 1.3; 15.1(A)
s 51	IT 1.3; 15.1(B)
s 52	IT 1.3; 15.1(A)
s 53	IT 1.3; 15.1(B)

2007 Income Tax Act – *cont.*

s 53(1)–(3)	IT 16.1
s 54	IT 1.3; 15.2
s 55	IT 1.3
s 56	IT 16.1
s 58	IT 1.2; 1.3; 18.1
s 61(2)	IT 14.3(A)(B)
s 62	IT 17.2
s 63	IT 14.4
s 64	IT 1.1(B); 14.1; 14.3(A)(B); 14.4; 17.3; 17.4; 29.5; 29.6; CGT 201.2; NIC 511.2
(2)	IT 14.2
s 71	IT 14.2
s 72	IT 14.3; 14.3(A)(B); 17.4; NIC 511.2
ss 73, 73	IT 14.3
s 83	IT 14.3(A)(B); NIC 511.2
ss 89–91	IT 14.4
ss 96–101	IT 20.2
ss 103–106	IT 17.3
ss 107–109	IT 17.4
ss 113A, 114	IT 17.3; 17.4
ss 118–124	IT 14.6
ss 125, 126	IT 20.2
s 127	IT 20.2
s 127ZA	IT 21.2
ss 127A, 127B	IT 14.6
ss 131, 132	IT 9.2(B); 14.5; CGT 216.3
ss 133–151	IT 134.5; CGT 216.3
ss 156, 157	IT 9
s 158	IT 9; 9.1(A)
(4)(5)	IT 9.1(B)
s 159	IT 9
(2)	IT 9; CGT 210.1; 210.2(B)
(4)	IT 9.2(B)
ss 160–162	IT 9
s 163	IT 9; CGT 210.3
ss 164, 165	IT 9
ss 166–168	IT 9; CGT 210.3
ss 169, 170	IT 9; 9.1(A); CGT 210.3
s 171	IT 9; CGT 210.3
ss 172–200	IT 9
s 201	IT 9; 9.1(B)
(6)	IT 9.2(A)
ss 202–208	IT 9
s 209	IT 9; 9.2(A)(B); CGT 210.2(A)
s 210	IT 9; 9.2(A); CGT 210.2(A)
(2)	IT 9.1(B)
ss 211, 212	IT 9
ss 213–217	IT 9; 9.2(B)
ss 218, 219	IT 9
s 220	IT 9; 9.2(B)
ss 221–233	IT 9
s 234	IT 9
(1)	IT 9.2(B)
s 235	IT 9; 9.2(A)(B)
ss 236–245	IT 9
s 246	IT 9; 9.2(A)
ss 247–257	IT 9

2007 Income Tax Act – *cont.*

ss 257A–257EG	IT 24.1
s 257AB(5)	CGT 227.3
s 257EA	CGT 227.3
ss 257FA, 257FB	CGT 227.2(B)
ss 257FC–257GI	IT 24.2(A)
s 257HA	IT 24.2(A)
ss 258–260	IT 31
ss 261–263	IT 31; 31.1(A)
ss 264, 265	IT 31
ss 266–270	IT 31; 31.1(B)
ss 271–332	IT 31
ss 414, 415	IT 5.1
s 423	IT 5.1; 5.1(C)
ss 424, 425	IT 5.1
ss 426, 427	IT 5.1(A)
ss 453–456	IT 15.2
s 460	IT 16.1
s 461	IT 11.1
ss 479–483	IT 26.2
ss 484–486	IT 26.2; 26.2(B)
s 487	IT 26.2
ss 491, 492	IT 26.2; 26.2(A)
ss 493–495	IT 26.2
ss 496–498	IT 26.2; 26.2(C)
s 503	IT 26.3(A)
ss 615–681	IT 2
s 643	IT 2.1
s 809B	IT 22.1; CGT 220.2; 225.1
s 809C	IT 22.1; CGT 225.1
s 809D	IT 22.1
s 809G	IT 22.1
s 809H	IT 22.1; CGT 225.1
s 809J	CGT 225.1
ss 809Q, 809R	IT 22.1
ss 809RA–809RD	IT 22.1
ss 810–828	IT 16.1
s 836	IT 15.1(B); CGT 217.2
s 837	CGT 217.2
ss 874–9380	CT 107.1
s 1005	IT 23.1(A)(B)
Sch 2 paras 14–17	IT 16.1
para 101	IT 15.2

2007 Finance Act

s 3	CT 119.1
s 27	CGT 207.1

2007 Pensions Act

s	NIC 501.1(B)

2008 Finance Act

s 8	CGT 228.1
s 10	IHT 308.1
s 31	IT 9
s 74	CT 101.2
s 77	IT 4.3
s 80(2)	IT 4.1(B)
(9)–(12)	IT 4.4
s 83	IT 4.5
s 86	IT 3.3
s 141	IHT 320; 320.2

2008 Finance Act – *cont.*
Sch 1 para 7 .... IT 1.1(E)
   para 20 .... IT 24.2
Sch 2 para 2 .... CGT 216.2
   para 22 ...... CGT 216.2; 228.2
       24 .... CGT 216.2
       25 .... CGT 211.5
       30 .... CGT 216.2
       37 .... IT 21.2
       43 .... CGT 216.4
       45 .... CGT 211.5
       56 ...... CGT 211.5; 216.2; 216.4
       59 .... CGT 214.2(A)
       60 .... CGT 214.2(A)
       65 ... CGT 205.2; 214.2(A)
   paras 85–87
       .... CGT 230.1
       98, 99
       .... CGT 216.3; 230.1
   para 100 .... CGT 216.3
Sch 3 para 6 .... CGT 211.3
       7 .. CGT 211.1(A)(B); 211.5
       8 .. CGT 211.1(A)(B); 211.5
Sch 4 para 2 .... IHT 308.1; 310.3; 310.3(A)–(C)
       9 ..... IHT 310.3; 310.3(A)
       10 .... IHT 310.3; 310.3(B)
   paras 120–125
       .... CGT 219.1(A)
Sch 19 .... IT 5.1(A)
Sch 24 .... CT 101.2
   para 3 .... CT 102.1

2009 Corporation Tax Act
s 8 .... CT 101.1; 119.1(C)
s 9 .... CT 112.1
s 10(1) .... CT 101.2
s 12 .... CT 112.1
s 18A .... CT 105.2; 105.2(A)(B)
ss 18A–18E .... CT 105.2
s 18F .... CT 105.2; 105.2(A)
ss 18G–18I .... CT 105.2
ss 18J–18N .... CT 105.2; 105.2(B)
ss 18O–18Q .... CT 105.2; 105.2(A)(B)
s 18R .... CT 105.2; 105.2(A)
s 18S .... CT 105.2
s 53 .... CT 101.2
s 56 .... CT 116.1
s 62–67 .... CGT 215.3(G)
ss 104A–104Y .... CT 117.1; 117.2
s 215, 216 .... CGT 215.3(C)
s 217, 218 ... CT 116.1; CGT 215.3(C)
s 219, 220 .... CT 116.1
ss 274–276 .... CT 116.1
ss 295–298 .... CT 113.1
s 299 .... CT 113.1; 113.2
ss 300, 301 .... CT 113.1
s 304 .... CT 113.1
ss 307–310 .... CT 113.1
s 328 .... CT 113.1
ss 726–744 .... CT 108.1

2009 Corporation Tax Act – *cont.*
ss 751–753 .... CT 108.2
ss 754–763 .... CT 108.3
s 849A .... CGT 213.4; 213.4(B)
ss 882–884 .... CGT 213.3(A)
s 1040A .... CT 117.1; 117.2
ss 1044–1062 .... CT 117.1
ss 1218–1231 .... CT 111.1
ss 1248, 1255 .... CT 111.1
s 1307 .... CT 101.2
Sch 1 paras 377, 378
   .... CGT 218.1
   para 536 .... CT 117.1

2009 Finance Act
s 4 .... IT 1.2; 5.1(C); 18.1(B); 27.2
s 6 .... IT 1.1; 18.1
s 27 .... IT 9; CT 27
s 31 .... CT 103.3(A)
s 71 .... IT 8.4
s 101 .... IT 12.1(A)(B)
s 102 .... IT 25.2(A)
s 107 .... IT 12.1(A)
s 122 .... IHT 302
Sch 2 paras 2–4 .... IT 1.1(E)
   para 6 .... IT 5.1(C)
   para 11 .... IT 18.1
   paras 15, 25
       .... IT 18.3
Sch 6 paras 1, 2 .... IT 13.1(B)
Sch 8 paras 1–5 ...... IT 9; CGT 210.3
   para 6 .... IT 9; 8.1(B)
       7 .... IT 9
       8 .... IT 31
   paras 11, 12
       .... IT 9
       13 .... IT 9; 9.1(B)
       14 .... IT 31
Sch 11 paras 7, 8 .... IT 4.3
   26–28
       .... IT 4.3
   para 47 .... CT 116.1
Sch 12 .... CT 103.3(A)
Sch 21 para 2 .... CT 113.1
Sch 27 para 5 .... CGT 225.1
Sch 35 .... IT 18.1
Sch 53 para 1 .... IT 12.1(B)
Sch 54 para 5 .... IT 25.2(A)
Sch 56 .... IT 12.1(A)

2010 Corporation Tax Act
s 18 .... CT 112.1; 119.1
ss 19–23 .... CT 119.1
s 24 .... CT 115.1; 119.2
ss 25–30 .... CT 119.1; 119.2
s 31 .... CT 119.1
s 32 .... CT 119.1; 119.2(A)
s 34(2) .... CT 112.1
s 37 .... CT 106.5; 109.2
   (3) .. CT 103.1; 114.1; 114.3(A)(B); 117.1
   (4) .... CT 114.3(A)

Table of Statutes

2010 Corporation Tax Act – *cont.*
- s 38 .... CT 114.3; 114.3(B)
- s 39 .... CT 109.2; 114.3; 114.3(A)
- ss 40–44 .... CT 114.3
- s 45 .... CT 106.2; 106.5; 114.2; 114.3(B); 117.1
- ss 62–67 .... CT 114.4
- ss 68–81 .... CT 114.4
- ss 82–86 .... CT 114.4; 116.1
- ss 87–90 .... CT 114.4
- ss 97, 98 .... CT 106.1
- s 99 .... CT 106.1; 106.2; 106.5
- ss 100–102 .... CT 106.1; 106.2
- s 103 .... CT 106.1; 106.2; 111.1
- s 104 .... CT 106.1; 106.2; 108.2
- s 105 .... CT 106.1; 106.2; 106.5
- ss 106–129 .... CT 106.1
- s 130 .... CT 106.1; 106.6
- s 131 .... CT 106.1
- s 132 ...... CT 106.1; 106.6; 106.6(D)
- s 133 ...... CT 106.1; 106.6; 106.6(B)
- ss 134–137 .... CT 106.1
- s 138 .... CT 106.1; 106.3; 106.4
- ss 139, 140 ... CT 106.1; 106.3; 106.4; 106.6(A)
- ss 141, 142 .... CT 106.1; 106.3; 106.4
- s 143 .... CT 106.1; 106.6(A)(C)
- s 144 .... CT 106.1; 106.6(D)
- s 145 .... CT 106.1
- s 146 .... CT 106.1; 106.6(B)
- s 147 .... CT 106.1
- s 148 .... CT 106.1; 106.6(B)
- ss 149, 150 .... CT 106.1
- s 151 .... CT 106.1; 106.6(C)
- s 152 .... CT 106.1
- s 153 .... CT 106.1; 106.6(C)
- ss 154–156 .... CT 106.1
- s 189 .... CT 114.1; 116.1
- s 190 .... CT 116.1
- s 439 .... CT 104.1(A)(C)
- ss 440–445 .... CT 104.1
- s 446 .... CT 104.1; 104.1(A)
- ss 447–449 .... CT 104.1
- s 450 .... CT 104.1; 104.1(B)(C)
- s 451 .... CT 104.1; 104.1(B)
- s 452 .... CT 104.1; 104.1(B)
- s 453 .... CT 104.1
- s 455 .... CT 104.2; 104.2(B)
- ss 456, 457 .... CT 104.2
- s 458 .... CT 104.2; 104.2(B)
- ss 459–464 .... CT 104.2
- s 464A .... CT 104.2; 104.2(A)
- s 464B .... CT 104.2
- ss 464C, 464D .... CT 104.2; 104.2(A)
- s 535 .... CT 103.3(E)
- ss 626–629 .... CT 112.1
- ss 677–703 .... CT 111.1
- ss 940A–944 .... CT 102.1; 114.5
- ss 945–947 . CT 102.1; 114.5; 114.5(A)
- ss 948–951 .... CT 102.1; 114.5
- s 952 .... CT 102.1; 114.5; 114.5(B)

2010 Corporation Tax Act – *cont.*
- s 953 .... CT 102.1; 114.5
- ss 963–966 .... CT 110.1(D)
- s 967 .... CT 107.1
- ss 1064–1069 .... CT 104.3
- s 1172 .... CT 101.2
- s 1223 .... CT 106.2
- Sch 1 para 117 .... CT 109.2
- para 155 .... CT 115.1
- para 604 .... CT 113.1

2010 Taxation (International and Other Provisions) Act
- ss 2–6 .... CT 105.1
- ss 18–20 .... IT 7.1(A); CT 105.1; CGT 209.1
- ss 21–30 .... IT 7.1(A); CGT 209.1
- ss 31–34 .... IT 7.1(A); CT 105.1; CGT 209.1
- s 35 .... IT 7.1(A); CGT 209.1
- s 36 .. IT 1.3(B); 7.1(A)(B); CGT 209.1
- ss 37–41 .... IT 7.1(A); CGT 209.1
- ss 42–56 .... CT 105.1
- s 113 .... CT 105.1
- ss 146–173 .... CT 120.1
- ss 174–178 .... CT 120.1; 120.1(B)
- ss 179, 180 .... CT 120.1
- ss 181–184 .... CT 120.1; 120.1(B)
- s 185 .... CT 120.1; 120.1(A)
- ss 186–230 .... CT 120.1
- ss 260–330 .... CT 120.1(B)

2010 Finance Act
- s 1 .... IT 1.2; 1.3
- s 3 .... CT 101.1
- s 4 .... CGT 211.1(B)
- s 5 .... IT 4.6; 4.7; CT 101.2
- s 25 .... IT 14.6
- s 37(1)(3) .... CGT 220.3
- s 53 .... IHT 320.1; 320.2; 320.3

2010 Finance (No 2) Act
- Sch 1 para 2 .... CGT 201.1; 228.1
- para 3 .... CGT 211.1(B)(C)
- para 4 .... CGT 211.1
- para 5 ..... CGT 211.1; 211.1(B)
- para 6 .... CGT 211.1
- para 7 .... CGT 211.1
- para 8 .... CGT 211.1
- para 10 ...... CGT 211.1; 211.5
- para 11 ...... CGT 211.1; 211.5
- para 12 ...... CGT 201.1; 228.1
- para 13 . CGT 201.1; 211.1(B)(C)
- para 14 .... CGT 211.1; 211.1(B)
- para 15 .... CGT 211.1
- paras 16, 17
.... CGT 211.1; 211.5
- para 18 ...... CGT 201.1; 228.1
- para 19 .... CGT 220.4
- para 22 .... CGT 218.1(A)

2010 Finance (No 3) Act
- s 6 .... IT 27.5

Table of Statutes

2011 Finance Act
- s 6 .... CT 101.1
- s 8 .... CGT 201.2
- s 9 .... CGT 211.1; 211.1(B)
- s 11 .... IT 4.6; 4.7
- s 12 .... IT 4.4
- s 42 .... IT 9
- s 43 .... CT 117.1
- s 44 .... CGT 202.2; 202.4
- s 46 .... CT 103.3(F)
- s 48 .... CT 105
- Sch 2 paras 15, 16
  - .... IT 27.2
  - paras 17, 18
  - .... IT 27.3
  - para 52 .... IT 27.2; 27.3
- Sch 5 para 3 .... CT 114.5
- Sch 7 paras 6, 8 .... CT 114.1
- Sch 9 para 1 .... CGT 202.2
  - para 2 .... CGT 202.2
  - para 3 .... CGT 202.2; 202.4
  - paras 4, 5 .... CGT 202.2
  - para 6 .... CGT 202.2; 202.4
- Sch 10 paras 3, 4 .... CT103.3(E)
  - para 9 .... CT103.3(E)
- Sch 11 .... CT 103.3(F)
- Sch 13 .... CT 105
  - para 4 .... CT 105.2(A)(B)
  - para 31 .... CT 105.2(A)
- Sch 14 para 2 .... IT 21.1; 21.2
  - paras 3–6 .... IT 21.2
  - paras 12–17
  - .... IT 21.2
- Sch 16 paras 43, 44
  - .... IT 18.2
  - para 45 .... IT 18.3
  - para 80 .... IT 18.2
  - para 84 .... IT 18.2
  - para 85 .... IT 18.3
  - para 104 .... IT 18.2
  - paras 73, 80
  - .... IT 18.2
- Sch 17 paras 3–17
  - .... IT 18.3
  - paras 26, 27
  - .... IT 18.3
  - paras 28, 29
  - .... IT 18.3; 18.3(C)
  - para 30 .... IT 18.3; 18.3(B)
  - paras 31, 32
  - .... IT 18.3
- Sch 18 para 2 .... IT 18.2; 18.2(B)
  - paras 12–14
  - .... IT 18.2; 18.2(B)

2012 Finance Act
- s 1 .... IT 26.2
- s 4 .... IT 21.2
- s 9 .... IT 1.3
- s 10 .... IT 14.6
- s 20 .... CT 117.1
- s 34 .... CGT 201.2

2012 Finance Act – cont.
- s 209 .... IHT 322.2
- Sch 1 paras 1, 3, 4, 7
  - .... IT 28.1
- Sch 3 .... CT 117.1
- Sch 6 para 1 .... IT 24.1; 24.2(A); CGT 227.3
  - para 3 ... IT 24.2(B); CGT 227.1; 227.2; 227.2(B)
  - paras 4, 5 .... CGT 227.3
  - paras 10–13 .... IT 9
  - paras 15–17 .... IT 31
  - para 23 .... CGT 227.1; 227.2
  - para 24 ...... IT 24.1; 24.2(A)(B)
- Sch 7 .... IT 9
  - paras 12, 23 .... IT 9.1(B)
- Sch 8 .... IT 31
- Sch 12 para 2 .... CGT 225.1
- Sch 20 para 3 ..... CT 105.2; 105.2(A)
  - para 4 .... CT 105.2
  - para 5 ..... CT 105.2; 105.2(A)
  - paras 6, 7 .... CT 105.2
  - para 55 .... CT 105.2; 105.2(A)
- Sch 33 .... IHT 322.2
  - para 1 .... IHT 322.2(A)(B)
  - para 4 ...... IHT 316; 316.2(B)
  - para 9 .... IHT 308
  - para 10 ..... IHT 308; 322.2(A)
- Sch 39 para 23 .... IT 13.4
  - paras 36, 37
  - .... IT 14.6
  - paras 40, 42
  - .... IT 14.6
  - para 43 .... CGT 218.1
  - para 44 .... CGT 218.1
  - paras 45–47
  - .... CGT 218.1
  - para 48 .... IT 23.1(A)

2013 Finance Act
- ss 1–3 .... IT 1.1
- s 7 .... IT 4.7; CT 101.2
- s 48 .... IT 18.2
- s 49 .... IT 18.3(A)
- s 56 .... IT 24.1
- s 57 .... CGT 227.3
- s 58 .... CGT 213.4; 213.4(A)
- s 59 .... CGT 213.4; 213.4(A)
- s 60 .... CGT 213.4; 213.4(A)
- s 60 .... CGT 213.4; 213.4(A)(B)
- s 229 .... CGT 220.1
- ss 177, 178 .... IHT310.4
- Sch 1 .... IT 4.7
- Sch 2 paras 2, 5 .... IT 4.7
- Sch 2para 17 .... IT 27.4
- Sch 2paras83–90 .... IT 27.4
- Sch 4 para 24 .... IT 27.4
- Sch 4para 32 .... IT 29.5; 29.6
- Sch 4para 39 .... IT 20.1
- Sch 4para 40 .... IT 21.3
- Sch 4paras 51, 52 .... IT 29.8

Table of Statutes

2013 Finance Act – *cont.*
Sch 4 para 56 ...... IT 10.1; 20.1; 21.3; 29.5; 29.6
Sch 4 para 57 .... IT 29.8
Sch 5 para 2 .... IT 30.1
    para 4 .... IT 22.1
    para 5 .... IT 30.1
    para 6 .... IT 22.1; 30.1
Sch 6 paras 5, 6, 8
.... IT 20.1
Sch 8 paras 3, 7 .... IT 13.3
Sch 15 .... CT 117.1; 117.2
Sch 22 .... IT 18.2
Sch 24 para 1 .. IT 27.5; CGT 211.1(C)
    para 3 .... CGT 211.1(C)
    paras 5, 6 .... IT 27.5
Sch 30 .... CT 104.2
    para 6 .... CT 104.2(A)
Sch 44 paras 2–5 .... IHT 323
    para 6 .... IHT 323; 324
    para 7 .... IHT 324; 324.4
    para 8 .... IHT 324
    para 9 ..... IHT 323; 324; 324.4
    para 10 .... IHT 324

2013 Finance Act – *cont.*
Sch 44 paras 14–19
.... CGT 228.2
Sch 45 para 77 .... IT 20.1
    para 86 .... IT 13.3
    paras 98, 99
.... CGT 225.1
    paras 109–115
.... CGT 219.1(A)
    para 119 .... CGT 219.1(A)
    para 152 .... IT 16.1; 22.1
    para 153 .... IT 13.3; 20.1; CGT 219.1(A)
Sch 46 paras 3–5 .... IT 22.1
    paras 25–27
.... IT 22.1
    para 35 .... IT 2.1; 8.1
    para 58 .... IT 2.1
    para 66 .... IT 16.1
    para 72 .... IT 2.1; 8.1; 16.1
    paras 92, 112
.... CGT 219.1(A)
Sch 49 .... CGT 220.1

Table of Statutory Instruments

1978/1689 Social Security (Categorisation of Earners) Regulations
Sch 3 para 2 .... NIC 502.4

1987/530 Income Tax (Entertainers and Sportsmen) Regulations
.... IT 16.2

1987/1130 Inheritance Tax (Double Charges Relief) Regulations
...... IHT 311; 311.1(B); 315; 322.1
Reg 4 .... IHT 315.1
Reg 5 .... IHT 311.1(B)
Reg 6 .... IHT 322.1
Reg 7 .... IHT 315.2

1988/1013 Personal Pension Schemes (Relief at Source) Regulations
.... IT 20.1(A)

1989/1297 Taxes (Interest Rate) Regulations .... CT 109; IHT 312

1992/3122 Value Added Tax (Cars) Order
Art 8(7) .... VAT 412.3

1993/2212 Taxes (Interest Rate) (Amendment No 3) Regulations
.... CT 109

1995/1268 Value Added Tax (Special Provisions) Order
Art 12(7) .... VAT 412.3
Art 13 .... VAT 412.2

1995/2518 Value Added Tax Regulations
Regs 66–75 .... VAT 411
Reg 73 .... VAT 403.1
Regs 99–109 .... VAT 408.1; 408.2
Regs 112–116 .... VAT 402.1
Regs 165–172E .... VAT 401.1
Regs 172F–172J .... VAT 405.1

1998/3175 Corporation Tax (Instalment Payments) Regulations
.... CT 109.1(A)(B); 110.1; 115.1

1998/3176 Taxes (Interest Rate) (Amendment No 2) Regulations
.... CT 109.1(A)(B); 110.1

1999/597 Income Tax (Indexation) Order
.... IT 1.3

1999/684 Income Tax (Cash Equivalent of Car Fuel Benefits) Order
.... IT 8.3(A)

1999/1928 Taxes (Interest Rate) (Amendment No 2) Regulations
.... CT 110.1(A)(B); 111.1

1999/1929 Corporation Tax (Instalment Payments) (Amendment) Regulations
.... CT 110.1(A)(B); 111.1; 119.1

1999/3120 Value Added Tax (Special Provisions) (Amendment) (No 2) Order
.... VAT 412.2

2000/727 Social Security Contributions (Intermediaries) Regulations
.... NIC 513.1

2000/2315 Personal Pension Schemes (Relief at Source) (Amendment) Regulations .... IT 18.1(A)

2001/1004 Social Security (Contributions) Regulations
Reg 1(2) .... NIC 502.7
Reg 2 .... NIC 512.1
Reg 3 .... NIC 512.1; 512.1(A)(B)
Reg 4 .... NIC 512.1; 512.1(C)
Reg 5 .... NIC 512.1
Reg 6 .... NIC 512.1
Reg 7 .... NIC 501.1; 512.1
Reg 8 . NIC 502.5; 508.2; 512.1; 512.3
Reg 9 .... NIC 512.1
Reg 12 .... NIC 504.2
Reg 14 .... NIC 502.1; 502.1(A)
Reg 15(1) .... NIC 502.2; 502.3; 502.4
Reg 18 .... NIC 512.2
Reg 19 .... NIC 512.3
Reg 21 .... NIC 503.1
Reg 22(2) .... NIC 508.1; 508.2
Regs 28, 29 ...... NIC 501.1; 501.1(A)
Reg 36 .... NIC 505.2(A)(B)
Reg 45 .... NIC 502.7; 511.1
Reg 52 .... NIC 515.1
Reg 68 .... NIC 510.1
Reg 84 .... NIC 510.1
Reg 90 .... NIC 510.2
Reg 94 .... NIC 507.1
Reg 95 .... NIC 510.2
Reg 100 .... NIC 503.2; 503.2(A)
Sch 3 Pt X para 2 .... NIC 508.1
Reg 90 .... NIC 510.2

2004/773 Retirement Benefits Schemes (Indexation of Earnings Cap) Order
.... IT 18.1(A)

2004/3161 Income Tax (Indexation) (No 2) Order .... IT 1.3

2005/720 Retirement Benefits Schemes (Indexation of Earnings Cap) Order
.... IT 18.1(A)

2006/912 Energy-Saving Items Regulations
.... IT 21.1

2006/1009 Social Security (Reduced Rates of Class 1 Contributions, Rebates and Minimum Contributions) Order
.... NIC 509.1

2007/107 Assisted Areas Order 2007
.... IT 3.1

2007/494 Registered Pension Schemes (Standard Lifetime and Annual Allowances) Order
.... IT 18.3

xxix

Table of Statutory Instruments

2007/945 Business Premises Renovation Allowances Regulations .... IT 3.1

2007/3278 Energy-Saving Items (Income Tax) Regulations .... IT 21.1

2009/730 Enactment of Extra-Statutory Concessions Order Art 4 .... CGT 217.1(B)

2010/922 Registered Pension Schemes (Standard Lifetime and Annual Allowances) Order .... IT 18.3

2011/701 Finance Act 2009, Sections 101 to 103 (Income Tax Self Assessment) (Appointed Days and Transitional and Consequential Provisions) Order .... IT 12.1(A)(B); 25.2(A)

2011/702 Finance Act 2009, Schedules 55 and 56 (Income Tax Self Assessment and Pension Schemes) (Appointed Days and Consequential and Savings Provisions) Order .... IT 12.1(A)

2011/896 Approved Mileage Payments Allowance (Rates) Regulations .... IT 8.2

2011/1037 Enactment of Extra-Statutory Concessions Order .... IT 21.1

2012/868 Business Premises Renovation Allowances (Amendment) Regulations .... IT 3.1

2012/915 Car Fuel Benefit Order .... IT 8.3(A)

2012/1359 Income Tax (Entertainers and Sportsmen) (Amendment) Regulations .... IT 16.2

2012/1360 Income Tax (Limits for Enterprise Management Incentives) Order .... IT 27.5

2012/3037 Car and Van Fuel Benefit Order .... IT 8.3(A)

2012/3047 Income Tax (Indexation) Order .... IT 1.1; 1.2; 1.3

2013/605 Income Tax (Removal of Ordinary Residence) Regulations .... IT 16.2

Income Tax

1. Allowances and Tax Rates
2. Accrued Income Scheme
3. Capital Allowances
4. Capital Allowances on Plant and Machinery
5. Charities
6. Deceased Estates
7. Double Tax Relief
8. Employment Income
9. Enterprise Investment Scheme
10. Herd Basis
11. Intellectual Property
12. Late Payment Interest and Penalties
13. Life Assurance Policies
14. Losses
15. Married Persons and Civil Partners
16. Non-Residents
17. Partnerships
18. Pension Provision
19. Personal Service Companies etc.
20. Post-Cessation Receipts and Expenditure
21. Property Income
22. Remittance Basis
23. Savings and Investment Income
24. Seed Enterprise Investment Scheme
25. Self-Assessment
26. Settlements
27. Share-Related Employment Income and Exemptions
28. Social Security Income
29. Trading Income
30. Trading Income — Cash Basis for Small Businesses
31. Venture Capital Trusts

1 Allowances and Tax Rates

Cross-reference. See also 15.1 MARRIED PERSONS AND CIVIL PARTNERS for transfer of married couple's allowance.

1.1 INCOME COMPONENTS AND RATES OF TAX

[*ITA 2007, ss 6–8, 10–14, 16, 18, 19, 23–25; ITTOIA 2005, s 397; FA 2013, ss 1–3; SI 2012 No 3047*]

(A) **Mixed income**

Victor is a single man born after 5 April 1948 and for ten years has traded as a sole proprietor of a retail outlet. Throughout, his accounts have been drawn up to 30 June, and his tax-adjusted profits for the year ended 30 June 2013 are £33,500. His other 2013/14 income is as follows:

	£
Building society interest (net)	2,000
Dividends from UK companies (net)	6,750
Interest on UK company loan stock (net)	1,200

His taxable income and tax liability are computed for 2013/14 as follows

	£	£
Trading income		33,500
Building society interest	2,000	
Add Tax deducted (£2,000 × $1/4$)	500	
		2,500
UK dividends	6,750	
Add Tax credit (£6,750 × $1/9$)	750	
		7,500
Loan stock interest	1,200	
Add Tax deducted (£1,200 × $1/4$)	300	
		1,500
Total and net income		45,000
Deduct Personal allowance		9,440
Taxable income		£35,560
Tax payable:		
24,060 @ 20% (basic rate on trading income)		4,810.00
4,000 @ 20% (basic rate on savings income)		800.00
3,950 @ 10% (dividend ordinary rate)		395.00

1.1 IT Allowances and Tax Rates

32,010	
3,550 @ 32.5% (dividend upper rate)	1,153.75
£35,560	7,158.75
Deduct Tax credits and tax deducted at source	1,550.00
Tax payable	£5,608.75

Note

(a) Chargeable 'savings income' is grossed up by reference to tax deducted at source at the basic rate (20%). UK dividend income carries a tax credit; the tax credit is a fixed proportion of the dividend (one-ninth) and is not repayable. The same applies to most dividends from non-UK resident companies.

The 10% starting rate for savings does not apply in this example as taxable income, other than dividend income and non-dividend 'savings income', exceeds the starting rate limit of £2,790 (for 2013/14). See also (C) below.

Income from dividends is charged at special rates. Where the income does not exceed the basic rate limit the rate is the 'dividend ordinary rate', 10% for 2013/14, so that the liability is met by the tax credit. To the extent that the income exceeds the basic rate limit but not the higher rate limit of £150,000, the rate is the 'dividend upper rate', 32.5% for 2013/14. To the extent that the income exceeds the higher rate limit, the rate is the 'dividend additional rate', 37.5% for 2013/14. In determining the extent to which dividend income does fall above the basic rate or higher rate limit, dividend income is treated as the top slice of income (with certain limited exceptions).

(B)

The facts are the same as in (A) above except that Victor's trading results for the year ended 30 June 2013 produce a tax-adjusted loss of £3,228. He also, however, commenced a separate partnership trade during 2013/14, his taxable profit for that tax year being £17,550. He makes a claim under *ITA 2007, s 64* to set off the 2013/14 loss against his other income for 2013/14.

His 2013/14 tax liability is computed as follows

	£
Trading income	17,550
Dividend Income and 'Savings Income'	11,500
Total income	29,050
Loss relief under *ITA 2007, s 64(2)(a)*	3,228
Net income	25,822
Personal Allowance	9,440
Taxable income	£16,382
Tax payable:	
4,882 @ 20%	976.40
4,000 @ 20%	800.00

Allowances and Tax Rates IT 1.1

7,500 @ 10%	750.00
16,382	2,526.40
Less: Tax credits and tax deducted at source	1,550.00
	£976.40

Note

(a) Although dividend income is generally regarded as the top slice of income and non-dividend 'savings income' as the next slice (see (A) above), this does not mean that the loss must be set against those types of income first. Deductions allowable in computing net income are treated as reducing income of different descriptions in the order which will result in the greatest reduction of the tax liability. [*ITA 2007, s 25(2)*]. Thus, the loss has been set against basic rate income; dividend income is left intact and is chargeable at 10% as taxable income does not exceed the basic rate limit of £32,010.

The 10% starting rate for savings continues not to apply. Even after setting off the trade loss, taxable income, other than dividend income and non-dividend 'savings income', still exceeds the starting rate limit of £2,790. See also (C) below.

(C) **Starting rate for savings**

(i) Lemon, a single man born after 5 April 1948, has earned income of £8,120, bank interest of £4,400 (net) and UK dividends of £450 for 2013/14.

His income tax position is as follows

	£
Earnings	8,120
Non-dividend savings income (£4,400 × 100/80)	5,500
Dividends + tax credits (£450 × 100/90)	500
Total and net income	14,120
Personal allowance	9,440
Taxable income	£4,680
Tax payable:	
2,790 @ 10% (starting rate for savings)	279.00
1,390 @ 20% (basic rate)	278.00
500 @ 10% (dividend ordinary rate)	50.00
	607.00
Less: Tax deducted at source and tax credits	1,150.00
Tax repayable	£543.00

1.1 IT   Allowances and Tax Rates

Notes

(a) To the extent that an individual's non-dividend 'savings income' does not exceed the starting rate limit, it is taxed at the starting rate for savings, which is 10%, instead of the basic rate. For 2013/14, the starting rate limit is £2,790. For the purpose of determining whether 'savings income' exceeds the starting rate limit, it is treated as the highest part of the individual's total income apart from dividend income and income chargeable under *ITEPA 2003, ss 401–416* (payments and benefits on termination of office or employment); most chargeable event gains on life policies etc. take priority over both dividend income and other non-dividend 'savings income'.

(b) The personal allowance is treated as reducing income of different descriptions in the order which will result in the greatest reduction of the tax liability. [*ITA 2007, s 25(2)*]. In this example, it is set firstly against earnings and then against non-dividend 'savings income', which will usually give the best result.

(c) '*Savings income*' includes interest, income from purchased life annuities, profits on deeply discounted securities, accrued income profits and chargeable event gains on life policies etc.

(ii) Orange, a single woman born in 1943, has a pension of £11,500, on which tax of £200 has been paid under PAYE, and building society interest of £4,000 (net) for 2013/14.

Her income tax position is as follows

	£
Pension income	11,500
Non-dividend savings income (£4,000 × 100/80)	5,000
Total and net income	16,500
Personal allowance	10,500
Taxable income	£6,000
Tax payable:	
1,000 @ 20% (basic rate on pension income)	200.00
1,790 @ 10% (starting rate for savings)	179.00
3,210 @ 20% (basic rate on 'savings income')	642.00
	1,021.00
Less: Tax deducted at source (including PAYE)	1,200.00
Tax repayable	£179.00

Note

(a) The building society interest is the highest part of the individual's income, and £1,790 of this interest is within the starting rate band of £2,790. The age-related personal allowance has been set against the pension income as this gives the best result.

(D) **Restriction on set-off of dividend tax credits**

For 2013/14, a widow, born in 1945, has a taxable pension of £8,685 and net dividend income of £31,005.

Allowances and Tax Rates IT 1.1

Her 2013/14 tax liability is computed as follows

	£	£
Pension income		8,685
Dividends	31,005	
Dividend tax credit ($^1/_9$)	3,445	34,450
Total income		43,135
Deduct Personal allowance		9,440
Taxable income		£33,695
No tax liability on non-dividend income (covered by personal allowance)		Nil
Tax liability on dividends:		
£32,010 at 10% (dividend ordinary rate)		3,201.00
£1,685 at 32.5% (dividend upper rate)		547.62
		3,748.62
Deduct Tax credit on dividends:		
£33,695 at 10% (note (*a*))		3,369.50
Income tax payable		£379.12

Notes

(a) Tax credits deductible are restricted to those on the amount of dividends brought into charge to tax. [*ITTOIA 2005, s 397(1)–(3)*]. In this case, £755 of dividends are covered by excess of personal allowance over non-dividend income.

(b) No age-related personal allowance is available — as total income is too far in excess of the £26,100 income limit. See **1.3** below.

(E) **Dividend additional rate**

A single woman aged 35 has employment income of £144,370 for 2013/14. She also receives UK dividends of £13,500 (with tax credit attached £1,500)

	£	£
Employment income		144,370
Dividends	13,500	
Dividend tax credit ($^1/_9$)	1,500	15,000
Total income		159,370
Deduct Personal allowance (note (*b*))		Nil
Taxable income		£159,370
Tax liability on non-dividend income:		
£32,010 at 20% (basic rate)		6,402.00
£112,360 at 40% (higher rate)		44,944.00

1.1 IT Allowances and Tax Rates

	51,346.00
Tax liability on dividend income: (£150,000 − £144,370 = £5,630)	
£5,630 at 32.5% (dividend upper rate)	1,829.75
£9,370 at 37.5% (dividend additional rate)	3,513.75
	56,689.50
Deduct Tax credit on dividends	£1,500.00
Income tax payable	£55,189.50

Note

(a) To the extent that it exceeds £150,000, taxable income is chargeable at the 45% additional rate of tax (50% before 2013/14). To the extent that it is dividend income, however, it is instead charged at the 37.5% dividend additional rate (42.5% before 2013/14). Dividend income is treated as the highest part of an individual's income. [*ITA 2007, ss 6, 8, 10, 16; FA 2009, s 6(1)–(3), (6), Sch 2 paras 2–4; FA 2012, s 1(1)(2)(3)(a)(6)*].

(b) No personal allowance is available — as total income is too far in excess of the £100,000 income limit. See **1.2** below.

1.2 RESTRICTION OF PERSONAL ALLOWANCE

[*ITA 2007, ss 35(2)–(4), 58; FA 2009, s 4(1)(5); SI 2012 No 3047*].

A single person born after 5 April 1948 has employment income of £114,000 for 2013/14 (and no other income) and makes Gift Aid donations of £4,800.

	£	£
Employment income		114,000
Total and net income		114,000
Deduct Personal allowance	9,440	
Less reduction for excess adjusted net income over £100,000 (1/2 × 8,000) (note (b))	4,000	£5,440
Taxable income		£108,560
Tax liability:		
£38,010 at 20% (note (c))		7,602.00
£70,550 at 40%		28,220.00
Income tax payable		£35,822.00

Notes

(a) The personal allowance is reduced by one-half of the excess of adjusted net income over £100,000.

(b) Net income of £114,000 is reduced to adjusted net income of £108,000 by deducting the grossed up amount of the Gift Aid donations (£4,800 x 100/80 = £6,000).

Allowances and Tax Rates IT 1.3

(c) Whilst the Gift Aid donations are deductible in arriving at adjusted net income, they are not deductible in arriving at taxable income. Instead, the basic rate band is extended by the grossed up amount of the donations. See **5.1(C)** CHARITIES.

1.3 AGE-RELATED ALLOWANCES

[*ITA 2007, ss 36, 37, 42–55, 58; FA 2012, s 4; SI 2011 No 2926; SI 2012 No 3047*]

(A)

In 2013/14, a single man born on 1 April 1948 received employment income of £25,020, net dividends of £900 and bank deposit interest of £1,600 net. His tax position is as follows.

	£	£
Employment income		25,020
Dividends	900	
Add Dividend tax credit £900 × $1/9$	100	1,000
Bank deposit interest	1,600	
Add Tax deducted £1,600 × $20/80$	400	2,000
Total and net income		28,020
Deduct		
Personal allowance	10,500	
Less Reduction for excess		
$1/2$ (28,020 − 26,100)	960	9,540
Taxable income		£18,480
Tax on £17,480 at 20% (basic rate)	3,496.00	
Tax on £1,000 at 10% (dividend ordinary rate)	100.00	
	3,596.00	
Less Dividend tax credits and tax at source	500.00	£3,496.00

Notes

(a) The taxpayer is entitled to an age-related personal allowance of £10,500 by virtue of his having been born before 6 April 1948 but after 5 April 1938. Had he been born before 6 April 1938, he would have been entitled to an age-related personal allowance of £10,660. In both cases, the allowance is subject to the income limit (£26,100 for 2013/14).

(b) If net income had been £200 greater in this example, the age-related personal allowance would have been reduced by a further £100 ($1/2$ × £200) to £9,440. It cannot be reduced below this figure, regardless of the amount of extra income, as this is the basic personal allowance for 2013/14.

1.3 IT Allowances and Tax Rates

(B)

In 2013/14, a single woman born before 6 April 1938 receives UK income of £23,700, comprising state and occupational pension, and foreign income from property of £4,000 on which foreign tax of £800 has been paid.

	£	£
Tax on total income		
Pension income		23,700
Property income (foreign tax £800)		4,000
		27,700
Deduct		
Personal allowance	10,660	
Less Reduction for excess ½ (27,700 − 26,100)	800	
		9,860
Taxable income		£17,840
Tax on £17,840 at 20%		£3,568.00
Tax on total income, excluding foreign income		
Pension income		23,700
Deduct Personal allowance		10,660
Taxable income		£13,040
Tax on £13,040 at 20%		£2,608.00

Note

(a) The difference between the computations is £960.00. As the foreign tax is less than this, full credit of £800 is available against UK tax payable, leaving tax payable of (£3,568.00 − £800) £2,768.00. If the foreign tax was £1,200, the credit would be limited to £960.00 and the balance of £240 would be unrelieved. [*TIOPA 2010, s 36*].

(C)

Mr and Mrs Brown are a married couple born in 1934 and 1942 respectively. Mr Brown's net income for 2013/14 amounts to £28,200 and Mrs Brown's to £31,900. Neither spouse has any dividend income or 'savings income'. Mrs Brown elected under *ITA 2007, s 47* before 6 April 2013 to be given half the basic married couple's allowance for 2013/14 onwards. The couple have been married for many years and have not elected to be brought within the rules for couples marrying on or after 5 December 2005.

Allowances and Tax Rates — IT 1.3

Taxable income and tax payable is calculated as follows

	Mr Brown £	Mrs Brown £
Net income	28,200	31,900
Deduct Personal allowances (see below)	9,610	9,440
Taxable income	£18,590	£22,460
Tax payable:		
18,590/22,460 @ 20%	3,718.00	4,492.00
Reduction for married couple's allowance:		
6,395/1,520 (see below) @ 10%	639.50	152.00
Total liabilities	£3,078.50	£4,340.00

Calculation of allowances

Unrestricted personal allowances		10,660	10,500
Deduct $^1/_2$ × £2,100/5,800 (i.e. excess over £26,100)		1,050	2,900
		£9,610	£7,600
Add back amount required to restore to level of normal allowance			1,840
			£9,440
Unrestricted married couple's allowance		7,915	
Deduct $^1/_2$ × £2,100 =	£1,050		
Less restriction in personal allowance	1,050	—	
		7,915	
Transfer from husband to wife (£3,040 × $^1/_2$)		(1,520)	£1,520
		£6,395	

Notes

(a) The restriction in the married couple's allowance is by reference to the husband's income only.

(b) The restriction of the married couple's allowance is itself restricted by the reduction in the personal allowance. [*ITA 2007, s 45(4)*].

(c) Married couple's allowance is available only where at least one of the spouses/civil partners was born before 6 April 1935. The transfer to the wife in this example under *ITA 2007, s 47* is restricted to one half of the basic allowance, i.e. the minimum amount below which the age-related allowance may not be reduced by reference to the income of the claimant. For 2013/14 this amount is £3,040. [*ITA 2007, ss 43, 47; SI 2012 No 3047*].

(d) If the wife, but not the husband, had been born before 6 April 1935, the husband would still qualify for the married couple's allowance. The *personal* allowance is, however, calculated by reference to the individual claimant's date of birth.

1.3 IT Allowances and Tax Rates

(D)

The facts are as in (C) above except that Mr and Mrs Brown have elected under *ITA 2007, s 44* to be treated in the same way as couples who married on or after 5 December 2005. The result of this, as regards the year 2013/14, is that the married couple's allowance is initially given to *Mrs* Brown as she has the higher net income for that year. They have elected under *ITA 2007, s 47* for half of the basic allowance to be then transferred to Mr Brown.

Taxable income and tax payable is calculated as follows

		Mr Brown £	Mrs Brown £
Net income		28,200	31,900
Deduct Personal allowances (as in (C) above)		9,610	9,440
Taxable income		£18,590	£22,460
Tax payable:			
18,590/22,460 @ 20%		3,718.00	4,492.00
Restriction for married couple's allowance:			
1,520/4,555 (see below) @ 10%		152.00	455.50
		£3,566.00	£4,036.50
Calculation of married couple's allowance			
Unrestricted allowance			7,915
Deduct ¹/₂ × £5,800 (i.e. excess over £26,100)	£2,900		
Less restriction in personal allowance			
(£2,900 − 1,840)	1,060		1,840
			6,075
Transfer from wife to husband (£3,040 × ¹/₂)		£1,520	(1,520)
			£4,555

Notes

(a) *ITA 2007, s 46* applies to all couples who get married on or after 5 December 2005 and to all civil partners. Couples who married before that date may elect into this regime; the election must be made before the start of the first tax year to which it is to have effect and is irrevocable. [*ITA 2007, ss 44, 46*].

(b) Under *section 46*, the married couple's allowance is given to the partner with the higher net income instead of automatically to the husband. The allowance is then restricted by reference to that partner's income. If, as in this example, the couple were married before 5 December 2005 and the wife has the higher net income, an election into the *section 46* regime may reduce the allowance. There are no known circumstances in which an election can result in an increased allowance.

(c) It remains possible for husband and wife (and civil partners) to elect to transfer half of the basic allowance between them.

2 Accrued Income Scheme

[*ITA 2007, ss 615–681*]

2.1 The following transactions take place between individuals during the year ended 5 April 2014.

Settlement day	Sale by	Purchase by	Securities
14.8.13	X (cum div)	Y	£4,000 6¼% Treasury Loan 2018
17.9.13	X (ex div)	P	£4,000 8% Treasury Loan 2016
4.4.14	S (cum div)	Y	£2,500 4% Treasury Loan 2015

Interest payment days are as follows

6¼% Treasury Loan 2018	25 May, 25 November
8% Treasury Loan 2016	27 March, 27 September
4% Treasury Loan 2015	7 March, 7 September

Both X and Y owned chargeable securities with a nominal value in excess of £5,000 at some time in either 2012/13 or 2013/14, and both are resident in the UK. P is not resident in the UK throughout 2013/14. The maximum value of securities held by S at any time in 2013/14 and 2014/15 is £4,000.

14.8.13 transaction

The transaction occurs in the interest period from 26.5.13 to 25.11.13 (inclusive).

Number of days in interest period	184
Number of days in interest period to 14.8.13	81
Interest payable on 25.11.13	£125

The deemed payment is

$$£125 \times \frac{81}{184} = £55$$

X is treated as receiving a payment of £55 on 25.11.13. Assuming no other transfers in this kind of security in the interest period, this will also be the figure of accrued income profit chargeable.

Y is treated as making a payment of £55. Assuming no other transfers in this kind of security in the interest period, this will also be the figure of accrued income loss to set against the interest of £125 he receives on 25.11.13. £70 remains taxable.

IT   Accrued Income Scheme

17.9.13 transaction

The transaction occurs in the interest period from 28.3.13 to 27.9.13 (inclusive).

Number of days in interest period	184
Number of days in interest period from 17.9.13	10
Interest payable on 27.9.13	£160

The deemed payment is

$$£160 \times \frac{10}{184} = £\underline{9}$$

X is treated as making a payment of £9. Assuming no other transfers in this kind of security in the interest period, this will also be the figure of accrued income loss to set against the interest of £160 he receives on 27.9.13. £151 remains taxable. P is an excluded transferee (see note (a)).

4.4.14 transaction

The transaction occurs in the interest period from 8.3.14 to 7.9.14 (inclusive)

Number of days in interest period	184
Number of days in interest period to 4.4.14	28
Interest payable on 7.9.14	£50

The deemed payment is

$$£50 \times \frac{28}{184} = £\underline{7}$$

S is an excluded transferor as his holdings do not exceed £5,000 at any time in 2013/14 or 2014/15 (the year in which the interest period ends).

Y is treated as making a payment of £7. Assuming no other transfers in this kind of security in the interest period, this will also be the figure of accrued income loss to set against the interest of £50 he receives on 7.9.14. £43 remains taxable.

Note

(a)   P is an excluded transferee as he is non-resident in the UK throughout the tax year in which the transfer is made (2013/14). Had that year been 2012/13 or an earlier year, he would have been excluded only if he were both non-UK resident throughout the year of transfer and not ordinarily resident in the UK during that year. Different rules apply where a non-UK resident is trading in the UK through a branch or agency. [*ITA 2007, s 643; FA 2013, Sch 46 paras 58, 72*].

3 Capital Allowances

Cross-reference. See also 4 CAPITAL ALLOWANCES ON PLANT AND MACHINERY.

3.1 BUSINESS PREMISES RENOVATION

[*CAA 2001, ss 360A–360Z4; SI 2007 Nos 107, 945; SI 2012 No 868*]

Mickey is a jeweller who has been in business for many years and makes up accounts to 30 June each year. On 1 July 2011, he purchases the freehold of a building in the Speke ward in Liverpool. The building has been empty since June 2008, having been used before that time as a pawnbrokers. In the year ended 30 June 2011, Mickey incurs capital expenditure of £40,000 in renovating the building for use as his business premises. Mickey claims a reduced business premises renovation initial allowance of 40% of the expenditure for the year ended 30 June 2011.

The renovation is completed on 1 August 2011, and Mickey starts to use the building for the purposes of his trade on that date. In September 2012 he sells the freehold for £260,000. Of the net sale proceeds, £45,000 can be attributed to assets representing the renovation expenditure.

Mickey's allowances are as follows

		£	Residue of expenditure £
2011/12	Qualifying expenditure		40,000
	Initial allowance (maximum 100%)	16,000	(16,000)
2012/13	Writing-down allowance		
	(25% of £40,000)	10,000	(10,000)
			14,000
2013/14	Writing-down allowance	—	—
	Sale proceeds		(45,000)
	Excess of sale proceeds over residue of expenditure		£31,000
	Balancing charge (restricted to allowances made, £16,000 + £10,000)		£26,000

Notes

(a) For expenditure incurred before 6 April 2017, subject to conditions, capital allowances (known as business premises renovation allowances) are available for qualifying expenditure incurred by individuals and companies on the conversion or renovation of vacant business premises in designated development areas of the UK

3.1 IT Capital Allowances

for the purpose of bringing those premises back into business use. The premises must have been unused for at least one year before the date the work begins. Certain trades are excluded.

(b) No writing-down allowance is available for the year ended 30 June 2011 as the building is not in use for the purposes of the trade (and hence is not qualifying business premises) on 30 June 2011. It becomes qualifying business premises on 1 August 2011, so that a writing-down allowance is available for the year ended 30 June 2012. Mickey does not hold the relevant interest in the building on 30 June 2013, having sold it in September 2012, so no writing-down allowance is available for the year ended 30 June 2013.

(c) A balancing adjustment is made for the chargeable period in which the relevant interest in the building is sold (or in which certain other events occur) if the sale (or other event) occurs within seven years of the after the time the building was first used, or suitable for letting, for qualifying purposes. There is no provision for the transfer of allowances to a purchaser. [*CAA 2001, ss 360M–360P*]. If the proceeds from the event are only partly attributable to assets representing expenditure for which a business premises renovation allowance can be made, only that part of the proceeds as is so attributable, on a just and reasonable apportionment, is brought into account. [*CAA 2001, s 360Z2*].

(d) If the person entitled to business premises renovation allowances or liable to charges carries on a trade or occupies the qualifying building for the purposes of a trade, profession or vocation, the allowances/charges are treated as expenses/receipts of the trade etc. Otherwise, allowances and charges are given effect by treating them as expenses/receipts of a UK property business. If the relevant interest in the building is not an asset of such a business, the claimant is treated as if he were carrying on such a business and allowances and charges made accordingly. [*CAA 2001, ss 360Z, 360Z1*].

3.2 DREDGING

[*CAA 2001, ss 484–489*]

D is the proprietor of an estuary maintenance business preparing accounts to 30 June. Expenditure qualifying for dredging allowances is incurred as follows

	£
Year ended 30.6.12	4,000
Year ended 30.6.13	5,000

On 2 January 2014, D sells the business to an unconnected third party.

Capital Allowances IT 3.3

The allowances available are

	Cost	Residue brought forward	Allowances WDA 4%	Residue carried forward
	£	£	£	£
2012/13 (year ended 30.6.12)				
2012	4,000	—	160	3,840
2013/14				
Year ended 30.6.13				
2012	4,000	3,840	160	3,680
2013	5,000	—	200	4,800
			£360	£8,480
Six months ended 2.1.14				
Balancing allowance note (a)			£8,480	
Total allowances 2013/14 (£360 + £8,480)			£8,840	

Note

(a) On permanent cessation of the trade by the person carrying it on, including a sale other than one falling within *CAA 2001, s 488(4)(5)*, a balancing allowance is given and is equal to the excess of expenditure over writing-down allowances previously made. There are no provisions for a balancing charge or a transfer of allowances to a purchaser.

3.3 ENTERPRISE ZONE BUILDINGS

[*CAA 2001, ss 281, 298–309; FA 2008, s 86*]

(A) **Allowances**

In 2008, J, a developer, incurs expenditure of £400,000 on the construction of a building in a designated enterprise zone. The whole of the expenditure was contracted for within ten years of the site's first being included in the zone. In January 2009, he sold the building unused to K for £600,000 (excluding land). In February 2009, K let the building to a trader who immediately brought it into use as a supermarket. K claimed a reduced initial allowance of £50,000. In May 2013, he sells the building to L for £650,000 (excluding land).

K's allowances are as follows

Residue of expenditure

3.3 IT Capital Allowances

			£	£
2008/09	Qualifying expenditure			600,000
	Initial allowance (maximum 100%)		50,000	
	Writing-down allowance 25% of £600,000		150,000	
	Total allowances due		200,000	(200,000)
2009/10	Writing-down allowance		150,000	(150,000)
				250,000
2010/11	Writing-down allowance		150,000	(150,000)
				100,000
2013/14	Sale proceeds			(650,000)
				£550,000
	Balancing charge (restricted to allowances given)			£500,000

Notes

(a) Allowances for buildings in enterprise zones were given for chargeable periods beginning before 6 April 2011 on commercial buildings as well as industrial buildings.

(b) Despite the abolition of allowances for chargeable periods beginning on or after 6 April 2011, a balancing charge occurs in the chargeable period 2013/14 because the building is sold within seven years after it was first used. This applies only to enterprise zone buildings.

(c) K's qualifying expenditure would normally be the lesser of cost of construction and the net price paid by him for the building. [*CAA 2001, s 295*]. However, on purchase unused from a developer, whose profit on sale is taxable as a trading profit, his qualifying expenditure is equal to the capital sum paid for the relevant interest (excluding the land). [*CAA 2001, s 296*].

(d) K's allowances and balancing charges are treated as expenses and receipts of a UK property business. [*CAA 2001, s 353*]. K could have claimed a 100% initial allowance in 2008/09 if he had so wished.

(B) **Expenditure only partly qualifying**

The facts are as in (A) above, except that, of the £400,000 construction expenditure actually incurred, only £360,000 was contracted for within ten years of the site's first being included in an enterprise zone, and the first sale occurred after the expiry of that ten-year period.

Capital Allowances IT 3.3

K's qualifying expenditure of £600,000 (arrived at as in (A) above) is divided into an enterprise zone element and a non-enterprise zone element. [*CAA 2001, s 302*].

The enterprise zone element is

$$£600,000 \times \frac{360,000}{400,000} = \underline{£540,000}$$

The non-enterprise zone element is

$$£600,000 - £540,000 = \underline{£60,000}$$

The non-enterprise zone element does not qualify for enterprise zone allowances. [*CAA 2001, s 302(2)*]. (It could have qualified for normal industrial buildings allowances if the building had been an industrial building.)

K's allowances are as follows

			Residue of expenditure
		£	£
2008/09	Qualifying expenditure (enterprise zone element)		540,000
	Initial allowance (maximum 100%)	50,000	
	Writing-down allowance (25% of £540,000)	135,000	
		185,000	(185,000)
2009/10	Writing-down allowance	135,000	(135,000)
			220,000
2010/11	Writing-down allowance	135,000	(135,000)
			85,000
2013/14	Sale proceeds £650,000 × $\frac{540,000}{600,000}$		(585,000)
			£500,000
	Balancing charge (restricted to allowances given)		£455,000

Note

(a) The apportionment of sale proceeds in 2013/14 is considered to be 'just and reasonable' as required by *CAA 2001, s 356*.

3.4 IT   Capital Allowances

3.4 MINERAL EXTRACTION

[*CAA 2001, Pt 5*]

X has for some years operated a mining business with two mineral sources, G and S. Accounts are prepared to 30 September. On 31 December 2012 the mineral deposits and mineworks at G are sold at market value to Z for £80,000 and £175,000 respectively. A new source, P, is purchased on 30 April 2013 for £170,000 (including land with an undeveloped market value of £70,000) and the following expenditure incurred before the end of the period of account ended 30 September 2013.

	£
Plant and machinery	40,000
Construction of administration office	25,000
Construction of mining works which are likely to have little value when mining ceases	50,000
Staff hostel	35,000
Winning access to the deposits	150,000
	£300,000

During the year to 30 September 2013, X incurred expenditure of £20,000 in seeking planning permission to mine a further plot of land, Source Q. Permission was refused.

Residue of expenditure brought forward (based on accounts to 30 September 2012)		£
Mineral exploration and access	– Source G	170,000
	– Source S	200,000
Mineral assets	– Source G	95,250
	– Source S	72,000

The mineral extraction allowances due for the year ending 30.9.13 are as follows.

Source G

	£	£
Mineral exploration and access		
WDV b/f	170,000	
Proceeds	175,000	
Balancing charge	£5,000	(5,000)
Mineral assets		
WDV b/f	95,250	
Proceeds	80,000	
Balancing allowance	£15,250	15,250
Total allowances		c/f 10,250
		b/f 10,250

Source S

Mineral exploration and access

Capital Allowances   IT 3.4

WDV b/f	200,000	
WDA 25%	(50,000)	50,000
WDV c/f	£150,000	
Mineral assets		
WDV b/f	72,000	
WDA 10%	(7,200)	7,200
WDV c/f	£64,800	

Source P
Mineral exploration and access

Expenditure	150,000	
WDA 25%	(37,500)	37,500
WDA c/f	£112,500	
Mineral assets		
Expenditure	100,000	
WDV 10%	(10,000)	10,000
WDV c/f	£90,000	
Mining works		
Expenditure	50,000	
WDA 25%	(12,500)	12,500
WDV c/f	£37,500	

Source Q
Mineral exploration and access

Expenditure	20,000	
WDA 25%	(5,000)	5,000
WDV c/f	£15,000	
Total allowances (net of charges)		£132,450

Notes

(a) Expenditure on the acquisition of mineral assets, which includes expenditure on the acquisition of, or of rights in or over, both the site of a source and of mineral deposits, qualifies for a 10% writing-down allowance. Other types of expenditure qualify for a 25% writing-down allowance. [*CAA 2001, s 418(1)*].

(b) Allowances are not due on either the office or staff hostel. The plant and machinery qualify for plant and machinery allowances under *CAA 2001, Pt 2* rather than for mineral extraction allowances.

(c) Abortive expenditure on seeking planning permission is qualifying expenditure by virtue of *CAA 2001, s 396(2)(3)* as if it were expenditure on mineral exploration and access.

(d) The undeveloped market value of land is excluded from qualifying expenditure and from disposal receipts. [*CAA 2001, ss 404, 424*].

3.5 IT   Capital Allowances

3.5 PATENT RIGHTS

[*CAA 2001, ss 464–483*]

P, who prepares accounts to 31 December, acquires two new patent rights for trading purposes

	Date	Term	Cost
Patent 1	19.4.12	15 years	£4,500
Patent 2	5.10.13	5 years	£8,000

On 1.12.13 P sold part of his rights under patent 1 for £2,000.

The allowances for each patent are

	Pool £	WDA £
Y/e 31.12.12		
Expenditure (patent 1)	4,500	
WDA 25%	(1,125)	£1,125
	3,375	
Y/e 31.12.13		
Expenditure (patent 2)	8,000	
Disposal proceeds (patent 1)	(2,000)	
	9,375	
WDA 25%	(2,344)	£2,344
WDV c/f	£7,031	

3.6 RESEARCH AND DEVELOPMENT

[*CAA 2001, ss 437–451*]

C is in business manufacturing and selling cosmetics, and he prepares accounts annually to 30 June. For the purposes of this trade, he built a new laboratory adjacent to his existing premises, incurring the following expenditure

		£
April 2011	Laboratory building	50,000
June 2011	Technical equipment	3,000
March 2012	Technical equipment	4,000
July 2012	Plant	2,500
August 2013	Extension to existing premises comprising 50% further laboratory area and 50% sales offices	30,000

In September 2012 a small fire destroyed an item of equipment originally costing £2,000 in June 2011; insurance recoveries totalled £3,000. In March 2013, the plant costing £2,500 in July 2012 was sold for £1,800.

Capital Allowances IT 3.6

The allowances due are

	£
Y/e 30.6.11	
Laboratory building	50,000
Technical equipment	3,000
	£53,000
Y/e 30.6.12	
Technical equipment	4,000
	£4,000
Y/e 30.6.13	
Net allowance on plant sold (note (a))	£700
Balancing charge on equipment destroyed (note (b))	(£2,000)
Y/e 30.6.14	
Extension (note (d))	£15,000

Notes

(a) As the plant was sold in the period of account in which the expenditure was incurred, the disposal value of £1,800 is set against the expenditure of £2,500, resulting in a net allowance of £700.

(b) The destruction of the equipment in the year to 30 June 2013 results in a balancing charge limited to the allowance given. The charge accrues in the period of account in which the event occurs.

(c) A capital gain of £1,000 (£3,000 − £2,000) will also have arisen on the destruction of equipment and insurance recovery. However, the gain will be exempt from capital gains tax under the chattels exemption. [*TCGA 1992, s 262*].

(d) Capital expenditure which is only partly for research and development is apportioned on a just basis to arrive at the amount qualifying for allowances. [*CAA 2001, s 439(4)*].

4 Capital Allowances on Plant and Machinery

Cross-reference. See also 30 TRADING INCOME — CASH BASIS FOR SMALL BUSINESSES.

4.1 PERIODS OF ACCOUNT

[*CAA 2001, s 6*]

(A) **General**

James commenced business on 1 October 2011 preparing accounts initially to 30 September. He changed his accounting date in 2013, preparing accounts for the 15 months to 31 December 2013. The following capital expenditure is incurred

	Plant	Car
	£	£
1 October 2011 to 5 April 2012	49,400	4,000 (no private use)
6 April 2012 to 30 September 2012	25,000	
1 October 2012 to 31 December 2013	7,500	
Year ended 31 December 2014	4,000	

An item of plant was sold for £500 (original cost £1,000) on 25 September 2013. All of the expenditure on plant additions is AIA qualifying expenditure. (AIA = Annual Investment Allowance.) The expenditure on the car is not special rate expenditure.

Profits *before* capital allowances but otherwise as adjusted for tax purposes are as follows

	£
Year ended 30 September 2012	96,000
Period ended 31 December 2013	81,000
Year ended 31 December 2014	100,000

4.1 IT Capital Allowances on Plant and Machinery

The capital allowances are

	AIA qualifying expenditure £	Main pool £	Allowances £
Year ended 30.9.12			
Qualifying expenditure	74,400	4,000	
AIA 100% (note (b))	(61,900)		61,900
Transfer to main pool	(12,500)	12,500	
		16,500	
WDA 20%		(3,135)	3,135
WDV at 30.9.11		13,365	
Total allowances			£65,035
15 months ended 31.12.13			
Additions	7,500	7,500	
AIA 100% (note (b))		(7,500)	7,500
Disposals		(500)	
		12,865	
WDA 18% x 15/12 (note (c))		(2,895)	2,895
WDV at 31.12.13		9,970	
Total allowances			£10,395
Year ended 31.12.14			
Additions	4,000	4,000	
AIA 100% (maximum £250,000)		(4,000)	4,000
		9,970	
WDA 18%		(1,795)	1,795
WDV at 31.12.14		£8,175	
Total allowances			£5,795

Taxable profits for the periods of account concerned are

	Before CAs £	CAs £	After CAs £
Year ended 30 September 2012	96,000	65.035	30,965
Period ended 31 December 2013	81,000	10,395	70,605
Year ended 31 December 2014	100,000	5,795	94,205

Taxable profits for the first four tax years of the business are

	£	£
2011/12 (1.10.11–5.4.12) (£30,965 × 6/12)		15,482

Capital Allowances on Plant and Machinery   IT 4.1

2012/13 (y/e 30.9.12)		30,965
2013/14 (1.10.12–31.12.13)	70,605	
Deduct Overlap relief £15,482 × 3/6 note (d)	7,741	
		62,864
2014/15 (y/e 31.12.14)		94,205

Notes

(a) Capital allowances are calculated by reference to periods of account and are treated as expenses of the trade or other qualifying activity. [*CAA 2001, ss 247–262, 352–355, 360Z, 391, 392, 393T, 450, 463, 478–480, 489, 529*]. For this purpose, a period of account may exceed 12 months (but cannot exceed 18 months — see (B) below).

(b) The maximum AIA for the 12-month period of account ending on 30 September 2012 is £62,500 ((£100,000 × 6/12) + (£25,000 × 6/12)). In practice, the apportionment should be made using the precise number of days falling before and on and after 6 April 2012. For convenience in this example, it is assumed that half the period of account falls before that date, which should give an approximately accurate result. The overriding rule (see also **4.6** below) is that no more than £12,500 (£25,000 × 6/12) of expenditure incurred after 5 April 2012 can qualify. All the expenditure incurred on or before that date can qualify as this does not cause the £62,500 maximum to be exceeded. The maximum AIA is therefore £12,500 + £49,400 = £61,900.

The maximum AIA for the 15-month period of account straddling 1 January 2013 and ending on 31 December 2013 is £256,250 ((£25,000 × 3/12) + (£250,000 × 12/12)), but is restricted to the actual amount of expenditure. In practice, the apportionment should ideally be made using the precise number of days falling before and on and after 1 January 2013; for convenience, the apportionment is made using months in this example. Whilst it does not affect this example due to the small amount of qualifying expenditure, note the overriding rule at **4.7** below regarding expenditure incurred in the part of the chargeable period falling before 1 January 2013.

(c) The rate of WDA for the 12-month period of account straddling 6 April 2012 is a hybrid rate of 19% computed as below. In practice, the formula should use the precise number of days falling before and on and after 6 April 2012. For convenience in this example, it is assumed that half the period of account falls before that date, which should give an approximately accurate result.

$$R = \left(20 \times \frac{6}{12}\right) + \left(18 \times \frac{6}{12}\right) = 19\%$$

Where a period of account exceeds 12 months as is the case with the 15-month period to 31 December 2013 in this example, WDAs are proportionately increased. [*CAA 2001, s 56(3)*].

(d) The overlap profit is £15,482 being the profit taxed twice under the commencement rules. This represents 6 months' profit (1 October 2011 to 5 April 2012). As the basis period for 2013/14 is 3 months greater than one year, 3/6 of the overlap profit is relieved in that year, the balance being carried forward. For further examples on the basis of assessment for businesses see **29.1–29.3** TRADING INCOME.

4.1 IT Capital Allowances on Plant and Machinery

(B) **Period of account exceeding 18 months**

Bianca commenced business on 1 October 2011 preparing accounts initially to 30 June. She changed her accounting date in 2013/14, preparing accounts for the 21 months to 31 March 2014. The following capital expenditure was incurred

	Plant £	Motor Car £
Period ended 30 June 2012	70,000	20,000 (no private use)
21 months to 31 March 2014	10,600	

Of the £70,000 of expenditure incurred in the 9-month accounting period to 30 June 2012, £8,000 was incurred after 5 April 2012. Of the £10,600 of expenditure incurred in the 21-month period of account to 31 March 2014, £3,600 was incurred in January 2013 and £7,000 in the nine months to 31 March 2014. Apart from the car, all expenditure is AIA qualifying expenditure. The expenditure on the car is special rate expenditure.

An item of plant was sold for £641 (original cost £1,100) on 3 November 2013.

Profits *before* capital allowances but otherwise as adjusted for tax purposes are as follows

	£
Period ended 30 June 2012	79,000
Period ended 31 March 2014	112,000

The capital allowances are

	AIA qualifying expenditure £	Main pool £	Car £	Total allowances £
9 months ended 30.6.12				
Qualifying expenditure	70,000		20,000	
AIA 100% (note (d))	(56,250)			56,250
	13,750			
	(13,750)	13,750		
WDA 19.33% ×9/12 (note (e))		(1,993)		2,400
WDA 9.33% × 9/12 (note (e))			(1,400)	1,400
WDV at 30.6.12		11,757	18,600	
Total allowances				£59,643
12 months ended 30.6.13				
Additions	3,600			
AIA 100% (maximum £137,500 (note (d))	(3,600)			3,600
WDA 18%		(2,116)		2,116
WDA 8%			(1,488)	1,488

Capital Allowances on Plant and Machinery IT 4.1

WDV at 30.6.13		9,641	17,112	
Total allowances				£7,204

9 months ended 31.3.14

Additions	7,000			
AIA 100% (maximum £250,000 × 9/12 = £187,500)	(7,000)			7,000
Disposals		(641)		
		9,000		
WDA 18% × 9/12		(1,215)		1,215
WDA 8% × 9/12			(1,027)	1,027
WDV at 31.3.14		£7,785	£16,085	
Total allowances				£9,242

Taxable profits for the periods of account concerned are

	Before CAs	CAs	After CAs
	£	£	£
Period ended 30 June 2012	79,000	59,643	19,357
Period ended 31 March 2014	112,000	(7,204 + 9,242)	95,554

Taxable profits for the first three tax years of the business are

	£	£
2011/12 (1.10.11 – 5.4.12) (£19,357 × 6/9)		12,904
2012/13 (1.10.11 – 30.9.12):		
1.10.11 – 30.6.12	19,357	
1.7.12 – 30.9.12 (£95,554 × 3/21)	13,651	
		33,008
2013/14 (1.10.12 – 31.3.14) (£95,554 × 18/21)	81,903	
Deduct Overlap relief (note (f))	(12,904)	
		68,999

Notes

(a) Where a period of account for capital allowances purposes would otherwise exceed 18 months, it is broken down into shorter periods, the first beginning on the first day of the actual period and each subsequent period beginning on an anniversary of the first day of the actual period. No period can therefore exceed 12 months. [*CAA 2001, s 6(6)*].

(b) The capital allowances computed for the notional periods of account referred to in (a) above are deductible in aggregate in arriving at the adjusted profit for the actual period of account.

4.1 IT Capital Allowances on Plant and Machinery

(c) A period of account exceeding 18 months cannot normally result in an immediate change of basis period, because of *ITTOIA 2005, ss 216, 217(1)(3)*. However, the conditions of *ITTOIA 2005, s 217* do not have to be satisfied if the change of accounting period occurs in the second or third tax year of a new business, as in this example.

(d) The maximum AIA for the 9-month period of account straddling 6 April 2012 is £56,250 ((£100,000 × 6/12) + (£25,000 × 3/12)). In practice, the apportionment should ideally be made using the precise number of days falling before and on and after 6 April 2012; for convenience, the apportionment is made using months in this example. There is an overriding rule (see **4.6** below) that no more than £6,250 (£25,000 × 3/12) of expenditure incurred after 5 April 2012 can qualify. However, this does not alter the maximum in this example as there is sufficient expenditure before 6 April to cover the shortfall; thus, £50,000 of the pre-6 April expenditure qualifies, as does £6,250 of the post-5 April expenditure.

The maximum AIA for the notional 12-month period of account straddling 1 January 2013 is calculated as in **4.7** below. The maximum is £137,500 ((£25,000 × 6/12) + (£250,000 × 6/12)).

(e) The WDAs for the 9-month period of account straddling 6 April 2012 and ending on 30 June 2012 are at a hybrid rate computed as follows. In practice, the formula should use the precise number of days falling before and on and after 6 April 2012. For convenience in this example, it is assumed that two-thirds of the period of account falls before that date, which should give an approximately accurate result.

$$R = \left(20 \times \frac{6}{9}\right) + \left(18 \times \frac{3}{9}\right) = 19.33\%$$

$$R = \left(10 \times \frac{6}{9}\right) + \left(8 \times \frac{3}{9}\right) = 9.33\%$$

As the period of account is less than 12 months, WDAs are proportionately reduced (see **11.24** above).

(f) In this example, the overlap profit is £12,904 being the profit taxed twice under the commencement rules. This represents 6 months' profit (1 October 2011 to 5 April 2012). As the basis period for 2013/14 is 6 months greater than one year, the whole of the overlap profit is relieved in that year. For further examples on the basis of assessment for businesses, including commencement and cessation rules, overlap relief and changes of accounting date, see **29.1–29.3** TRADING INCOME.

4.2 SUCCESSIONS

[*CAA 2001, ss 265–267, 268, 559*]

Michael, who had been in business for a number of years, decided to retire, and he transferred the business, as a gift, to his son, Alec, on 1 May 2013. Accounts, prepared by both Michael and Alec to 30 April annually, reveal the following expenditure on, and proceeds of, plant and machinery.

Capital Allowances on Plant and Machinery IT 4.2

	Expenditure £	(Disposal Proceeds) £
Michael Period 1.5.12 – 30.4.13	7,200	–
Alec Period 1.5.13 – 30.4.14	5,000	(600)

The plant and machinery disposed of by Alec was an item transferred to him by Michael. The market value of plant and machinery at 1.5.13 totalled £18,000. In no case did an item's market value exceed its cost. The written-down value brought forward at 1.5.12 was £10,000.

The capital allowances are as follows.

(i) No election under CAA 2001, s 266

	AIA qualifying expenditure £	Main pool £	Total allowances £
Michael			
Period of account y/e 30.4.13			
WDV b/f at 1.5.12		10,000	
Additions		7,200	
Disposals (at market value)		(18,000)	
		(800)	
Balancing charge		800	£(800)
Alec			
Period of account y/e 30.4.14			
Additions qualifying for AIA	5,000		
AIA 100%	(5,000)	—	5,000
Other additions		18,000	
Disposals		(600)	
		17,400	
WDA 18%		(3,132)	3,132
WDV at 30.4.14		£14,268	
Total allowances			£8,132

4.2 IT Capital Allowances on Plant and Machinery

Note

(a) If no election is made under *CAA 2001, s 266* (see (ii) below), plant and machinery is treated as sold by the predecessor to the successor at market value, but no annual investment allowance is due to Alec on the assets transferred. [*CAA 2001, s 265*]. Similar rules apply for other assets. [*CAA 2001, s 559*]. No annual investment allowance is due for expenditure incurred in the period of account at the end of which Michael permanently ceases to carry on the trade. [*CAA 2001, ss 38B, 46(2)*].

(ii) **Election under CAA 2001, s 266**

	AIA qualifying expenditure £	Main pool £	Total allowances £
Michael			
Period of account y/e 30.4.13			
WDV b/f at 1.5.12		10,000	
Additions		7,200	
Disposals (at written-down value)		(17,200)	
Balancing allowance/charge		Nil	Nil
Alec			
Period of account y/e 30.4.14			
Additions qualifying for AIA	5,000		
AIA 100%	(5,000)	—	5,000
Other additions		17,200	
Disposals		(600)	
		16,600	
WDA 18%		(2,988)	2,988
WDV at 30.4.14		£13,612	
Total allowances			£7,988

Notes

(a) Under *CAA 2001, s 267*, plant and machinery passing to the successor is deemed to have been sold by the predecessor to the successor at such a price as to leave no balancing allowance or balancing charge. An election must be made (under *CAA 2001, s 266*) for these provisions to apply.

(b) An election under *CAA 2001, s 266* may be made only between connected persons, as defined by *section 266(5)*, must be made jointly by predecessor and successor and must be made within two years of the succession, i.e. by 1 May 2015 in this example.

(c) Annual investment allowances are not available to the successor on plant and machinery transferred under a *CAA 2001, s 266* election (by virtue of *CAA 2001, ss 214, 217*).

(d) For certain assets other than plant and machinery, a similar election is available under *CAA 2001, s 569* for certain transfers between connected persons.

4.3 POOLING, ANNUAL INVESTMENT ALLOWANCE, WRITING-DOWN ALLOWANCES, CARS, PARTIAL NON-BUSINESS USE, ACQUISITIONS FROM CONNECTED PERSONS AND BALANCING ADJUSTMENTS

A has for some years been in business as a builder and demolition contractor. He makes up his accounts to 5 April. The accounts for the year to 5 April 2014 reveal the following additions and disposals.

	£
Additions	
Plant	
Wagon	30,000
Crusher	80,000
Concrete mixer	40,000
Excavator 1	32,000
Excavator 2	50,000
Dumper Truck	5,000
Bulldozer	20,000
Fittings	
Office furniture	£28,000
Motor Vehicles	
Land Rover	6,000
Van	5,000
Car 2	21,000
Car 3	2,000
Car 4	15,000

Disposals	Cost	Proceeds
	£	£
Excavator 1	32,000	30,000
Digger loader	15,000	4,000
Car 1 (purchased before 6.4.09)	14,200	3,600
Fittings	3,500	500

The dumper truck was bought second-hand from Q, brother of A, but had not been used in a trade or other qualifying activity. The truck had originally cost Q £6,000, but its market value at sale was only £2,000.

4.3 IT Capital Allowances on Plant and Machinery

Excavator 1 was sold without having been brought into use.

The bulldozer and Car 3 were both purchased from P, father of A and had originally cost P £25,000 and £3,500 respectively. Both assets had been used for the purposes of a qualifying activity. In both cases the price paid by A was less than the market value.

Car 1 sold and the new Car 2 are both used for private motoring by A. Private use has always been 30%. Car 2 has CO_2 emissions of over 130g/km. Car 3 is occasionally borrowed by A's daughter, and the private use proportion is 20%. Car 3 has CO_2 emissions of less than 130g/km.

Car 4 was purchased new and unused on 1 July 2013 and is used for business purposes only. It is a car with low CO_2 emissions and qualifies for 100% first-year allowances under *CAA 2001, s 45D*.

The written-down values at 5 April 2013 of the main plant and machinery pool and Car 1 are £80,500 and £3,225 respectively.

The capital allowances for 12-month period of account to 5.4.14 are as follows

	Expenditure qualifying for AIA	Main pool	Car 2 partial use pool	Car 3 partial use pool	Expensive car pool (Car 1)	Total allowances
	£	£	£	£	£	£
WDV b/f		80,500			3,225	
Additions						
Wagon	30,000	30,000				
Crusher	80,000	80,000				
Concrete mixer	40,000	40,000				
Excavator 1 (note (a))	32,000	32,000				
Excavator 2	50,000	50,000				
Dumper truck (notes (b)(c))		2,000				
Bulldozer (notes (b)(d))		20,000				
Furniture	28,000	28,000				
Land Rover and van	11,000	11,000				
Cars		—	21,000	2,000		
	£271,000					
Car 4	15,000					
FYA 100%	15,000					15,000
AIA (100% on £250,000)		(250,000)				250,000

Capital Allowances on Plant and Machinery   IT 4.3

Disposals				
Excavator	(30,000)			
Digger	(4,000)			
Fittings	(500)			
Audi				(3,600)
	89,000	21,000	2,000	(£375)
WDA (18%)	(16,020)		(360)	16,380
WDA (8%)		(1,680)		1,680
Private use restriction:				
Car 2 — £1,680 @ 30%				(504)
Car 3 — £360 @ 20%	–	–	–	(72)
WDV c/f	£72,980	£19,320	£1,640	
Total allowances				£282,484
Balancing charge (Car 1) £375 less 30% private use				£263

Notes

(a) The annual investment allowance (AIA) and writing-down allowances are available even though an item of plant or machinery is disposed of without being brought into use, always provided that the expenditure is, respectively, AIA qualifying expenditure and general qualifying expenditure.

(b) If an AIA is made in respect of an amount of AIA qualifying expenditure, the expenditure is nevertheless added to the appropriate pool (or pools). Such allocation is necessary to enable a disposal value to be properly brought into account when a disposal event occurs in relation to the item in question. Following the allocation, the available qualifying expenditure in the pool (or in each pool) is reduced by the amount of the AIA on the expenditure allocated. [*CAA 2001, s 58(4A)*]. It follows that any excess of the AIA qualifying expenditure over the AIA made will qualify for WDAs beginning with the chargeable period in which the expenditure is incurred.

(c) No AIA is available in respect of an item of plant or machinery purchased from a connected person (within *CAA 2001, s 575*). [*CAA 2001, ss 213, 214, 217*].

(d) Qualifying expenditure (and AIA qualifying expenditure) on the dumper truck is restricted to the lowest of

   (i)   market value;

   (ii) capital expenditure incurred by the vendor (or, if lower, by a person connected with him);

   (iii) capital expenditure incurred by the purchaser.

   [*CAA 2001, ss 213, 214, 218(3)*].

4.3 IT   Capital Allowances on Plant and Machinery

(e) Qualifying expenditure on the bulldozer is the lesser of A's actual expenditure and the disposal value brought into account in the vendor's computations. [*CAA 2001, ss 213, 214, 218(2)*]. (The vendor's disposal value would have been market value but for the fact that the purchaser is himself entitled to claim capital allowances on the acquisition. [*CAA 2001, s 61(2)(4)*].) A's qualifying expenditure is thus equal to his actual expenditure. The same applies to the purchase of Car 3.

(f) Cars 2 and 3 are allocated to separate single asset pools by virtue their being partly used for non-business purposes. [*CAA 2001, s 206*]. Car 2 qualifies for writing-down allowances at the special rate of 8% because of its CO_2 emissions level. [*CAA 2001, ss 104A, 104AA; FA 2009, Sch 11 paras 7, 8, 26–28; FA 2013, s 68(3)(6)(8)*]. See note (e) above as regards the amount of qualifying expenditure to be brought into account in respect of Car 3. Car 4 qualifies for 100% first-year allowances under *CAA 2001, s 45D*; if the full 100% had not been claimed, the balance of the expenditure would have entered the main pool.

4.4   SHORT-LIFE ASSETS

[*CAA 2001, ss 83–89; FA 2011, s 12*]

A prepares trading accounts to 30 September each year and buys and sells machines for use in the trade as follows

	Cost	Date of acquisition	Disposal proceeds	Date of disposal
Machine X	£40,000	30.4.08	£13,000	1.12.09
Machine Y	£25,000	1.9.08	£4,000	1.12.12
Machine Z	£35,000	15.12.12	N/A	N/A

A elects under *CAA 2001, s 83* for these machines to be treated as short-life assets. It is assumed for the purposes of the example that no annual investment allowance is claimed for any of the expenditure. His pool of qualifying expenditure brought forward at the beginning of period of account 1.10.07–30.9.08 is £80,000.

A's capital allowances are as follows

	Main pool	Short-life asset pools Machine X	Short-life asset pools Machine Y	Total allowances
	£	£	£	£
Period of account 1.10.07–30.9.08				
WDV b/f	80,000			
Additions		40,000	25,000	
WDA 22.57% (note (e))	(18,056)	(9,028)	(5,643)	£32,727
	61,944	30,972	19,357	

Capital Allowances on Plant and Machinery IT 4.4

Period of account
1.10.08–30.9.09
WDA 20%	(12,389)	(6,194)	(3,871)	£22,454
	49,555	24,778	15,486	

Period of account
1.10.09–30.9.10
Disposal		(13,000)		
Balancing allowance		£11,778		11,778
WDA 20%	(9,911)		(3,097)	13,008
				£24,786
	39,644	–	12,389	

Period of account
1.10.10–30.9.11
WDA 20%	(7,929)		(2,478)	£10,407
	31,715		9,911	

Period of account
1.10.11–30.9.12
WDA 19.03% (note (e))	(6,035)		(1,886)	£7,921
	25,680		8,025	

Period of account
1.10.12–30.9.13
Transfer to main pool	8,025		(8,025)	
	33,705		—	
Disposal	(4,000)			
	29,705			
		Machine Z		
Addition		35,000		
WDA 18%	(5,347)	(6,300)		£11,647
WDV c/f	£24,358	£28,700		

Notes

(a) Only plant and machinery which is not specified in *CAA 2001, s 84* is eligible to be treated as short-life assets.

(b) Where separate identification of short-life assets is impracticable, a form of pooling may be adopted (HMRC Statement of Practice SP 1/86).

(c) The chargeable period in which the expenditure on the first two machines is incurred in this example is the period of account 1.10.07–30.9.08. The fourth anniversary of the end of that chargeable period is 30.9.12. The balance of

4.4 IT Capital Allowances on Plant and Machinery

expenditure on Machine Y is thus transferred to the main pool in the period of account 1.10.12–30.9.13, this being the first chargeable period ending after 30.9.12. [*CAA 2001, s 86(2)(3)*].

(d) The expenditure on Machine Z is incurred after 5 April 2011, so an eight-year cut-off applies. [*FA 2011, s 12*]. If the machine is not disposed of in the meantime, the balance of expenditure will be transferred to the main pool in the period of account 1.10.21–30.9.22.

(e) The hybrid rate of writing-down allowance for the year to 30 September 2008 is 22.57%, computed as follows (where 188 is the number of days from 1 October 2007 to 5 April 2008, 178 is the number of days from 6 April 2008 to 30 September 2008 and 366 is the total number of days in the period of account).

$$R = \left(25 \times \frac{188}{366}\right) + \left(20 \times \frac{178}{366}\right) = 22.57\%$$

[*FA 2008, s 80(9)–(12)*].

The hybrid rate of writing-down allowance for the year to 30 September 2012 is 19.03%, computed as follows (where 188 is the number of days from 1 October 2011 to 5 April 2012, 178 is the number of days from 6 April 2012 to 30 September 2012 and 366 is the total number of days in the period of account).

$$R = \left(20 \times \frac{188}{366}\right) + \left(18 \times \frac{178}{366}\right) = 19.03\%$$

4.5 LONG-LIFE ASSETS AND SPECIAL RATE POOL

[*CAA 2001, ss 90–104, 104A–104E*]

B prepares trading accounts to 31 December. In the year to 31 December 2007, he has new factory premises built for use in his trade, which include a building mainly in use as offices (on which 20% of the cost of the premises is expended). Industrial buildings allowances are available on the construction expenditure. The main plant and machinery pool written-down value at 1 January 2007 is £800,000, and the disposal value brought into account in respect of plant and machinery on his previous premises is £720,000. Machines installed in the new factory cost £920,000. No first-year allowances are available.

B also claims, for the year to 31 December 2007, plant and machinery allowances for expenditure of £520,000 incurred on fixtures integral to the new premises, which are agreed to have an expected life in excess of 25 years. Of this expenditure, it is agreed £120,000 should be apportioned to the offices.

On 1 May 2008 B incurs additional expenditure on upgrading the fixtures of £19,000, none of it relating to office fixtures.

On 1 May 2013 he moves to new premises, disposing of the old premises for a consideration including £425,000 relating to the integral fixtures (of which £95,000 relates to the office fixtures) and £510,000 relating to other plant and machinery.

Plant and machinery in the new premises costs £1,760,000, of which £200,000 is agreed to be long-life asset expenditure and £600,000 relates to integral features as defined by *CAA 2001, s 33A*. The full £1,760,000 is AIA (annual investment allowance) qualifying expenditure.

Capital Allowances on Plant and Machinery   IT 4.5

The plant and machinery allowances computations for relevant periods are as follows

	Main pool £	Long-life asset pool £	Special rate pool £	Total allowances
Year ending 31.12.07				
WDV b/f	800,000	—		
Additions (see note (b))	1,040,000	400,000		
Disposals	(720,000)	—		
	1,120,000	400,000		
WDA 25%/6%	280,000	24,000		304,000
WDV c/f	840,000	376,000		
Year ending 31.12.08				
Addition (see note (c))	—	19,000		
	840,000	395,000		
WDA (see note (d))	179,004	35,353		214,357
	660,996	359,647		
Transfer to special rate pool	—	359,647	359,647	
WDV c/f	660,996	—	359,647	
b/f	660,996	—	359,647	
Year ending 31.12.09				
WDA (see note (d))	132,199		35,965	168,164
WDV c/f	528,797		323,682	
Year ending 31.12.10				
WDA (see note (d))	105,759		32,368	138,127
WDV c/f	423,038		291,314	
Year ending 31.12.11				
WDA (see note (d))	84,607		29,131	£138,127
WDV c/f	338,431		262,183	
Year ending 31.12.12				
Additions	960,000		800,000	
	1,298,431		1,062,183	
AIA 100% (see note (g))			18,442	18,442
			1,043,741	
Disposals	(605,000)		(330,000)	
	693,431		713,741	
WDA (see note (e))	128,493		60,811	189,304
				£207,746
WDV c/f	564,938		652,930	
Year ending 31.12.13				
WDA (see note (h))	101,689		52,234	£153,923

39

4.5 IT Capital Allowances on Plant and Machinery

WDV c/f	£463,249	£600,696

Notes

(a) Long-life asset expenditure incurred on or before 5 April 2008 was allocated to a class pool known as the long-life asset pool. Long-life asset expenditure incurred after 5 April 2008, is allocated to the special rate pool in *CAA 2001, s 104C*.

(b) Expenditure on fixtures provided for use in offices is excluded from being on long-life assets (regardless of whether the office building itself attracts industrial buildings allowances because it represents not more than 25% of the overall cost of premises otherwise qualifying). (Where incurred after 5 April 2008, such expenditure is nevertheless special rate expenditure if it relates to integral features as defined by *CAA 2001, s 33A*.)

(c) Additional expenditure on existing long-life assets is within the provisions even if within the annual £100,000 *de minimis* limit.

(d) The WDAs in the main pool and long-asset pool are at a hybrid rate for periods of account straddling 5 April 2008, calculated as follows.

Main pool (where 96 is the number of days from 1 January 2008 to 5 April 2008, 270 is the number of days from 6 April 2008 to 31 December 2008 and 366 is the total number of days in the period of account)

$$R = \left(25 \times \frac{96}{366}\right) + \left(20 \times \frac{270}{366}\right) = 21.31\%$$

[*FA 2008, s 80(9)–(12)*].

Long-life asset pool

$$R = \left(6 \times \frac{96}{366}\right) + \left(10 \times \frac{270}{366}\right) = 8.95\%$$

[*FA 2008, s 83(1)–(3)*].

For the three years to 31 December 2011, the rate of WDA in the main pool is 20% p.a.. The rate of WDA in the special rate pool is 10% p.a. from the outset. [*CAA 2001, ss 56(1), 56A, 104D*].

(e) The WDAs in the main pool and special rate pool are at hybrid rates for periods of account straddling 5 April 2012. [*FA 2011, s 10*]. The rates are calculated as follows.

Main pool (where 96 is the number of days from 1 January 2012 to 5 April 2012, 270 is the number of days from 6 April 2012 to 31 December 2012 and 366 is the total number of days in the period of account):

$$R = \left(20 \times \frac{96}{366}\right) + \left(18 \times \frac{270}{366}\right) = 18.53\%$$

Special rate pool:

$$R = \left(10 \times \frac{96}{366}\right) + \left(8 \times \frac{270}{366}\right) = 8.52\%$$

(f) The balance of the long-life asset pool at the end of the period of account straddling 5 April 2008 is transferred to the special rate pool, and the long-life asset pool ceases to exist. [*FA 2008, s 83(4), (5)*].

(g) The annual investment allowance (AIA) is restricted to the first £25,000 of AIA qualifying expenditure incurred on and after 6 April 2012. However, for chargeable periods straddling 6 April 2012, the rule as regards expenditure incurred in the part of the chargeable period falling after 5 April 2012 is that no more than the appropriate proportion of £25,000 can qualify for the AIA (see also **4.6** below). The appropriate proportion is (where 270 is the number of days from 6 April 2012 to 31 December 2012 and 366 is the total number of days in the period of account):

$$£25,000 \times \frac{270}{366} = 18,442$$

The AIA has been allocated in this example to special rate expenditure as this maximises the WDA available in subsequent years.

(h) For the year to 31 December 2013, the rate of WDA in the main pool is 18% p.a. The rate of WDA in the special rate pool is 8% p.a.

4.6 ANNUAL INVESTMENT ALLOWANCE — PERIODS STRADDLING 6 APRIL 2012

[*CAA 2001, ss 38A, 38B, 51A; FA 2010, s 5; FA 2011, s 11*].

L is a trader making up accounts to 31 October each year. For the year ended 31 October 2012, he incurs expenditure of £72,000 on plant and machinery. £20,000 of this amount was incurred before 6 April 2012. All the expenditure is AIA qualifying expenditure.

L's maximum annual investment allowance for the year ended 31 October 2012 is computed as follows

Period 1.11.11 to 5.4.12 (157 days)

$$\text{Maximum} \quad £100,000 \times \frac{157}{366} \qquad \qquad 42,896$$

Period 6.4.12 to 31.10.12 (209 days)

$$\text{Maximum} \quad £25,000 \times \frac{209}{366} \qquad \qquad \underline{14,276}$$

Maximum qualifying for AIAs for the year £57,172

Further adjustment

4.6 IT Capital Allowances on Plant and Machinery

However, there is an overriding rule, as regards expenditure incurred in the part of the period of account falling after 5 April 2012, that no more than the appropriate proportion of £25,000 (£14,276 in this example) can qualify for the AIA.

Therefore, the expenditure of £20,000 for the period 1.11.11 to 5.4.12 qualifies in full, but only £14,276 of the expenditure of £52,000 incurred after 5.4.12 qualifies. The maximum AIA for the year is £34,276 (20,000 + 14,276).

If the total expenditure of £72,000 had been split as to £52,000 incurred on or before 5 April 2012 and £20,000 thereafter, £57,172 would have qualified for AIAs.

4.7 ANNUAL INVESTMENT ALLOWANCE — PERIODS STRADDLING 1 JANUARY 2013

[*CAA 2001, ss 38A, 38B, 51A; FA 2010, s 5; FA 2011, s 11; FA 2013, s 7, Sch 1*].

(A) Periods not also spanning 6 April 2012

M is a trader making up accounts to 30 September each year. For the year ended 30 September 2013, he incurs expenditure of £162,000 on plant and machinery. £40,000 of this amount was incurred before 1 January 2013. All the expenditure is AIA qualifying expenditure.

M's maximum annual investment allowance for the year ended 30 September 2013 is computed as follows

Period 1.10.12 to 31.12.12 (92 days)

$$\text{Maximum} \quad £25,000 \times \frac{92}{365} \qquad \qquad 6,301$$

Period 1.1.13 to 30.9.13 (273 days)

$$\text{Maximum} \quad £250,000 \times \frac{273}{365} \qquad \qquad \underline{186,986}$$

Maximum qualifying for AIAs for the year $\qquad \qquad \underline{£193,287}$

Further adjustment

However, there is an overriding rule, as regards expenditure incurred in the part of the period of account falling before 1 January 2013, that no more than no more than £25,000 of such expenditure can qualify for the AIA.

Therefore, the expenditure of £122,000 for the period 1.1.13 to 30.9.13 qualifies in full, but only £25,000 of the expenditure of £40,000 incurred before 1.1.13 qualifies. The maximum AIA for the year is £147,000 (25,000 + 122,000).

If the total expenditure of £162,000 had been split as to £25,000 incurred before 1 January 2013 and £137,000 thereafter, it would all have qualified for AIAs.

Capital Allowances on Plant and Machinery   IT 4.7

(B) **Periods spanning both 6 April 2012 and 1 January 2013**

An individual trading as Damnation prepares accounts to the end of January each year. For the year ended 31 January 2013, Damnation incurs expenditure of £63,000 on plant and machinery. £20,000 of this amount was incurred before 6 April 2012, £21,000 in the period 6 April 2012 to 31 December 2012 and £22,000 in the month of January 2013. All the expenditure is AIA qualifying expenditure.

Damnation's maximum annual investment allowance for the year ended 31 January 2013 is computed as follows

Period 1.2.12 to 5.4.12 (65 days)

$$\text{Maximum } £100,000 \times \frac{65}{366} \qquad 17,759$$

Period 6.4.12 to 31.12.12 (270 days)

$$\text{Maximum } £25,000 \times \frac{270}{366} \qquad 18,443$$

Period 1.1.13 to 31.1.13 (31 days)

$$\text{Maximum } £250,000 \times \frac{31}{366} \qquad 21,175$$

Maximum qualifying for AIAs for the year £57,377

Consideration of further adjustments

However, there are three overriding rules to be considered.

The first overriding rule is that, as regards expenditure incurred before 6.4.12, the maximum that can qualify for the AIA is calculated as if the increase from £25,000 to £250,000 had not taken place. This brings into account the rules in **4.6** above for periods straddling 6 April 2012. For Damnation, this maximum is: (£100,000 x 65/366) + (£25,000 x 301/366) = £38,319.

The second overriding rule is that, as regards expenditure incurred in the period 6.4.12 to 31.12.12, the maximum that can qualify for the AIA is: A – B, where:

A = the amount that would have been the maximum for the period 6.4.12 to 31.1.13 if the increase from £25,000 to £250,000 had not taken place; and

B = the amount (if any) by which the AIA expenditure incurred before 6.4.12 (and in respect of which an AIA claim is actually made) exceeds what would be the maximum allowance for the period 1.2.12 to 5.4.12 if it were treated as a separate chargeable period.

For Damnation, A = (£25,000 x 301/366) = £20,560. On the assumption that Damnation claims AIA for the full £20,000 of expenditure incurred before 6.4.12, B = (£20,000 – £17,759) = £2,241. (The maximum allowance for the period 1.2.12 to 5.4.12 if it were treated as a separate chargeable period is £17,759 (£100,000 x 65/366).) Therefore, A – B = (£20,560 – £2,241) = £18,319.

4.7 IT Capital Allowances on Plant and Machinery

The third overriding rule is that, as regards expenditure incurred after 31.12.12, the maximum that can qualify for the AIA is the sum of each maximum allowance that would be found if the periods 6.4.12 to 31.12.12 and 1.1.13 to 31.1.13 were each treated as separate chargeable periods. For Damnation, this sum is: (£25,000 x 270/366) + (£250,000 x 31/366) = £39,618.

So for Damnation the maximum that can qualify for the AIA in respect of the three periods in question are, respectively, £38,319, £18,319 and £39,618. But this does not alter the fact that the maximum AIA that Damnation can claim for the full 12-month period ending on 31 January 2013 is £57,377 as already calculated above before applying the overriding rules. As Damnation has already claimed £20,000 for the first period and is limited to £18,319 for the second, it can claim a further £19,058, making £57,377 in all.

4.8 VAT CAPITAL GOODS SCHEME

[*CAA 2001, ss 234–246, 546–551*]

T Ltd carries on a trade which is partially exempt for VAT purposes, and draws up accounts to 31 March each year. Its partial exemption year also runs to 31 March. On 1 May 2008, the company acquired computer equipment at a cost of £100,000 plus VAT of £17,500. The company had a written-down value of £40,000 on its plant and machinery main pool at 1 April 2008 and, for the purposes of this example, it is assumed that there are no other acquisitions and no disposals during the period covered.

T Ltd's claimable percentage of non-attributable input tax for the partial exemption years ended 31 March 2009, 2010, 2011 and 2012 is as follows

Year ended	
31.3.09	75%
31.3.10	80%
31.3.11	65%
31.3.12	65%

The input tax position is as follows

	Computer
Year ended 31.3.09 Initial input tax claim: £17,500 × 75%	£13,125
Year ended 31.3.10 Additional VAT rebate: $\frac{17{,}500}{5} \times (80 - 75)\%$	£175
Year ended 31.3.11 Additional VAT liability: $\frac{17{,}500}{5} \times (75 - 65)\%$	£350

Capital Allowances on Plant and Machinery   IT 4.8

Year ended 31.3.12
Additional VAT liability:

$$\frac{17,500}{5} \times (75-65)\% \qquad \underline{£350}$$

T Ltd deals with the appropriate VAT capital goods scheme adjustments in its quarterly VAT return to 30 September following each partial exemption year.

The capital allowances computations are as follows

Plant and machinery

	Qualifying for AIAs £	Main pool £	Total allowances £
Year to 31.3.09			
WDV at 1.4.08		40,000	
Addition (£100,000 + £(17,500 – 13,125))	104,375		
AIA 100% (maximum £50,000)	(50,000)	54,375	50,000
		94,375	
WDA 20%		(18,875)	18,875
			£68,875
		75,500	
Year to 31.3.10			
WDA 20%		(15,100)	£15,100
		60,400	
Year to 31.3.11			
Disposal value		(175)	
		60,225	
WDA 20%		(12,045)	£12,045
		c/f 38,180	
		b/f 38,180	
Year to 31.3.12			
Addition	350		
AIA 100% (maximum £100,000)	(350)	—	350
WDA 20%		(7,636)	7,636

4.8 IT Capital Allowances on Plant and Machinery

Plant and machinery

		30,544	—
			£7,986
Year to 31.3.13			
Addition	350		
AIA 100% (maximum £25,000)	(350)	—	350
WDA 18%		(5,498)	5,498
WDV at 31.3.13		£25,046	—
			£5,848

Notes

(a) For the purpose of determining the chargeable period in which capital allowances are to be adjusted by reference to any additional VAT rebate/liability, the rebate/liability is treated as accruing on the last day of the VAT return period in which the adjustment is made (i.e. the return for the quarter to 30 September in the chargeable period). [*CAA 2001, s 549*].

(b) Where expenditure was AIA qualifying expenditure (i.e. it qualified for the annual investment allowance), any additional VAT liability incurred in respect of that expenditure at a time when the plant or machinery is provided for the purposes of the qualifying activity, is also AIA qualifying expenditure — for the chargeable period in which the liability accrues. [*CAA 2001, s 236(3A)–(3C)*].

5 Charities

5.1 DONATIONS TO CHARITY

[*ITA 2007, ss 414, 415, 423–425*]

(A) **Higher rate taxpayer**

Ronan, a single man born after 5 April 1948, has total income of £42,875 for 2013/14, which consists entirely of employment income. During that year, he makes a number of payments to charity, all of them qualifying donations, amounting in total to £600.

Ronan's income tax liability for 2013/14 is as follows

	£
Total and net income	42,875
Less Personal allowance	9,440
Taxable income	£33,435
Tax liability	
32,760 at 20%	6,552.00
675 at 40%	270.00
£33,435	£6,822.00

Notes

(a) The basic rate limit of £32,010 is increased by the grossed up amount of the qualifying donations (£600 × 100/80 = £750) and becomes £32,760. Ronan thereby saves tax of £150 (£750 × 20% (40% − 20%)). The charities will reclaim basic rate tax of £150 (£750 × 20%) and will thus receive £750 in all. The net cost to Ronan is £450 (£600 − £150), a saving of 40%. (The tax relief can, in fact, exceed 40% where the effect of extending the basic rate limit is that an additional amount of dividend income falls within the basic rate band and is taxed at 10% instead of at 32.5% (see (B) below).

(b) Gift aid donations may, by election, be treated as made in the preceding year of assessment. The election must be made on or before the date the donor submits his tax return for that preceding year and not later than 31 January following that year. An election cannot be made if insufficient income tax or capital gains tax was payable for the preceding year to cover the tax deducted from the payment. [*ITA 2007, ss 426, 427*].

(B) **Higher rate taxpayer with dividend income**

The facts are as in (A) above except that £10,000 of Ronan's income is UK dividend income.

5.1 IT Charities

Ronan's income tax liability for 2013/14 is as follows

	£
Employment income	32,875
Dividend income (inclusive of tax credits)	10,000
Total and net income	42,875
Less Personal allowance	9,440
Taxable income	£33,435

Tax liability		
23,435	at 20%	4,687.00
9,325	at 10%	932.50
32,760		
675	at 32.5%	219.37
£33,435		£5,838.87

Notes

(a) As in (A) above, the basic rate limit (£32,010) is increased by the grossed up amount of the qualifying donations (£750) and thus becomes £32,760. But this time the tax saving is £168.75; this reflects the fact that the donation has the effect of pushing £750 of dividend income back into the basic rate band, a saving of 22.5% (32.5% − 10%) instead of the usual 20% (40% − 20%). Ronan's relief at source is still £150 (£750 − £600). His total relief is thus £318.75 which gives him total relief of 42.5% (not 40%) on the grossed up amount of the gift (£750).

(b) The tax liability will of course be reduced by tax credits of £1,000 attached to the dividends.

(C) **Additional rate taxpayer**

Rikki, a single man born after 5 April 1948, has total income of £175,000 for 2013/14, none of which is dividend income. During that year, he makes qualifying donations to charity of £2,400.

Rikki's income tax liability for 2013/14 is as follows

	£
Total and net income	175,000
Less Personal allowance (note (b))	Nil
Taxable income	£175,000

Tax liability		
35,010	at 20%	7,002.00
117,990	at 40%	47,196.00
22,000	at 45%	9,900.00

Charities IT 5.1

£175,000   £64,098.00

Notes

(a) Both the basic rate limit of £32,010 and the higher rate limit of £150,000 are increased by the grossed up amount of the qualifying donations (£2,400 × 100/80 = £3,000) and become £35,010 and £153,000 respectively. Rikki thereby saves tax of £750 (£3,000 × 25% (45% − 20%)). [ITA 2007, s 414(2)(b); FA 2009, Sch 2 para 6]. The charities will reclaim basic rate tax of £600 (£3,000 × 20%) and will thus receive £3,000 in all. The net cost to Rikki is £1,650 (£2,400 − £750), a saving of 45%.

(b) No personal allowance is available in this example as income is too far above the £100,000 income limit. [ITA 2007, s 35; FA 2009, s 4(1)(4)].

(D) **Low income taxpayer**

Rod, a single person born in 1947, has a State pension of £7,850 and UK dividends of £2,700 (with tax credits of £300) for 2013/14. He makes a qualifying donation of £400 to charity.

Rod's income tax liability for 2013/14 is as follows

		£
Pension income		7,850
Dividends plus tax credits		3,000
Total and net income		10,850
Less Personal allowance	10,500	
Restricted by (see note (a))	650	9,850
Taxable income		£1,000
Tax liability		
1,000 at 10%		100.00
Deduct tax credits on dividends (see note (b))		100.00
		Nil

Notes

(a) The personal allowance is restricted by such amount as is necessary to leave tax of £100.00 in charge, this being the amount of basic rate tax deemed to have been deducted at source from the qualifying donation (£400 × 20/80 = £100). [ITA 2007, s 423].

(b) Although dividend tax credits of £300 are available, the deduction is limited to 10% of the taxable income (as dividend tax credits are not repayable).

6 Deceased Estates

[*ITTOIA 2005, ss 649–680A, 681, 682*]

6.1 ESTATE INCOME: ABSOLUTE INTEREST

C died on 5 July 2011 leaving his estate of £400,000 divisible equally between his three children. The income arising and administration expenses paid in the administration period which ends on 25 January 2014 are as follows

	\multicolumn{2}{c}{*Period to 5.4.12*}	\multicolumn{2}{c}{*Year to 5.4.13*}	\multicolumn{2}{c}{*Period to 25.1.14*}
	£	£	£	£	£	£
UK dividends (net)		16,875		9,900		3,375
Administration expenses chargeable to income		(1,500)		(750)		(300)
		15,375		9,150		3,075
Other income (gross)	10,000		3,200		975	
Basic rate tax thereon payable by executors	(2,000)		(640)		(195)	
		8,000		2,560		780
Net residuary income		£23,375		£11,710		£3,855
Each child's share		£7,792		£3,903		£1,285

Dates and amounts of payments to each child are as follows

	Payment
	£
30.4.12	5,000
16.10.12	3,500
21.6.13	2,500
22.1.14	1,000
30.7.14	980

Each child's assumed income entitlement is as follows

	2011/12	2012/13	2013/14
	£	£	£
Cumulative income entitlement (net)	7,792	11,695	12,980
Deduct net equivalents of amounts taxed in previous years	Nil	Nil	8,500
Assumed income entitlement	£7,792	£11,695	£4,480

6.1 IT Deceased Estates

For all years other than the final tax year (i.e. the year in which the administration period ends), compare the assumed income entitlement with the payments made.

	2011/12	2012/13
Assumed income entitlement	£7,792	£11,695
Payments made	Nil	£8,500
Lower amount is the taxable amount (subject to grossing up)	Nil	£8,500

For the final tax year (2013/14), the taxable amount (subject to grossing up) is the amount of the assumed income entitlement (£4,480).

The children's income from the estate for tax purposes is as follows

	2011/12	2012/13	2013/14
Each child's share of income (net)	Nil	£8,500	£4,480
Each child's share of basic rate income	Nil	3,250*	260
Basic rate tax	Nil	880	65
Gross basic rate income	Nil	£4,400	£325
* £(8,000 + 2,560) × 1/3 = £3,520.			
Each child's share of dividend income	Nil	4,980	4,220
Dividend tax credit	Nil	553	469
Gross dividend income	Nil	£5,533	£4,689

Notes

(a) A beneficiary with an absolute interest is chargeable to income tax on income treated as arising in a tax year from the interest if he has an 'assumed income entitlement' (see *ITTOIA 2005, s 665*) for the year and a payment is made in respect of the interest in the year and before the end of the administration period. For the year in which the administration period ends (the '*final tax year*'), income is treated as arising if the beneficiary has an assumed income entitlement for the year (whether or not any payments are made). [*ITTOIA 2005, s 652*].

(b) Payments to a beneficiary of an estate are deemed to be made out of his share of income bearing tax at the basic rate in priority to his share of income bearing tax at the dividend ordinary rate. [*ITTOIA 2005, s 679*]. Therefore, administration expenses chargeable to income are effectively relieved primarily against dividend income.

(c) Each beneficiary would receive tax certificates (Forms R185 (Estate Income)) showing the gross amount of his entitlement and the tax paid by the personal representatives. Where the estate has dividend income bearing tax at the dividend ordinary rate, the tax certificate shows such income separately from income which has borne tax at the basic rate.

(d) In the hands of a beneficiary, estate income which has borne tax at the dividend ordinary rate is treated as dividend income. The beneficiary will have a further liability only to the extent that such income exceeds the basic rate limit. [*ITTOIA 2005, s 680A*]. Dividend tax credits are not, however, repayable.

Deceased Estates **IT 6.2**

(e) The beneficiaries' shares of income are grossed up at the rate for the year in which the income is treated as arising to them, rather than, if different, the year in which the income is received, and tax accounted for, by the trustees. [*ITTOIA 2005, s 656*].

6.2 ESTATE INCOME: LIMITED INTEREST

Mrs D died on 5 January 2007 leaving her whole estate with a life interest to her husband and then the capital to her children on his death. The administration of the estate was completed on 7 February 2009. Mr D received payments on account of income of £1,200 on 30 September 2007, £2,500 on 31 December 2008, £1,050 on 7 February 2009 and £340 on 31 May 2009.

The actual income and deductible expenses of the estate were as follows

	2006/07 (from 6.1.06) £	2007/08 £	2008/09 (to 7.2.09) £
Interest received (net)	750	2,400	2,000
Other income (gross)	400	600	200
Basic rate tax thereon	(88)	(132)	(40)
Expenses	(150)	(450)	(400)
Net income available for distribution	£912	£2,418	£1,760

D's income from the estate for tax purposes is calculated as follows

	2006/07	2007/08 Basic rate income	2007/08 Savings rate income	2008/09 Basic rate income
	£	£	£	£
Net income	Nil	780[*]	420[*]	3,890
Basic rate tax		220	105	972
Savings rate tax	—	—	—	—
Gross income	Nil	£1,000	£525	£4,862

[*] The payments to the beneficiary in each year prior to 2008/09 must be allocated between (i) income bearing tax at the basic rate and (ii) income bearing tax at the savings rate, (i) taking priority over (ii). Total basic rate income for 2006/07 and 2007/08 is £780 (£400 − £600 − £88 − £132), so £780 of the £1,200 payment in 2007/08 is deemed to have been made out of basic rate income.

Notes

(a) The £340 paid to D in May 2009 remains payable on completion of administration and is thus treated as income of the beneficiary for the tax year in which the administration period ends, i.e. 2008/09. [*ITTOIA 2005, ss 654(3), 661*].

(b) See also notes (*b*) to (*e*) to **6.1** above.

6.2 IT Deceased Estates

(c) For 2008/09, D is also likely to have taxable income from his life interest in his wife's settlement. This will be income covering the period 8 February 2009 to 5 April 2009. It does not enter into the above calculations, but is dealt with as in **26.3**(A) SETTLEMENTS.

(d) Had the death and all other events occurred, say, five years later, the computation would have proceeded in the same way but without the added complication of distinguishing between basic rate income and savings rate income.

7 Double Tax Relief

7.1 RELIEF BY CREDIT

[*TIOPA 2010, ss 18–41*].

(A)

A single man has, for 2013/14, UK earnings of £20,895 and foreign income from property of £2,000 on which foreign tax of £300 has been paid. He is entitled to the personal allowance of £9,440.

(i) *Tax on total income*

	£
Employment income	20,895
Income from property (foreign tax £300)	2,000
	22,895
Personal allowance	9,440
Taxable income	£13,455
Tax on £13,455 @ 20%	£2,691.00

(ii) *Tax on total income less foreign income*

	£
Employment income	20,895
Personal allowance	9,440
Taxable income	£11,455
Tax on £11,455 @ 20%	£2,291.00

The difference in tax between (i) and (ii) is £400. The foreign tax is less than this and full credit of £300 is available against the UK tax payable. If the foreign tax was £600, the credit would be limited to £400 and the balance of £200 would be unrelieved.

(B)

A UK resident has the following income, allowances and UK tax liability for the year 2013/14 before double tax relief

	£
Earned income	
UK directorship	24,075
USA directorship (foreign tax £1,200)	6,000
Dutch partnership (foreign tax £3,750)	7,500
	37,575

7.1 IT Double Tax Relief

Unearned income	
UK dividends and tax credits	5,600
Foreign bank interest (foreign tax £300)	2,000
Total income	45,175
Deduct Personal allowance	9,440
Taxable income	£35,735
Tax on £30,135 at basic rate (20%)	6,027.00
£1,875 at dividend ordinary rate (10%)	187.50
£3,725 at dividend upper rate (32.5%)	1,210.62
Tax borne before double tax relief	£7,425.12

The maximum double tax relief is obtained by progressively taking relief for each foreign source with the source with the highest rate of foreign tax being eliminated first. [*TIOPA 2010, s 36*].

	£	£	£
Taxable income from all sources	35,735	35,735	35,735
Deduct foreign income			
Dutch partnership	(7,500)	(7,500)	(7,500)
USA directorship	—	(6,000)	(6,000)
Dividends	—	—	(2,000)
	£28,235	£22,235	£20,235
Tax thereon (see note (a))	5,087.00	3,887.00	3,487.00
Tax on income before eliminating foreign source under review	7,425.12	5,087.00	3,887.00
Tax attributable to that source (A)	£2,338.12	£1,200.00	£400.00
Foreign tax suffered (B)	£3,750.00	£1,200.00	£300.00
Double tax relief i.e. lesser of (A) and (B)	£2,338.12	£1,200.00	£300.00

The UK income tax borne after credit for double tax relief is	
As computed before double tax relief	£7,425.12
Deduct Double tax relief	3,838.12
	£3,587.00

Notes

(a) The recalculation of tax after each element of foreign income has been deducted is as follows

Double Tax Relief IT 7.1

	£	£	£
Non-dividend income	32,075	26,075	24,075
Deduct Personal allowance	9,440	9,440	9,440
	£22,635	£16,635	£14,635
Tax at basic rate (20%) on	22,635	16,635	14,635
Tax at dividend ordinary rate (10%) on	5,600	5,600	5,600
	£28,235	£22,235	£20,235
Tax at basic rate (20%)	4,527.00	3,327.00	2,927.00
Tax at dividend ordinary rate (10%)	560.00	560.00	560.00
	£5,087.00	£3,887.00	£3,487.00

(b) The UK tax borne is partly satisfied by tax credits of £560 on UK dividends. This, together with any UK tax paid under PAYE will be deducted from the tax borne of £3,587.00 in arriving at the net liability. However, the dividend tax credits are not repayable.

8 Employment Income

8.1 DUTIES PERFORMED ABROAD — TRAVEL COSTS AND EXPENSES

[*ITEPA 2003, ss 370, 371; FA 2013, Sch 46 paras 35, 72*]

M, a married man resident in the UK, is employed by Bigbuild Ltd in Milnrow at a salary of £40,000 per annum and is involved in the management of the following construction projects.

29.8.13 – 30.11.13	Office block in Philippines
9.12.13 – 15.1.14	Factory in Germany
19.3.14 – 27.6.14	Housing development in Spain

Details of travel expenses incurred in 2013/14 are

		By M £	Reimbursed By Bigbuild £	By Bigbuild £
28. 8.13	Milnrow – Heathrow Airport (M)	40		
29. 8.13	Heathrow – Philippines (M)			400
20.10.13	Milnrow – Philippines (wife and children)			1,000
30.10.13	Philippines – Milnrow (wife and children)			1,000
30.11.13	Philippines – Milnrow (M)	500	500	
9.12.13	Milnrow – Manchester Airport (M)	10	10	
9.12.13	Manchester – Germany (M)			100
10.12.13	Milnrow – Germany (wife and children)			300
3. 1.14	Germany – Milnrow (wife and children)	300	300	
15. 1.14	Germany – Milnrow (M)			100
19. 3.14	Milnrow – Spain (M)	150	150	
31.3.14	Milnrow – Spain (wife)	60		150
		£1,060	£960	£3,050

8.1 IT Employment Income

M's 2013/14 taxable income is as follows

	£	£
Salary		40,000
Cost of expenses incurred by Bigbuild		3,050
Reimbursed travel expenses		960
		39,010
Allowable part of expenses incurred by Bigbuild (note (a))	2,750	
Allowable expenses incurred by M (note (a))	700	
Personal allowance	9,440	12,890
		£26,120

Note

(a) A deduction is allowed for travelling expenses of the employee from any place in the UK to take up the overseas employment. In addition where the employee is out of the UK for 60 days or more continuously, an allowance is available for up to two outward and two return trips per fiscal year for the employee's wife and minor children provided the expense is borne or reimbursed by the employer. As M is away for less than 60 days in Germany, he cannot deduct the cost of his family's Christmas and New Year trip. The part of the cost of his wife's trip to Spain not reimbursed cannot be deducted.

8.2 ALLOWABLE DEDUCTIONS

(A) **Mileage allowances**

[*ITEPA 2003, ss 229–236; SI 2011 No 896*]

D is employed as a buyer by CB Ltd and uses his own car for business. CB Ltd pays its employees a standard mileage allowance of 62 pence per business mile for 2013/14. D's business mileage is 18,000 in 2013/14.

The amount to be included in D's taxable employment income for 2013/14 is as follows

	£	£
Mileage allowances received 18,000 × 62p		11,160
Tax free rates:		
First 10,000 business miles at 45p	4,500	
Balance of 8,000 miles at 25p	2,000	6,500
Taxable amount		£4,660

Notes

(a) Mileage allowance payments are taxable only to the extent that, in total for the year, they exceed the approved rates. For 2012/13 onwards the approved rates for cars and vans are 45 pence per mile for the first 10,000 miles and 25 pence per mile thereafter. The same rates apply to all cars and vans, regardless of cylinder capacity. [*ITEPA 2003, ss 229, 230; SI 2011 No 896*].

(b) Where no mileage allowance payments are made, or payments are made at a rate lower than the approved rates, the employee may claim a deduction ('mileage allowance relief') for business mileage of an amount equal to the approved rates or, as the case may be, equal to the excess of the approved rates over the payments. [*ITEPA 2003, ss 231, 232*].

(c) In addition to the mileage allowances, employers can make 'approved passenger payments', taxable only to the extent that they exceed 5 pence per mile. If no such payment is made, however, the employee may not claim a deduction as in (*b*) above. [*ITEPA 2003, ss 233, 234*].

(d) Relief as in (a) and (b) above is also available in respect of business use of a cycle or motorcycle. The approved rates are 20 pence per mile for cycles and 24 pence per mile for motorcycles.

(e) No other method can be used to calculate relief for business use of an employee's own vehicle, and capital allowances are not available. [*CAA 2001, s 36(1)(a)*].

(B) **Travelling expenses generally**

[*ITEPA 2003, ss 336–340*]

Three employees of Fixit Ltd, which has offices in Central London and a main depot in Chelmsford in Essex, incur travelling expenses as follows in 2013/14.

(1) A, who lives in Surrey, normally works in the London office, travelling in by train. She has to attend a monthly meeting of managers in Chelmsford, to which she travels direct by car. She is able to claim a deduction for the costs of travel to Chelmsford.

(2) B, who lives in North London and normally drives to work in the Chelmsford office, occasionally calls in at the London office to pick up urgent packages. He also frequently visits, on his way to the Chelmsford office, a customer whose offices are close to Fixit Ltd in Chelmsford, to check on work in progress. He is allowed the costs of travel on days when he visits the London office. It is unlikely that he will be allowed the costs of travel when he visits the customer in Chelmsford; an employee cannot turn what is really an ordinary commuting journey into a business journey simply by arranging a business appointment along the way (HMRC Employment Income Manual EIM32060).

(3) C is an operative living in a defined area of Kent, in which he has responsibility for serving all the company's customers. He occasionally calls at the Chelmsford office to discuss new contracts, but generally arranges call-outs by telephone. He is allowed in full the costs of travel within the defined area, the whole of which is defined as his 'permanent workplace'. He is also allowed the costs of travel to the Chelmsford office, as this is not a permanent workplace.

8.3 IT   Employment Income

8.3 DIRECTORS AND EMPLOYEES (OTHER THAN LOWER-PAID EMPLOYEES) — BENEFITS CODE

(A) **Cars and fuel**

[*ITEPA 2003, ss 114–153*]

(i)

A, B and C are employees of D Ltd. Each earns at least £8,500 per annum and each is provided with a company car throughout 2013/14. The company also bears at least part of the cost of petrol for private motoring.

A is provided with a 1,800 cc car first registered in January 2011 with a list price (including VAT, car tax (but not road tax), delivery charges and standard accessories) of £19,000. The car was made available to A in April 2011. It has a diesel engine and a CO_2 emissions figure of 185g/km. An immobilisor was fitted in September 2011 at a cost of £200. A is required to pay the company £250 per year as a condition of using the car for private motoring, and duly pays this amount.

B is provided with a 1,400 cc car first registered in March 2010 with a list price of £9,000. It has an emissions figure of 90g/km. B was required to make a capital contribution of £1,000 on provision of the car in January 2012. B leaves the company in March 2014 and returns the car to D Ltd on 16 March. B was required to pay the company £50 per year as a condition of using the car for private motoring, and duly paid this amount.

C is provided with a luxury car first registered in February 2012 with a list price of £88,000 (which includes the list price of non-standard accessories). He made a capital contribution of £3,000 in 2011/12. The car's CO_2 emissions figure is 280g/km.

Car and fuel benefits for 2013/14 are as follows

	A	B	C
	£	£	£
List price	19,000	9,000	88,000
Later accessories	200	—	—
	19,200		
Capital contributions	—	(1,000)	(3,000)
Price of car	£19,200	£8,000	£85,000
Cash equivalent — 32% (29% + 3% (including diesel supplement)	6,144		
— 10%		800	
— 35%			29,750
Deduction for unavailability (£800 × 20/365)		(44)	
		756	
Contribution for private use	(250)	(50)	—
Car benefit	5,894	706	29,750
Fuel benefit (£21,100 @ 32%)	6,752		

(£21,100 @ 10%)		2,110	
(£21,100 @ 35%)			7,385
Deduction for unavailability			
(£2,110 × 20/365)		(116)	
Total car and fuel benefits	£12,646	£2,700	£37,135

Notes

(a) For cars which have an approved carbon dioxide emissions figure, the benefit is a percentage of the car's list price determined by reference to the level of those emissions. [*ITEPA 2003, ss 133–142*].

(b) The price of the car is ascertained under *ITEPA 2003, ss 122–132*.

(c) The fuel benefit charge is computed by taking the car benefit percentage ascertained in (a) above and applying it to a set figure of £21,100 (£20,200 for 2012/13). [*ITEPA 2003, ss 149–153; SI 2012 Nos 915, 3037*].

(ii)

J is Managing Director of K Ltd and during the year ended 5 April 2014 the company provided two cars for his use. Car 1 was a two-year old car (2,200 cc with CO2 emissions of 240g/km and a list price of £20,000) and it was used by J for both business and private purposes until 31 October 2013 when it was written off as a result of an accident. J was subsequently prosecuted for dangerous driving, banned for one year and incurred legal costs of £800 which were ultimately paid for by K Ltd. In the period 6 April 2013 to 31 October 2013 J had paid the company £30 per month as a contribution towards private fuel. J was then provided with the use of a new 2-litre car (Car 2) and, since at first he had injuries which prevented him from driving and later lost his licence, a chauffeur. This replacement car was to be used for business purposes only.

J's benefits for 2013/14 relating to the cars are

	£
Car 1	
Car benefit £20,000 @ 35%	7,000
Fuel benefit £21,100 @ 35%	7,385
	£14,385
Proportion for period 6.4.13–31.10.13	
($^{209}/_{365}$ × £14,385)	8,237
Legal costs	800
Car 2	
Annual scale charge	—
Provision of chauffeur	—
	£9,037

8.3 IT   Employment Income

Notes

(a) For 2013/14 the percentage used to compute the car and fuel benefits is 11% at a carbon dioxide emissions level of 95g/km plus 1% for each additional 5g/km up to a maximum of 35%. The maximum is reached at 215g/km.

(b) The car benefit and car fuel scale charges for Car 1 are reduced because the car was not available for use for part of the year. [*ITEPA 2003, ss 143, 152*].

(c) Since J makes a contribution only towards private fuel as distinct from private use, a reduction in the car benefit under *ITEPA 2003, s 144* will not be available. As J is not *required* to make good the *whole* of the expense incurred by K Ltd in providing fuel for private use, his contributions do not reduce the fuel benefit. [*ITEPA 2003, s 151*].

(d) The legal costs will be taxable as a benefit following *Rendell v Went HL 1964, 41 TC 641*. No relief is available under *ITEPA 2003, ss 346–350* (employee liabilities) as the expenses are incurred in connection with a criminal conviction. [*ITEPA 2003, s 346(2)*].

(e) Since Car 2 is not available for private use, no benefits will arise [*ITEPA 2003, ss 114, 118*]. Although a benefit in respect of the chauffeur's wages will arise under *ITEPA 2003, s 239(4)(5)*), a claim under *ITEPA 2003, s 336* (relief for necessary expenses) will eliminate the liability.

(f) K Ltd will be liable to employers' Class 1A NIC for 2013/14 in respect of Car 1, under *Social Security Contributions and Benefits Act 1992, s 10*.

(B)   **Vans**

[*ITEPA 2003, ss 154–164, 170(1A)(2)(5)*]

W is an employee of C Ltd, earning £37,000 per annum. From 1 October 2013 to 5 April 2014, W is provided by his employer with exclusive use of a one-year old company van (Van A) on terms such that the restricted private use requirements are not met and which provide for a deduction of £4 per month to be made from his net salary at the end of each month in consideration for private use. Van A was off the road and incapable of use for a three-week period in January 2014; no replacement was provided.

X, Y and Z are also employees of C Ltd, each earning £32,500 per annum. Throughout 2013/14, a single two-year old company van (Van B) is made available to the three of them. The terms are such that the restricted private use requirements are met in relation to X but not in relation to Y and Z. No payment for private use was required from any of them. Van B was damaged and incapable of use for 40 consecutive days in February/ March 2014; no replacement was provided. The facts show that a just and reasonable allocation of the benefit for 2013/14 is 0% to X (whose private use was insignificant), 60% to Y and 40% to Z.

Both vans have a normal laden weight not exceeding 3,500 kilograms.

It is not the policy of C Ltd to provide fuel for private travel in its vans. All employees are required to make good the full cost of any fuel used for private purposes and have done so.

The taxable benefits to W, X, Y and Z for 2013/14 of company vans are calculated as follows.

£

W

Cash equivalent of benefit before adjustment	3,000
Exclude Period of unavailability (see note below):	

$$£3,000 \times \frac{178}{365} \quad (6.4.13 - 30.9.13)$$

	1,464
	1,536
Deduct Payment for private use (6 × £4 per month)	24
Cash equivalent of benefit	£1,512

X

Cash equivalent of benefit	Nil

Y

Cash equivalent of benefit before adjustment	3,000
Exclude Period of unavailability:	

$$£3,000 \times \frac{40}{365}$$

	329
	2,671
Exclude Reduction for sharing (40%)	1,068
Cash equivalent of benefit	£1,603

Z

Cash equivalent of benefit before adjustment	3,000
Exclude Period of unavailability (same as for Y):	329
	2,671
Exclude Reduction for sharing (60%)	1,603
Cash equivalent of benefit	£1,068

Notes

(a) In W's case, the period of unavailability in January 2014 does not count towards the reduction as it is a period of less than 30 consecutive days.

(b) No fuel benefit arises in this example due to C Ltd's policy on fuel for private travel and the fact that the employees have reimbursed the company for any private fuel used.

8.3 IT   Employment Income

(C)   **Assets given and leased**

[*ITEPA 2003, ss 203–208*]

During 2013/14 P Ltd transferred to R a television set which it had previously leased to him for a nominal rent of £2 per month. The company also leased a suit to R under the same arrangements. R's salary is £35,000 p.a.

Television

First leased to R in April 2012 (when its market value was £560); transferred to R on 6 March 2014 for £50, the market value at that time being £175.

R's benefits are	£	£
2012/13		
Cost of benefit 20% × £560		112
Deduct Rent paid by R		24
Cash equivalent of benefit		£88
2013/14		
Cost of benefit 20% × £560 × $^{11}/_{12}$		103
Deduct Rent paid by R (11 months)		22
Cash equivalent of benefit		81
Greater of		
(i) Market value at transfer	175	
Deduct Price paid by R	50	
	£125	
and		
(ii) Original market value	560	
Deduct Cost of benefits note (b)	215	
	345	
Deduct Price paid by R	50	
	£295	
		295
Total		£376

Suit

First leased to R on 6 November 2013 (when its market value was £340).

R's benefit for 2013/14 is		
Cost of benefit 20% × £340 × $^{5}/_{12}$		28
Deduct Rent paid by R (5 months)		10
Cash equivalent of benefit		£18

Employment Income IT 8.3

Notes

(a) Where appropriate, e.g. where an asset is not available for the whole of the tax year or where it is available to more than one person, only a corresponding proportion of the cost of the benefit is brought in. See *ITEPA 2003, s 204* and HMRC Employment Income Manual EIM21200 *et seq.*

(b) On the transfer of the television set, the cost of the benefits to date (£112 + £103), not the cash equivalents, is deducted from the original market value. [*ITEPA 2003, s 206*].

(c) It is assumed that the television set and suit have been bought by P Ltd and are not goods provided from within its own business. If the latter was the case, R would be taxed on the marginal or additional cost to P Ltd in providing the benefit (*Pepper v Hart* HL 1992, 65 TC 421).

(D) **Cheap loan arrangements**

[*ITEPA 2003, ss 173–191*]

D, who is an employee of A Ltd earning £40,000 per annum, obtained a loan of £10,000 from the company on 10 October 2007 for the purpose of buying a car. Interest at a nominal rate is charged annually on the outstanding balance while the principal is repayable by instalments of £1,000 on 31 December and 30 June commencing 31 December 2007. The interest paid by D in 2007/08 amounted to £50 and in 2008/09 to £250. The official rate of interest is 6.25% p.a. until 28 February 2009 and 4.75% p.a. thereafter. The average rate for 2008/09 is 6.1%.

D will be chargeable for 2007/08 as follows

Normal method (averaging)

		£
Average balance for period $\dfrac{£10,000 + £9,000}{2}$		£9,500
£9,500 × $^{5}/_{12}$		£3,958
£3,958 × 6.25%		247
Deduct Interest paid in year		50
Cash equivalent of loan benefit		£197

Alternative method

Period	Balance of loan in period	Interest at official rate on balance	
	£		£
10.10.07 – 31.12.07	10,000	£10,000 × 6.25% × $^{83}/_{365}$	142
1.1.08 – 5.4.08	9,000	£9,000 × 6.25% × $^{95}/_{365}$	146

8.3 IT   Employment Income

	288
Deduct Interest paid in year	50
Cash equivalent of loan benefit	£238
Amount chargeable to tax note (b)	£238

D will be chargeable for 2008/09 as follows

Normal method (averaging)   £

$$\text{Average balance for year } \frac{£9{,}000 + £7{,}000}{2} \qquad £8{,}000$$

£8,000 × 6.1%	488
Deduct Interest paid in year	250
Cash equivalent of loan benefit	£238

Alternative method

Period	Balance of loan in period	Interest at official rate on balance	
	£		£
6.4.08 – 30.6.08	9,000	£9,000 × 6.25% × $^{86}/_{365}$	132
1.7.08 – 31.12.08	8,000	£8,000 × 6.25% × $^{184}/_{365}$	252
1.1.09 – 28.2.09	7,000	£7,000 × 6.25% × $^{59}/_{365}$	71
1.3.09 – 5.4.09	7,000	£7,000 × 4.75% × $^{95}/_{365}$	33
			488
Deduct Interest paid in year			250
Cash equivalent of loan benefit			£238
Amount chargeable to tax note (b)			£238

Notes

(a) The period 10 October 2007 to 5 April 2008 is, for the purpose of calculating the average balance, five complete months (months begin on the sixth day of each calendar month). However, for the purpose of applying interest rates, the actual number of days (178) during which the loan was outstanding is taken into account.

(b) HMRC will probably require the alternative method to be applied for 2007/08. For 2008/09, both methods happen to give the same result.

(c) Note that a loan is exempt from the beneficial loan provisions for a tax year if it and other employment-related loans (excluding qualifying loans) do not exceed £5,000 in aggregate at any time in the year. [*ITEPA 2003, s 180*]. This de minimis is to be doubled to £10,000 for 2014/15 onwards (www.hmrc.gov.uk/budget2013/ootlar -main.pdf at para 2.9).

(d) There is no taxable benefit in respect of a loan where, if interest were paid on it, the whole of the interest would qualify for tax relief. [*ITEPA 2003, s 178*]. Where such interest only partly qualifies, a benefit continues to arise, with relief being given for the qualifying part of the interest.

(e) In order for interest paid by the employee to be taken into account, it need not be paid *in* the tax year, only *for* the tax year. See HMRC Employment Income Manual, EIM26250–26258 for a useful discussion on this.

(f) This example illustrates the year 2008/09 as that was the latest year in which the official rate was changed in-year. The principles continue to apply for subsequent years.

8.4 BENEFITS — LIVING ACCOMMODATION

[*ITEPA 2003, ss 97–113, 313–315; FA 2009, s 71*]

(A) **Expenses**

N is employed by the G Property Co Ltd, earning £13,850 p.a. He occupies, rent-free, the basement flat of a block of flats for which he is employed as caretaker/security officer. The annual value of the flat is determined at £250. In 2013/14, G Ltd incurred the following expenditure on the flat

	£
Heat and light	700
Decoration	330
Repairs	210
Cleaning	160
	£1,400
Conversion of large bedroom into two smaller bedrooms	£3,000

In addition, the company pays N's council tax which amounts to £500.

As the company does not have a pension scheme, N pays a stakeholder pension premium of £160 net of tax (equivalent to £200 gross) into a registered scheme on 31 October 2013, but, apart from his personal allowance, he has no other reliefs.

N's taxable income for 2013/14 is

	£
Salary	13,850
Annual value of flat	—
Heat and light, decoration, repairs, cleaning	
£1,400 restricted to (note (c))	1,365
	15,215
Deduct Personal allowance	9,440

8.4 IT Employment Income

       Taxable   £5,775

Notes

(a) N is not chargeable to income tax on the annual value of the flat if he can show that it is necessary for the proper performance of his duties for him to reside in the accommodation. [*ITEPA 2003, s 99(1)*]. He might equally well be able to claim under *ITEPA 2003, s 99(2)*.

(b) The structural alterations costing £3,000 will not be regarded as a benefit. [*ITEPA 2003, s 313*].

(c) The earnings treated as having arisen in respect of the heat and light, decoration, repairs and cleaning costs will be restricted by *ITEPA 2003, s 315* to the lesser of

    (i)   the expenses incurred   £1,400
    (ii)   10% × £13,650 (net earnings)   £1,250

The contribution to a registered pension scheme is deductible in arriving at net earnings for this purpose. [*ITEPA 2003, s 315(5)*]. (The contribution is not shown above as a deduction from taxable income as basic rate relief has been given at source and higher/additional rate relief is not applicable.)

(d) Where the benefit of living accommodation is exempt under *ITEPA 2003, s 99(1), s 99(2) or s 100* (accommodation provided as result of security threat), the payment by the employer of the employee's council tax (and/or water rates) is also exempt. [*ITEPA 2003, s 314*].

(B) **Normal and additional charge**

S, the founder and managing director of S Ltd, a successful transport company, has since April 2008 occupied a house owned by S Ltd. The house was acquired by S Ltd in August 2002 for £150,000 and, since acquisition, but before 6 April 2012, £80,000 has been spent by S Ltd on alterations and improvements to the house. The gross annual value of the house for rating purposes before 1 April 1990 (when the community charge replaced general rates) was £1,663. S pays annual rental of £2,000 to the company for 2013/14 only. He pays all expenses relating to the property.

S's taxable benefits in respect of his occupation of the house for 2012/13 and 2013/14 are as follows

	£	£
2012/13		
Gross annual value		1,663
Additional charge		
Acquisition cost of house	150,000	
Cost of improvements	80,000	
	230,000	
Deduct	75,000	

Additional value		£155,000		
Additional value at 4%	note (b)			6,200
				£7,863
2013/14				
Gross annual value	note (a)			Nil
Additional charge				
Acquisition cost of house		150,000		
Cost of improvements		80,000		
		230,000		
Deduct		75,000		
Additional value		£155,000		
Additional value at 4%	note (b)			6,200
				6,200
Rental payable by S		2,000		
Deduct Gross annual value		1,663		
				337
				£5,863

Notes

(a) No taxable gross annual value arises in 2013/14 because the rental of £2,000 payable by S exceeds the gross annual value of £1,663. The excess is deductible from the amount of the benefit arising under the additional charge.

(b) The percentage to be used in determining the amount of the benefit is that in force for the purposes of taxing cheap loan arrangements (see **8.3(D)** above) at the beginning of the tax year.

(c) If S had moved into the house on, say, 6 April 2009 (more than six years after its acquisition by S Ltd), market value at that date would be substituted for cost plus improvements to date. If, however, original cost plus cost of improvements had not exceeded £75,000, the additional charge would not apply (regardless of market value at the date of first occupation by S). [*ITEPA 2003, s 107*].

8.5 REMOVAL BENEFITS AND EXPENSES, INCLUDING CHEAP LOAN ARRANGEMENTS

[*ITEPA 2003, ss 271–289*]

Mr R E Locate lives in Chelsea and is employed as a store manager by T Ltd, a department store chain, at one of their London branches. In June 2013, he is asked by T Ltd to take up a similar position at their main Birmingham store with effect from 1 September 2013. The company agrees to pay Mr Locate's expenses, up to a ceiling of £7,500, in connection with his moving house to the Birmingham area. In the event, the expenses paid or reimbursed by the company amount to £7,000, all paid in 2013, all eligible expenses within *ITEPA 2003, ss 272, 277–285* and all reasonably incurred by the employee in connection with his change of residence. As he is unable to move into his new home until 15 September 2013, T Ltd provides Mr Locate with temporary living accommodation near his new place of employment. The accommodation is rented by the company and would give rise to a taxable benefit on the employee of £300 under *ITEPA 2003, s 105*, but no charge under *ITEPA 2003, s 106* (see **8.4** above).

8.5 IT Employment Income

T Ltd also provides Mr Locate with an interest-free bridging loan of £50,000 in connection with the change of residence. The loan is made on 1 September 2013 and is repaid on 10 April 2014 when the sale of the employee's former residence is completed. The official rate of interest under *ITEPA 2003, s 181* is assumed to remain at 4% throughout.

Mr Locate's salary for 2013/14 amounts to £40,000.

Mr Locate's taxable benefits for 2013/14 in respect of removal expenses and benefits plus beneficial loans are calculated as follows

	£
Qualifying removal expenses	7,000
Qualifying removal benefits	300
	£7,300

The total is less than the qualifying limit of £8,000 under *ITEPA 2003, s 287(1)* and is thus exempt from tax by virtue of *ITEPA 2003, s 271(1)*.

Cheap loan arrangements

The interest-free loan is treated by *ITEPA 2003, s 289* as having been made on a date later than that on which it was actually made, as follows.

$$\text{Number of days in the 'exempted discharge period'} = \frac{A}{B \times C} \times 365$$

A = 700 (unused qualifying limit, i.e. £8,000 - £7,300)

B = 50,000 (maximum loan outstanding between the actual date of the loan, 1.9.13, and 5.4.15, the latter being the 'limitation day' — see *ITEPA 2003, s 274* and note (a) below)

C = 4% (the official rate of interest as at the actual date of the loan, 1.9.13, disregarding any subsequent changes of rate)

$$\frac{700}{50,000 \times 4\%} \times 365$$

= 127.75 rounded up to 128 days

[*ITEPA 2003, s 288(4)*].

The 'exempted discharge period' of 128 days runs from 1.9.13 to 6.1.14 inclusive. The loan is deemed to have been made on 6.1.14. [*ITEPA 2003, s 289(1)–(3)*].

Calculation of benefit:

(i) Averaging method

$$\frac{£50{,}000 + £50{,}000}{2} \times \frac{3}{12} \times 4\% = \qquad \underline{£500}$$

(ii) Alternative method
6.1.14–5.4.14 = 90 days

$$£50{,}000 \times 4\% \times {}^{90}/_{365} \qquad \underline{£493}$$

Amount chargeable to tax (on the assumption
that the averaging method is applied) £500

Notes

(a) Eligible expenses and benefits which are reasonably incurred or provided in connection with the change in the employee's residence are qualifying expenses or benefits only if they are incurred or provided on or before the end of the tax year following that in which the employment, new duties or duties at the new location commence, i.e. by 5 April 2015 in this example.

(b) 'Subsistence' provided for the employee is an eligible benefit by virtue of *ITEPA 2003, s 281(4)*. For this purpose, 'subsistence' includes temporary living accommodation as well as food and drink. [*ITEPA 2003, s 281(6)*].

(c) See also 8.3(D) above as regards beneficial loans.

8.6 BENEFITS — MEDICAL INSURANCE, VOUCHERS ETC.

(A)

T earns £6,000 p.a. and during the year ended 5 April 2014 his employer provided him with, or paid on his behalf, or reimbursed, the following

	£
BUPA contributions (self and family) of which 25% reimbursed by T	600
Special medical insurance for overseas business visit lasting four nights	250
Voucher exchangeable for rail season ticket	500
Gift token exchangeable for goods at local department store	75
Holiday pay scheme voucher, exchangeable for cash	350
Overnight incidental expenses (telephone, laundry etc.) relating to above-mentioned overseas trip	36

The rail ticket voucher was purchased in March 2013 but was not handed to T until after 6 April 2013. The holiday pay voucher was received by T in June 2013 at which time PAYE was applied. The gift token was received in December 2013.

8.6 IT   Employment Income

T's assessable chargeable earnings for 2013/14 are

	£
Salary	6,000
Rail ticket voucher	500
Gift token	75
Holiday pay scheme voucher	350
	£6,925

Notes

(a) T is not a director or an employee earning £8,500 a year or more and so the BUPA contributions are not a chargeable benefit. [*ITEPA 2003, ss 201, 216*].

(b) The rail ticket voucher is chargeable in 2013/14 being the later of the year of receipt by the employee and the year of expense incurred by the employer. [*ITEPA 2003, s 88*].

(c) The gift token is a non-cash voucher chargeable under *ITEPA 2003, s 87*.

(d) The holiday pay voucher, being a 'cash voucher' within *ITEPA 2003, s 75* is taxable under PAYE by virtue of *ITEPA 2003, s 693*.

(e) The reimbursement of incidental overnight expenses is not taxable as the amount does not exceed £10 for each night of absence (£5 for absences within the UK). [*ITEPA 2003, ss 240, 241*].

(B)

Instead of earning £6,000 as in (A) above, T has a salary of £7,500 p.a.

T's chargeable earnings for 2013/14 are

	£
Salary	7,500
BUPA contributions (£600 less 25% reimbursed)	450
Rail ticket voucher	500
Gift token	75
Holiday pay scheme voucher	350
	£8,875

Notes

(a) All chargeable benefits and expenses payments, before relief for business expenditure, are taken into account in determining whether or not the £8,500 limit has been reached. [*ITEPA 2003, s 218*].

(b) The special medical insurance for the overseas business trip is exempted from charge by *ITEPA 2003, s 325*.

9 Enterprise Investment Scheme

[*ITA 2007, ss 156–257; TCGA 1992, ss 150A, 150B; FA 2009, s 27, Sch 8 paras 1–7, 11–13; FA 2011, s 42; FA 2012, Sch 6 paras 10–13, Sch 7*]

9.1 CONDITIONS FOR AND FORM OF RELIEF

(A)

Mr Jones is a married man with a salary of £182,500 for 2012/13 and no other income. He is not entitled to married couple's allowance. For 2012/13, he is entitled to full income tax relief on an investment of £200,000 in a venture capital trust.

In 2012/13 he subscribes for ordinary shares in two unquoted companies issuing shares under the enterprise investment scheme (EIS).

A Ltd was formed by some people in Mr Jones' neighbourhood to publish a local newspaper. 200,000 ordinary £1 shares were issued at par in August 2012 and the company started trading in September 2012. Mr Jones subscribed for 16,000 of the shares. Mr Jones becomes a director of A Ltd in September 2012, and receives director's fees of £2,248 in 2012/13, a level of remuneration which is considered reasonable for services rendered by him to the company in his capacity as a director.

B Ltd, which is controlled by an old friend of Mr Jones, has acquired the rights to manufacture in the UK a new type of industrial cleaning solvent and requires additional finance. Mr Jones subscribed for 8,000 ordinary £1 shares at a premium of £1.50 per share in October 2012. The issue increases the company's issued share capital to 25,000 ordinary £1 shares.

Mr Jones will obtain tax relief in 2012/13 as follows

Amount eligible for relief

		£
A Ltd	notes (a) and (b)	16,000
B Ltd	note (c)	Nil
Total (being less than the maximum of £1,000,000)		£16,000

	£
Salary	182,500
Director's remuneration (A Ltd)	2,248
Total income	184,748
Personal allowance (restricted due to level of income)	Nil
Taxable income	£184,748
Tax payable:	
34,370 @ 20%	6,874.00
115,630 @ 40%	46,252.00
34,748 @ 50%	17,374.00

9.1 IT   Enterprise Investment Scheme

	70,500.00
VCT relief £200,000 @ 30%	60,000
	10,500
Deduct EIS relief £16,000 @ 30%	4,800.00
Net tax liability 2012/13	£5,700.00

Notes

(a) Mr Jones is entitled to relief on the full amount of his investment in A Ltd regardless of the amount of relief claimed by other investors.

(b) The fact that Mr Jones becomes a paid director of A Ltd *after* an issue to him of eligible shares does not prevent his qualifying for relief in respect of those shares providing his remuneration as a director is reasonable and he is not otherwise connected with the company. [*ITA 2007, s 169*].

(c) Mr Jones is not entitled to relief against his income for his investment of £20,000 in B Ltd. As a result of the share issue he owns more than 30% of the issued ordinary share capital (8,000 out of 25,000 shares) and is therefore regarded as connected with the company and denied relief. [*ITA 2007, s 170*].

(d) EIS relief is given at the EIS rate of tax (30%) and by way of an income tax reduction. The relief cannot exceed what would otherwise be the income tax liability (no restriction being necessary in this example). For this purpose, the income tax liability is before taking into account any married couple's allowance, double tax relief and certain other specified items. However, the VCT investment relief must be deducted before the EIS relief. [*ITA 2007, ss 26, 27, 29, 158*].

(B)

In 2013/14 Mr Jones subscribes for shares in three more unquoted companies trading in the UK and issuing shares under the EIS.

C Ltd is a local company engaged in the manufacture of car components. It issues a further 540,000 ordinary £1 shares at £2 per share in June 2013 and Mr Jones subscribes for 14,800 shares costing £29,600, increasing his stake in the company to 10%. He had originally held 24,300 shares, acquired by purchase at arm's length in May 2011 for £32,400.

D Ltd has been trading as a restaurateur for several years and requires an injection of capital to finance a new restaurant. Mr Jones and three other unconnected individuals each subscribe for 75,000 ordinary £1 shares at par in November 2013. The balance of 480,000 shares are held by Mr Jones' sister and niece. D Ltd has the equivalent of 80 full-time employees in November 2013 when the new shares are issued.

E Ltd is an electronics company, with 60 employees, controlled by two cousins of Mr Jones. The company has not issued any shares in the previous twelve months but is now seeking £5 million extra capital for expansion, and raises it via the EIS. Mr Jones subscribes for 950,000 ordinary £1 shares at par in December 2013.

Mr Jones' salary is increased by bonus to £265,000 for 2013/14. His director's fees from A Ltd amount to £4,056, which again is considered reasonable for services rendered. He makes a claim to treat 9,500 of his C Ltd shares (costing £19,000) to be regarded as issued in 2012/13, thus eliminating his income tax liability for that year.

Enterprise Investment Scheme   IT 9.1

Mr Jones will obtain tax relief as follows

2012/13

C Ltd note (a) £19,000 @ 30% = £5,700

2013/14

Amount eligible for relief

	£
C Ltd (£29,600 − £19,000 carried back)	10,600
D Ltd	75,000
E Ltd	950,000
Total amount subscribed	£1,035,600

But amount eligible for relief restricted to subscriptions of £1,000,000

Relief given

	£
Salary	265,000
Director's remuneration	4,056
Total income	269,056
Personal allowance (restricted due to level of income)	Nil
Taxable income	£269,056

Tax payable:

32,010 @ 20%	6,402.00
117,990 @ 40%	47,196.00
119,056 @ 50%	59,528.00
	113,126.00

Deduct EIS relief:
£1,000,000 @ 30% = £300,000, but
restricted to 113,126.00
Net tax liability 2013/14 Nil

Attribution of relief to shares   note (b)

£

CLtd shares $\dfrac{10,600}{1,035,600} \times £113,126$ 1,158

9.1 IT Enterprise Investment Scheme

$$\text{DLtd shares } \frac{75{,}000}{1{,}035{,}600} \times £113{,}126 \qquad 8{,}193$$

$$\text{ELtd shares } \frac{950{,}000}{1{,}035{,}600} \times £113{,}126 \qquad \underline{103{,}775}$$

$$\underline{\underline{£113{,}126}}$$

Notes

(a) The investor may claim relief as if any number of the shares had been issued in the preceding tax year. The only restriction (not relevant in this example) is that relief in any one tax year may not be given on subscriptions of more than the annual maximum for that year. The relief will be given in addition to that previously claimed for 2012/13 (see (A) above). [*ITA 2007, s 158(4); FA 2009, Sch 8 paras 6, 13*].

(b) Relief is restricted in this example by (i) the £1,000,000 maximum, (ii) the available EIS rate (i.e. 30%) and (iii) an insufficiency in Mr Jones' tax liability. The relief attributable to each issue of shares (which will be relevant in the event of a disposal of the shares or withdrawal of relief — see **9.2** below) is found by apportioning the income tax reduction by reference to the amounts subscribed for each issue. (For this purpose, 9,500 of the C Ltd shares are regarded as having been separately issued in the previous year.) The relief so attributed to each issue is then apportioned equally between all the shares comprised in that issue. [*ITA 2007, ss 201, 210(2)*].

(c) An issuing company under the EIS scheme must have fewer than the equivalent of 250 full-time employees when the EIS shares are issued. [*ITA 2007, s 186A; FA 2012, Sch 7 paras 12, 23*].

9.2 WITHDRAWAL OF RELIEF/GAINS AND LOSSES ON EIS SHARES

(A)

In June 2014, Mr Jones, the investor in **9.1** above, sells 38,100 ordinary £1 shares in C Ltd (see **9.1**(B) above), in an arm's length transaction, for £90,000, leaving him with 1,000 shares.

The position is as follows
Income Tax

2012/13 £

Relief attributable to 9,500 shares treated as issued in 2012/13:
9,500 shares at £2 per share = £19,000 @ 30% 5,700

$$\text{Consideration received } \left(\frac{9{,}500}{38{,}100} \times £90{,}000 \right) = £22{,}441 \text{ @ } 30\% \qquad \underline{6{,}732}$$

Excess of tax at the EIS rate on consideration over relief £1,032

Relief withdrawn by assessment £5,700

	£
2013/14	
Relief attributable to 4,300 shares	
4,300/5,300 × £1,158	939
Consideration received	–
$\left(\dfrac{4,300}{38,100} \times £90,000\right) = £10,157 \times 939/(1,000 @ 30\%) = £31,791 @ 30\%$	9,537
Excess of tax at the EIS rate on adjusted consideration over relief	£8,598
Relief withdrawn by assessment	£939

Capital Gains Tax

2014/15	£	£
Disposal proceeds (38,100 shares)		90,000
Cost: 24,300 shares acquired May 2011	32,400	
13,800 shares acquired June 2013	27,600	60,000
Chargeable gain		£30,000

Notes

(a) For both income tax and capital gains tax purposes, a disposal is matched with acquisitions on a first in/first out basis. [*ITA 2007, s 246*]. Thus, the 38,100 shares sold in June 2014 are matched with 24,300 shares purchased in May 2011 and with 13,800 of the 14,800 EIS shares subscribed for in June 2013. For these purposes, 9,500 of the EIS shares are treated as having been issued in 2012/13 (by virtue of Mr Jones' carry-back claim — see note (a) to **9.1(B)** above). [*ITA 2007, s 201(6)*]. Therefore, those shares are treated as disposed of in priority to those on which relief was given in 2013/14.

(b) Following the disposal, Mr Jones is left with 1,000 shares in C Ltd acquired in June 2013 for £2,000, to which the EIS relief attributable is £219 (1,158 – 939).

(c) EIS relief is withdrawn if shares are disposed of before the end of the requisite three-year period. In this example, relief attributable to the shares sold is fully withdrawn as consideration received, reduced as illustrated, exceeds the relief attributable. See (B) below for where the reverse applies. The consideration is reduced where the relief attributable (A) is less than tax at the 'EIS original rate' on the amount subscribed (B), and is so reduced by applying the fraction A/B. [*ITA 2007, ss 209, 210*]. The '*EIS original rate*' is the EIS rate for the tax year for which the relief was obtained, i.e. 30% for 2012/13 and 2013/14.

(d) Relief is withdrawn by means of an assessment for the year(s) in which relief was given. [*ITA 2007, s 235*].

(e) The capital gain on the disposal is fully chargeable as the EIS shares are not held for the requisite three-year period.

9.2 IT Enterprise Investment Scheme

(B)

In December 2014 Mr Jones disposes of his 75,000 ordinary £1 shares in D Ltd (see **9.1(B)** above), in an arm's length transaction, for £60,000.

The position is as follows
Income Tax

2013/14

	£
Relief attributable to shares sold	8,193

$$£60,000 \times \frac{8,193}{£75,000 \times 30\%} = £21,848 \text{ @ } 30\% \qquad 6,554$$

Excess of relief over tax at the EIS rate on adjusted consideration	£1,639
Relief withdrawn by assessment	£6,554

Capital Gains Tax

2014/15

	£	£
Disposal proceeds (December 2014)		60,000
Cost (November 2013)	75,000	
Less Relief attributable to shares:		
£8,193 − £6,554	1,639	
		73,341
Allowable loss		£13,341

Notes

(a) See notes (*b*) and (*c*) to (A) above.

(b) The EIS relief withdrawn is limited to tax at the EIS original rate (see note (c) to (A) above) on the consideration received, reduced as illustrated. If the disposal had been made otherwise than by way of a bargain made at arm's length, the full relief would have been withdrawn. [*ITA 2007, s 209*].

(c) An allowable loss may arise for capital gains tax purposes on a disposal of EIS shares, whether or not the disposal occurs within the requisite three-year period. In computing such a loss, the allowable cost is reduced by EIS relief attributable to the shares (and not withdrawn). [*TCGA 1992, s 150A(1)*].

(d) A loss, as computed for capital gains tax purposes, may be relieved against income on a claim under *ITA 2007, s 132* (share loss relief — see **14.5 LOSSES**). [*ITA 2007, s 131*].

(C)

(i) In September 2014, Mr Jones receives from E Ltd (one of the companies in **9.1(B)** above) an asset with a market value of £38,000 but for which he pays the company only £2,000.

Enterprise Investment Scheme IT 9.2

(ii) In March 2017, Mr Jones sells his 950,000 shares in E Ltd for their market value of £1,190,000.

Income Tax

(i) The difference of £36,000 between the market value of the asset and the consideration given for it represents value (which is not insignificant value) received by the investor from the company within the period beginning one year before the issue of the shares and ending three years after the issue (or three years after the commencement of trade, if later). The value received (reduced in like manner as is mentioned in note (b) to (A) above) is compared to the relief attributable to the shares.

2013/14

	£
Relief attributable to 950,000 E Ltd shares (see 9.1(B) above)	103,775
Value received	
$£36,000 \times \dfrac{103,775}{£950,000 \times 30\%} = £13,108 @ 30\%$	3,932
Excess of relief over value received	**£99,843**
Relief withdrawn by assessment	**£3,932**

[ITA 2007, ss 159(4), 213–217, 220, 234(1), 235].

(ii) As Mr Jones holds the shares for the requisite three-year period, there is no withdrawal of relief on disposal.

Capital Gains Tax

As Mr Jones holds the shares for the requisite three-year period, and EIS relief has not been fully withdrawn, any gain on disposal is generally exempt from capital gains tax (although this does not prevent an allowable loss from arising). [TCGA 1992, s 150A(2)(2A)]. A proportion of the gain could become chargeable under TCGA 1992, s 150A(3) where the relief given was less than tax at the EIS rate on the amount subscribed but this does not apply where, as in the case of Mr Jones, the relief fell to be restricted due to his having insufficient income tax liability to cover it. [TCGA 1992, s 150A(3)]. A proportion of the gain does, however, become chargeable where value is received leading to a part-withdrawal of relief. [TCGA 1992, s 150B].

2016/17

	£
Disposal proceeds (March 2017)	1,190,000
Cost (December 2013)	950,000
Gain	240,000

Chargeable gain =

$$\text{gain} \times \dfrac{\text{Relief withdrawn}}{\text{Relief attributable (before reduction)}}$$

9.2 IT   Enterprise Investment Scheme

i.e.

$$£240,000 \times \frac{3,932}{103,775} \qquad £9,093$$

Exempt gain £(240,000 − 9,093)   £230,097

10 Herd Basis

[*ITTOIA 2005, ss 111–129*]

10.1 A farmer acquires a dairy herd and elects for the herd basis to apply. The movements in the herd and the tax treatment are as follows

Year 1

	No	Value £
Mature		
Bought @ £150	70	10,500
Bought in calf @ £180		
(Market value of calf £35)	5	900
Immature		
Bought @ £75	15	1,125

Herd Account		£
70	Friesians	10,500
5	Friesians in calf (5 × £(180 − 35))	725
75	Closing balance	£11,225

Trading Account		£
5	Calves (5 × £35)	175
15	Immature Friesians	1,125
	Debit to profit and loss account	£1,300

Year 2

	No	Value £
Mature		
Bought @ £185	15	2,775
Sold @ £200	10	2,000
Died	3	—
Immature		
Born	52	—
Matured @ 60% of market value of £200 note (a)	12	1,440

IT   Herd Basis

Herd Account

		£	£
75	Opening balance		11,225
	Increase in herd		
15	Purchases	2,775	
12	Transferred from trading stock	1,440	
27		4,215	
(13)	Replacement cost £4,215 × 13/27	2,029	
14	Non-replacement animals cost		2,186
89	Closing balance		£13,411

Trading Account

	£
Sale of 10 mature cows replaced	(2,000)
Transfer to herd — 14 animals	(1,440)
Cost of 13 mature cows purchased to replace those sold/deceased ($^{13}/_{15}$ × £2,775)	2,405
Net credit to profit and loss account note (b)	£(1,035)

Year 3

	No	Value £
Mature		
Jerseys bought @ £250	70	17,500
Friesians slaughtered @ £175 (market value £185)	52	9,100
Immature		
Friesians born	20	—
Matured		
Friesians @ 60% of market value of £190 note (a)	15	1,710

Herd Account

			£
89	Opening balance		13,411
	Increase in herd		
18	Jerseys		4,500
52	Improvement Jerseys@	250	
less	Market value of Friesians	185	
		—	
52@		65	3,380

Herd Basis IT 10.1

		Transfer from trading stock	
	15	Friesians	1,710
	122	Closing balance	£23,001

Trading Account	£
Compensation	(9,100)
Transfer to herd	(1,710)
Purchase of replacements note (c) (52 × £185)	9,620
Net credit to profit and loss account	£(1,190)

Year 4

The farmer ceases dairy farming and sells his whole herd.

	No	Value £
Mature		
Jersey sold @ £320	70	22,400
Friesians sold @ £200	52	10,400
Immature		
Friesians sold @ £100	65	6,500

Herd Account		£
	Opening balance	23,001
52	Friesians	
70	Jerseys	
(122)	Sales	(32,800)
—	Profit on sale note (d)	£(9,799)

Trading Account	£
Sale of 65 immature Friesians	(6,500)
Credit to profit and loss account	£(6,500)

Notes

(a) The use of 60% of market value was originally by agreement between the National Farmers' Union and HMRC (see now HMRC Business Income Manual BIM55410 at paragraph 7.2). Alternatively, the actual cost of breeding or purchase and rearing could be used.

(b) As the cost of rearing the 12 cows to maturity will already have been debited to the profit and loss account, no additional entry is required to reflect that cost. Due to the fact that the animals were in opening stock at valuation and will not be in closing stock, the trading account will in effect be debited with that valuation.

IT   Herd Basis

(c) The cost of the replacements is restricted to the cost of replacing like with like.

(d) Provided these animals are not replaced by a herd of the same type within five years the proceeds will be tax-free.

(e) The herd basis is not available when profits are calculated using the cash basis for small businesses. [*ITTOIA 2005, s 111A; FA 2013, Sch 4 paras 24, 56*].

11 Intellectual Property

Cross-reference. See 3.5 CAPITAL ALLOWANCES for allowances for patent rights.

11.1 PATENT ROYALTIES

[*ITA 2007, s 461*].

An inventor received £24,920 after deduction of tax at source (i.e. £31,150 gross) on 1 June 2013, for the use of his patent over a four-year period ending on that date. He is a single man and his only other income for the four years was a salary as set out below.

In the absence of spreading provisions, the assessments for the four years to 5 April 2014 are

Tax year	2010/11	2010/11	2012/13	2013/14
	£	£	£	£
Salary	17,100	19,100	20,100	19,075
Patent rights	—	—	—	31,150
	17,100	19,100	20,100	50,225
Personal allowance	6,475	7,475	8,105	9,440
Taxable income	£10,625	£11,625	£11,995	£40,785
Tax thereon	2,125.00	2,325.00	2,399.00	9,912.00
Less tax deducted at source	—	—	—	6,230.00
	£2,125.00	£2,325.00	£2,399.00	£3,682.00
Total tax payable				£10,531.00

The inventor may however claim under *ITA 2007, s 461* for the liability for 2013/14 to be limited to the tax payable if the royalties had been spread over the four-year period to which they relate. The tax payable would then have been

	£	£	£	£
Salary	17,100	19,100	20,100	19,075
Patent rights	7,787	7,787	7,787	7,787
	24,887	26,887	27,887	26,862
Personal allowance	6,475	7,475	8,105	9,440
Taxable income	£18,412	£19,412	£19,782	£17,422
Tax thereon	£3,682.40	£3,882.40	£3,956.40	£3,484.40
Total tax thereon				15,005.60
Less tax deducted at source				6,230.00
Total tax payable				£8,775.60

A claim is beneficial in this case as spreading would reduce the liability by £1,755.40. Upon a claim being made, the saving will be given effect by means of a tax reduction for the year in which the royalty is received (2013/14 in this example). Tax reductions are given effect at Step 6 of the calculation of income tax liability at *ITA 2007, s 23*.

12 Late Payment Interest and Penalties

12.1 PAYMENTS UNDER SELF-ASSESSMENT

(A) **Interest and penalties arising on late payment**

[*FA 2009, ss 101, 107, Sch 56; SI 2011 Nos 701, 702*]

Mrs Worthington is a self-employed cook. Her self-assessment for 2010/11 shows a net income tax liability of £9,000. She makes the following interim payments for 2011/12:

31 January 2012	£4,500
31 July 2012	£4,500

Mrs Worthington's profits increase, and her self-assessment liability for 2011/12 amounts to £12,000. Mrs Worthington does not pay the additional income tax of £3,000 until 26 August 2013.

Mrs Worthington will have a liability to interest on overdue tax computed as follows

		£
31.1.13 – 25.8.13	£3,000 × 3% × $^{206}/_{365}$	50.79

In addition as the tax is paid more than 30 days late a late payment penalty will arise on 3 March 2013 of £3,000 × 5% = £150.

As the tax is still unpaid more than five months after the initial penalty is incurred, a further late payment penalty will arise on 3 August 2013 of £3,000 × 5% = £150. See also note (b).

Notes

(a) Interest accrues from the due date until date of payment. [*FA 2009, s 101(3)(4)*].

(b) If the tax had remained unpaid on 3 February 2014 (i.e. eleven months after the initial penalty was incurred), there would have been a third late payment penalty of 5% of the amount unpaid). [*FA 2009, Sch 56 para 3*].

(c) A late payment penalty may arise in respect of unpaid tax due in respect of a final payment of income tax or capital gains tax under *TMA 1970, s 59B*. For other circumstances in which a late payment penalty may arise, see the Table in *FA 2009, Sch 56 para 1*.

(d) Late payment interest will accrue on an unpaid late payment penalty with effect from the expiry of 30 days beginning with the date of the notice imposing the penalty. [*FA 2009, s 101, Sch 56 para 11; SI 2011 No 701, Art 2*].

12.1 IT   Late Payment Interest and Penalties

(B)   **Interest arising on insufficient interim payment**

[*FA 2009, s 101, Sch 53 para 1; SI 2011 No 701*]

Mr Jones is a self-employed butcher with no other income or capital gains who draws up accounts to 31 October each year. His liability under self-assessment for 2011/12 amounts to £25,000. Mr Jones forecasts that his profits for the accounting period ended 31 October 2012 will result in a liability under self-assessment of £10,000 for 2012/13. He makes a claim to that effect under *TMA 1970, s 59A(4)* and duly pays £5,000 each on 31 January 2013 and 31 July 2013. However, actual profits are in excess of his expectations and result in a self-assessment liability of £16,000. Mr Jones pays an additional £6,000 income tax on 25 January 2014.

For each interim payment Mr Jones' interest will be calculated on the difference between £5,000 and the lesser of:

£8,000 being the sum of £5,000 (actual interim payment) and £3,000 (50% of the final tax payment); and

£12,500 being the interim payment based on the preceding year's tax liability.

Interest will be as follows[*]

First interim payment		
31.1.13 – 24.1.14	£3,000 × 3% × $^{359}/_{365}$	**£88.52**
Second interim payment		
31.7.13 – 24.1.14	£3,000 × 3% × $^{178}/_{365}$	**£43.89**

---

[*]   Assuming no changes in interest rates before 25 January 2013

13 Life Assurance Policies

13.1 LIFE ASSURANCE GAINS AND NON-QUALIFYING POLICIES
[*ITTOIA 2005, ss 461–546*]

(A) **Top slicing relief — single chargeable event**

A single policyholder realises, in 2013/14, a gain of £2,600 on a non-qualifying policy which has been in existence for $2^{1}/_{2}$ years. Her other income for 2013/14 comprises employment income of £36,475 and dividends amounting to £3,895 (inclusive of dividend tax credits).

The tax chargeable on the gain is calculated as follows

	Normal basis	Top slicing relief claim
	£	£
Policy gain	2,600	1,300
Earnings	36,475	36,475
Dividends	3,895	3,895
	42,970	41,670
Personal allowance	9,440	9,440
	£33,530	£32,230

	Normal basis	Top slicing relief claim
	£	£
Tax applicable to policy gain		
Higher rate		
£1,520 at 40%	608.00	—
£220 at 40%	—	88.00
	608.00	88.00
Deduct		
Basic rate		
£1,520 at 20%	304.00	—
£220 at 20%	—	44.00
		£44.00
Appropriate multiple 2 × £44.00		£88.00
Tax chargeable lower of	£304.00 and	£88.00

13.1 IT   Life Assurance Policies

Top slicing relief (£304.00 − £88.00) =   £216.00

Tax payable is therefore as follows

27,035 @ 20%		5,407.00
3,895 @ 10%		389.50
1,080 @ 20% (policy gain at basic rate)		216.00
32,010		
1,520 @ 40% (policy gain at higher rate)		608.00
£33,530		
		6,620.50
Deduct: Top slicing relief (as above)		216.00
		6,404.50
Deduct: Tax credits on dividends (£3,895 @ 10%)	389.50	
Basic rate of tax on policy gain (£2,600 @ 20%)	520.00	909.50
Tax liability (subject to PAYE deductions)		£5,495.00

Notes

(a) Tax is calculated by treating the policy gain as the top slice of income. Under the top slicing relief calculation, the total policy gain is divided by the number of complete years the policy has run (two) and the resulting tax multiplied by the same factor.

(b) If a qualifying policy is replaced by a new qualifying policy on a different life or lives then, if certain conditions are met, no chargeable event occurs on the surrender of the earlier policy. [*ITTOIA 2005, s 542*].

(c) Gains on certain offshore policies do not carry a notional tax credit, though top slicing relief is computed as if a notional tax credit were available. [*ITTOIA 2005, s 531*]. A similar rule applies to gains on policies issued by friendly societies as part of their tax exempt life or endowment business.

(B) **Top slicing relief — multiple chargeable events in same tax year**

[*ITTOIA 2005, s 537*]

On 1 May 2013, a policyholder realises a gain of £10,000 on the maturity of a four-year non-qualifying policy. On 1 March 2014, he realises a gain of £12,000 on the surrender of a non-qualifying policy which he took out on 1 October 2007. For 2013/14, his *taxable* income excluding the two policy gains is £30,810.

Tax on policy gains without top slicing relief

1,200 @ 20% (basic rate)		240.00
20,800 @ 40%		8,320.00
£22,000		8,560.00

Life Assurance Policies IT 13.2

Deduct Basic rate tax (£22,000 × 20%)	4,400.00
Tax payable on policy gains	£4,160.00

Tax on policy gains with top slicing relief

£10,000 divided by 4 years =	2,500	
£12,000 divided by 6 years =	2,000	
	£4,500	

Tax on £4,500 as top slice of income:

1,200 @ 20% (basic rate)		240.00
3,300 @ 40%		1,320.00
£4,500		1,560.00
Deduct Basic rate tax (£4,500 × 20%)		900.00
		£660.00

$$£660.00 \times \frac{2,500}{4,500} = £366.67. \quad £366.67 \times 4 = \qquad 1,466.68$$

$$£660.00 \times \frac{2,000}{4,500} = £293.33. \quad £293.33 \times 6 = \qquad 1,760.00$$

Tax payable on policy gains	£3,226.68

Note

(a) The basic rate limit for 2013/14 is £32,010, so the amount of policy gains falling within the basic rate band in this case is £1,200 (£32,010 − £30,810).

13.2 PARTIAL SURRENDERS OF LIFE POLICIES ETC.

[ITTOIA 2005, s 507]

Sheridan takes out a policy on 4 February 2006 for a single premium of £15,000. The contract permits periodical withdrawals.

(i) Sheridan draws £750 p.a. on 4 February in each subsequent year.

There is no taxable gain because at the end of each insurance year the total value of rights surrendered (VRS) does not exceed the total allowable payments (TAP).

	£	
At 3.2.10 withdrawals have been	2,250	(VRS)
Deduct 4 × 1/20 of the sums paid in	3,000	(TAP)
	No gain	

13.2 IT   Life Assurance Policies

(ii) On 20.7.10 Sheridan withdraws an additional £3,500.

	£	
At 3.2.11 withdrawals have been	6,500	(VRS)
Deduct 5 × ¹/₂₀ of the sums paid in	3,750	(TAP)
Chargeable 2010/11	£2,750	

(iii) Sheridan makes no annual withdrawal on 4.2.11 but on 4.2.12 makes a withdrawal of £1,000.

In the year 2012/13 the position is

	£	£	
At 3.2.13 withdrawals have been		7,500	
Deduct Withdrawals at last charge		6,500	
		1,000	(VRS)
Deduct 7 × ¹/₂₀ of the sums paid in	5,250		
less amount deducted at last charge	3,750		
		1,500	(TAP)
		No gain	

(iv) Sheridan surrenders the policy on 1.7.13 for £13,250, having made a further £1,000 withdrawal on 4.2.13.

In the year 2013/14, the position is

	£	£
Proceeds on surrender		13,250
Previous withdrawals		8,500
		21,750
Deduct Premium paid	15,000	
Gains previously charged	2,750	
		17,750
Chargeable 2013/14		£4,000

Notes

(a) VRS is the total of all surrenders, withdrawals etc. for each insurance year since commencement *less* the total of such values which have been brought into account in earlier chargeable events.

(b) TAP is the total of annual fractions of one-twentieth (with a maximum of 20 twentieths) of the premiums, lump sums etc. paid for each insurance year since commencement *less* the total of such fractions which have been brought into account in earlier chargeable events.

Life Assurance Policies IT 13.3

(c) The chargeable event gain is generally treated as arising at the end of the insurance year and is thus chargeable to income for the tax year in which the insurance year ends. [*ITTOIA 2005, s 509*].

(d) An insurance year is a year ending twelve months from the commencement of the policy or from an anniversary thereof. [*ITTOIA 2005, s 499*].

(e) The gain on final surrender of the policy is calculated under *ITTOIA 2005, s 491*.

(f) The gains in (ii) and (iv) above are subject to any available top slicing relief (see **13.1** above).

13.3 ADJUSTMENTS FOR PERIODS OF NON-UK RESIDENCE

[*ITTOIA 2005, s 528; FA 2013, Sch 8 paras 3, 7, Sch 45 paras 86(2)–(6), 153(2)*]

Churchill took out a life policy on 1 May 2007 paying premiums of £100 per month. On 1 May 2013 he exercised a right under the policy to vary the policy so as to increase the benefits payable under it; the premiums then increase to £120 per month. On 31 March 2014 Churchill assigns all the rights under the policy to an unconnected third party for £10,000. Churchill was non-resident in the UK throughout the three years 2008/09 to 2010/11 but UK resident throughout 2007/08, 2011/12 and 2012/13 and also UK resident for 2013/14. Subject to the chargeable event gain, his income for 2013/14 amounts to £41,350, consisting entirely of employment income.

The chargeable event gain is calculated as follows

Total benefit value (assignment proceeds)
Total allowable deductions (premiums paid):
    1.5.07–1.4.13 (£100 x 72 months)
    1.5.13–1.3.14 (£120 x 11 months)
Chargeable event gain
Reduction for periods of non-UK residence (note (b)):

$$£1,480 \times \frac{1,095 \ (6.4.08 - 5.4.11)}{2,525 \ (1.5.07 - 31.3.14)}$$

Taxable gain

Top slicing relief is calculated as follows

	Normal basis	Top slicing relief claim
	£	£
Taxable gain (note (c))	838	279
Earnings	41,350	41,350
	42,188	41,629
Personal allowance	9,440	9,440
	£32,748	£32,189

13.3 IT   Life Assurance Policies

	Normal basis £	Top slicing relief claim £
Tax applicable to policy gain		
Higher rate		
£738 at 40%	295.20	—
£179 at 40%	—	71.60
	295.20	71.60
Deduct		
Basic rate		
£738 at 20%	147.60	—
£179 at 20%	—	35.80
		£35.80
Appropriate multiple 3 × £35.80 (note (c))		£107.40
Tax chargeable lower of	£147.60 and	£107.40
Top slicing relief (£147.60 − £107.40) =	£40.20	

Notes

(a) As regards policies issued in respect of insurances made on or after 6 April 2013, a chargeable event gain is reduced to take account of any periods during which the policyholder was not resident in the UK. The reduction also applies in relation to an insurance made before 6 April 2013 if, on or after that date, the policy is varied so as to increase the benefits (an exercise of rights conferred by the policy being treated for this purpose as a variation), is assigned (in whole or in part) or becomes held as security for a debt.

(b) In the reduction fraction, the numerator is the number of days in the 'material interest period' when the individual was not UK resident. The denominator is the total number of days in the material interest period. The '*material interest period*' is broadly the policy period, i.e. the period for which the policy has run before the chargeable event occurs; see *ITTOIA 2005, s 528(5)(10)* for the full definition.

(c) In computing top slicing relief, the total policy gain is normally divided by the number of *complete* years the policy has run (6 years in this example) and the resulting tax multiplied by the same factor — see **13.1(A)** above. However, where a reduction has been made for periods of non-UK residence, that number is itself reduced by the number of complete years consisting wholly of days of non-UK residence (3 years in this example). Therefore, a factor of 3 (6 minus 3) applies in this example. [*ITTOIA 2005, s 536(6)–(8); FA 2013, Sch 8 paras 5, 7, Sch 45 paras 88(2)(3), 153(2)*].

(d) The calculation of tax payable would then proceed as in **13.1(A)** above with the top slicing relief given as a tax reduction.

Life Assurance Policies IT 13.4

13.4 LIFE ASSURANCE PREMIUM RELIEF (OBSOLESCENT)

[*ICTA 1988, ss 266, 274*]

Life assurance premiums totalling £2,100 (net) are paid in 2013/14 by a married woman on pre-14 March 1984 qualifying life policies in respect of her own life and that of her husband. Her income amounts to £11,700.

Calculation of limit of admissible premiums

Total income	£11,700
Limit is greater of $1/6$ thereof (£1,950) and £1,500	£1,950
Gross premiums paid — £2,100 × $\dfrac{100}{87.5}$	£2,400
Income tax relief on payments made £2,400 × 12 $1/2$%	300
Admissible premium relief £1,950 × 12 $1/2$%	244
Income tax relief clawed back	£56

Note

(a) Relief for premiums paid on qualifying life assurance policies is available only for insurances made before 14 March 1984. The relief is repealed altogether with effect for premiums due and payable on or after 6 April 2015 or due and payable before that date but paid on or after 6 July 2015. [*ICTA 1988, s 266; FA 2012, Sch 39 para 23*].

14 Losses

Cross-references. See also **18.2–18.4** PARTNERSHIPS, and see **26.2** SELF-ASSESSMENT for the method of giving effect under self-assessment to the carry-back of losses to earlier years of assessment.

14.1 SET-OFF OF TRADING LOSSES AGAINST GENERAL INCOME

[*ITA 2007, ss 61(2), 64, 65*]

L, a single woman, commences to trade on 1 July 2009, preparing accounts to 30 June, and has the following results (as adjusted for tax purposes) for the first four years.

	Profit/(loss) £
Year ended 30 June 2010	18,000
Year ended 30 June 2011	6,000
Year ended 30 June 2012	(2,000)
Year ended 30 June 2013	(14,000)

L has other income of £12,000 for 2012/13 and £19,000 for 2013/14, having had no other income in the earlier years.

The taxable profits for the first four tax years of the business are as follows

	£
2009/10 (1.7.09–5.4.10) (£18,000 × $^9/_{12}$)	13,500*
2010/11 (y/e 30.6.10)	18,000
2011/12 (y/e 30.6.11)	6,000
2012/13 (y/e 30.6.12)	Nil
2013/14 (y/e 30.6.13)	Nil

* Overlap relief accruing – £13,500.

L claims relief under *ITA 2007, s 64(2)(a)* (set-off against income of the same year) for the 2012/13 loss (£2,000). She also claims relief under *ITA 2007, s 64(2)(b)* (set-off against income of the preceding year) for the 2013/14 loss (£14,000), with a further claim being made under *ITA 2007, s 64(2)(a)* for the balance of that loss.

The tax position for 2012/13 and 2013/14 is as follows

	£
2012/13	
Total income before loss relief	12,000
Deduct Claim under *ITA 2007, s 64(2)(a) note (b)*	2,000
	10,000
Deduct Claim under *ITA 2007, s 64(2)(b)*	10,000

14.1 IT Losses

Net income	Nil

2013/14

Total income before loss relief	19,000
Deduct Claim under *ITA 2007, s 64(2)(a)*	4,000
Net income	15,000
Deduct Personal allowance	9,440
Taxable income	£5,560

Loss utilisation

	£
2012/13	
Loss available under *ITA 2007, s 64(2)(a)*	2,000
Deduct Utilised in 2012/13	2,000
Loss available under *ITA 2007, s 64(2)(b)*	14,000
Deduct Utilised in 2012/13	10,000
Loss available for relief in 2013/14 under *ITA 2007, s 64(2)(a)*	£4,000
2013/14	
Balance of loss available under *ITA 2007, s 64(2)(a)*	4,000
Deduct Utilised in 2013/14	4,000

Notes

(a) Under *ITA 2007, s 64*, relief is available for the tax year in which the loss arises (*section 64(2)(a)*) or the immediately preceding year (*section 64(2)(b)*).

(b) Where losses of two different years are set against the income of one tax year, then, regardless of the order of claims, relief for the current year's loss is given in priority to that for the following year's loss. [*ITA 2007, s 65(2)–(4)*]. This is beneficial to the taxpayer in this example as it leaves £4,000 of the 2013/14 loss to be relieved in that year.

(c) See **14.3** below for losses in the opening years of a business.

14.2 SET-OFF OF TRADING LOSSES ETC. AGAINST CAPITAL GAINS

[*ITA 2007, s 71; TCGA 1992, ss 261B, 261C*]

M has carried on a trade for some years, preparing accounts to 30 June each year. For the year ended 30 June 2013 he makes a trading loss of £17,000. His assessable profit for 2012/13 is £5,000 and his other income for both 2012/13 and 2013/14 amounts to £2,000. He makes a capital gain of £16,000 and a capital loss of £1,000 for 2013/14 and has capital

Losses IT 14.2

losses brought forward of £10,700. M makes claims for loss relief, against income of 2012/13 and income and gains of 2013/14, under *ITA 2007, s 64(2)(b), s 64(2)(a)* and *TCGA 1992, s 261B*.

Calculation of 'relevant amount'

	£
Trading loss — year ended 30.6.13	17,000
Relieved against other income for 2013/14	(2,000)
Relieved against income for 2012/13	(7,000)
Relevant amount	£8,000

Calculation of 'maximum amount'

	£
Gains for 2013/14	16,000
Deduct Losses for 2013/14	(1,000)
Unrelieved losses brought forward	(10,700)
Maximum amount	£4,300

Relief under *TCGA 1992, s 261B*

	£	£
Gains for the year		16,000
Losses for the year	1,000	
Relief under *TCGA 1992, s 261B*	4,300	
		5,300
Gain (covered by annual exemption)		£10,700
Capital losses brought forward and carried forward		£10,700

Loss memorandum

	£
Trading loss	17,000
Claimed under *ITA 2007, s 64(2)(a)*	(2,000)
Claimed under *ITA 2007, s 64(2)(b)*	(7,000)
Claimed under *TCGA 1992, s 261B*	(4,300)
Unutilised loss	£3,700

14.2 IT Losses

Notes

(a) Where relief is available under *ITA 2007, s 64* (set-off against general income) for a tax year and either a claim is made under that *section* or the person's total income for the year is nil, a claim may also be made to treat an amount of trading loss (determined as above) as an allowable capital loss for the year.

(b) The amount to be set against gains is restricted to so much of the 'relevant amount' as does not exceed the 'maximum amount'. The '*relevant amount*' is so much of the loss that cannot be set against income for the year and has not been otherwise relieved. The '*maximum amount*' is the amount chargeable to capital gains tax for the year, ignoring the annual exemption and the effect of *TCGA 1992, s 261B* itself.

(c) Capital losses brought forward are deducted in ascertaining the 'maximum amount', and thus the relief due under *TCGA 1992, s 261B*, but the relief itself is treated as an allowable loss for the year of claim and thus given in priority to capital losses brought forward.

(d) In this example, £200 of the capital gains tax annual exemption of £10,900 is wasted, but the brought forward capital losses are preserved for carry-forward against gains of future years. If M had *not* made the claim under *TCGA 1992, s 261B*, his net gains for the year of £15,000 would have been reduced to the annual exempt amount by deducting £4,100 of the losses brought forward. Only £6,600 of capital losses would remain available for carry-forward against future gains and a further £4,300 of trading losses would have been available for carry-forward against future trading profits. So the effect of the claim is to preserve capital losses at the expense of trading losses.

14.3 LOSSES IN EARLY YEARS OF A BUSINESS

(A) Losses carried back three years

[*ITA 2007, ss 72–74*]

F, a single person, commences to trade on 1 December 2010, preparing accounts to 30 November. The first four years of trading produce losses of £12,000, £9,000, £2,000 and £1,000 respectively, these figures being as adjusted for tax purposes. For each of the four tax years 2007/08 to 2010/11, F had other income of £8,000.

The losses for tax purposes are as follows

		£	£
2010/11	(1.12.10–5.4.11) (£12,000 × 4/12)		4,000
2011/12	(y/e 30.11.11)	12,000	
	Less already allocated to 2010/11	4,000	8,000
2012/13	(y/e 30.11.12)		9,000
2013/14	(y/e 30.11.13)		2,000
2014/15	(y/e 30.11.14) note (b)		1,000

Losses IT 14.3

Loss relief under *ITA 2007, s 72* is available as follows

	Losses available			
	2010/11 £	2011/12 £	2012/13 £	2013/14 £
Losses available	4,000	8,000	9,000	2,000
Set against total income				
2007/08	4,000	—	—	—
2008/09	—	8,000	—	—
2009/10	—	—	8,000	—
2010/11	—	—	1,000	2,000
	£4,000	£8,000	£9,000	£2,000

Revised total income is thus £4,000 for 2007/08, nil for 2008/09 and 2009/10 and £5,000 for 2010/11.

Notes

(a) Losses are computed by reference to the same basis periods as profits. Where any part of a loss would otherwise fall to be included in the computations for two successive tax years (as is the case for 2010/11 and 2011/12 in this example), that part is excluded from the computation for the second of those years. [*ITA 2007, s 61(2)*].

(b) The loss for the year ended 30 November 2014 in this example is not available for relief under *ITA 2007, s 72* as it does not fall into the first four *tax years* of the business (even though it is incurred in the first four years of trading). It is of course available for relief under *ITA 2007, s 64* (depending on the level of other income for 2013/14 and 2014/15) or for carry-forward under *ITA 2007, s 83*.

(B) **Computation of losses in early years**

Q commenced trading on 1 February 2013 and prepared accounts to 31 December. He made a trading loss of £20,900 in the eleven months to 31 December 2013 and profits of £18,000 and £16,000 in the years to 31 December 2014 and 2015 respectively. He has substantial other income for 2012/13 and 2013/14 and makes claims under *ITA 2007, s 64* for both years.

Taxable profits/(allowable losses) are as follows

		£	£
2012/13	(1.2.13–5.4.13) (£20,900) × $^2/_{11}$		(3,800)
2013/14	(1.2.13–31.1.14)		
	1.2.13–31.12.13	(20,900)	
	Less already allocated to 2012/13	3,800	
		(17,100)	
	1.1.14–31.1.14 £18,000 × $^1/_{12}$	1,500	

14.3 IT   Losses

		(15,600)
2014/15	(y/e 31.12.14)	18,000
	(Overlap relief accruing — £1,500)	
2015/16	(y/e 31.12.15)	16,000

Notes

(a) Losses are computed by reference to the same basis periods as profits. Where any part of a loss would otherwise fall to be included in the computations for two successive tax years (as is the case for 2012/13 and 2013/14 in this example), that part is excluded from the computation for the second of those years. [*ITA 2007, s 61(2)*].

(b) Losses available for relief for 2012/13 and 2013/14 are £3,800 and £15,600 respectively. If both years' losses are carried forward under *ITA 2007, s 83* instead of being set against other income (under either *ITA 2007, s 64* or *s 72*), the aggregate loss of £19,400 will extinguish the 2014/15 profit and reduce the 2015/16 profit by £1,400. Note that although the actual loss was £20,900, there is no further amount available for carry-forward: the difference of £1,500 has been used in aggregation in 2013/14.

(c) The net profit for the first three accounting periods is £13,100 (£18,000 + £16,000 − £20,900). The net taxable profit for the first four tax years is £14,600 (£18,000 + £16,000 − £3,800 − £15,600). The difference of £1,500 represents the overlap relief accrued, which will be given on cessation or on a change of accounting date resulting in a basis period of more than one year. Note that the overlap profit of £1,500 is by reference to an overlap period of *three* months, i.e. 1.2.13 to 5.4.13 (two months — overlap profit nil) and 1.1.14 to 31.1.14 (one month — overlap profit £1,500).

14.4   TERMINAL LOSS RELIEF

[*ITA 2007, ss 63, 89–91*]

B, a trader with a 30 September year end, ceases to trade on 30 June 2013. Tax-adjusted results for his last two periods of account are as follows

	Trading profit/(loss) £
Year ended 30 September 2012	28,000
Nine months to 30 June 2013	(9,000)

The terminal loss relief available is as follows

	£	£
2013/14 (6.4.13 – 30.6.13)		
£9,000 × ³/₉		3,000
plus unused overlap relief		2,000
Terminal loss		5,000

                                                            Losses   IT 14.5

2012/13 (1.7.12 – 5.4.13)
   1.10.12 – 5.4.13 £ 9,000 × ⁶/₉   6,000
   1.7.12 – 30.9.12 (£28,000) × ³/₁₂ (7,000)
              (1,000)
Terminal loss   Nil
Terminal loss relief   £5,000

Notes

(a) In determining the terminal loss arising in a part of the final twelve months (a terminal loss period) that falls into any one tax year, a profit made in that period must be netted off against a loss in that period. In this example, no loss has been incurred in the terminal loss period that falls within 2012/13. However, two different tax years are looked at separately, so that the 'net profit' of £1,000 arising in the terminal loss period falling within 2012/13 does not have to be netted off against the 2013/14 loss and is instead disregarded.

(b) Available overlap relief is given as a deduction in computing the profit or loss of the final *tax year* and is thus included in a terminal loss in full. It does not fall to be apportioned between tax years in the same way as a loss sustained for a *period of account*.

(c) The losses which do not form part of the terminal loss claim may be relieved under *ITA 2007, s 64*, and in practice, where other income is sufficient, the whole of the losses would in many cases be claimed under *section 64*.

14.5 SHARE LOSS RELIEF

[*ITA 2007, ss 131–151*]

Over the years, X has acquired a number of shareholdings in unquoted companies and suffers the following losses.

(i) 500 shares in A Ltd (a qualifying trading company) which X subscribed for in 1996. Allowable loss for CGT purposes on liquidation in June 2012 — £12,000.

(ii) 500 shares in B Ltd which X subscribed for in 1997 at £10 per share. B Ltd traded as builders until 2004 when it changed its trade to that of buying and selling land. X received an arm's length offer for the shares of £3 per share in May 2012 which he accepted.

(iii) In 1995, X subscribed for 2,000 shares in C Ltd at £50 per share. In 1999, his aunt gave him a further 1,000 shares. The market value of the shares at that time was £60 per share. The company has been a qualifying trading company since 1991 but has fallen on hard times recently. X was offered £20 per share in June 2013 and accepted it to the extent of 1,500 shares.

The treatment of these losses in relation to income tax would be as follows

(i) Loss claim — *ITA 2007, s 132*, 2012/13 or 2011/12 — £12,000.

(ii) No loss claim possible under *ITA 2007, s 132* as the company does not meet the trading requirement.

(iii) *Step 1.* Compute the allowable loss for capital gains tax purposes.

14.5 IT Losses

Share pool

	Shares	Qualifying expenditure
		£
1995 subscription	2,000	100,000
1999 acquisition	1,000	60,000
	3,000	160,000
2013 disposal	(1,500)	(80,000)
Pool carried forward	1,500	£80,000

	£
Disposal consideration 1,500 × £20	30,000
Allowable cost $\dfrac{1,500}{3,000}$ × £160,000	80,000
Allowable capital loss	£50,000

Step 2. Applying a LIFO basis, identify the qualifying shares (500) and the non-qualifying shares (1,000) comprised in the disposal.

Step 3. Calculate the proportion of the loss attributable to the qualifying shares.

Loss referable to 500 qualifying shares 500/1,500 × £50,000   £16,667

Step 4. Compare the loss in *Step 3* with the actual cost of the qualifying shares, *viz.*

Cost of 500 qualifying shares 500/2,000 × £100,000   £25,000

No restriction is necessary as the cost of the qualifying shares exceeds the loss in *Step 3*.

Loss claim — *ITA 2007, s 132* for 2013/14 or 2012/13 — £16,667

(The loss not relieved against income (£50,000 - £16,667 = £33,333) remains an allowable loss for capital gains tax purposes.)

X makes all possible claims under *ITA 2007, s 132* so as to obtain relief against the earliest possible income. He is a single man and has total income of £7,000 for 2011/12, £11,500 for 2012/13 and £10,000 for 2013/14.

The losses available are as follows

	2012/13 disposals	2013/14 disposals
	£	£
A Ltd shares	12,000	
C Ltd shares		16,667

Losses   IT 14.5

Claims are made as follows

	£
2011/12	
Total income	7,000
Claim under *ITA 2007, s 132(1)(b)*	(7,000)
Net income	Nil
2012/13	
Total income	11,500
Claim under *ITA 2007, s 132(1)(a)* note (b)	(5,000)
	6,500
Claim under *ITA 2007, s 132(1)(b)*	(6,500)
Net income	Nil
2013/14	
Total income	10,000
Claim under *ITA 2007, s 132(1)(a)*	(10,000)
Net income	Nil

Loss utilisation

	£
2012/13 loss	
Loss available	12,000
Relief claimed for 2011/12 *(ITA 2007, s 132(1)(b))*	(7,000)
Relief claimed for 2012/13 *(ITA 2007, s 132(1)(a))*	(5,000)
2013/14 loss	
Loss available	16,667
Relief claimed for 2012/13 *(ITA 2007, s 132(1)(b))*	(6,500)
Relief claimed for 2013/14 *(ITA 2007, s 132(1)(a))*	(10,000)
Unused balance note (c)	£167

Notes

(a)   Losses may be set against current year's income *(ITA 2007, s 132(1)(a))* or preceding year's income *(ITA 2007, s 132(1)(b))*. In this example, losses have been set against preceding year's income first, as X wished to obtain relief against earliest possible income, but this need not be the case.

(b)   Where two years' losses are set against one year's income, the current year's loss is relieved in priority to that of the following year. [*ITA 2007, s 133(3)*].

14.5 IT Losses

(c) The unused balance of the 2013/14 loss cannot be relieved under *ITA 2007, s 132* due to insufficiency of income and therefore reverts to being a capital loss available to reduce chargeable gains.

14.6 PROPERTY BUSINESS LOSSES

[*ITA 2007, ss 120–124*]

Simon owns the freehold of a four-storey building. The ground floor is let to a firm of undertakers, but the upper storeys are empty. Simon incurs expenditure of £10,000 in each of the two years ended 5 April 2012 and 5 April 2013 on converting the upper floors of the building into flats. This expenditure qualified for flat conversion allowances under *CAA 2001, ss 393A–393W*, and Simon claimed the full initial allowance of 100% for 2011/12 and 2013/14 but is entitled to no other capital allowances. Simon makes the following taxable profits and losses in respect of his UK property business:

	Profit/(loss) before capital allowances £	Capital allowances £	Profit/(loss) after capital allowances £
2011/12	(2,000)	(10,000)	(12,000)
2012/13	5,000	(10,000)	(5,000)
2013/14	8,000	—	8,000

Simon has other income of £5,000 for 2011/12, £20,000 for 2012/13 and £25,000 for 2013/14. He makes a claim under *ITA 2007, s 120* in respect of the property business loss for 2011/12 to set against income of 2011/12 first, with any remaining amount to be set against income of 2012/13. He claims under *ITA 2007, s 120* for the 2012/13 loss to be set against other income of 2012/13.

The tax position for 2011/12 to 2013/14 is as follows.

	£
2011/12	
Total income	5,000
Deduct claim under *ITA 2007, s 120* note (a)	(5,000)
Net income	Nil

	£
2012/13	
Total income	20,000
Deduct claims under *ITA 2007, s 120* note (b)	
2011/12 loss	(5,000)
2012/13 loss	(5,000)
Net income	£10,000

Losses IT 14.6

	£	£
2013/14		
Property income	8,000	
Deduct 2011/12 loss b/fwd	(2,000)	6,000
Other income		25,000
Net income		£31,000

Loss utilisation

	£
Loss for 2011/12	12,000
Used in 2011/12 under *ITA 2007, s 120*	(5,000)
Used in 2012/13 under *ITA 2007, s 120*	(5,000)
Used in 2013/14 under *ITA 2007, s 118*	(2,000)
Loss for 2012/13	5,000
Used in 2012/13 under *ITA 2007, s 120*	(5,000)

Notes

(a) The amount of relief for 2011/12 in respect of the 2011/12 loss under *ITA 2007, s 120* is the lowest of:

   (i) income of 2011/12 = £5,000;

   (ii) the property business loss for 2011/12 = £12,000; and

   (iii) the net capital allowances (after deducting any balancing charges) for 2011/12 = £10,000.

   Relief is therefore restricted to £5,000. In practice, Simon would be likely to claim relief for the 2011/12 loss for 2012/13 only, to avoid wasting personal allowances.

(b) The amount of relief for 2012/13 in respect of the 2011/12 loss under *ITA 2007, s 120* is the balance of the lower of (ii) and (iii) in note (a) above after deducting the relief given in 2011/12 (i.e. £5,000), or where lower the income of 2012/13.

   The amount of relief for 2012/13 in respect of the 2012/13 loss under *ITA 2007, s 120* is the lowest of:

   (A) income of the year less relief given for 2012/13 in respect of the 2011/12 loss (£20,000 − £5,000) = £15,000;

   (B) the property business loss for 2012/13 = £5,000; and

   (C) the net capital allowances for 2012/13 = £10,000.

   Relief is therefore restricted to £5,000.

(c) A claim under *ITA 2007, s 120* must be made on or before the first anniversary of 31 January following the tax year for which relief is claimed.

14.6 IT Losses

(d) Any balance of a property business loss not claimed under *ITA 2007, s 120* is carried forward to be set against profits of the UK property business of subsequent years, earliest first. [*ITA 2007, ss 118, 119*].

(e) Where a UK property business is carried on in relation to land consisting of or including an agricultural estate, a claim may be made under *ITA 2007, s 120* as above to the extent that the loss consists of 'allowable agricultural expenses', being expenses attributable to the estate which are deductible in respect of maintenance, repairs, insurance or management of the estate (and not in respect of interest on a loan). [*ITA 2007, ss 122, 123, 127B; FA 2012, s 10*]. In computing the amount of relief, the amount in (ii) in note (a) above would then be the net capital allowances plus the allowable agricultural expenses.

(f) A restriction applies if a loss arises in connection with tax avoidance arrangements on or after 24 March 2010 and there is a net amount of capital allowances. No property loss relief against general income may be given to the person making the loss for so much of the available loss relief as is attributable to a plant and machinery annual investment allowance. [*ITA 2007, s 127A; FA 2010, s 25*].

(g) Flat conversion allowances are abolished with effect for expenditure incurred on or after 6 April 2013. Writing-down allowances on earlier expenditure also cease to be available for 2013/14 onwards. [*FA 2012, Sch 39 paras 36, 37, 40, 42*].

15 Married Persons and Civil Partners

15.1 TRANSFER OF PERSONAL RELIEFS

(A) **Election to transfer basic married couple's allowance**

[*ITA 2007, ss 45, 47–50*]

Before 6 April 2013, Mr and Mrs Scarlet made a joint election under *ITA 2007, s 48* to transfer from husband to wife the whole of the basic married couple's allowance with effect for 2013/14 and later years. Mr Scarlet was born on 29 May 1934 and his wife on 6 January 1952. The couple married before 5 December 2005 and have not made the joint election under *ITA 2007, s 44* to be treated in the same way as couples marrying on or after that date. For 2013/14, their income is as follows.

	Mr Scarlet	Mrs Scarlet
	£	£
Employment income	—	33,930
Pension income	6,620	—
Dividends (net)	2,250	3,240
Building society interest (net)	8,000	1,232

The couple's tax position for 2013/14 is as follows

	£	£
Employment income	—	35,265
Pension income	6,620	
Dividends plus tax credits	2,500	3,600
Building society interest (gross)	10,000	1,540
Total and net income	19,120	40,405
Deduct Personal allowance	10,660	9,440
Taxable income	£8,460	£30,965

Tax payable:
2,790 @ 10% (starting rate for savings)	279.00	
3,170 @ 20% (basic rate on savings income)	634.00	
2,500 @ 10% (dividend ordinary rate)	250.00	
27,365 @ 20% (basic rate)		5,473.00
3,600 @ 10% (dividend ordinary rate)		360.00
	1,163.00	5,833.00

Deduct Married couple's allowance (£7,915):

15.1 IT Married Persons and Civil Partners

£4,875 @ 10%	487.50	
£3,040 @ 10%		304.00
Total tax liabilities	675.50	5,529.00
Deduct Dividend tax credits	(250.00)	(360.00)
Tax on building society interest	(2,000.00)	(308.00)
Net tax (repayment)/liability (subject to Mrs Scarlet's PAYE deductions)	(£1,574.50)	£4,861.00

Notes

(a) Married couple's allowance is available only where one of the spouses/civil partners was born before 6 April 1935.

(b) A wife can elect to receive half the basic married couple's allowance (i.e. the minimum amount below which the age-related allowance may not be reduced by reference to the income of the claimant) or, as illustrated in this example, husband and wife can jointly elect for the whole of the basic amount to be allocated to the wife. An election is not dependent on levels of income but, except for the year of marriage, must be made before the start of the first year for which it is to apply (e.g. before 6 April 2013 to have effect for 2013/14). [*ITA 2007, ss 47–50*].

(c) If the wife's income is too low to fully utilise the married couple's allowance allocated to her, she may transfer the excess allowance back to the husband. [*ITA 2007, s 52*]. The transfer operates in the same way as a transfer of surplus married couple's allowance from husband to wife — see (B) below.

(d) As the married couple's allowance attracts tax relief at a fixed rate of 10%, an election to transfer the basic allowance does not normally save any tax, although the election may have cash flow advantages where the wife pays tax under PAYE and the husband does not.

(e) Civil partners and couples who marry on or after 5 December 2005 (or who married before that date and elect into the new rules) are also able to transfer the basic married couple's allowance between them. [*ITA 2007, ss 47–50*].

(B) Transfer of surplus married couple's allowance

[*ITA 2007, ss 45, 51, 53*]

Mr Grey, who was born on 19 July 1933, has pension income of £8,680 and building society interest of £1,040 (net) for 2013/14 and his wife, who was born in 1953, has a salary of £19,405 and building society interest of £2,000 (net). Mr and Mrs Grey receive interest of £2,240 (net) in 2013/14 from a bank deposit account in their joint names. The couple have not made the joint election under *ITA 2007, s 44* to be treated in the same way as couples who marry on or after 5 December 2005. Neither have they made the election at (A) above to transfer the basic married couple's allowance between them. Mr Grey gives notice under *ITA 2007, s 51* to transfer the unused balance of his married couple's allowance for 2013/14 to his wife.

Married Persons and Civil Partners IT 15.1

The couple's tax position for 2013/14 is as follows

	Mr Grey	Mrs Grey
	£	£
Employment income	—	19,405
Pension income	8,680	—
Building society interest (gross)	1,300	2,500
Bank deposit interest (gross) (note (b))	1,400	1,400
Total and net income	11,380	23,305
Deduct Personal allowance	10,660	9,440
Taxable income	£720	£13,865
Tax payable:		
720 @ 10% (starting rate for savings)	72.00	
13,865 @ 20% (basic rate)	—	2,773.00
	72.00	2,773.00
Deduct Married couple's allowance		
7,915 @ 10% = £791.50, but restricted to	72.00	
Deduct Excess married couple's allowance (note (b))	—	719.50
Total tax liabilities	Nil	2,053.50
Deduct Tax at source:		
Building society interest	(260.00)	(500.00)
Bank deposit interest	(280.00)	(280.00)
Net tax (repayment)/liability (subject to PAYE)	£(540.00)	£1,273.50

Notes

(a) Where the married couple's allowance is restricted to the amount that reduces the tax liability to nil (or where no married couple's allowance can be given as there is no tax liability), the unused part of the allowance (or all of it) can be transferred to the spouse. Married couple's allowance is available only where one of the spouses/civil partners was born before 6 April 1935.

(b) Mr Grey's 'comparable tax liability' (see *ITA 2007, s 53(1)–(3)*) is £72.00. Thus the excess married couple's allowance is £719.50 (£791.50 - £72.00).

(c) Income from property held in their joint names is normally divided equally between husband and wife (and civil partners). [*ITA 2007, s 836*]. Note that certain gifts and settlements between spouses (and civil partners) of property from which income arises are not valid transfers of income. [*ITTOIA 2005, s 626*]. This applies where the donor retains an interest in the property. Outright gifts comprising both income and capital should not be caught.

(d) Civil partners and couples who marry on or after 5 December 2005 (or who married before that date and elect into the new rules) are also able to transfer surplus married couple's allowance between them.

15.2 IT   Married Persons and Civil Partners

15.2 MAINTENANCE PAYMENTS

[*ITA 2007, ss 453–456, Sch 2 para 101*]

Mr Green, who was born on 7 October 1933, separated from his wife in June 2000 and, under a Court Order dated 15 July 2001, pays maintenance of £300 per month to his ex-wife and £100 per month to his daughter, payments being due on the first of each calendar month commencing 1 August 2001. Mr Green has pension income of £16,830 and net dividends of £4,500 for 2013/14. He re-marries on 6 October 2013.

		£	£
2013/14			
Mr Green			
Earned income			16,830
Dividends		4,500	
Add Dividend tax credits (£4,500 × $^1/_9$)		500	5,000
Total and net income			21,830
Deduct Personal allowance			10,660
Taxable income			£11,170
Tax payable:			
6,170	@ 20% (basic rate)		1,234.00
5,000	@ 10% (dividend ordinary rate)		500.00
			1,734.00
Deduct	Maintenance relief — wife:		
	£3,600 paid, but restricted to £3,040 @ 10%		304.00
			1,430.00
Deduct	Married couple's allowance		
	£7,915 × $^6/_{12}$ = £3,958 @ 10%		395.80
Total tax liability			1,034.20
Deduct Dividend tax credits			500.00
Net liability (subject to PAYE deductions)			£534.20

Notes

(a)   Relief for qualifying maintenance payments is restricted to cases where at least one of the parties was aged 65 or over on 5 April 2000. The relief is restricted to an amount equal to a percentage of the basic married couple's allowance for the year. No relief is due for other maintenance payments. Relief is given by way of income tax reduction and is restricted to 10%.

(b)   Maintenance payments are exempt from tax in the hands of the recipient.

(c)   Tax relief for maintenance payments does not affect entitlement to the married couple's allowance either in the year of re-marriage or in later years. The allowance for the year of re-marriage is restricted in the normal way under *ITA 2007, s 54*.

16 Non-Residents

16.1 LIMIT ON LIABILITY TO INCOME TAX

[*ITA 2007, ss 56, 460, 810–828, Sch 2 paras 14–17; ITTOIA 2005, s 397(1)(4); FA 2013, Sch 45 para 152(5), Sch 46 paras 66, 72*]

Hugh and Elizabeth are non-UK residents throughout 2013/14. They are each entitled to a UK personal allowance under *ITA 2007, s 56*. Their tax liabilities on total UK income for 2013/14, disregarding the limit under *ITA 2007, s 811*, are as follows

	Hugh £	Elizabeth £
Net rental income (received gross)	2,500	6,300
Bank interest (received gross)	11,730	3,950
Dividends	3,600	—
Dividend tax credits	400	—
Total UK income	18,230	10,250
Deduct Personal allowance	9,440	9,440
Taxable UK income	£8,790	£810
Tax on total UK income:		
£2,790/810 @ 10% (starting rate for savings)	279.00	81.00
£2,000 @ 20% (basic rate on interest)	400.00	
£4,000 @ 10% (dividend ordinary rate)	400.00	
	1,079.00	81.00
Deduct Dividend tax credits	400.00	
	£679.00	£81.00

But tax is limited under *ITA 2007, s 811* as follows

	£	£
Property income	2,500	6,300
(Bank interest and dividends are 'disregarded income'.)		
£2,500/6,300 @ 20% (basic rate)	£500.00	£1,260.00

Notes

(a) 'Disregarded income' includes interest and other annual payments, dividends from UK resident companies, purchased life annuity payments, profits from deeply discounted securities, distributions from unit trusts, some social security benefits (including state pensions), retirement annuities, certain UK-sourced employment-related annuities and any other income so designated by the Treasury, but generally excluding income from non-UK sources. [*ITA 2007, s 813*].

16.1 IT   Non-Residents

(b)   Hugh's UK income tax liability is therefore restricted to £500.00 (plus £400.00 in dividend tax credits, which cannot be reclaimed). The total of £900.00 is less than the figure of £1,079.00 in the normal computation and means that Hugh has to pay only £500.00 to HMRC as opposed to £679.00. Elizabeth's liability is not reduced under *ITA 2007, s 811* and is thus £81.00.

16.2 NON-RESIDENT ENTERTAINERS AND SPORTSMEN

[*ITA 2007, ss 965–970; ITTOIA 2005, ss 13, 14; SI 1987 No 530; SI 2012 No 1359; SI 2013 No 605, Regs 2, 3*]

G, a professional golfer who is not resident in the UK, visits the UK in July 2013 to play in a tournament from which he earns £80,000 in appearance and prize money. He directs that the money be paid to a non-resident company which he controls. During his visit, he receives £8,000 from a UK television company for a series of interviews and £15,000 from a national newspaper for a number of exclusive articles. He arranges for 22.5% of the latter sum to be paid direct to his agent, also non-resident and who pays tax on his income at a rate not exceeding 25%, who arranged the deal. G incurs allowable expenses of £14,000 in connection with the trip. He has no other taxable income in the UK during 2013/14. He does not qualify for UK personal reliefs.

G's UK tax position for 2013/14 is as follows

		Taxable income	Tax withheld at source
		£	£
Prize and appearance money	note (b)	80,000	16,000
Fee from television company	note (c)	8,000	—
Fee for newspaper articles	note (d)	15,000	3,000
		103,000	19,000
Deduct Expenses		14,000	
		£89,000	

Tax payable		£	
32,010 at 20%		6,402	
56,990 at 40%		22,976	
£89,000		29,198	
Tax payable			£10,198

Notes

(a)   G is considered to have carried on a trade in the UK in respect of the payments received, or deemed to have been received, by him in connection with his UK activities. The trade is distinct from any other trade carried on by him. [*ITTOIA 2005, s 13*].

(b) A payment to a company under the entertainer's (or sportsman's) control (defined in accordance with *ICTA 1988, s 416(1)–(6)*) is treated as a payment to him and withholding tax at the basic rate must be deducted at source. [*ITTOIA 2005, s 14; SI 1987 No 530, Reg 7*].

(c) No withholding tax falls to be deducted from the television company fee as it does not exceed the de minimis limit. [*SI 1987 No 530, Reg 4(3)*]. The limit used to be £1,000 but was increased, for payments made on or after 1 July 2012, to the amount of the basic personal allowance for the year in question (£9,440 for 2013/14). [*SI 2012 No 1359*].

(d) Although a percentage of the fee for newspaper articles was paid not to G but to his agent, it falls to be treated as G's income and is subject to withholding tax by virtue of his agent's being non-resident in the UK and liable to tax at a rate not exceeding 25% in his country of residence. [*SI 1987 No 530, Reg 7(2)(b)*].

(e) It is assumed in the above example that G would not have been able to agree with HMRC a reduced rate of withholding tax. He could have attempted to do so by making written application, under *SI 1987 No 530, Reg 5*, not later than 30 days before any payment fell to be made. However, the total reduced tax payment must represent, as nearly as can be, the actual liability of the performer.

17 Partnerships

17.1 BASIS OF ASSESSMENT

[*ITTOIA 2005, ss 846–856*].

(A) Changes in partners etc.

P and Q commenced trading in partnership on 1 July 2009, making up accounts to 30 June. Under the partnership agreement P is to receive a salary of £10,000 per year and Q a salary of £5,000. Profits are to be shared in the ratio 3:2. On 1 July 2012 R becomes a partner, and profits for the year to 30 June 2013 are shared in the ratio 2:2:1 (P and Q continuing to receive their salaries). On 30 June 2013 P leaves the partnership and profits are thereafter shared between Q and R in the ratio 2:1 (Q continuing to receive his salary).

Results for relevant years up to 30 June 2014 are as follows

Year ended	Partners' salaries			Adjusted Profit
	P	Q	R	
	£	£	£	£
30.6.10	10,000	5,000	—	30,000
30.6.11	10,000	5,000	—	35,000
30.6.12	10,000	5,000	—	38,000
30.6.13	10,000	5,000	—	51,000
30.6.14	—	5,000	—	47,000

The adjusted profit figures above are after adding back partners' salaries, which are not deductible for tax purposes.

The tax position for the years 2009/10 to 2014/15 is as follows

	P	Q	R
	£	£	£
2009/10			
1.7.09–5.4.10			
Profits £(30,000 − 15,000) × $^9/_{12}$	6,750	4,500	
Salaries × $^9/_{12}$	7,500	3,750	
Trading income	£14,250	£8,250	
2010/11			
Y/e 30.6.10			
Profits £(30,000 − 15,000)	9,000	6,000	
Salaries	10,000	5,000	
Trading income	£19,000*	£11,000*	

119

17.1 IT   Partnerships

*Overlap relief accrued:
(1.7.09–5.4.10)   £14,250   £8,250

2011/12
Y/e 30.6.11
Profits £(35,000 − 15,000)   12,000   8,000
Salaries   10,000   5,000
Trading income   £22,000   £13,000

2012/13
Y/e 30.6.12
Profits £(38,000 − 15,000)   13,800   9,200
Salaries   10,000   5,000
                                                 £23,800   £14,200
1.7.12–5.4.13
Profits £(51,000 − 15,000) × $1/5$ × $9/12$ 5,400
Trading income   £23,800   £14,200   £5,400

2013/14
Y/e 30.6.13
Profits £(51,000 − 15,000)   14,400   14,400   7,200
Salaries   10,000   5,000   —
                                                  24,400   £19,400   7,200
Less overlap relief
(see 2010/11)   14,250   —   —
Trading income   £10,150   £19,400   £7,200*
*Overlap relief accrued:
(1.7.12–5.4.13)   £5,400

2014/15
Y/e 30.6.14
Profits £(47,000 − 5,000)   28,000   14,000
Salaries   5,000   —
Trading income   £33,000   £14,000

Notes

(a) On a partnership change (e.g. the admission or retirement of a partner), the partnership is automatically regarded as continuing, providing there is at least one continuing partner.

(b) Profits are allocated between partners for tax purposes in accordance with the profit-sharing ratios in force during a period of account. Each partner is taxed on his own share, the partnership not being treated as a separate entity. The normal

Partnerships IT 17.1

rules used to determine the basis periods for the early years and closing years of a business apply to individuals joining or leaving a partnership. [*ITTOIA 2005, ss 850(1), 852, 853*].

(B) **Partnership trading and investment income**

X and Y begin to trade in partnership on 1 July 2009 preparing first accounts to 30 September 2010 and sharing profits equally. Z joins the firm as an equal partner on 1 October 2011. Y leaves the firm on 31 March 2013. Accounts are prepared to that date to ascertain Y's entitlement but the accounting date then reverts to 30 September and the partnership does not give notice to HMRC of a change of accounting date, so there is no change of basis period. In addition to trading profits, the partnership had a source of lettings income which ceased in September 2012 and is in receipt of both taxed and untaxed interest, the latter from a source commencing in October 2010. Taxed interest is received on 31 March each year. Relevant figures as adjusted for tax purposes are as follows.

	Trading income	Property income	Savings income (untaxed interest)	Savings income (taxed interest) (gross)
	£	£	£	£
15 months to 30.9.10	30,000	4,500	—	750
Year to 30.9.11	24,000	5,000	1,000	1,500
Year to 30.9.12	39,000	3,000	600	300
6 months to 31.3.13	19,500	—	225	165
6 months to 30.9.13	14,000	—	140	—

The partners' shares of taxable income from the partnership for the years 2009/10 to 2013/14 are as follows

Trading income

	X	Y	Z
	£	£	£
2009/10			
1.7.09–5.4.10 (£30,000 × 9/15)	9,000	9,000	
2010/11			
1.10.09–30.9.10 (£30,000 × 12/15)	12,000*	12,000*	
* Overlap relief accrued			
1.10.09–5.4.10 (£30,000 × 6/15)	(6,000)	(6,000)	
2011/12			
Y/e 30.9.11	12,000	12,000	

17.1 IT   Partnerships

1.10.11–5.4.12
($£39,000 \times {}^6/_{12} \times {}^1/_3$)   6,500

2012/13
Y/e 30.9.12   13,000   13,000   13,000*
1.10.12–31.3.13   6,500
                                                                                     19,500
Less overlap relief   (6,000)
                                                                                     13,500

* Overlap relief accrued
1.10.11–5.4.12 (as above)   (6,500)

2013/14
Y/e 30.9.13
1.10.12–31.3.13   6,500   6,500
1.4.13–30.9.13   7,000   7,000
                                                                        13,500   13,500

Property income
2009/10
1.7.09–5.4.10 ($£4,500 \times {}^9/_{15}$)   1,350   1,350

2010/11
1.10.09–30.9.10 ($£4,500 \times {}^{12}/_{15}$)   1,800*   1,800*

* Overlap relief accrued
1.10.09–5.4.10 ($£4,500 \times {}^6/_{15}$)   (900)   (900)

2011/12
Y/e 30.9.11   2,500   2,500

1.10.11–5.4.12
($£3,000 \times {}^6/_{12} \times {}^1/_3$)   500

2012/13
Y/e 30.9.12   1,000   1,000   1,000*
1.10.12–31.3.13   —
                                                                                       1,000
Less overlap relief   (900)
                                                                                         100

Partnerships   IT 17.1

* Overlap relief accrued
1.10.11–5.4.12 (as above) (500)

Savings income (untaxed)
2011/12
Y/e 30.9.11   500   500

1.10.11–5.4.12
(£600 × ⁶/₁₂ × ¹/₃)   100

2012/13
Y/e 30.9.12   200   200   200*
1.10.12–31.3.13   75
                                                     275

* Overlap relief accrued
1.10.11–5.4.12 (as above)   (100)

2013/14
Y/e 30.9.13
1.10.12–31.3.13   75   75
1.4.13–30.9.13   70   70
                                         145   145

Savings income (taxed)

2009/10 (received 31.3.10)   375   375

2010/11 (received 31.3.11)   750   750

2011/12 (received 31.3.12)   100   100   100

2012/13 (received 31.3.13)   55   55   55

2013/14   ***   —   ***
*** Each to be based on one-half of interest received 31.3.14.

Notes

(a)   As regards trading profits, see also (A) above.

(b)   Untaxed investment income of a trading or professional partnership is taxed by reference to the same periods as the trading or professional profits with the same rules as to overlap relief, changes of accounting date (not illustrated here) etc. For this purpose, all sources of such income are regarded as a single source which

17.1 IT   Partnerships

commences when a partner joins the partnership and ceases when he leaves (regardless of when any source actually commences or ceases). Thus, the basis of assessment for any tax year will always follow that for the trading or professional income source. [*ITTOIA 2005, ss 851, 854, 855*].

(c) Any excess of investment income overlap relief over untaxed investment income for the tax year in which the relief falls to be given is deductible in arriving at the partner's total income for that year (not illustrated in this example). [*ITTOIA 2005, s 856*].

(d) The above rules do not apply to taxed investment income, which is taxed on a fiscal year basis as for an individual but is apportioned between partners according to their shares for the period of account in which the income arises. Nor do those rules apply to untaxed income receivable by a partnership not carrying on a trade or profession, such income being taxable on a fiscal year basis as for an individual.

(e) For convenience, income for accounting periods has been apportioned to tax years on a time basis in this example. However, *ITTOIA 2005, s 203* strictly permits a time basis to be used only where 'it is necessary'. It may be more appropriate to apportion untaxed interest, for example, according to the dates when it was received. For instance, if the £600 interest received in the year to 30 September 2012 had been received as to, say, £100 on 31 December 2011 and £500 on 30 June 2012, Z's taxable interest for 2011/12 (and his overlap relief) could be taken as a one-third share of £100 rather than a one-third share of £600 × 6/12.

17.2 UNUSUAL ALLOCATIONS OF PROFITS/LOSSES BETWEEN PARTNERS

[*ITTOIA 2005, s 850(2)–(5)*].

J, K and L are full equity partners, sharing profits and losses equally and preparing accounts to 30 April. The partnership agreement also makes provision for partners' salaries, and for the year to 30 April 2013, J and K are entitled to salaries of £12,000 and £5,000 respectively. However, the firm has an unexpectedly bad year and makes a loss of £13,000, this being the tax-adjusted figure after adding back non-deductible partners' salaries.

The initial allocation between partners is as follows

	Total	J	K	L
	£	£	£	£
Partnership loss	(13,000)			
Allocate salaries	17,000	12,000	5,000	—
Loss after salaries	(£30,000)	(10,000)	(10,000)	(10,000)
Allocation of loss	(£13,000)	2,000	(£5,000)	(£10,000)

A reallocation must be made as follows

For tax purposes, a profit cannot be allocated to one partner (in this case J) if the partnership as a whole has made a tax loss. (Similarly, if the partnership had made a tax profit, no partner could have a tax loss.) J's allocation must be reduced to nil and the profit initially allocated to K and L must be proportionately reduced as follows.

$$\text{K's loss} = £13,000 \times \frac{5,000}{5,000 + 10,000} = \underline{£4,333}$$

Partnerships   IT 17.3

$$\text{L's loss} = £13{,}000 \times \frac{10{,}000}{5{,}000 + 10{,}000} = £8{,}667$$

	Total	J	K	L
Final allocation	(£13,000)	Nil	(£4,333)	(£8,667)

Note

(a) The losses allocated to K and L are losses of the basis period for 2013/14 and are therefore tax losses of that year. [*ITA 2007, s 62*]. It is up to each of K and L individually to decide what to do with his allocated loss, e.g. carry it forward, set it off against other income etc.

17.3 LIMITED PARTNERSHIPS — LOSSES

[*ITA 2007, ss 103–106, 113A, 114*]

R and S, who have been trading in partnership for several years preparing accounts to 30 June, share profits and losses equally. S is a limited partner.

For the year ended 30 June 2013, the partnership made a loss of £12,000. Other relevant details are as follows

	R £	S £
Other income 2013/14	10,000	8,000
Capital and accumulated profits At 30.6.13	4,000	5,000

R and S may claim loss relief under ITA 2007, s 64 for 2013/14 as follows

	R £	S £
Other income	10,000	8,000
Share of partnership loss (restricted for S)	(6,000)	(5,000)
	£4,000	£3,000
Loss carried forward against future partnership trading profits	—	£1,000

Notes

(a) The amount of partnership loss which a limited partner may set against general income and gains is restricted to the amount of his 'contribution to the firm' (broadly his capital contribution and accumulated profits) at the end of the basis period for the tax year in which the loss is sustained.

17.3 IT Partnerships

(b) Certain amounts must be excluded from a limited partner's contribution for these purposes, where the cost of providing those amounts is or could be borne by another person.

(c) The relief a limited partner can claim (against general income and gains) for what remains of the loss after applying the above restrictions is capped at £25,000. [*ITA 2007, ss 103, 103C, 103D; ITTOIA 2005, s 863(2)*].

17.4 LIMITED LIABILITY PARTNERSHIPS — LOSSES

[*ITA 2007, ss 107–109, 113A(2)–(4), 114; LLPA 2000, s 10(1)*]

Mr Wainwright becomes a member of a limited liability trading partnership on 6 April 2011. The partnership prepares accounts to 5 April each year. He introduces capital of £20,000 into the partnership on 6 April 2011, and on 1 April 2014 he makes a further capital contribution of £12,000.

His share of the partnership's trading losses are as follows

Y/e 5 April 2012	£12,000
Y/e 5 April 2013	£12,000
Y/e 5 April 2014	£6,000

Mr Wainwright claims relief under *ITA 2007, s 64* for these losses against his general income. The amounts available are as follows:

	£	£
2011/12		
Share of loss y/e 5.4.12		12,000
Capital contribution 6.4.11		20,000
Unrelieved capital contribution c/fwd		£8,000
ITA 2007, s 64 relief available		£12,000
2012/13		
Share of loss y/e 5.4.13		12,000
Unrelieved capital contribution b/fwd		8,000
Total unrelieved loss c/fwd		£4,000
ITA 2007, s 64 relief available		£8,000
2013/14		
Share of loss y/e 5.4.14	6,000	
Total unrelieved loss b/fwd	4,000	10,000
Capital contribution 1.4.14		12,000
Unrelieved capital contribution c/fwd		£2,000
ITA 2007, s 64 relief available		£10,000

Partnerships IT 17.4

Notes

(a) The amounts of partnership trading loss which a member of a limited liability partnership may set against general income and gains are restricted to the amount of his 'contribution to the LLP' (as defined) at the end of the basis period for the tax year in which the loss is sustained.

(b) Amounts relating to a trade carried on by a member of a limited liability partnership which are prevented from being given or allowed by (a) above are referred to as the member's 'total unrelieved loss'. In each subsequent tax year in which the member continues to carry on the trade and any of the total unrelieved loss remains outstanding, the balance of the total unrelieved loss is treated for the purposes of *ITA 2007, s 64*, *ITA 2007, s 72* and *TCGA 1992, s 261B*, and for the purposes of (a) above, as having been made in that subsequent tax year.

(c) 'Contribution to the LLP' falls to be restricted as in note (b) to **17.3** above.

18 Pension Provision

18.1 RELIEF FOR CONTRIBUTIONS BY INDIVIDUAL MEMBERS

[*FA 2004, ss 188–195, 195A, Sch 36 paras 39, 40; ITA 2007, s 58; FA 2009, s 6(5)(6), Sch 2 para 11*]

(A) Henry

Henry, a single man born after 5 April 1948, carries on a trade in the UK in which he makes an allowable loss of £1,000 for 2011/12 (for which he claims relief against 2010/11 income), a taxable profit of £17,000 for 2012/13 and a taxable profit of £43,000 for 2013/14. His only other income consists of building society interest of £5,600 (net) and UK dividends of £900; these figures remain constant for the three years in question. He makes net contributions to a registered pension scheme of £2,400 during the tax year 2011/12 and £4,000 during each of the tax years 2012/13 and 2013/14.

Henry's tax liabilities are as follows.

2011/12

		£
Trading income		Nil
Taxed interest £5,600 × $^{100}/_{80}$		7,000
UK dividends £900 × $^{100}/_{90}$		1,000
Total and net income		8,000
Less Personal Allowance		7,475
Taxable Income		£525
Tax Liability		
525	@ 10% (dividend ordinary rate)	52.50
Deduct	tax credits on dividends	(52.50)
	tax paid at source on interest	(1,400.00)
		£(1,400.00)

Henry is entitled to an income tax repayment of £1,400.00. (Dividend tax credits can be offset only to the extent that the dividends are chargeable to tax, and the excess cannot be repaid.) Henry has made gross pension contributions of £3,000 (£2,400 × 100/80). As his gross contributions do not exceed £3,600, he is entitled to tax relief even though he has no relevant UK earnings for the year. He is not required to repay the basic rate tax of £600 withheld at source from the contributions.

2012/13

	£
Trading income	17,000
Taxed interest (as before)	7,000

18.1 IT Pension Provision

UK dividends (as before)	1,000
Total and net income	25,000
Less Personal Allowance	8,105
Taxable Income	£16,895

Tax Liability		
15,895	@ 20% (basic rate)	3,179.00
1,000	@ 10% (dividend ordinary rate)	100.00
£16,895		
		3,279.00
Deduct	tax paid at source on interest	(1,400.00)
	tax credits on dividends	(100.00)
		£1,779.00

Henry has made gross pension contributions of £5,000 (£4,000 × 100/80). His relevant UK earnings are £17,000, which is more than sufficient to cover the gross contributions. He is entitled to full tax relief, which he has already obtained by deduction at source.

2013/14

	£
Trading income	43,000
Taxed interest (as before)	7,000
UK dividends (as before)	1,000
Total and net income	51,000
Less Personal Allowance	9,440
Taxable Income	£41,560

Tax Liability		
37,010	@ 20% (basic rate)	7,402.00
3,550	@ 40% (higher rate)	1,420.00
1,000	@ 32.5% (dividend upper rate)	325.00
£41,560		9,147.00
Deduct	tax paid at source on interest	(1,400.00)
	tax credits on dividends	(100.00)
		£7,647.00

Henry has made gross pension contributions of £5,000 (£4,000 × 100/80). His relevant UK earnings are £43,000, which is more than sufficient to cover the gross contributions. He has obtained basic rate tax relief at 20% by deduction at source. He obtains higher rate relief by extension of the basic rate band; the normal basic rate limit of £32,010 is increased by £5,000 to £37,010. Without that increase, £1,550 of trading income and an additional £3,450 of taxed interest would have been taxable at 40% instead of 20% (a 20% saving). (Above the normal basic rate limit, the rate at which the pension contributions save tax will depend on the mix of taxable income, i.e. the extent to which it is dividend income or other income.)

Pension Provision IT 18.1

Notes

(a) A 'relevant UK individual' (see *FA 2004, s 189(1)*) is entitled to relief on contributions to a registered pension scheme up to the total amount of his 'relevant UK earnings' (see *FA 2004, s 189(2)(3)*) within the charge to income tax for the year. Provided, however, the scheme operates tax relief at source, contributions of up to £3,600 (gross) attract relief even if total relevant UK earnings are less than that amount or if there are no such earnings.

(b) Provided the individual has sufficient relevant UK earnings to cover them there is no upper limit on the contributions that can be relieved in each year. Tax relief may, however, be effectively clawed back by the application of the lifetime allowance charge and/or the annual allowance charge.

(B) **Celia**

Celia is a self-employed professional with taxable profits of £200,000 for the year to 30 April 2013. She has bank deposit interest of £3,200 (net) for 2013/14. She makes net contributions to a registered pension scheme of £16,000 during the tax year ending on 5 April 2014.

Celia's 2013/14 income tax liability is computed as follows.

	£
Professional income	200,000
Taxed interest (£3,200 x 100/80)	4,000
Total and net income	204,000
Less Personal Allowance (note (b))	—
Taxable Income	£204,000
Tax Liability	
52,010 @ 20% (basic rate)	10,402.00
117,990 @ 40% (higher rate)	47,196.00
34,000 @ 45% (additional rate)	15,300.00
£204,000	
	72,898.00
Deduct tax paid at source on interest	(800.00)
	£72,098.00

Notes

(a) Celia has made gross pension contributions of £20,000 (£16,000 × 100/80) and has obtained basic rate relief at source. She obtains additional rate relief by extension of the basic rate band; the normal basic rate limit of £32,010 is increased by £20,000 to £52,010. The higher rate limit of £150,000 is increased by the same amount, so that the higher rate band remains at £117,990. Without these adjustments, an additional £20,000 of income would have been taxable at 45% instead of 20% (a 25% saving).

18.1 IT   Pension Provision

    (b)   No personal allowance is due as income is too far in excess of the £100,000 limit. [*ITA 2007, s 35(2)–(4); FA 2009, s 4(1)(4)*].

18.2 LIFETIME ALLOWANCE

[*FA 2004, ss 214–226; FA 2011, Sch 16 paras 43, 44, 73, 80, 84, 104, Sch 18 paras 2, 12, 13; FA 2013, s 48, Sch 22*]

(A)   **With no enhancement factor**

Aisleyne starts to receive a pension from a registered pension scheme (a benefit crystallisation event) on 1 November 2006. The amount of benefit crystallised is £500,000. Aisleyne is entitled to the standard lifetime allowance of £1.5 million (for 2006/07). Thus, the crystallisation event does not give rise to a lifetime allowance charge, but Aisleyne has used up one-third of her lifetime allowance.

Aisleyne is also a member of another registered pension scheme, from which she receives a lump sum on 1 August 2013 and starts to draw a pension; these are benefit crystallisation events. The total amount of benefit crystallised is £900,000. The standard lifetime allowance for 2013/14 is £1.5 million. Aisleyne's unused lifetime allowance is two-thirds of this, i.e. £1 million. Thus, the crystallisation event does not give rise to a lifetime allowance charge, and Aisleyne has now used up 93.333% (to three decimal places) of her lifetime allowance (33.333% + 60% (0.9/1.5 × 100)).

(B)   **With an enhancement factor**

(i) Shabnam notified HMRC of her intention to benefit from **primary protection** by reference to relevant pre-2006/07 accrued pension rights of £2.5 million, and HMRC duly certified that she is entitled to a lifetime allowance enhancement factor of 0.667 ((£2.5 million – 1.5 million)/£1.5 million). This means that Shabnam can have benefits of 1.667 times the standard lifetime allowance before incurring any liability to the lifetime allowance charge.

In 2013/14 Shabnam receives a lump sum from the registered scheme and starts to draw a pension; these are benefit crystallisation events. The total amount of benefit crystallised is £2.95 million. Shabnam's enhanced lifetime allowance in 2013/14 is £3 million (£1.8 million × 1.667) (see note (d)). Therefore, she will not become liable to the lifetime allowance charge.

(ii) Winston has primary protection by reference to relevant pre-2006/07 accrued pension rights of £2.25 million and has a lifetime allowance enhancement factor of 0.5 ((£2.25 million – 1.5 million)/£1.5 million). In 2011/12, he took benefits valued at £0.9 million. At this time his enhanced lifetime allowance was £2.7 million (£1.8 million × 1.5), so the benefit crystallisation did not give rise to a lifetime allowance charge.

In 2014/15 Winston takes the remainder of his benefits then worth £1.9 million. The standard lifetime allowance is then £1.25 million. Winston's enhanced lifetime allowance remains at £2.7 million (£1.8 million × 1.5) (see note (d)).

The amount of lifetime allowance used up by Winston''s 2011/12 benefit crystallisation is found by multiplying the then crystalised amount of £0.9 million by:

$$\frac{SLA \text{ at time of current } (2014/15) \text{ event} \quad \text{(but see note (e))}}{SLA \text{ at time of previous } (2011/12) \text{ event}}$$

So the used amount is:

$$£900,000 \times \frac{1.5}{1.8} = £750,000$$

Winston has used up £0.75 million and has £1.95 million (£2.7 million − £0.75 million) still available. As Winston's 2014/15 benefit crystallisation is worth £1.9 million, he does not become liable to the lifetime allowance charge.

Notes

(a) Any excess of crystallised benefits over the unused lifetime allowance is chargeable to income tax at 55% if paid as a lump sum or at 25% otherwise. The charge is not dependent upon any person's being resident or domiciled in the UK. Although chargeable to income tax, the chargeable amount is not treated for any tax purposes as income, which means that, for example, losses, reliefs and allowances cannot be set against it and it does not count as income for the purposes of any double tax treaty.

(b) The tax will normally be paid by the scheme administrator. It will usually be recovered by deduction from the benefits paid by the scheme to the individual. If instead it is paid out of scheme funds, the tax itself is added to the chargeable amount. Eg, see HMRC Registered Pension Schemes Manual RPSM 11105260.

(c) See *FA 2004, Sch 36 paras 7–11D* as regards primary protection under the transitional rules for pension rights accrued at 5 April 2006.

(d) Despite the fall in the standard lifetime allowance from £1.8 million to £1.5 million and then to £1.25 million, where an individual's lifetime allowance falls to be enhanced under primary protection for 2012/13 or any subsequent year, the amount of the enhancement is computed by applying the primary protection factor to a lifetime allowance of £1.8 million (as long as this remains greater than the actual lifetime allowance). [*FA 2004, s 218(5B); FA 2011, Sch 18 paras 2(3), 13*].

(e) When calculating the availability of the lifetime allowance for an individual with primary protection, where a benefit crystallisation event has previously occurred and a further benefit crystallisation event occurs on or after 6 April 2014, then in calculating the adjustment of the used amount, the current standard lifetime allowance (£1.25 million for 2014/15) is replaced by £1.5 million if greater. This ensures that those with primary protection do not benefit from an increase in their available lifetime allowance if the current standard lifetime allowance is less than £1,500,000 when the adjustment is made. [*FA 2004, s 219(5A); FA 2013, Sch 22 para 7*].

18.3 ANNUAL ALLOWANCE

[*FA 2004, ss 227–238A; FA 2009, Sch 2 paras 15, 25; FA 2011, Sch 16 paras 45, 85, Sch 17 paras 3–17, 26, 27–32; FA 2013, s 49; SI 2007 No 494; SI 2010 No 922, Reg 3*]

(A) **Carry-forward of annual allowance**

Lily is self-employed and joins a registered pension scheme for the first time on 1 July 2011. The scheme's annual pension input period coincides with the fiscal year. Lily has fluctuating business profits and makes contributions to the scheme under deduction of basic rate tax at source as follows.

18.3 IT   Pension Provision

2011/12	£6,400 net (£8,000 gross)
2012/13	£48,000 net (£60,000 gross)
2013/14	£24,000 net (£30,000 gross)
2014/15	£52,000 net (£65,000 gross)
2015/16	£68,800 net (£86,000 gross)

No-one else makes contributions to Lily's pension arrangement under the scheme. Lily's total pension input amount for each year will be equal to the gross amount of her contributions. For each year, she will receive higher and additional rate tax relief, where appropriate, on the gross amount of her contributions provided she has sufficient relevant UK earnings to cover that amount, which it is assumed she does.

For 2011/12, Lily has unused annual allowance of £42,000 (£50,000 – £8,000). Note that if her total pension input had exceeded the annual allowance, there would have been no question of her bringing forward any unused annual allowance from earlier years as she was not a member of a registered pension scheme in those years.

For 2012/13, she has excess pension input amounts of £10,000 (£50,000 – £60,000). In the absence of a carry-forward facility, she would have been liable to an annual allowance charge on £10,000 at her marginal rate of tax for the year. However, £10,000 of her unused allowance for 2011/12 is brought forward to extinguish her liability. She still has £32,000 unused allowance remaining from 2011/12.

For 2013/14, she has unused annual allowance of £20,000 (£50,000 – £30,000).

For 2014/15, she has excess pension input amounts of £25,000 (£40,000 – £65,000). £25,000 of her unused allowance for 2011/12 is brought forward to extinguish her liability.

For 2015/16, Lily has excess pension input amounts of £46,000 (£40,000 – £86,000). Although £7,000 of her 2011/12 annual allowance remains unused, it cannot be carried forward more than three years. However, her unused allowance of £20,000 for 2013/14 is available in full. She is liable to an annual allowance charge on £26,000 at her marginal rate of tax for the year and has no more unused allowance to carry forward.

Pension Provision   IT 18.3

The position can be summarised as follows

Annual allowance	Pension input amounts	Unused allowance b/fwd	Chargeable amount	Unused allowance c/fwd	Cumulative unused allowance c/fwd
	£	£	£	£	£	£
2011/12	(50,000)	8,000		Nil	42,000	42,000
2012/13	(50,000)	60,000	(10,000)	Nil		32,000
2013/14	(50,000)	30,000		Nil	20,000	52,000
2014/15	(40,000)	65,000	(25,000)	Nil		27,000
					3 year dropout	(7,000)
						20,000
2015/16	(40,000)	86,000	(20,000)	26,000		Nil

Notes

(a) A carry-forward facility was introduced by *FA 2011* whereby any unused part of the annual allowance for a tax year can be carried forward for up to three tax years. The first year for which unused allowance can be carried forward is 2008/09, but see (B) below as regards carry-forward from 2008/09, 2009/10 and/or 2010/11. Unused annual allowance is available for carry-forward only if it arises during a tax year in which the individual is a member of a registered pension scheme. If the amount of the annual allowance exceeds the total pension input amount (broadly the pension savings) for that year, the excess is unused allowance.

(b) The current year's annual allowance is deemed to be used first. If this is insufficient to avoid an annual allowance charge, any unused annual allowance from the three previous years can then be used; the earliest year's unused allowance is used first and so on. The carry-forward is automatic and does not have to be claimed.

(c) For 2014/15 onwards the annual allowance is reduced from £50,000 to £40,000. [*FA 2013, s 49*].

(B) **Carry-forward of annual allowance from before 2011/12 (transitional)**

Alfie is a company director and has been a member of his employer's final salary scheme (a registered pension scheme) for a number of years. The scheme's annual pension input period coincides with the fiscal year. Alfie's total pension input amounts for the three years preceding 2011/12 were as follows.

	£
2008/09	39,000
2009/10	44,000
2010/11	46,000

18.3 IT   Pension Provision

For each of these years, Alfie's total pension input amounts were clearly well within his annual allowance, so there was no annual allowance charge. Alfie's total pension input amounts for the next two years are as follows.

	£
2011/12	55,500
2012/13	55,000

For 2011/12, in the absence of a carry-forward facility, Alfie would have been liable to an annual allowance charge on £5,500 at his marginal rate of tax for the year. Similarly, he would have been liable on £5,000 for 2012/13. In order to ascertain whether he has any unused annual allowance to bring forward to 2011/12 and beyond, his annual allowance is assumed to have been £50,000 for each of the years 2008/09 to 2010/11, and his total pension input amount for each of those years must be recomputed using post-2010/11 valuation methods. Alfie's revised total pension input amounts for those three years are as follows (and note that these figures are purely for illustration purposes and not necessarily realistic).

	£
2008/09	44,000
2009/10	49,000
2010/11	51,000

The position can now be summarised as follows (bearing in mind that the annual allowance and pension input amounts for years prior to 2011/12 are assumed figures only).

	Annual allowance	Pension input amounts	Unused allowance b/fwd	Chargeable amount	Unused allowance c/fwd	Cumulative unused allowance c/fwd
	£	£	£	£	£	£
2008/09	(50,000)	44,000		Nil	6,000	6,000
2009/10	(50,000)	49,000		Nil	1,000	7,000
2010/11	(50,000)	51,000		Nil		7,000
2011/12	(50,000)	55,500	(5,500)	Nil		1,500
				3 year dropout		(500)
						1,000
2012/13	(50,000)	55,000	(1,000)	4,000		Nil

Notes

(a)   For the purpose of carrying forward unused annual allowances from 2008/09, 2009/10 and/or 2010/11, the unused amount is computed under post-2010/11 rules. Therefore, it is assumed for this purpose only that the annual allowance was

Pension Provision   IT 18.3

only £50,000 for each of those years, and that pension input amounts for those years are to be calculated as if the post-2010/11 rules had already been in place. [*FA 2011, Sch 17 para 30*].

(b) HMRC announced a change of practice on 25 November 2011 and this example reflects this. Although in 2010/11 the assumed pension input amounts exceed the assumed annual allowance, none of the cumulative unused allowance brought forward need be set against this excess. This is in contrast to the position for 2011/12 and subsequent years. (HMRC Registered Pension Schemes Manual RPSM06108030).

(C) **Annual allowance for transitional pension input periods**

(i) Say the transitional pension input period (see note (a)) is the twelve months to 31 May 2011. Say there are pension savings of £100,000 in the period 1 June 2010 to 13 October 2010 (period A) and £110,000 in the period 14 October 2010 to 31 May 2011 (period B). Assume there is no unused annual allowance available for carry-forward to 2011/12. The savings for period A are less than £255,000 and no charge arises. The savings for period B exceed £50,000 and there will be an annual allowance charge for 2011/12 on the excess of £60,000, notwithstanding that savings for the whole of the transitional pension input period are less than £255,000.

(ii) Say the transitional pension input period is again the twelve months to 31 May 2011. Say there are pension savings of £300,000 in the period 1 June 2010 to 13 October 2010 (period A) and £120,000 in the period 14 October 2010 to 31 May 2011 (period B). Assume there is no unused annual allowance available for carry-forward to 2011/12. The savings for period B exceed £50,000 and there will be an annual allowance charge on the excess of £70,000. The savings for period A are compared to an annual allowance of £255,000 of which £50,000 has been used in period B. The annual allowance charge for period A is £300,000 − (£255,000 − £50,000) = £95,000. The total annual allowance charge for 2011/12 is on £165,000.

(iii) Say the transitional pension input period is again the twelve months to 31 May 2011. Say there are pension savings of £300,000 in the period 1 June 2010 to 13 October 2010 (period A) but only £40,000 in the period 14 October 2010 to 31 May 2011 (period B). Assume there is unused annual allowance of £20,000 available for carry-forward to 2011/12. The savings for period B are less than £50,000 and there will be no annual allowance charge. The savings for period A are compared to an annual allowance of £255,000 of which £40,000 has been used in period B. The annual allowance charge for period A is £300,000 − (£255,000 − £40,000) = £85,000. The total annual allowance charge for 2011/12 is on £85,000 − £20,000 brought forward = £65,000.

Note

(a) There are transitional rules for pension input periods starting before 14 October 2010 and ending in 2011/12 (transitional pension input periods). In order to avoid an annual allowance charge:

- the pension savings for the transitional pension input period must not exceed £255,000; and

- the pension savings for that part of the transitional pension input period that begins on 14 October 2010 must not exceed £50,000.

[*FA 2011, Sch 17 paras 28, 29*].

19 Personal Service Companies etc.

[*ITEPA 2003, ss 48–61; ITTOIA 2005, ss 163, 164*]

19.1 CALCULATION OF DEEMED EMPLOYMENT PAYMENT

Harry is a systems analyst trading through his own personal service company, ABC Ltd, in which he owns 99% of the ordinary shares. During 2013/14, he is engaged at different times by two independent companies, DEF Ltd and GHJ Ltd (the client companies), in each case under a contract between the client company and ABC Ltd. It is accepted that each engagement is in the nature of employment and is within the special tax and NIC rules for personal service companies and other intermediaries. ABC Ltd is paid £40,000 by DEF Ltd and £20,000 by GHJ Ltd for the services provided by Harry.

For 2013/14, Harry draws a salary of £28,000 from ABC Ltd which is taxed under PAYE and on which employer's NICs of, say, £2,800 are due. He is also provided with a company car on which the taxable benefit is £4,000 and on which Class 1A NICs of, say, £550 are due. ABC Ltd makes pension contributions of £3,100 into a registered pension scheme on Harry's behalf and reimburses expenses of £1,500 which, if Harry had been employed directly by the client companies, would have been qualifying travelling expenses within *ITEPA 2003, ss 337–340*. It pays a salary of £7,700 to Harry's wife who acts as company secretary and administrator.

ABC Ltd is deemed to make a payment to Harry on 5 April 2014, chargeable to tax as employment income and computed as follows

			£	£	£
Step (1)	Total amount from relevant engagements				60,000
	Deduct 5%				3,000
					57,000
Step (2)	*Add* payments and other benefits received other than from ABC Ltd				—
Step (3)	*Deduct*	(a) Expenses	1,500		
		(b) Capital allowances	—		
		(c) Pension contributions	3,100	4,600	
Step (4)	*Deduct*	Salary	28,000		
		Benefits	4,000		
		Employer's Class 1 NICs	2,800		
		Employer's Class 1A NICs	550	35,350	39,950
					£17,050

Deemed employment payment £17,050 × $\dfrac{100}{113.8}$ 14,982

19.1 IT Personal Service Companies etc.

Employer's NICs due on deemed payment £14,982 @ 13.8%		2,068
Total as above		£17,050

Notes

(a) The salary paid by ABC Ltd to Harry's wife is not deductible in arriving at the deemed employment payment, except to the extent that it, and other expenses of the company, are covered by the 5% deduction at Step (1) above. (The salary may of course be deductible in computing ABC Ltd's taxable business profits.) The 5% deduction is a standard allowance intended to cover the company's running costs and is given automatically, regardless of the actual occurrence or amount of such costs. It is computed purely for the purpose of determining the deemed employment payment and is not deductible in computing ABC Ltd's taxable business profits.

(b) The deemed employment payment is generally treated in the same way as an actual payment of remuneration, so that the normal PAYE provisions apply. Subject to special rules where the intermediary is a partnership, the payment (and the related employer's NICs) is an allowable expense in computing the taxable business profits of the intermediary for the period of account in which it is deemed to be made (and for no other period). [*ITEPA 2003, s 56; ITTOIA 2005, ss 163, 164*].

20 Post-Cessation Receipts and Expenditure

20.1 POST-CESSATION RECEIPTS

[*ITTOIA 2005, ss 241–257; FA 2013, Sch 4 paras 39(2), 56, Sch 5 paras 4, 6, Sch 45 paras 77, 153(2)*].

A trader retired and closed down his trade on 31 March 2013 and, in the year 2013/14, the following subsequent events occurred.

(i) He paid a former customer £100 as compensation for defective work.

(ii) In the accounts at the date of closure a specific provision was made against a debt for £722 and in addition there was a general bad debt provision of £2,000. All debts were recovered in full.

(iii) Stock in trade incorrectly taken to be valueless at the date of cessation was sold for £215.

(iv) He eventually sold a piece of machinery six months after cessation for £136. This had been valued at nil at cessation.

(v) At 31 March 2013, after obtaining maximum loss relief, there was a trading loss of £333 unrelieved.

The above will be subject to income tax for 2013/14 as follows

		£	£
Sales			215
Bad debts recovered			722
			937
Deduct	Compensation payment	100	
	Balance of losses	197	
			297
Taxable post-cessation receipts			£640

Notes

(a) The proceeds of sale of the plant are taken into the final capital allowances computation, i.e. for 2012/13 [*CAA 2001, s 61(2)*] and the loss carried forward of £333 has been reduced by the balancing charge to £197.

(b) An election could be made under *ITTOIA 2005, s 257* for the post-cessation receipts to be treated as having been received on the date of cessation and thus chargeable at 2012/13 rates. See also *TMA 1970, Sch 1B para 5*.

20.2 POST-CESSATION EXPENDITURE

[*ITA 2007, ss 96–101, 125, 126; TCGA 1992, ss 261D, 261E; ITTOIA 2005, ss 248(3)(4), 250, 255(4); FA 2012, s 9*]

20.2 IT Post-Cessation Receipts and Expenditure

Simcock ceased trading in October 2012. In 2013/14, the following events occur in connection with his former trade.

(i) Simcock pays a former customer £9,250 by way of damages for defective work carried out by him in the course of the trade.

(ii) He incurs legal fees of £800 in connection with the above claim.

(iii) He incurs debt collection fees of £200 in connection with trade debts outstanding at cessation and which were taken into account as receipts in computing profits.

(iv) He writes off a trade debt of £500, giving HMRC notice of his having done so.

(v) He incurs legal fees of £175 in relation to a debt of £1,000 owing by him to a supplier which, although disputed, was taken into account as an expense in computing his trading profits.

(vi) He eventually agrees to pay £500 in full settlement of his liability in respect of the debt in (v) above, paying £250 in March 2014 and the remaining £250 in May 2014.

In 2014/15, Simcock receives £3,000 from his insurers in full settlement of their liability with regard to the expense incurred in (i) above.

For 2013/14, Simcock's total income before taking account of the above events is £9,000 and he also has capital gains of £12,100 (with £1,000 capital losses brought forward from 2012/13).

Simcock makes a claim under *ITA 2007, s 96* (relief for post-cessation expenditure) for 2013/14 and a simultaneous claim under *TCGA 1992, s 261D* to have any excess relief set against capital gains.

Simcock's tax position for 2013/14 is as follows

		£	£
Income			
Total income before claim under *ITA 2007, s 96*			9,000
Deduct Post-cessation expenditure			
(i)		9,250	
(ii)		800	
(iii)		200	
(iv)		500	
(v)	not allowable under these rules	—	
(vi)	*less* unpaid expenses at 5.4.14	(750)	
		10,000	
Restricted to total income		(9,000)	(9,000)
Excess relief		£1,000	
Capital gains			
Gains before losses brought forward and annual exemption			12,100
Deduct Post-cessation expenditure (excess as above)			1,000
Net gains for the year			11,100

Post-Cessation Receipts and Expenditure IT 20.2

Losses brought forward	1,000	
Used in 2013/14	200	200
Carried forward	£800	—
Net gains (covered by annual exemption)		£10,900

For 2014/15, Simcock will have taxable post-cessation receipts of £3,000 arising from the insurance recovery. He will be able to offset expenses of £175 under (v) above, which, whilst not within these rules, should qualify as a deduction against post-cessation receipts. He will also have post-cessation expenditure of £250 in respect of the further payment in 2014/15 under (vi) above, the 2013/14 post-cessation expenditure having been restricted by at least that amount (see note (b)).

Notes

(a) Under *ITA 2007, s 96* relief is available against total income for specified types of expenditure and for bad debts where the expenditure is incurred or the debt proves to be bad within seven years after the date of cessation of the trade, profession or vocation. Any excess can be claimed against chargeable gains for the year. Any remaining excess relief cannot be carried forward against total income or gains of a subsequent year but is available as a deduction against any future post-cessation receipts.

(b) Allowable post-cessation expenditure is restricted to the extent that any expenses were taken into account in computing profits but remained unpaid at the end of the year to which the claim relates. Any subsequent payment is itself treated as a post-cessation expense to the extent that the unpaid expense previously caused post-cessation expenditure to be restricted.

21 Property Income

Cross-references. See **14.6** LOSSES for property business losses.

[*ITTOIA 2005, Pt 3*]

21.1 GENERAL

[*ITTOIA 2005, ss 263–275, 308A–308C; SI 2011 No 1037, Arts 11(2), 13*]

Mrs A inherited a furnished cottage in a picturesque coastal village and she and her husband decided to spend their own holiday there during the month of July and to make the cottage available for letting to other holidaymakers during the remainder of the year. The rent charged was £500 per month from June to September inclusive and £350 per month for the remainder of the year. Mrs A has no other letting income.

During 2013/14 the house was occupied from April until October, lay vacant during November, December and January and was let again for February and March. In March 2014, the tenant defaulted on two weeks' rent, which proved impossible to collect.

Several lettings were for periods of more than 31 days.

Expenses were as follows:

Business rates £480, Water rates £84, Electricity £420 (£400 received from tenants through coin operated meters), Advertising £100, Cleaning between lettings £180, House contents insurance £72, Repairs £120.

In September 2013, Mrs A incurred capital expenditure of £2,250 on insulating the loft.

The letting does not constitute a trade. The cottage does not qualify for relief as 'furnished holiday accommodation' under **22.2** below.

The property income computation for 2013/14 is as follows

		£	£
Rent receivable (3 × £500 + 5 × £350)			3,250
Business rates note (d)		480	
Water rates ($^{11}/_{12}$ × £84)		77	
Electricity ($^{11}/_{12}$ × 420) − 400		(15)	
Advertising		100	
Cleaning $^8/_9$ × 180		160	
Insurance $^{11}/_{12}$ × 72		66	
Repairs $^{11}/_{12}$ × 120		110	
Bad debt written off		125	
Wear and tear allowance:			
(£3,250 − £557) × 10%	note (c)	269	
Loft insulation note (e)		1,500	2,872
			£378

21.1 IT Property Income

Notes

(a) All letting income from UK property, whether furnished or unfurnished, is taxed as income from a single UK property business carried on by the landlord. The profits of that business are computed according to trading income principles as if the business were a trade.

(b) Although property income is computed similarly to trading income, it retains its nature as investment income as opposed to earnings and does not count as relevant earnings for pension contribution purposes (subject to the rules for furnished holiday lettings — see **21.2** below).

(c) Expenses paid by the landlord that, in the case of a furnished letting, would normally borne by the tenants are deducted from rents received in computing the 10% wear and tear allowance. The most common examples are rates, water rates and council tax. A landlord must make an election if he is to take the wear and tear allowance for a tax year; the election must be made no later than the first anniversary of 31 January following that tax year. [*ITTOIA 2005, ss 308A–308C*].

(d) As the business rates relate entirely to the letting, no apportionment is considered appropriate.

(e) For capital expenditure incurred within any year up to and including 2014/15 on the acquisition, and installation in the dwelling-house, of a 'qualifying energy-saving item' (as defined), a maximum deduction of £1,500 per dwelling-house is available in computing the profits of a property business for income tax purposes. [*ITTOIA 2005, ss 312–314; SI 2007 No 3278*].

(f) As the gross rental income is less than the VAT registration threshold (£79,000 for 2013/14), it will be sufficient to include in the self-assessment tax return only the following figures

	£
Rent received	3,250
Expenses	2,872
Net income	£378

The detailed accounts will, of course, still have to be prepared in order to arrive at the above summary. (see www.hmrc.gov.uk/factsheet/three-line-account.pdf).

21.2 FURNISHED HOLIDAY LETTINGS

[*ITA 2007, ss 127, 127ZA; ITTOIA 2005, ss 322–326, 326A, 327, 328, 328A, 328B; FA 2011, Sch 14 paras 2–6, 12(2)(3)(5)(6), 13*]

Mr B owns and lets out furnished holiday cottages. None is ever let to the same person for more than 31 consecutive days. Three cottages have been owned for many years but Rose Cottage was acquired on 1 June 2013 (and first let on that day) while Ivy Cottage was sold on 30 June 2013 (and last let on that day).

In 2013/14 days available for letting and days let are as follows

	Days available	Days let
Honeysuckle Cottage	270	240

Primrose Cottage	195	150
Bluebell Cottage	225	90
Rose Cottage	225	90
Ivy Cottage	30	5

Additional information

Rose Cottage was let for 45 days between 6 April and 31 May 2014.

Ivy Cottage was let for 103 days in the period 1 July 2012 to 5 April 2013 and was available for letting for 180 days in that period.

Qualification as 'furnished holiday accommodation'

Honeysuckle Cottage qualifies as it meets both the 210-day availability test and the 105-day letting test.

Primrose Cottage does *not* qualify although it is let for more than 105 days as it fails to satisfy the 210-day test. Averaging (see below) is only possible where it is the 105-day test which is not satisfied.

Bluebell Cottage does not qualify by itself as it fails the 105-day test. However, it may be included in an averaging election.

Rose Cottage qualifies as furnished holiday accommodation. It was acquired on 1 June 2013 so qualification in 2013/14 is determined by reference to the period of twelve months beginning on the day it was first let, in which it was let for a total of 135 days.

Ivy Cottage was sold on 30 June 2013 so qualification is determined by reference to the period from 1 July 2012 to 30 June 2013 (the last day of letting). It qualifies as it was available for letting for 210 days and let for 108 in this period.

Averaging election for 2013/14

	Days let
Honeysuckle Cottage	240
Bluebell Cottage	90
Rose Cottage	135
Ivy Cottage	108

$$\frac{240 + 90 + 135 + 108}{4} = 143.25 \text{ days} \quad \text{note (c)}$$

Notes

(a) Income from the commercial letting of furnished holiday accommodation is treated as trading income for certain limited purposes; in particular it counts as relevant UK earnings for the purpose of obtaining relief for contributions to a registered pension scheme.

(b) In addition, the commercial letting of furnished holiday accommodation is treated as a trade for the purpose of various capital gains tax reliefs including ENTREPRENEURS' RELIEF (CGT 211) and business assets gifts hold-over relief (see CGT 213 HOLD-OVER RELIEFS). [*TCGA 1992, ss 241, 241A; FA 2011, Sch 14 paras 14–17*].

21.2 IT Property Income

(c) All four cottages included in the averaging election now qualify as furnished holiday accommodation as each is deemed to have been let for 143.25 days in the year 2013/14.

(d) If Bluebell cottage had still not qualified as a result of averaging but qualified in 2012/13, it would have been possible to make a 'period of grace' election, provided there had been a genuine intention to meet the 105-day letting condition for 2013/14. [*ITTOIA 2005, s 326A; FA 2011, Sch 14 para 2(5), 6*].

21.3 'RENT-A-ROOM' RELIEF

[*ITTOIA 2005, ss 784–802; FA 2013, Sch 4 paras 40, 56*]

Frankie and Johnny are single persons sharing a house as their main residence. They have for some years taken in lodgers to supplement their income. As Frankie contributed the greater part of the purchase price of the house, she and Johnny have an agreement to share the rental income in the ratio 2:1, although expenses are shared equally.

For the year ended 5 April 2008, gross rents amounted to £5,700 and allowable expenses were £1,100. In the year ended 5 April 2009, the pair face a heavy repair bill after uninsured damage to one of the rooms. Gross rents for that year amount to £3,600 and expenses to £4,400. For the years ended 5 April 2010 and 5 April 2011, gross rents are £6,600 and expenses £2,200, and for the year ended 5 April 2012 they are £6,000 and £2,500 respectively. For the year ended 5 April 2013 they are £8,100 and £4,500 respectively. For the year ended 5 April 2014, they are £9,000 and £3,000 respectively.

For 2007/08, the position is as follows

Normal computation of property income

	Frankie £	Johnny £
Gross rents (y/e 5.4.08)	3,800	1,900
Allowable expenses	550	550
Net rents	£3,250	£1,350

Johnny's share of *gross* rents is less than his one half share (£2,125) of the basic amount (£4,250). It is assumed that he would not make the election for full rent-a-room relief not to apply. His share of net rents is thus treated as nil.

Frankie's share of gross rents exceeds £2,125, so full rent-a-room relief cannot apply. She can, however, elect to apply the alternative method of calculation. Under that method, she is taxed on the excess of *gross* rents over £2,125. It is assumed that she will make the election as she will then be taxed on £1,675 rather than £3,250.

For 2008/09, the position is as follows

Normal computation of property income

	Frankie £	Johnny £
Gross rents (y/e 5.4.09)	2,400	1,200
Allowable expenses	2,200	2,200
Net rents / (loss)	£200	£(1,000)

Johnny's share of gross rents continues to be less than £2,125. Under full rent-a-room relief, his share of net rents will be treated as nil. However, he will obtain no relief, by carry-forward or otherwise, for his loss. In order to preserve his loss, he could elect for full rent-a-room relief not to apply, the election having effect for 2008/09 only.

Frankie's share of gross rents exceeds £2,125. Therefore, her previous election for the alternative method will not be treated as automatically withdrawn. She will be taxed under the alternative method on £275 (£2,400 – £2,125). However, this is greater than the amount taxable on the normal property income computation (£200), so it is assumed she would withdraw the election with effect for 2008/09 and subsequent years. The notice of withdrawal does not prejudice the making of a fresh election for 2009/10 or any subsequent year.

For 2009/10, the position is as follows

Normal computation of property income

	Frankie £	Johnny £
Gross rents (y/e 5.4.10)	4,400	2,200
Allowable expenses	1,100	1,100
Net rents	£3,300	£1,100

Johnny's share of gross rents now exceeds £2,125, so full rent-a-room relief will not apply. He could elect for the alternative method to apply, and his chargeable income will then be reduced to £75 (£2,200 – £2,125). This is further reduced to nil by the bringing forward of his £1,000 loss for 2008/09. If Johnny did not make the election, his chargeable income would be £100 with the whole of his 2008/09 loss having been utilised.

Frankie can make a fresh election for the alternative method, with effect from 2009/10, and she will then be taxed on £2,275 (£4,400 – £2,125).

For 2010/11, the position is as follows

The normal computation of property income is as for 2009/10. Assuming Frankie and Johnny both elected to apply the alternative method for 2009/10, the elections will continue to apply for 2010/11, so that their respective chargeable property incomes are £2,275 and £75. Johnny's profit is reduced to nil by the brought forward balance of £925 of the 2008/09 loss (of which the balance of £850 is carried forward to 2011/12).

21.3 IT Property Income

For 2011/12, the position is as follows

Normal computation of property income

	Frankie £	Johnny £
Gross rents (y/e 5.4.12)	4,000	2,000
Allowable expenses	1,250	1,250
Net rents	£2,750	£750

Johnny's share of gross rents is now below £2,125, so that the election to apply the alternative method is treated as having been withdrawn, and full rent-a-room relief applies instead (assuming no election to disapply it). The balance of £850 of his 2008/09 loss is carried forward to 2012/13. Frankie's election to apply the alternative method will continue to have effect (unless withdrawn), so that her chargeable property income will be £1,875 (£4,000 − £2,125).

For 2012/13, the position is as follows

Normal computation of property income

	Frankie £	Johnny £
Gross rents (y/e 5.4.13)	5,400	2,700
Allowable expenses	2,250	2,250
Net rents	£3,150	£450

For both Frankie and Johnny their share of gross rents now exceeds £2,125, so that full rent-a-room relief will not apply, and since their share of the expenses also exceeds £2,125, the election to apply the alternative method will be unfavourable. It is therefore assumed that Frankie withdraws her election (by 31 January 2015). They are accordingly both charged to tax on the basis of the normal property income computation, with Johnny's £850 loss brought forward being set against his share, the balance of £400 being carried forward to 2013/14.

For 2013/14, the position is as follows

Normal computation of property income

	Frankie £	Johnny £
Gross rents (y/e 5.4.14)	6,000	3,000
Allowable expenses	1,500	1,500
Net rents	£4,500	£1,500

Both could now elect to apply the alternative method of calculation (the election to be made by 31 January 2016). Frankie's chargeable property income will be reduced to £3,875 (£6,000 − £2,125). Johnny's chargeable property income will be reduced to £875 (£3,000 − £2,125) and further reduced to £475 by the balance of his brought forward losses from 2008/09.

Notes

(a) Rent-a-room relief covers receipts for meals, cleaning, laundry etc. as well as sums (i.e. rents) received for the use of the furnished accommodation. It applies equally where the provision of accommodation and services is chargeable as trading income or as miscellaneous income. [*ITTOIA 2005, s 786*].

(b) Where receipts accrue to more than one person in respect of the same residence in one income period, each of those persons who is a qualifying individual is entitled to a limit of one half of the 'basic amount' for the relevant tax year. The basic amount is £4,250. [*ITTOIA 2005, ss 789, 790; SI 1996 No 2953*].

21.4 PREMIUMS ETC. ON LEASES OF UP TO 50 YEARS

[*ITTOIA 2005, ss 276–307*]

Cross-reference. See also CGT 213.3(C)(H)(J) LAND.

(A)

Mr Green grants a 30-year lease of premises to a trader, Mr Indigo, on 1 March 2014 for a premium of £35,000.

The amount to be included in the profits of Mr Green's property business for 2013/14 is as follows

$$P \times \frac{50 - Y}{50}$$

where

P = the amount of the premium, and

Y = the number of complete periods of 12 months (other than the first) comprised in the effective duration of the lease.

[*ITTOIA 2005, s 277*].

Thus

$$£35,000 \times \frac{50 - 29}{50} = \underline{£14,700}$$

(B) Allowance to lessee carrying on trade etc.

[*ITTOIA 2005, ss 60–67*]

Assuming the same figures as in (A) above and that Mr Indigo prepares accounts to 31 March

Chargeable premium	£14,700
Number of days comprised in the lease period	10,957

21.4 IT   Property Income

The lessee will obtain relief as follows

$$\frac{£14,700}{10,957} = £1.34 \text{ per day treated as a deductible expense.}$$

i.e. £42 for period of account to 31.3.14 and £489 for period of account to 31.3.15 and so on.

(C) **Grant of sub-lease**

[*ITTOIA 2005, ss 64, 287, 288*]

On 1 May 2015, Mr Indigo in (A) and (B) above finds that the leased premises are now surplus to his trading requirements, and he grants a 10-year sub-lease at a premium of £12,500.

The amount to be included in the profits of Mr Indigo's property business for 2015/16 is computed as follows

	£
Chargeable premium before reduction	
$£12,500 \times \dfrac{50-9}{50} =$	10,250
Reduced by £14,700 × ¹⁰/₃₀	4,900
Reduced chargeable premium	£5,350

The chargeable sub-lease premium is reduced by reference to the premium chargeable on the landlord.

The number of days in the 10-year receipt period of the sub-lease is 3,652. The daily amount of the relief given is therefore £4,900 divided by 3,652 = £1.34. This equals the daily expense computed in (B) above; as there is no deficit, Mr Indigo is not entitled to any deduction under (B) above for any of the 3,652 qualifying days covered by the sublease.

Supposing Mr Indigo had been able to obtain a premium of only £5,000 for the 10-year sub-lease. The amount to be included as a receipt in computing the profits of his property business for 2015/16 would then be as follows.

	£
Chargeable premium before reduction	
$£5,000 \times \dfrac{50-9}{50} =$	4,100
Reduced by	
$£14,700 \times \dfrac{10}{30} = £4,900$ but restricted to	4,100
	Nil

The daily amount of the relief given is now £4,100 divided by 3,652 = £1.12. This is less than the daily expense of £1.34 computed in (B) above, the deficit being £0.22. Mr Indigo would be entitled to a deduction of £0.22 under (B) above for each of the 3,652 qualifying days covered by the sub-lease.

22 Remittance Basis

22.1 REMITTANCES FROM MIXED FUNDS

[*ITA 2007, ss 809Q, 809R; FA 2013, Sch 6 para 5*]

Van Helsing is resident, but not domiciled, in the UK. He has regular employment in both the UK and Transylvania and some non-UK shareholdings. He maintains a single bank account in Transylvania which he opened in August 2012. Previously all his transactions went through a UK bank account; part of his UK salary after tax continues to be paid into that account. Van Helsing has made a claim to pay UK tax on the remittance basis for 2012/13 and 2013/14.

Van Helsing's Transylvanian bank account statements show the following

		Debit £	Credit £	Balance £
30 August 2012	UK salary (part)		4,200	4,200
15 September 2012	overseas salary		12,000	16,200
30 September 2012	UK salary (part)		4,200	20,400
10 October 2012	overseas dividends		11,000	31,400
30 October 2012	UK salary (part)		4,200	35,600
30 November 2012	UK salary (part)		4,200	39,800
15 December 2012	overseas salary		12,000	51,800
30 December 2012	UK salary (part)		4,200	56,000
30 January 2013	UK salary (part)		4,500	60,500
28 February 2013	UK salary (part)		4,500	65,000
15 March 2013	overseas salary		12,000	77,000
30 March 2013	UK salary (part)		4,500	81,500
8 April 2013	overseas dividends		21,500	103,000
30 April 2013	UK salary (part)		4,500	107,500
30 April 2013	bank interest		6,000	113,500
15 May 2013	sale proceeds of overseas shareholding		794,000	907,500

22.1 IT   Remittance Basis

		Debit £	Credit £	Balance £
30 May 2013	UK salary (part)		4,500	912,000
15 June 2013	overseas salary		13,000	925,000
21 June 2013	transfer to UK bank account	450,000		475,000

All amounts of overseas income other than the bank interest were subject to deduction of tax at source in their country of origin. The investment sold in January 2013 was originally inherited from Van Helsing's great aunt's estate; the chargeable gain on disposal is £350,000.

Applying the rules in ITA 2007, s 809Q(3)

Step 1

For each of the categories of income and capital in paragraphs (a) to (i) below, find the amount of income or capital for the tax year in question in the mixed fund immediately before the transfer to the UK. The tax year in question is the tax year in which the transfer occurs, i.e. 2013/14. The categories are:

(a) employment income (other than income within (b), (c) or (f));

(b) relevant foreign earnings (other than income within (f));

(c) foreign specific employment income (other than income within (f));

(d) relevant foreign income (other than income within (g));

(e) foreign chargeable gains (other than gains within (h));

(f) employment income subject to a foreign tax;

(g) relevant foreign income subject to a foreign tax;

(h) foreign chargeable gains subject to a foreign tax;

(i) income or capital not within any of the above.

		£
employment income not subject to a foreign tax — (a) above	UK salary	9,000
relevant foreign income not subject to a foreign tax — (d) above	bank interest	6,000
foreign chargeable gains not subject to a foreign tax — (e) above	overseas shareholding	350,000
employment income subject to a foreign tax — (f) above	overseas salary	13,000
relevant foreign income subject to a foreign tax — (g) above	overseas dividends	Nil
		£378,000

Step 2

Identify the earliest category which has an amount of income or gain in the mixed fund. This is category (a) which has £9,000.

Step 3

As the amount of the transfer is greater than the amount identified at Step 2 the amount of the transfer is treated as reduced by the amount identified in Step 2.

£450,000 − £9,000 = £441,000

Step 4

Repeat Steps 2 & 3 for each category in turn until the transfer is reduced to nil or all categories are exhausted.

£441,000 − £6,000 − £350,000 − £13,000 = £72,000

Step 5

As the amount of the transfer is not exhausted, repeat steps 1 to 4 but this time in relation to the immediately preceding year, i.e. 2012/13.

		£
employment income not subject to a foreign tax — (a) above	UK salary	34,500
employment income subject to a foreign tax — (f) above	overseas salary	36,000
relevant foreign income subject to a foreign tax — (g) above	overseas dividends	32,500
		£102,500

Applying Steps 1 to 4 for 2012/13, all of the income in categories (a) and (f) and £1,500 of the income in category (g) is matched with the transfer.

£72,000 − £34,500 − £36,000 − £1,500 = Nil

Outcome

The £450,000 transfer is therefore regarded as a remittance of:

	2013/14 £	2012/13 £	Total £
UK employment income − category (a)	9,000	34,500	43,500
relevant foreign income not subject to foreign tax — category (d)	6,000		6,000
foreign chargeable gains not subject to foreign tax — category (e)	350,000		350,000

	2013/14 £	2012/13 £	Total £
employment income subject to a foreign tax — category (f)	13,000	36,000	49,000
relevant foreign income subject to a foreign tax — category (g)		1,500	1,500
			£450,000

Conclusions

All of Van Helsing's UK employment income for both years to date (£43,500) is included in the transfer. This is not a taxable remittance as it is taxable in the UK on an arising basis.

22.1 IT   Remittance Basis

£56,500 of overseas income is included in the transfer and treated as remitted to the UK. It is chargeable income for 2013/14, the year in which it is remitted, with credit being available under the double tax relief provisions for foreign taxes paid.

The remaining £350,000 of the £450,000 transfer is taxable as a chargeable gain for 2013/14, the year in which it is remitted.

The balance of £475,000 carried forward in the Transylvanian bank account consists of £31,000 of 2012/13 overseas dividends and £444,000 (£794,000 – £350,000) of capital originally represented by the overseas shareholding sold in May 2013. The capital is 'clean capital', having come from an inheritance, and will not be chargeable to tax when remitted to the UK.

Notes

(a) The remittance basis can only apply to an individual for a particular tax year if, , for that tax year (or, for 2012/13 and earlier years, in that tax year), the individual is (i) resident in the UK, but *either* (ii) not domiciled in the UK or (iii) (in relation to income and gains for 2012/13 and earlier years) not ordinarily resident in the UK. In most cases it requires the making of a claim; there are certain exceptions where the amounts involved are small. [*ITA 2007, ss 809B–809D; FA 2013, Sch 45 para 152(2)–(4), Sch 46 paras 3–5, 25, 27*].

(b) The abolition of the concept of ordinary residence for 2013/14 onwards means that the remittance basis no longer applies on the grounds that an individual is not ordinarily resident in the UK. However, transitional provisions have effect where an individual was resident in the UK for 2012/13 but was not ordinarily resident there at the end of that year. These provisions are intended to reflect the fact that an individual, unless having established an intention to settle in the UK, would have been regarded as not ordinarily resident for a maximum of three years of UK residence (typically straddling four tax years). See *FA 2013, Sch 46 para 26*.

(c) Where, for any tax year, an individual makes a *claim* for the remittance basis to apply, he loses entitlement to UK personal reliefs for that year and, if he is a 'long-term UK resident' (as defined), he is also liable to an additional tax charge of £30,000 or in some cases £50,000. [*ITA 2007, ss 809G, 809H*].

(d) All chargeable income and gains are taxable for the year in which they are remitted and not, if different, the year in which they arose. [*ITEPA 2003, s 22; ITTOIA 2005, s 832; TCGA 1992, s 12*].

(e) If Van Helsing had claimed the remittance basis for 2013/14 but not for 2012/13, his 2012/13 foreign income would have been taxed on the arising basis in that year and would not have been taxable when remitted. If, on the other hand, he had claimed the remittance basis for 2012/13 but not for 2013/14, his 2012/13 foreign income would still have been chargeable when remitted in 2013/14 or any later year.

(f) In practice, and subject to conditions, for the years 2009/10 to 2012/13 inclusive HMRC accepted that, notwithstanding the statutory rules illustrated in this example, individuals performing the duties of a *single* employment both inside and outside the UK could, if they wished, calculate their tax liability by reference to the total amount transferred out of a mixed fund during a tax year, rather than by reference to individual transfers. The statutory rules were then applied to the total amount transferred out of the fund to the UK in the tax year as if it were a single transfer. (HMRC SP 1/09). The practice is given statutory effect with effect in relation to transfers from a mixed fund that are made in the tax year 2013/14 or any subsequent year. The mixed fund account must not be credited with anything other than earnings from the employment, any consideration for the disposal of employment-related securities/options and interest on the account. [*ITA 2007, ss 809RA–809RD; FA 2013, Sch 6 paras 6, 8*].

23 Savings and Investment Income

23.1 DEEPLY DISCOUNTED SECURITIES

[*ITTOIA 2005, ss 427–460*]

(A) **Profit on disposal.**

On 28 June 2002 Mr Knight subscribed for £10,000 3% loan stock issued by DDS plc at a price of £55 per £100 stock incurring costs of £60. He sold these same securities on 6 April 2013 for £80 per £100 stock and incurred costs of £80. The 3% loan stock in DDS plc is quoted on the Stock Exchange, was issued on 1 July 2000 at £80 and is redeemable on 30 June 2030 at £100.

Mr Knight's tax position for 2013/14 on the disposal is

			£	£
Disposal proceeds				8,000
Less acquisition cost				5,500
				2,500
Deduct Costs of disposal	note (b)		80	
Costs of acquisition	note (b)		60	140
Taxable income				£2,360

Notes

(a) Subject to certain exceptions, a security is a '*deeply discounted security*' if, at the time it is issued, the amount payable on maturity (or any possible occasion of redemption) exceeds (or may exceed) the issue price by more than R × 0.5% × Y, where R is the amount payable on maturity etc. and Y is the period between issue and redemption, expressed in years (and fractions of years) but with a maximum value of 30. In this example, R = £100 and Y = 30. £100 × 0.5% × 30 = £15. The difference between issue price and redemption price is £20. Thus, the loan stock is a deeply discounted security. Exceptions include company shares, gilts (but not strips), excluded indexed securities, life assurance policies, capital redemption policies and securities issued under the same prospectus as other securities issued previously but not themselves deeply discounted securities. [*ITTOIA 2005, ss 430–436*].

(b) Subject to note (c), relief is available for costs incurred in connection with the acquisition of the security or with its transfer or redemption, but only if incurred before 27 March 2003 or, if incurred on or after that date, the person transferring or redeeming the security had held it continuously since before that date *and* the security was listed on a recognised stock exchange (within *ITA 2007, s 1005*) at some time before that date. [*FA 1996, Sch 13 para 1(2)–(4); ITTOIA 2005, ss 453, 455*].

(c) Such costs as are referred to in note (b) will not be deductible where incurred on or after 6 April 2015. [*ITTOIA 2005, s 455; FA 2012, Sch 39 para 48*].

23.1 IT   Savings and Investment Income

(B)   **Loss on disposal.**

On the assumption that Mr Knight sells the loan stock for £40 per £100 stock instead of £80 per £100 stock the following will apply:

Mr Knight's tax position for 2013/14 on the disposal is

		£	£
Disposal proceeds			4,000
Less acquisition cost			5,500
			1,500
Deduct Costs of disposal		80	
Costs of acquisition		60	140
Allowable loss			£1,640

Notes

(a)   Mr Knight will be able to claim loss relief of £1,640 as a deduction in computing net income for 2013/14. The relief must be claimed no later than 31 January 2016.

(b)   Loss relief is available only if the person sustaining the loss had held the security continuously since before 27 March 2003 *and* the security was listed on a recognised stock exchange (within *ITA 2007, s 1005*) at some time before that date. [*ITTOIA 2005, ss 453, 454*].

24 Seed Enterprise Investment Scheme

24.1 INCOME TAX INVESTMENT RELIEF

[*ITA 2007, ss 257A–257EG; FA 2012, Sch 6 paras 1, 24; FA 2013, s 56(4)(6)*].

For 2013/14 Ben has taxable earnings of £225,000, dividends of £18,000 and taxed interest of £12,000 (net). He makes the following qualifying investments by subscription in companies issuing shares via the Seed Enterprise Investment Scheme (SEIS).

	Date shares acquired	Shares acquired (all at par)	Acquisition cost £
X Ltd	25 August 2013	10,000 ordinary £1	10,000
Y Ltd	15 December 2013	40,000 ordinary 50p	20,000
Z Ltd	1 February 2014	30,000 ordinary £1	30,000
			£60,000

On 29 April 2013 Ben also made a qualifying investment of £5,000 under the enterprise investment scheme (EIS).

Ben's investment in Z Ltd represents 25% of that company's issued share capital. He becomes a director of the company and receives director's fees of £6,000 in 2013/14. This is in addition to his earnings quoted above.

Ben will obtain tax relief for 2013/14 as follows

Amount eligible for SEIS relief

	£
X Ltd	10,000
Y Ltd	20,000
Z Ltd note (c)	30,000
Total (being less than the maximum of £100,000)	£60,000

24.1 IT Seed Enterprise Investment Scheme

			£
Earnings (including director's fees)			231,000
Dividends		18,000	
Add Dividend tax credits		2,000	20,000
Taxed interest (gross)			15,000
Total income			266,000
Personal allowance (restricted due to level of income)			Nil
Taxable income			£266,000
Tax payable:			
32,010	@ 20%		6,402.00
117,990	@ 40%		47,196.00
96,000	@ 45%		43,200.00
20,000	@ 37.5% (dividend additional rate)		7,400.00
			104,198.00
Deduct EIS relief £5,000 @ 30%			1,500.00
			102,698.00
Deduct SEIS relief £60,000 @ 50%			30,000.00
			72,698.00
Deduct	dividend tax credits	2,000.00	
	tax on interest	3,000.00	5,000.00
Net tax liability 2013/14 (subject to PAYE deductions)			£67,698.00

Notes

(a) The SEIS is a tax-advantaged venture capital scheme which has effect in relation to shares issued to individuals on or after 6 April 2012. Income tax relief is available for investment in small companies (i.e. those with 25 or fewer employees and assets of up to £200,000) that are carrying on, or preparing to carry on, a new qualifying business. The relief is available on share subscriptions of up to £100,000 per individual per tax year. The shares must be retained for at least three years.

(b) SEIS relief is given at the SEIS rate of tax (50%) and by way of an income tax reduction. The relief cannot exceed what would otherwise be the income tax liability (no restriction being necessary in this example). For this purpose, the income tax liability is before taking into account any married couple's allowance, double tax relief and certain other specified items. However, the EIS investment relief must be deducted before the SEIS relief. [*ITA 2007, ss 26, 27, 29, 257AB; FA 2012, Sch 6 paras 1, 8, 9, 24*].

(c) The fact that Ben is a director of Z Ltd and in receipt of director's remuneration does not invalidate his claim for relief. If, however, he had been an employee *other than a director* of the company at any time in the requisite three-year holding period, he would not have been eligible for SEIS income tax relief. [*ITA 2007, ss 257AC, 257BA; FA 2012, Sch 6 paras 1, 24*].

(d) Though not illustrated in this example, any amount of SEIS investment relief can be carried back to the preceding tax year, provided the £100,000 maximum is not thereby exceeded for that year. No relief can be carried back from 2012/13 to 2011/12.

24.2 WITHDRAWAL OF RELIEF/CAPITAL LOSSES

(A) **Withdrawal of income tax relief**

[*ITA 2007, ss 257F–257GI, 257HA; FA 2012, Sch 6 paras 1, 24*].

On 1 March 2016 Ben, the investor in **24.1** above, needs to raise some funds urgently and sells half his X Ltd shares at arm's length to another shareholder for £4,250.

The position is as follows

SEIS investment relief falls to be reduced or withdrawn as the shares have not been held for the requisite period of three years.

The tax reduction in 2013/14 is attributed to the three share issues subscribed for according to the amounts claimed for each issue.

The relief attributable to the 10,000 X Ltd shares subscribed for is 10,000/60,000 x £30,000 = £5,000.

The relief attributable to the 5,000 shares sold is therefore £2,500.

If the relief attributable is greater than an amount equal to tax at the SEIS rate on the disposal consideration, the relief is reduced by that amount. Otherwise, the relief is withdrawn in full.

Tax at the SEIS rate on the disposal consideration:

50% x £4,250 = £2,125

This is less than £2,500 so the relief given is reduced by £2,125 by the making of an assessment to income tax for 2013/14.

Notes

(a) If the disposal had not been at arm's length, the relief would have been withdrawn in full.

(b) The disposal consideration would fall to be treated as reduced for the purposes of the above calculation where the relief attributable (A) is less than tax at the SEIS rate on the amount subscribed (B). It is so reduced by applying the fraction A/B. [*ITA 2007, ss 209, 210*]. This works the same way as for withdrawal of relief under the EIS scheme; see **9.2** ENTERPRISE INVESTMENT SCHEME for an illustration.

24.2 IT   Seed Enterprise Investment Scheme

(B) **Capital losses**

[*TCGA 1992, s 150E; FA 2012, Sch 6 paras 3, 24*].

The disposal in (A) above is also a disposal for capital gains tax purposes.

The capital gains position is as follows

2015/16

	£	£
Disposal proceeds (March 2016)		4,250
Cost (August 2013)	5,000	
Less Relief attributable to shares:		
£2,500 − £2,125	375	
		4,625
Allowable loss		£375

Note

(a)   An allowable loss may arise for capital gains tax purposes on a disposal of SEIS shares, whether or not the disposal occurs within the requisite three-year period. In computing such a loss, the allowable cost is reduced by SEIS relief attributable to the shares (and not withdrawn).

25 Self-Assessment

Cross-references. See also **12.1** LATE PAYMENT INTEREST AND PENALTIES.

25.1 CALCULATION OF INTERIM PAYMENTS

[*TMA 1970, s 59A*]

For 2012/13, Kylie's self-assessment shows the following.

	£
Gross income tax liability	8,664
Capital gains tax liability	2,122
Class 4 NIC liability	198
PAYE tax deducted (all relating to 2012/13)	3,740
Tax credits on dividends received	200
Tax deducted from interest received	300

The payments on account for 2013/14 (unless, on a claim, Kylie chooses to pay different amounts) are based on relevant amounts as follows.

	£
Income tax (£8,664 − £3,740 − £200 − £300 =)	4,424
Class 4 NIC	198

Half of the relevant amounts is due on each of 31 January 2014 and 31 July 2014. No payment on account is required in respect of capital gains tax liability.

25.2 CLAIMS INVOLVING MORE THAN ONE YEAR

[*TMA 1970, s 42(11A), Sch 1B*]

(A) **Carry-back claim made after 31 January in the later year**

Ant files his 2012/13 tax return at the end of January 2014. His self-assessment shows an income tax liability of £8,640, of which £2,400 represents higher rate tax charged on the top £6,000 of income. Ant subsequently makes a claim to carry back from 2013/14 (the later year) to 2012/13 a trading loss of £5,000 for the year to 31 December 2013, producing a tax saving of £2,000 (£5,000 @ 40%). All tax due has been paid on the due dates.

If the claim is made on, say, 1 April 2014, a repayment of £2,000 will be made.

If the claim is made on, say, 1 July 2014, the relief of £2,000 will be set against the second 2013/14 interim payment on account (POA) of £4,320 (half of £8,640) due on 31 July 2014 (see note (a)).

If the claim is made on, say, 1 September 2014, and the 31 July 2014 POA has been duly made, a repayment of £2,000 will be made. If the claim is made on 1 September 2014, and the 31 July 2014 POA has *not* been made, the relief of £2,000 will be set against the POA (see note (a)), which is then regarded to that extent as having been paid on 1 September 2014 (see note (b)).

25.2 IT Self-Assessment

In no case will repayment interest be due, as the relief is given before 31 January 2015 (see note (c)).

As he has made no trading profit for 2013/14, Ant might make a separate claim to reduce or dispense with his POAs for that year (see *TMA 1970, s 59A(3)(4)*).

Notes

(a) Once a valid claim involving more than one year, e.g. a carry-back claim, has been made, HMRC will give effect to it as soon as possible, subject to the following policies:

- no repayment of tax will be made for the earlier year unless tax for the earlier year has been paid in full; and

- where liability for any year is outstanding (or will become due within 35 days after HMRC process the claim), relief will be given by set-off rather than by repayment.

(Revenue Tax Bulletins December 1996 361–365, June 1997 p 443; HMRC Business Income Manual BIM75050).

(b) Where the tax saving arising from a loss carry-back claim is set against an outstanding tax liability, the effective date of settlement of that liability, for the purpose of calculating any charge to interest on overdue tax or any surcharge, is the date on which the valid carry-back claim is made (Revenue Tax Bulletins December 1996 p 364, August 2001 p 879).

(c) On a repayment or set-off arising from a loss carry-back claim, repayment interest accrues only from 31 January following the later year (i.e. the year of loss). It follows that if the repayment or set-off is made before 31 January 2015, no repayment interest will be due. [*FA 2009, s 102, Sch 54 para 7; SI 2011 No 701, Arts 3, 4*].

(d) For loss relief carry-backs generally, see **14.1, 14.3, 14.4** LOSSES.

(B) **Carry-back claim made after 31 July but before 31 January in the later year**

Dec files his 2012/13 tax return in October 2013. On 1 November 2013, he makes a claim to carry back from 2013/14 (the later year) to 2012/13 a trading loss of £5,000 for the year to 30 April 2013. Dec's POAs for 2012/13 (based on his 2011/12 liability) were £3,000 each. All tax due has been paid on the due dates.

What if Dec's self-assessment for 2012/13 shows an income tax liability of £8,640, of which £2,400 represents higher rate tax charged on the top £6,000 of income? The loss produces a tax saving of £2,000 (£5,000 @ 40%). This will be available to set off against the 2012/13 balancing payment (due on 31 January 2014), reducing it from £2,640 to £640. The 2013/14 POAs will be £4,320 each.

What if Dec's self-assessment for 2012/13 shows an income tax liability of £5,500, which represents tax charged at 20%? The 2012/13 POAs will have been adjusted to £2,750 each, and repayments made of £250 in respect of each POA. The loss produces a tax saving of £1,000 (£5,000 @ 20%). As all the tax for 2012/13 has been paid and there are no outstanding liabilities for any year, the £1,000 will be repaid. No repayment interest is due. The 2013/14 POAs will be £2,750 each.

Say the carry-back claim had instead been made on 3 January 2014 (assuming all other facts are as immediately above), the £1,000 tax saving would have been set against the first 2013/14 POA of £2,750 due on 31 January 2014, reducing it to £1,750.

As he has made no trading profit for 2013/14, Dec might make a separate claim to reduce or dispense with his POAs for that year (see *TMA 1970, s 59A(3)(4)*).

(C) **Carry-back claim made before 31 July in the later year**

The facts are as in (B) above except that Dec files his 2012/13 return on 25 April 2013 and makes his carry-back claim on 31 May 2013. As accounts for the year to 30 April 2013 are not finalised at this stage, the trading loss of £5,000 is a 'best estimate' but does turn out to be an accurate figure. Dec could not have made the claim in the return as the period of account in which the loss is sustained had not yet come to an end when he filed the return.

What if Dec's self-assessment for 2012/13 shows an income tax liability of £8,640, which £2,400 represents higher rate tax charged on the top £6,000 of income? The loss produces a tax saving of £2,000 (£5,000 @ 40%). This will be available to set off against the 2012/13 balancing payment (due on 31 January 2014), reducing it from £2,640 to £640. The 2013/14 POAs will be £4,320 each.

What if Dec's self-assessment for 2012/13 shows an income tax liability of £5,500, which represents tax charged at 20%? The 2012/13 POAs will be adjusted to £2,750 each and there will be no balancing payment due on 31 January 2014. A repayment of £250 will be made from the first POA paid on 31 January 2013. The tax saving of £1,000 (£5,000 @ 20%) will be set against the second POA due on 31 July 2013, reducing it from £2,750 to £1,750. The 2013/14 POAs will be £2,750 each.

What if the facts were as immediately above but Dec has failed to pay the first POA for 2012/13 due on 31 January 2013? The tax saving of £1,000 (£5,000 @ 20%) will be set against this outstanding liability, reducing the payment required from £2,750 (originally £3,000) to £1,750. The effective date of payment for interest purposes is 31 May 2013, the date of the valid claim (see note (b) to (A) above). The balance of £1,750 is already overdue, and a further POA of £2,750 is due on 31 July 2013. No balancing payment for 2012/13 is due on 31 January 2014. The 2013/14 POAs will be £2,750 each.

As he has made no trading profit for 2013/14, Dec might make a separate claim to reduce or dispense with his POAs for that year (see *TMA 1970, s 59A(3)(4)*).

26 Settlements

26.1 TAX PAYABLE BY TRUSTEES

A is sole life-tenant of a settlement which has income and expenses in the year 2013/14 as follows

	£	£
Property income		500
Taxed investment income (tax deducted at source £300)		1,500
Dividends	900	
Add Dividend tax credits	100	
		1,000
		£3,000
Expenses chargeable to income		£400

The tax payable by the trustees under self-assessment will be £100 (£500 at 20%). The expenses are not deductible in arriving at the tax payable by the trustees. The starting rate for savings applies only to individual taxpayers and not to trustees, although the 10% dividend ordinary rate does apply to trustees.

Notes

(a) By prior arrangement, where there is a sole life-tenant in a trust, HMRC may allow the interest to be assessed directly on that beneficiary.

(b) For treatment of the trust income in the hands of the beneficiary, see **26.3(A)** below.

26.2 SPECIAL TRUST RATES OF TAX

[*ITA 2007, ss 9, 479–487, 491–498; ITTOIA 2005, ss 399(4)–(6), 400(4)(5); FA 2012, s 1(3)(6)*]

(A) 'Basic rate' band

For 2013/14, a small discretionary trust has property income of £500, building society interest of £240 (net of £60 tax deducted at source) and UK dividends of £450 (carrying a tax credit of £50). It has no other income or expenses. The settlor has made no other settlements.

The tax liability of the trust for 2013/14 is as follows

	£
'Basic rate' band	
Property income — £500 @ 20%	100.00

26.2 IT Settlements

Gross interest — £300 @ 20%	60.00
Dividends and tax credits — (£180 × $^{100}/_{90}$) = £200 @ 10%	20.00
	£180.00
Income exceeding 'basic rate' band	
Dividends and tax credits — (£270 × $^{100}/_{90}$) = £300 @ 37.5%	112.50
	292.50
Less: Tax deducted at source	(60.00)
Dividend tax credits	(50.00)
Net tax liability	£182.50

Notes

(a) The property income and building society interest form the lowest slice of the total income; thus, it all falls within the 'basic rate' band and is charged at basic rate. £800 of the £1,000 'basic rate' band is now used up; thus, £200 of the dividend income falls within the 'basic rate' band and is charged at the dividend ordinary rate. The remainder of the dividend income is charged at the dividend trust rate.

(b) Note that if the trustees were to distribute the whole of the net income of £1,007.50 (£500 + £240 + £450 − £182.50) to beneficiaries, they will have further tax to pay (assuming no balance, or insufficient balance, brought forward from earlier years in the trustees' tax pool). The total tax payable will be £824.32 (£1,007.50 × 45/55), from which can be deducted tax paid of £242.50 (£100.00 + £60.00 + (£112.50 − £30.00)), leaving a further £581.82 to pay (if no balance is brought forward in the pool). See also note (c) to (B) below and, for an illustration of the pool, (C) below.

(c) The 'basic rate' band of £1,000 is divided between all settlements made by the same settlor, subject to a minimum band of £200 for each settlement. [*ITA 2007, ss 491, 492*].

(B) **General**

An accumulation and maintenance settlement set up by W for his grandchildren in 1995 now comprises quoted investments and an industrial property. The property is let to an engineering company. Charges for rates, electricity etc. are paid by the trust and recharged yearly in arrears to the tenant. As a result of the delay in recovering the service costs, the settlement incurs overdraft interest. There are no other settlements in existence in relation to which W is the settlor.

The relevant figures for the year ended 5 April 2014 are as follows

	£
Property rents	40,500
UK dividends (including tax credits of £500)	5,000
Taxed interest (tax deducted at source £700)	3,500
	£49,000
Trust administration expenses — proportion chargeable to income	1,350
Overdraft interest	1,050

Settlements IT 26.2

£2,400

Tax is payable by the trustees of a discretionary trust (including an accumulation and maintenance trust) at the trust rate (45%) or, in the case of dividend income, at the dividend trust rate (37.5%).

The tax liability of the trust for 2013/14 is as follows

	£	£
Property income £1,000 at 20%	200	
£39,500 at 45%	17,775	17,975
Taxed interest £3,500 at 25% (45 – 20)		875
Net dividends	4,500	
Deduct Expenses	(2,400)	
	£2,100	
£2,100 grossed at $^{100}/_{90}$ = £2,333 @ 27.5%(37.5 – 10)		641
Tax payable by self-assessment		19,491
Add: Tax deducted at source		700
Dividend tax credits		500
Total tax borne		£20,691

Notes

(a) Expenses (including in this example the overdraft interest) are set firstly against UK dividends and similar income, then against dividends from non-UK resident companies (not illustrated in this example), then against other savings income and finally against non-savings income. [*ITA 2007, ss 484–486*]. In this example, all the expenses are set against UK dividends, the effect being that the total expenses, grossed up at 10%, save tax at 27.5% (the difference between the dividend ordinary rate and dividend trust rate), equal to £866.67.

(b) The net income available for distribution to the beneficiaries, at the trustees' discretion, will be £25,909 (£49,000 – £20,691 – £2,400).

(c) Of the tax borne, only £20,191 goes into the trustees' tax pool. Tax credits on dividends cannot enter the pool. Unless there is sufficient balance brought forward from earlier years, the effect is that if the whole of the distributable income is in fact distributed, there will be insufficient tax in the pool to frank the distribution (£25,909 × 45/55 = £21,198) and the trustees will have a further liability which they may not have the funds to settle. For an illustration, see (C) below.

(d) The property income and savings income form the lowest slice of the total income. Thus, the first £1,000 of such income falls within the 'basic rate' band; as it is basic rate income by nature, that £1,000 is chargeable at the basic rate of 20%.

(e) See note (*c*) to (A) above as regards the 'basic rate' band.

(f) For treatment of the trust income in the hands of a beneficiary, see **26.3(B)** below.

26.2 IT   Settlements

(C)   **Trustees' tax**

[*ITA 2007, ss 496–498*]

The property of the XYZ discretionary trust consists entirely of UK shares. For 2013/14, the trustees receive net dividends of £9,950 and the trust expenses consist of professional fees of £500. The trustees have distributed to beneficiaries all available income arising before 6 April 2013, and there is no balance brought forward in the trustees' tax pool created under *ITA 2007, s 497*. There are no other settlements in existence in relation to which the settlor of the XYZ trust is the settlor.

The trustees' tax liabilities for 2013/14 are computed as follows

	£
Net income	9,950
Less expenses	500
	£9,450
	£9,450
£9,450 grossed at $^{100}/_{90}$	£10,500
Tax at 10% (dividend ordinary rate) on £1,000	100
Tax at 37.5% (dividend trust rate) on £9,500	3,563
Less tax credits @ 10% on £10,500	(1,050)
Tax payable by trustees' self-assessment	£2,613
Distributable income: £(9,450 − 2,613)	£6,837
Tax added to trustees' tax pool (Y) (note (a))	£2,612.50
Position if all income distributed	
Beneficiaries' income	6,837.50
Add tax at $^{45}/_{55}$ (see **26.3(B)** below) (X)	5,594.32
Beneficiaries' gross income	£12,431.82
Additional tax due from trustees (X) − (Y) note (b)	£2,981.82
Optimum position	
Income distributed (£9,450 net income @ 55%)	5,197.50
Tax credit $^{45}/_{55}$	4,252.50
Beneficiaries' gross income	£9,450.00
Additional tax due from trustees £(4,252.50 − 2,612.50)	£1,640.00
Funds available £(6,837.50 − 5,197.50)	£1,640.00

Notes

(a)   Tax credits on UK dividends cannot form part of the trustees' tax pool, so cannot be used to frank distributions. Tax paid at the dividend ordinary rate cannot go into the pool either. This effectively restricts the amount that can be paid out to beneficiaries. The additional 27.5% tax paid by the trustees on grossed-up dividends, i.e. the difference between the dividend ordinary and trust rates (£9,500 @ 27.5%), does go into the pool.

(b) If the trustees distribute the whole of the net income, they will have no funds available from income to pay the additional tax due of £2,981.82.

26.3 INCOME OF BENEFICIARIES

(A) **Interests in possession**

A, as sole life-tenant of the settlement in **26.1** above, is absolutely entitled to receive the whole settlement income.

A's income from the trust for 2013/14 is computed as follows

	£	£	£
Trust dividend income plus tax credits	1,000		
Trust savings income		1,500	
Other trust income			500
Deduct: dividend ordinary rate tax (10%)	(100)		
basic rate tax (20%)	—	(300)	(100)
	900	1,200	400
Deduct Expenses (note (b))	400	—	—
Net income entitlement	£500	£1,200	£400

Beneficiary's entitlement

Grossed-up amounts:				
	£500 × $^{100}/_{90}$	£555.56		
	£1,200 × $^{100}/_{80}$		£1,500.00	
	£400 × $^{100}/_{80}$			£500.00
Tax deducted at source		£55.56	£300.00	£100.00

Notes

(a) This income falls to be included in A's return even if it is not actually paid to him, as he is absolutely entitled to it. He will receive a tax certificate (form R185 (Trust Income)) from the trust agents, showing three figures each for gross income, tax deducted and net income, as illustrated above.

(b) Trust expenses are deductible firstly from UK dividends and similar income, then from dividends from non-UK resident companies (not illustrated in this example), then from savings income and finally from non-savings income. [*ITA 2007, s 503*].

(c) That part of A's trust income which is represented by dividend income is treated as dividend income in his hands. It is thus chargeable at the dividend ordinary rate, the liability being satisfied by the 10% dividend tax credit, except to the extent, if any, that it exceeds his basic rate limit. The tax credit is not repayable if the income is covered by allowances. Similarly, that part of A's trust income which is represented

26.3 IT Settlements

by savings income is treated as savings income in his hands. It will thus qualify wholly or partly for the 10% starting rate for savings to the extent (if any) that A's other taxable income is less than the starting rate limit of £2,790.

(B) **Accumulation or discretionary trusts**

M, the 17-year old grandson of W, is one of the five beneficiaries to whom the trustees can pay the settlement income in **26.2(B)** above. The trustees make a payment of £5,500 to M on 31 January 2014. He has no other income in the year 2013/14.

M's income from the trust is

	£
Net income	5,500.00
Tax at $^{45}/_{55}$	4,500.00
Gross income	£10,000.00

He can claim a tax repayment for 2013/14 of

	£
Total income	10,000
Deduct Personal allowance	9,440
	£560

Tax payable:	
£560 × 20% (basic rate)	112.00
Tax accounted for by trustees	4,500.00
Repayment due	£4,388.00

Notes

(a) If no income was actually paid to M from the settlement, nothing would fall to be included in his return.

(b) Unlike the position with interest in possession trusts (see (A) above), no distinction is made between dividend income, non-dividend savings income and other income in the beneficiary's hands, the full amount of the payment to him being treated as having suffered tax at a single rate of 45% in the hands of the trustees. The beneficiary is not entitled to the starting rate for savings as a payment from a discretionary trust is not savings income in his hands.

(c) For treatment of trust income where the beneficiary is an infant under a parent's settlement, see **26.4** below.

Settlements   IT 26.5

26.4 SETTLEMENT BY PARENT IN FAVOUR OF OWN CHILD

[*ITTOIA 2005, ss 629, 631, 632, Sch 2 para 133*]

L set up an accumulation and maintenance trust for his two children, aged 5 and 3, in 1998. On 31 December 1999 and 31 December 2000, school fees of £990 were paid on behalf of each child. In January 2014 the trust was wound up and the assets transferred to the two beneficiaries, then aged 21 and 19, in equal shares. At that time there was £6,000 of undistributed income.

The income to be treated as the settlor's income will be as follows

1999/2000	$£1,980 \times \dfrac{100}{66}$	£3,000
2000/01	$£1,980 \times \dfrac{100}{66}$	£3,000
2013/14	note (b)	Nil

Notes

(a) The payments for 1999/2000 and 2000/01 are grossed up in accordance with the 'rate applicable to trusts' for each of those years, i.e. 34%.

(b) Income is not treated as that of the parent settlor if, at the time of payment, the children have either married or reached the age of eighteen.

26.5 LOANS BY SETTLEMENT TO SETTLOR

[*ITTOIA 2005, ss 633–638*]

The trustees of a settlement with undistributed income of £1,375 at 5 April 2010 made a loan of £20,000 to B, the settlor, on 30 September 2010.

B repays the loan on 31 December 2013. Undistributed income of £3,500 arose in 2010/11, £6,500 in 2011/12, £4,500 in 2012/13 and £4,200 in 2013/14. The trustees duly settle all their liabilities to tax on trust income.

The following income amounts will be treated as part of B's total income

		£
2010/11	$£4,875 \times {}^{100}/_{50}$	9,750
2011/12	$£6,500 \times {}^{100}/_{50}$	13,000
2012/13	$£4,500 \times {}^{100}/_{50}$	9,000
2013/14	$£4,125 \times {}^{100}/_{55}$ note (b)	7,500

The notional tax credit available to B is

26.5 IT Settlements

		£	£
2010/11	£1,375 × 100/60 at 40% note (c)	916.67	
	£3,500 × 100/50 at 50%	3,500.00	4,416.67
2011/12	£13,000 at 50%		6,500.00
2012/13	£9,000 at 50%		4,500.00
2013/14	£7,500 at 45%		3,375.00

Notes

(a) Where in any tax year the trustees of a settlement pay any capital sum (including by way of loan) to the settlor, a corresponding amount (grossed up at the trust rate) is treated as income of the settlor to the extent that it falls within the amount of available income in the settlement up to the end of that tax year or, to the extent that it does not fall within that amount, to the end of the next and subsequent tax years (up to a maximum of ten years).

(b) The amount treated as income in 2013/14 is limited to the amount of the loan less amounts previously treated as income (£20,000 − (£4,875 + £6,500 + £4,500)).

(c) B's notional tax credit for 2010/11 would otherwise be £9,750 @ 50% = £4,875, but is restricted by the fact that £1,375 of the net income attributed to him for that year arose before 6 April 2010 and thus at a time when the trust rate was 40%

27 Share-Related Employment Income and Exemptions

27.1 SHARE OPTIONS — CHARGE TO TAX

[*ITEPA 2003, ss 471–484*]

An employee is granted an option exercisable within 5 years to buy 1,000 shares at £5 each. The option costs 50p per share. He exercises the option on 15 June 2013 when the shares are worth £7.50. The option is not granted under an approved scheme. The employee does not incur any expenses in connection with the acquisition of the shares.

The amount taxable as employment income in 2013/14 is as follows

	£	£
Open market value of shares 1,000 × £7.50		7,500
Price paid 1,000 × £5 − shares	5,000	
1,000 × 50p − option	500	
		5,500
Amount taxable as employment income		£2,000

Notes

(a) The result would be the same if, instead of exercising the option, the employee transferred his option to a third party for £2,500.

(b) The capital gains tax base cost of the shares will be £7,500 being the aggregate of the price paid for the shares, the price paid for the options and the amount chargeable to income tax. [*TCGA 1992, ss 119A, 144(3)*].

(c) A share option acquired on or after 2 December 2004 is taken outside these rules (and into the convertible shares regime at **27.3** below) if it is a right to acquire securities that is itself acquired pursuant to a right or opportunity made available under arrangements having as one of their main purposes the avoidance of tax or national insurance contributions. This may also apply to a share option acquired before 2 December 2004 if 'something is done on or after that date as part of the arrangements under which it was made available'. [*ITEPA 2003, s 420(8)*].

27.2 RESTRICTED SHARES

[*ITEPA 2003, ss 422–432; FA 2011, Sch 2 paras 15, 16, 52*]

Edward and Andrew are employees of Perks Ltd.

Edward is given 2,000 shares in the company on 1 October 2009 on the understanding that he cannot sell them for at least three years. This has the practical effect of restricting the market value by 30 pence per share.

Andrew is given 3,000 shares in the company on the same date on the understanding that they will be forfeited if he leaves the company before 1 January 2014. This has the practical effect of restricting the market value by 50 pence per share. Andrew does not leave the company and thus holds the shares with full rights as from 1 January 2014.

27.2 IT Share-Related Employment Income and Exemptions

The above awards are not made under an approved scheme.

The market value per share, disregarding the above restrictions, is as follows.

At 1.10.09	£2.00
At 1.10.12	£4.00
At 1.1.14	£5.00

The following amounts are chargeable to tax as employment income

2009/10

Edward — 2,000 × £1.70 (restricted market value at 1.10.09) =   £3,400

Andrew — no charge, as provision for forfeiture persists for no more than five years (see *ITEPA 2003, s 425*)   Nil

2012/13

Edward — chargeable event occurs on 1.10.12 when the shares cease to be restricted shares.

Taxable amount = UMV × (IUP − PCP − OP) − CE (see *ITEPA 2003, s 428*)
UMV (Unrestricted Market Value) = (2,000 × £4)   £8,000

$$\text{IUP (Initial Uncharged Proportion)} = \frac{4,000\,(2,000 \times £2) - 3,400}{4,000}$$

PCP (Previously Charged Proportion) = Nil (as there has been no previous chargeable event)
OP (Outstanding Proportion) = Nil (as unrestricted market value and actual market value are the same after the event)
CE (employee's expenses) = Nil
Taxable amount = £8,000 × 15% (600/4,000) =   £1,200

2013/14

Edward — chargeable event occurs on 1.1.14 when the shares cease to be restricted shares.
Taxable amount = UMV × (IUP − PCP − OP) − CE
UMV = (3,000 × £5)   £15,000

$$\text{IUP (Initial Uncharged Proportion)} = \frac{6,000\,(3,000 \times £2) - \text{Nil}}{6,000}$$

Other values = Nil
Taxable amount = £15,000 × 100% (6,000/6,000) =   £15,000

Share-Related Employment Income and Exemptions   IT 27.3

Available elections and their effect

Andrew could have elected, jointly with his employer, to disapply the exemption on acquisition. The election would have had to be made by 15 October 2009. [*ITEPA 2003, s 425*]. The chargeable amount for 2009/10 would have been 3,000 × £1.50 = £4,500. The chargeable amount in 2013/14 would then have been £15,000 × 25% (1,500/6,000) = £3,750.

Edward and/or Andrew could also (or alternatively) have elected, jointly with the employer, to ignore the restrictions in computing the chargeable amount on acquisition. The election(s) would have had to be made by 15 October 2009. [*ITEPA 2003, s 431*]. The chargeable amounts for 2009/10 would have been £4,000 for Edward (2,000 × £2) and £6,000 for Andrew (3,000 × £2) but there would have been no further charge in subsequent years.

Note

(a) The elections mentioned above are implemented by way of an agreement (between employer and employee), in a form approved by HMRC; there is no requirement for them to be submitted to HMRC. Once made, the elections are irrevocable.

27.3 CONVERTIBLE SHARES

[*ITEPA 2003, ss 435–444; FA 2011, Sch 2 paras 17, 18, 52*]

Missy is an employee of XYZ Ltd. Under an unapproved employee share scheme, she is awarded 1,000 'B' shares in the company on 1 December 2011 which are convertible in exactly two years' time into 1,200 'A' shares. Under the terms of the scheme, Missy is required to pay the company £150 for the conversion. She duly converts the shares on 1 December 2013. Relevant market values (MV) per share are as follows.

MV per 'B' share at 1.12.11 with right to convert after 2 years	£2.00
MV per 'B' share at 1.12.11 ignoring right to convert	£1.80
MV per 'A' share at 1.12.13	£3.75
MV per 'B' share at 1.12.13 ignoring right to convert	£3.00

Chargeable amount on acquisition of 'B' shares (2011/12)

1,000 × £1.80 (conversion right ignored — *ITEPA 2003, s 437*)	£1,800

Chargeable amount on conversion into 'A' shares (2013/14) *(ITEPA 2003, ss 440, 441)*

	£	£
1,200 × £3.75 (MV of 'A' shares)		4,500
Less 1,000 × £3.00 (MV of 'B' shares)	3,000	
Consideration given for the conversion	150	3,150
Chargeable amount		£1,350

27.3 IT   Share-Related Employment Income and Exemptions

Note

(a)   Immediately after the conversion, Missy has shares worth £4,500 for which she has paid £150, a benefit of £4,350 of which only £3,150 has been taxed. The capital growth in the 'B' shares between acquisition and conversion is not charged to income tax.

27.4 APPROVED SHARE INCENTIVE PLANS

[*ITEPA 2003, ss 488–515, Sch 2*]

GB plc operates a share incentive plan approved by HMRC in August 2013. The plan provides for free shares, partnership shares, matching shares and dividend shares. The following table illustrates the permissible benefits and the tax position of participating employees as regards each of these kinds of share.

	Free shares	Partnership shares	Matching shares	Dividend shares
Brief description	Shares appropriated (without payment) to employees	Shares acquired on employees' behalf from sums deducted from their salary	Shares appropriated (without payment) to employees in proportion to their partnership shares	Shares acquired on employees' behalf out of dividends received on their plan shares
Maximum limits per participant	Shares worth £3,000 (per tax year) at time of award	Salary deductions per month must be lower of £1,500 per tax year and 10% of salary (plan may specify lower limits)	Two matching shares for each partnership share acquired (plan may specify lower ratio)	No statutory limit but the amount of cash dividends to be reinvested (or how such an amount is to be determined) is at the direction of the company (and see note (b)).
Minimum limits — note (a)	N/A	£10 on any occasion or such lesser amount as is specified in the plan	N/A	N/A
Holding period (i.e. period during which shares must remain in plan) — note (c)	As specified by company — must be at least three years but not more than five, from time of award	None — employee may withdraw shares from plan at any time (see below for tax position)	As specified by company — must be at least three years but not more than five, from time of award	Three years from acquisition

182

Share-Related Employment Income and Exemptions   IT 27.4

Tax on award of shares	None	None — deductions from salary allowable for income tax	None	None — dividends applied in acquiring shares are not taxable
Income tax on shares leaving the plan (note (d)) within less than three years of award (subject to note (e))	On market value of shares when they leave the plan	On market value of shares when they leave the plan	On market value of shares when they leave the plan	Original dividend becomes taxable, but in tax year in which shares leave plan
Income tax on shares leaving the plan (note (d)) after three years or more, but less than five years, after award (subject to note (e))	On lower of market value at time of award and market value on leaving the plan	On lower of salary used to acquire the shares and market value on leaving the plan	On lower of market value at time of award and market value on leaving the plan	None
Income tax on shares leaving the plan (note (d)) five or more years after award	None	None	None	None
Capital gains tax on shares leaving the plan (note (d)) at any time—note (g)	None	None	None	None

Notes

(a)   It is at the option of the company whether or not to include in the plan a minimum limit for partnership shares. [*ITEPA 2003, Sch 2 para 47*].

(b)   For 2012/13 and earlier years, the maximum dividend reinvestment per participant per tax year was limited to £1,500. Before 17 July 2013, it was not possible to specify that only some of the cash dividends be reinvested. A plan approved before 17 July 2013 which provides for reinvestment has effect on and after that date with any modifications needed to reflect the change of law. A direction given before that date is to be treated on and after that date, unless modified, as requiring the reinvestment of all the cash dividends. To the extent that cash dividends are not required to be reinvested, they must be paid over to the participants. [*ITEPA 2003, Sch 2 paras 62–69; ITTOIA 2005, s 397A(7); FA 2013, Sch 2 paras 83–90*].

27.4 IT   Share-Related Employment Income and Exemptions

(c) Shares appropriated to employees, or acquired on their behalf, are held within the plan by trustees until leaving the plan as in (d)) below. In all cases, the stipulated holding period automatically ends if the participating employee ceases to be in relevant employment. [*ITEPA 2003, Sch 2 paras 36, 61, 67*].

(d) References to shares leaving the plan are to their ceasing to be subject to the plan. Shares cease to be subject to the plan if they are withdrawn by the participant (i.e. transferred by the plan trustees on his instructions or sold by them on his instructions and his account) or the participant leaves the relevant employment. [*ITEPA 2003, Sch 2 paras 95–97*].

(e) There is no income tax charge on shares ceasing to be subject to the plan *at any time* by reason of the participant's ceasing to be in relevant employment due to death, injury, disability, redundancy, retirement and other specified reasons beyond his control. [*ITEPA 2003, s 498, Sch 2 paras 98, 99; FA 2013, Sch 2 paras 2, 5, 17(1)*].

(f) The income tax exemptions do not apply if the shares are awarded or acquired under arrangements one of the main purposes of which is the avoidance of tax or national insurance contributions. [*ITEPA 2003, s 489(4)*].

(g) For capital gains tax purposes, shares ceasing to be subject to the plan at any time are deemed to have been disposed of and immediately reacquired by the participant at that time at their then market value, but no chargeable gain or allowable loss arises on that deemed disposal. [*TCGA 1992, Sch 7D para 5*].

27.5 ENTERPRISE MANAGEMENT INCENTIVES

[*ITEPA 2003, ss 527–541, Sch 5; F(No 3)A 2010, s 6; SI 2012 No 1360*]

Keyman, an executive director of HIP Company Ltd, is granted on 1 September 2011, by reason of his employment, an option, exercisable within ten years, to acquire 8,000 ordinary shares in the company at £2.50 per share. No price is payable for the option itself. The market value of the company's ordinary shares at the date the option is granted is £3.50 per share. Keyman exercises the option on 11 October 2012 when the market value is £4.50 per share. On 19 September 2013, he sells half his holding (i.e. 4,000 shares) for net proceeds of £24,900. No other options have been granted to Keyman by reason of his employment with the company.

HIP Company Ltd is a qualifying company for the purposes of the Enterprise Management Incentives provisions, and gives HMRC notice of the grant of the option by 1 December 2011 (i.e. within 92 days). It obtained a Stock Market quotation in March 2013. Keyman is an eligible employee and, at the time of grant, the total value of shares in the company in respect of which options existed was well below £3 million.

Income tax

2011/12

No charge arises on receipt of the option. [*ITEPA 2003, ss 475, 528*].

Share-Related Employment Income and Exemptions IT 27.5

2012/13

Charge on exercise of option (note (c))

Lower of

		£
Market value of 8,000 shares at time option granted (8,000 × £3.50)	£28,000	
Market value of 8,000 shares at time option exercised (8,000 × £4.50)	£36,000	28,000
Deduct Option Price (8,000 × £2.50)		20,000
Amount chargeable to income tax as employment income		£8,000

Capital gains tax
2013/14

	£	£
Net disposal proceeds (4,000 shares)		24,900
Deduct Cost of shares (4,000 × £2.50)	10,000	
Amount charged to income tax: (note (c)) £8,000 × 4,000/8,000	4,000	14,000
Chargeable gain (equal to annual exemption)		£10,900

Notes

(a) Under the Enterprise Management Incentives provisions, the company may be quoted or unquoted but must be an independent company carrying on (or preparing to carry on) a qualifying trade, whose gross assets do not exceed £30 million and which has less than 250 full-time employees and a permanent establishment in the UK. Broadly, an employee is eligible if he is employed by the company for at least 25 hours per week or, if less, at least 75% of his total working time, and he controls no more than 30% of the company's ordinary share capital.

(b) Companies are able to grant options over shares worth (at time of grant) up to £250,000 (£120,000 before 16 June 2012) to eligible employees.

(c) The discount (i.e. the excess of market value at date of grant over the aggregate of any amount paid for the option itself and the option price) is chargeable to income tax under *ITEPA 2003, s 476*. If market value had fallen by the time of exercise, the amount so chargeable is reduced (or extinguished) accordingly. [*ITEPA 2003, s 531*]. The amount chargeable to income tax is deductible for capital gains tax purposes by virtue of *TCGA 1992, s 119A*. It is allocated pro rata to the shares sold, under the normal part disposal rules for shares.

(d) If the option had been an unapproved share option, the income tax charge would have been on £16,000 (£36,000 – £20,000) (see computation at **27.1** above).

(e) Where the option is exercised on or after 6 April 2012 and the shares are disposed of on or after 6 April 2013, chargeable gains realised on shares acquired by the exercise of qualifying options may be eligible for capital gains tax entrepreneurs' relief. The twelve-month minimum holding period required for entrepreneurs' relief begins

27.5 IT Share-Related Employment Income and Exemptions

when the option is granted rather than when the shares are acquired. The normal requirement for entrepreneurs' relief that the individual must hold at least 5% of the company's ordinary share capital does not apply. [*TCGA 1992, s 169I(7A)–(7R); FA 2013, Sch 24 paras 1, 5, 6*].

# 28 Social Security Income

28.1 HIGH INCOME CHILD BENEFIT CHARGE

[*ITEPA 2003, ss 681B–681H; Social Security Administration Act 1992, s 13A; Social Security Administration (Northern Ireland) Act 1992, s 11A; FA 2012, Sch 1 paras 1, 3, 4, 7*].

Jill is a single parent of one child and is entitled to child benefit of £20.30 per week throughout 2012/13 and 2013/14. Her adjusted net income is less than £50,000 for both those tax years. On 4 May 2013 she moves in with her boyfriend Jack, who has an adjusted net income of £56,344 for 2013/14. They continue to live together beyond 5 April 2014.

The income tax consequences for 2012/13 and 2013/14 are as follows

Jill has no liability to the high income child benefit charge for either year as her adjusted net income does not exceed £50,000. Jack is liable to the charge in respect of Jill's child benefit entitlement for the week beginning Monday 6 May 2013 and all subsequent weeks throughout the tax year 2013/14.

The charge is 1% of the amount of child benefit entitlement for every £100 of the chargeable person's adjusted net income above £50,000. The amount of the charge on Jack is computed as follows. Child benefit entitlement for the 48 weeks beginning Monday 6 May 2013 is £20.30 x 48 = £974.40 which is rounded down to £974. Adjusted net income is rounded down to £56,300. The tax charge is:

£974 x 1% x 6,300/100 = £613.62

This is rounded down to £613, which is added to Jack's income tax liability for the year.

Notes

(a) With effect on and after 7 January 2013, an income tax charge (the '*high income child benefit charge*') is imposed on an individual whose adjusted net income exceeds £50,000 in a tax year and who is, or whose partner is, in receipt of child benefit. In the event that both partners have an adjusted net income that exceeds £50,000, the charge applies only to the partner with the highest income.

(b) The maximum charge is an amount equal to the full amount of child benefit entitlement and applies where the chargeable person's adjusted net income is £60,000 or more.

(c) Child benefit itself remains non-taxable but the high income child benefit charge effectively claws back the benefit from high income taxpayers.

(d) Adjusted net income is broadly taxable income before deducting personal reliefs but adjusted by deducting the gross equivalent of any Gift Aid donations or any pension contributions paid net of basic rate tax. [*ITA 2007, s 58*].

29 Trading Income

Cross-reference. See also **30 TRADING INCOME — CASH BASIS FOR SMALL BUSINESSES**.

29.1 OPENING YEARS OF ASSESSMENT

[*ITTOIA 2005, ss 199, 200, 204*].

Simon commences trade on 1 September 2012 and prepares accounts to 30 April, starting with an eight-month period of account to 30 April 2013. His profits (as adjusted for tax purposes) for the first three periods of account are as follows

	£
Eight months to 30 April 2013	24,000
Year to 30 April 2014	39,000
Year to 30 April 2015	40,000

His taxable profits for the first four tax years are as follows

	Basis period		£	£
2012/13	1.9.12 – 5.4.13	£24,000 × $^7/_8$		21,000
2013/14	1.9.12 – 31.8.13:			
	1.9.12 – 30.4.13		24,000	
	1.5.13 – 31.8.13	£39,000 × $^4/_{12}$	13,000	
				37,000
2014/15	Y/e 30.4.14			39,000
2015/16	Y/e 30.4.15			40,000

Overlap relief accrued:	
1.9.12 – 5.4.13 – 7 months	21,000
1.5.13 – 31.8.13 – 4 months	13,000
Total overlap relief accrued note (b)	£34,000

Notes

(a) The taxable profits for the first tax year are those from the commencement date to 5 April. [*ITTOIA 2005, s 199(1)*]. In the second tax year, the period from commencement to the accounting date in that year is less than 12 months, so the basis period is the 12 months from commencement. [*ITTOIA 2005, s 200(2)*]. In the third tax year, there is a period of account of 12 months to the normal accounting date, so the basis period is that period of account. [*ITTOIA 2005, s 198*]. Assessments then continue on that basis.

29.1 IT   Trading Income

(b) The overlap relief accrued (by reference to an aggregate overlap period of 11 months) will be given on cessation (see **29.3** below) or on a change of accounting date resulting in a basis period exceeding 12 months (the relief given depending on the extent of the excess) (see **29.2(B)** below).

29.2 CHANGE OF ACCOUNTING DATE

[*ITTOIA 2005, ss 214–220*]

(A) **Change to a date earlier in the tax year**

Miranda commenced trade on 1 September 2010, preparing accounts to 31 August. In 2013, she changes her accounting date to 31 May, preparing accounts for the nine months to 31 May 2013. The conditions of *ITTOIA 2005, s 217* are satisfied in relation to the change. Her profits (as adjusted for tax purposes) are as follows

	£
Year ended 31 August 2011	18,000
Year ended 31 August 2012	21,500
Nine months to 31 May 2013	17,000
Year ended 31 May 2014	23,000

Taxable profits for the first five tax years are as follows

	Basis period		£	£
2010/11	1.9.10 – 5.4.11	£18,000 × $^7/_{12}$		10,500
2011/12	Y/e 31.8.11			18,000
2012/13	Y/e 31.8.12			21,500
2013/14	1.6.12 – 31.5.13:			
	1.6.12 – 31.8.12	£21,500 × $^3/_{12}$	5,375	
	1.9.12 – 31.5.13		17,000	
				22,375
2014/15	Y/e 31.5.14			23,000

Overlap relief accrued:
1.9.10 – 5.4.11 — 7 months	10,500
1.6.12 – 31.8.12 — 3 months	5,375
Total overlap relief accrued note (c)	£15,875

Notes

(a) For a change of accounting date to result in a change of basis period, the conditions in *ITTOIA 2005, s 217* must normally be satisfied. [*ITTOIA 2005, s 216*].

Trading Income IT 29.2

(b) In this example, the 'relevant period' is that from 1 September 2012 (the day following the end of the basis period for 2012/13) to 31 May 2013 (the new accounting date in the year 2013/14 — the year of change). As the relevant period is less than 12 months, the basis period for 2013/14 is the 12 months ending on the new accounting date. [*ITTOIA 2005, s 216(2)*].

(c) The overlap relief accrued (by reference to an aggregate overlap period of 10 months) will be given on cessation (see **29.3** below) or on a change of accounting date resulting in a basis period exceeding 12 months (the relief given depending on the extent of the excess) (see (B) below).

(B) **Change to a date later in the tax year**

Dennis starts a business on 1 July 2010, preparing accounts to 30 June. In 2013, he changes his accounting date to 31 December, preparing accounts for the six months to 31 December 2013. The conditions of *ITTOIA 2005, s 217* are satisfied in relation to the change. His profits (as adjusted for tax purposes) are as follows

	£
Year ended 30 June 2011	18,000
Year ended 30 June 2012	21,500
Year ended 30 June 2013	23,000
Six months to 31 December 2013	12,000
Year ended 31 December 2014	27,000

Taxable profits for the first five years are as follows

	Basis period		£	£
2010/11	1.7.10 – 5.4.11	£18,000 × 9/12		13,500
2011/12	Y/e 30.6.11			18,000
2012/13	Y/e 30.6.12			21,500
2013/14	1.7.12 – 31.12.13:			
	1.7.12 – 30.6.13		23,000	
	1.7.13 – 31.12.13		12,000	
			35,000	
	Deduct Overlap relief		9,000	
				26,000
2014/15	Y/e 31.12.14			27,000

Overlap relief accrued:
1.7.10 – 5.4.11 — 9 months	13,500
Less utilised in 2013/14 — 6 months	9,000
Carried forward — 3 months	£4,500

29.2 IT   Trading Income

Utilisation of overlap relief in 2013/14

$$\text{Apply the formula: } A \times \frac{B - C}{D}$$

where

A = aggregate overlap relief accrued (£13,500);

B = length of basis period for 2013/14 (18 months);

C = 12 months; and

D = the length of the overlap period(s) by reference to which the aggregate overlap profits accrued (9 months).

Thus, the deduction to be given in computing profits for 2013/14 is

$$£13,500 \times \frac{18 - 12}{9} = £9,000$$

Notes

(a) For a change of accounting date to result in a change of basis period, the conditions in *ITTOIA 2005, s 217* must normally be satisfied. [*ITTOIA 2005, s 216*].

(b) In this example, the 'relevant period' is that from 1 July 2012 (the day following the end of the basis period for 2012/13) to 31 December 2013 (the new accounting date in the year 2013/14 — the year of change). As the relevant period is more than 12 months, the basis period for 2013/14 is equal to the relevant period. [*ITTOIA 2005, s 216(3)*]. Note that a basis period of 18 months results in this case, even though accounts were prepared for a period of only 6 months to the new date.

(c) The overlap relief accrued (by reference to an overlap period of 9 months) is given on cessation (see **29.3** below) or, as in this example, on a change of accounting date resulting in a basis period exceeding 12 months (the relief given depending on the extent of the excess). The balance of overlap relief (£4,500) is carried forward for future relief on the happening of such an event. [*ITTOIA 2005, s 220*]. If Dennis had changed his accounting date to 31 March or 5 April (instead of 31 December), the overlap relief of £13,500 would have been given in full in 2013/14.

(C) **Change of accounting date carried forward**

[*ITTOIA 2005, s 219*]

Sharon has been trading since 1 September 1992, preparing accounts to 31 August. She has transitional overlap relief of £21,000 brought forward by reference to an overlap period of seven months. She decides to change her accounting date to 30 April, preparing accounts for a period of 20 months from 1 September 2010 to 30 April 2012. Results for relevant periods of account are as follows.

Trading Income IT 29.2

	£
Year ended 31 August 2010	60,000
1 September 2010 to 30 April 2012 (20 months)	90,000
Year ended 30 April 2013	67,500
Year ended 30 April 2014	73,500

The first year of change is 2011/12 being the first year in which accounts are not made up to the old date of 31 August. [*ITTOIA 2005, s 214(1)*]. However, a period of account exceeding 18 months cannot result in a change of basis period. [*ITTOIA 2005, s 217(1)(3)*]. The position is then looked at with regard to 2012/13, but again the period of account ending with the new date in that year, 30 April 2012, is a period exceeding 18 months, so the basis period cannot change. Moving on to 2013/14, however, there is a period of account of less than 18 months to the new date in that year, i.e. the year to 30 April 2013, so there *can* be a change of basis period provided the other conditions of *ITTOIA 2005, s 217* are satisfied.

The assessments are as follows

	Basis period		£	£
2010/11	Y/e 31.8.10			60,000
2011/12	1.9.10 – 31.8.11	(90,000 × $^{12}/_{20}$)		54,000
2012/13	1.9.11 – 31.8.12			
	1.9.11 – 30.4.12	(£90,000 × $^{8}/_{20}$)	36,000	
	1.5.12 – 31.8.12	(£67,500 × $^{4}/_{12}$)	22,500	58,500
2013/14	1.5.12 – 30.4.13*			67,500
2014/15	Y/e 30.4.14			73,500

* The relevant period is the 8 months from 1.9.12 – 30.4.13. As this is less than 12 months, the basis period for 2013/14 is the 12 months ending on 30.4.13, the new date in the year.

Notes

(a) The period 1.5.12 – 31.8.12 is an overlap period of 4 months for which there is an overlap profit of £22,500 (as computed for the 2012/13 assessment). Thus, the aggregate overlap profit carried forward is increased to £43,500 by reference to an overlap period of 11 months.

(b) The fact that the original overlap relief is transitional relief (applicable only to businesses commenced before 6 April 1994) is of no relevance. Such relief is carried forward, and eventually relieved, in the same way as any other overlap relief.

(c) For the calculation of capital allowances for a period of account exceeding 18 months, see **4.1(B)** CAPITAL ALLOWANCES ON PLANT AND MACHINERY.

29.3 IT Trading Income

29.3 CLOSING YEAR OF ASSESSMENT

[*ITTOIA 2005, s 202*].

Robin commenced to trade on 1 May 2009, preparing accounts to 30 April. He permanently ceases to trade on 30 June 2013, preparing accounts for the two months to that date. His profits (as adjusted for tax purposes) are as follows

	£
Year ended 30 April 2010	24,000
Year ended 30 April 2011	48,000
Year ended 30 April 2012	96,000
Year ended 30 April 2013	36,000
Two months ended 30 June 2013	5,000
	£209,000

Taxable profits for the five tax years of trading are as follows

	Basis period		£	£
2009/10	1.5.09 – 5.4.10	(£24,000 × $^{11}/_{12}$)		22,000
2010/11	Y/e 30.4.10			24,000
2011/12	Y/e 30.4.11			48,000
2012/13	Y/e 30.4.12			96,000
2013/14	1.5.12 – 30.6.13:			
	1.5.12 – 30.4.13		36,000	
	1.5.13 – 30.6.13		5,000	
			41,000	
	Deduct Overlap relief		22,000	19,000
				£209,000

Overlap relief accrued:
1.5.09 – 5.4.10 — 11 months	22,000
Utilised in 2013/14	(22,000)

Notes

(a) The basis period for the tax year of cessation is the period beginning immediately after the end of the basis period for the penultimate tax year and ending on the date of cessation. Note that profits taxed over the lifetime of the business equate to profits earned (as adjusted for tax purposes).

(b) The overlap relief accrued as a result of the application of the opening years rules is given in full on cessation (in the absence of an earlier change of accounting date resulting in a basis period exceeding 12 months — see **29.2(B)** above). [*ITTOIA 2005, s 205*].

29.4 PROFIT COMPUTATIONS

A UK trader commences trading on 1 October 2012. His profit and loss account for the year to 30 September 2013 is

	£	£
Sales		110,000
Deduct Purchases	75,000	
Less Stock and work in progress at 30.9.13	15,000	
		60,000
Gross profit		50,000
Deduct		
Salaries (all paid by 30.6.14)	15,600	
Rent and rates	2,400	
Telephone	500	
Heat and light	650	
Depreciation	1,000	
Motor expenses	2,700	
Entertainment	600	
Bank interest	900	
Hire-purchase interest	250	
Repairs and renewals	1,000	
Accountant's fee	500	
Bad debts	200	
Sundries	700	
		27,000
Net profit		23,000
Gain on sale of fixed asset		300
Rent received		500
Bank interest received (net)		150
Profit		£23,950

Further Information

(i) Rent and rates. £200 of the rates bill relates to the period from 1.6.12 to 30.9.12.

(ii) Telephone. Telephone bills for the trader's private telephone (included in the accounts) amount to £150. It is estimated that 40% of these calls are for business purposes.

29.4 IT Trading Income

(iii) Motor expenses. All the motor expenses are in respect of the proprietor's car. 40% of the annual mileage relates to private use and home to business use.

(iv) Entertainment

		£
Staff		100
UK customers		450
Overseas customers		50
		£600

(v) Hire-purchase interest. This is in respect of the owner's car.
(vi) Repairs and renewals. There is an improvement element of 20% included.
(vii) Bad debts. This is a specific write-off.
(viii) Sundries. Included is £250 being the cost of obtaining a bank loan to finance business expenditure, £200 for agent's fees in obtaining a patent for trading purposes and a £50 inducement to a local official.
(ix) Other. The proprietor obtained goods for his own use from the business costing £400 (resale value £500) without payment.
(x) Capital allowances for the year to 30 September 2013 amount to £1,520.

Computation of taxable trading income — Year to 30.9.13

		£	£
Profit per the accounts			23,950
Add			
Repairs — improvement element			200
Hire-purchase interest (40% private)			100
Entertainment	note (e)		500
Motor expenses (40% private)			1,080
Depreciation			1,000
Telephone (60% × £150)			90
Goods for own use			500
Illegal payment	note (g)		50
			27,470
Deduct			
Bank interest received (savings and investment income)		150	
Rent received (property income)		500	
Gain on sale of fixed asset		300	
			950
			26,520
Less Capital allowances			1,520
Chargeable trading income			£25,000

Trading Income IT 29.5

Notes

(a) Costs of obtaining loan finance are specifically allowable. [*ITTOIA 2005, s 58*].

(b) Capital allowances are deductible as a trading expense.

(c) The adjusted profit of £25,000 would be subject to the commencement provisions for assessment purposes. See **29.1** above.

(d) Pre-trading expenses are treated as incurred on the day on which trade is commenced if they are incurred within seven years of the commencement and would have been allowable if incurred after commencement. [*ITTOIA 2005, s 57*].

(e) All entertainment expenses, other than staff entertaining, are non-deductible. [*ITTOIA 2005, ss 45–47*].

(f) If wages and salaries remain unpaid nine months after the end of the period of account, they are disallowed. A deduction is then allowable for the period of account in which they are paid. [*ITTOIA 2005, ss 36, 37*].

(g) Trading stock appropriated for personal use must be accounted for at market value. [*ITTOIA 2005, s 172B*].

(h) Expenditure in making a payment which itself constitutes the commission of a criminal offence (or would do if made in the UK) is specifically disallowed. This includes payments which are contrary to the Prevention of Corruption Acts (Revenue Press Release 11 June 1993). [*ITTOIA 2005, s 55*].

29.5 CREATIVE ARTISTS — AVERAGING

[*ITTOIA 2005, ss 221–225*]

Richard is an established author by profession and has the following profits/losses as adjusted for income tax purposes (including a deduction for capital allowances) for the five years mentioned.

Year ended	Schedule D, Case II profit/loss £
31.12.09	35,000
31.12.10	30,000
31.12.11	6,000
31.12.12	25,000
31.12.13	(2,000)

Averaged profits for all years would be

		No averaging claims £	Averaging claims for all possible years £
2009/10	note (a)	35,000	35,000

29.5 IT Trading Income

2010/11	note (b)	30,000	18,000
2011/12	note (c)	6,000	20,250
2012/13	note (d)	25,000	11,375
2013/14	note (d)	Nil	11,375
		£96,000	£96,000

Notes

(a) 2009/10   35,000
    2010/11   30,000
              £65,000

As £30,000 is not less than 75% of £35,000, no averaging claim is possible.

(b) 2010/11   30,000
    2011/12   6,000
              £36,000 ÷ 2 = £18,000

As £6,000 does not exceed 70% of £30,000, straight averaging applies. Still no claim can be made to average 2010/11 (as adjusted) with 2009/10, even though this would now be possible purely on the figures.

(c) 2011/12   18,000
    2012/13   25,000
              £43,000

As £18,000 exceeds 70% of £25,000 (but is less than 75%), the adjustment proceeds as follows

Difference £7,000 × 3	21,000	
Deduct 75% × £25,000	18,750	
Adjustment	2,250	(2,250)
Existing 2011/12	18,000	
Existing 2012/13		25,000
Averaged profits 2011/12 & 2012/13	£20,250	£22,750

(d) 2012/13   22,750
    2013/14   Nil
              £22,750 ÷ 2 = £11,375

The loss of £2,000 for 2013/14 does not enter into the averaging claim, but is available to reduce either the 2012/13 or the 2013/14 averaged profits of £11,375 on a claim under *ITA 2007, s 64* (see **14.1** LOSSES).

The 2013/14 averaged profits of £11,375 may themselves be averaged with 2014/15 profits if the 75% rule is satisfied. Any loss claim against income of 2013/14 is disregarded for this purpose.

Trading Income   IT 29.6

(e) Averaging does not apply in calculating profits using the cash basis for small businesses. [*ITTOIA 2005, ss 221–221A; FA 2013, Sch 4 paras 32, 56*].

29.6 FARMING AND MARKET GARDENING — AVERAGING
[*ITTOIA 2005, ss 221–225*]

A, who has been farming for several years, earns the following profits as adjusted for income tax purposes.

Year ended	Schedule D, Case I Profit/(loss) £
30.9.06	8,500
30.9.07	12,000
30.9.08	15,000
30.9.09	10,000
30.9.10	4,000
30.9.11	(1,000)
30.9.12	(10,000)
30.9.13	1,600

Averaged profits for all years would be

		No averaging claims £	Averaging claims for all years £
2006/07	note (a)	8,500	10,000
2007/08	notes (a)(b)	12,000	12,750
2008/09	notes (b)(c)	15,000	12,750
2009/10	notes (c)(d)	10,000	7,000
2010/11	notes (d)(e)	4,000	3,500
2011/12	notes (e)(f)	Nil	1,750
2012/13	notes (g)(h)	Nil	1,750
2013/14	note (j)	1,600	1,600
		£51,100	£51,100

Notes

(a) 2006/07   8,500
    2007/08   _12,000_
              £20,500

As £8,500 exceeds $^7/_{10}$ of £ 12,000 but does not exceed $^3/_4$, the adjustment is computed as follows

29.6 IT   Trading Income

Difference £3,500 × 3	10,500	
Deduct ³/₄ × £12,000	9,000	
Adjustment	1,500	(1,500)
Existing 2006/07	8,500	
Existing 2007/08		12,000
Revised averaged profits 2006/07 & 2007/08	£10,000	£10,500

(b) 2007/08   10,500
     2008/09   15,000
                    £25,500 ÷ 2 = £12,750

As £10,500 does not exceed ⁷/₁₀ of £15,000, the straight average applies.

(c) 2008/09   12,750
     2009/10   10,000
                    £22,750

As £10,000 is not less than ³/₄ of £12,750, no averaging is permitted.

(d) 2009/10   10,000
     2010/11   4,000
                    £14,000 ÷ 2 = £7,000

As £4,000 does not exceed ⁷/₁₀ of £10,000, the straight average applies.

(e) 2010/11   7,000
     2011/12   Nil
                    £7,000 ÷ 2 = £3,500

(f) The loss for the year to 30 September 2011 is not taken into account for averaging, but would be available to eliminate the averaged profits for 2011/12 on a claim under *ITA 2007, s 64*.

(g) 2011/12   3,500
     2012/13   Nil
                    £3,500 ÷ 2 = £1,750

(h) The loss for the year to 30 September 2012 is not taken into account for averaging, but would be available to set off against the balance of the averaged profits for 2011/12 and against the averaged profits for 2012/13 on a claim under *ITA 2007, s 64*, with the balance being carried forward.

(j) 2012/13   1,750

2013/14	1,600
	£3,350

As £1,600 is not less than 3/4 of £1,750, no averaging is permitted.

(k) Averaging does not apply in calculating profits using the cash basis for small businesses. [*ITTOIA 2005, ss 221–221A; FA 2013, Sch 4 paras 32, 56*].

29.7 FINANCE LEASES

(*SSAP 21; HMRC Statement of Practice SP 3/91*)

Jones prepares accounts annually to 31 March. On 1 April 2009 he entered into a five-year finance lease to acquire new machinery at an annual rental of £6,600 payable quarterly in advance.

The fair value (cash price) of the machinery at the inception of the lease is £25,000, being a close approximation to the present value of the minimum lease rentals. This is capitalised in the balance sheet in accordance with Statement of Standard Accounting Practice (SSAP) 21, and depreciation is charged on a straight line basis at the rate of 20% per annum on the fair value. Rentals are treated as comprising a finance charge element and a capital repayment element.

The total lease rentals are £6,600 × 5 = £33,000, giving a finance charge of £(33,000 − 25,000) = £8,000.

Note that the lease cannot be a long funding lease within the rules at *ITTOIA 2005, ss 148A–148J* as its term does not exceed five years.

29.7 IT Trading Income

The finance charge is allocated over the period of the lease using the sum of digits method, as follows

Quarter	Number of rentals not yet due	×	Finance charge / Sum of no of rentals	=	Finance charge per annum £
1	19			= 800	
2	18			= 758	
3	17			= 716	
4	16			= 674	2,948
5	15			= 632	
6	14			= 589	
7	13			= 547	
8	12			= 505	2,273
9	11		× 8,000/190	= 463	
10	10			= 421	
11	9			= 379	
12	8			= 337	1,600
13	7			= 295	
14	6			= 253	
15	5			= 211	
16	4			= 168	927
17	3			= 126	
18	2			= 84	
19	1			= 42	
20	–			= –	252
	190				£8,000

The deduction in each year's accounts, and the allowable deduction for tax purposes, for depreciation and finance charges over the period of the lease will therefore be as follows

Accounting year ended 31 March

	20010 £	2011 £	2012 £	2013 £	2014 £	Total £
Depreciation	5,000	5,000	5,000	5,000	5,000	
Finance charge	2,948	2,273	1,600	927	252	
	£7,948	£7,273	£6,600	£5,927	£5,252	£33,000
Compared to actual rentals paid of	£6,600	£6,600	£6,600	£6,600	£6,600	£33,000

Notes

(a) As the rentals are payable in advance, the final payment in quarter 20 will have no finance charge allocated to it. If the rentals had been payable in arrears, a finance charge would have been allocated to quarter 20, and the charge allocated to quarter 1 would have been 20 units instead of 19, with consequential changes to all the other quarters.

(b) The sum of the number of rentals may be computed by using the formula

$$\frac{n(n+1)}{2}$$

where n is the number of quarters in question. Hence in this case n = 19 (see note (*a*)) and thus

$$\frac{19 \times 20}{2} = 190.$$

(c) Under HMRC Statement of Practice SP 3/91, HMRC will normally allow tax relief to a lessee for amounts charged in the accounts in respect of finance charges if they are dealt with in accordance with SSAP 21. A finance lease exists under SSAP 21 where substantially all the risks and rewards of ownership, other than legal title, are transferred to the lessee, with generally the present value of the minimum lease payments (including initial payment) amounting to 90% or more of the fair value of the leased asset. Any other lease is an operating lease.

(d) SSAP 21 permits three methods of calculating finance lease charges, i.e. straight line, actuarial and sum of digits (the so-called 'rule of 78'). The sum of digits method is a close approximation to an actuarial calculation where the lease period is normally less than eight years and interest rates are not too high.

(e) SP 3/91 additionally allows a deduction in the accounts for depreciation charged in respect of assets acquired under finance leases, provided that the rate of depreciation used is calculated on normal commercial principles (SSAP 12). Depreciation should be charged either over the period of the lease or the useful life of the asset, whichever is the shorter.

(f) In *Threlfall v Jones CA 1993*, 66 TC 77, it was held that payments under finance leases had to be accounted for in accordance with accounting standards as they were the ordinary way to ascertain profits or losses for tax purposes.

29.8 ADJUSTMENT ON CHANGE OF BASIS — BARRISTERS

[*ITTOIA 2005*, ss 227, 228, 231, 238, 239]

Olivia commenced practice as a barrister on 1 October 2003, preparing accounts to 30 June on a cash basis as permitted by *ITTOIA 2005, s 160* (and earlier equivalents). As required by that *section*, she switches to an earnings basis for the year to 30 June 2011, preparing accounts in accordance with *ITTOIA 2005, s 25* (note (a)). She accordingly brings in opening work-in-progress of £43,000, opening debtors of £10,000 (for fees billed, but not received, before 1 July 2010) and opening creditors of £2,000 (for expenses invoiced to her, but not paid, before 1 July 2010). She also brings in a £1,000 opening creditor for cash received in advance (and included in the accounts to 30 June 2010) in respect of a fee billed in the year to 30 June 2011.

29.8 IT Trading Income

Without an adjustment, the £43,000 opening work-in-progress would be relieved twice and the £10,000 fees reflected in debtors would never be taxed. On the other hand, the expenses of £2,000 would never be relieved and the £1,000 payment in advance would be taxed twice.

The adjustment income required to be brought into account under ITTOIA 2005, s 232 is

£(43,000 + 10,000) − £(2,000 + 1,000) = £50,000

(i) Olivia's profits before capital allowances and balancing charges are as follows.

	£
Y/e 30 June 2011	30,000
Y/e 30 June 2012	45,000
Y/e 30 June 2013	40,000
Y/e 30 June 2014	48,000
Y/e 30 June 2015	52,000
Y/e 30 June 2016	56,000
Y/e 30 June 2017	47,000
Y/e 30 June 2018	51,000
Y/e 30 June 2019	53,000
Y/e 30 June 2020	46,000

The £50,000 adjustment will be taxed as follows

		£
2011/12	(£30,000 × 10%)	3,000
2012/13	(£45,000 × 10%)	4,500
2013/14	(£40,000 × 10%)	4,000
2014/15	(£48,000 × 10%)	4,800
2015/16	(£50,000 × 10%)	5,000
2016/17	(£50,000 × 10%)	5,000
2017/18	(£47,000 × 10%)	4,700
2018/19	(£50,000 × 10%)	5,000
2019/20	(£50,000 × 10%)	5,000
2020/21	(balance)	9,000
		£50,000

(ii) Supposing Olivia ceased to practice on 30 June 2013. The catching-up charge would be taxed as above for years up to and including 2013/14. Thereafter, it would be £5,000 for each of the six years up to and including 2019/20, leaving a balance of £8,500 to be taxed in 2020/21.

(iii) Supposing that Olivia continued to practice as in (i) above but she had extraordinary expenditure in the year to 30 June 2017 and made a tax loss of £9,000 (after capital allowances) instead of the profit in (i) above, all figures for other years remaining the same. The catching-up charge for 2017/18 would then be nil (i.e. 10% of nil profits). On the assumption that her other income is covered by her personal allowance, she might elect to increase the catching-up charge by £9,000 (see note (c)), so as to relieve the loss in that year by means of a claim under *ITA 2007, s 64*.

The £50,000 adjustment will then be taxed as follows

		£
2011/12	(£30,000 × 10%)	3,000
2012/13	(£45,000 × 10%)	4,500
2013/14	(£40,000 × 10%)	4,000
2014/15	(£48,000 × 10%)	4,800
2015/16	(£50,000 × 10%)	5,000
2016/17	(£50,000 × 10%)	5,000
2017/18	(nil + £9,000)	9,000
2018/19	(£20,000 × 10%) note (d)	2,000
2019/20	(£20,000 × 10%) note (d)	2,000
2020/21	(balance)	10,700
		£50,000

Notes

(a) *ITTOIA 2005, s 25* requires that profits be calculated in accordance with generally accepted accounting practice (GAAP), subject to any adjustment required or authorised by law in calculating profits for income tax purposes. This in turn requires (among other things) profits to be calculated on an earnings basis rather than a cash basis. For 2012/13 and earlier years (and see note (e) below), *ITTOIA 2005, s 160* provides an exemption for barristers for periods of account ending no more than seven years after they commence practice. The exemption is not compulsory but once a particular basis has been adopted it must be applied consistently.

(b) Adjustment income is treated as arising on the last day of the first period of account for which the new basis is adopted. [*ITTOIA 2005, s 232*].

(c) The election in (iii) above must be made in writing on or before the first anniversary of 31 January following the tax year for which the charge is to be increased. [*ITTOIA 2005, s 239(2)*].

(d) In (iii) above, for years subsequent to 2017/18 (apart from the tenth year) the catch-up charge is calculated as if the adjustment income (£50,000) were reduced by £9,000 (the additional amount taxed in 2017/18) multiplied by 10 and divided by 3 (the number of tax years remaining). Thus the maximum charge for 2018/19 and 2019/20 is 10% of £20,000 (the revised amount of adjustment income) as this is less than 10% of profits.

(e) *ITTOIA 2005, s 160* is repealed for 2013/14 onwards in light of the introduction of the cash basis for small businesses. By way of transition, where a barrister's profits for a period of account ending in the tax year 2012/13 were calculated under *section 160*, they can continue to be so calculated for any subsequent period of account for which *section 160* would have been applied had it not been repealed, i.e.

29.8 IT   Trading Income

any periods within the seven years mentioned in (a) above above, assuming the barrister does not choose to adopt an earnings basis before the end of those seven years. [*ITTOIA 2005, s 160; FA 2013, Sch 4 paras 51, 56, 57(1)*].

The spreading rules illustrated in this example are also repealed for 2013/14 onwards but the repeal does not apply in a case where, as in this example, advantage was taken of *ITTOIA 2005, s 160* for any period(s) of account ending in or before the tax year 2012/13. [*ITTOIA 2005, ss 238, 239; FA 2013, Sch 4 paras 52, 56, 57(2)*].

29.9   FOSTER CARE RELIEF

[*ITTOIA 2005, ss 803–828*]

Dave and Holly, a couple living together, provide foster care by way of trade. Each prepares accounts to 31 December. Foster children are placed with them by their local authority. During the year 2013, they provide care to a twelve-year old (child 1) for the full 52 weeks and to a nine-year old (child 2) for 15 weeks. Their total foster care receipts for the year (before deduction of expenses) are £25,000 each. Their allowable expenses are £14,000 each.

Each of Dave and Holly's individual limits for 2013/14 is computed as follows

		£
Fixed amount for 2013/14: £10,000 ÷ 2		5,000
Amounts per child (y/e 31.12.13):	child 1 (52 × £250)	13,000
	child 2 (15 × £200)	3,000
		£21,000

For 2013/14, their income tax position is as follows

Normal trading income computation

	Dave	Holly
	£	£
Total foster care receipts (y/e 31.12.13)	25,000	25,000
Allowable expenses	14,000	14,000
Net taxable profit (subject to below)	£11,000	£11,000

Alternative calculation under ITTOIA 2005, ss 815–819

Each could now elect, under *ITTOIA 2005, s 818*, for his or her taxable profits from foster care to be taken as the excess of total foster care receipts over his or her individual limit computed as above. Such an election for any tax year must be made on or before the first anniversary of 31 January following that year and has effect for that tax year only. Under the election, Dave and Holly's taxable profits for 2013/14 will each be reduced to £4,000 (£25,000 - £21,000).

Notes

(a) Foster care receipts are exempt if they do not exceed a limit computed by reference to the individual recipient. If, as in this example, they do exceed that limit, and the recipient so elects, they are subject to the alternative computation above. It is up to each individual recipient whether or not to make the election.

(b) Some HMRC offices are believed to have taken the view that, in a case such as that illustrated in this example, the amounts per child must be divided between the couple instead of being available separately to each individual. In this example, this would have the effect of reducing each individual's limit by £8,000. In the author's opinion, the legislation does not support such a view. If, however, a couple were trading in partnership (clearly not the case here) it does then become arguable that the partnership takes the place of the individual for the purpose of computing the limits, in which case only one amount per child would be available to the partnership.

29.10 CEMETERIES AND CREMATORIA

[*ITTOIA 2005, ss 169–172*]

GE, who operates a funeral service, owns a cemetery for which accounts to 31 December are prepared. The accounts to 31.12.13 reveal the following

(i)	Cost of land representing 110 grave spaces sold in period	£3,400
(ii)	Number of grave spaces remaining	275
(iii)	Residual capital expenditure on buildings and other land unsuitable for interments	£18,250

	The allowances available are	£
(A)	Item (i)	3,400
(B)	$\dfrac{110}{110 + 275} \times £18,250$	5,214
		£8,614

Note

(a) £8,614 will be allowed as a deduction in computing GE's trading profits for the period of account ending on 31 December 2013.

30 Trading Income — Cash Basis for Small Businesses

Cross-reference. See also **29** TRADING INCOME.

30.1 CASH BASIS

[*ITTOIA 2005, ss 25A, 31A–31F; FA 2013, Sch 4*]

Keith has been running a one-man business for a number of years, preparing accounts to 30 September. For the year ended 30 September 2013, his turnover is £77,000 and he elects for his trading profits to be calculated on the cash basis for 2013/14 onwards as provided for by *ITTOIA 2005, s 25A*. His accounts for the year ended 30 September 2012 showed closing stock of £6,300, trade and other creditors of £2,400 and trade debtors of £300.

Keith uses a motor vehicle in the business. On 15 October 2012 he sold his car (Vehicle 1) for £1,400 to an unconnected individual and purchased instead a van (Vehicle 2) for £3,500. Expenditure in connection with Vehicle 1 for the period from 1 October to date of sale amounted to £300, and it had always been accepted that the car was used as to 20% for private purposes. Keith chooses to use the fixed rate deduction scheme (under *ITTOIA 2005, ss 94D–94G*) to calculate allowable expenditure on Vehicle 2. Business mileage was 6,200 miles for the period from date of purchase to 30 September 2013.

Keith also uses a room in his home as an office, working there for 60 hours each month. He chooses to use the fixed rate deduction scheme (under *ITTOIA 2005, s 94H*) to calculate allowable expenditure for use of home for business purposes.

Keith pays out £27,000 on purchases and £4,400 on business overheads in the year to 30 September 2013. The business overheads are all allowable revenue expenses but the figure excludes bank overdraft interest and all expenses connected with the car and van. In addition, Keith spends £2,094 on office furniture and equipment; it is accepted that this is capital expenditure. In the year to 30 September 2013, he is charged interest of £700 on a bank overdraft; the bank account in question includes some personal as well as business transactions.

At 30 September 2012, there were written-down values of £1,560 on the plant and machinery general pool and £2,200 on the pool for Vehicle 1 (which is a single asset pool due to the private use). The general pool includes a computer used only for business purposes which Keith sells for £150 in June 2013 to a fellow he knows from his local public house.

An adjustment expense required to be brought into account under ITTOIA 2005, s 233 as follows

Without an adjustment, the value of £6,300 placed on the previous year's closing stock would be taxed twice, once in the previous year and again when the stock is sold. The £300 brought forward as trade debts would also be taxed twice, once in the previous year and again when the debts are settled. Similarly, the £2,400 brought forward as trade and other creditors would be relieved twice. See note (d).

The adjustment expense is: £(6,300 + 300) – £2,400 = £4,200.

This is treated as an expense of the trade arising on the last day of the year ending 30.9.13, i.e. the first period of account for which the new basis is adopted.

30.1 IT   Trading Income — Cash Basis for Small Businesses

The capital allowances computation for 2013/14 is as follows

	Main pool £	Vehicle 1 £	Allowances £
Year ended 30.9.13			
WDV at 30.9.12	1,560	2,200	
Expenditure removed from pool (note (e))	(1,560)	–	
WDV brought forward at 1.10.12	Nil	2,200	
Disposal proceeds		(1,400)	
		800	
Private use adjustment 20%		(160)	
Balancing allowance		£640	640
Total allowances			£640
WDV carried forward		Nil	

The allowable expenditure for Vehicle 2 is

$$M \times R$$

where M is the number of miles of business journeys made by a person (other than as a passenger) using the vehicle in the period; and

R is the rate applicable for that kind of vehicle. The rate applicable to a goods vehicle is 45p per mile up to 10,000 miles and 25p thereafter. See note (f).

6,200 x 45p = £2,790.

The allowable expenditure for use of home as business is as follows

The amount of the fixed rate deduction for the period is the sum of the applicable amounts for each month (or part of a month) falling within the period. The applicable amounts is based on the number of hours worked; it is £18 where the number of hours worked is 51 hours or more but less than 101 hours. See note (f).

£18 x 12 months = £216.

Taxable profits for the year to 30.9.13 are computed as follows

	£	£
Turnover		77,000
Deduct Purchases		27,000
Gross profit		50,000
Deduct		
Business overheads	4,400	
Expenses relating to Vehicle 1 (£300 x 80% business use)	240	

Trading Income — Cash Basis for Small Businesses IT 30.1

Fixed rate deduction for Vehicle 2 (see above)	2,790	
Fixed rate deduction for use of home as business (see above)	216	
Capital expenditure on office furniture and equipment (note (g))	3,654	
Interest (note (h))	500	
Adjustment expense (see above)	4,200	
		16,000
		34,000
Add Capital receipt (note (i))		150
Net profit		34,150
Deduct Capital allowances on Vehicle 1 (see above)		640
Taxable profit		£33,510

Notes

(a) The cash basis has effect for 2013/14 onwards. It is optional, and is available to unincorporated trades, professions and vocations (including those carried on in partnership) with an annual turnover not exceeding the VAT registration threshold (currently £79,000). For recipients of Universal Credit, the turnover threshold is twice the VAT registration threshold. Certain types of business are excluded from using the cash basis (see *ITTOIA 2005, s 31C*). Businesses must leave the cash basis the year after their receipts exceed twice the VAT registration threshold.

(b) The cash basis is an alternative to preparing accounts for tax purposes on an earnings basis and in accordance with generally accepted accounting practice (GAAP).

(c) In practice, elections to adopt the cash basis will be made via the self-assessment tax return by ticking a box (HMRC Technical Note, 28 March 2013, Chapter 2 para 4).

(d) An adjustment must be made upon entering or leaving the cash basis in the same way as for any other change of accounting basis. [*ITTOIA 2005, s 227A; FA 2013, Sch 4 paras 36, 56*]. This is to ensure that no receipt is taxed twice and no allowable payment is deducted twice, and similarly that neither receipts nor payments fall out of tax.

(e) No capital allowances are available to a person carrying on a trade in relation to which a cash basis election is in force, other than an allowance for capital expenditure on a car.

When a person enters the cash basis for a tax year (Year Z), any qualifying expenditure on plant or machinery which is unrelieved at the end of the basis period for the preceding tax year (Year Y) is allowable as a deduction under the cash basis in Year Z. The rule does not apply where the asset had not been fully paid for as at the end of the basis period for Year Y. [*ITTOIA 2005, ss 240A–240D; FA 2013, Sch 4 paras 38, 56*]. See also note (g) below.

(f) The fixed rate deduction schemes are available for 2013/14 onwards. Each scheme is entirely optional and is not restricted to those using the cash basis. If a fixed rate deduction is made for a period of account in respect of qualifying expenditure incurred in relation to a particular vehicle, no other deduction is allowed for such qualifying expenditure. As regards subsequent periods of account, the fixed rate deduction scheme is then compulsory for that vehicle for every period for which it

30.1 IT Trading Income — Cash Basis for Small Businesses

is used for the purposes of the trade. 'Qualifying expenditure', in relation to a vehicle, means expenditure incurred in respect of the acquisition, ownership, hire, leasing or use of the vehicle (other than incidental expenses incurred in connection with a particular journey). [*ITTOIA 2005, ss 94B–94I; CAA 2001, s 38ZA; FA 2013, Sch 5 paras 2, 5, 6*].

For cars and goods vehicles, the 10,000 mile limit for the 45p rate takes into account the business mileage of *all* such vehicles used in the trade for which a fixed rate deduction is made; it is not 10,000 miles per vehicle.

(g) A deduction is allowed for expenditure that would otherwise be qualifying expenditure for the purposes of capital allowances on plant and machinery, but no deduction is allowed for other items of a capital nature. Capital expenditure on the provision of a car (as defined and excluding a goods vehicle) is non-deductible. [*ITTOIA 2005, s 33A; FA 2013, Sch 4 paras 8, 56*].

The deduction of £3,654 for capital expenditure in this example comprises both the plant and machinery bought in the year (other than the van) and the written-down value for capital allowances of plant and machinery bought in earlier years (see note (e) above). No deduction can be made for capital expenditure on the van due to the use of the fixed rate deduction scheme.

(h) Interest paid is deductible up to a limit of £500. It does not matter whether or not the interest was paid wholly and exclusively for the purposes of the trade. [*ITTOIA 2005, ss 51A, 57B; FA 2013, Sch 4 paras 10, 14, 56*].

(i) Any proceeds on the disposal of an asset must be brought into account as a receipt if expenditure on its acquisition was brought into account in calculating profits on the cash basis (or would have been so brought into account if a cash basis election had been in force at the time the expenditure was paid). [*ITTOIA 2005, s 96A; FA 2013, Sch 4 paras 20, 56*].

31 Venture Capital Trusts

[*ITA 2007, ss 258–332; TCGA 1992, ss 151A, 151B, Sch 5C; FA 2009, s 27, Sch 8 paras 9, 14; FA 2012, Sch 6 paras 15–17, Sch 8*]

31.1 INCOME TAX INVESTMENT RELIEF

(A) Form of relief

On 1 May 2013, Miss K, who has annual earnings of £80,000, subscribes for 100,000 eligible £1 shares issued at par to raise money by VCT plc, an approved venture capital trust. On 1 September 2013 she purchases a further 225,000 £1 shares in VCT plc for £175,000 on the open market. The VCT makes no distribution in 2013/14. Miss K's other income for 2013/14 consists of dividends of £17,496. PAYE tax deducted is £21,822.00.

Miss K's tax computation for 2013/14 is as follows

		£	£
Employment income			80,000
Dividends		17,496	
Add Dividend tax credits		1,944	19,440
Total and net income			99,440
Deduct Personal allowance			9,440
Taxable income			£90,000
Tax payable:			
32,010	@ 20%		6,402.00
38,550	@ 40%		15,420.00
19,440	@ 32.5% (dividend upper rate)		6,318.00
90,000			28,140.00
Deduct	VCT investment relief:		
	£100,000 @ 30% = £30,000 but restricted to		28,140.00
Income tax liability			Nil
Deduct: PAYE			21,822.00
Income tax repayable			£21,822.00

Notes

(a) VCT investment relief is available at the rate of 30% on the amount *subscribed for* up to a maximum subscription of £200,000 per tax year. The relief is restricted to the income tax liability (before taking into account certain reductions etc.). [*ITA 2007, ss 261–263*].

(b) Dividend tax credits are not repayable.

31.1 IT   Venture Capital Trusts

(B)   Withdrawal of relief

[*ITA 2007, ss 266–270*]

On 1 May 2015, Miss K in (A) above, who has since 2013/14 neither acquired nor disposed of any shares in VCT plc, gives 62,500 shares to her son. On 1 January 2016, she disposes of the remaining 262,500 shares on the open market for £212,500.

The relief given as in (A) above is withdrawn as follows

Disposal on 1 May 2015

The shares disposed of are identified, on a first in, first out basis, with 62,500 of the 100,000 shares subscribed for in May 2013. Since the disposal was not at arm's length, the relief given on those shares is fully withdrawn.

$$\text{Relief withdrawn } \frac{62,500}{100,000} \times £28,140 = \quad \underline{£17,587}$$

Disposal on 1 January 2016

The balance of £10,553 of the relief originally given was in respect of 37,500 of the 262,500 shares disposed of. The disposal consideration for those 37,500 shares is

$$£212,500 \times \frac{37,500}{262,500} = \quad \underline{£30,357}$$

As the disposal was at arm's length, the relief withdrawn is the lesser of the relief originally given and 30% of the consideration received, i.e. 30% of £30,357 = £9,107. Relief withdrawn is therefore £9,107.

The 2013/14 assessment on relief withdrawn will therefore charge tax of £(17,587 + 9,107)   £26,694

Notes

(a)   VCT investment relief is withdrawn on a disposal (or deemed disposal) within five years following the issue of the shares. Withdrawal of relief is by assessment for the tax year for which the relief was given.

(b)   If the disposal is at arm's length, the relief given by reference to those shares is reduced by the appropriate percentage of the consideration received for the disposal and is withdrawn entirely if thereby reduced to nil. The appropriate percentage is 30% in relation to shares issued in 2006/07 or any subsequent year, i.e. the rate at which investment relief was available.

Venture Capital Trusts   IT 31.2

31.2 INCOME TAX DIVIDEND RELIEF

On 1 June 2012, W, who is unmarried, subscribes for 100,000 eligible £1 shares issued at par to raise money by XYZ plc, an approved venture capital trust. On 1 October 2012, he purchases on the open market a further 200,000 shares in XYZ plc for £120,000. On 30 June 2013 W receives a distribution from XYZ plc of 2p per share. W's other income in 2013/14 is a salary of £84,000 and net dividends from other companies of £18,000. Tax paid under PAYE amounts to £23,422.

W's taxable distribution from XYZ plc is arrived at as follows

The shares in XYZ plc were acquired in 2012/13 for £220,000. Distributions in respect of shares representing the £20,000 excess over the permitted maximum are not exempt. The 100,000 shares first acquired for £100,000 are first identified, so that the shares representing the excess are one-sixth of the 200,000 shares subsequently acquired for £120,000, i.e. 33,333 of those shares. The taxable dividend is therefore 33,333 @ 2p per share = £666.66. The dividend on the balance of 266,667 shares (266,667 @ 2p = £5,333.34) is exempt.

W's tax computation for 2013/14 is as follows

	£	£
Employment income		84,000
Dividends (other than from XYZ plc)	18,000	
Add Dividend tax credits ($^1/_9$)	2,000	20,000
Taxable dividends from XYZ plc	666	
Add Dividend tax credits ($^1/_9$)	74	740
Total and net income		104,740
Deduct Personal allowance	9,440	
Restricted by excess of income over £100,000: (£4,740 x /)	£2,370	£7,070
Taxable income		£97,670
Tax payable:		
32,010 @ 20%		6,402.00
44,920 @ 40%		17,968.00
20,740 @ 32.5% (dividend upper rate)		6,740.50
97,670		31,110.50
Deduct: Dividend tax credits	2,074.00	
PAYE	23,422.00	25,496.00
Net income tax liability		£5,614.50

Notes

(a) Dividends paid to a qualifying individual from a VCT are exempt from tax to the extent that they are made in respect of shares *acquired* (not necessarily subscribed for) for up to £200,000 in any tax year [*ITTOIA 2005, ss 709–712*]. Dividend tax credits relating to such shares are not repayable.

31.2 IT   Venture Capital Trusts

(b) The personal allowance is reduced by one-half of the excess of 'adjusted net income' over £100,000. [*ITA 2007, s 35; FA 2009, s 4(1)(4)*]. *'Adjusted net income'* is broadly net income less the grossed up amount of any allowable pension contributions and Gift Aid donations. [*ITA 2007, s 58*].

31.3 CAPITAL GAINS TAX RELIEF ON DISPOSAL

On the disposals in 31.1(B) above, a chargeable gain or allowable loss arises only on the disposal of shares acquired in excess of the permitted maximum (£200,000) for 2013/14. The 100,000 shares first acquired for £100,000 are first identified, so that the shares representing the excess are three-sevenths (75,000/175,000) of the 225,000 shares acquired for £175,000 on 1 September 2013, i.e. 96,429 of those shares. The disposal identified with those shares (on a first in, first out basis) is a corresponding proportion of the 262,500 shares disposed of for a consideration of £212,500 on 1 January 2016.

Miss K's capital gains tax computation for 2015/16 is therefore as follows

	£
Disposal consideration for 96,429 shares: $£212,500 \times \dfrac{96,429}{262,500} =$	78,061
Deduct Cost of 96,429 shares: $£175,000 \times \dfrac{96,429}{225,000} =$	75,000
Chargeable gain	£3,061

Notes

(a) On disposals by an individual of VCT shares (whether or not they were subscribed for), capital gains are exempt and losses not allowable to the extent that the shares disposed of were not acquired in excess of the £200,000 maximum in any tax year. [*TCGA 1992, s 151A*].

(b) The capital gains tax share identification provisions are disapplied as regards VCT shares within the above exemption. [*TCGA 1992, s 151B(1)*].

Corporation Tax

101	Accounting Periods
102	Capital Allowances
103	Capital Gains
104	Close Companies
105	Double Tax Relief
106	Group Relief
107	Income Tax in relation to a Company
108	Intangible Assets
109	Interest on Overpaid Tax
110	Interest on Unpaid Tax
111	Investment Companies and Investment Business
112	Liquidation
113	Loan Relationships
114	Losses
115	Payment of Tax
116	Profit Computations
117	Research and Development
118	Returns
119	Small Profits — Reduced Rates
120	Transfer Pricing

101 Accounting Periods

101.1 EFFECT OF AN ACCOUNTING PERIOD OVERLAPPING TWO FINANCIAL YEARS HAVING DIFFERENT RATES OF CORPORATION TAX

[*CTA 2009, ss 5, 6, 8; FA 2010, s 3; FA 2011, s 6*]

For the year ended 30 June 2011, the following information is relevant to A Ltd, a company with no associated companies.

	£
Trading income	200,600
UK property income	35,000
Income from non-trading loan relationships	30,000

The small profits rate of corporation tax for the financial year 2010 is 21% and the rate for the financial year 2011 is 20%.

The corporation tax computation of A Ltd for the 12-month accounting period ended on 30.6.11 is

		£
Trading income		200,600
UK property income		35,000
Income from non-trading loan relationships		30,000
Total taxable profits		£265,600
Total profits apportioned		
1.7.10 – 31.3.11	$9/12 \times £265,600$	£199,200
1.4.11 – 30.6.11	$3/12 \times £265,600$	£66,400
Tax chargeable		
21% × £199,200		41,832
20% × £66,400		13,280
Total tax charge		£55,112

Note

(a) Where an accounting period does not coincide with a financial year, apportionment is necessary to calculate the tax payable. Apportionment is on a time basis, between the financial years which overlap the accounting period. Corporation tax is then charged on each proportion so computed at the rate fixed for the financial year concerned. [*CTA 2009, s 8*].

101.2 CT Accounting Periods

101.2 PERIODS OF ACCOUNT EXCEEDING 12 MONTHS

[*CTA 2009, ss 10(1), 53, 1307; CTA 2010, s 1172*]

B Ltd prepares accounts for 16 months ending on 31 March 2014. The following information is relevant

	£
Profit for 16 months	450,000
Capital gain (after indexation) arising on 1.6.13	100,000
Tax written down value of plant and machinery main pool At 1.12.12	40,000
Plant purchased 1.2.13	200,000
Plant purchased 1.2.14	246,000
Proceeds of plant sold 31.12.13 (less than cost)	4,000

B Ltd has no associated companies

B Ltd will be chargeable to corporation tax as follows

	Accounting period 12 months to 30.11.13	Accounting period 4 months to 31.3.14
	£	£
Adjusted profits (apportioned 12:4)	712,500	237,500
Capital allowances	(207,200)	(93,568)
Trading income	505,300	143,932
Chargeable gain	100,000	—
Chargeable profits	£605,300	£143,932

Notes

(a) Capital allowances
12 months to 30.11.13

	AIA	Main pool	Allowances
	£	£	£
Main pool		40,000	
Additions	200,000	—	
AIA	(200,000)		200,000
		40,000	
WDA 18%		(7,200)	7,200
Total allowances			£207,200
WDV c/f		£32,800	

4 months to 31 March 2014

	AIA	Main pool	Allowances
	£	£	£
WDV b/f		32,800	
Additions	82,000	164,000	
Disposals		(4,000)	
AIA	(82,000)		82,000
		192,800	
WDA 18% x 4/12		(11,568)	11,568
Total allowances			£93,568
WDV c/f		£181,232	

Writing-down allowances, but not first-year allowances, are a proportionately reduced percentage of 18% if the accounting period is only part of a year. [*CAA 2001, s 56(3)*].

Annual investment allowance on £250,000 (£25,000 for expenditure incurred before 1 January 2013) is available in a 12-month period. It is proportionately reduced for shorter periods or where there are related companies. [*CAA 2001, s 51A; FA 2008, s 74, Sch 24; FA 2010, s 5; FA 2013, s 7*]. See IT 4 CAPITAL ALLOWANCES ON PLANT AND MACHINERY.

(b) The capital gain is not apportioned on a time basis, but is included for the period in which it arises. [*TCGA 1992, s 8(1)*].

(c) The tax for the two accounting periods ended 30.11.13 and 31.3.14 will be due for payment on 1.9.14 and 1.1.15 respectively. [*TMA 1970, s 59D*]. The CT return(s) for both accounting periods will be due by 31.3.15, i.e. the first anniversary of the last day of the sixteen-month period of account, or, if later, three months after the issue of the notice requiring the return. [*FA 1998, Sch 18 para 14*]. See also 121 RETURNS.

102 Capital Allowances

102.1 TRANSFER OF TRADE WITHIN GROUP: PERIOD OF ACCOUNT EXCEEDING 12 MONTHS

[*CTA 2010, ss 938–953; ICTA 1988, s 343; CAA 2001, ss 55, 56, 310–313*]

A Ltd owns 80% of the ordinary share capital of both B Ltd and C Ltd, the latter companies carrying on similar trades.

A Ltd and C Ltd prepare accounts annually to 31 July. B Ltd which previously prepared accounts to 30 April each year has prepared accounts for 15 months ending on 31 July 2013.

On 31 December 2012, C Ltd transferred the whole of its trade to B Ltd under circumstances covered by *CTA 2010, ss 938–953*.

The following information is relevant to B Ltd

		£
Trading profit for 15 months to 31.7.13		200,000
1.5.12	Tax written-down value of plant and machinery main pool	10,800
11.6.12	Plant purchased	3,000
3.9.12	Plant purchased	2,000
4.10.12	Plant sold (original cost £9,000)	6,800
1.3.13	Plant purchased	8,000
10.5.13	Plant sold (original cost £40,000)	9,560
15.6.13	Plant purchased	30,000
1.8.12	Tax written-down value of plant and machinery main pool owned by C Ltd	9,216

B Ltd will have chargeable profits as follows

	Accounting period 12 months to 30.4.13	Accounting period 3 months to 31.7.13
	£	£
Trading profits	160,000	40,000
Capital allowances on plant and machinery	(14,231)	(30,078)
Chargeable profits	£145,769	£9,922

102.1 CT   Capital Allowances

Capital allowances

Plant and machinery
12 months to 30.4.13

	AIA £	Main pool £	Total allowances £
WDV b/f		10,800	
Additions	13,000		
Transfer from C Ltd note (a)		8,525	
		19,325	
Disposals		(6,800)	
		12,525	
AIA £13,000 × 100% (note (e))	(13,000)		13,000
WDA on assets transferred from C Ltd £8,525 × 18% × 4/12 note (a)		(511)	511
WDA on balance of expenditure £(12,525 − 8,525) × 18%		(720)	720
WDV c/f		£11,294	
Total allowances			£14,231

3 months to 31.7.13

	AIA £	Main Pool £	Total allowances £
WDV b/f		11,295	
Additions	30,000		
Disposals		(9,560)	
		1,735	
AIA (note (e))	(30,000)		30,000
WDA (18% × 3/12)		(78)	78
WDV c/f		£1,657	—

224

3 months to 31.7.13

	AIA	Main Pool	Total allowances
	£	£	£
Total allowances			£30,078

Notes

(a) Where a trade is transferred part-way through an accounting period, HMRC take the view that writing-down allowances are calculated for the predecessor for a notional accounting period ending on the date of the transfer. The successor is then treated, in relation to the assets transferred, as having a chargeable period starting on that date and running to the end of its accounting period. (HMRC Capital Allowances Manual CA 15400.)

	£
The transfer value of machinery and plant obtained from C Ltd is	
Tax written-down value at 1.8.12	9,216
WDA due to C Ltd (£9,216 × 18% × $^5/_{12}$)	691
	£8,525

(b) The 'successor' company (B Ltd) is entitled to the capital allowances which the 'predecessor' company (C Ltd) would have been able to claim if it had continued to trade. [*CTA 2010, s 948(2)*].

(c) No annual investment allowance, first-year or initial allowance is available to the successor on assets transferred to it by the predecessor. [*CTA 2010, s 948(3)*].

(d) Writing-down allowances are reduced proportionately where the accounting period is less than one year. [*CAA 2001, ss 56(3), 310(2)*].

(e) A Ltd's group is entitled to only one annual investment allowance between all the companies, which can be allocated as the companies think fit. [*CAA 2001, s 51C*]. For the year ended 30 April 2013 it is assumed that C Ltd is allocated £13,000 to allow all of its expenditure in the period to qualify. For the three months to 31 July 2013 it is assumed that C Ltd is allocated £30,000 to allow all of its expenditure in the period to qualify.

102.2 NO CLAIM FOR ANNUAL INVESTMENT, FIRST-YEAR AND WRITING-DOWN ALLOWANCES

[*CAA 2001, ss 52(4), 56(5)*]

D Ltd is a company with one wholly-owned subsidiary, E Ltd, and no other associated companies. Both companies prepare accounts to 30 September. For the year ended 30 September 2013, D Ltd has trading profits of £100,000 before capital allowances, whilst E Ltd incurs a trading loss of £100,000. E Ltd also incurred trading losses in the previous year and is unlikely to have any taxable profits in the foreseeable future. D Ltd spent £50,000 on plant and machinery on 26 March 2013 which qualifies for annual investment allowance at 100%. There was a written-down value of £70,000 on the plant and machinery main pool at 1 October 2013 and there were no disposals during the year.

102.2 CT   Capital Allowances

Assuming a group relief claim is made under *CTA 2010, s 130* and that D Ltd claims the full capital allowances to which it is entitled, D Ltd's trading profits computation for the year to 30 September 2013 will be as follows

	£
Trading profit	100,000
Less capital allowances (see below)	62,600
	37,400
Less loss surrendered by E Ltd	37,400
Taxable profit	Nil

E Ltd has unrelieved losses carried forward of £62,600 which will not be relieved in the foreseeable future.

D Ltd's capital allowances computation is as follows

	AIA	Main pool	Total allowances
	£	£	£
WDV b/f		70,000	
Additions	50,000		
AIA	50,000	—	50,000
		70,000	
WDA 18%		(12,600)	12,600
WDV c/f		57,400	—
Total allowances			£62,600

If D Ltd does not claim capital allowances, the position is as follows

	£
Trading profit	100,000
Less loss surrendered by E Ltd	100,000
Taxable profit	Nil

Capital Allowances   CT 102.2

Capital allowances computation

	Expenditure qualifying for AIA £	Main pool £	Total allowances £
WDV b/f		70,000	
Additions	—	50,000	—
		120,000	
WDA – not claimed		—	—
WDV c/f		£120,000	
Total allowances			Nil

Notes

(a) A company may claim the whole, a part, or none of the allowances to which it is entitled. [*CAA 2001, ss 52(4), 56(5)*]. If a company does not claim annual investment allowance or claims part only, where available, the balance of the expenditure qualifies for writing-down allowances in the same accounting period. Capital allowances claims may be withdrawn within the same time limits as apply to the making of claims. [*FA 1998, s 117, Sch 18 paras 78–83*].

(b) As a result of the allowances not being claimed, all of E Ltd's current year losses have been relieved, and D Ltd has a higher written-down value to carry forward on its plant and machinery main pool.

(c) See **106 GROUP RELIEF** for group relief generally.

103 Capital Gains

103.1 CAPITAL LOSSES

[*TCGA 1992, s 8(1)*]

P Ltd has the following capital gains/(losses)

Year ended		£
31.7.10	Gains	27,000
	Losses	(7,000)
31.7.11	Losses	(12,000)
31.7.12	Gains	5,000
	Losses	(13,000)
31.7.13	Gains	40,000
	Losses	(30,000)

The gains and losses would be dealt with as follows in the CT computations of P Ltd

	£	Gain assessable £
31.7.10		
Gains chargeable to CT		£20,000
31.7.11		
Unrelieved losses carried forward	£(12,000)	Nil
31.7.12		
Losses (net)	8,000	Nil
Add Unrelieved losses brought forward	12,000	
Unrelieved losses carried forward	£(20,000)	
31.7.13		
Chargeable gains (net)	10,000	
Deduct Unrelieved losses brought forward	20,000	
Unrelieved losses carried forward	£(10,000)	Nil

Notes

(a) Unrelieved losses cannot be set off against trading profits, but are available to relieve future gains.

(b) Gains otherwise chargeable to CT may be covered by trading losses for the same accounting period or trading losses carried back from a succeeding period under *CTA 2010, s 37(3)*—see **114 LOSSES**.

(c) See also **103.3(A)** below.

103.2 CT   Capital Gains

103.2 CLOSE COMPANY TRANSFERRING ASSET AT UNDERVALUE
[TCGA 1992, s 125]

(A)

G Ltd (a close company) sold a building in 2012 to an associated company Q Ltd, which is not a member of the same group as G Ltd, at a price below market value at the time. Relevant values relating to the asset were

	£
Cost 1998	45,000
Market value at date of disposal	95,000
Sale proceeds received	75,000

The issued share capital of G Ltd was held at the time of disposal as follows

	£1 ordinary shares	Value prior to sale of asset £
C	25,000	50,000
D	30,000	60,000
E	20,000	40,000
F	25,000	50,000
	100,000	£200,000

Sale proceeds on subsequent sale (at market value) in July 2013 of C's total shareholding (originally purchased at £0.80 per share in 1992) in G Ltd were £55,000.

G Ltd's chargeable gain on the sale of the building in 2012 is

	£
Market value (note (b))	95,000
Cost	45,000
Unindexed gain	50,000
Indexation allowance at, say, 40% on £45,000	18,000
Chargeable gain	£32,000

C's gain on the disposal of the shares in 2013 is

		£	£
Sale proceeds			55,000
Deduct Allowable cost:			
	Purchase price (25,000 × £0.80)	20,000	
	Less Apportioned undervalue (note (a))	5,000	15,000
Chargeable gain			£40,000

230

Notes

(a) The apportionment of undervalue on disposal is

	£
Market value at time of sale	95,000
Deduct Sale proceeds	75,000
	£20,000

	Proportion of shareholding	Value apportioned
		£
C	$^{25}/_{100} \times £20,000$	5,000
D	$^{30}/_{100} \times £20,000$	6,000
E	$^{20}/_{100} \times £20,000$	4,000
F	$^{25}/_{100} \times £20,000$	5,000
		£20,000

(b) In the computation of the company's gain, market value is substituted for proceeds under *TCGA 1992, s 17*.

(c) Transfers of assets on or before 31 March 1982 are disregarded in respect of disposals after 5 April 1988 to which re-basing applies (not illustrated in this example). [*TCGA 1992, s 125(1)(5)*].

(B)

Assume the same facts as in (A) above except that the building had a market value of £155,000 at the date of disposal and C subsequently sold his shares for their market value of £40,000. Assume now also that C purchased his shares at £0.70 per share before 31 March 1982 and that their value on that date was £21,000.

G Ltd's chargeable gain will be computed under the same principles as in (A) above.
C's gain on the disposal of the shares will be as follows

			£	£
Sale proceeds				40,000
Deduct Allowable cost:				
	31 March 1982 value		21,000	
	Less Apportioned undervalue	(note (a))	20,000	
				1,000
Chargeable gain				£39,000

103.2 CT Capital Gains

Notes

(a) The apportionment of undervalue on disposal is

	£
Market value at time of sale	155,000
Deduct Sale proceeds	75,000
	£80,000

Proportion of shareholding		Value apportioned £
C	$^{25}/_{100} \times £80,000$	20,000
D	$^{30}/_{100} \times £80,000$	24,000
E	$^{20}/_{100} \times £80,000$	16,000
F	$^{25}/_{100} \times £80,000$	20,000
		£80,000

(b) See also note (c) to (A) above.

103.3 GROUPS OF COMPANIES

(A) **Re-allocation of gains and losses within a group**

[*TCGA 1992, ss 171A–171C; FA 2009, s 31, Sch 12*]

A Ltd and B Ltd are members of the same group of companies, preparing accounts each year to 31 March. On 30 September 2013, A Ltd sold an asset (asset 1) to an unconnected third party for £100,000. The asset had been acquired in June 2008 for £40,000. On 29 January 2014 B Ltd sold an asset (asset 2), which had cost £70,000 in January 2006, for £50,000 to C Ltd, an unconnected third party. B Ltd incurred costs on the disposal of £2,000. Neither company disposes of any other assets in the year ended 31 March 2014.

A Ltd and B Ltd jointly elect before 31 March 2016 under *TCGA 1992, s 171A* for the chargeable gain or loss on asset 2 to be treated as accruing to company A at the time it would otherwise have accrued to B.

The chargeable gains computations for the year ended 31 March 2014 for A Ltd and B Ltd are as follows.

B Ltd

Deemed disposal of asset 2 in April 2013: consideration deemed to be such that neither gain nor loss arises.

	£
Deemed consideration	84,000
Cost of asset to B Ltd	70,000
Indexation allowance £70,000 × say 20%	14,000
Gain	—

A Ltd

Disposal of asset 1 in September 2013

	£
Consideration	100,000
Cost	40,000
Indexation allowance £40,000 × say 10%	4,000
Chargeable gain	£56,000

Disposal of asset 2 in January 2014

	£
Consideration	50,000
Cost to A Ltd	70,000
Cost of disposal incurred by B Ltd	2,000
Allowable loss	£(22,000)

103.3 CT   Capital Gains

Net chargeable gains £56,000 − £22,000 = £34,000

Note

(a) The election under *TCGA 1992, s 171A* must be made in writing to HMRC within two years after the end of the accounting period of A Ltd in which the gain accrued. The election can only be made if a disposal of asset 2 by B Ltd to A Ltd would have been a no gain, no loss disposal within *TCGA 1992, s 171*.

(B) **Intra-group transfers of assets which are trading stock of one company but not of the other — transfer from a 'capital asset' company to a 'trading stock' company**

[*TCGA 1992, ss 161, 173(1)*]

In June 2013, X Ltd transfers an item classed as a fixed asset to another group company Y Ltd, which treats it as trading stock.

The following information is relevant

	Case (i) £	Case (ii) £
Original cost (after 31.3.82)	100,000	100,000
Market value at date of transfer	120,000	40,000
Eventual sale proceeds	140,000	140,000
Indexation allowance due on original cost at date of transfer	17,000	17,000

The position of Y Ltd will be as follows if there is no election under *TCGA 1992, s 161(3)*

Chargeable gain/(allowable loss) on appropriation		
Market value	120,000	40,000
Deemed cost of asset (note (a))	117,000	117,000
Gain/(loss)	3,000	(77,000)
Deduct Indexation allowance included in cost (note (b))	—	17,000
Chargeable gain/(allowable loss)	£3,000	£(60,000)
Trading profit at date of sale		
Sale proceeds	140,000	140,000
Deemed cost of asset	120,000	40,000
Trading profit	£20,000	£100,000

Capital Gains   CT 103.3

With an election under *TCGA 1992, s 161(3)*

No chargeable gain or allowable loss arises on appropriation

	£	£	£	£
Trading profit at date of sale				
Sale proceeds		140,000		140,000
Market value at appropriation	120,000		40,000	
Adjustment for (gain)/loss otherwise (chargeable)/allowable	(3,000)	117,000	60,000	100,000
Trading profit		£23,000		£40,000

Notes

(a) The intra-group transfer by X Ltd to Y Ltd is treated as a disposal on which neither a gain nor a loss accrues after taking account of any indexation allowance due. X Ltd has no liability on the transfer and Y Ltd has a deemed acquisition cost of £117,000 on the appropriation to stock. [*TCGA 1992, ss 56(2), 171(1)*].

(b) The indexation allowance on a no gain/no loss transfer must be excluded on a subsequent disposal to the extent that it would otherwise contribute to an allowable loss. [*TCGA 1992, s 56(3)*].

(C) **Intra-group transfers of assets which are trading stock of one company but not of the other — transfer from a 'trading stock' company to a 'capital asset' company**

[*TCGA 1992, ss 161, 173(2)*]

P Ltd acquires from another group company Q Ltd as a fixed asset an item previously treated as trading stock.

	£
Cost to Q Ltd (after 31.3.82)	100,000
Market value at date of transfer	150,000
Eventual sale proceeds	200,000
Indexation allowance due on transfer value from date of transfer to date of sale	10,000

103.3 CT   Capital Gains

The group will have the following trading profits and chargeable gains

	£	£
Q Ltd trading profit [*TCGA 1992, s 161(2)*]		
Deemed sale proceeds		150,000
Cost to Q Ltd		100,000
Trading profit		£50,000
P Ltd chargeable gain [*TCGA 1992, s 171(1)*]		
Sale proceeds		200,000
Cost of asset	150,000	
Indexation allowance	10,000	
		160,000
Chargeable gain		£40,000

(D) **Rollover relief on the replacement of business assets**

[*TCGA 1992, ss 152, 153, 155, 175*]

M Ltd and N Ltd are 75% subsidiaries of H Ltd. On 1 February 2012 M Ltd sold a showroom for £200,000, realising a chargeable gain of £110,000. N Ltd purchased a factory for £150,000 in March 2014, within three years after the date of sale of the showroom.

Rollover relief could be claimed as follows

	£	£
Gain otherwise chargeable to corporation tax		110,000
Deduct Unrelieved gain:		
Sale proceeds	200,000	
Less Amount reinvested	150,000	
Chargeable gain	£50,000	50,000
Rollover relief		£60,000
New base cost of factory		
Purchase price		150,000
Deduct Rollover relief		60,000
		£90,000

Notes

(a)   To qualify for relief, the two companies concerned need not be members of the same group throughout the period between the transactions but each must be a member at the time of its own particular transaction.

Capital Gains   CT 103.3

(b) N Ltd will be entitled to indexation allowance, based on the deemed cost of £90,000, on a subsequent sale (to the extent that such sale produces an unindexed gain).

(c) See also CGT 205.2 ASSETS HELD ON 31 MARCH 1982 and CGT 226 ROLLOVER RELIEF.

(E) **Degrouping charge**

A Ltd had the following transactions

1.3.80 Purchased a freehold property £10,000.

31.3.82 Market value £25,000.

1.3.86 Purchased the entire share capital of B Ltd for £120,000.

1.12.07 Sold the freehold to B Ltd for £20,000 (market value £80,000).

31.9.13 Sold its shares in B Ltd (at which time B Ltd continued to own the freehold property) for £1 million.

Both companies prepare accounts to 30 April.

Relevant values of the RPI are: March 1982: 79.44, March 1986 96.73, December 2007: 210.9, September 2013 (assumed) 246.4.

The taxation consequences are

(i) There will be no chargeable gain on A Ltd's disposal of the property to B Ltd as the disposal is one on which, after taking account of indexation allowance, neither gain nor loss arises. [*TCGA 1992, ss 56(2), 171(1)*].

Indexation factor (210.9 − 79.44)/79.44 = 1.655

	£
Cost to A Ltd	10,000
Indexation allowance £25,000 × 1.655 (note (a))	41,375
Deemed cost to B Ltd	£51,375

(ii) On the sale of A Ltd's shares in B Ltd on 31.9.13 (i.e. within six years after the transaction in (i) above), *A Ltd* will have a deemed disposal as follows.

103.3 CT   Capital Gains

Deemed disposal on 1.12.07

	£	£	£
Market value at 1.12.07		80,000	80,000
Cost (as above)	51,375		
Less indexation to date	41,375		
		10,000	
Market value at 31.3.82		–	25,000
Unindexed gain		70,000	55,000
Indexation allowance			
£25,000 × 1.655		41,375	41,375
Indexed gain		£28,625	£13,625
Deemed gain			£13,625

The deemed gain is not charged to corporation tax directly, but is treated as follows.

A Ltd's chargeable gain on disposal of B Ltd shares on 31.9.13

	£
Consideration	1,000,000
Add degrouping gain	13,625
	1,013,625
Less acquisition cost	120,000
Uninexed gain	893,625
Indexation allowance (246.4 – 96.73/96.73) × £120,000	185,640
Chargeable gain subject to note (b)	£707,985

Notes

(a) Where the conditions listed below are satisfied, a degrouping gain or loss is not treated as a separate gain or loss accruing to the transferee company, but instead the gain or loss accruing on a 'group disposal' (see below) is adjusted to take account of the degrouping gain or loss. The conditions are as follows:

  (A) the transferee company ceases to be a member of the group as a result of one or more disposals ('*group disposals*') by a group member of the transferee's shares or those of another group member;

  (B) either:

   (i) the company making the group disposal (or, if there is more than one such disposal, at least one of them) is UK resident at the time of disposal, the shares are within the charge to corporation tax (or would be but for the substantial shareholdings exemption — see 103.4), or any part of the gains or loss on the disposal (or at least one of them) is treated as accruing to a person under *TCGA 1992, s 13(2)* (attribution of gains to members of non-resident companies), or

Capital Gains CT 103.3

   (ii) had (i) above applied to the group disposal or to each of them, any gain arising would not have been a chargeable gain as a result of the substantial shareholdings exemption; and

 (C) *CTA 2010, s 535* (UK real estate investment trusts: exemption of gains) would not apply to the degrouping gain or loss.

Where the conditions are satisfied, a chargeable gain or allowable loss on a single group disposal is calculated by adding any degrouping gain which would otherwise have arisen but for these provisions to the consideration for the group disposal (and a degrouping loss is treated as an allowable deduction).

[*TCGA 1992, s 179(3A)–(3H); FA 2011, Sch 10 para 3(6)*].

(b) Where a company is treated as making a gain under the degrouping charge provisions or such a gain is taken into account in calculating a gain on a disposal of shares as illustrated in this example, a claim can be made to defer part of the gain. Where the degrouping gain is taken into account in calculating a gain on a disposal of shares, the claim can be made by the company making the share disposal or, if there is more than one such disposal, the companies making those disposals acting jointly. In any other case the claim is to be made by the company to whom the degrouping gain is deemed to accrue. The effect is to reduce the amount of the gain by the amount specified in the claim. The reduction must be just and reasonable with regard, in particular, to any transaction as a direct or indirect result of which the asset to which the gain relates was acquired. Where a gain is reduced in this way, the consideration for the deemed reacquisition of the asset by the transferee company is taken to be its market value less the amount of the adjustment to the gain. In effect the part of the gain excluded is deferred until final disposal of the asset by the transferee company (to whom the liability will then fall). [*TCGA 1992, s 179ZA; FA 2011, Sch 10 paras 4, 9(1)*].

(F) **Restriction on set-off of pre-entry losses on or after 19 July 2011**

[*TCGA 1992, s 177A, Sch 7A; FA 2011, s 46, Sch 11*]

The entire share capital of House Ltd is acquired by Wooster Ltd, the holding company of a group, on 1 January 2010. At that date, House Ltd is trading as a gun seller and has an unrelieved allowable pre-entry loss of £150,000. House Ltd makes no further disposals of assets until, in its accounting period ended 31 March 2014, it disposes of four assets as follows.

	Date of acquisition	Chargeable gain/(allowable loss)
Asset A	31/3/08	£50,000
Asset B	1/5/11	£30,000
Asset C	1/11/10	£100,000
Asset D	8/6/06	£(25,000)

Asset B was acquired from an unconnected company and has been used throughout the period of House Ltd's ownership for the purposes of the company's gun selling trade. Asset C is a building which has been leased to an unconnected company throughout. House Ltd had not carried on a property business before acquiring the asset.

103.3 CT Capital Gains

House Ltd's total taxable gains for the year ended 31 March 2014 are as follows.

	£	£
Asset A (note (b))		
Chargeable gain	50,000	
Less pre-entry loss (part)	(50,000)	—
Asset B (note (b))		
Chargeable gain	30,000	
Less pre-entry loss (part)	(30,000)	—
Asset C (note (b))		
Chargeable gain	100,000	
Less loss on Asset D (note (b))	(25,000)	75,000
Total taxable gains		£75,000

The pre-entry loss has been utilised as follows.

	£
Loss brought forward	150,000
Set against gain on Asset A	50,000
Set against gain on Asset B	30,000
Unrelieved loss carried forward	£70,000

Notes

(a) Broadly, the provisions of *TCGA 1992, Sch 7A* restrict the use of losses realised by a company before it joins a group and remaining unrelieved at that time. Such pre-entry losses can be set only against gains on assets held by the company at the time it joined the group or subsequently acquired by the company from outside the group and used by it in a continuing trade.

(b) The pre-entry loss in this example can be set off against the gain on Asset A as Asset A was owned by House Ltd before it joined Wooster Ltd's group. The loss can also be set off against the gain on Asset B as although Asset B was acquired by House Ltd after it joined the group it was acquired by the company from outside the group and has been used by it in a continuing trade throughout its period of ownership. Asset C fails to meet either of these conditions and so the loss cannot be set against the gain arising on its disposal.

(c) Although Asset D was acquired before House Ltd joined the group, the loss is not a pre-entry loss because it accrues on or after 19 July 2011. Had Asset D been disposed of before that date, the pre-entry proportion of the loss would have been subject to the pre-entry loss restrictions until that date. The loss would have been treated on and after that date as if it had accrued immediately before the company became a member of the group (and therefore as a pre-entry loss).

Capital Gains   CT 103.4

(d) The provisions do not apply where *TCGA 1992, s 184A* (restrictions on buying losses: avoidance schemes) applies. [*TCGA 1992, Sch 7A para 1(1); FA 2006, s 70(3)*].

103.4 SUBSTANTIAL SHAREHOLDING EXEMPTION

[*TCGA 1992, Sch 7AC*]

Swallow Ltd acquired 1,500 shares in Summer Ltd in April 1994. Swallow Ltd holds no other investments in any company, has been a trading company throughout its existence, and is not a member of a group. Summer Ltd has 10,000 issued shares and has been a trading company since its formation. Swallow Ltd makes the following disposals of Summer Ltd shares.

31 May 2012	600 shares
30 April 2013	400 shares
30 June 2013	500 shares

The effect of the disposals for the purposes of corporation tax on chargeable gains is as follows

31 May 2012 disposal

Swallow Ltd has held at least 10% of the ordinary share capital of Summer Ltd throughout the two years prior to the disposal. The disposal is therefore of part of a substantial shareholding and no chargeable gain or allowable loss arises on the disposal.

30 April 2013 disposal

Although Swallow Ltd did not hold at least 10% of the shares in Summer Ltd immediately before the disposal (the remaining holding being only 900 of 10,000 shares), there is a twelve month period beginning within two years prior to the disposal throughout which it did hold at least 10%. That period is 1 June 2011 to 31 May 2012. Accordingly, the substantial shareholding exemption applies and no chargeable gain or allowable loss arises on the disposal.

30 June 2013 disposal

Swallow Ltd holds only 5% of the share capital of Summer Ltd immediately before the disposal. In the period from 1 July 2011 to 30 June 2013, the company held at least 10% of Summer Ltd's shares only from 1 July 2011 to 31 May 20121. This is not a continuous twelve month period beginning within two years prior to the disposal, and therefore the substantial shareholding exemption will not apply. A gain on the disposal of 500 shares will be a chargeable gain, and a loss an allowable loss.

Note

(a) A gain on a disposal by a trading company of shares in another trading company is not a chargeable gain (and a loss is not an allowable loss) if, broadly, the company held at least 10% of the other company's ordinary share capital throughout a twelve month period beginning within two years prior to the disposal.

104 Close Companies

104.1 CLOSE COMPANY — DEFINITION

[*CTA 2010, ss 439–453*]

(A)

A plc is a quoted company whose ordinary share capital is owned as follows

		%
B	a director	10
C	wife of B	5
D	father of B	4
E		17
F	business partner of E	2
G	a director	10
H		8
I Ltd	a non-close company	30
J		7
100	other shareholders	7
		100

It can be shown that A plc is a close company by considering the following three steps

(i) Is A plc controlled by five or fewer participators or by its directors?

		%	%
I Ltd			30
B	own shares	10	
	C's shares	5	
	D's shares	4	
			19
E	own shares	17	
	F's shares	2	
			19
			68

As A plc is controlled by three participators, the initial conclusion is that the company is close. [*CTA 2010, s 439(2)*].

(ii) Is A plc a quoted company, with at least 35% of the voting power owned by the public?

%

104.1 CT   Close Companies

I Ltd		30
J		7
100	other shareholders	7
		44

As at least 35% of the voting power is owned by the public it appears that A plc is exempt from close company status, subject to step (iii). [*CTA 2010, s 446(1)*].

(iii) Is more than 85% of the voting power in A plc owned by its principal members?

	%
I Ltd	30
B	19
E	19
G	10
H	8
	86

Because the principal members own more than 85% of the voting power A plc is a close company. [*CTA 2010, s 446(2)-(4)*].

Note

(a) Although J owns more than 5% of the share capital, he is not a principal member because five other persons each hold more than J's 7% and so themselves constitute the principal members. [*CTA 2010, s 446(4)*].

(B)

The ordinary share capital of A Ltd (an unquoted company) is owned as follows

		%
B	a director	9
C	son of B	9
D	works manager	5
E	wife of D	15
F	a director	9
G	a director	1
H	a director	1
J	a director	1
K	a director	1
49	other shareholders with 1% each	49
		100

Close Companies CT 104.1

A Ltd is a close company because it is controlled by its directors, thus

			%	%
B	own shares		9	
	C's shares		9	
				18
D	own shares		5	
	E's shares		15	
				20
F				9
G				1
H				1
J				1
K				1
				51

Note

(a) A manager is deemed to be a director if he and his associates own 20% or more of the ordinary share capital. [*CTA 2010, s 452(2)*].

(C)

The ordinary share capital of A Ltd is owned as follows

		%
B	a director	9
C	a director	9
D	a director	9
E		9
F		9
G Ltd	a close company	8
47	other shareholders with 1% each	47
		100

The ordinary share capital of G Ltd is owned as follows

		%
B	a director	50
C	a director	50
		100

A Ltd is not a close company under the control test because it is not under the control of five or fewer participators. The five largest shareholdings comprise only 45% of the share capital. [*CTA 2010, ss 439(2), 450(3)*].

104.1 CT   Close Companies

A Ltd is a close company under the distribution of assets test because B and C would each become entitled to one-half of G Ltd's share of the assets of A Ltd. [*CTA 2010, s 439(3)*]. The shares of assets attributable to the five largest shareholdings become

			%	%
B	own share		9	
	50% of G Ltd's share		4	
				13
C	own share		9	
	50% of G Ltd's share		4	
				13
D				9
E				9
F				9
				53

(D)

A Ltd is an unquoted company with the following capital structure, owned as shown

	£1 ordinary shares	£1 non-participating preference shares (no votes attached)
B	6,000	—
C	15,000	25,000
D	6,000	19,000
E	5,000	10,000
F	1,600	13,000
G	2,000	—
Other shareholders owning less than 1,000 shares each	64,400	33,000
	100,000	100,000

The company is close by reference to share capital as follows

	Control by votes	Control of issued capital
B	6,000	6,000
C	15,000	40,000
D	6,000	25,000
E	5,000	15,000
F	—	14,600
G	2,000	—
	34,000	100,600

Note

(a) Control of the company includes control of more than one-half of

    (i) voting power; or

    (ii) issued share capital.

[*CTA 2010, s 450(3)*].

104.2 LOANS TO PARTICIPATORS

[*CTA 2010, ss 455–464D; FA 2013, Sch 30*]

(A)

P is a participator in Q Ltd, a close company which makes up accounts to 30 September. Q Ltd loaned P £80,000 on 29 August 2011. On 24 May 2013 P repays the loan.

The effect of these transactions on Q Ltd is as follows

1 July 2012	The company is liable to pay corporation tax of £80,000 × 25%	£20,000
30 June 2014	On a claim, Q Ltd is entitled to a repayment of	£20,000

Notes

(a) An amount equal to 25% of the loan must be self-assessed by the company as if it were corporation tax chargeable for the accounting period in which the loan was made.

(b) The tax is due on the day following the expiry of nine months after the end of the accounting period in which the loan or advance was made.

(c) Where loans or advances, made in an accounting period ended on or after 31 March 1996, are repaid after the due date on which tax is charged, relief by claim in respect of the repayment is not given at any time before the expiry of nine months from the end of the accounting period in which the repayment takes place.

(d) Where a loan is repaid on or after 20 March 2013, the tax, or part of the tax, is not repaid if either:

- within a period of 30 days, a repayment of £5,000 or more is made by a participator and the company makes further chargeable payments (i.e. loans or benefits chargeable under *CTA 2010, s 464A*) of at least £5,000 to the participator, provided that the further chargeable payments are made in an accounting period after that in which the original loan was made; or

- the amount outstanding is at least £15,000, arrangements have been made at the time of the repayment for one or more chargeable payments to be made to replace some or all of the loan, and further chargeable payments of at least £5,000 are made by the company to the participator.

104.2 CT   Close Companies

In either case, the repayment is treated as a repayment of the further chargeable payments and only any excess amount is treated as a repayment of the original loan.

[*CTA 2010, ss 464C, 464D; FA 2013, Sch 30 para 6*].

(B)

T is a participator in (but not an employee of) V Ltd, a close company. V Ltd loaned T £100,000 on 10 May 2011. On 2 March 2012, T repays £73,000 and on 15 February 2013, V Ltd agrees to waive the balance of the loan. V Ltd has a year end of 31 March and is not a large company for instalment payment purposes. T is a higher rate (but not an additional rate) taxpayer for 2012/13.

The effect of these transactions is as follows

V Ltd

On 1.1.13	The company becomes liable to pay corporation tax of (£100,000 − £73,000) £27,000 × 25%	£6,750
On 31.12.13	The company is due a repayment of £27,000 × 25%	£6,750

T

On 15.2.13	T's 2012/13 taxable income is increased by £27,000 × $^{10}/_9$	£30,000
	And	
	he is credited with dividend ordinary rate tax paid of £30,000 at 10%	£3,000
	As T pays tax at the higher rate, the deemed income will be subject to tax at the dividend upper rate of 32.5% on £30,000	9,750
	Less: tax credit (as above)	3,000
	T's tax liability	£6,750

Notes

(a)   Where a loan or advance which gave rise to a charge under *CTA 2010, s 455* is released or written off, a claim can be made for repayment of the tax. [*CTA 2010, s 458(2)(b)*].

(b)   Companies are required to include *section 455* tax in their self-assessment.

104.3 BENEFITS IN KIND FOR PARTICIPATORS

[*CTA 2010, ss 1064–1069*]

R is a participator in S Ltd, a close company, but he is neither a director nor an employee earning £8,500 a year or more. For the whole of 2013/14, S Ltd provided R with a new petrol fuelled car of which the 'price' for tax purposes (i.e. under *ITEPA 2003, ss 122–124*) was £21,200, and the carbon dioxide emission figure for which was 230g/km. R was required to, and did, pay S Ltd £500 a year for the use of the car. The cost of providing the car, charged in S Ltd's accounts for its year ended 31 March 2014, was £5,000.

Deemed distribution

If the benefit of the car were assessable to tax as income from employment, the cash equivalent would be

	£
£21,200 @ 35%	7,420
Less contribution	500
	£6,920

S Ltd is treated as making a distribution of £6,920 to R.

Tax credit £6,920 × $1/9$ (note (a))	£769
Income of R for 2013/14 £6,920 × $10/9$	£7,689

Note

(a) The credit is non-repayable but satisfies the liability to the dividend ordinary rate (10%) on the grossed up amount and is set against a liability arising at the dividend upper rate (32.5%) or additional rate (37.5%).

S Ltd's taxable profits

In computing S Ltd's profits chargeable to corporation tax, the actual expenditure charged (£5,000) must be added back.

105 Double Tax Relief

105.1 MEASURE OF RELIEF

[*TIOPA 2010, ss 2–6, 18–20, 31–34, 42–56*]

The following facts relate to A Ltd's accounting period for the year ended 31 March 2014.

	£
Trading profits	1,500,000
Overseas chargeable gain (tax 40%)	80,000

A Ltd's tax liability is

	Trading income	Overseas gain	Total
	£	£	£
Profits	1,500,000	80,000	1,580,000
CT at 23%	345,000	18,400	363,400
Relief for foreign tax (note (a))	—	(18,400)	(18,400)
	£345,000	—	£345,000

Note

(a) The maximum amount of relief for foreign tax is the amount of the gain multiplied by the company's corporation tax rate (£80,000 × 23% = £18,400). [*TIOPA 2010, s 42*]. The unrelieved foreign tax (£32,000 – £18,400 = £13,600) cannot be relieved by way of deduction from the gain under *TIOPA 2010, s 113*. [*TIOPA 2010, s 31*].

105.2 EXEMPTION FOR PROFITS OF FOREIGN PERMANENT ESTABLISHMENTS

[*CTA 2009, ss 18A–18S; FA 2011, s 48, Sch 13; FA 2012, Sch 20 paras 3–7, 55*]

(A) Exclusion of permanent establishment profits

Wiggo Ltd is a UK company trading as a bike wholesaler. The company also operates through a permanent establishment in Tourland and has made an election under *CTA 2009, s 18A* which took effect at the start of the accounting period ending 31 December 2013. For the accounting period ending 31 December 2013, Wiggo Ltd's total taxable profits, before applying the foreign permanent establishments exemption, consists of trading profits of £5,000,000 and non-trading loan relationships income of £120,000. The company had no opening negative amount (see (B) below) and its foreign permanent establishments amount for the accounting period is calculated as follows.

105.2 CT Double Tax Relief

	£
Profits amount	
Trading profits	250,000
Losses amount	
Non-trading loan relationship deficit	(40,000)
Foreign permanent establishments amount	£210,000

Exemption adjustments under *CTA 2009, s 18A* are made to Wiggo Ltd's total taxable profits for the year ended 31 December 2013 are made as follows.

	£	£
Trading profits	5,000,000	
Less Tourland trading profits	(250,000)	4,750,000
Non-trading loan relationship income	120,000	
Add Tourland non-trading loan relationship deficit	40,000	160,000
Total taxable profits		£4,910,000

Notes

(a) With effect from 19 July 2011, a company can make an election for profits arising from its foreign permanent establishments, including chargeable gains, to be exempt from corporation tax (and for losses from those permanent establishments to be excluded). Orginally, only UK resident companies could make an election but, with effect from 1 January 2013, an election can now also be made by a non-UK resident company which expects to become UK resident. An election will apply to all accounting periods of the company beginning on or after the 'relevant day'. For this purpose, the 'relevant day' is the day on which, at the time of the election, the next or first accounting period is expected to begin or, in the case of a non-resident company, the day on which the company becomes UK resident. If, in the event, an accounting period begins before and ends on or after the relevant day, then for corporation tax purposes that period is treated as two accounting periods, the first ending immediately before the relevant day and the second starting on that day. Profits and losses are to be apportioned to the two periods on a just and reasonable basis. An election can only be revoked before the relevant day; otherwise it is irrevocable. [*CTA 2009, ss 18A(1)–(3), 18F; FA 2011, Sch 13 paras 4, 31; FA 2012, Sch 20 paras 3, 5, 55*].

(b) The '*foreign permanent establishments amount*' is the aggregate of the 'profits amount' for each territory outside the UK in which the company carries on, or has carried on, business through a permanent establishment, less the aggregate of the 'losses amount' for each such territory. Where there is a double tax treaty between the territory and the UK which includes a provision non-discrimination provision, the '*profits amount*' is the profits which would be taken to be attributable to the permanent establishment in ascertaining the amount of any credit relief for foreign tax. The '*losses amount*' is calculated on the same basis. If an amount of credit relief does not depend on the profits taken to be attributable to the permanent establishment because, under the treaty, the foreign tax is not charged by reference to such profits, then only profits which would be taken to be attributable to the permanent establishment if the foreign tax were charged by reference to such profits are included in the profits amount (and only such losses are included in the losses amount). Where there is no such treaty, the profits amount and losses amount are the amounts which would be taken to be so attributable to the permanent establishment if there were such a treaty and it was in the terms of the OECD model tax convention. [*CTA 2009, ss 18A(4)–(10), 18R; FA 2011, Sch 13 para 4*].

(c) Although profits amounts and losses amounts are aggregated in computing the foreign permanent establishments amount, they nevertheless retain their identity for the purpose of making the necessary adjustments to the company's total taxable profits.

(B) **Pre-entry losses**

A company with three foreign permanent establishments makes an election under *CTA 2009, s 18A* which takes effect for the accounting period ending 31 December 2016. The profits amounts and losses amounts (excluding chargeable gains and allowable losses) for the three territories in the preceding six years are as follows.

Year ended 31 December	Territory 1	Territory 2	Territory 3	Foreign permanent establishments amount
2010	2,000	0	(6,000)	(4,000)
2011	1,000	(2,000)	1,000	0
2012	(5,000)	(2,000)	2,000	(5,000)
2013	2,000	4,000	(3,000)	3,000
2014	(10,000)	1,000	2,000	(7,000)
2015	2,000	2,000	2,000	6,000
Opening negative amount				£7,000

The opening negative amount must be extinguished by matching with the aggregate profits amount (see note (b) to (A) above) for each subsequent accounting period, starting with the first period for which the election takes effect (i.e. the year ended 31 December 2016). No adjustments can be made to the company's total taxable profits under *CTA 2009, s 18A* until the opening negative amount has been so extinguished.

Alternatively, the company could have elected for the opening negative amount for territory 1 to be streamed, so that it need be matched only with profits amounts for that territory. The opening negative amount is calculated as follows.

Year ended 31 December	Territory 1
2010	2,000
2011	1,000
2012	(5,000)
2013	2,000
2014	(10,000)
2015	2,000

105.2 CT   Double Tax Relief

Total   (£11,000)

The streamed negative amount for that territory is the lower of £11,000 and the aggregate total opening negative amount, i.e. £7,000. The company streams no other territory, so the residual negative amount is the difference between the aggregate negative amount £7,000 and the streamed negative amount £7,000, i.e. nil. The profits amounts for Territory 1 must therefore be matched with the negative amount £7,000 before exemption can apply (i.e. the first £7,000 of such amounts are not exempt), but there is no restriction on exemption for profits amounts of Territories 2 and 3.

Notes

(a)   Where losses have arisen in any of the company's foreign permanent establishments in the six-year period ending at the end of the accounting period in which the election is made, and those losses have not been eliminated by profits from those establishments before the end of that period, then the company will have an 'opening negative amount' and no adjustments can be made to the company's total taxable profits until that amount has been eliminated. The *'opening negative amount'* is ascertained by calculating the foreign permanent establishments amount (excluding chargeable gains and allowable losses) for each accounting period ending less than six years before the end of the accounting period in which the election is made and for that accounting period. The earliest negative amount is carried forward to the next period where it is either increased by another negative amount or reduced or eliminated by a positive amount, but not so as to cause the result to be positive. This process continues through each accounting period and if there is a negative amount remaining after applying it to the last period, that amount is the opening negative amount. The period for which this process must be carried out is extended if there is a losses amount of more than £50 million in an accounting period beginning within the six-year period ending on 18 July 2011, if that period would not otherwise fall within the normal six-year period. Where the period is extended in this way, the process must be carried out for the period of the losses amount and each subsequent accounting period up to and including that in which the election is made. [*CTA 2009, ss 18J, 18K; FA 2011, Sch 13 paras 4, 31, 34*].

(b)   Alternatively, the company can elect for the opening negative amount to be streamed. If such an election is made then, in effect, the above provisions are applied separately to losses in a particular territory so that they do not delay the application of the exemption to other permanent establishments which would otherwise have no, or a shorter, transitional period. The election must be made at the same time as the exemption election and can only be revoked before the first accounting period to which the exemption election applies. It must specify the territories which are to be streamed. Where not all of the negative opening amount is streamed in this way, the residual amount must be eliminated against the residual profits amounts (i.e. for each accounting period, the total profits amount less the streamed profits amounts) in the same way. [*CTA 2009, ss 18L–18N; FA 2011, Sch 13 para 4*].

106 Group Relief

106.1 CALCULATION OF GROUP RELIEF

[*CTA 2010, ss 97–156*]

(A)

A Ltd has a subsidiary company, B Ltd, in which it owns 75% of the ordinary share capital. Relevant information for the year ended 31 March 2014 is as follows

		£
A Ltd	Trading profit	30,000
	Property income	10,000
	Chargeable gain	15,000
	Qualifying charitable donations	2,000
B Ltd	Trading loss	48,000
	Qualifying charitable donations	2,000

In addition, B Ltd has trading losses brought forward of £25,000.

Group relief is available as follows

	£	£
A Ltd		
Trading profit		30,000
Property income		10,000
Chargeable gain		15,000
		55,000
Deduct Charitable donation		2,000
Profits		53,000
Deduct Loss surrendered by B Ltd		50,000
Chargeable profits		£3,000
B Ltd		
Losses brought forward		25,000
Trading loss for the year	48,000	
Charitable donation	2,000	
	50,000	
Deduct Loss surrendered to A Ltd	50,000	—
Losses carried forward		£25,000

106.1 CT   Group Relief

(B)

A Ltd has two wholly owned subsidiaries B Ltd and C Ltd. There are no other associated companies. Results for the year ended 31 March 2014 are as follows

	£
A Ltd	
Trading profit	485,000
Chargeable gains	75,000
B Ltd	
Trading loss	92,000
Income from non-trading loan relationship	6,000
Qualifying charitable donations	4,000
C Ltd	
Trading profit	124,500
Property income	7,500

Disregarding group relief, the computation for each company is as follows

A Ltd	
Total profits	£560,000
Corporation tax: (note (a))	
£560,000 at 23%	128,800
B Ltd	
Total profits	6,000
Less: trading loss set against profits	6,000
Corporation tax liability	Nil
Trading loss unrelieved (£92,000 − £6,000)	86,000
Qualifying charitable donations	4,000
Loss available for group relief	£90,000
C Ltd	
Total profits	£132,000
Corporation tax: (note (a))	
£132,000 at 23%	30,360
Less: 3/400 × (£500,000 − £132,000) =	2,760
Corporation tax payable	£27,600

256

B Ltd surrenders its losses by group relief, £58,000 to A Ltd, £32,000 to C Ltd. The computations are then revised as follows

A Ltd

	£
Total profits	560,000
Less: group relief	58,000
Profits chargeable to corporation tax	£502,000
Corporation tax: (note (a))	
£502,000 at 23%	£115,460

B Ltd

Loss available for group relief	90,000
Less: losses surrendered	90,000

C Ltd

Total profits	132,000
Less: group relief	32,000
Profits chargeable to corporation tax	£100,000
Corporation tax: (note (a))	
£100,000 at 20%	£20,000

Notes

(a) The upper and lower limits for profits to be chargeable at the small profits rate (£1,500,000 and £300,000) are divided by one plus the number of associated companies. They are thus £500,000 and £100,000 in this case.

(b) The surrenders as above achieve the maximum tax saving. Any switch of relief from A Ltd to C Ltd saves tax in C Ltd at 20% but at the cost of extra tax in A Ltd at 23%. Any switch from C Ltd to A Ltd saves tax in A Ltd at 23% but at the cost of extra tax in C Ltd at the effective marginal rate of 23.75%.

106.2 KINDS OF GROUP RELIEF

[*CTA 2010, s 99(1)(2), 100–104*]

A Ltd is an investment company which has three trading subsidiaries, B Ltd, C Ltd and D Ltd in which it owns 100% of the share capital. The companies have the following results for the two years ending 31 March 2014.

		Year ended 31.3.12	Year ended 31.3.13
		£	£
A Ltd	Profits	10,000	20,000
	Management expenses	(20,000)	(50,000)
B Ltd	Trading loss	(10,000)	(10,000)

106.2 CT   Group Relief

	Year ended 31.3.12 £	Year ended 31.3.13 £
Property income (after capital allowances)		30,000
Non-trading loan relationship deficit		(10,000)
C Ltd Trading profit/(loss)	(10,000)	30,000
Property income		1,000
Capital allowances — trading assets		(5,000)
— property assets		(2,000)
Management expenses		(40,000)
D Ltd Profits		70,000

Group relief may be claimed for trading losses, management expenses, property business losses and charges on income, as follows

		Year ended 31.3.13 £	Year ended 31.3.14 £
A Ltd			
Profits		10,000	20,000
Management expenses		(20,000)	(50,000)
Excess management expenses		(10,000)	(30,000)
Deduct Surrendered to D Ltd		—	30,000
Management expenses carried forward to year ended 31.3.14	(note (a))	£(10,000)	—
B Ltd			
Trading loss brought forward		—	(10,000)
Trading loss		(10,000)	(10,000)
Trading loss carried forward		£(10,000)	—
			(20,000)
Deduct Surrendered to D Ltd	(note (b))		10,000
Trading loss carried forward (not available for group relief or set-off against non-trading income)			£(10,000)
Non-trading loan relationship deficit	(note (b))		(10,000)
Deduct Surrendered to D Ltd			10,000
Profits chargeable to corporation tax			£30,000

C Ltd

Group Relief CT 106.2

	Year ended 31.3.13 £	Year ended 31.3.14 £
Trading loss brought forward	—	(10,000)
Trading loss	(10,000)	
Trading loss carried forward	£(10,000)	
Trading profit (£30,000) *less* trade capital allowances (£5,000)		25,000
		15,000
UK property income (£1,000) less UK property capital allowances (£2,000) less		
surrendered to D Ltd (£1,000) (note (c))		—
		15,000
Management expenses (£40,000) less surrendered to D Ltd (£15,000) (note (c))		(25,000)
Management expenses carried forward		£(10,000)

D Ltd — year ended 31.3.14	£	£
Profits		70,000
Deduct Surrendered by A Ltd	30,000	
Surrendered by B Ltd		
trading loss	10,000	
loan relationship deficit	10,000	
Surrendered by C Ltd		
UK property losses and management expenses	16,000	66,000
Profits chargeable to corporation tax		£4,000

Notes

(a) It is not possible in the year ended 31 March 2014 to deduct the excess management expenses brought forward from the year ended 31 March 2013 before deducting the current year management expenses to arrive at the amount available for group relief. The excess management expenses of £10,000 arising in the year ended 31 March 2013 are carried forward to the year ended 31 March 2014 but may not be surrendered and are, therefore, treated as carried forward from the year ended 31 March 2014. [*CTA 2010, ss 103, 1223*].

(b) Although a company might normally relieve a trading loss and a non-trading loan relationship deficit against other income of the year before surrendering the loss or deficit, it is not obliged to do so. Thus, B Ltd could have reduced its chargeable profits in the year ended 31 March 2013 by £20,000 instead of surrendering that amount to D Ltd. [*CTA 2010, s 99(3)*].

106.2 CT   Group Relief

(c) Qualifying charitable donations, UK property losses, management expenses and non-trading losses on intangible assets can be surrendered as group relief only to the extent that in aggregate they exceed the surrendering company's 'gross profits' for the accounting period. The 'gross profits' of the accounting period are, broadly, the profits of the period without any deduction for any amounts qualifying for group relief relating to that period or any amounts of any other period. [CTA 2010, ss 99(4), 105]. Therefore, the amount which C Ltd can surrender as group relief is restricted as follows

Management expenses	40,000
UK property loss	1,000
	41,000
Deduct gross profits (before *CTA 2010, s 45* relief)	25,000
Group relief	£16,000

The amount surrendered is taken to consist first of qualifying charitable donations, then of UK property losses, then of management expenses, and finally of losses on intangible assets. The amount surrendered by C Ltd is therefore identified as the UK property loss of £1,000 and management expenses of £15,000.

C Ltd's management expenses have been relieved as follows

Management expenses	40,000
Deduct Management expenses relieved against income	(15,000)
Surrendered to D Ltd	(15,000)
Excess management expenses carried forward	£10,000

106.3 'OVERLAPPING PERIODS'

[*CTA 2010, ss 138–142*]

D Ltd has several wholly owned subsidiaries, including E Ltd and F Ltd. D Ltd prepares accounts to 30 September, the other two companies to 31 December. Their results were as follows

			£
D Ltd	year ended 30.9.13	loss	(240,000)
E Ltd	year ended 31.12.13	profit	120,000
F Ltd	year ended 31.12.13	profit	150,000

D Ltd makes a profit for the year ended 30.9.14.

The overlapping period is the nine months to 30.9.13. The surrenderable amount of D Ltd's loss for the overlapping period is $9/12 \times £240,000 = £180,000$. D Ltd surrenders the loss as follows

(i)   Surrender to E Ltd — see note (a)

   Surrender the smaller of: £

Unused part of the surrenderable amount for the overlapping period			180,000
Unrelieved part of E Ltd's total profits for the overlapping period	$^9/_{12} \times £120{,}000$		90,000
Surrender			£90,000

(ii) Surrender to F Ltd — see note (b)

		£	£
Surrender the smaller of:			
Unused part of the surrenderable amount for the overlapping period			
surrenderable amount		180,000	
deduct amount surrendered to E Ltd		90,000	90,000
Unrelieved part of F Ltd's total profits for the overlapping period	$^9/_{12} \times £150{,}000$		112,500
Surrender			£90,000

Notes

(a) The effect of the rules is to restrict the overall surrender by D Ltd to $^9/_{12}$ of its loss for the year ended 30 September 2013.

(b) Where more than one claim relates to the whole or part of the same overlapping period, the claims must be considered in the order in which they are made (determined by the date on which the claim ceases to be capable of being withdrawn). Where, as in this case, two or more claims are deemed to be made at the same time, they are treated as made in such order as the companies involved may elect. In the absence of such an election, HMRC may direct. [*CTA 2010, ss 139–141*].

106.4 COMPANIES JOINING OR LEAVING THE GROUP

[*CTA 2010, ss 138–142*]

On 1 April 2013 B Ltd was held as to 90% by A Ltd and 10% by a non-resident.

On 1 September 2013 C Ltd became a 75% subsidiary of A Ltd.

On 31 December 2013 A Ltd sells 30% of the shares in B Ltd (retaining 60%). A Ltd, B Ltd and C Ltd all prepare accounts to 31 March each year. During the year ended 31 March 2014 the results of the companies are as follows

A Ltd	Profit	£60,000
B Ltd	Loss	£(240,000)
C Ltd	Profit	£30,000

106.4 CT   Group Relief

Group relief for the loss sustained by B Ltd in the year ended 31.3.14 is available as follows

Overlapping periods					
Loss making period	1.4.13	30.6.13	1.9.13	31.12.13	31.3.14

Period for which B Ltd was a '75% subsiduary' of A Ltd ⊢————— 9 months —————⊣

Period for which B Ltd and C Ltd were '75% subsiduaries' of A Ltd ⊢ 4 months ⊣

Calculation of loss relieved
(i) Against profits of A Ltd

Smaller of:
Unused part of the surrenderable amount
for the overlapping period $9/12 \times £240,000$ £180,000
Unrelieved part of A Ltd's total profits for
the overlapping period $9/12 \times £60,000$ £45,000
Therefore, loss relieved   £45,000

(ii) Against profits of C Ltd

		£	£
Unused part of the surrenderable amount for the overlapping period			
surrenderable amount	$4/12 \times £240,000$	80,000	
deduct proportion of amount surrendered to A Ltd relating to overlapping period	$4/9 \times £45,000$	20,000	60,000
Unrelieved part of C Ltd's total profits for the overlapping period	$4/12 \times £30,000$		10,000
Therefore, loss relieved			£10,000

Summary

	A Ltd	B Ltd	C Ltd
	£	£	£
Profit/(loss)	60,000	(240,000)	30,000
Group relief (claim)/surrender	(45,000)	55,000	(10,000)
Chargeable profit/(loss carried forward)	£15,000	£(185,000)	£20,000

Notes

(a) When a company joins or leaves a group, the profit or loss is apportioned on a time basis unless this method would work unreasonably or unjustly. In the latter event a just and reasonable method of apportionment must be used. [*CTA 2010, s 141(3)*].

(b) See notes (a) and (b) to **106.3** above.

106.5 RELATIONSHIP TO OTHER RELIEFS

[*CTA 2010, ss 37, 45, 99, 105*]

B Ltd is a subsidiary of A Ltd and commenced trading on 1 April 2004. Both companies prepare accounts to 31 March each year. The results for the three years ended 31 March 2014 were as follows.

				£
A Ltd ended 31 March year		2012	Loss	(4,000)
		2013	Loss	(3,000)
		2014	Loss	(5,000)
B Ltd year ended 31 March		2012	Loss	(5,000)
		2013	Profit	10,000
		2014	Loss	(20,000)
		2012	UK property income	1,000
		2013	UK property income	1,000
		2014	UK property income	1,000
		2014	Chargeable gains	5,000

The losses can be used as follows

	Year ended 31.3.12 £	Year ended 31.3.13 £	Year ended 31.3.14 £
B Ltd			
Trading profit/(loss)	(5,000)	10,000	(20,000)
Trading income	—	10,000	—
CTA 2010, s 45 loss relief	—	(4,000)	—
UK property income	1,000	1,000	1,000
Income	1,000	7,000	1,000
Chargeable gains	—	—	5,000
CTA 2010, s 37(3)(a) loss relief	(1,000)	—	(6,000)
Profits subject to group relief	—	7,000	—
Losses surrendered by A Ltd	—	(3,000)	—

106.5 CT   Group Relief

	Year ended 31.3.12 £	Year ended 31.3.13 £	Year ended 31.3.14 £
	—	4,000	—
CTA 2010, s 37(3)(b) loss relief	—	(4,000)	—
Chargeable profits	—	—	—
Losses brought forward	—	(4,000)	—
Loss of the period	(5,000)	—	(20,000)
CTA 2010, s 45 relief	—	4,000	—
CTA 2010, s 37(3)(a) relief	1,000	—	6,000
CTA 2010, s 37(3)(b) relief	—	—	4,000
Losses carried forward	£(4,000)	—	£(10,000)
A Ltd			
Trading loss	4,000	3,000	5,000
Deduct Surrendered to B Ltd	—	(3,000)	—
	4,000	—	5,000
Loss brought forward	—	4,000	4,000
Loss (not available for group relief) carried forward	£4,000	£4,000	£9,000

Note

(a)   Losses brought forward from previous periods must be used before claiming group relief, as must losses incurred in the current period and available for set-off under *CTA 2010, s 37(3)(a)*. However, group relief takes priority to losses carried back from subsequent periods under *CTA 2010, s 37(3)(b)*.

106.6 CONSORTIUM RELIEF

(A)   **Loss by company owned by consortium**

[*CTA 2010, ss 130, 132, 133*]

On 1 April 2013 the share capital of E Ltd was owned as follows

	%
A Ltd	40
B Ltd	40
C Ltd	20
	100

All the companies were UK resident for tax purposes.

Group Relief CT 106.6

During the year ended 31 March 2014 the following events took place

| On 1.7.13 | D Ltd bought | 20% from A Ltd |
| On 1.10.13 | C Ltd bought | 10% from B Ltd |

The companies had the following results for the year ended 31 March 2014

		£
A Ltd	Profit	40,000
B Ltd	Profit	33,000
C Ltd	Profit	10,000
D Ltd	Profit	18,000
E Ltd	Loss	(100,000)

All the member companies claim consortium relief in respect of the loss sustained by E Ltd. The companies elect that the claims be treated as made first by A Ltd, then by B Ltd, C Ltd and finally by D Ltd. For each company the consortium relief available is the lowest of the following three amounts:

(i) the unused part of the surrenderable amount for the overlapping period;

(ii) the unrelieved part of the claimant company's total profits for the overlapping period; and

(iii) the surrenderable amount for the overlapping period multiplied by the claimant member's share in the consortium in that period.

[CTA 2010, ss 139, 140, 143]

A Ltd

The overlapping period is the twelve months to 31.3.14. The amounts are

	£
(i)	100,000
(ii)	40,000
(iii) $100,000 \times 25\% \ (40\% \times {}^{3}/_{12} + 20\% \times {}^{9}/_{12})$	25,000
Therefore, loss relieved	£25,000

B Ltd

The overlapping period is the twelve months to 31.3.14. The amounts are

	£	£
(i) Surrenderable amount	100,000	
Deduct loss previously surrendered	25,000	75,000
(ii)		33,000
(iii) $100,000 \times 35\% \ (40\% \times {}^{6}/_{12} + 30\% \times {}^{6}/_{12})$		35,000

106.6 CT   Group Relief

Therefore, loss relieved   £33,000

C Ltd

The overlapping period is the twelve months to 31.3.14. The amounts are

		£	£
(i)	Surrenderable amount	100,000	
	Deduct losses previously surrendered (£25,000 + £33,000)	58,000	42,000
(ii)			10,000
(iii)	$100,000 \times 25\%$ ($20\% \times {}^6/_{12} + 30\% \times {}^6/_{12}$)		25,000
	Therefore, loss relieved		£10,000

D Ltd

As D Ltd only became a member of the consortium on 1.7.13, the overlapping period is the nine months to 31.3.14. The amounts are

		£	£
(i)	Surrenderable amount $100,000 \times {}^9/_{12}$	75,000	
	Deduct ${}^9/_{12} \times$ losses previously surrendered (£25,000 + £33,000 + £10,000)	51,000	24,000
(ii)	$18,000 \times {}^9/_{12}$		13,500
(iii)	$100,000 \times {}^9/_{12} \times 20\%$		15,000
	Therefore, loss relieved		£13,500

Summary

	A Ltd £	B Ltd £	C Ltd £	D Ltd £
Profits for the year ended 31.3.14	40,000	33,000	10,000	18,000
Deduct Loss surrendered by E Ltd	(25,000)	(33,000)	(10,000)	(13,500)
Chargeable profits	£15,000	—	—	£4,500

E Ltd

		£	£
Loss for the year ended 31.3.14			100,000
Deduct Loss surrendered to	A Ltd	(25,000)	
	B Ltd	(33,000)	

		£	£
	C Ltd	(10,000)	
	D Ltd	(13,500)	(81,500)
Not available for consortium relief			£18,500

(B) **Loss by company owned by consortium: claim by member of consortium company's group**

[CTA 2010, ss 133, 146, 148]

A Ltd owns 100% of the share capital of B Ltd

B Ltd owns 40% of the share capital of D Ltd

C Ltd owns 60% of the share capital of D Ltd

D Ltd owns 100% of the share capital of E Ltd

D Ltd owns 100% of the share capital of F Ltd

This can be shown as follows

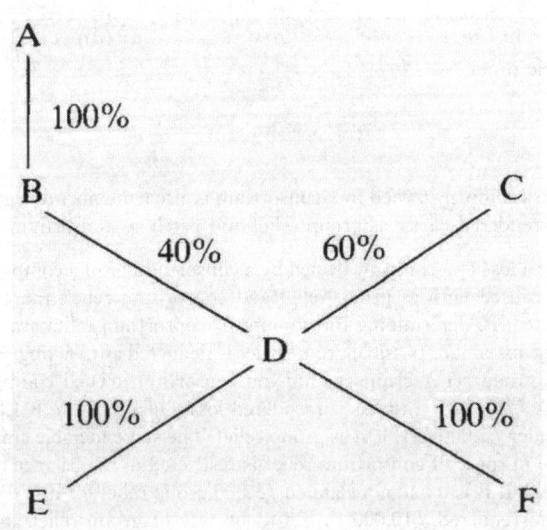

There are two groups, A and B, and D, E and F. D is owned by a consortium of B and C. This relationship has existed for a number of years with all companies having the same accounting periods. None of the companies has any losses brought forward.

The companies have the following results for year ended 31 July 2013

A Ltd	£100,000 profit
B Ltd	£(30,000) loss
C Ltd	£Nil
D Ltd	£(20,000) loss
E Ltd	£10,000 profit
F Ltd	£(3,000) loss

106.6 CT   Group Relief

E Ltd claims group relief as follows

			£	£
Profit				10,000
Deduct Group relief: loss surrendered by F Ltd	(note (b))	3,000	
Group relief: loss surrendered by D Ltd	(note (b))	7,000	(10,000)
				—

A Ltd can claim group relief and consortium relief as follows

			£	£
Profit				100,000
Deduct Group relief: loss surrendered by B Ltd	(note (c))	30,000	
Consortium relief: loss surrendered by D Ltd	(note (d))	5,200	(35,200)
Chargeable profit				£64,800

Notes

(a)   Where a company owned by a consortium is also a member of a group, its losses may be surrendered partly as group relief and partly as consortium relief.

(b)   Where a loss of a company owned by a consortium or of a company within its group may be used both as group relief and consortium relief, the consortium relief is restricted. In determining the amount of consortium relief available, it is assumed that the maximum possible group relief is deducted after taking account of any other actual group relief claims within the consortium owned company's group. [*CTA 2010, s 148*]. As F Ltd has surrendered losses of £3,000 to E Ltd, D Ltd can only surrender £7,000 to E Ltd as group relief. The surrenderable amount for the period for the purpose of consortium relief is restricted to the balance of D Ltd's loss, i.e. £13,000. If E Ltd had not claimed £3,000 group relief for F Ltd's loss, D Ltd could have surrendered £10,000 to E Ltd by way of group relief and this would have reduced D Ltd's surrenderable amount for consortium relief purposes to £10,000.

(c)   Group relief available to A Ltd is the lower of £100,000 and £30,000.

(d)   Consortium relief available to A Ltd is the lower of £13,000 (the unused surrenderable amount for the period), £70,000 (its unrelieved profits for the period (£100,000 less £30,000 group relief previously claimed) and £5,200 (40% of £13,000). The relief available to A Ltd is the same as that which B Ltd could have claimed if it had had sufficient profits. A Ltd could also have claimed consortium relief in respect of F Ltd's loss if that had exceeded the £10,000 necessary to cover E Ltd's profit. [*CTA 2010, s 133(1), 146*].

Group Relief CT 106.6

(C) **Loss by subsidiary of company owned by consortium**

[CTA 2010, ss 143, 151(4), 153(3)]

Throughout 2013 the share capital of E Ltd was owned as follows

	%
A Ltd	35
B Ltd	30
C Ltd	25
D Ltd	10
	100

E Ltd owned 90% of the share capital of F Ltd, a trading company. The companies had the following results for the year ended 31 December 2013.

		£
A Ltd	Profit	100,000
B Ltd	Loss	(40,000)
C Ltd	Profit	30,000
D Ltd	Profit	80,000
E Ltd	Profit	40,000
F Ltd	Loss	(240,000)

All the above companies were UK resident for tax purposes.

Group relief of £40,000 of the loss sustained by F Ltd is claimed by E Ltd (note (c)).

Consortium relief for the loss sustained by F Ltd would be available as follows

	A Ltd	B Ltd	C Ltd	D Ltd
	£	£	£	£
Profits for the year ended 31.12.13	100,000	—	30,000	80,000
Deduct Loss surrendered by				
F Ltd (note (a))	(70,000)	—	(30,000)	(20,000)
Chargeable profits	£30,000	—	—	£60,000

	Losses
	£ £

F Ltd

Loss for the year ended 31.12.123	240,000
Deduct Loss surrendered to E Ltd	(40,000)
Available for consortium relief	200,000
Deduct Loss surrendered to A Ltd	(70,000)

106.6 CT   Group Relief

	C Ltd	(30,000)	
	D Ltd	(20,000)	(120,000)
Losses carried forward			£80,000

Notes

(a) Loss relief for each consortium member is the lower of

    (i) the unused part of the surrenderable amount for the year;

    (ii) the unrelieved part of the claimant company's total profits for the year; and

    (iii) the surrenderable amount for the year multiplied by the claimant member's share in the consortium.

In this instance, the order in which the claims are deemed to be made does not affect the amounts which can be claimed, as (i) is greater than (ii) and (iii) in all cases.

(b) The surrenderable amount (see note (c)) multiplied by the share in the consortium appropriate to each member is

	%	£
A Ltd	35	70,000
B Ltd	30	60,000
C Ltd	25	50,000
D Ltd	10	20,000
	100	£200,000

(c) The loss available for consortium relief (the surrenderable amount) is reduced by any potentially available group relief. See also notes (a) and (b) to (B) above.

(D) **Loss by consortium member**

[CTA 2010, ss 132, 144]

A Ltd, B Ltd, C Ltd and D Ltd have for many years held 40%, 30%, 20% and 10% respectively of the ordinary share capital of E Ltd. All five companies are UK resident and have always previously had taxable profits. However, for the year ending 30 June 2013 D Ltd has a tax loss of £100,000, followed by taxable profits of £40,000 for the subsequent year. E Ltd's taxable profits are £80,000 and £140,000 for the two years ending 31 December 2012 and 31 December 2013 respectively.

With the consent of A Ltd, B Ltd and C Ltd, D Ltd can (if it wishes) surrender the following part of its loss of £100,000 to E Ltd (assuming no other group/consortium relief claims are made involving either company)

    Overlapping period 1.7.12 to 31.12.12

    Unused part of the surrenderable amount for
the overlapping period $^6/_{12}$ × £100,000   £50,000

    Unrelieved part of E Ltd's total profits for the

Group Relief CT 106.6

overlapping period	$^6/_{12} \times £80,000$	£40,000
E Ltd's total profits for the overlapping period multiplied by D Ltd's share in consortium	$^6/_{12} \times £80,000 \times 10\%$	£4,000

Overlapping period 1.1.13 to 30.6.13

Unused part of the surrenderable amount for the overlapping period	$^6/_{12} \times £100,000$	£50,000
Unrelieved part of E Ltd's total profits for the overlapping period	$^6/_{12} \times £140,000$	£70,000
E Ltd's total profits for the overlapping period multiplied by D Ltd's share in consortium	$^6/_{12} \times £140,000 \times 10\%$	£7,000

The lowest figures for the two periods are £4,000 and £7,000.

Therefore, E Ltd can claim £4,000 of D Ltd's loss against its own profits for the year ended 31.12.12 and £7,000 against its profits for the year ending 31.12.13.

107 Income Tax in Relation to a Company

107.1 ACCOUNTING FOR INCOME TAX ON RECEIPTS AND PAYMENTS

[*ITA 2007, ss 874–938; CTA 2010, s 967*]

S Ltd, a company with two associated companies, prepares accounts each year to 31 October. During the two years ending 31 October 2013 it pays and receives several sums (not being interest) from which basic rate income tax is deducted.

The following items are shown net

	Receipts £	Payments £
21.12.11		8,000
4.1.12	4,000	
9.8.12	8,000	
24.10.12	12,000	
25.3.13		8,000
14.8.13		9,600

The adjusted profits (*before* taking account of the gross equivalents of the above amounts) were

	£
Year ended 31.10.12	630,000
Year ended 31.10.13	860,000

107.1 CT Income Tax in Relation to a Company

S Ltd will use the following figures in connection with the CT61 returns rendered to HMRC and will also be able to set off against its corporation tax liability the income tax suffered as shown

Return period		Payments	Receipts	Cumulative payments less receipts	Income tax paid/ (repaid) with return
Year ended 31.10.12		£	£	£	£
1.11.11 to 31.12.11		8,000		8,000	2,000
1.1.12 to 31.3.12			4,000	4,000	(1,000)
1.4.12 to 30.6.12	(No return)			4,000	
1.7.12 to 30.9.12			8,000	(4,000)	(1,000)
1.10.12 to 31.10.12			12,000	(16,000)	–
Year ended 31.10.13					
1.11.12 to 31.12.12	(No return)				
1.1.13 to 31.3.13		8,000		8,000	2,000
1.4.13 to 30.6.13	(No return)			8,000	
1.7.13 to 30.9.13	(No return)	9,600		17,600	2,400
1.10.13 to 31.10.13	(No return)			17,600	–
					£4,400

Taxable profits

	Year ended 31.10.12	Year ended 31.10.13
	£	£
Adjusted profits as stated	630,000	860,000
Add Cumulative receipts		
£16,000 + tax £4,000	20,000	
Deduct Cumulative payments		
£17,600 + tax of £4,400	–	22,000
Taxable profits	£650,000	£838,000

Income Tax in Relation to a Company   CT 107.1

Tax payable

		Year ended 31.10.12 £	Year ended 31.10.13 £
CT @ 26%/24%/23% on profits		161,416	196,231
Deduct Income tax suffered	(note (a))	4,000	—
Net liability		£157,416	£196,231

Notes

(a) This represents tax suffered on receipts, less that which has been offset against tax deducted from payments.

	£
Tax on receipts	6,000
Tax deducted from payments and recovered from HMRC	2,000
	£4,000

(b) Payments made by companies under the following provisions do not have to be made under deduction of income tax where the company reasonably believes that, at the time of payment, the recipient is a UK company (or a partnership of such companies), a non-UK resident company trading in the UK through a permanent establishment and in computing whose profits the payment falls to be brought into account or one of certain specified bodies or persons. The provisions concerned are:

   (i) *ITA 2007, s 874(2)* (payments of yearly interest);

   (ii) *ITA 2007, s 889(4)* (payments in respect of building society securities);

   (iii) *ITA 2007, s 901(4)* (annual payments by persons other than companies);

   (iv) *ITA 2007, s 903(7)* (patent royalties);

   (v) *ITA 2007, s 906(5)* (royalty payments etc. where the owner lives abroad);

   (vi) *ITA 2007, s 910(2)* (proceeds of sale of patent rights paid to non-UK residents);

   (vii) *ITA 2007, s 919(2)* (manufactured interest on UK securities: payments to UK residents etc.); and

   (viii) *ITA 2007, s 928(2)* (chargeable payments connected with exempt distributions).

108 Intangible Assets

108.1 DEBITS AND CREDITS

[*CTA 2009, 726–744*]

(A) **Writing-down on accounting basis**

On 1 April 2010, Oval Ltd purchased an intangible asset from an unrelated company, Edgbaston Ltd, for £100,000. The asset is to be used for trading purposes and has a remaining useful economic life of 15 years. The cost of the asset is capitalised in Oval Ltd's accounts and in accordance with generally accepted accounting practice is amortised on a straight-line basis over the remaining 15 year life. On 1 April 2013, the company sells the asset to another unrelated company, Riverside Ltd, for £150,000.

Oval Ltd will bring into account for tax purposes the following debits and credits in respect of the intangible asset.

	£
Y/e 31.3.11	
Cost of asset	100,000
Debit for year (1/15 of cost)	(6,667)
WDV at 31.3.11	93,333
Y/e 31.3.12	
Debit for year (1/15 of cost)	(6,667)
WDV at 31.3.12	86,666
Y/e 31.3.13	
Debit for year (1/15 of cost)	(6,667)
WDV at 31.3.13	£80,000
Y/e 31.3.14	
Proceeds of realisation	150,000
Less Tax written-down value	80,000
Taxable credit	£70,000

As the asset was held for trading purposes, the debits of £6,667 for each of the years ended 31 March 2011, 2012 and 2013 are allowable trading deductions, and the credit of £70,000 for the year ended 31 March 2014 is a trading receipt.

Note

(a) See **108.3** below for the rollover relief available on reinvestment of disposal proceeds in new intangible assets.

108.1 CT   Intangible Assets

(B) **Writing-down at fixed rate**

On 1 January 2011, M Ltd, which draws up accounts each year to 31 December, purchases the trade of X Ltd, an unrelated company. It is agreed that, of the purchase price, £500,000 is allocated to X Ltd's brand name, which is particularly well established in the UK and the USA. The brand name is considered to have an indefinite economic life and accordingly the expenditure is not amortised in M Ltd's accounts. Before 31 December 2013 M Ltd elects to write down the cost at the fixed rate of 4% per year. On 1 January 2013, M Ltd sells its rights to the brand name in the USA for £400,000 to Z plc, an unrelated company. £250,000 of the book value of the brand name in the accounts is set off against the disposal, giving an accounting profit of £150,000, and leaving the remaining book value as £250,000. On 1 January 2015, M Ltd sells the remaining rights in the brand name to Z plc for £200,000.

M Ltd must bring into account in calculating its trading profits the following debits and credits in respect of the brand name.

	£
Y/e 31.12.11	
Cost of brand name	500,000
Debit for year (4% of cost)	(20,000)
WDV at 31.12.11	480,000
Y/e 31.12.12	
Debit for year (4% of cost)	(20,000)
WDV at 31.12.12	£460,000
Y/e 31.12.13	
Part-realisation proceeds	400,000
Less Adjusted WDV (note (b))	230,000
Gain on part realisation (credit)	£170,000
Adjusted WDV of asset after part realisation (note (c))	230,000
Debit for year (4% of cost of remaining asset (note (d))	(10,000)
WDV at 31.12.13	220,000
Y/e 31.12.14	
Debit for year (4% of remaining cost)	(10,000)
WDV at 31.12.14	£210,000
Y/e 31.12.15	
Realisation proceeds	200,000
Less WDV at 31.12.14	210,000
Loss on realisation (debit)	£(10,000)

Intangible Assets CT 108.2

Notes

(a) A company may elect for the tax cost of an intangible asset to be written down for tax purposes at a fixed rate. The election must be made in writing to HMRC within two years after the end of the accounting period in which the asset is created or acquired by the company and is irrevocable. Where the election is made, a debit of 4% of the cost (or, if less, the balance of the written-down value) is brought into account in each accounting period beginning with that in which the expenditure is incurred. The debit is proportionately reduced for accounting periods of less than twelve months. [*CTA 2009, ss 730, 731*].

(b) On the part realisation of an asset, a proportion of the written-down value of the asset is deducted from the proceeds to arrive at the amount of the credit or debit arising. The proportion is that given by dividing the reduction in accounting value (i.e. the accounting value immediately before the realisation less the accounting value immediately afterwards) by the accounting value immediately before the realisation. [*CTA 2009, s 737*]. In this case, the reduction in accounting value is (£500,000 − £250,000) = £250,000, and the accounting value immediately before the realisation is £500,000. The amount to be deducted from the proceeds in this case is therefore £460,000 × (£250,000/£500,000) = £230,000.

(c) Following a part realisation, the written-down value of the remaining part of the asset is reduced to that proportion of it that is equal to the accounting value immediately after the realisation divided by the accounting value immediately before the realisation. [*CTA 2009, s 744*]. In this case, therefore, the adjusted written-down value is £460,000 × (£250,000/£500,000) = £230,000.

(d) Following a part realisation, the fixed rate debit is calculated by reference to 4% of the value of the asset recognised for accounting purposes immediately after the realisation (plus the cost of any subsequent capitalised expenditure on the asset). [*CTA 2009, s 731(6)*].

108.2 NON-TRADING LOSS ON INTANGIBLE ASSETS

[*CTA 2009, ss 751–753*]

A Ltd is an investment company drawing up accounts each year to 31 March. The following figures are relevant for the two years ended 31 March 2013 and 2014.

	Y/e 31.3.13 £	Y/e 31.3.14 £
UK property income	15,000	16,000
Income from non-trading loan relationships	5,000	20,000
Overseas income (foreign tax paid £3,800)	20,000	—
Management expenses	5,000	5,000
Non-trading profit/(loss) on intangible fixed assets	(55,000)	11,000

A Ltd wishes to make the most tax-efficient use of the non-trading loss, and so makes a claim to set off £15,000 against profits of the year ended 31 March 2013 under *CTA 2009, s 753(1)*. The corporation tax computations for the two years ended 31 March 2014 are as follows.

108.2 CT Intangible Assets

Y/e 31.3.13

	£
UK property income	15,000
Income from non-trading loan relationships	5,000
overseas income	20,000
	40,000
Deduct Management expenses	5,000
Non-trading loss	15,000
Profits chargeable to CT	£20,000
Corporation tax: £20,000 @ 20%	4,000
Deduct Double tax relief	3,800
Corporation tax payable	200

Y/e 31.3.14

	£
UK property income	16,000
Income from non-trading loan relationships	20,000
Income from non-trading intangible assets (see below)	—
	36,000
Deduct Management expenses	5,000
Non-trading loss	29,000
Profits chargeable to CT	£2,000
Corporation tax: £2,000 @ 20%	£400

Use of non-trading loss

	£
Loss y/e 31.3.13	55,000
Set-off against profits for y/e 31.3.13	15,000
Carry-forward as non-trading debit	£40,000

Y/e 31.3.14

Non-trading profit of period	11,000
Deduct Non-trading debit brought forward	40,000
Non-trading loss set off against profits for y/e 31.3.14	£29,000

Intangible Assets CT 108.3

Notes

(a) A non-trading loss on intangible fixed assets for an accounting period may be set off against the company's total profits for the period. The company must make a claim for relief within two years after the end of the accounting period, or within such further period as HMRC may allow. Relief for the whole or part of the loss may be claimed in this way. [*CTA 2009, s 753(1)(2)*].

(b) A non-trading loss may alternatively be surrendered as group relief. See **106.2** GROUP RELIEF.

(c) To the extent that a non-trading loss is not set off against profits of the current accounting period or surrendered as group relief, it is carried forward to the next accounting period and treated as a non-trading debit of that period. [*CTA 2009, s 753(3)*]. The carried-forward loss is therefore included in the computation of any profit or loss on intangible fixed assets for that period. Where a loss results, the whole loss is available for set-off against total profits of the period. However, the debit carried forward must be excluded from the loss for the period in calculating any amount available for surrender as group relief. [*CTA 2010, s 104(2)*].

108.3 ROLLOVER RELIEF ON REINVESTMENT

[*CTA 2009, ss 754–763*]

Oval Ltd, the company in **108.1(A)** above, purchases a new intangible fixed asset (asset 2) on 1 April 2014 for £165,000 and claims rollover relief in respect of the asset disposed of in that example (referred to below as asset 1).

The effect of the claim for tax purposes is as follows.

	£
Disposal proceeds of asset 1	150,000
Tax cost of asset 1	100,000
Rollover relief available	£50,000

The taxable credit on disposal of asset 1 for the year ended 31.3.14 is therefore recalculated as follows

	£
Proceeds of realisation	150,000
Less Tax written-down value	80,000
Amount rolled over	50,000
Taxable credit	£20,000

The cost for tax purposes of asset 2 is adjusted as follows

	£
Cost of asset 2	165,000
Less amount rolled over on asset 1	50,000
Adjusted cost for tax purposes	£115,000

108.3 CT   Intangible Assets

Notes

(a)   A company which realises a chargeable intangible asset and incurs expenditure on other chargeable intangible assets within the period beginning one year before the date of realisation and ending three years after that date, may, subject to meeting detailed conditions, claim rollover relief under *CTA 2009, Pt 8 Ch 7*. The claim must specify the old assets to which the claim relates, the expenditure on other assets by reference to which relief is claimed, and the amount of relief claimed. [*CTA 2009, s 757*].

(b)   On making the claim, the proceeds of realisation of the old asset and the cost recognised for tax purposes of the other assets are both reduced by the amount available for relief. Where the expenditure on the other assets is equal to or exceeds the realisation proceeds the amount available for relief is the excess of the proceeds over the tax cost of the original asset. Where the expenditure on other assets is less than the realisation proceeds, the amount available for relief is the excess of the expenditure over the tax cost of the original asset. The relief does not affect the tax treatment of the other parties to the transactions. [*CTA 2009, s 758*].

(c)   In this case, the relief available is £50,000, leaving £20,000 of the gain on realisation chargeable. This effectively recovers the debits previously given in respect of the asset (£6,667 × 3 = £20,000, see **108.1(A)** above). Only the profit element is rolled over.

109 Interest on Overpaid Tax

[*ICTA 1988, ss 825, 826; FA 1989, s 178; FA 1991, Sch 15 para 22, 23; SI 1989 No 1297; SI 1993 No 2212*]

109.1 (A) REPAYMENT OF TAX: GENERAL

[*SI 1998 No 3175 and SI 1998 No 3176*]

X Ltd prepares accounts to 31 December. On 15 June 2013 it submits its tax return for the year ended 31 December 2012 showing a corporation tax liability for the period of £14,000, and accompanied by a payment of £7,000. On 1 October 2013 it makes a further payment of £7,000. It subsequently submits an amended return showing a reduced liability of £12,500, and £1,500 is repaid to the company on 1 December 2013.

X Ltd will be entitled to interest on overpaid tax, calculated as follows

		£
15.6.13 to 30.9.13	£7,000 × 0.5% × $^{108}/_{365}$ =	10.36
1.10.13 to 30.11.13	£1,500 × 0.5% × $^{86}/_{365}$ =	1.77
Total interest		**£12.13**

Note

(a) The rate of interest on corporation tax paid early is the special (usually) higher rate applying to overpaid instalment payments (see (B) below). The special rate does not apply to overpaid tax after nine months after the end of the accounting period, from which date the (usually) lower normal rate applies. At the time of writing the two rates were the same: 0.5%. This is the minimum possible rate.

(B) REPAYMENT OF TAX: INSTALMENT PAYMENTS

[*SI 1998 No 3175 and SI 1998 No 3176*]

Z Ltd has no associated companies and had taxable profits in excess of £1,500,000 for the year ended 31 March 2011. For the year ending 31 March 2012, Z Ltd pays £143,000 for the first instalment on 30 September 2011, this being equivalent to a quarter of its estimated corporation tax liability of £572,000. The same amount is paid on the due dates for the second and third instalments and on 5 July 2012 for the fourth instalment. On 3 September 2013, the tax liability is agreed at £506,800 and £65,200 is repaid to the company on 22 September 2013.

The rates of interest are assumed to remain unchanged after 29 September 2009.

The interest on overpaid tax is calculated as follows

Instalments due on quarter dates £506,800 × $^1/_4$ = £126,700

Interest on overpaid tax

£

109.1 CT Interest on Overpaid Tax

14 October 2011 to 13 January 2012
143,000 − 126,700 = £16,300 @ 0.5% × $^{91}/_{365}$ 20.32

14 January 2012 to 13 April 2012
286,000 − 253,400 = £32,600 @ 0.5% × $^{90}/_{365}$ 40.19

14 April 2012 to 5 July 2012
429,000 − 380,100 = £48,900 @ 0.5% × $^{83}/_{365}$ 55.60

6 July 2012 to 13 July 2012
572,000 − 380,100 = £191,900 @ 0.5% × $^{8}/_{365}$ 21.03

14 July 2012 to 31 December 2012
572,000 − 506,800 = £65,200 @ 0.5% × $^{169}/_{365}$ 150.94

1 January 2013 to 21 September 2013
572,000 − 506,800 = £65,200 @ 0.5% × $^{264}/_{365}$ 235.79

    £523.87

Notes

(a) Interest will not be payable before the due date of the first instalment.

(b) A special (usually) higher rate of interest for instalment payments applies from the date the excess arises to the earlier of nine months after the end of the accounting period and the date the tax is repaid. Interest is calculated using the usually lower normal rate from the date of nine months after the end of the accounting period to the date of issue of the repayment order. At the time of writing the two rates were the same: 0.5%. This is the minimum possible rate.

(c) Debit interest works in the same way as the credit interest illustrated in this example (see 110.1(C)). For example, had Z Ltd paid less than the amount of tax due at any one of the above dates, the interest payable would be worked out on the same basis but using the relevant interest rates for unpaid tax.

109.2 REPAYMENT ARISING FROM CARRY-BACK OF LOSSES UNDER *CTA 2010*, *SS 37, 39*: TERMINAL LOSSES

Y Ltd prepares accounts to 31 December. It has chargeable profits of £100,000 and £60,000 for the years to 31 December 2011 and 2012 respectively and duly pays corporation tax of £21,000 and £12,150 on 1 October 2012 and 1 October 2013 respectively. The company ceases trading on 31 July 2013 and incurs a loss in its last period of £80,000. It claims loss relief under *CTA 2010, ss 37, 39* against profits of previous accounting periods. As a result of the claim, it receives a corporation tax repayment of £16,350 on 25 July 2014 comprising £4,200 for the year to 31 December 2011 and £12,150 for the year to 31 December 2012.

Interest on Overpaid Tax   CT 109.2

Interest on overpaid tax is calculated as follows

On tax of £12,150 for year ended 31.12.12:

Date of payment	1 October 2013
Material date	1 October 2013
Interest runs from	1 October 2013

Interest runs to 25 July 2014, a total of 298 days.

On tax of £4,200 for year ended 31.12.11:

Date of payment		1 October 2012
Material date	(note (a))	1 May 2014
Interest runs from		1 May 2014

Interest runs to 25 July 2014, a total of 85 days.

Notes

(a) Where, under a *section 37* claim, a loss is carried back to an accounting period not falling wholly within the twelve months preceding the period of loss, the resulting corporation tax repayment is effectively treated as a repayment of tax paid for the period *in* which the loss is incurred, rather than for the period *to* which the loss is carried back. [*ICTA 1988, s 826(7A); CTA 2010, Sch 1 para 117*].

(b) HMRC use a denominator of 365 in calculations of repayment interest regardless of whether or not a leap year is involved.

110 Interest on Unpaid Tax

110.1 SELF-ASSESSMENT

[*TMA 1970, s 87A; SI 1998, No 3175; SI 1998 No 3176; SI 1999 No 1928; SI 1999 No 1929*]

(A) General

S Ltd (which has no associated companies) prepares accounts to 31 July. On 31 May 2013, it makes a payment of £80,000 in respect of its corporation tax liability for the year to 31 July 2012, the due date being 1 May 2013. On completing its corporation tax return, the company ascertains its total tax liability for the year to be £105,000 and makes a further payment of £25,000 on 16 July 2013. The final CT liability is agreed at £107,500 on 27 November 2013 and the company pays a further £2,500 on 5 January 2014.

It is assumed that the interest rates remain unchanged after 29 September 2009.

Interest on unpaid tax will be payable as follows

1.5.13 to 31.5.13	£80,000 × 3% × $^{30}/_{366}$	=	196.72
1.5.13 to 16.7.13	£25,000 × 3% × $^{76}/_{366}$	=	155.73
1.5.13 to 5.1.14	£2,500 × 3% × $^{248}/_{366}$	=	50.81
Total interest charge			£403.26

Note

(a) HMRC use a denominator of 366 in calculations of interest on unpaid tax regardless of whether or not a leap year is involved.

(B) Refund of interest charged

On 1 November 2013, T Ltd pays corporation tax of £100,000 for its year ended 31 December 2012. The due date for payment was 1 October 2013. The liability is finally agreed at £80,000 and a repayment of £20,000 is made to T Ltd on 1 May 2014.

The interest position will be as follows

(i) T Ltd will be charged interest on £100,000 for the period 1.10.13 to 1.11.13 (31 days). The charge will be raised following payment of the £100,000 on 1.11.13.

£100,000 × 3% × $^{31}/_{366}$ = £254.09

(ii) The company will be entitled to interest on overpaid tax of £20,000 for the period 1.11.13 (date of payment) to 1.5.14 (date of repayment) (181 days).

£20,000 × 0.5% × $^{181}/_{365}$ = £49.58

(iii) T Ltd will also receive a refund of interest charged on £20,000 for the period 1.10.14 to 1.11.14.

110.1 CT   Interest on Unpaid Tax

£20,000 × 3% × $^{31}/_{366}$ = £50.82

(C) **Instalment payments**

R Ltd has no associated companies and had taxable profits in excess of £1,500,000 for the year ended 31 March 2011. For the year ending 31 March 2012, R Ltd makes instalment payments of £110,000 (this being equivalent to a quarter of its estimated corporation tax liability of £440,000) on the first three due dates. The last instalment is not paid until 24 July 2012. On 3 September 2013, the tax liability is finally agreed at £524,800. R Ltd pays the balance due of £84,800 on 10 September 2013.

The rates of interest are assumed, for the purposes of this example, to remain unchanged after 29 September 2009.

The interest on unpaid tax is calculated as follows

Instalments due on quarter dates £524,800 × 1/4 = £131,200

	£
14 October 2011 to 13 January 2012 131,200 − 110,000 = £21,200 @ 1.5% × $^{91}/_{366}$	79.06
14 January 2012 to 13 April 2012 262,400 − 220,000 = £42,400 @ 1.5% × $^{89}/_{366}$	154.65
14 April 2012 to 13 July 2012 393,600 − 330,000 = £63,600 @ 1.5% × $^{91}/_{366}$	237.85
14 July 2012 to 23 July 2012 524,800 − 330,000 = £194,800 @ 1.5% × $^{10}/_{366}$	80.05
24 July 2012 to 31 December 2012 524,800 − 440,000 = £84,800 @ 1.5% × $^{161}/_{366}$	561.07
1 January 2013 to 9 September 2013 524,800 − 440,000 = £84,800 @ 3% × $^{252}/_{366}$	1,751.60
Interest on underpaid tax	£2,864.28

Notes

(a) A special lower rate of interest for instalment payments applies from the due date of payment to the earlier of nine months after the end of the accounting period and the date the tax is paid. Interest is calculated using the higher normal rate from the date of nine months after the end of the accounting period to the date the tax is paid.

(b) Credit interest works in the same way as the debit interest illustrated in this example (see 109.1(B)). For example, had R Ltd paid more than the amount of tax due at any one of the above dates, the interest payable by HMRC would be worked out on the same basis but using the relevant interest rates for overpaid tax.

Interest on Unpaid Tax CT 110.1

(D) **Surrenders of tax refunds within a group of companies**

[CTA 2010, ss 963–966; FA 1989, s 102]

V Ltd has had, for some years, a 75% subsidiary, W Ltd, and both prepare accounts to 30 October. On 1 August 2012 (the due date), both companies make payments on account of their CT liabilities for the year ended 30 October 2011. V Ltd pays £250,000 and W Ltd pays £150,000. In July 2013, the liabilities are eventually agreed at £200,000 and £180,000 respectively. Before any tax repayment is made to V Ltd, the two companies jointly give notice under CTA 2010, s 963(2) that £30,000 of the £50,000 tax repayment due to V Ltd is to be surrendered to W Ltd. W Ltd makes a payment of £20,000 to V Ltd in consideration for the tax refund surrendered.

It is assumed that the rates of interest on overdue tax and overpaid tax are, respectively, 3% and 0.5% throughout.

If no surrender had been made, and all outstanding tax payments/repayments made on, say, 1 August 2013, the interest position would have been as follows

		£
V Ltd Interest on CT repayment of £50,000 for the period 1.8.12 to 1.8.13	£50,000 × 0.5% =	250
W Ltd Interest on late paid CT of £30,000 for the period 1.8.12 to 1.8.13	£30,000 × 3% =	900
Net interest payable by the group		£650

The surrender has the following consequences

(i) Only £20,000 of the repayment (the unsurrendered amount) is actually made, and is made to V Ltd together with interest of £100 (at 0.5% for 365 days).

(ii) V Ltd, the surrendering company, is treated as having received a CT repayment of £30,000 (the surrendered amount) on the 'relevant date' which in this case is the normal due date of 1.8.12 V Ltd having made its CT payment on time. V Ltd is thus not entitled to any interest on this amount.

(iii) W Ltd, the recipient company, is deemed to have paid CT of £30,000 on the 'relevant date', 1.8.12 as above. It thus incurs no interest charge.

(iv) The group has turned a net interest charge of £650 into a net interest receipt of £100, a saving of £750. This arises from the differential in the rates of interest charged on unpaid and overpaid tax. (The surrendered amount £30,000 × 2.5% (3 − 0.5) × 365 days = £750.)

(v) The payment of £20,000 by W Ltd to V Ltd, not being a payment in excess of the surrendered refund, has no tax effect on either company.

110.1 CT   Interest on Unpaid Tax

Note

(a) V Ltd could have given notice to surrender its full refund of £50,000 to W Ltd, instead of just £30,000. There would, in fact, have been no point in doing so, but if W Ltd had made its original CT payment later than the due date, so as to incur an interest charge on the £150,000 originally paid, a full surrender would have produced a saving as the amount surrendered would be treated as having been paid on the due date.

111 Investment Companies and Investment Business

111.1 MANAGEMENT EXPENSES

[*CTA 2009 ss 1218–1220, 1248; CAA 2001, ss 18, 253*]

XYZ Ltd, an investment company, rents out rooms, halls and equipment to conference providers. It makes up accounts to 31 March. The following details are relevant

	31.3.12 £	31.3.13 £
Rents receivable	38,000	107,000
Interest receivable accrued gross	10,000	5,000
Chargeable gains	18,000	48,000
Management expenses		
attributable to property	20,000	25,000
attributable to management	50,000	40,000
Capital allowances		
attributable to property	1,000	500
attributable to management	2,000	1,000

The corporation tax computations are as follows
Year ended 31.3.12

	£	£
Property income		
Rents		38,000
Deduct Capital allowances	1,000	
Management expenses	20,000	(21,000)
		17,000
Non-trading loan relationships		10,000
Chargeable gains		18,000
		45,000
Deduct Management expenses	50,000	
Capital allowances	2,000	(52,000)
Unrelieved balance carried forward		£(7,000)

111.1 CT Investment Companies and Investment Business

Year ended 31.3.13

		£	£
Property income			
Rents			107,000
Deduct	Capital allowances	500	
	Management expenses	25,000	(25,500)
			81,500
Non-trading loan relationships			5,000
Chargeable gains			48,000
			£134,500
Deduct	Management expenses	40,000	
	Capital allowances	1,000	
	Unrelieved balance from previous accounting period	7,000	(48,000)
Profit chargeable to CT			£86,500

On 1 April 2013, XYZ Ltd diversified and began to provide conference services itself. The following details are relevant for the year ending 31 March 2014.

	31.3.14
	£
Income from conferences	65,000
Rents receivable	40,000
Interest receivable accrued (gross)	5,000
Conference costs	22,000
Management expenses	
attributable to property	20,000
attributable to management	73,000
Capital allowances	
attributable to conferences	2,000
attributable to property	400
attributable to management	800

Investment Companies and Investment Business — CT 111.1

The corporation tax computations are as follows.
Year ended 31.3.14

	£	£	£
Trading income			65,000
Deduct Conference costs		22,000	
Capital allowances		2,000	
			(24,000)
			41,000
Property income			
Rents		40,000	
Deduct Capital allowances	400		
Management expenses	20,000	(20,400)	
			19,600
Income from non-trading loan relationships			5,000
Deduct Management expenses	73,000		
Capital allowances	800		
			(73,800)
Unrelieved balance carried forward			£(8,200)

Notes

(a) Relief for management expenses is available to companies with investment business whether or not they are investment companies. Such expenses are deductible for corporation tax purposes for the accounting period in which they are charged to the accounts. [*CTA 2009, ss 1218–1231, 1248, 1255*]. A company with investment business is defined as 'any company whose business consists wholly or partly in the making of investments'. [*CTA 2009, s 1218*]. (It will include, for example, a trading company with shares in subsidiary companies.)

(b) The excess management expenses (including capital allowances) in the accounting period ended 31.3.12 are carried forward to the accounting period ended 31.3.13 and are set against total profits of that period. If profits in the year ended 31.3.13 had been insufficient, the excess management expenses could have been carried forward to subsequent periods until fully used. Similarly, the excess management expenses in the accounting period ended 31.3.14 can be carried forward to subsequent accounting periods. See also note (d) below.

(c) Management expenses brought forward from earlier accounting periods cannot be included in a group relief claim. [*CTA 2010, s 103(2)*].

(d) Surplus management expenses may not be carried forward if there is a change of ownership of a company with investment business and one of the following occurs:

   (i) a significant increase (as defined) in the company's capital after the change of ownership,

111.1 CT   Investment Companies and Investment Business

(ii) a major change in the nature or conduct of the business of the company in the period beginning three years before the change and ending three years after,

(iii) a considerable revival of the company's business which before the change was small or negligible.

[*CTA 2010, ss 677–703*].

112 Liquidation

112.1 ACCOUNTING PERIODS IN A LIQUIDATION

[*CTA 2009, ss 9, 12; CTA 2010, ss 626–629*]

On 31 August 2012 a resolution was passed to wind up X Ltd. The company's normal accounting date was 31 December.

It was later agreed between the liquidator and HMRC that 31 January 2014 would be the assumed date of completion of winding-up. The actual date of completion is 30 April 2015.

The last accounting period of the company before liquidation is

1.1.12 to 31.8.12	—	8 months

The accounting periods during the liquidation are as follows

1.9.12 to 31.8.13	—	12 months
1.9.13 to 31.1.14	—	5 months
1.2.14 to 31.1.15	—	12 months
1.2.15 to 30.4.15	—	3 months

Notes

(a) If the rate for the financial year in which the winding-up is completed (the 'final year') has not been fixed or proposed by Budget resolution before completion of the winding-up, the rate for thepenultimate financial year will apply to the income of that year. In this case, the final and penultimate financial years for the above accounting periods are 2015 and 2014 respectively.

(b) If the company is a close company, it may be unable, following the commencement of winding-up, to comply with *CTA 2010, s 34(2)*. It would then be a close investment-holding company (CIC) and liable to the full rate of corporation tax whatever the level of profits. This does not apply to the accounting period beginning on commencement of the winding-up providing the company was not a CIC for the accounting period immediately before the commencement of the winding-up; however, a company which had ceased to trade before commencement of winding-up is unlikely to be able to satisfy this condition. [*CTA 2010, ss 18(b), 34*].

113 Loan Relationships

113.1 TRADING PURPOSE

[*CTA 2009 ss 295–301, 304, 307–310, 328; FA 2009, Sch 21 para 2; CTA 2010, Sch 1 para 604; FA 2011, Sch 7 paras 6, 8*]

A Ltd requires additional trade finance and on 1 January 2013 enters into an agreement with XY Bank plc to borrow £100,000 for 3 years. Interest is payable every 6 months commencing 1 July 2013 at 6% per annum. Legal fees and negotiation expenses in respect of this loan paid in December 2012 amount to £2,800. The company's accounting reference date is 31 March and it adopts an amortised cost basis for all loan relationships.

A Ltd's accounts for the year ended 31 March 2013 show the following

	£	£
Turnover		1,400,000
Purchases and expenses		
(all allowable for corporation tax purposes)	900,000	
Finance Charges		
XY Bank plc – interest to 31 March 2013	1,500	
Legal fees and negotiation expenses	2,800	
Depreciation*	120,000	
		1,024,300
Net profit per accounts		£375,700

* Capital allowances for the same year are £95,000.

The company's corporation tax computation for the same period is as follows

	£
Net profit per accounts	375,700
Add: Depreciation	120,000
Less: Capital allowances	(95,000)
Adjusted profit for corporation tax purposes	£400,700

For corporation tax purposes the accrued interest on the loan with XY Bank plc taken out for trading purposes is treated as a trading expense.

113.1 CT Loan Relationships

The profit and loss charge for each of the following accounting periods will be

	Year ended 31.3.13 £	Year ended 31.3.14 £	Year ended 31.3.15 £	Year ended 31.3.16 £
'Debits'				
Expenses	2,800	—	—	—
Interest payable	1,500	6,000	6,000	4,500

This conforms to the amortised cost basis of accounting as interest will be allocated to the period to which it relates.

Notes

(a) A company has a loan relationship whenever it stands in the position of debtor or creditor in respect of a money debt. (A money debt being any debt not arising in the normal course of purchase and sale of goods and services for resale.) [*CTA 2009 ss 302, 303*].

(b) The taxation of the loan relationship follows accounts drawn up in accordance with generally accepted accounting practice, using either an amortised cost basis or fair value basis of accounting. [*CTA 2009, ss 307–310*].

(c) Interest payments on current loans for trading purposes are treated as a trading expense. [*CTA 2009, ss 296, 297, 301*].

113.2 NON-TRADING PURPOSES

Tradissimo Ltd, a trading company, bought £10,000 nominal of gilt edged securities at £94 per £100 nominal stock as a speculative venture on 1 January 2011. The gilts will be redeemed on 1 January 2014 at par. Interest at 5% is payable annually on 31 December each year. The company uses an amortised cost accounting method for all its loan relationships. The accounting reference date is 31 March.

As the purchase of the gilt-edged security does not relate to the company's trade, its income and expenditure is chargeable as income from a non-trading loan relationship. In addition to the interest the company will also be taxable on the discount which will be spread over three years.

	Year ended 31.3.11 £	Year ended 31.3.12 £	Year ended 31.3.13 £	Year ended 31.3.14 £
'Credits'				
Interest received	125	500	500	375
Discount	50	200	200	150
Income from non-trading loan relationships	£175	£700	£700	£525

Note

(a) Profits and losses from non-trading loan relationships are taxable as income from non-trading loan relationships. [*CTA 2009, s 299*].

113.3 NON-TRADING DEFICIT ON A LOAN RELATIONSHIP

[*CTA 2009, ss 456–463*]

The Beta Trading Co Ltd, which is a single company and not part of a group, made a loan to the PQR Company Ltd. This transaction did not form part of Beta's normal trade. PQR Company Ltd defaults on the loan on 1 October 2012 leaving a balance of £8,500 due to The Beta Trading Co Ltd. The accounting reference date is 31 March.

The Beta Trading Co Ltd's computations for relevant years are as follows

	Year ended 31.3.11 £	Year ended 31.3.12 £	Year ended 31.3.13 £	Year ended 31.3.14 £
Trading income	10,000	11,000	800	12,000
Non-trading loan relationship income	2,000	2,000	100	400

The £8,500 debit is set against the non-trading loan relationship credit of £100 in the year ending 31 March 2013 and the remaining deficit of £8,400 may be relieved in whole or in part in three different ways (group relief not being available).

		£
Non-trading deficit		8,400
1.	Set off against total profits of the year ended 31 March 2013	(800)
2.	Carry back against profits from non-trading loan relationships of the preceding accounting period	(2,000)
3.	Carry forward against non-trading profits of the company for year ended 31 March 2014	(400)
	Net deficit to carry forward against subsequent non-trading profits	£5,200

Notes

(a) Relief for a non-trading deficit may be claimed (to the extent not already surrendered as group relief) either:

    (i) by set-off against profits of the company of whatever description for the deficit period; or

    (ii) by carry back and set-off against profits of the preceding accounting period arising from non-trading loan relationships.

113.3 CT Loan Relationships

(b) Where relief is not claimed as in (a) above, the non-trading deficit is automatically carried forward for set-off against non-trading profits of the subsequent accounting period, subject to a claim for it to be not so carried forward, in which case it is treated as a non-trading deficit of that period to be carried forward for offset against non-trading profits of succeeding accounting periods.

(c) The £5,200 deficit balance (which income from non trading loan relationships for the year ended 31 March 2014 is insufficient to relieve) will be carried forward for relief against non-trading profits of the next and subsequent accounting periods subject to a claim as in (b) above. [*CTA 2009, s 457(1)(2)*].

114 Losses

114.1 CURRENT YEAR SET-OFF OF TRADING LOSSES

[*CTA 2010, s 37(3)(a)*]

A Ltd is a trading company with investment business (see **111.1** INVESTMENT COMPANIES AND INVESTMENT BUSINESS). Its results for the year ended 31 March 2014 show

	£
Trading loss	(100,000)
Property income	30,000
Income from non-trading loan relationships	40,000
Chargeable gains	72,000
Management expenses	(20,000)
Qualifying charitable donations	(10,000)

The loss may be relieved as follows

	£
Property income	30,000
Income from non-trading loan relationships	40,000
Chargeable gains	72,000
	142,000
Deduct Management expenses	(20,000)
	122,000
Deduct Trading loss	(100,000)
	22,000
Deduct Qualifying charitable donations	(10,000)
Taxable total profits	£12,000

Note

(a) Loss relief (other than group relief) against profits for the current year is given in priority to qualifying charitable donations. [*CTA 2010, s 189(1)(3)*].

114.2 CARRY-FORWARD OF TRADING LOSSES

[*CTA 2010, s 45*]

B Ltd has carried on the same trade for many years. The results for the years ended 30 September 2011, 2012 and 2013 are shown below

114.2 CT   Losses

	2011 £	2012 £	2013 £
Trading profit/(loss)	(25,000)	10,000	5,000
Property income	3,000	1,000	2,000
Income from non-trading loan relationships	2,000	2,000	3,000
Chargeable gains	5,600	4,700	4,000

B Ltd may claim under *CTA 2010, s 37* to set off the trading loss against other profits of the same accounting period. Assuming the claim is made (and that no claim is made to carry back the balance of the loss), the loss will be set off as follows

Year ended 30 September 2011

	£	Loss memo-randum £
Trading loss		(25,000)
Property income	3,000	
Income from non-trading loan relationships	2,000	
Chargeable gains	5,600	
	10,600	
Deduct Trading loss	(10,600)	10,600
Taxable total profits	—	
		(14,400)

Year ended 30 September 2012

	£	£
Trading income	10,000	
Deduct Loss brought forward	(10,000)	10,000
	—	(4,400)
Property income	1,000	
Income from non-trading loan relationships	2,000	
Chargeable gains	4,700	
Taxable total profits	7,700	

Year ended 30 September 2013

	£	£
Trading income	5,000	
Deduct Loss brought forward	(4,400)	4,400
	600	
Property income	2,000	
Income from non-trading loan relationships	3,000	
Chargeable gains	4,000	
Taxable total profits	9,600	

Losses CT 114.3

114.3 CARRY-BACK OF TRADING LOSSES
[*CTA 2010, ss 37–44*]

(A) **Terminal losses**

X Ltd has the following results for the two years ending 31 December 2011 and 2012 and its final period to 30 September 2013 when it ceases trading.

	31.12.11 £	31.12.12 £	30.9.13 £
Trading profit/(loss)	30,000	4,500	(30,000)
Property income	1,000	1,000	3,000
Income from non-trading loan relationships	500	500	4,000
Chargeable gains	—	1,500	2,250
Management expenses	—	(4,000)	(4,000)

The loss can be relieved as follows	£	Loss memorandum £
Period ended 30 September 2013		
Trading loss		(30,000)
Property income	3,000	
Income from non-trading loan relationships	4,000	
Chargeable gains	2,250	
	9,250	
Deduct Management expenses	(4,000)	
Trading loss (*CTA 2010, s 37(3)(a)*)	(5,250)	5,250
Taxable total profits	—	
		(24,750)
Year ended 31 December 2012		
Trading income	4,500	
Property income	1,000	
Income from non-trading loan relationships	500	
Chargeable gains	1,500	
	7,500	
Deduct Management expenses	(4,000)	
	3,500	
Deduct Loss carried back	(3,500)	3,500
(*CTA 2010, ss 37(3)(b), 39*)		
Taxable total profits	—	
		£(21,250)

114.3 CT Losses

Year ended 31 December 2011

Trading income	30,000	
Property income	1,000	
Income from non-trading loan relationships	500	
	31,500	
Deduct Loss carried back	21,250	21,250
(CTA 2010, ss 37(3)(b), 39)		–
Taxable total profits	£10,250	
Losses remaining (note (a))		=

Notes

(a) Where a loss is incurred in the accounting period in which the trade is discontinued, it may be carried back for three years prior to the period in which the loss occurred. In this example, the losses are fully utilised in the year ended 31 December 2011 but if this were not the case, they could have been carried back to the year ended 31 December 2010. Similar relief is available where the loss is incurred in an accounting period ending within the 12 months immediately before the cessation but in this case the three year carry-back is limited to an apportioned part of the loss for that penultimate period. This apportionment is on a time basis, by reference to the proportion of the accounting period falling within the final 12-month period. The balance attributable to the earlier part of the accounting period can be carried back one year in the normal way. [*CTA 2010, s 39*].

(b) Losses must be set against current year profits before being carried back. If carried back, they must be carried back to the full extent possible, i.e. if losses are not fully relieved in the immediately preceding period, any balance must then be carried back to the period before that, and so on. [*CTA 2010, s 37(3)(4)*].

Losses CT 114.3

(B) **Accounting periods of different lengths**

Y Ltd, which previously made up accounts to 31 March, changed its accounting date to 31 December. Its results for the three accounting periods up to 31 December 2013 were as follows

	12 months 31.3.12 £	9 months 31.12.12 £	12 months 31.12.13 £
Trading profit/(loss)	5,500	9,000	(66,000)
Income from non-trading loan relationships	2,500	3,000	—
Chargeable gains	—	—	2,000

Y Ltd makes all available loss relief claims so as to obtain relief against the earliest possible profits.

The computations are summarised as follows

	12 months 31.3.12 £	9 months 31.12.12 £	12 months 31.12.13 £
Trading income	5,500	9,000	—
Income from non-trading loan relationships	2,500	3,000	—
Chargeable gains	—	—	2,000
	8,000	12,000	2,000
Loss relief			
CTA 2010, s 37(3)(a)			(2,000)
CTA 2010, s 37(3)(b)	(2,000)	(12,000)	—
Taxable total profits	£6,000	—	—

Loss memoranda

	12 months 31.12.13 £
Trading loss	66,000
Relieved against current year profits	(2,000)
Relieved by carry-back:	
To p/e 31.12.12	(12,000)
To y/e 31.3.12	(2,000)
Carried forward under *CTA 2010, s 45*	£50,000

114.3 CT Losses

Note

(a) Relief under *CTA 2010, s 37(3)(b)* (carry-back of losses) is not restricted by reference to the length of the accounting period of loss. However, where a loss is carried back to an accounting period falling partly outside the carry-back period, relief is restricted to an appropriate proportion of profits. [*CTA 2010, s 38*]. In this example, the one-year period, as regards the loss for the year to 31 December 2013, begins on 1 January 2012 and, therefore, only three-twelfths of the profit for the year to 31 March 2012 can be relieved.

114.4 LOSSES ON UNLISTED SHARES

[*CTA 2010, ss 68–90*]

Z Ltd has been an investment company since its incorporation in 1973. It is not part of a trading group and has no associated companies. It makes up accounts to 31 December. On 6 February 2013, Z Ltd disposed of part of its holding of shares in T Ltd for full market value. Z Ltd makes no global re-basing election under *TCGA 1992, s 35(5)*.

Details of disposal	
Contract date	6.2.13
Shares sold	2,000 Ord
Proceeds (after expenses)	£4,500

Z acquired its shares in T Ltd as follows

				£
6.4.81 subscribed for	1,000	shares	cost (with expenses)	5,000
6.4.91 acquired	1,500	shares	cost (with expenses)	4,000
	2,500			£9,000

T Ltd shares were valued at £3 per share at 31 March 1982. T Ltd has been a UK resident trading company since 1980. Its shares are not quoted on a recognised stock exchange.

Z Ltd may claim that part of the loss incurred be set off against its income as follows

Identification on last in, first out basis

(i) Shares acquired 6.4.91 (not subscribed for)

£

Proceeds of 1,500 shares

$$\frac{1,500}{2,000} \times £4,500 \qquad 3,375$$

Cost of 1,500 shares	(4,000)
Capital loss *not* available for set-off against income	£(625)

		Cost basis £	31.3.82 value basis £
(ii) Shares acquired 6.4.81 (subscribed for)			
Proceeds of 500 shares	$\frac{500}{2{,}000} \times £4{,}500$	1,125	1,125
Cost of 500 shares		(2,500)	
31.3.82 value		—	(1,500)
		£(1,375)	£(375)
Capital loss available for set-off against income			£(375)

Notes

(a) A claim under *CTA 2010, s 70* is restricted to the loss in respect of the shares *subscribed* for.

(b) The claim must be submitted within two years of the end of the accounting period in which the loss was incurred.

(c) The loss of £375 is available primarily against income of the year ended 31 December 2013, with any balance being available against, broadly speaking, income of the 12 months ended 31 December 2012.

(d) See IT 14.5 LOSSES and CGT 216.3 LOSSES for further examples on this topic.

114.5 RESTRICTION OF TRADING LOSSES ON RECONSTRUCTION WITHOUT CHANGE OF OWNERSHIP

[*CTA 2010, ss 940A–953; FA 2011, Sch 5 para 3*]

(A) **Transfer of trade**

A Ltd and B Ltd are two wholly-owned subsidiaries of X Ltd. All are within the charge to corporation tax, although A Ltd has accumulated trading losses brought forward and unrelieved of £200,000 and has not paid tax for several years. As part of a group reorganisation, A Ltd's trade is transferred to B Ltd on 31 October 2013.

A Ltd's balance sheet immediately before the transfer is as follows

	£		£
Share capital	100,000	Property	90,000
Debenture secured on property	50,000	Plant	20,000
		Stock	130,000
Group loan	10,000	Trade debtors	120,000
Trade creditors	300,000		
Bank overdraft	60,000		

114.5 CT   Losses

	520,000	
Deficit on reserves	(160,000)	
	£360,000	£360,000

Book values represent the approximate open market values of assets. B Ltd takes over the stock and plant to continue the trade, paying £150,000 to A Ltd and taking over £15,000 of trade creditors relating to stock. A Ltd is to collect outstanding debts and pay remaining creditors.

B Ltd becomes entitled to A Ltd's trading losses as follows.

Amount 'A' (i.e. broadly A Ltd's assets not transferred to B Ltd plus any consideration given for the transfer (in this case nil))

	£
Freehold property (£90,000 − £50,000)	40,000
Trade debtors	120,000
Consideration from B Ltd	150,000
	£310,000

Amount 'L' (i.e. A Ltd's liabilities not transferred to B Ltd)

	£
Bank overdraft	60,000
Group loan	10,000
Trade creditors (£300,000 − £15,000)	285,000
	£355,000

Trading losses transferable with trade

£200,000 − £(355,000 − 310,000) = £155,000

Notes

(a)   Where amount L exceeds amount A the amount of relief given to the successor for losses of the predecessor carried forward is reduced by the excess of L over A. [*CTA 2010, ss 945–947*].

(b)   Assets taken over by the successor to the trade are not included in amount A. Loan stock is not included in amount L, but where the loan is secured on an asset which is not transferred, the value of the asset is reduced by the amount secured.

(c)   The assumption by B Ltd of liability for £15,000 of trade creditors does not constitute the giving of consideration and is not, therefore, a included in amount A. Amount L is, however, reduced by the amount taken over.

Losses   CT 114.5

(B) **Transfer of part of a trade**

D Ltd and E Ltd are wholly-owned subsidiaries of X Ltd. On 1 November 2013 D Ltd transfers the manufacturing part of what has been an integrated trade to E Ltd. D Ltd has accumulated trading losses brought forward and unrelieved of £150,000, of which £50,000 are attributable to the manufacturing operations.

Immediately before the transfer D Ltd's balance sheet is as follows

	£			£
Share capital	100,000	Property	— shops	110,000
Share premium	18,000		— factory	70,000
Loan stock	50,000	Plant		45,000
Trade creditors	290,000	Vehicles		20,000
Bank overdraft	42,000	Stock		30,000
	500,000	Trade debtors		65,000
Deficit on reserves	(160,000)			
	£340,000			£340,000

Book values represent the approximate open market value of assets. E Ltd takes over the manufacturing business together with the factory, plant and £18,000 of stock for a total consideration of £134,000.

Approximately 60% of D Ltd's turnover relates to manufacturing, and it is agreed that trade debtors and creditors are proportional to turnover.

Amount A (see A above) apportioned to the trade transferred is

	£
Trade debtors (60%)	39,000
Consideration received from E Ltd	134,000
	£173,000

Amount L apportioned to the trade is

	£
Trade creditors (60%)	174,000
Overdraft (33%) note (a)	14,000
	£188,000

Tax losses transferable are restricted to

£50,000 − £(188,000 − 173,000) = £35,000

114.5 CT   Losses

Notes

(a) On the transfer of part of a trade, such apportionments of receipts, expenses, assets or liabilities are made as may be just and reasonable. [*CTA 2010, s 952(1)*]. It is assumed that it is reasonable to apportion trade debtors and creditors in proportion to turnover and the overdraft in proportion to losses.

(b) Loan stock, share premium and share capital are not relevant liabilities unless they have arisen in replacing relevant liabilities within the preceding year.

(c) If the trade were transferred as a whole for market value of the assets, no restriction would apply to the losses transferable.

114.6 PROPERTY BUSINESS LOSSES

[*CTA 2010, ss 62–67*]

JW Ltd, an investment company, has the following results for the three years ended 30 April 2013:

	y/e 30.4.11 £	y/e 30.4.12 £	y/e 30.4.13 £
Income from non-trading loan relationships	6,000	6,000	6,000
Property profit/(loss)	(7,500)	2,000	(8,500)
Management expenses	300	300	500

In view of the continuing losses, JW Ltd closes down its UK property business on 30 April 2013. It sells its properties in the year ended 30 April 2014, realising chargeable gains of £155,000. The company has income from non-trading loan relationships for that year of £6,000 and incurs management expenses of £600.

The company's profits chargeable to corporation tax for the four years are as follows.

	£	£
y/e 30.4.11		
Income from non-trading loan relationships		6,000
Deduct management expenses	300	
Property loss (restricted)	5,700	6,000
Taxable total profits		Nil
y/e 30.4.12		
Income from non-trading loan relationships		6,000
Property income		2,000
		8,000
Deduct management expenses	300	

Property loss (y/e 30.4.11)	1,800	2,100
Taxable total profits		£5,900

y/e 30.4.13

Income from non-trading loan relationships		6,000
Deduct management expenses	500	
Property loss (restricted)	5,500	6,000
Taxable total profits		Nil

y/e 30.4.14

Income from non-trading loan relationships	6,000
Chargeable gains	155,000
	161,000
Deduct management expenses	3,600
Taxable total profits	£157,400

Loss memorandum

	£
Loss for y/e 30.4.11	7,500
Used y/e 30.4.11	5,700
Used y/e 30.4.12	1,800
	Nil

	£
Loss for y/e 30.4.13	8,500
Used y/e 30.4.13	5,500
Carried forward as management expenses (relieved y/e 30.4.14)	£3,000

Notes

(a) Relief for UK property business losses is only available where the UK property business is carried on as a commercial business or in the exercise of a statutory function.

(b) As A Ltd is a company with investment business, on ceasing the UK property business, the unrelieved losses of £3,000 are treated as excess management expenses. [*CTA 2010, s 63*].

115 Payment of Tax

Cross-reference. See **109.1** and **110.1** for interest on overpaid and unpaid tax, and **118.1** and **118.2** for returns and filing dates.

115.1 PAYMENTS BY LARGE COMPANIES

[*TMA 1970, ss 59D, 59E; CTA 2010, Sch 1 para 155; SI 1998 No 3175; SI 1999 No 1929*]

(A) Large companies

BG Ltd, which has five associated companies, draws up accounts to 31 December each year. Its taxable profits and tax liabilities are as follows

Accounting period ended	Profits £	Tax £
31.12.07	240,000	22,500
31.12.08	260,000	20,000
31.12.09	275,000	25,000
31.12.10	255,000	9,500
31.12.11	270,000	68,000
31.12.12	260,000	60,000
31.12.13	200,000	40,000

Assuming that the upper limit does not change, it will be as follows

£1,500,000 ÷ 6 = £250,000

Year ended 31.12.07

The company is not large as its profits do not exceed the upper limit.

Year ended 31.12.08

Although the company's profits exceed the upper limit, it will not have to make quarterly instalments payments because it was not large during the previous twelve months.

Year ended 31.12.09

The company is a large company in this period as it would have been a large company in the previous year but for the exclusion in *SI 1998 No 3175, reg 3*.

Year ended 31.12.10

Although the company's profits exceed the upper limit, its tax liability does not exceed £10,000 so it is not a large company.

Year ended 31.12.11

Although the company's profits exceed the upper limit, it will not have to make quarterly instalment payments because it was not large during the previous twelve months.

115.1 CT   Payment of Tax

Year ended 31.12.12

The company is a large company in this period as it would have been a large company in the previous year but for the exclusion in *SI 1998 No 3175, reg 3*.

Year ended 31.12.13

The company is not large as its profits do not exceed the upper limit.

Notes

(a) A company is 'large' for the purpose of quarterly instalment payments (see B below) if its augmented profits for an accounting period exceed the *CTA 2010, s 24* 'upper limit' which is in force at the end of that period. This is currently £1,500,000 divided by one plus the number of associated companies. It is proportionately reduced where the accounting period is less than 12 months. 'Augmented profits' mean total profits chargeable to corporation tax plus franked investment income received otherwise than from other group members.

(b) A company is not large in an accounting period for which its total corporation tax liability (reduced by any deductions from payments in the period under the construction industry tax scheme) does not exceed £10,000, proportionately reduced if the accounting period is less than twelve months, or if its profits do not exceed £10,000,000 provided it was not a large company (disregarding this exclusion) in the previous 12-month period.

(B) Instalment payments

HP Ltd, a large company, draws up accounts to 30 September each year. The company's return for the year ended 30 September 2013 shows total taxable profits of £4,000,000 and corporation tax payable £1,080,000.

Tax is due and payable by the company for the year ended 30 September 2013 as follows.

Instalments due:	£
14.4.13	270,000
14.7.13	270,000
14.10.13	270,000
14.1.14	270,000
	£1,080,000

Notes

(a) Large companies (see A above) are required to pay corporation tax by instalments. Instalments are due at intervals of three months commencing six months and thirteen days from the start of the accounting period and culminating three months and fourteen days from its end. Therefore, for a twelve-month accounting period there will be four instalments.

(b) Instalment payments are calculated by reference to the total liability of the accounting period to which they relate. Where four instalments are due, each will be one quarter of the liability. Each instalment is calculated by reference to the formula

Payment of Tax CT 115.1

$3 \times CTI/n$ where CTI is the total liability and n is the number of whole months in the accounting period plus the 'relevant decimal' (which adjusts for any odd days in the period). Clearly, an estimate of the liability will be required for making instalments before the final liability is known. Where those estimates turn out to be incorrect, interest will be charged to the extent that the instalment payments were insufficient (and interest will be paid on overpayments). Top-up payments may be made at any time. Where the company has grounds for believing that its instalment payments were excessive it may claim a repayment. For interest on instalment payments see **109.1(B)** INTEREST ON OVERPAID TAX and **110.1(C)** INTEREST ON UNPAID TAX.

116 Profit Computations

116.1 COMPUTATIONS

Y Ltd's accounts for the 12 months to 31 December 2013 show the following.

	£		£
Wages and salaries	77,500	Gross trading profit	209,160
Rent, rates and insurance	5,000	Net rents	1,510
Motor expenses	8,000	Government securities	340
Car hire	6,000	Dividend from UK company	
Legal expenses	2,000	(received 30.9.13)	4,500
Directors' remuneration	22,875	Profit on sale of investment	5,500
Audit and accountancy	2,500		
Miscellaneous expenses	2,600		
Debenture finance charges	2,450		
Ordinary dividend paid	15,000		
Depreciation	6,125		
Premium on lease written off	14,000		
Net profit	56,960		
	£221,010		£221,010

Analysis of various items gave the following additional information

(i) Legal expenses:

	£
Re staff service agreements	250
Re debt collecting	600
Re new issue of debentures (see (viii) below)	1,150
	£2,000

Miscellaneous expenses:	£
Staff outing	400
Subscriptions: Chamber of Commerce	250
Political party	100
Interest on overdue tax	250
Contribution to training and enterprise council	350
Charitable donation to trade benevolent fund	150
Qualifying charitable donations	1,100
	£2,600

(ii) On 1 July 2013, Y Ltd was granted a lease on office accommodation for a period of seven years from that date for which it paid a premium of £14,000.

(iii) Car hire of £6,000 represents the hire, under a contract dated 1 July 2013, of a car with emissions 180g/km.

116.1 CT   Profit Computations

(iv) All wages and salaries were paid during the period of account apart from directors' bonuses of £20,000, accrued in the accounts, voted at the AGM on 1 November 2014 and not previously paid or credited to directors' accounts with the company.

(v) Profit on sale of investment is the unindexed gain arising from the sale of quoted securities on 28 February 2013. The chargeable gain after indexation is £2,070.

(vi) Capital allowances for the year to 31 December 2013 are £10,000.

(vii) Debenture finance charges relate to £50,000 nominal stock issued on 1 January 2013 for trade finance at £96 per £100, carrying interest at 4.5% payable annually in arrears, for redemption 31 December 2020. The charge to profit and loss comprises interest of £2,250 and redemption reserve costs of £200 on a straight line basis. As these are arrived at under an amortised cost basis, the charges are allowable for tax purposes. The issue costs included in legal expenses (see (i) above) are also allowable.

The £340 Government securities credit relates to £4,000 nominal stock acquired in May 2012 at £4,040 with two years to redemption. It represents gross interest £360 less £20 premium amortisation charge on a straight line basis. It is thus properly chargeable as income from a non-trading loan relationship. The interest was received gross on 31 March and 30 September.

The corporation tax computation is as follows

		£	£
Net profit			56,960
Add			
Depreciation		6,125	
Directors' remuneration	(note (a))	20,000	
Subscription to political party		100	
Charitable donations	(notes (c) and (d))	1,100	
Car hire	(note (e))	900	
Dividend paid		15,000	
Premium on lease written off		14,000	
Interest on overdue tax (note (g))		250	57,475
			114,435
Deduct			
Net rents		1,510	
Government securities		340	
Dividend received		4,500	
Profit on sale of investment		5,500	11,850
			102,585
Deduct			
Capital allowances		10,000	
Allowance for lease premium			

Profit Computations CT 116.1

$$\frac{1}{7} \times 14,000 - \left(\frac{7-1}{50} \times £14,000\right) \times \frac{6}{12} \qquad \underline{880}$$

	10,880
CT trading profit	91,705
Income from non-trading loan relationships (note (g))	90
Property Income	1,510
Chargeable gains	2,070
	95,375
Deduct Qualifying charitable donations	1,100
(note (d))	–
Profits chargeable to corporation tax	£94,275

Notes

(a) Director's remuneration of £20,000 is disallowed as it remained unpaid nine months after the end of the period of account. It will, however, be allowable in the tax computation for the year to 31 December 2014, i.e. the period of account in which it is paid. See also *CTA 2009, s 1289; ITEPA 2003, s 18*.

(b) The contribution to a training and enterprise council is allowable under *CTA 2009, ss 82–86*.

(c) The charitable donation to trade benevolent fund is allowable under *CTA 2009, s 1300*.

(d) The qualifying charitable donations are deducted from the company's total profits under the Gift Aid provisions. [*CTA 2010, ss 189, 190*].

(e) The allowable proportion of the car hire expenditure is £6,000@85%

[*CTA 2009, s 56; FA 2009 Sch 11 para 47*].

(f) The proportion of the lease premium allowable is calculated under *CTA 2009 ss 217–220*.

(g) Interest on the overdue tax is treated as a non-trading loan relationship debit. The income from non-trading loan relationships for the year ended 31 December 2013 is therefore (£340 − £250 =) £90.

117 Research and Development

117.1 SMALL OR MEDIUM-SIZED ENTERPRISE

[*CTA 2009, ss 104B, 1044–1062; FA 2011, s 43; FA 2012, s 20, Sch 3; FA 2013, Sch 15 paras 12–15, 27–29*]

D Ltd is a small or medium-sized enterprise established on 1 January 2013. The company incurs qualifying research and development expenditure of £80,000 in the year ended 31 December 2013, in addition to other revenue expenditure of £50,000 (all of which would have been allowable expenditure had the company been trading). The company's total PAYE and NIC liabilities for payment periods ending in the accounting period are £14,000. On 1 January 2014 D Ltd commences a trade derived from the research and development expenditure, making a taxable profit (before adjustment for research and development relief or pre-trading expenditure) of £160,000 for the year ended 31 December 2014. Further qualifying research and development expenditure is incurred in that year of £41,000. If the company does not make a claim under *CTA 2009, s 104A* (see note (c) below) he corporation tax position is as follows.

Y/e 31.12.13

D Ltd may elect, by 31 December 2015, to be treated as having incurred a trading loss in the period of an amount equal to 225% of the qualifying research and development expenditure, i.e. £180,000 (£80,000 × 225%). There are then four possible alternatives open to D Ltd to make use of the loss. It may:

(1)   set the loss against other profits for the accounting period under *CTA 2010, s 37(3)(a)*;

(2)   surrender the loss as group relief;

(3)   claim a research and development tax credit equal to 11% of the loss (as reduced by any part of it relieved under (1) or (2)) or, if less, equal to the company's PAYE and NIC liabilities for payment periods ending in the accounting period; or

(4)   carry the loss forward for set-off against future trading income under *CTA 2010, s 45*.

D Ltd claims a tax credit as in (3) above in respect of the deemed loss for the year ended 31 December 2013. The maximum credit would be £180,000 × 11% = £19,800, but is restricted to £14,000, being the company's total PAYE and NIC liabilities for payment periods ending in the accounting period. Accordingly, part of the loss can still be carried forward (as in (4) above), amounting to £52,728 (£180,000 − (£14,000 × 100/11)).

Y/e 31.12.14

D Ltd claims for the qualifying research and development expenditure to be treated as if it were 225% of the actual amount, i.e. £92,250. The company's taxable trading profits for the year are therefore as follows.

	£
Adjusted profit as above	160,000
Less Research and development relief	51,250

117.1 CT   Research and Development

Other pre-trading expenditure	50,000
Trading profits	58,750
Less Loss brought forward	52,728
Trading profits chargeable to CT	£6,022

Notes

(a)   Relief for expenditure on research and development is available for expenditure of a revenue nature incurred by a 'small or medium-sized' company on qualifying 'research and development'. A 'small or medium-sized' enterprise is one that has less than 500 employees and either or both annual turnover not exceeding 100 million euros and annual balance sheet total not exceeding 86 million euros. A company is generally excluded if any company in which it holds, or which holds in it, more than 25% of the capital or voting rights, is not a small or medium-sized enterprise. For accounting periods ending before 1 April 2012 the company had to incur research and development expenditure of at least £10,000 (reduced pro-rata for accounting periods of less than 12 months) to qualify for enhanced relief.
For qualifying research and development expenditure incurred on or after 1 April 2012, where a claim is made, the expenditure is to be treated as if it were 225% of the actual amount. [*CTA 2009, s 1044; FA 2011, s 43(3)(13); FA 2012, Sch 3 para 2*].

(b)   Research and development relief for large companies (i.e. companies which are not small or medium-sized enterprises as defined in (a) above) is also available. Where such companies incur qualifying research and development expenditure they may claim an additional trading deduction of an amount equal to 30% of the expenditure. [*CTA 2009 ss 1040, 1064-1054*]. Tax credits, as claimed by D Ltd for the year ended 31 December 2013, are not available to such companies.

(c)   *FA 2013* introduced a new scheme for 'above the line' research and development tax credits which may be claimed by companies for expenditure incurred on or after 1 April 2013. The new scheme initially runs alongside the existing research and development reliefs, but those reliefs cease to be available for expenditure incurred on or after 1 April 2016. A company cannot claim relief under both schemes for the same expenditure, and once a company has made a claim under the new scheme it can make no further claims under the existing schemes. [*CTA 2009, ss 104A–104Y, 1040A; FA 2013, Sch 15*]. See further 117.2 below.

117.2 ABOVE THE LINE R&D EXPENDITURE CREDITS

[*CTA 2009, ss 104A–104Y; FA 2013, Sch 15*].

R Ltd, a large company has trade profits of £6,000,000 before deducting research and development expenditure of £2,000,000 for the year ended 31 March 2014. The research and development expenditure is qualifying expenditure for the purposes of both the above the line (ATL) expenditure credit and large companies' R&D relief. R Ltd's corporation tax liability will be as follows, depending on which type of claim it makes.

Research and Development   CT 117.2

	Claim for ATL R&D credit	No claim	Claim for large companies' R&D relief
	£'000	£'000	£'000
Trade profits before R&D expenditure	6,000	6,000	6,000
Qualifying R&D expenditure	(2,000)	(2,000)	(2,000)
	4,000		
R&D expenditure credit ('above the line')	200	—	—
Additional R&D expenditure relief	—	—	(600)
Trade profits	4,200	4,000	3,400
Corporation tax at 23%	966	920	782
Deduct R&D expenditure credit (ATL)	(200)	—	—
Corporation tax payable	766	920	782

Notes

(a) *FA 2013* introduced a new scheme for 'above the line' research and development tax credits which may be claimed by companies for expenditure incurred on or after 1 April 2013. The new scheme initially runs alongside the existing research and development reliefs, but those reliefs cease to be available for expenditure incurred on or after 1 April 2016. A company cannot claim relief under both schemes for the same expenditure, and once a company has made a claim under the new scheme it can make no further claims under the existing schemes. [*CTA 2009, ss 104A–104Y, 1040A; FA 2013, Sch 15*].

(b) Where a company claims ATL R&D expenditure credit, the amount of the credit is included as a receipt in the company's tax computation. The amount of the credit is 10% of the qualifying expenditure (49% in the case of a ring fence trade). [*CTA 2009, ss 104A, 104M; FA 2013, Sch 15 para 1*]. The tax credit is set off against the company's corporation tax liability for the period. If the credit exceeds the corporation tax liability then a set order of set applies, which allows for it to be surrendered as group relief, as well as carried forward, or back, against the company's tax liability for other accounting periods. See *CTA 2009, s 104N*.

118 Returns

118.1 RETURN PERIODS
[*FA 1998, Sch 18 paras 3–7*]

(A)

Aquarius Ltd has always prepared its accounts to 31 October. In 2013, it changes its accounting date, preparing accounts for the nine months to 31 July 2013. On 31 January 2013, HMRC issues a notice specifying a return period of 1 November 2011 to 31 October 2012. On 31 January 2014, they issue a notice specifying a return period of 1 November 2012 to 31 October 2013.

In respect of the first-mentioned notice, Aquarius Ltd is required to make a return for the period 1.11.11 to 31.10.12 accompanied by accounts and tax computations for that period.

In respect of the second of the above-mentioned notices, the company is required to make a return for the period 1.11.12 to 31.7.13 accompanied by accounts and tax computations for that period. [*FA 1998, Sch 18 para 5(1)(2)*].

(B)

Pisces Ltd has always prepared its accounts to 31 December. In 2013, it changes its accounting date, preparing accounts for the nine months to 30 September 2013. On 15 December 2013, HMRC issue a notice specifying a return period of 1 October 2012 to 30 September 2013.

Pisces Ltd is required to make returns both for the period 1.1.12 to 31.12.12 and for the period 1.1.13 to 30.9.13, each return being accompanied by accounts and tax computations for the period covered by it. [*FA 1998, Sch 18 para 5(1)(2)*].

(C)

Aries Ltd has always prepared accounts to 31 October. After 2012, it changes its accounting date, preparing accounts for the fifteen months to 31 January 2014. On 21 August 2013, HMRC issue a notice specifying a return period of 1 November 2011 to 31 October 2012. On 31 January 2013, they issue a notice specifying a return period of 1 November 2012 to 31 October 2013.

In respect of the first-mentioned notice, Aries Ltd is required to make a return for the period 1.11.11 to 31.10.12 accompanied by accounts and tax computations for that period.

In respect of the second of the above-mentioned notices, the company is required to make a return for the accounting period 1.11.12 to 31.10.13, accompanied by accounts and tax computations for the period of account 1.11.12 to 31.1.14. [*FA 1998, Sch 18 para 5(1)(3)*].

(D)

Taurus Ltd has always prepared accounts to 31 October. After 2012, it changes its accounting date, preparing accounts for the fifteen months to 31 January 2014. On 31 January 2013, HMRC issue a notice specifying a return period of 1 November 2011 to 31 October 2012. On 1 April 2013, HMRC issue a notice specifying a return period of 1 November 2012 to 31 January 2013.

118.1 CT Returns

In respect of the first-mentioned notice, the position is as in (C) above.

In respect of the second of the above-mentioned notices, Taurus Ltd is not required to make a return, but should notify HMRC of the correct accounting dates and periods. [*FA 1998, Sch 18 para 5(3)(5)*].

(E)

Gemini Ltd was incorporated on 1 July 2010 but remains dormant until 1 April 2012 when it begins to trade. The first trading accounts are prepared for the year to 31 March 2013 and the company retains that accounting date. On 1 May 2014, HMRC issue notices specifying return periods of 1 July 2010 to 30 June 2011, 1 July 2011 to 30 June 2012, 1 July 2012 to 30 June 2013 and 1 July 2013 to 31 March 2014.

In respect of the notice for the period 1.7.10 to 30.6.11, Gemini Ltd is required to make a return for that period.

In respect of the notice for the period 1.7.11 to 30.6.12, the company is required to make a return for the period 1.7.11 to 31.3.12.

In respect of the notice for the period 1.7.12 to 30.6.13, the company is required to make a return for the period 1.4.12 to 31.3.13 accompanied by accounts and tax computations for that period.

In respect of the notice for the period 1.7.13 to 31.3.14, the company is required to make a return for the period 1.4.12 to 31.3.13 accompanied by accounts and tax computations for that period. [*FA 1998, Sch 18 para 5(1)(2)*].

118.2 FILING DATES

[*FA 1998, Sch 18 para 14*]

The final dates for the filing with HMRC of the returns in **118.1** above, and for the payment of corporation tax (assuming none of the companies concerned falls within the definition of a 'large company' to which the instalment payment provisions apply—see **115.1** PAYMENT OF TAX), are as follows

Return period	Filing date		Payment date (note (f))
119.1(A) above			
1.11.11 – 31.10.12	31.10.13	(note (a))	1.8.13
1.11.12 – 31.7.13	31.7.14		1.5.14
119.1(B) above			
1.1.12 – 31.12.12	15.3.14	(note (b))	1.10.13
1.1.13 – 30.9.13	30.9.14		1.7.14
119.1(C) above			
1.11.11 – 31.10.12	21.11.13	(note (b))	1.8.13
1.11.12 – 31.10.13	31.1.15	(note (c))	1.8.14

Returns   CT 118.2

Return period	Filing date	Payment date
119.1(D) above		
1.11.11 – 31.10.12	31.10.13	1.8.13
119.1(E) above		
1.7.10 – 30.6.11	1.8.14	—
1.7.11 – 31.3.12	1.8.14	—
1.4.12 – 31.3.13	1.8.14	1.1.14
1.4.13 – 31.3.14	31.3.15	1.1.15

Notes

(a) The normal filing date is the first anniversary of the last day of the return period.

(b) If later than the date in (a) above (or, where relevant, (c) below), the filing date is three months after the date on which the notice is issued by the Inspector.

(c) Where a company's period of account extends beyond the end of the return period, the filing date is extended to the first anniversary of the last day of that period of account. This is subject to a limit of 30 months from the beginning of the period of account, although this would come into play only in the exceptional case where accounts are prepared for a period exceeding 18 months.

(d) The time allowed for filing returns is effectively extended to the time allowed under the *Companies Act 2006* if this would give a later filing date than under (a)–(c) above. [*FA 1998, Sch 18 para 19*]. This will not be so in the majority of cases.

(e) HMRC may grant an extension, on an application by the company, if they are satisfied that the company has a 'reasonable excuse' for not being able to meet the filing date under (a)–(c) above. [*TMA 1970, s 118(2)*].

(f) Nothing in (a)–(e) above affects a company's liability to pay corporation tax within nine months and one day following the end of an accounting period. [*TMA 1970, s 59D(1)*]. See **115** PAYMENT OF TAX for the instalment payment provisions applicable to large companies.

119 Small Profits—Reduced Rates

119.1 REDUCED RATE IF PROFITS £300,000 OR LESS — MARGINAL RELIEF
[*CTA 2010, ss 18–32*]

(A)

In its accounting period 1 April 2013 to 31 March 2014, X Ltd, a trading company, has chargeable profits of £300,000 and also has franked investment income of £75,000 (representing net distributions received of £67,500). X Ltd has no associated companies.

Corporation tax payable is calculated as follows

	£
Corporation tax at full rate of 23% on £300,000	69,000
3/400 × £(1,500,000 − 375,000) × 300,000/375,000	6,750
Corporation tax payable	£62,250

Note

(a) Marginal relief applies as the augmented profits (i.e. the total taxable profits plus franked investment income) fall between the lower and upper limits of £300,000 and £1,500,000 respectively.

(B)

In its accounting period 1 April 2013 to 31 March 2014, Y Ltd, a trading company, has chargeable profits of £375,000, but has no franked investment income. Y Ltd has no associated companies.

Corporation tax payable is calculated as follows

	£
Corporation tax at full rate of 23% on £375,000	86,250
3/400 × £(1,500,000 − 375,000)	8,438
Corporation tax payable	£77,812

Note

(a) An alternative method of calculation, where there is no franked investment income, is to apply small companies rate up to the small companies rate limit and marginal rate (23.75% for FY 2013) to the balance of profits. Thus

119.1 CT   Small Profits—Reduced Rates

	£
£300,000 at 20%	60,000
75,000 at 23.75%	17,812
£375,000	£77,812

(C) Changes in the marginal relief fraction

[*CTA 2009, s 8(1)(2)(5)*]

In its accounting period 1 January 2013 to 31 December 2013, Z Ltd had chargeable profits of £540,000 and franked investment income of £60,000. Z Ltd had no associated companies.

Corporation tax payable is calculated as follows

Part of the accounting period falling in financial year 2012

		£	£
Augmented profits	3/12 × £600,000 = £150,000		
Taxable total profits	3/12 × £540,000 = £135,000		
Lower limit	= £75,000 (note (b))		
Corporation tax at full rate			
£135,000 at 24%		32,400	
Less marginal relief			
1/100 × (375,000 – 150,000) × 135,000/150,000		2,025	30,375

Part of the accounting period falling in financial year 2013

Augmented profits	9/12 × £600,000 = £450,000		
Taxable total profits	9/12 × £540,000 = £405,000		
Lower limit	= £225,000 (note (b))		
Corporation tax at full rate			
£405,000 at 23%		93,150	
Less marginal relief			
3/400 × (1,125,000 – 450,000) × 405,000/450,000		4,556	88,594
Corporation tax payable			£118,969

Small Profits—Reduced Rates CT 119.2

Notes

(a) Where the marginal relief fraction changes from one financial year to the next, an accounting period which overlaps the end of the first such year is treated as if the part before and the part after were separate accounting periods.

(b) The upper and lower limits are proportionately reduced for an actual or notional accounting period of less than twelve months.

Upper limit

Financial year 2012 $^{3}/_{12}$ × £1,500,000 = £375,000

Financial year 2013 $^{9}/_{12}$ × £1,500,000 = £1,125,000

Lower limit

Financial year 2012 $^{3}/_{12}$ × £300,000 = £75,000

Financial year 2013 $^{9}/_{12}$ × £300,000 = £225,000

119.2 A COMPANY WITH AN ASSOCIATED COMPANY OR COMPANIES

[*CTA 2010, ss 24–30*]

(A)

C Ltd has a 51% subsidiary, D Ltd. Both companies are resident in the UK. C Ltd had previously prepared accounts to 31 March but changes its accounting date and prepares accounts for the nine-month period to 31 December 2013. Its chargeable profits for that period amount to £480,000. It also receives franked investment income of £84,000 including £24,000 representing dividends from D Ltd. At no time in the accounting period to 31 December 2013 does C Ltd have any active associated companies other than D Ltd.

Corporation tax payable by C Ltd for the period to 31 December 2013 is calculated as follows

	£
Corporation tax at full rate of 23% on £480,000	110,400
3/400 × (562,500 − 540,000) × 480,000/540,000	150
Corporation tax payable	£110,250

Notes

(a) The upper and lower limits are proportionately reduced for accounting periods of less than twelve months and further reduced where the company has associated companies (other than dormant ones) at any time during the accounting period.

Upper limit

$^{9}/_{12}$ × $^{1}/_{2}$ × £1,500,000 = £562,500

Lower limit

$^{9}/_{12}$ × $^{1}/_{2}$ × £300,000 = £112,500

119.2 CT Small Profits—Reduced Rates

(b) Augmented profits for these purposes do not include distributions from within the group. [*CTA 2010, s 32*]. Thus, the £24,000 franked investment income received from D Ltd is omitted from the calculations in this example.

(B) **Changes in upper and lower limits**

A Ltd has chargeable profits of £200,000 for the 12-month accounting period ended 30 September 1994 and has no franked investment income. It had no associated company until 1 March 1994 when all of its share capital was acquired by a company, B Ltd, with three wholly-owned subsidiaries, of which one was dormant throughout the 12-month period and another was resident overseas. B Ltd acquired a further active subsidiary on 1 May 1994.

Corporation tax payable by A Ltd is calculated as follows

Part of the accounting period falling in financial year 1993

		£	£
Profits $^6/_{12}$ × £200,000	= £100,000		
Lower limit	= £31,250 (note (b))		
Upper limit	= £156,250 (note (b))		
Corporation tax at full rate			
£100,000 at 33%		33,000	
Less marginal relief			
$^1/_{50}$ × £(156,250 − 100,000)		1,125	31,875

Part of the accounting period falling in financial year 1994

Profits $^6/_{12}$ × £200,000	= £100,000		
Lower limit	= £30,000 (note (b))		
Upper limit	= £150,000 (note (b))		
Corporation tax at full rate			
£100,000 at 33%		33,000	
Less marginal relief			
$^1/_{50}$ × £(150,000 − 100,000)		1,000	32,000
Corporation tax payable			£63,875

Notes

(a) Where the upper and lower limits change from one financial year to the next, an accounting period which overlaps the end of the first such year is treated as if the part before and the part after were separate accounting periods.

Small Profits—Reduced Rates   CT 119.2

(b) The limits are proportionately reduced for an actual or notional accounting period of less than twelve months and also where the company has associated companies (other than dormant ones) at any time during the accounting period.

Upper limit

Financial year 1993 $^6/_{12} \times ^1/_4 \times £1,250,000 = £156,250$

Financial year 1994 $^6/_{12} \times ^1/_5 \times £1,500,000 = £150,000$

Lower limit

Financial year 1993 $^6/_{12} \times ^1/_4 \times £250,000 = £31,250$

Financial year 1994 $^6/_{12} \times ^1/_5 \times £300,000 = £30,000$

(c) Small profits relief and marginal relief are not given automatically, but must be claimed. The claim must include a statement of the number of associated companies, or a statement that there were none, in the relevant accounting period. (Revenue Statement of Practice SP 1/91). The claim may be made by completing the relevant boxes of the corporation tax return.

120 Transfer Pricing

120.1 ADJUSTMENTS FOR TRANSFER PRICING

[*TIOPA 2010, ss 146–230*].

(A) **Transfer pricing adjustment**

A Ltd provides management and administrative services to a number of its wholly-owned subsidiaries. All companies in the group have accounting periods ending on 31 March and do not qualify as small or medium-sized enterprises for transfer pricing purposes. For the accounting period ending 31 March 2014, A Ltd makes a charge for its management and administrative services to B Ltd of £450,000. Following an enquiry into A Ltd's return for that period, it is agreed that the arm's length value of the services to A Ltd was £600,000. An adjustment is accordingly made of £150,000 to increase A Ltd's taxable profits by that amount.

B Ltd can claim to apply a corresponding adjustment (see note (c) below) to reduce its taxable profits for the same period by £150,000 (increasing its deductible expenses to £600,000). B Ltd may also make a balancing payment to A Ltd of up to £150,000 without it being treated as a distribution or otherwise taken into account for tax purposes.

Notes

(a) The transfer pricing rules apply broadly where transactions between connected parties take place at other than arm's length prices conferring an advantage to the parties in terms of a reduction in the liability to UK tax. A transfer pricing adjustment may then be made to restore the tax position to what it would have been had the transaction been at arm's length. The regime applies to both UK and cross-border transactions. Dormant companies and small and medium-sized enterprises will, in most circumstances, be exempt from applying the transfer pricing and thin capitalisation rules. Where an adjustment is required by the provisions to increase the profits of one party, the corresponding adjustment provisions apply so that the connected UK party can make a compensating reduction in their taxable profits, and provisions allow for a 'balancing payment' to be made tax-free up to the amount of the compensating adjustment.

(b) A 'dormant' company is one which is dormant (under the *Companies Act 2006, s 1169*) throughout the accounting period ending on 31 March 2004 (or if there is no such accounting period, the three-month period ending on that date); and has continued to be dormant at all times since the end of that period apart from any transfer pricing adjustments. Very broadly, a small enterprise is defined as a business with less than 50 employees and either turnover or assets of less than €10 million and a small or medium-sized enterprise as a business with less than 250 employees and either turnover of less than €50 million or assets of less than €43 million. A medium-sized enterprise can still be subject to a transfer pricing notice.

(c) Where a transfer pricing adjustment has been made by the advantaged party (either in the return or following a determination) the disadvantaged party may claim a corresponding adjustment in applying the arm's length rule rather than the actual provision. Claims must be made within two years of the making of the return or the giving of the notice taking account of the determination, and a claim based on a

120.1 CT   Transfer Pricing

return which is subsequently the subject of such a notice may be amended within two years of the giving of the notice. (These time limits may be extended in certain cases where HMRC fails to give proper notice to disadvantaged persons under *TIOPA 2010, s 185*.)

(d) Where a transfer pricing adjustment is made, the disadvantaged company may make a corresponding balancing payment to the advantaged company. Provided the balancing payment does not exceed the amount of the 'available compensating adjustment', it is not taken into account when computing profits or losses for tax purposes or regarded as a distribution or charge on income. The *'available compensating adjustment'* is the difference between the profits and losses of the disadvantaged company computed on the basis of the actual provision and computed for the purposes of making a compensating adjustment (see note (c) above).

(B) **Transfer pricing and thin capitalisation**

On 1 July 2013, B Ltd is granted a loan of £5,000,000 at 6% interest p.a. from an unassociated bank. The loan is guaranteed by B Ltd's parent company, G plc. Both companies draw up accounts for the year ended 30 June and neither company qualifies as a small or medium-sized enterprise for transfer pricing purposes. Following an enquiry into B Ltd's return for the accounting period ending 30 June 2014, HMRC successfully maintain that, in the absence of the guarantee from G plc, the bank would not have advanced more than £1,000,000 to B Ltd. Accordingly, an adjustment is made to increase B Ltd's profits for the period by £240,000 in disallowing the interest on £4,000,000 of the loan.

G plc could make a claim (or B Ltd could claim on its behalf) for a corresponding adjustment before or after the transfer pricing adjustment is made in B Ltd's return, or following the determination so that it is treated as having paid the interest subject to the disallowance. Accordingly, provided the interest in G plc's case would not be subject to a transfer pricing adjustment, G plc could claim a deduction for £240,000 in respect of the interest paid by B Ltd. G plc can make a balancing payment of up to £240,000 to B Ltd without it being treated as a distribution or charge on income or otherwise taken into account for tax purposes.

Notes

(a) A compensating adjustment may be claimed by the disadvantaged party or by the advantaged person on his behalf before or after the arm's length provision has been applied in the case of the advantaged party (in his return or following a determination). Where a transfer pricing adjustment to disallow interest follows from the provision of a guarantee, the guarantor can claim a compensating adjustment as if it was the borrower and had paid the interest subject to the disallowance, and adjust its accounts accordingly. A claim can also be made by the lender on behalf of the guarantor. Claims must be made or amended before the expiry of the time limits in note (c) to (A) above.

(b) Where a transfer pricing adjustment applies to disallow interest and the lender claims a compensating adjustment under either *TIOPA 2010, ss 174–178* or *ss 181–184*, the interest disallowed as a deduction for the borrower is correspondingly not treated as from non-trading loan relationships income for the lending company.

(c) Where a transfer pricing adjustment applies in the case of the advantaged company, the guarantor company may make a corresponding balancing payment to the borrower. Provided such a balancing payment does not in aggregate exceed the

Transfer Pricing CT 120.1

amount of the compensating adjustment, it is not taken into account for corporation tax purposes when computing profits or losses of the guarantor or the borrower, or regarded as a distribution or charge on income. The compensating adjustment in this case is the total reduction in interest or other amounts payable under the loan subject to the guarantee (and thus treated as paid by the guarantor).

(d) See also the worldwide debt cap provisions of *TIOPA 2010, ss 260–350* under which interest relief in the UK for large groups (as defined) is restricted. The application of those provisions does not form a safe harbour for thin capitalisation purposes.

(e) See also the notes to (A) above.

Capital Gains Tax

201	Annual Rates and Exemptions
202	Anti-Avoidance
203	Assets
204	Assets held on 6 April 1965
205	Assets held on 31 March 1982
206	Capital Sums Derived from Assets
207	Companies
208	Computation of Gains and Losses
209	Double Tax Relief
210	Enterprise Investment Scheme
211	Entrepreneurs' Relief
212	Exemptions and Reliefs
213	Hold-Over Reliefs
214	Indexation
215	Land
216	Losses
217	Married Persons and Civil Partners
218	Mineral Royalties
219	Offshore Settlements
220	Overseas Matters
221	Partnerships
222	Payment of Tax
223	Private Residences
224	Qualifying Corporate Bonds
225	Remittance Basis
226	Rollover Relief — Replacement of Business Assets
227	Seed Enterprise Investment Scheme
228	Settlements
229	Shares and Securities
230	Shares and Securities — Identification Rules
231	Wasting Assets

201 Annual Rates and Exemptions

201.1 RATES OF TAX

[*TCGA 1992, ss 4, 4A; F(No 2)A 2010, Sch 1 para 2*]

(A)

Patsy, who is under 65, owns an established business and has taxable profits of £37,000 for her accounting year ended 5 April 2014. She has no other income for 2013/14 but she makes a chargeable gain (before deduction of the annual exemption) of £30,000. The gain does not qualify for entrepreneurs' relief. Patsy's capital gains tax liability for 2013/14 is computed as follows.

	£
Trade profits	37,000
Deduct Personal allowance	9,440
Step 3 income	£27,560
Unused part of the basic rate band (£32,010 – £27,560)	£4,450

	£
Chargeable gain	30,000
Deduct Annual exemption	10,900
Taxable gain	£19,100
Capital gains tax payable	

		£
4,450	@ 18%	801.00
14,650	@ 28%	4,102.00
£19,100		£4,903.00

Notes

(a) An individual's gains are chargeable at a rate of 18%. However, to any extent that gains, if treated as the top slice of income, exceed the basic rate limit (£32,010 for 2013/14), they are chargeable at 28%.

(b) See **211 ENTREPRENEURS' RELIEF** for the 10% rate applicable to gains in respect of which a claim to such relief is made.

(B)

Bradley, who is under 65, owns an established business and has taxable profits of £40,000 for his accounting year ended 31 March 2014. He has no other income for 2013/14 but he makes two chargeable gains (before deducting the annual exemption) of £17,000 each. One of the gains qualifies for entrepreneurs' relief. His capital gains tax liability for 2013/14 is computed as follows.

CGT   Annual Rates and Exemptions

Disposal qualifying for entrepreneurs' relief

	£
Chargeable gain £17,000 × 10%	£1,700

Disposal not qualifying for entrepreneurs' relief

Chargeable gain	17,000
Deduct Annual exemption	10,900
Taxable gain	£6,100
Capital gains tax £6,100 × 28%	£1,708
Total capital gains tax for 2013/14 (£1,700 + £1,708)	£3,408

Notes

(a) Gains qualifying for entrepreneurs' relief are treated as the lowest part of the gains for the year. The unused part of the basic rate band (£1,450) is set against the gain qualifying for entrepreneurs' relief even though it does not affect the rate of tax for that gain. The whole of the gain not qualifying for entrepreneurs' relief is therefore chargeable to tax at 28%.

(b) It is assumed that Bradley sets his annual exemption against the gain chargeable at 28% as this achieves the greater tax saving.

201.2 ANNUAL EXEMPTION

[*TCGA 1992, s 2(2)(4)–(8), s 3; FA 2008, s 8, Sch 2 paras 2, 24, 26, 56, Sch 7 para 56; FA 2011, s 8; FA 2012, s 34*]

(A) Interaction with losses

For 2013/14, R has chargeable gains of £16,900 and allowable losses of £4,000. He also has allowable losses of £14,000 brought forward.

	£
Adjusted net gains (£16,600 − £4,000)	12,900
Losses brought forward (part)	2,000
	10,900
Annual exempt amount	10,900
Taxable gains	Nil
Losses brought forward	14,000
Less utilised in 2013/14	2,000
Losses carried forward	£12,000

Annual Rates and Exemptions CGT 201.2

(B) **Interaction with losses and settlement gains attributed under TCGA 1992, s 87**

(i)

For 2013/14, P has the same gains and losses (including brought-forward losses) as R above, but is also a beneficiary of an offshore trust. Trust gains of £12,000 are attributed to her for 2013/14 under *TCGA 1992, s 87*.

	£
Adjusted net gains (£16,900 − £4,000 + £10,900 (note (a))	23,800
Losses brought forward (part)	12,900
	10,900
Annual exempt amount	10,900
	Nil
Add: section 87 gains not brought in above	1,100
Taxable gains	£1,100
Losses brought forward	14,000
Less utilised in 2013/14	12,900
Losses carried forward	£1,100

(ii)

Q is in the same position as P except that his attributed gains are only £6,300.

	£
Adjusted net gains (£16,900 − £4,000 + £6,300)	19,200
Losses brought forward (part)	8,300
	10,900
Annual exempt amount	10,900
Taxable gains	Nil
Losses brought forward	14,000
Less utilised in 2013/14	8,300
Losses carried forward	£5,700

Notes

(a) Attributed gains (as in (b) below) are included in adjusted net gains *only* to the extent that they do not exceed the annual exempt amount. Such gains cannot be covered by personal losses. The exempt amount is effectively allocated to attributed gains in priority to personal gains.

(b) For the purposes of (a) above, 'attributed gains' include non-resident settlement gains attributed to a beneficiary under *TCGA 1992, s 87* (as in this example) and those similarly attributed under *TCGA 1992, s 89(2)*.

202 Anti-Avoidance

202.1 VALUE SHIFTING

[*TCGA 1992, s 29*]

Jak owns all the 1,000 £1 ordinary shares of K Ltd. The shares were acquired on subscription in 1978 for £1,000 and had a value of £65,250 on 31 March 1982. In December 2013, the trustees of Jak's family settlement subscribed at par for 250 £1 ordinary shares in K Ltd, thereby acquiring 20% of the voting power in the company.

It is agreed that the value per share of Jak's holding immediately before the December 2013 share issue was £175 and immediately afterwards was £150. The value per share of the trust's holding, on issue, was £97 per share.

The proceeds of the deemed disposal are computed as follows

Value passing out of Jak's 1,000 shares is £25,000 (1,000 × £25 per share (£175 − £150)).

Value passing into the trust's 250 shares is £24,250 (250 × £97 per share) *less* the subscription price paid of £250 (250 × £1 per share) = £24,000.

The proceeds of the deemed disposal are equal to the value passing into the new shares, i.e. £24,000. (The trust's acquisition cost is £24,250, i.e. actual plus deemed consideration given.)

The disposal is a part disposal (see **208.2** COMPUTATION OF GAINS AND LOSSES), the value of the part retained being £150,000 (1,000 × £150 per share).

Jak will have a capital gain for 2013/14 as follows

	£
Proceeds of deemed disposal	24,000
Allowable cost $\dfrac{24,000}{24,000 + 150,000} \times £65,250$	9,000
Chargeable gain	£15,000

Note

(a) The legislation taxes the amount of value passing *into* the transferee holdings, not (if different) the amount passing from the transferor. The deemed proceeds are thus equal to the value received by the transferee(s). See HMRC Capital Gains Manual CG 58855.

202.2 CGT   Anti-Avoidance

202.2 VALUE-SHIFTING TO GIVE TAX-FREE BENEFIT

[*TCGA 1992, s 30, Sch 11 para 10(1); FA 2011, s 44, Sch 9 paras 1, 6*]

M owns the whole of the issued share capital in C Ltd, an unquoted company. He is also a director of the company. M receives an offer from a public company for his shares. Prior to sale, C Ltd pays M £30,000 for loss of his office as director. M then sells the shares for £100,000.

On the sale of M's shares, HMRC may seek to adjust the consideration in computing M's chargeable gain on the grounds that M has received a tax-free benefit and the value of his shares has thereby been materially reduced.

202.3 ASSETS DISPOSED OF IN A SERIES OF TRANSACTIONS

[*TCGA 1992, ss 19, 20*]

L purchased a set of 6 antique chairs in June 1991 at a cost of £12,000. He gave 2 chairs to his daughter in February 2008, another pair to his son in November 2010, and sold the final pair to his brother for their market value in August 2013.

The market value of the chairs at the relevant dates were

	2 chairs £	4 chairs £	6 chairs £
February 2008	6,000	14,000	26,000
November 2010	7,800	18,000	34,200
August 2013	10,400	24,000	46,200

The indexation factor for June 1991 to April 1998 is 0.213.

The capital gains tax computations are as follows
February 2008

Disposal to daughter

Deemed consideration	£6,000

As the consideration does not exceed £6,000, the disposal is covered by the chattel exemption (see note (a)).

November 2010

(i) 2007/08 disposal to daughter recomputed

Original market value (deemed disposal consideration at February 2008)	£6,000
Reasonable proportion of aggregate market value as at February 2008 of all assets disposed of to date	
£14,000 × 2/4	£7,000

Anti-Avoidance   CGT 202.3

	£
Deemed consideration (greater of £6,000 and £7,000)	7,000

$$\text{Cost} \frac{7,000}{7,000 + 14,000} \times £12,000 \qquad 4,000$$

Unindexed gain	3,000
Indexation allowance £4,000 × 0.213	852
Chargeable gain 2007/08 (subject to taper relief)	£2,148

(ii) 2010/11 disposal to son

Original market value (deemed disposal consideration)	£7,800
Reasonable proportion of aggregate market value as at November 2010 of all assets disposed of to date	
£18,000 × ²/₄	£9,000

	£
Deemed consideration (greater of £7,800 and £9,000)	9,000

$$\text{Cost} \frac{9,000}{9,000 + 7,800} \times (£12,000 - £4,000) \qquad 4,286$$

Chargeable gain 2010/11	£4,714

August 2013

(i) Gain on 2007/08 disposal to daughter recomputed

Original market value (deemed consideration in recomputation at November 2010)	£7,000
Reasonable proportion of aggregate market value as at February 2008 of all assets disposed of to date	
£26,000 × ²/₆	£8,667

	£
Deemed consideration (greater of £7,000 and £8,667)	8,667

$$\text{Cost} \frac{8,667}{8,667 + 14,000} \times £12,000 \qquad 4,588$$

202.3 CGT   Anti-Avoidance

Unindexed gain	4,079
Indexation allowance £4,588 × 0.213	977
Revised chargeable gain 2007/08 (subject to taper relief)	£3,102

(ii) Gain on 2010/11 disposal to son recomputed

Original market value (deemed consideration in computation at November 2010)	£9,000
Reasonable proportion of aggregate market value as at November 2010 of all assets disposed of to date	
£34,200 × $^2/_6$	£11,400
	£
Deemed consideration (greater of £9,000 and £11,400)	11,400
Cost $\dfrac{11,400}{11,400 + 7,800} \times (£12,000 - £4,588)$	4,401
	—
Revised chargeable gain 2010/11	£6,999

(iii) Gain on 2013/14 disposal to brother

Original market value (actual consideration)	£10,400
Reasonable proportion of aggregate market value as at August 2013 of all assets disposed of to date	
£46,200 × $^2/_6$	£15,400
	£
Deemed consideration (greater of £10,400 and £15,400)	15,400
Cost (£12,000 − £4,588 − £4,401)	3,011
Chargeable gain 2013/14	£12,389

Notes

(a) The disposal in February 2008 is at first covered by the chattel exemption of £6,000. As the second disposal in November 2010 is to a person connected with the recipient of the first disposal, the two must then be looked at together for the purposes of the chattel exemption, and, as the combined proceeds exceed the chattel exemption limit, the exemption is not available. [*TCGA 1992, s 262*]. See also **212.1(C)** EXEMPTIONS AND RELIEFS.

(b) The three disposals are linked transactions within *TCGA 1992, s 19* as they are made by the same transferor to persons with whom he is connected, and take place within a six-year period.

(c) It is assumed in the above example that it is 'reasonable' to apportion the aggregate market value in proportion to the number of items. In other instances a different basis may be needed to give the 'reasonable' apportionment required by *TCGA 1992, s 20(4)*.

202.4 DEPRECIATORY TRANSACTIONS: GROUPS OF COMPANIES

[*TCGA 1992, s 176; FA 2011, s 44, Sch 9 paras 3, 6*]

G Ltd owns 100% of the share capital of Q Ltd, which it acquired in June 1989 for £75,000. Q Ltd owns land which it purchased in 1985 for £50,000. In 2009, the land, then with a market value of £120,000, was transferred to G Ltd for £50,000. In April 2013, Q Ltd was put into liquidation, and G Ltd received liquidation distributions totalling £30,000.

The loss on the Q Ltd shares is £45,000 (£75,000 − £30,000). The whole or part of the loss is likely to be disallowed on the grounds that it resulted from the depreciatory transaction involving the transfer of land at less than market value.

Note

(a) Where the ultimate disposal of the shares or securities takes place on or after 19 July 2011, only depreciatory transactions occurring in the six years ending with that disposal are taken into account. Previously any such transactions occurring on or after 31 March 1982 were taken into account.

203 Assets

203.1 OPTIONS

[*TCGA 1992*, ss 44, 46, 144, 144ZA–144ZD, 145]

Cross-reference. See also 231.2 WASTING ASSETS.

On 1 February 2009 F granted an option to G for £10,000 to acquire freehold land bought by F for £50,000 in September 1996. The option is for a period of 5 years, and the option price is £100,000 plus 1% thereof for each month since the option was granted. On 1 February 2011, G sold the option to H for £20,000. On 30 June 2013, H exercises the option and pays F £141,000 for the land. Neither G nor H intended to use the land for the purposes of a trade.

2009 Grant of option by F

	£
Disposal proceeds	10,000
Allowable cost	—
Chargeable gain 2008/09	£10,000

2011 Disposal of option by G

	£	£
Disposal proceeds		20,000
Allowable cost	10,000	
Less: Wasted — £10,000 × $^2/_5$	4,000	6,000
Chargeable gain 2010/11		£14,000

2013 Exercise of option

(i) Earlier assessment on F vacated
(ii) Aggregate disposal proceeds
(£10,000 + £141,000)   151,000
Allowable cost of land   50,000
Chargeable gain (on F) 2013/14   £101,000

H's allowable expenditure is

Cost of option	20,000
Cost of land	141,000
	£161,000

203.1 CGT Assets

Note

(a) The wasting asset rules (see **231** WASTING ASSETS) apply on the disposal of the option by G (though certain options are exempted from these rules — see *TCGA 1992, s 144*). As these rules can only apply on a disposal, they cannot apply on the exercise of the option by H (as the exercise of an option is not treated as a disposal), so his acquisition cost remains intact.

204 Assets held on 6 April 1965

Note

The general re-basing rule for ASSETS HELD ON 31 MARCH 1982 (205) applies automatically and without exception for capital gains tax purposes, so that special rules for assets held on 6 April 1965 are not required. Accordingly, the provisions in this chapter apply only for the purposes of corporation tax on chargeable gains. [*TCGA 1992, s 35(9)*].

204.1 QUOTED SHARES AND SECURITIES
[*TCGA 1992, s 109(4)(5), Sch 2 paras 1–8*]

(A) **Basic computation of gain**

H Ltd acquired 3,000 U plc ordinary shares in 1962 for £15,000. Their market value was £10 per share on 6 April 1965 and £12 per share on 31 March 1982. In September 2013, H Ltd sells 2,000 of the shares for £40 per share. For the purpose only of this example, it is assumed that the indexation factor for March 1982 to September 2013 is 2.100.

	£	£	£
Sale proceeds	80,000	80,000	80,000
Cost	10,000		
6 April 1965 value		20,000	
31 March 1982 value	—	—	24,000
Unindexed gain	70,000	60,000	56,000
Indexation allowance:			
£24,000 × 2.100	50,400	50,400	50,400
Indexed gain	£19,600	£9,600	£5,600
Chargeable gain			£5,600

Notes

(a) The comparison is firstly between the gain arrived at by deducting cost and that arrived at by deducting 6 April 1965 value. The smaller of the two gains is taken. If, however, an election had been made under either *TCGA 1992, Sch 2 para 4* or *TCGA 1992, s 109(4)* for 6 April 1965 value to be used in computing all gains and losses on quoted shares held at that date, this comparison need not be made and the taxable gain, subject to (c) below, would be £9,600.

(b) The second comparison is between the figure arrived at in (a) above and the gain using 31 March 1982 value. As the latter is smaller, it is substituted for the figure in (b) above by virtue of *TCGA 1992, s 35(2)*. If, however, an election had been made under *TCGA 1992, s 35(5)* for 31 March 1982 value to be used in computing all gains and losses on assets held at that date, neither this comparison nor that in (a) above need be made and the taxable gain would still be £5,600.

(c) Indexation is based on 31 March 1982 value in all three calculations as this gives the greater allowance. [*TCGA 1992, s 55(1)(2)*].

204.1 CGT   Assets held on 6 April 1965

    (d)   All comparisons are between gains *after* indexation.

(B) **Basic computation—no gain/no loss disposals**

J Ltd acquired a holding of quoted shares in 1956 for £1,000. The market value of the holding at 6 April 1965 and 31 March 1982 respectively was £19,000 and £20,000. J Ltd sells the holding in September 2013 for £18,000. For the purpose of this example only, it is assumed that the indexation factor for the period March 1982 to September 2013 is 2.100.

(i) Assuming no elections made to use 1965 value or 1982 value

	£	£
Sale proceeds	18,000	18,000
Cost	1,000	
6 April 1965 value	—	19,000
Unindexed gain/(loss)	17,000	(1,000)
Indexation allowance:		
£20,000 × 2.100 (see below) = £42,000 but restricted to	17,000	—
Indexed gain/(loss)	Nil	£(1,000)
Chargeable gain/allowable loss		Nil

As one computation shows no gain/no loss and the other a loss, the disposal is a no gain/no loss disposal. [*TCGA 1992, Sch 2 para 2(1)*]. There is no need to compute the gain or loss using 31 March 1982 value as re-basing cannot disturb a no gain/no loss position. [*TCGA 1992, s 35(3)(c)*].

(ii) Election made to use 6 April 1965 value

	£	£
Sale proceeds	18,000	18,000
6 April 1965 value	19,000	
31 March 1982 value	—	20,000
(Loss)	(1,000)	(2,000)
Allowable loss	£1,000	

The allowable loss is £1,000 as re-basing cannot increase a loss. [*TCGA 1992, s 35(3)(b)*].

(iii) Election made to use 31 March 1982 value

There is an allowable loss of £2,000.

Assets held on 6 April 1965   CGT 204.1

(C) **Parts of holding acquired at different times**

L Ltd has the following transactions in shares of A plc, a quoted company

Date	Number of shares bought/(sold)	Cost/(proceeds)
9.1.57	1,500	1,050
10.11.62	750	600
15.7.69	1,200	3,000
12.10.80	1,400	5,000
16.12.83	850	5,950
17.9.95	1,150	5,200
19.12.13	(6,000)	(75,000)
	850	

Market value of A shares at 6 April 1965 was £1.60

Market value of A shares at 31 March 1982 was £4.00

Indexation factors		
March 1982 to December 2013 (assumed)		1.850
December 1983 to April 1985		0.091
April 1985 to September 1995		0.589
September 1995 to December 2013 (assumed)		0.450

(i) No election made to substitute 1965 market value

Identify 6,000 shares sold as follows

Section 104 holding	Shares	Qualifying Expenditure £	Indexed Pool £
16.12.83 acquisition	850	5,950	5,950
£5,950 × 0.091	—	—	541
6.4.85 pool	850	5,950	6,491
Indexed rise: April 1985 to September 1995			
£6,491 × 0.589			3,823
17.9.95 acquisition	1,150	5,200	5,200
	2,000	11,150	15,514
Indexed rise: September 1995 to December 2013			
£15,514 × 0.450			6,981
			22,495
19.12.13 disposal	(2,000)	(11,150)	(22,495)
Balance of pool	—	—	—

355

204.1 CGT Assets held on 6 April 1965

	£
Sale proceeds (2,000 × £12.50)	25,000
Cost (as above)	11,150
Unindexed gain	13,850
Indexation allowance (£22,495 − £11,150)	11,345
Chargeable gain	£2,505

1982 holding

	£	£
Sale proceeds (1,200 + 1,400) × £12.50	32,500	32,500
Cost (£3,000 + £5,000)	8,000	
Market value 31.3.82 (2,600 × £4)	—	10,400
Unindexed gain	24,500	22,100
Indexation allowance £10,400 × 1.850	19,240	19,240
Gain after indexation	£5,260	£2,860

Chargeable gain £2,860

10.11.62 acquisition

	£	£	£
Sale proceeds (750 × £12.50)	9,375	9,375	9,375
Cost	600		
Market value 6.4.65 (750 × £1.60)		1,200	
Market value 31.3.82 (750 × £4)	—	—	3,000
Unindexed gain	8,775	8,175	6,375
Indexation allowance £3,000 × 1.850	5,550	5,550	5,550
Gain after indexation	£3,225	£2,625	£825

Chargeable gain £825

9.1.57 acquisition (part)

	£	£	£
Sale proceeds (650 × £12.50)	8,125	8,125	8,125
Cost (650 × £0.70)	455		
Market value 6.4.65 (650 × £1.60)		1,040	
Market value 31.3.82 (650 × £4)	—	—	2,600
Unindexed gain	7,670	7,085	5,525
Indexation allowance £2,600 × 1.850	4,810	4,810	4,810
Gain after indexation	£2,860	£2,275	£715

Chargeable gain £715

Assets held on 6 April 1965   CGT 204.1

Summary of chargeable gains	Number of shares	Chargeable gain
		£
Section 104 holding	2,000	2,505
1982 holding	2,600	2,860
10.11.62 acquisition	750	825
9.1.57 acquisition (part)	650	715
	6,000	£6,905

Remaining shares
850 acquired on 9.1.57 for £595

(ii) Election made to substitute 1965 market value

Identify 6,000 shares as follows

Section 104 holding
Disposal of 2,000 shares as in (i) above   £2,505

1982 holding	Shares		Pool cost
			£
9.1.57	1,500 × £1.60		2,400
10.11.62	750 × £1.60		1,200
15.7.69	1,200		3,000
12.10.80	1,400		5,000
	4,850		11,600
19.12.13 disposal	4,000	4,000/4,850 × £11,600	9,567
Remaining shares	850		£2,033

	£	£
Sale proceeds (4,000 × £12.50)	50,000	50,000
Cost (as above)	9,567	
Market value 31.3.82 (4,000 × £4)		16,000
Unindexed gain	40,433	34,000
Indexation allowance £16,000 × 1.850	29,600	29,600
Gain after indexation	£10,833	£4,400
Chargeable gain		£4,400

204.1 CGT   Assets held on 6 April 1965

Summary of chargeable gains/allowable losses	Number of shares	Chargeable gain/ (loss) £
Section 104 holding	2,000	2,505
1982 holding	4,000	4,400
	6,000	£6,905

Notes

(a) Because re-basing to 31 March 1982 applies in this case, the result is the same whether or not the election to substitute 6 April 1965 value has been made, but with a lower 31 March 1982 value the computations could produce differing overall gains/losses.

(b) Note that indexation is based on 31 March 1982 value whenever this gives the greater allowance.

204.2 LAND REFLECTING DEVELOPMENT VALUE

[TCGA 1992, Sch 2 paras 9–15]

K Ltd sells a building plot, on which planning permission has just been obtained, in November 2013 for £200,000. The company acquired the plot in 1958 when its value was £2,000. The market value was £5,000 at 6 April 1965 and £10,000 at 31 March 1982, and the current use value in November 2013 is £15,000. For the purpose only of this example, the indexation factor for March 1982 to November 2013 is 2.150.

	£	£	£
Sale proceeds	200,000	200,000	200,000
Cost	2,000		
Market value 6.4.65		5,000	
Market value 31.3.82	–	–	10,000
Unindexed gain	198,000	195,000	190,000
Indexation allowance			
£10,000 × 2.150	21,500	21,500	21,500
Gain after indexation	£176,500	£173,500	£168,500
Chargeable gain			£168,5000

Notes

(a) Time apportionment would have substantially reduced the gain of £176,500, using cost, such that re-basing to 31 March 1982 would have given a greater gain than that based on cost and would not therefore have applied. However, as the plot has been sold for a price in excess of its current use value, no time apportionment can be claimed.

(b) Gains must be compared after applying the indexation allowance, which is based on 31 March 1982 value, this being greater than either cost or 6 April 1965 value.

(c) In this case, the gain is computed in accordance with the rules in 205 ASSETS HELD ON 31 MARCH 1982 as the gain by reference to 31 March 1982 value is lower than the gain by reference to 6 April 1965 value which in turn is lower than the gain by reference to cost.

204.3 OTHER ASSETS

[*TCGA 1992, Sch 2 paras 16–19*]

(A) **Chattels**

M Ltd purchased a painting in 1942 for £5,000 to hang on the boardroom wall. On 5 October 2013 the company sold the painting for £370,000 net. The painting's value was £129,000 at 6 April 1965, but only £125,000 at 31 March 1982. For the purpose only of this example, it is assumed that the indexation factor for March 1982 to October 2013 is 1.847.

(i) Time apportionment

Period of ownership since 6 April 1945	(note (a))	68 years 6 months
Period of ownership since 6 April 1965		48 years 6 months
		£
Unindexed gain (£370,000 − £5,000)		365,000
Indexation allowance £125,000 × 1.847	(note (b))	230,875
		£134,125
Gain after indexation £134,124 × (48y 6m/68y 6m) (note (c))		£94,964

(ii) Election for 6.4.65 value

		£
Sale proceeds		370,000
Market value 6.4.65		129,000
Unindexed gain		241,000
Indexation allowance £129,000 × 1.847	(note (b))	238,263
Gain after indexation		£2,737

Election for 6.4.65 value is beneficial, subject to re-basing.

(iii) Re-basing to 1982

		£
Sale proceeds		370,000
Market value 31.3.82		125,000
Unindexed gain		245,000
Indexation allowance £129,000 × 1.847	(note (b))	238,263
Gain after indexation		£6,737

204.3 CGT   Assets held on 6 April 1965

Re-basing cannot increase a gain. [*TCGA 1992, s 35(3)(a)*]. Therefore, the gain of £2,737 stands and the election for 6.4.65 value is beneficial.

Notes

(a)   Under time apportionment, the period of ownership is limited to that after 5 April 1945.

(b)   In (i) above, indexation is based on 31.3.82 value, being greater than cost — it cannot be based on 6 April 1965 value as this does not enter into the calculation. In (ii), indexation is on the higher of 31.3.82 value and 6.4.65 value. This is also the case in (iii) as one is comparing the position using 6.4.65 value and 31.3.82 value. See *TCGA 1992, s 55(1)(2)*.

(c)   The time apportionment calculation is applied to the gain *after* indexation (*Smith v Schofield HL 1993, 65 TC 669, [1993] STC 268*).

(B) **Land and buildings**

X Ltd acquired land on 5 June 1960 for £7,250. The company acquired access land adjoining the property for £2,750 on 1 January 1961 and, having obtained planning consent, on 30 July 1963 incurred expenditure of £15,000 in building houses on the land, which were let. On 6 September 2013, X Ltd sells the houses with vacant possession for £400,000, net of expenses. The value of the houses and land is £20,000 at 6 April 1965 and £100,000 at 31 March 1982. For the purpose only of this example, it is assumed that the indexation factor for March 1982 to September 2013 is 1.820.

The gain using time apportionment is

		£	£
Net proceeds of sale			400,000
Deduct Cost of land		7,250	
Cost of addition		2,750	
Cost of building		15,000	25,000
Unindexed gain			375,000
Indexation allowance £100,000 × 1.820			182,000
Gain after indexation			£193,000

Apportion to allowable expenditure   (note (c))

	£	£
(i) Land 7,250 / 25,000 × £193,000	55,970	
Time apportion £55,970 × (48y 5m/53y 3m)		50,890
(ii) Addition 2,750 / 25,000 × £193,000	21,230	

Assets held on 6 April 1965   CGT 204.3

    Time apportion £21,230 × (48y 5m/52y 8m)   19,517

    (iii) Building 15,000/25,000 × £193,000   115,800

    Time apportion £115,800 × (48y 5m/50y 1m)   111,946
    Gain after indexation and time apportionment   £182,353

The gain using re-basing to 1982 is

	£
Net proceeds of sale	400,000
Market value at 31.3.82	100,000
Unindexed gain	300,000
Indexation allowance	
£100,000 × 1.820	182,000
Gain	£118,000
Chargeable gain	**£118,000**

Notes

(a)   An election for 6 April 1965 valuation could not be favourable, even were it not for the effect of re-basing, as the value is less than historic costs.

(b)   It is the gain/loss *after* time apportionment that is compared with the gain/loss produced by re-basing. [*TCGA 1992, Sch 3 para 6*].

(c)   The time apportionment calculation is applied to the gain *after* indexation (*Smith v Schofield HL 1993, 65 TC 669, [1993] STC 268*).

(C)   Unquoted shares

On 6 April 1953, A Ltd acquired 5,000 shares in C Ltd, an unquoted company, for £15,201. At 6 April 1965, the value of the holding was £15,000. A Ltd sells the shares (its entire holding in the company) on 6 April 2013 for £95,000. The indexation factor for the period March 1982 to April 2013 is 2.141. No election for universal 31 March 1982 re-basing is made but the market value of the holding at that date is agreed at £17,000.

The gain using time apportionment is as follows

Total period of ownership:	60 years
Period after 6 April 1965:	48 years

	£
Proceeds	95,000
Cost	15,201
Unindexed gain	79,799

204.3 CGT   Assets held on 6 April 1965

Indexation allowance:	
31.3.82 value £17,000 × 2.141	36,397
Gain after indexation	£43,402
Gain after time apportionment: £43,402 × 48/60	£34,722

The gain with an election to use 6.4.65 value is as follows

	£
Proceeds	95,000
6.4.65 value	15,000
Unindexed gain	80,000
Indexation allowance:	
31.3.82 value £17,000 × 2.141	36,397
Gain after indexation	£43,603

The gain with re-basing to 1982 is as follows

	£
Proceeds	95,000
31.3.82 value	17,000
Unindexed gain	78,000
Indexation allowance:	
31.3.82 value £17,000 × 2.141	36,397
Gain after indexation	£41,603

Time apportionment is more beneficial than an election for 6 April 1965 value. Re-basing does not apply as it cannot increase a gain. The chargeable gain is therefore £34,722.

(D)   **Unquoted shares — share exchange before 6 April 1965**

   [*TCGA 1992, Sch 2 para 19(1)(3)*]

   N Ltd purchased 5,000 £1 ordinary shares in R Ltd, an unquoted company, on 1 January 1961. The purchase price was £3 per share, a total of £15,000. On 1 December 1964, R Ltd was acquired by D Ltd, an unquoted company, as a result of which N Ltd received 10,000 8% convertible preference shares in D Ltd in exchange for its holding of R shares. In November 2013, N Ltd sold the D Ltd shares for £8.45 per share. The market value of the D Ltd shares was £2.03 per share at 6 April 1965 but only £1.50 per share at 31 March 1982. For the purpose only of this example, it is assumed that the indexation factor for March 1982 to November 2013 is 1.820.

   The gain, disregarding re-basing, is

		£
Disposal consideration	10,000 at £8.45	84,500

Assets held on 6 April 1965   CGT 204.3

Allowable cost	10,000 at £2.03	20,300
Unindexed gain		64,200
Indexation allowance £20,300 × 1.820		36,946
Gain after indexation		£27,254

The gain using re-basing to 1982 is

	£
Disposal consideration (as above)	84,500
Market value 31.3.82 10,000 at £1.50	15,000
Unindexed gain	69,500
Indexation allowance £20,300 × 1.820	36,946
Gain after indexation	£32,554
The overall result is	
Chargeable gain	£27,254

Notes

(a) Subject to re-basing, allowable cost *must* be taken as 6.4.65 value.

(b) Indexation is based on the greater of 31.3.82 value and 6.4.65 value. [*TCGA 1992, s 55(1)(2)*].

(c) Where the effect of re-basing would be to increase a gain, re-basing does not apply (but see note (e) below). [*TCGA 1992, s 35(3)(a)*].

(d) By concession (ESC D10), tax is not charged on a disposal of the *entire* new shareholding on more than the actual gain realised, i.e. by reference to original cost but without time apportionment.

(E) **Unquoted shares — share exchange after 5 April 1965**

[*TCGA 1992, Sch 2 para 19(2)(3)*]

S Ltd acquired 10,000 £1 ordinary shares in L Ltd for £5,000 on 31 May 1959. The shares are not quoted, and their value at 6 April 1965 was £6,000. On 1 September 1989, the shares were acquired by R plc, in exchange for its own ordinary shares on the basis of 1 for 2. The offer valued L ordinary shares at £2.23 per share. In February 2014, S Ltd sells its 5,000 R shares for £14.60 per share. The agreed value of the L Ltd shares at 31 March 1982 was £2.05 per share.

Indexation factors	March 1982 to September 1989	0.468
	September 1989 to February 2014 (assumed)	0.895
	March 1982 to February 2014 (assumed)	1.900

204.3 CGT   Assets held on 6 April 1965

The gain without re-basing to 1982 is computed as follows

(i) Using time apportionment

Deemed disposal at 1.9.89:

	£
Proceeds (market value £2.23 × 10,000)	22,300
Cost	5,000
Unindexed gain	17,300
Indexation allowance	
MV 31.3.82 10,000 × £2.05 × 0.468	9,594
Gain after indexation	£7,706
Gain after time apportionment:	
£7,706 × (27y 5m/33y 3m)	
$£7{,}706 \times \dfrac{26\text{y } 5\text{m}}{32\text{y } 3\text{m}}$	£6,354

Actual disposal in February 2014:

	£
Proceeds 5,000 × £14.60	73,000
Deemed acquisition cost at 1.9.89	22,300
Unindexed gain	50,700
Indexation allowance £22,300 × 0.895	19,959
Gain after indexation	£30,741
Total gain £(6,354 + 30,741)	£37,095

(ii) With election for 6.4.65 value

	£
Disposal consideration	73,000
Allowable cost	6,000
Unindexed gain	67,000
Indexation allowance 10,000 × £2.05 × 1.900	38,950
Gain	£28,050

Subject to re-basing, the election is beneficial.

The gain using re-basing to 1982 is

	£
Disposal consideration	73,000
Market value 31.3.82 10,000 × £2.05	20,500

Assets held on 6 April 1965   CGT 204.3

Unindexed gain	52,500
Indexation allowance £20,500 × 1.900	38,950
Gain after indexation	£13,550
The overall result is	
Chargeable gain	£13,550

Re-basing applies as it produces a smaller gain than that using 6 April 1965 value.

Notes

(a) The deemed disposal on 1 September 1989 is *only* for the purposes of *TCGA 1992, Sch 2 para 16* (time apportionment).

(b) If an election is made for 6 April 1965 value, no valuation is required at 1 September 1989.

(F) **Part disposals after 5 April 1965**

[*TCGA 1992, s 42, Sch 2 para 16(8)*]

H Ltd bought land for £15,000 on 31 October 1960. Its value at 6 April 1965 was £17,200. On 1 February 1988, H Ltd sold part of the land for £50,000, the balance being then worth £200,000. On 9 April 2013, H Ltd sells the remaining land for £450,000. The agreed value of the total estate at 31 March 1982 was £150,000 and H Ltd made a claim on the February 1988 disposal for that value to be used for indexation purposes under the law then in force.

Indexation factors	March 1982 to February 1988	0.305
	March 1982 to April 2013	2.141

1988 disposal

	£
Proceeds of part disposal	50,000
Deduct allowable cost $\dfrac{50,000}{50,000 + 200,000} \times £15,000$	3,000
Unindexed gain	47,000
Indexation allowance £150,000 × $\dfrac{50,000}{50,000 + 200,000}$ × £30,000	
£30,000 × 0.305	9,150
Gain after indexation	£37,850

204.3 CGT   Assets held on 6 April 1965

Time apportionment

$$\text{Chargeable gain } \frac{22y\ 10m}{27y\ 3m} \times £37{,}850 \qquad \underline{£31{,}715}$$

If an election were made to substitute 6 April 1965 valuation, the computation would be

	£
Proceeds of part disposal	50,000

$$\text{Deduct allowable cost } \frac{50{,}000}{50{,}000 + 200{,}000} \times £17{,}200 \qquad \underline{3{,}440}$$

Unindexed gain	46,560

$$\text{Indexation allowance } £150{,}000 \times \frac{50{,}000}{50{,}000 + 200{,}000} \times £30{,}000$$

£30,000 × 0.305	9,150
Chargeable gain	£37,410

An election would not be beneficial.

2013 disposal
The gain without re-basing to 1982 is as follows

Computation of entire gain over period of ownership:

	£
Proceeds	450,000
Cost £(15,000 − 3,000)	12,000
Unindexed gain	438,000
Indexation allowance	
MV 31.3.82 £(150,000 − 30,000) × 2.141	256,920
Gain after indexation	£181,080 (A)

Computation of gain for period 31.10.60 - 1.2.88:

	£
Market value at date of part disposal	200,000
Cost £(15,000 − 3,000)	12,000
Unindexed gain	188,000
Indexation allowance £(150,000 − 30,000) × 0.305	36,600
Gain after indexation	£151,400 (B)

Assets held on 6 April 1965   CGT 204.3

$$\text{Time apportionment } £151,400 \times \frac{22y\ 10m}{27y\ 3m} \qquad \underline{£126,861} \ \text{(C)}$$

Balance of gain (1.2.88 to 9.4.13) ((A) − (B))	£29,680 (D)
Chargeable gain (subject to re-basing) ((C) + (D))	£166,541

The gain using re-basing to 1982 is as follows

		£
Disposal proceeds		450,000
Market value 31.3.82 $£150,000 \times \dfrac{12,000}{15,000}$	(note (b))	120,000
Unindexed gain		330,000
Indexation allowance £120,000 × 2.141		256,920
Gain after indexation		£73,080

The overall result is

Chargeable gain	£73,0800

Re-basing applies as it produces neither a larger gain nor a loss.

Notes

(a) The deemed disposal on 1 February 1988 is only for the purposes of *TCGA 1992, Sch 2 para 16(3)–(5)* (time apportionment). For re-basing purposes, the asset is still regarded as having been held at 31 March 1982.

(b) Where there has been a part disposal after 31 March 1982 and before 6 April 1988 of an asset held at 31 March 1982, the proportion of 31 March 1982 value to be brought into account in the re-basing calculation is that which the cost previously unallowed bears to the total cost, giving the same effect as if re-basing had applied to the part disposal. [*TCGA 1992, Sch 3 para 4(1)*].

(c) HMRC will also accept an alternative basis of calculation on the part disposal of land. Under this method, the part disposed of is treated as a separate asset and any fair and reasonable method of apportioning part of the total cost to it will be accepted e.g. a reasonable valuation of that part at the acquisition date. (HMRC Statement of Practice SP D1.)

(d) The time apportionment calculation is applied to the gain *after* indexation (*Smith v Schofield HL 1993*, 65 TC 669, [1993] STC 268).

205 Assets held on 31 March 1982

205.1 CAPITAL GAINS TAX

[*TCGA 1992, s 35(1)(2)*]

Robbie sells an asset (which is neither tangible movable property nor otherwise exempt) on 25 April 2013 for £200,000. He had purchased the asset in 1979 for £50,000, and its value at 31 March 1982 was £42,000. The chargeable gain on the asset is computed as follows.

	£
Sale proceeds	200,000
31.3.1982 value	42,000
Chargeable gain 2013/14	£158,000

Notes

(a) The asset is deemed to have been sold and immediately re-acquired at its market value at 31 March 1982. For capital gains tax purposes (i.e. in relation to disposals by individuals, trustees and personal representatives), this rule (known as 're-basing') applies to all disposals. [*TCGA 1992, s 35(1)(2)*].

(b) Exceptions to re-basing apply for the purposes of corporation tax on chargeable gains. See 205.2 below.

205.2 CORPORATION TAX

[*TCGA 1992, s 35, Sch 3*]

(A)

R Ltd purchased a painting on 1 October 1979 for £50,000 (including costs of acquisition) and sold it at auction for £260,000 (net of selling expenses) on 15 August 2013. Its value at 31 March 1982 was £70,000 and the indexation factor for the period March 1982 to August 2013 is assumed, for the purpose only of this example, to be 1.820.

	£	£
Net sale proceeds	260,000	260,000
Cost	50,000	
Market value 31.3.82	—	70,000
Unindexed gain	210,000	190,000
Indexation allowance £70,000 × 1.820	127,400	127,400
Gain after indexation	£82,600	£62,600
		—
Chargeable gain		£62,600

205.2 CGT Assets held on 31 March 1982

Notes

(a) The asset is deemed to have been sold and immediately re-acquired at its market value at 31 March 1982. [*TCGA 1992, s 35(1)(2)*].

(b) Re-basing does not apply if it would produce a larger gain or larger loss than would otherwise be the case, nor if it would turn a gain into a loss or vice versa, nor if the disposal would otherwise be a no gain/no loss disposal. [*TCGA 1992, s 35(3)(4)*].

(c) An *irrevocable* election may be made to treat, broadly speaking, *all* assets held on 31 March 1982 as having been sold and re-acquired at their market value on that date, in which case the restrictions in (b) above will not apply. [*TCGA 1992, s 35(5)*]. If the election had been made in this example, the gain would still be £62,600, but there would have been no need to compute the gain by reference to cost and make a comparison with that using re-basing.

There are some minor exclusions from the rule that the election must extend to all assets. [*TCGA 1992, Sch 3 para 7*]. There are also special rules for groups of companies. [*TCGA 1992, Sch 3 paras 8, 9*].

(d) Indexation is automatically based on 31 March 1982 value, without the need to claim such treatment, unless a greater allowance would be produced by reference to cost. [*TCGA 1992, s 55(1)(2)*]. See also **214.1(C) INDEXATION**.

(e) See also **204 ASSETS HELD ON 6 APRIL 1965** for the general application of the re-basing provisions to such assets. See **214.2(A)(C) INDEXATION** for the position as regards an asset acquired by means of a no gain/no loss transfer from a person who held it at 31 March 1982.

(f) For capital gains tax purposes (i.e. in relation to disposals by individuals, trustees and personal representatives), re-basing applies to all disposals with no exceptions. See **205.1** above.

(B)

The facts are as in (A) above, except that net sale proceeds amount to £60,000.

	£	£
Net sale proceeds	60,000	60,000
Cost	50,000	
Market value 31.3.82	—	70,000
Unindexed gain/(loss)	10,000	(10,000)
Indexation allowance (as in (A))		
but restricted to	10,000	—
Gain/(loss)	Nil	£(10,000)
Chargeable gain/(allowable loss)	Nil	

Notes

(a) Re-basing does not apply as it cannot disturb a no gain/no loss position. [*TCGA 1992, s 35(3)(c)*].

Assets held on 31 March 1982 CGT 205.2

(b) (b) A universal re-basing election under *TCGA 1992, s 35(5)* would produce an allowable loss of £10,000 (but must extend to all assets).

(c) See **205.1** above for the application of re-basing for capital gains tax purposes.

(C)

The facts are as in (A) above, except that net sale proceeds amount to £185,000.

	£	£
Net sale proceeds	185,000	185,000
Cost	50,000	
Market value 31.3.82	–	70,000
Unindexed gain	135,000	115,000
Indexation allowance (as in (A))	127,400	
Indexation allowance (as in (A)) but restricted to	–	115,000
Gain	£7,600	Nil
Chargeable gain/(allowable loss)		Nil

Note

(a) Re-basing applies as it produces a no gain/no loss position compared to a gain otherwise.

(D)

A Ltd acquired a holding of D plc quoted shares for £11,000 net in January 1980. At 31 March 1982, their value had fallen to £8,000. On 29 April 2013, A Ltd sold the entire holding for £50,000 net. The indexation factor for the period March 1982 to April 2013 is 2.141.

	£	£
Proceeds	50,000	50,000
Cost	11,000	
Market value 31.3.82	–	8,000
Unindexed gain	39,000	42,000
Indexation allowance £11,000 × 2.141	23,551	23,551
Gain after indexation	£15,449	£18,449
Chargeable gain		£15,449

Notes

(a) Re-basing does not apply as its effect would be to increase a gain.

(b) Indexation is based on cost as that is greater than 31 March 1982 value.

205.2 CGT Assets held on 31 March 1982

(c) If a universal re-basing election had been made (under *TCGA 1992, s 35(5)*), the chargeable gain would have been £18,449.

(E)

C Ltd acquired a holding of E Ltd shares for £14,000 net in January 1980. At 31 March 1982, their value stood at £17,000. C Ltd sold the shares in April 2013 for £10,000 net.

	£	£
Proceeds	10,000	10,000
Cost	14,000	
Market value 31.3.82	—	17,000
Unindexed loss (no indexation due)	£4,000	£7,000
Allowable loss	£4,000	

Notes

(a) Re-basing does not apply as its effect would be to increase a loss.

(b) Indexation is not available in either calculation as it cannot increase a loss.

(c) If a universal re-basing election had been made (under *TCGA 1992, s 35(5)*), the allowable loss would have been £7,000, but the election must extend to all assets.

205.3 DEFERRED CHARGES ON GAINS BEFORE 31 MARCH 1982

[*TCGA 1992, s 36, Sch 4*]

K Ltd, a farming company, purchased farmland for £25,000 in 1975. The company sold the land in August 1984 for £45,000 but purchased further farmland in September 1984 for £50,000 and claimed rollover relief in respect of the disposal of the original farmland. K Ltd sells the replacement farmland in April 2013 for £250,000 and claims relief under *TCGA 1992, Sch 4*. The relevant indexation factors are

March 1982 to August 1984	0.133
September 1984 to April 2013	1.769

The gain on the original farmland is rolled over as follows

	£
Allowable cost	25,000
Indexation allowance £25,000 × 0.133	3,325
	28,325
Actual consideration	45,000
Chargeable gain rolled over	£16,675
Cost of replacement farmland	50,000
Deduct amount rolled over	16,675

Assets held on 31 March 1982   CGT 205.3

Deemed allowable cost £33,325

K Ltd's chargeable gain on disposal of the replacement farmland in April 2013 is as follows

	£	£
Proceeds		250,000
Deemed allowable cost	33,325	
Add one-half of rolled-over gain	8,338	
	41,663	
Indexation allowance £41,663 × 1.769	73,702	115,365
Chargeable gain		£134,635

Notes

(a) K Ltd cannot benefit from re-basing to 1982 as it did not hold the replacement farmland on 31 March 1982. Instead, the company claims relief under *TCGA 1992, s 36, Sch 4* so that the reduction in the cost of the replacement farmland resulting from the rollover relief on the original farmland is itself reduced by one half. [*TCGA 1992, Sch 4 para 1*].

(b) Relief under *TCGA 1992, Sch 4* must be claimed within two years of the end of the accounting period in which the ultimate disposal takes place. [*TCGA 1992, Sch 4 para 9*].

(c) The relief applies only for the purposes of corporation tax on chargeable gains. [*TCGA 1992, s 36, Sch 4 para A1*].

(d) For further rollover relief examples, see **226 ROLLOVER RELIEF — REPLACEMENT OF BUSINESS ASSETS**.

206 Capital Sums Derived from Assets

206.1 GENERAL

[*TCGA 1992, s 22(1)*]

A Ltd holds the remainder of a 99-year lease of land, under which it has mineral rights. The lease, which commenced in 1995, was acquired in April 2004 by assignment for £80,000. Following a proposal to extract minerals, the freeholder pays A Ltd £100,000 in June 2013 in consideration of relinquishing the mineral rights, in order to prevent such development. The value of the lease after the alteration is £150,000.

	£
Disposal proceeds	100,000
Allowable cost $\dfrac{100{,}000}{100{,}000 + 150{,}000} \times £80{,}000$	32,000
Gain subject to indexation from April 2004 to June 2013	£68,000

206.2 DEFERRED CONSIDERATION

Z owns 2,000 £1 ordinary shares in B Ltd, for which he subscribed at par in August 2000. On 31 March 2009, he and the other shareholders in B Ltd sold their shares to another company for £10 per share plus a further unquantified cash amount calculated by means of a formula relating to the future profits of B Ltd. The value in March 2009 of the deferred consideration was estimated at £2 per share. On 30 April 2013, Z receives a further £4.20 per share under the sale agreement.

2008/09

		£	£
Disposal proceeds	2,000 at £10	20,000	
Value of rights	2,000 at £2	4,000	24,000
Cost of acquisition			2,000
Chargeable gain			£22,000

2013/14

	£
Disposal of rights to deferred consideration	
Proceeds 2,000 × £4.20	8,400
Deemed cost of acquiring rights	4,000
Chargeable gain	£4,400

206.2 CGT   Capital Sums Derived from Assets

Notes

(a) A right to unquantified and contingent future consideration on the disposal of an asset is itself an asset, and the future consideration when received is a capital sum derived from that asset (*Marren v Ingles HL 1980, 54 TC 76* and *Marson v Marriage Ch D 1979, 54 TC 59*).

(b) See **229.4** SHARES AND SECURITIES for the position where deferred consideration is to be satisfied in shares and/or debentures in the acquiring company.

(c) See also **216.4** LOSSES for the election to treat a loss on disposal of a right to deferred unascertainable consideration as accruing in an earlier year.

206.3 RECEIPT OF COMPENSATION

[*TCGA 1992, ss 22, 23*]

(A)

C owns a freehold warehouse which is badly damaged by fire as a result of inflammable goods having been inadequately packaged. The value of the warehouse after the fire is £90,000, and it cost £120,000 in 1994. The owner of the goods is held liable for the damage and pays C £60,000 compensation in October 2013.

	£
Disposal proceeds	60,000
Allowable cost $\dfrac{60,000}{60,000 + 90,000} \times £120,000$	48,000
Chargeable gain 2013/14	£12,000

(B) Restoration using insurance moneys

A diamond necklace owned by D cost £100,000 in 2005. D is involved in a motor accident in which the necklace is damaged. Its value is reduced to £80,000. D receives £40,000 under an insurance policy in May 2013 and spends £45,000 on having the necklace restored.

(i) *No claim under TCGA 1992, s 23*

	£
Disposal proceeds	40,000
Allowable cost $\dfrac{40,000}{40,000 + 80,000} \times £100,000$	33,333
Chargeable gain 2013/14	£6,667
Allowable cost in relation to subsequent disposal	
£100,000 − £33,333 + £45,000	£111,667

(ii) *Claim under TCGA 1992, s 23*

No chargeable gain arises in 2013/14	
Allowable cost originally	100,000
Deduct Amount received on claim	40,000
	60,000
Add Expenditure on restoration	45,000
Allowable cost in relation to subsequent disposal	£105,000

(C) **Part application of capital sum received**

E Ltd is the owner of a large estate consisting mainly of parkland which it acquired for £150,000 in August 1993. It grants a one-year licence in August 2013 to an exploration company to prospect for minerals, in consideration for a capital sum of £50,000. The exploration proves unsuccessful and on expiry of the licence E Ltd spends £20,000 on restoration of the drilling sites to their former state. The market value of the estate after granting the licence is £350,000, and it is £400,000 after restoration.

(i) *No claim under TCGA 1992, s 23(3)*

	£
Disposal proceeds	50,000
Deduct Allowable cost $\dfrac{50,000}{50,000 + 350,000} \times £150,000$	18,750
Gain subject to indexation from August 1993 to August 2013	£31,250
Allowable expenditure remaining	
£150,000 − £18,750 + £20,000	£151,250

(ii) *Claim made under TCGA 1992, s 23(3)*

	£
Deemed disposal proceeds (£50,000 − £20,000)	30,000
Deduct	
Allowable cost $\dfrac{30,000}{30,000 + 400,000} \times £(150,000 + 20,000)$	11,860
Gain subject to indexation to August 2013	£18,140
Allowable expenditure remaining	
£150,000 − £20,000 − £11,860 + £20,000	£138,140

206.3 CGT   Capital Sums Derived from Assets

(D) **Capital sum exceeding allowable expenditure**

F inherited a painting in 1980 when it was valued at £2,000. Its value at 31 March 1982 was £3,000. In March 1987, by which time its value had increased considerably, the painting suffered damage whilst on loan to an art gallery and F received £10,000 compensation. The value of the painting was then £30,000. It then cost F £9,800 to have the painting restored. In June 2013, he sells the painting for £50,000.

(i) *No election under TCGA 1992, s 23(2)*

	£
Disposal proceeds March 1987	10,000
Allowable cost $\dfrac{10,000}{10,000 + 30,000} \times £2,000$	500
Gain subject to indexation 1986/87	£9,500
Allowable cost in relation to subsequent disposal	
£2,000 − £500 + £9,800	£11,300

	£
Disposal proceeds June 2013	50,000
Allowable cost with re-basing	
$£3,000 \times \dfrac{30,000}{10,000 + 30,000} = £2,250 + £9,800$	12,050
Chargeable gain 2013/14	£37,950

(ii) *Election under TCGA 1992, s 23(2)*

	£
Disposal proceeds March 1987	10,000
Less allowable expenditure	2,000
Gain subject to indexation 1986/87	£8,000
Allowable cost in relation to subsequent disposal	
£2,000 − £2,000 + £9,800	£9,800

	£
Disposal proceeds June 2013	50,000
Allowable cost with re-basing (note (b))	
£3,000 − £2,000 + £9,800	10,800
Chargeable gain 2013/14	£39,200

Capital Sums Derived from Assets   CGT 206.3

Notes

(a) For capital gains tax purposes (i.e. in relation to disposals by individuals, trustees and personal representatives), re-basing applies to all disposals with no exceptions. See **205.1** ASSETS HELD ON **31** MARCH **1982**.

(b) Where there is a disposal after 5 April 1989 to which re-basing applies and, if re-basing had not applied, the allowable expenditure would have fallen to be reduced under *TCGA 1992, s 23(2)* by reference to a capital sum received after 31 March 1982 but before 6 April 1988, the 31 March 1982 value is reduced by the amount previously allowed against the capital sum. [*TCGA 1992, Sch 3 para 4(2)*].

207 Companies

Cross-references. See also **CT 104** CAPITAL GAINS.

207.1 CAPITAL LOSSES

P Ltd, which makes up accounts to 30 June annually, changes its accounting date to 31 December. It makes up 18-month accounts to 31 December 2013, and its chargeable gains and allowable losses are as follows

	Gains/(losses) £
31.7.12	4,600
19.10.12	11,500
1.12.12	3,500
28.3.13	(8,300)
21.7.13	8,500
1.9.13	(25,000)
20.12.13	7,000

The period of account is split into two accounting periods

1.7.12 – 30.6.13
Net chargeable gain £11,300

1.7.13 – 31.12.13
Net allowable loss £9,500

Notes

(a) The loss cannot be set off against the £11,300 net gain in the earlier accounting period (but *can* be carried forward against subsequent gains).

(b) A loss accruing to a company is not an allowable loss if it arises directly or indirectly in consequence of, or otherwise in connection with, any arrangements one of the main purposes of which is to secure a tax advantage. [*TCGA 1992, ss 8(2), 16A*].

(c) For a further example, see CT **104.1** CAPITAL GAINS.

208 Computation of Gains and Losses

208.1 ALLOWABLE AND NON-ALLOWABLE EXPENDITURE

(A) **Allowable expenditure**

[*TCGA 1992, s 38*]

In 2013/14 T sold a house which he had owned since 1991 and which was let throughout the period of ownership (other than as furnished holiday accommodation). The house cost £34,000, with legal costs of £900, in June 1991. T spent £2,000 on initial dilapidations in July 1991. In November 1998, he added an extension at a cost of £5,500 for which he received a local authority grant of £2,500 on completion. Legal costs of £500 were incurred on obtaining vacant possession at the end of the final tenancy in May 2013. The sale proceeds were £170,000 before deducting incidental costs (including valuation fees) of £1,200.

	£	£	£
Sale proceeds		170,000	
Deduct Costs of sale		1,200	168,800
Cost of house		34,000	
Add Incidental costs of purchase		900	
		34,900	
Improvement costs:			
Initial dilapidations (note (a))	2,000		
Extension, less grant	3,000	5,000	
Cost of obtaining vacant possession (enhancement cost)		500	40,400
Chargeable gain 2013/14			£128,400

Note

(a) It is assumed that the cost of the initial dilapidations were disallowed for income tax purposes under the rule in *Law Shipping Co Ltd v CIR, CS 1923, 12 TC 621*. If any of the expenditure had been so allowed, a deduction would to that extent be precluded as an allowable deduction for CGT purposes by *TCGA 1992, s 39*.

(B) **Non-allowable expenditure — capital allowances**

[*TCGA 1992, s 41*]

S Ltd acquired land in March 2006 for £90,000 on which it constructed a factory for use in its manufacturing trade. The cost of construction was £45,000 incurred in June 2006. In April 2013, the company sold the freehold factory for £140,000, of which £100,000 related

208.1 CGT   Computation of Gains and Losses

to the land and £40,000 to the building. Industrial buildings allowances of £9,000 had been given and, as the sale occurred after 20 March 2007, there was no balancing adjustment. For the purposes of this example, it is assumed that the indexation factor for the period March 2006 to April 2013 is 0.171.

	Land		Building
	£	£	£
Disposal consideration	100,000		40,000
Allowable cost	90,000	45,000	
Deduct net allowances given	–	9,000	36,000
Unindexed gain	10,000		4,000
Indexation allowance:			
£90,000 × 0.171 = £15,390, but restricted to	10,000		
£36,000 × 0.171 = £6,156, but restricted to	–		4,000
Chargeable gain/(allowable loss)	Nil		Nil

(C)   Enhancement expenditure

[*TCGA 1992, s 38*]

Mr Hopkins bought a second home in August 1978 for £15,000. Mr Hopkins' neighbour, Mr Douglas, claimed that part of the garden of the house belonged to him. Mr Hopkins won the court case resulting, but incurred legal fees of £5,000 in September 1985.

In 2000 Mr Hopkins had a tennis court built for £5,000, but this was demolished in 2007.

Mr Hopkins sold the house in November 2013 for £126,000. It was agreed that the value of the house at 31 March 1982 was £25,000. The house has never been treated as Mr Hopkins' main residence.

The chargeable gain is as follows.

	£
Sale consideration	126,000
Less 31 March 1982 value	25,000
Legal fees re boundary dispute	5,000
Chargeable gain	£96,000

Notes

(a)   The expenditure on the tennis court in 2000 is not allowable as it is not reflected in the state or nature of the asset at the time of disposal in November 2013 as required by *TCGA 1992, s 38(1)(b)*. HMRC consider that the demolition of the tennis court is not within *TCGA 1992, s 24(1)* as it is not the 'entire loss, destruction, dissipation or extinction' of an asset because it is not an 'asset': it is only part of an asset, the land (see HMRC Capital Gains Manual CG 15190).

(b)   Expenditure wholly and exclusively incurred in establishing, preserving or defending title to, or to a right over, an asset is allowable expenditure. [*TCGA 1992, s 38(1)(b)*].

Computation of Gains and Losses   CGT 208.2

208.2 PART DISPOSALS

[*TCGA 1992, s 42*]

NOTE.
See also **215.1** LAND for small part disposals of land.

(A)

T purchased a 300-acre estate in March 1988 for £1m plus legal and other costs of £50,000. In January 1991 he spent £47,000 on improvements to the main house on the estate (not his main residence), which he sells in September 2013 for £660,000. The costs of sale are £40,000. The value of the remaining land is £2.34m.

	£	£
Sale proceeds		660,000
Deduct incidental costs		40,000
		620,000
Cost £1,050,000 × $\frac{660,000}{660,000 + 2,340,000}$	231,000	
Improvement costs	47,000	278,000
Chargeable gain		£342,000

Note

(a) The improvements expenditure is not apportioned as it relates entirely to the part of the estate being sold. [*TCGA 1992, s 42(4)*].

(B)

U inherited some land at a probate value of £500,000 in November 1981. Its market value at 31 March 1982 was £540,000. In November 1987, he sold part of the land for £240,000, the remaining land then being worth £480,000. He sells the remaining land in April 2013 for £600,000.

The gain, subject to indexation, on the part disposal in November 1987 is

	£
Proceeds	240,000
Cost £500,000 × $\frac{240,000}{240,000 + 480,000}$	166,667
Gain subject to indexation	£73,333

208.2 CGT Computation of Gains and Losses

The gain on the disposal in April 2013 is

	£
Proceeds	600,000
Market value 31.3.82 $£540,000 \times \dfrac{480,000}{240,000 + 480,000}$	360,000
Chargeable gain	£240,000

Notes

(a) Where re-basing applies and there has been a part disposal after 31 March 1982 and before 6 April 1988, the proportion of 31 March 1982 value to be brought into account on the ultimate disposal is the same as the proportion of cost not allowed on the part disposal, as if the re-basing provisions had applied to the part disposal. [*TCGA 1992, Sch 3 para 4(1)*].

(b) For capital gains tax purposes (i.e. in relation to disposals by individuals, trustees and personal representatives), re-basing applies to all disposals with no exceptions. See **205.1** ASSETS HELD ON 31 MARCH 1982.

(C)

V bought the film rights of a novel for £50,000 in May 2008. A one-third share of the rights was sold to W Ltd in March 2009 for £20,000, when the rights retained had a value of £45,000. In December 2013, V's rights were sold to a film company for £100,000 plus a right to royalties, such right being estimated to be worth £150,000.

March 2009

	£
Sale proceeds	20,000
Cost $£50,000 \times \dfrac{20,000}{20,000 + 45,000}$	15,385
Chargeable gain 2008/09	4,615

December 2013

	£
Sale proceeds (£100,000 + £150,000)	250,000
Cost (£50,000 − £15,385)	34,615
Chargeable gain 2013/14	£215,385

Note

(a) The right to royalties is itself an asset and could be the subject of a future disposal by V. See **206.2** CAPITAL SUMS DERIVED FROM ASSETS and, where applicable, **231** WASTING ASSETS.

(D)

C inherited land valued at £72,000 in May 1989. He granted rights of way over the land to a neighbouring landowner in March 1994, in consideration for a parcel of land adjacent to his, valued at £21,000. The value of the original land, subject to the right of way, was then £147,000. In March 2014, C sold the whole of the land for £170,000.

Indexation factor May 1989 to March 1994	0.239

Part disposal in March 1994 £

Disposal consideration		21,000
Allowable expenditure		
$\dfrac{21,000}{21,000 + 147,000} \times £72,000$		9,000
Unindexed gain		12,000
Indexation allowance £9,000 × 0.239		2,151
Chargeable gain 1993/94		£9,849

Disposal in March 2014 £

Disposal consideration			170,000
Deduct Original land £(72,000 − 9,000)		63,000	
Addition		21,000	84,000
Chargeable gain 2013/14			£86,000

Notes

(a) It is assumed that the additional land is merged with the existing land to give a single asset.

(b) A claim under *TCGA 1992, s 242* (small part disposals of land — see **215.1** LAND) could not be made in respect of the March 1994 part disposal as the consideration exceeded £20,000.

209 Double Tax Relief

209.1 RELIEF BY CREDIT

[*TIOPA 2010, ss 18–41*]

Lyra, a higher rate income tax payer, has the following chargeable gains for 2013/14.

UK gain	£30,000	
Foreign gain	16,000	(Foreign tax £6,400)

Lyra claims credit relief for the foreign tax paid. Her capital gains tax liability for 2013/14 is as follows.

	UK gain	Foreign gain
	£	£
Chargeable gain	30,000	16,000
Less annual exempt amount	10,600	—
Gain chargeable to tax	19,400	16,000
Capital gains tax: £19,400/£16,000 × 28%	5,432	4,480
Less credit for foreign tax	—	4,480
Tax payable	£5,432	Nil

Notes

(a) No relief is available for the excess of the foreign tax over the CGT liability in respect of the foreign gain (£6,400 – £4,480 = £1,920).

(b) Strictly, the double tax relief is limited to the difference between the total CGT liability for the year before relief (i.e. £9,912) and what the CGT liability would be if the foreign gain were excluded (i.e. £5,432) [*TIOPA 2010, s 40*]. In practice, the effect of this provision is that the annual exempt amount is allocated against the UK gain. If Lyra had been a basic rate income tax payer, any unused part of the basic rate band would likewise have been allocated against the UK gain in priority to the foreign gain (gains within that unused part being chargeable to CGT at 18%).

(c) A claim for credit relief must normally be made not more than four years after the end of the tax year for which the gain is chargeable. The claim deadline is extended to 31 January following the tax year in which the foreign tax is paid, where this is later than the above deadline [*TIOPA 2010, s 19*].

210 Enterprise Investment Scheme

Cross-reference. See also **IT 8.2** ENTERPRISE INVESTMENT SCHEME.

210.1 DISPOSAL OF EIS SHARES MORE THAN THREE YEARS AFTER ISSUE

[*TCGA 1992, s 150A(2)(3); ITA 2007, s 159(2)*]

On 8 November 2010 P subscribes £675,000 for 450,000 shares in the EIS company, S Ltd, and obtains the maximum EIS income tax relief of £100,000 (£500,000 × 20%) for 2010/11. On 3 April 2015 he sells the entire holding for £1,395,000.

The chargeable gain arising is calculated as follows

	£
Disposal proceeds	1,395,000
Cost	675,000
Gain	720,000
Less TCGA 1992, s 150A(2)(3) exemption	
£720,000 × $\frac{100,000}{135,000}$ (note(b))	533,334
Chargeable gain 2014/15	£186,666

Notes

(a) Gains arising on the sale more than three years after issue of shares qualifying for EIS income tax relief are not chargeable gains unless the EIS relief is fully withdrawn before disposal. The exemption begins three years after the date of commencement of the qualifying trade if this is later than three years after issue.

(b) Where the income tax relief is not given on the full EIS subscription (otherwise than because of insufficient income), capital gains tax relief is given on a proportion of the gain on the disposal or part disposal.

The gain is reduced by the multiple A/B where

A = the actual income tax reduction and

B = the tax at the basic rate for the year of relief on the amount subscribed for the issue.

A = £500,000 × 20% = £100,000

B = £675,000 × 20% = £135,000

(c) For shares issued in 2011/12 onwards, the rate of income tax EIS relief is increased to 30%. For 2012/13 onwards, the maximum amount on which income tax relief can be obtained is increased to £1 million.

210.2 CGT Enterprise Investment Scheme

210.2 LOSS ON DISPOSAL OF EIS SHARES

[TCGA 1992, s 150A(1)(2A)]

(A) Disposal more than three years after issue

Assuming the facts otherwise remain the same as in 210.1 above but that the shares are sold for £450,000 on 3 April 2015.

The allowable loss arising is calculated as follows

	£	£
Disposal proceeds		450,000
Less Cost	675,000	
Less Income tax relief given (and not withdrawn)	100,000	575,000
Allowable loss 2014/15		£125,000

Note

(a) Any loss arising is reduced by deducting the amount of the EIS relief (given and not withdrawn) from the acquisition cost. On the question of income tax withdrawal, see note (b) to (B) below.

(B) Disposal within three years of issue

The facts are otherwise as in (A) above except that the shares are sold in an arm's length bargain on 6 April 2013, i.e. within three years after their issue.

Income tax relief given for 2010/11 is withdrawn as follows

Relief attributable (£500,000 @ 20%) £100,000 (1)

Consideration

$$£450,000 \times \frac{100,000 \ (£500,000 \ @ \ 20\%)}{135,000 \ (£675,000 \ @ \ 20\%)} \ @ \ 20\% \quad £66,666 \ (2)$$

The amount at (1) is greater than that at (2), so income tax relief of £66,666 is withdrawn. [ITA 2007, ss 209, 210].

The relief not withdrawn is therefore £(100,000 − 66,666) = £33,334

Enterprise Investment Scheme   CGT 210.3

The allowable loss arising is calculated as follows

	£	£
Disposal proceeds		450,000
Less Cost	675,000	
Less Income tax relief not withdrawn	33,334	641,666
Allowable loss 2013/14		£191,666

Notes

(a) For the purposes of computing an allowable loss, the consideration is reduced by the relief attributable to the shares. [*TCGA 1992, s 150A(1)*]. The relief attributable is that remaining following any withdrawal of relief.

(b) A withdrawal of income tax relief arises on a disposal of EIS shares within period A under *ITA 2007, s 159(2)*, i.e. within three years after their issue or, if later, within the period ending immediately before the third anniversary of the date of commencement of the qualifying trade. [*ITA 2007, s 209*].

210.3 EIS DEFERRAL RELIEF

[*TCGA 1992, Sch 5B; FA 2009, Sch 8 paras 1–5*]

On 1 June 2013, X realises a gain of £300,000 on the disposal of an asset he had owned since September 2005. X makes no other disposals in 2013/14. On 1 February 2015, X acquires by subscription 65% of the issued ordinary share capital of ABC Ltd at a total subscription price of £248,000. This is a qualifying investment for the purposes of EIS deferral relief. X makes a claim to defer the maximum £248,000 of the June 2012 gain against the qualifying investment.

On 1 July 2019, X sells 40% of his holding in ABC Ltd for £199,200. He makes no other disposals in 2019/20.

X's CGT position for 2013/14 is as follows

	£
Gain	300,000
Less EIS deferral relief	248,000
	52,000
Less annual exemption	10,900
Taxable gain 2013/14	£41,100

X's CGT position for 2019/20 is as follows

	£
Gain on ABC Ltd shares	
Disposal proceeds	199,200
Less cost (£248,000 @ 40%)	99,200

210.3 CGT   Enterprise Investment Scheme

Chargeable gain	£100,000
Deferred gain brought into charge	
Total gain deferred	£248,000
Clawback restricted to expenditure to which disposal relates	£99,200
Taxable gains 2019/20 (subject to annual exemption) (£100,000 + £99,200)	£199,200
Gain remaining deferred until any future chargeable event (£248,000 − £99,200)	£148,800

Notes

(a) No part of X's subscription for ABC Ltd shares can qualify for EIS income tax relief. X is connected with the company by virtue of his shareholding being greater than 30%. (In practice, the holdings of his associates, e.g. wife and children, must also be taken into account in applying the 30% limit.) [*ITA 2007, ss 163, 166–171*].

(b) As the ABC Ltd shares do not qualify for income tax relief, there is no CGT exemption for the gain arising on disposal even though the shares were held for the requisite three-year period.

(c) Where a disposal would potentially qualify for both ENTREPRENEURS' RELIEF (211) and EIS deferral relief, the taxpayer must choose between the reliefs. He will either pay tax immediately on the gain at 10% if he chooses entrepreneurs' relief or will defer the gain and pay tax at 18% or 28% when it comes back into charge. Where a gain exceeds the £10 million lifetime limit for entrepreneurs' relief it will be possible to claim entrepreneurs' relief on the gain up to the limit and to defer the gain above the limit under the EIS rules. See *TCGA 1992, Sch 5B para 1(5A)*.

211 Entrepreneurs' Relief

211.1 COMPUTATION OF RELIEF

[*TCGA 1992, ss 169L–169M; FA 2010, s 4; F(No 2)A 2010, Sch 1 paras 4–8, 10, 11, 14–17; FA 2011, s 9*]

(A) Basic computation

In May 2013, Mr Henry sells his business, Joe's Toys, which he has owned since 1998, realising the following chargeable gains and allowable loss.

	Gain/(loss) £
Goodwill	700,000
Freehold shop 1	200,000
Freehold shop 2	200,000
Freehold shop 3	(150,000)

Mr Henry claims entrepreneurs' relief in respect of the sale of the business. He makes no other disposals in 2012/13 and has made no previous claim to entrepreneurs' relief.

Mr Henry's capital gains tax liability for 2013/14 is calculated as follows.

	£
Gains qualifying for entrepreneurs' relief	
Goodwill	700,000
Freehold shop 1	200,000
Freehold shop 2	200,000
	1,100,000
Less Loss on freehold shop 3	150,000
Deemed chargeable gain qualifying for entrepreneurs' relief	950,000
Annual exemption	10,900
Gain chargeable to tax	£939,100
Capital gains tax payable (£939,100 × 10%)	£93,910

Notes

(a) Entrepreneurs' relief can be claimed in respect of 'qualifying business disposals' (as defined in *TCGA 1992, ss 169H–169K*) made on or after 6 April 2008. Relief can also apply to certain chargeable gains deferred before that date which are deemed to accrue on or after that date — see *FA 2008, Sch 3 paras 7, 8*. The relief applies for capital gains tax purposes only and is not available to companies. For disposals on or after 23 June 2010, relief is given by deducting the aggregate losses arising on the

211.1 CGT   Entrepreneurs' Relief

disposal from the aggregate gains and, where the resulting amount is positive, charging it to tax at 10%. Previously, relief was given by deducting the aggregate losses arising on the disposal from the aggregate gains and, where the resulting amount was positive, reducing it by 4/9ths.

(b) Entrepreneurs' relief must be claimed on or before the first anniversary of the 31 January following the tax year in which the qualifying business disposal is made. In the case of a disposal of trust business assets, the claim must be made jointly by the trustees and the qualifying beneficiary. [*TCGA 1992, s 169M(1)–(3); FA 2008, Sch 3 para 2*]. Mr Henry must therefore make a claim on or before 31 January 2016.

(c) Where a disposal on or after 23 June 2010 would potentially qualify for both entrepreneurs' relief and EIS deferral relief, the taxpayer must choose between the reliefs. He will either pay tax immediately on the gain at 10% if he chooses entrepreneurs' relief or will defer the gain and pay tax at 18% or 28% when it comes back into charge. Where a gain exceeds the £10 million lifetime limit for entrepreneurs' relief it will be possible to claim entrepreneurs' relief on the gain up to the limit and to defer the gain above the limit under the EIS rules. See *TCGA 1992, Sch 5B para 1(5A)*. Previously it was possible to claim entrepreneurs' relief and then defer the gain as reduced by 4/9ths.

(B) Lifetime limit

In August 2013 Mr Robertson sells his entire shareholding in Robbie Ltd, realising a gain of £10,050,000, which qualifies for entrepreneurs' relief. Mr Robertson makes no other disposals in 2013/14 and has made no previous disposals qualifying for entrepreneurs' relief. He is an additional rate income tax payer for 2013/14.

Mr Robertson's capital gains tax liability for 2013/14 is calculated as follows.

	£
Deemed chargeable gain qualifying for entrepreneurs' relief (subject to lifetime limit £10,000,000)	10,050,000
Annual exemption	10,900
Gain chargeable to tax	£10,039,100
Capital gains tax payable	
£10,000,000 × 10%	1,000,000
£39,100 × 28%	10,948
	£1,010,948

Notes

(a) Entrepreneurs' relief is subject to a lifetime limit of £10 million (£5 million for disposals before 6 April 2011; £2 million for disposals before 23 June 2010; £1 million for disposals before 6 April 2010). The amount to which relief would otherwise apply in respect of a qualifying business disposal is added to any amounts to which relief applied in respect of earlier qualifying business disposals. Where the total exceeds the limit, only so much (if any) of the amount to which relief would

Entrepreneurs' Relief CGT 211.1

otherwise apply in respect of the current disposal as, together with the earlier amounts, does not exceed the limit qualifies for the 10% rate (or $^4/_9$ths reduction). Any part of the deemed gain excluded by the application of this rule is chargeable at the normal rates of CGT.

Where one of the previous lower lifetime limits was exceeded on disposals made before the increases, no further relief can be obtained for those disposals following the increases. Relief can, however, be obtained for qualifying business disposals on or after the dates of increase up to the appropriate new limit. See (D) below.

[*TCGA 1992, s 169N; FA 2008, Sch 3 para 2; FA 2010, s 4; F(No 2)A 2010, Sch 1 paras 5, 14; FA 2011, s 9*].

(b) Disposals before 6 April 2008 do not affect the lifetime limit except in the case of deferred gains on which entrepreneurs' relief is claimed under the transitional rules of *FA 2008, Sch 3 paras 7, 8*.

(c) The annual exemption of £10,900 is allocated against the part of the gain chargeable to tax at 28% as this gives the greater tax saving. [*TCGA 1992, s 4B: F(No 2)A 2010, Sch 1 paras 3, 13*].

(C) **Lifetime limit — further example**

In May 2013, Mr Helm sells his entire shareholding in Levon Ltd for £400,000. He had acquired the shares in March 2001 for £150,000 and has been a director of the company since that time. Levon Ltd is a trading company and qualifies as Mr Helm's personal company. He makes no other disposals in 2013/14 and claims entrepreneurs' relief in respect of the gain on the shares. He has made no previous entrepreneurs' relief claims.

Mr Helm's capital gains tax liability for 2013/14 is calculated as follows.

	£
Sale proceeds	400,000
Cost	150,000
Chargeable gain qualifying for entrepreneurs' relief	250,000
Annual exemption	10,900
Gain chargeable to tax 2013/14	£239,100
Capital gains tax payable (£239,100 × 10%)	£23,910

Following the disposal of his shares in Levon Ltd, Mr Helm buys a 25% shareholding in Amy Ltd, another trading company, for £200,000, and starts work as a director of the company. He continues as a director of the company until May 2017 when he sells his entire shareholding for £10,100,000. He claims entrepreneurs' relief in respect of the disposal. He makes no other disposals in 2017/18, but pays income tax at the additional rate. It is assumed for the purpose of this example only that the annual exemption for 2017/18 is £12,000 and the rates of tax remain as for 2013/14.

Mr Helm's capital gains tax liability for 2017/18 is calculated as follows.

	£
Sale proceeds	10,100,000

211.1 CGT Entrepreneurs' Relief

Cost	200,000
Chargeable gain qualifying for entrepreneurs' relief (subject to lifetime limit £10,000,000)	9,900,000
Annual exemption	12,000
Taxable gain 2017/18	£9,888,000
Capital gains tax payable (note (a))	
£9,750,000 × 10%	975,000
£138,000 × 28%	38,640
	£1,013,640

Notes

(a) The lifetime limit applies to restrict the amount of the gain in 2017/18 which qualifies for entrepreneurs' relief as follows. Of the limit of £10,000,000, £250,000 was used in 2013/14 leaving (£10,000,000 - £250,000 =) £9,750,000 unused. As the otherwise qualifying gain for 2017/18 is greater than the unused part of the limit, entrepreneurs' relief is restricted to £9,750,000.

(b) For a disposal of shares or securities (other than EMI shares — see (c) below) in a company to qualify for entrepreneurs' relief, the company must be the taxpayer's 'personal company' and must be either a 'trading company' or the 'holding company of a trading group' (both as defined). The taxpayer must be an officer or employee of the company or, where the company is a member of a trading group, of one or more companies which are members of the group. For this purpose, an individual's *'personal company'* is a company in which he holds at least 5% of the ordinary share capital (within *ITA 2007, s 989*) and in which he is able to exercise at least 5% of the voting rights by virtue of that holding. These conditions must be met throughout the one-year period ending with the date of disposal (or the one-year period ending with the date, within three years before the disposal, on which the company ceases to be a trading company without continuing to be or becoming a member of a trading group or ceases to be a member of a trading group without continuing to be or becoming a trading company). [*TCGA 1992, ss 169I, 169S(2)–(5); FA 2013, Sch 24 para 1*].

(c) A disposal of shares in a company on or after 6 April 2013 also qualifies for entrepreneurs' relief if the shares were acquired on or after 6 April 2012 as a result of the exercise of an option under the enterprise management incentives (EMI) scheme and the company is either a 'trading company' or the 'holding company of a trading group' (both as defined). The taxpayer must be an officer or employee of the company or, where the company is a member of a trading group, of one or more companies which are members of the group. These conditions must be met throughout the one-year period ending with the date of disposal (or the one-year period ending with the date, within three years before the disposal, on which the company ceases to be a trading company without continuing to be or becoming a member of a trading group or ceases to be a member of a trading group without continuing to be or becoming a trading company). The taxpayer does not have to have held the shares throughout the one year period, but the EMI option must have been granted on or before the first day of that period. For shares acquired on or after 6 April 2012 and before 6 April 2013 the taxpayer must elect before 31 January 2014 for the shares to qualify for entrepreneurs' relief if he disposed of any shares of the same class in 2012/13. [*TCGA 1992, s 169I; FA 2013, Sch 24 paras 1, 5*].

(d) The annual exemption of £12,000 is allocated against the part of the gain chargeable to tax at 28% as this gives the greater tax saving. [*TCGA 1992, s 4B: F(No 2)A 2010, Sch 1 paras 3, 13*].

(D) Change in lifetime limit

If, in (C) above, Mr Helm's initial gain had been in May 2010 and had been, say, £2,500,000, his entrepreneurs' relief would have been restricted to the then lifetime limit of £2 million. Following the increases in the lifetime limit to £5 million with effect for disposals on or after 23 June 2010 and to £10 milliion for disposals on or after 6 April 2011, no further relief would have been due in respect of the 2010/11 gain. On the disposal in 2017/18, however, his unused lifetime limit would be £8 million (i.e. the new limit of £10 million less the £2 million in respect of which relief had previously been given).

211.2 PARTNERSHIPS

[*TCGA 1992, s 169I(8)*]

Martha has been a member of a trading partnership for ten years. In November 2013 she retires from the partnership and sells her interest in the partnership assets to the other partners, realising the following chargeable gains.

	£
Goodwill	100,000
Property	150,000
	£250,000

Martha claims entrepreneurs' relief in respect of the sale. She makes no other disposals in 2013/14 and has made no previous entrepreneurs' relief claims.

Martha's capital gains tax liability for 2013/14 is calculated as follows.

Gains qualifying for entrepreneurs' relief	£
Goodwill	100,000
Property	150,000
Deemed chargeable gain qualifying for entrepreneurs' relief	250,000
Annual exemption	10,900
Gain chargeable to tax	£239,100
Capital gains tax payable (£239,100 × 10%)	£23,910

Note

(a) A disposal by an individual of the whole or part of his interest in the assets of a partnership is treated for entrepreneurs' relief purposes as a disposal by him of the whole or part of the partnership business and may therefore be a qualifying business disposal where the necessary conditions are satisfied. [*TCGA 1992, s 169I(8)(b)*].

211.3 CGT   Entrepreneurs' Relief

211.3 ASSOCIATED DISPOSALS

[*TCGA 1992, ss 169K, 169P*]

The facts are as in 211.2 above, except that Martha also sells an office which she owns personally and has let to the partnership rent-free since she first purchased it in 2004. The office has been used by the partnership for trade purposes throughout. The chargeable gain on the sale of the office is £56,000 and Martha claims entrepreneurs' relief.

Martha's capital gains tax liability for 2013/14 is calculated as follows.

Gains qualifying for entrepreneurs' relief	£
Goodwill	100,000
Property	150,000
Office	56,000
Deemed chargeable gain qualifying for entrepreneurs' relief	306,000
Annual exemption	10,900
Gain chargeable to tax	£295,100
Capital gains tax payable (£295,100 × 10%)	£29,510

Notes

(a) Where an individual makes a disposal of either all or part of his interest in the assets of a partnership or shares in or securities of a company (or an interest in such shares or securities) which qualifies for entrepreneurs' relief, an associated disposal of assets owned personally also qualifies for relief. The assets which are disposed of must have been in use for the purposes of the business of the partnership or company (or, where the company is a member of a trading group, the business of a member of the trading group) throughout the one-year period ending with the earlier of the date of the disposal of the partnership assets or shares etc. and the cessation of the business of the partnership or company. The disposal must be made as part of the individual's withdrawal from participation in the business. [*TCGA 1992, s 169K*].

(b) Entrepreneurs' relief in respect of an associated disposal is restricted where the assets were in use for the purposes of the business only for part of the period of ownership; where only part of the assets are in use for business purposes for that period; where the individual is concerned in carrying on the business (personally, in partnership or as an officer or employee of his personal company) for only part of the period in which the assets are in use for the purposes of the business; and where, for any part of the period for which the assets are in use for the purposes of the business (but ignoring any part of the period which falls before 6 April 2008), their availability is dependent on the payment of rent (which term includes any form of consideration given for the use of an asset). Relief is applied only to such part of the gain as is just and reasonable. [*TCGA 1992, ss 169P, 169S(5)*].

211.4 REORGANISATIONS ETC.

[*TCGA 1992, s 169Q*]

Mr Prosser is a shareholder in Oyster Ltd, a trading company which qualifies as his personal company for the purposes of entrepreneurs' relief. He acquired the shares in March 2002 for £150,000 and has been a director of the company since that time. In January 2014, the shareholders of Oyster Ltd accept an offer by a public company, Lobster plc, and Mr Prosser receives shares in Lobster plc in exchange for his entire shareholding in Oyster Ltd. His Lobster plc shares are valued at £550,000 at the time of the exchange, and the company does not qualify as his personal company. Mr Prosser makes no other disposals in 2013/14 and has made no previous claims to entrepreneurs' relief.

If Mr Prosser elects under *TCGA 1992, s 169Q* to disapply *TCGA 1992, s 127* in respect of the share exchange and claims entrepreneurs' relief in respect of the gain on the Oyster Ltd shares, his capital gains tax liability for 2013/14 is calculated as follows.

	£
Sale proceeds	550,000
Cost	150,000
Chargeable gain qualifying for entrepreneurs' relief	400,000
Annual exemption	10,900
Gain chargeable to tax	£389,100
Capital gains tax payable (£389,100 × 10%)	£38,910

Notes

(a) Where an exchange of securities (within *TCGA 1992, s 135*) takes place and *TCGA 1992, s 127* would otherwise apply to treat the 'original shares' and the 'new holding' (as defined for the purposes of that section) as the same asset, an election can be made to disapply that section so that entrepreneurs' relief can be claimed in respect of the disposal of the original shares.

(b) The election must be made on or before the first anniversary of the 31 January following the tax year in which the reorganisation takes place. In this case, therefore, the claim must be made by 31 January 2016 (which is the same date by which the claim to entrepreneurs' relief must be made). An election takes effect only where a claim to entrepreneurs' relief is also made; without such a claim, the election has no effect.

(c) Mr Prosser cannot claim entrepreneurs' relief on an eventual disposal of his shares in Lobster plc. If he had not made an election under *TCGA 1992, s 169Q* the opportunity to claim relief would have been lost.

(d) The above provisions apply also to reorganisations within *TCGA 1992, s 126* and to schemes of reconstruction within *TCGA 1992, s 136* to which *TCGA 1992, s 127* applies.

211.5 TRANSITIONAL PROVISIONS FOR DEFERRED GAINS

[*FA 2008, Sch 3 para 8*]

In May 2006, Charlotte sells her entire shareholding in Gochenauer Ltd, realising a gain (before taper relief) of £137,000. The gain would have qualified for entrepreneurs' relief had it then been available. In August 2006, Charlotte acquires by subscription 51% of the issued ordinary share capital of Thorn Ltd for £137,000. This is a qualifying investment for the purposes of EIS deferral relief and Charlotte makes a claim to defer the whole of the May 2006 gain.

211.5 CGT   Entrepreneurs' Relief

On 1 May 2013, Charlotte sells her shares in Thorn Ltd, realising a chargeable gain of £80,000, which qualifies for entrepreneurs' relief. She makes no other disposals in 2013/14 and has made no previous entrepreneur's relief claims.

If Charlotte claims entrepreneurs' relief in respect of both the deferred May 2006 gain and the May 2013 gain, her CGT position for 2013/14 is as follows.

	£
Deferred May 2006 gain brought into charge	137,000
May 2013 gain	80,000
Chargeable gains qualifying for entrepreneurs' relief	217,000
Annual exemption	10,900
Gain chargeable to tax	£206,100
Capital gains tax payable (£206,100 × 10%)	£20,610

Notes

(a) Entrepreneurs' relief can be claimed where a chargeable gain which would have accrued before 6 April 2008 has been deferred under either the ENTERPRISE INVESTMENT SCHEME (210) or venture capital trusts scheme and there is a 'chargeable event' on or after that date in relation to any of the shares by virtue of which the original gain was deferred. [FA 2008, Sch 3 para 8; F(No 2)A 2010, Sch 1 paras 11, 17].

(b) See 210.3 ENTERPRISE INVESTMENT SCHEME for a further example of EIS deferral relief.

(c) Taper relief is not available in respect of the deferred May 2006 gain when brought into charge after 5 April 2008, as the relief is abolished for gains accruing *or treated as accruing* after that date. [FA 2008, Sch 2 paras 25, 45, 56(3)].

(d) Transitional provisions also apply where a chargeable gain is deemed to accrue to an individual on a disposal on or after 6 April 2008 under *TCGA 1992, s 116(10)(b)* (see 223.2 QUALIFYING CORPORATE BONDS) by reason of a reorganisation to which that individual was a party and which took place before that date. [FA 2008, Sch 3 para 7; F(No 2)A 2010, Sch 1 paras 10, 16].

212 Exemptions and Reliefs

Cross-references. See also 224 PRIVATE RESIDENCES, 225 QUALIFYING CORPORATE BONDS and 231 WASTING ASSETS.

212.1 CHATTELS

(A) **Marginal relief**

[*TCGA 1992, s 262(2)*]

On 1 April 1988, Y acquired by inheritance a painting valued for probate at £900. He sold it for £7,200 on 30 October 2013, incurring costs of £150.

	£	£
Disposal proceeds	7,200	
Incidental costs	150	7,050
Acquisition cost		900
Chargeable gain		£6,150
Marginal relief		
Chargeable gain limited to ⁵/₃ × (£7,200 − £6,000)		£2,000

(B) **Loss relief**

[*TCGA 1992, s 262(3)*]

Z bought a piece of antique jewellery for £7,000 in February 1991. In January 2014, he is forced to sell it, but at auction it realises only £1,500 and Z incurs costs of £100.

	£	£
Deemed disposal consideration		6,000
Cost of disposal	100	
Cost of acquisition	7,000	7,100
Allowable loss		£1,100

Note

(a) Where the disposal consideration for tangible movable property is less than £6,000 and there would otherwise be a loss, the consideration is deemed to be £6,000.

(C) **Partial disposal of assets forming sets**

[*TCGA 1992, s 262(4)*]

212.1 CGT   Exemptions and Reliefs

AB purchased a set of six 18th century dining chairs in 1985 for £1,200. After incurring restoration costs of £300 in 1991, he sold two of them in March 2009 to an unconnected person for £2,900. In August 2013, he sold the other four to the same buyer for £4,900.

The two disposals are treated as one for the purposes of the chattel exemption and marginal relief, the consideration for which is £7,800. Marginal relief on this basis would give a total chargeable gain of £3,000([£7,800 − £6,000] x $^5/_3$ which is to be compared with the following:

March 2009	£	£
Disposal proceeds		2,900
Acquisition cost	1,200	
Enhancement cost	300	
	1,500	
Cost of two chairs sold £1,500 × $^2/_6$		500
Chargeable gain		£2,400

August 2013	£
Disposal proceeds	4,900
Cost £1,500 × $^4/_6$	1,000
Chargeable gain	£3,900
Total chargeable gains (£2,400 + £3,900)	£6,300

The total gain of £6,300 compares with a gain of £3,000 using marginal relief. Marginal relief is therefore effective and the total chargeable gain is £3,000.

The gain is apportioned to tax years as follows (note (b))

2008/09	£3,000 × $\dfrac{2,900}{7,800}$ =	£1,115
2013/14	£3,000 × $\dfrac{4,900}{7,800}$ =	£1,885

Notes

(a)   Prior to the second disposal, the first disposal would have been exempt, the proceeds being within the £6,000 chattel exemption.

(b)   The gain as reduced by marginal relief is apportioned between tax years in the same ratio as the proportion of total sale proceeds applicable to each year (HMRC Capital Gains Manual, CG 76637).

(c)   See also **202.4** ANTI-AVOIDANCE.

213 Hold-Over Reliefs

213.1 RELIEF FOR GIFTS

[*TCGA 1992, s 260*]

(A) Chargeable lifetime transfers

B owns a house which he has not occupied as a private residence. He purchased the house for £15,200 inclusive of costs in 1979 and in January 2014 he gives it to a discretionary trust of which he is the settlor. The settlement is not a settlor-interested settlement for the purposes of *TCGA 1992, ss 169B–169G*. The market value of the house is agreed to be £200,000 at the date of transfer, and B incurs transfer costs of £1,000. The house had a value of £21,000 at 31 March 1982.

	£
Disposal consideration	200,000
Deduct Costs of disposal	1,000
	199,000
Market value 31.3.82	21,000
Chargeable gain	£178,000

If B elects under *TCGA 1992, s 260*, his chargeable gain is reduced to nil, and the trustees' acquisition cost of the house is treated as £22,000 (£200,000 - £178,000).

Notes

(a) Relief under *TCGA 1992, s 260* is restricted, generally, to transfers which are, or would but for annual exemptions be, chargeable lifetime transfers for inheritance tax purposes.

(b) Separate rules apply to transfers of assets between MARRIED PERSONS AND CIVIL PARTNERS **(217)**.

(c) Relief under *TCGA 1992, s 260* is not available on a disposal to the trustees of a settlor-interested settlement (as defined). [*TCGA 1992, ss 169B–169G*].

(B) Disposal consideration

[*TCGA 1992, s 260(5)*]

The facts are as in (A) above except that B sells the house to the trustees for £30,000.

213.1 CGT Hold-Over Reliefs

	£	£
Chargeable gain (as above) (note (a))		178,000
Deduct		
Actual consideration passing	30,000	
B's allowable costs	(22,000)	
		8,000
Held-over gain		£170,000
(i) B's chargeable gain is reduced to £178,000 − £170,000		£8,000
(ii) The trustees' allowable cost is reduced to £200,000 − £170,000		£30,000

Note

(a) The disposal consideration is taken as the open market value of the house at the date of disposal because B and the trustees are connected persons. Thus, the computation of the gain is as in (A) above.

(C) **Relief for IHT**

[*TCGA 1992, s 260(7)*]

The facts are as in (A) above. Before transferring the house, B had made substantial chargeable transfers. Inheritance tax of £20,000 is payable on the transfer. The trustees sell the house in December 2014 for £195,000.

	£	£
Disposal proceeds		195,000
Acquisition cost	200,000	
Deduct held-over gain	178,000	
		22,000
Gain		173,000
IHT attributable to earlier transfer		20,000
Chargeable gain		£153,000

Notes

(a) Where the IHT attributable to the earlier transfer is greater than the gain, the IHT deduction is limited to the amount of the gain and cannot create or increase a loss. [*TCGA 1992, s 260(7)*].

(b) A similar inheritance tax relief operates where the original gain was held over under *TCGA 1992, s 165* or *FA 1980, s 79*. [*TCGA 1992, ss 67, 165(10)*].

213.2 RELIEF FOR GIFTS OF BUSINESS ASSETS

[*TCGA 1992, s 165, Sch 7*]

Zoë owns a freehold property which she lets to the family trading company, Sphere Ltd, in which she and her father each own half the shares and voting rights. Zoë inherited the property in April 1990 at a probate value of £50,000, and since then the whole of the property has been used for the purposes of the company's trade. In November 2013, Zoë transfers the property to her boyfriend. Its market value at that time is £115,000. The intention is that he should give sufficient consideration to leave Zoë with a chargeable gain exactly equal to the annual exempt amount (there being no other disposals in 2013/14).

Actual consideration should be £60,900 as shown by the following computation

	£
Deemed consideration	115,000
Deduct: Cost	50,000
Unrelieved gain	65,000
Held-over gain (see below)	54,100
Chargeable gain covered by annual exemption	£10,900

Computation of held over gain

	£	£
Unrelieved gain		65,000
Actual consideration	60,900	
Less allowable expenditure	50,000	10,900
Held-over gain		£54,100

Note

(a) On a subsequent disposal of the property, the allowable expenditure would be £60,900 (deemed proceeds of £115,000 less held-over gain of £54,100).

213.3 TRANSFER OF BUSINESS TO A COMPANY

(A) Incorporation relief

[*TCGA 1992, s 162*]

W carries on an antiquarian bookselling business. He decides to form an unquoted company, P Ltd, to carry on the business. He transfers, in May 2013, the whole of the business undertaking, assets and liabilities to P Ltd, in consideration for the issue of shares, plus an amount left outstanding on interest-free loan. W becomes a director of P Ltd. The business assets and liabilities transferred are valued as follows

213.3 CGT   Hold-Over Reliefs

		Value	Chargeable gain
	£	£	£
Freehold shop premises (acquired in 1990)		80,000	52,000
Goodwill		36,000	26,000
Fixtures and fittings		4,000	—
Trading stock		52,000	—
Debtors		28,000	—
		200,000	
Mortgage on shop	50,000		
Trade creditors	20,000	70,000	—
		£130,000	£78,000

The company issues 100,000 £1 ordinary shares, valued at par, to W in May 2013, and the amount left outstanding is £30,000. W does not elect to disapply incorporation relief. In January 2014, W sells 20,000 of his shares for £45,000 to X. W's remaining shareholding is then worth, say, £155,000. It is assumed that W has made no previous disposals qualifying for ENTREPRENEURS' RELIEF (211)

(i)   *Amount of chargeable gain rolled over on transfer of the business*

$$\frac{100,000}{130,000} \times £78,000 \qquad\qquad £60,000$$

Of the chargeable gain, £18,000 (£78,000 - £60,000) remains taxable and is subject to ENTREPRENEURS' RELIEF (211).

The allowable cost of W's shares is £40,000 (£100,000 - £60,000).

(ii)   *On the sale of shares to X, W realises a chargeable gain*

	£
Disposal consideration	45,000
Allowable cost £40,000 × $\frac{45,000}{45,000 + 155,000}$	9,000
Chargeable gain (no entrepreneurs' relief as shares held less than 12 months)	£36,000

Notes

(a)   Relief under *TCGA 1992, s 162* is given automatically and without the need for a claim (but see (B) below).

(b)   In the hands of the company, the goodwill will not qualify for the special treatment of intangible assets of companies in *CTA 2009, Pt 8*, because it was acquired from a related party and was created before 1 April 2002 (by virtue of the business having been carried on before that date). [*CTA 2009, ss 882–884*].

Hold-Over Reliefs CGT 213.3

(B) **Election to disapply incorporation relief**

[*TCGA 1992, s 162A; FA 2002, s 49*] The facts are as in (A) above, except that W considers an election under *TCGA 1992, s162A* to disapply *TCGA 1992, s 162*. With an election, the computations in (A) are revised as follows.

(i) *Chargeable gain on transfer of the business*

	£
Chargeable gain	78,000

(ii) *Chargeable gain on sale of shares*

	£
Disposal consideration	45,000
Allowable cost $£100,000 \times \dfrac{45,000}{45,000 + 155,000}$	22,500
Chargeable gain (no entrepreneurs' relief as shares held less than 12 months)	£22,500

On the face of it, the election is not beneficial, producing aggregate gains of £100,500 (£78,000 + £22,500) as against £54,000 (£18,000 + £36,000) in (A) above.

If, however, W then sells his remaining 80,000 shares for £155,000 in, say, May 2014, he will have, as illustrated below, a chargeable gain for 2014/15 of £124,000 without the election or £77,500 with the election. There is now a substantial overall saving if the election is made. If W had retained the shares for at least one year, such that entrepreneurs' relief would have been available on sale, the election would have been neutral, the relief forgone on incorporation having been fully recovered.

213.3 CGT   Hold-Over Reliefs

Chargeable gain on sale of 80,000 shares in May 2014

Without the election

	£
Disposal consideration	155,000
Allowable cost (£40,000 − £9,000)	31,000
Chargeable gain (no entrepreneurs' relief as shares held less than 12 months)	£124,000

With the election

	£
Disposal consideration	155,000
Allowable cost (£100,000 − £22,500)	77,500
Chargeable gain (no entrepreneurs' relief as shares held less than 12 months)	£77,500

Note

(a) On a transfer (of a business) that is otherwise within the scope of *TCGA 1992, s 162* at (A) above the transferor may make an election under *TCGA 1992, s 162A* to forgo incorporation relief.

213.4 DISINCORPORATION RELIEF

[*TCGA 1992, ss 162B, 162C; CTA 2009, s 849A; FA 2013, ss 58–61*]

(A) **Goodwill outside intangible assets regime**

W has owned all of the shares in B Ltd since the company was set up and began trading in 2000. On 31 July 2013, B Ltd transfers the trade as a going concern to W. The assets of the trade include land with a market value of £35,000 and goodwill with a market value of £27,000. The land cost £12,000 in 2000 and the goodwill, being internally generated, has no acquisition cost for chargeable gains purposes.

If W and B Ltd jointly make a claim for disincorporation relief before 31 July 2015, B Ltd's chargeable gains computation on the transfer is as follows.

Land

	£
Deemed disposal consideration	12,000
Deduct Costs of acquisition	12,000
Chargeable gain	£Nil

Goodwill

	£
Deemed disposal consideration	Nil
Deduct Costs of acquisition	Nil
Chargeable gain	£Nil

W's acquisition costs for the purposes of capital gains tax are £12,000 for the land and £Nil for the goodwill.

Notes

(a) A claim to disincorporation relief must be made jointly by the company and all of the shareholders to whom the business is transferred. A claim is irrevocable and must be made within the two years beginning with the date of the transfer of the company's business. [*FA 2013, s 60*].

(b) A transfer of a business from a company to some or all of its shareholders qualifies for disincorporation relief if the business is transferred as a going concern and it is transferred together with all of the business assets (or all the assets other than cash). All of the shareholders to whom the business is transferred must be individuals and must have held shares in the company throughout the twelve months ending with the date of the transfer. The qualifying assets (see (c) below) must have a combined market value not exceeding £100,000. The business must be transferred between 1 April 2013 and 31 March 2018 inclusive. [*FA 2013, ss 58(1), 59(1)–(6)*].

(c) Qualifying assets are goodwill and interests in land which are not held as trading stock. [*FA 2013, s 59(10)*]. Goodwill within the INTANGIBLE ASSETS (CT 109) regime in the hands of the company is subject to specific rules under that regime. See (B) below. In this case, the goodwill is excluded from the intangible assets regime because the company's trade was carried on before 1 April 2002.

(d) Where a claim to disincorporation relief is made, the disposal consideration for each of the qualifying assets (and the shareholder's acquisition cost) is deemed to be equal to the lower of the allowable expenditure on the disposal and the market value of the asset. [*TCGA 1992, s 162B; FA 2013, s 61(1)*]. Where the market value is less than the allowable expenditure, the result is that an allowable loss accrues to the company; otherwise neither a gain nor a loss arises.

(B) **Goodwill within intangible assets regime**

[*TCGA 1992, s 260(5)*]

The facts are as in (A) above except that B Ltd was set up and the trade commenced in 2004.

If W and B Ltd jointly make a claim for disincorporation relief before 31 July 2015, B Ltd's chargeable gains computation on the transfer of the land is as follows.

	£
Deemed disposal consideration	12,000
Deduct Costs of acquisition	12,000
Chargeable gain	£Nil

213.4 CGT   Hold-Over Reliefs

W's acquisition cost for the purposes of capital gains tax is £12,000.

The goodwill falls within the INTANGIBLE ASSETS (CT 109) regime in the hands of the company. If a disincorporation relief claim is made, the realisation proceeds of the goodwill are treated as nil (see note (a)). W's acquisition cost for the purposes of capital gains tax is equal to the value at which the goodwill is treated as transferred by the company under the intangible assets regime, i.e. nil.

Note

(a) Where a claim to disincorporation relief is made and goodwill within the INTANGIBLE ASSETS (CT 109) regime is one of the qualifying assets, that regime applies to the company as follows:

- if the goodwill has been written-down for corporation tax purposes, the transfer is treated as being at the lower of the tax written-down value and the market value of the goodwill;

- if the goodwill has not been written down but is shown in the conmpany's balance sheet, the transfer is treated as being at the lower of cost and market value;

- if the goodwill is not shown in the balance sheet, the transfer is treated as made for realisation proceeds of nil.

[*CTA 2009, s 849A; FA 2013, s 61(5)*].

214 Indexation

Note

Indexation allowance is available only for the purposes of corporation tax on chargeable gains.

214.1 INDEXATION ALLOWANCE — GENERAL RULES

[*TCGA 1992, ss 53–56*]

(A) **Calculation of indexation factor — companies**

M Ltd bought a freehold factory in December 1984 for £500,000. Further buildings are erected at a cost of £200,000 in May 1992. In May 2013 the factory is sold for £2m. The retail price index (RPI) was re-based in January 1987 from 394.5 to 100 and the relevant values are as follows

December 1984	358.5
May 1992	139.3
May 2013	250.0

	£	£
Disposal consideration		2,000,000
Deduct Cost of factory and site	500,000	
Cost of additions	200,000	700,000
Unindexed gain		1,300,000
Indexation allowance		

(i) Factory and site

Indexation factor

$$\left(\frac{394.5 \times 250.0}{358.5}\right) - 100 = 175.1\%$$

Indexed rise

£500,000 × 1.751   875,500

(ii) Additions

Indexation factor

$$\frac{250.0 - 139.3}{139.3} = 0.795$$

Indexed rise

£200,000 × 0.795   159,000   1,034,500

214.1 CGT   Indexation

Gain chargeable to corporation tax   £265,500

Note

(a)   Alternatively the indexation factor on the pre-January 1987 expenditure can be calculated using the revised RPI figures so that, for example,

December 1984	=	90.87
May 2013	=	250.0

$$\text{Indexation from December 1984 to May 2013} = \frac{250.0 - 90.87}{90.87} = 1.751$$

(B) **Disposal of asset held on 31 March 1982**

X Ltd acquired an asset for £6,000 in August 1979. The company sold it for £27,000 in December 2013. The agreed market value of the asset at 31 March 1982 is £7,500. For the purpose only of this example, the indexation factor for March 1982 to December 2013 is 2.100.

	£	£
Disposal consideration	27,000	27,000
Deduct Cost	6,000	
Market value 31.3.82	—	7,500
Unindexed gain	21,000	19,500
Indexation allowance £7,500 × 2.100	15,750	15,750
Gain after indexation	£5,250	£3,750
Chargeable gain		£3,750

Notes

(a)   In both the calculation using cost and that using 31 March 1982 value, indexation is automatically based on 31 March 1982 value. If, however, a greater allowance would have been produced by basing indexation on cost, that would automatically have applied instead. If, however, an irrevocable election were to be made under *TCGA 1992, s 35(5)* for all assets to be treated as sold and re-acquired at 31 March 1982, indexation must then be based on 31 March 1982 value whether it is beneficial or not. [*TCGA 1992, s 55(1)(2)*].

(b)   See also **205.1 ASSETS HELD ON 31 MARCH 1982**.

Indexation   CGT 214.2

(C) **Losses — indexation allowance restriction**

[*TCGA 1992, s 53(1)(b)(2A); FA 1994, s 93(1)–(3)(11)*]

In June 1990, M Ltd had purchased two assets, each for £25,000. In September 2013, the company sells the assets for £30,000 (A) and £23,000 (B) respectively. Incidental costs of purchase and sale are ignored for the purposes of this example. For the purpose only of this example, the indexation factor for the period June 1990 to September 2013 is assumed to be 0.710.

The gains/losses on the sales are as follows

	(A) £	(B) £
Proceeds	30,000	23,000
Cost	25,000	25,000
Unindexed gain/(loss)	5,000	(2,000)
Indexation allowance £25,000 × 0.710 = £17,750 but restricted to	(5,000)	Nil
Chargeable gain/(allowable loss)	Nil	£(2,000)

Note

(a) Indexation allowance can reduce an unindexed gain to nil but cannot create or increase a loss.

214.2 NO GAIN/NO LOSS TRANSFERS

(A) **Transfers between spouses or civil partners before 6 April 2008 — asset acquired by first spouse before 1 April 1982 — gain on ultimate disposal after 5 April 2008**

[*TCGA 1992, s 35A, s 52A, s 55(5)(6), s 56(2), s 58; FA 2008, Sch 2 paras 59, 60, 65(2), 71, 78, 83; SI 2005 No 3229, Reg 107*]

Mr N inherited a country cottage in 1977 at a probate value of £12,000. Its market value at 31 March 1982 was £30,000. In July 1988, Mr N incurred enhancement expenditure of £5,000 on the cottage. In May 1990, he gave the cottage to his wife. In November 2013, Mrs N sells it for £205,000. At no time was the cottage the main residence of either spouse. The relevant indexation factors are as follows

March 1982 to May 1990	0.589
July 1988 to May 1990	0.183

(i) *Disposal in May 1990*

Consideration deemed to be such that neither gain nor loss arises.

£   £

214.2 CGT Indexation

Cost of cottage to Mr N		12,000
Enhancement expenditure		5,000
		17,000
Indexation allowance:		
£30,000 × 0.589	17,670	
£5,000 × 0.183	915	18,585
Cost of cottage to Mrs N		£35,585

(ii) *Disposal in November 2013*

Re-computation of Mrs N's acquisition cost

	£
Market value 31.3.82	30,000
Enhancement expenditure	5,000
	35,000
Indexation allowance (as above)	18,585
Cost of cottage to Mrs N	£53,585

Mrs N's chargeable gain

	£
Sale proceeds	205,000
Deduct cost	53,585
Chargeable gain 2013/14	£151,415

Notes

(a) The cottage having been acquired by Mrs N by means of a no gain/no loss disposal from her husband to which re-basing did not apply, in computing the gain on her disposal of the cottage after 5 April 2008 re-basing is assumed to have applied to the no gain/no loss disposal. [*TCGA 1992, s 35A; FA 2008, Sch 2 paras 59, 71*]. Therefore, in computing the gain or loss on the post-5 April 2008 disposal, the allowable expenditure includes the value of the cottage at 31 March 1982 and the indexation allowance due for the period from that date to the date on which Mrs N acquired the cottage (May 1990). This rule does not affect the position of Mr N.

(b) Indexation allowance is abolished for capital gains tax purposes (i.e. for disposals by individuals, trustees and personal representatives) for disposals on or after 6 April 2008. [*TCGA 1992, s 52A; FA 2008, Sch 2 paras 78, 83*]. No indexation allowance is due therefore on the disposal by Mrs N, but as a result of the rule in note (a) above, she effectively obtains indexation allowance up to the date on which she acquired the cottage (or April 1998 if earlier).

(c) See also (B) below and **217 MARRIED PERSONS AND CIVIL PARTNERS**.

Indexation   CGT 214.2

(B) **Transfers between spouses or civil partners before 6 April 2008 — asset acquired by first spouse after 31 March 1982 — gain on ultimate disposal after 5 April 2008**

[*TCGA 1992, s 56(2)*]

The facts are as in (A) above except that Mr N inherited the cottage in April 1982 at a probate value of £30,000. The relevant indexation factors are

April 1982 to May 1990	0.557
July 1988 to May 1990	0.183

(i) *Disposal in May 1990*

Consideration deemed to be such that neither gain nor loss arises.

	£	£
Cost of cottage to Mr N		30,000
Enhancement expenditure		5,000
		35,000
Indexation allowance:		
£30,000 × 0.557	16,710	
£5,000 × 0.183	915	17,625
Cost of cottage to Mrs N		£52,625

(ii) *Disposal in November 2013*

	£
Sale proceeds	205,000
Cost (as above)	52,625
Chargeable gain 2013/14	£152,375

Notes

(a) For further examples on transfers between spouses or civil partners, see (A) above and **217 MARRIED PERSONS AND CIVIL PARTNERS**.

(b) See note (b) to (A) above.

(C) **Intra-group transfers — asset acquired by group before 1 April 1982**

[*TCGA 1992, s 55(5)–(9), s 56(2), s 171*]

J Ltd and K Ltd are 75% subsidiaries of H Ltd. J Ltd acquired a property in 1980 for £20,000. Its market value at 31 March 1982 was £25,000. In May 1990, J Ltd transferred the property to K Ltd. In May 2013, K Ltd sells the property outside the group. The sale proceeds are (1) £80,000, (2) £18,000 or (3) £29,000. The relevant indexation factors are as follows

214.2 CGT   Indexation

March 1982 to May 1990	0.589
March 1982 to May 2013	2.147

(i) *Disposal in May 1990*

Consideration deemed to be such that neither gain nor loss arises.

	£
Cost of asset to J Ltd	20,000
Indexation allowance £25,000 × 0.589	14,725
Cost of asset to K Ltd	£34,725

(ii) *Disposal in May 2013*

(1)   Proceeds £80,000

	£	£	£
Proceeds		80,000	80,000
Cost	34,725		
Deduct Indexation allowance previously given	14,725	(20,000)	
Market value 31.3.82		–	(25,000)
Unindexed gain		60,000	55,000
Indexation allowance £25,000 × 2.147		53,675	53,675
Gain after indexation		£6,325	£1,325
Chargeable gain			£1,325

(2)   Proceeds £18,000

	£	£	£
Proceeds		18,000	18,000
Cost	34,725		
Deduct Indexation allowance previously given	14,725	(20,000)	
Market value 31.3.82		–	(25,000)
		(2,000)	(7,000)
Add Rolled-up indexation		(14,725)	(14,725)
Loss after rolled-up indexation		£(16,725)	£(21,725)
Allowable loss		£16,725	

Indexation CGT 214.2

(3)   Proceeds £29,000

	£	£	£
Proceeds		29,000	29,000
Cost	34,725		
Deduct Indexation allowance previously given	14,725		
	(20,000)		
Market value 31.3.82		—	(25,000)
Unindexed gain		9,000	4,000
Indexation allowance:			
£25,000 × 2.147 = £53,675 but restricted to		(9,000)	(4,000)
		Nil	Nil
Excess of rolled-up indexation (£14,725) over indexation allowance given above		(5,725)	(10,725)
Loss after rolled-up indexation		£(5,725)	£(10,725)
Allowable loss		£5,725	

Notes

(a) Having acquired the property by means of a no gain/no loss disposal from J Ltd, who held it at 31 March 1982, K Ltd is deemed to have held the asset at 31 March 1982 for the purposes of the re-basing provisions, and also the provisions under which indexation allowance is computed using value at 31 March 1982. [*TCGA 1992, s 55(5)(6), Sch 3 para 1*].

(b) In (2) and (3) above, as the ultimate disposal is after 29 November 1993 and indexation allowance is either unavailable in (2) above or restricted in (3) above, special provisions enable the person making the disposal to obtain the benefit of any indexation allowance already accrued on no gain/no loss transfers made *before* 30 November 1993 (called 'rolled-up indexation'). [*TCGA 1992, s 55(7)–(9)*].

(D) **Intra-group transfers — asset acquired by group after 31 March 1982 — loss on ultimate disposal**

[*TCGA 1992, s 56(2)–(4), s 171*]

L Ltd, M Ltd and N Ltd are members of a 75% group of companies. L Ltd acquired a property in June 1990 for £50,000 and transferred it to M Ltd in June 1993. M Ltd transferred the property to N Ltd in June 1996, and N Ltd sold it outside the group in June 2013 for £55,000. The relevant indexation factors are as follows

June 1990 to June 1993	0.113
June 1993 to June 1996	0.085

214.2 CGT Indexation

(i) *Disposal in June 1993*

Consideration deemed to be such that neither gain nor loss arises.

	£
Cost of asset to L Ltd	50,000
Indexation allowance £50,000 × 0.113	5,650
Cost of asset to M Ltd	£55,650

(ii) *Disposal in June 1996*

	£
Cost of asset to M Ltd	55,650
Indexation allowance £55,650 × 0.085	4,730
Cost of asset to N Ltd	£60,380

(iii) *Disposal in June 2013*

	£
Proceeds	55,000
Cost (as above)	60,380
Loss before adjustment under *TCGA 1992, s 56(3)*	5,380
Deduct Indexation on June 1996 disposal	4,730
Allowable loss	£650

Note

(a) Where a loss accrues on the ultimate disposal, it is reduced by any indexation allowance included in the cost of the asset by virtue of a no gain/no loss disposal made *after* 29 November 1993. If this adjustment would otherwise convert a loss into a gain, the disposal is treated as giving rise to neither a gain nor a loss. [*TCGA 1992, s 56(3)*].

215 Land

215.1 SMALL PART DISPOSALS

[*TCGA 1992, s 242*]

C owns farmland which cost £134,000 in May 1988. In February 1996, a small plot of land is exchanged with an adjoining landowner for another piece of land. The value placed on the transaction is £18,000. The value of the remaining estate excluding the new piece of land is estimated at £250,000. In March 2014, C sells the whole estate for £300,000. He makes no other disposals in 2013/14. The indexation factor for May 1988 to February 1996 is 0.421

(i) **No claim made under TCGA 1992, s 242(2)**

		£	£
(a)	*Disposal in February 1996*		
	Disposal proceeds		18,000
	Allowable cost $\dfrac{18,000}{18,000 + 250,000} \times £134,000$		9,000
	Unindexed gain		9,000
	Indexation allowance £9,000 × 0.421		3,789
	Chargeable gain 1995/96		£5,211
(b)	*Disposal in March 2014*		
	Disposal proceeds		300,000
	Allowable cost		
	Original land £(134,000 − 9,000)	125,000	
	Exchanged land	18,000	143,000
	Chargeable gain 2013/14		£157,000

(ii) **Claim made under TCGA 1992, s 242(2)**

		£	£
(a)	*No disposal in February 1996*		
	Allowable cost of original land		134,000
	Deduct Disposal proceeds		18,000
	Adjusted allowable cost		£116,000
	Allowable cost of additional land		£18,000

215.1 CGT Land

(b) Disposal in March 2014

Disposal proceeds		300,000
Allowable cost		
Original land	116,000	
Additional land	18,000	134,000
Chargeable gain 2013/14		£166,000

Notes

(a) A claim under *TCGA 1992, s 242* may be made where the consideration for the part disposal does not exceed one-fifth of the value of the whole, up to a maximum of £20,000.

(b) If the second disposal had also been made in 1995/96 no claim under *section 242(2)* could have been made on the part disposal as proceeds of all disposals of land in the year would have exceeded £20,000.

(c) If the original land had been held at 31 March 1982 and the part disposal took place after that date, the disposal proceeds, on a claim under *section 242(2)*, would be deducted from the 31 March 1982 value for the purpose of the re-basing provisions.

215.2 COMPULSORY PURCHASE

[*TCGA 1992, ss 243–248*]

(A) **Rollover where new land acquired**

(i) *Rollover not claimed*

D owns freehold land purchased for £77,000 in 1978. Part of the land is made the subject of a compulsory purchase order. The compensation of £70,000 is agreed on 10 August 2013. The market value of the remaining land is £175,000. The value of the total freehold land at 31 March 1982 was £98,000.

	£
Disposal consideration	70,000
Market value 31.3.82	
$£98,000 \times \dfrac{70,000}{70,000 + 175,000}$	28,000
Chargeable gain 2013/14	£42,000

(ii) *Rollover claimed under TCGA 1992, s 247*

If, in (i), D acquires new land costing, say, £80,000 in, say, December 2013, relief may be claimed as follows.

	£
Allowable cost of land compulsorily purchased	28,000
Actual consideration	70,000
Chargeable gain rolled over	£42,000
Allowable cost of new land (£80,000 − £42,000)	£38,000

(B) **Small disposals**

(i) *No rollover relief claimed*

T inherited land in June 1988 at a probate value of £290,000. Under a compulsory purchase order, a part of the land is acquired for highway improvements. Compensation of £32,000 and a further £10,000 for severance, neither sum including any amount in respect of loss of profits, is agreed on 14 May 2013. The value of the remaining land is £900,000. Prior to the compulsory purchase, the value of all the land had been £950,000.

	£
Total consideration for disposal (£32,000 + £10,000)	42,000
Deduct Allowable cost $\dfrac{42,000}{42,000 + 900,000} \times £290,000$	12,930
Chargeable gain 2013/14	£29,070

(ii) *Rollover relief claimed under TCGA 1992, s 243*

Total consideration for disposal is £42,000, less than 5% of the value of the estate before the disposal (£950,000). T may therefore claim that the consideration be deducted from the allowable cost of the estate.

Revised allowable cost (£290,000 − £42,000)	£248,000

No chargeable gain then arises in 2013/14.

Note

(a) HMRC additionally regard consideration of £3,000 or less as 'small', whether or not it would pass the 5% test illustrated here. (Revenue Tax Bulletin February 1997, p 397).

215.3 LEASES

(A) **Short leases which are not initially wasting assets**

[*TCGA 1992, Sch 8 para 1*]

On 31 August 2008, N purchased the remaining term of a lease of commercial premises for £55,000. The lease was subject to a 25-year sub-lease granted on 1 July 1986 at a fixed rental of £1,000 a year. The market rental was estimated at £15,000 a year. The term of the lease

215.3 CGT   Land

held by N is 60 years from 1 April 1984. The value of the lease in 2011, when the sub-lease expired, was estimated at 31 August 2008 as being £70,000. Immediately upon expiry of the sub-lease, N has refurbishment work done at a cost of £50,000, of which £40,000 qualifies as enhancement expenditure. On 31 March 2014, N sells the lease for £130,000.

Term of lease at date of expiry of sub-lease	32 years 9 months
Relevant percentage $89.354 + {}^9/_{12} \times (90.280 - 89.354)$	90.049%
Term of lease at date of assignment	30 years
Relevant percentage	87.330%

	£	£
Disposal consideration		130,000
Deduct Allowable cost	55,000	
Enhancement costs	40,000	
	95,000	
Less Wasted		
$\dfrac{90.049 - 87.330}{90.049} \times 95,000$	2,868	
		92,132
Chargeable gain 2013/14		£37,868

Note

(a)   The head-lease becomes a wasting asset on the expiry of the sub-lease. [*TCGA 1992, Sch 8 para 1(2)*].

(B)   **Grant of long lease**

[*TCGA 1992, s 42, Sch 8 para 2*]

In 1982, K acquired a long lease by assignment for £44,000. At the time he acquired it, the lease had an unexpired term of 87 years. On 10 April 2013, he granted a 55-year sublease for a premium of £110,000 and a peppercorn rent. The value of the reversion plus the capitalised value of the rents is £10,000. The value of the lease at 31 March 1982 was estimated at £54,000.

	£
Disposal consideration	110,000
Market value 31.3.82	
$£54,000 \times \dfrac{110,000}{110,000 + 10,000}$	49,500

Land   CGT 215.3

Chargeable gain 2013/14	£60,500

(C) **Grant of short lease**

[*TCGA 1992, Sch 8 paras 2, 5; ITTOIA 2005, ss 277–281; CTA 2009, ss 215–218*]

L is the owner of a freehold factory which he leases for a term of 25 years commencing in December 2013. The cost of the factory was £100,000 in April 1999. The lease is granted for a premium of £30,000 and an annual rent. The reversion to the lease plus the capitalised value of the rents amount to £120,000.

	£	£
Amount chargeable to income tax		
Amount of premium		30,000
Deduct Excluded $\dfrac{25-1}{50} \times £30{,}000$		14,400
Amount chargeable to income tax		£15,600
Chargeable gain		
Premium received	30,000	
Deduct Charged to income tax	15,600	
		14,400
Allowable cost $\dfrac{14{,}400}{30{,}000 + 120{,}000} \times £100{,}000$		9,600
Chargeable gain 2013/14		£4,800

Notes

(a)   A short lease is one the duration of which, at the time of grant, does not exceed 50 years.

(b)   The amount chargeable to income tax is not deducted from the amount of premium appearing in the denominator of the CGT apportionment fraction.

(D) **Disposal by assignment of short lease: without enhancement expenditure**

[*TCGA 1992, Sch 8 para 1*]

X buys a lease for £200,000 on 1 October 2009. The lease commenced on 1 June 2000 for a term of 60 years. X assigns the lease for £300,000 at the end of March 2014.

Term of lease unexpired at date of acquisition	50 years 8 months

215.3 CGT Land

    Relevant percentage   100%

    Term of lease unexpired at date of assignment   46 years 2 months
    Relevant percentage 98.490 + $^2/_{12}$ × (98.902 − 98.490)   98.559%

	£	£
Disposal consideration		300,000
Allowable cost	200,000	
Deduct Wasted $\dfrac{100 - 98.559}{100} \times £200,000$	2,882	
		197,118
Chargeable gain 2013/14		£102,882

(E) **Disposal by assignment of short lease held at 31 March 1982**

[*TCGA 1992, s 35, Sch 8 para 1*]

A Ltd buys a lease for £100,000 on 1 March 1982. The lease commenced on 31 March 1972 for a term of 60 years. Its value at 31 March 1982 was estimated at £104,000. On 31 March 2014 A Ltd assigns the lease for £270,000. For the purposes only of this example, the indexation factor for the period March 1982 to March 2014 is taken to be 1.890.

(i) *The computation without re-basing to 1982 is as follows*

    Term of lease unexpired at date of acquisition (1.3.82)   50 years 1 month
    Relevant percentage   100%

    Term of lease unexpired at date of assignment   18 years 0 months
    Relevant percentage   68.697%

	£	£
Disposal consideration		270,000
Cost	100,000	
Deduct Wasted $\dfrac{100 - 68.697}{100} \times £100,000$	31,303	68,697
Unindexed gain		201,303
Indexation allowance (see (ii) below)		135,031
Gain after indexation		£66,272

(ii) *The computation with re-basing to 1982 is as follows*

Term of lease unexpired at deemed date of acquisition (31.3.82)	50 years
Relevant percentage	100%
Term of lease unexpired at date of assignment	18 years
Relevant percentage	68.697%

	£	£
Disposal consideration		270,000
Market value 31.3.82	104,000	
Deduct Wasted $\dfrac{100 - 68.697}{100} \times £104{,}000$	32,555	71,445
Unindexed gain		198,555
Indexation allowance £71,445 × 1.890		135,031
Gain after indexation		£63,524
Chargeable gain		£63,524

Notes

(a) A Ltd is deemed, under *TCGA 1992, s 35*, to have disposed of and immediately re-acquired the lease on 31 March 1982 at its market value at that date.

(b) Both calculations produce a gain with the re-basing calculation producing the smaller gain. Therefore, re-basing applies. [*TCGA 1992, s 35(2)(3)(a)*].

(c) Indexation is based, in both calculations, on the assumption that the asset was sold and re-acquired at market value on 31 March 1982 since this gives a greater allowance than if based on original cost as reduced by the wasting asset provisions. [*TCGA 1992, s 55(1)(2)*].

(F) **Disposal by assignment of short lease: with enhancement expenditure**

[*TCGA 1992, Sch 8 para 1*]

D Ltd acquires the lease of office premises for £100,000 on 1 July 2005. On 1 January 2007, the company contracts for complete refurbishment of the premises at a total cost of £180,000, of which £120,000 can be regarded as capital enhancement expenditure. The work is done at the beginning of January 2007, and the money is payable in equal tranches in March 2007 and May 2007. The lease is for a term of 50 years commencing 1 April 1998. On 1 January 2014, the lease is assigned to a new lessee for £450,000.

Indexation factors (assumed)	July 2005 to January 2014	0.250
	March 2007 to January 2014	0.180
	May 2007 to January 2014	0.170

215.3 CGT Land

Term of lease unexpired at date of acquisition		42 years 9 months	
Relevant percentage 96.593 + $^9/_{12}$ × (97.107 − 96.593)		96.978%	
Term of lease unexpired at date of expenditure incurred (January 2007 — see note (a))		41 years 3 months	
Relevant percentage 96.041 + $^3/_{12}$ × (96.593 − 96.041)		96.179%	
Term of lease unexpired at date of assignment		34 years 3 months	
Relevant percentage 91.156 + $^3/_{12}$ × (91.981 − 91.156)		91.362%	

	£	£	£
Disposal consideration			450,000
Cost of acquisition	100,000		
Deduct Wasted			
$\dfrac{96.978 - 91.362}{96.978} \times 100{,}000$	5,791	94,209	
Enhancement expenditure	120,000		
Deduct Wasted			
$\dfrac{96.179 - 91.362}{96.179} \times 120{,}000$	6,010	113,990	208,199
Unindexed gain			241,801
Indexation allowance			
Cost of lease £94,209 × 0.250		23,552	
Enhancement costs			
March 2007 £56,995 × 0.180		10,259	
May 2007 £56,995 × 0.170		9,689	
			43,500
Chargeable gain			£198,301

Note

(a) The wasting provisions apply to enhancement expenditure by reference to the time when it is first reflected in the nature of the lease. The indexation provisions apply by reference to the date the expenditure became due and payable. [*TCGA 1992, s 54(4)(b), Sch 8 para 1(4)(b)*].

Land CGT 215.3

(G) **Disposal of short lease where premium partly relieved as trading deduction**

[*ITTOIA 2005, ss 60–67; CTA 2009, ss 62–67*]

Butcher acquired a 36-year lease of shop premises from Baker on 1 July 2006 at a premium of £33,000. Butcher prepares trading accounts to 30 June each year. On 1 July 2013, when the unexpired term of the lease is 29 years and property values have risen sharply in the locality, he assigns the lease for £76,000. He makes no other chargeable disposals in 2013/14.

The annual trading deduction under *ITTOIA 2005, ss 60–67* is computed as follows

	£
Premium on 36-year lease	33,000
Deduct (36 − 1) × 2% × £33,000	23,100
Premium chargeable on Baker	£9,900

In addition to actual rent payable under the lease, Butcher is entitled to a deduction in computing trading profits in respect of the part of the premium chargeable on Baker, accruing on a day-to-day basis for up to 36 years, of

$$\frac{£9,900}{36} = £275 \text{ p.a.}$$

In his seven accounting years to 30 June 2013, Butcher has thus received a total deduction of (£275 × 7) = £1,925

The chargeable gain on disposal of the lease in July 2013 is computed as below.

Term of lease unexpired at date of acquisition	36 years
Relevant percentage	92.761%
Term of lease unexpired at date of disposal	29 years
Relevant percentage	86.226%

	£	£
Disposal consideration		76,000
Cost of acquisition	33,000	
Deduct Income tax relief given (see above)	1,925	(note (a))
	31,075	
Deduct Wasted $\dfrac{92.761 - 86.226}{92.761} \times £31,075$	2,189	28,886
Chargeable gain		47,114
Deduct Annual exemption		10,600

429

215.3 CGT   Land

Taxable gains 2013/14 .... £36,514

Notes

(a) The allowable expenditure for CGT is reduced, by virtue of *TCGA 1992, s 39* (exclusion of double relief), by the amount on which income tax relief has been given. This reduction is made *before* the wasting asset reduction required by *TCGA 1992, Sch 8 para 1(4)* (HMRC Capital Gains Manual CG 71201).

(b) For further examples on the *income tax* treatment of lease premiums, see (C) above, (H) and (J) below, and **IT 21.4** PROPERTY INCOME.

(H) **Sub-lease granted out of short lease: premium not less than potential premium**

[*TCGA 1992, Sch 8 paras 4, 5*]

On 1 November 2011, S purchased a lease of shop premises then having 50 years to run for a premium of £100,000 and an annual rental of £40,000. After occupying the premises for the purposes of his own business, S granted a sub-lease to N Ltd. The sub-lease was for a term of 21 years commencing on 1 August 2013, for a premium of £50,000 and an annual rental of £30,000. It is agreed that, had the rent under the sub-lease been £40,000, the premium obtainable would have been £20,000.

Term of lease at date granted	50 years
Relevant percentage	100%
Term of lease at date sub-lease granted	48 years 3 months
Relevant percentage 99.289 + $^3/_{12}$ × (99.657 − 99.289)	99.381%
Term of lease at date sub-lease expires	27 years 3 months
Relevant percentage 83.816 + $^3/_{12}$ × (85.053 − 83.816)	84.125%

Premium chargeable to income tax on S

	£
Amount of premium	50,000
Deduct $\dfrac{21-1}{50} \times £50,000$	20,000
Amount chargeable	£30,000

Chargeable gain

Disposal consideration	50,000
Allowable expenditure	
$£100,000 \times \dfrac{99.381 - 84.125}{100}$	15,256

Chargeable gain	34,744
Deduct Amount chargeable to income tax	30,000
Net chargeable gain 2013/14	£4,744

Note

(a)   If the amount chargeable to income tax had exceeded the chargeable gain, the net gain would have been nil. The deduction cannot create or increase a loss. [*TCGA 1992, Sch 8 para 5(2)*].

(J)   **Sub-lease granted out of short lease: premium less than potential premium**

[*TCGA 1992, Sch 8 paras 4, 5*]

C bought a lease of a house on 1 May 2009, when the unexpired term was 49 years. The cost of the lease was £20,000, and the ground rent payable is £500 p.a. C then let the house on a monthly tenancy until 30 November 2013 when he granted a 10-year lease for a premium of £5,000 and an annual rent of £8,000. Had the rent under the sub-lease been £500 a year, the premium obtainable would have been £40,000. C does not at any time occupy the house as a private residence.

Term of lease at date of acquisition	49 years
Relevant percentage	99.657%
Term of lease when sub-lease granted	44 years 5 months
Relevant percentage $97.595 + {}^{5}/_{12} \times (98.059 - 97.595)$	97.788%
Term of lease when sub-lease expires	34 years 5 months
Relevant percentage $91.156 + {}^{5}/_{12} \times (91.981 - 91.156)$	91.500%

Amount chargeable to income tax	£
Amount of premium	5,000
Deduct Exclusion $\dfrac{10-1}{50} \times £5,000$	900
Chargeable to income tax	£4,100
Chargeable gain	
Disposal consideration	5,000
Deduct Allowable expenditure	

215.3 CGT   Land

$$£20{,}000 \times \frac{97.788 - 91.500}{99.657} \times \frac{5{,}000}{40{,}000} \qquad 158$$

Gain	4,842
Deduct Amount chargeable to income tax	4,100
Net chargeable gain 2013/14	£742

Note

(a)   If the amount chargeable to income tax had exceeded the chargeable gain, the net gain would have been nil. The deduction cannot create or increase a loss. [*TCGA 1992, Sch 8 para 5(2)*].

216 Losses

Cross-references. See **IT 13.2** LOSSES for the set-off of trading losses against chargeable gains made by individuals. See **201.2** ANNUAL RATES AND EXEMPTIONS for the interaction between losses and the annual exemption.

216.1 RELIEF FOR ALLOWABLE LOSSES

[*TCGA 1992, ss 2, 24, 62(2)*].

(A) General

On 30 April 2013 Q sells for £40,000 a part of the land which he owns. The market value of the remaining estate is £160,000. Q bought the land for £250,000 in March 1996.

	£
Disposal consideration	40,000
Allowable cost $\dfrac{40,000}{40,000 + 160,000} \times £250,000$	50,000
Allowable loss	£10,000

(B) Asset of negligible value

In June 2013, John sells an asset, realising a chargeable gain of £25,000. In December 2013, John learns that his shareholding in Jones Ltd has become worthless. He acquired the shares in 1995 for their then market value of £15,000. John makes no other disposals in 2013/14.

If John makes a claim under *TCGA 1992, s 24* no later than 5 April 2016, then his capital gains tax computation for 2013/14 is as follows.

	£
Chargeable gain	25,000
Less allowable loss	15,000
	10,000
Less annual exemption (£10,600 restricted to)	10,000
Gains chargeable to tax 2013/14	Nil

Notes

(a) Where the owner of an asset which has become of 'negligible value' makes a claim to that effect he is treated as if he had sold, and immediately reacquired, the asset for a consideration of an amount equal to the value specified in the claim. Such a claim can also be made if the disposal by which the claimant acquired the asset was a no gain/no loss disposal at the time of which the asset was of negligible value and, between the time at which the asset became of negligible value and that disposal, any other disposal of the asset was a no gain/no loss disposal. The deemed sale is treated

216.1 CGT Losses

as having occurred at the time of the claim or at an earlier time specified in the claim. An earlier time can be specified only if the claimant owned the asset at that time, the asset had become of negligible value at that time and that time is not more than two years before the beginning of the tax year in which the claim is made or, for corporation tax, is on or after the first day of the earliest accounting period ending not more than two years before the time of the claim. [*TCGA 1992, s 24; SI 2009 No 730, Art 4*].

(b) *'Negligible value'* is not defined but is taken by HMRC to mean 'worth next to nothing' (HMRC Capital Gains Manual CG 13124).

(C) Loss carried back from year of death

Rick dies on 30 March 2014. Before his death, he makes one disposal in 2013/14, realising an allowable loss of £20,000. In 2012/13 and 2011/12 he had realised chargeable gains of £16,000 and £26,000 respectively.

Following Rick's death his capital gains position for 2011/12 and 2012/13 is revised as follows.

	£
2012/13	
Chargeable gain	16,000
Less 2013/14 allowable loss carried back (part)	5,400
	10,600
Less annual exemption	10,600
Gains chargeable to tax 2012/13	Nil
2011/12	
Chargeable gain	26,000
Less 2013/14 allowable loss carried back (remainder)	14,600
	11,400
Less annual exemption	10,100
Taxable gain 2011/12	£1,300

Notes

(a) Allowable losses in excess of chargeable gains incurred by the deceased in the tax year in which death occurs can be carried back and set off against chargeable gains in the three preceding tax years. Chargeable gains accruing in a later year must be relieved before those of an earlier year. Losses carried back cannot be set against gains treated under *TCGA 1992, s 87* or *s 89(2)* as accruing to the individual as a beneficiary of a non-UK resident settlement. [*TCGA 1992, s 62(2)(2A)*].

(b) Any remaining unused losses *cannot* be carried forward and set off against gains made by the personal representatives or legatees.

216.2 PERSONAL LOSSES SET AGAINST ATTRIBUTED SETTLEMENT GAINS

[*TCGA 1992, ss 2(2)–(7), 86; FA 2008, Sch 2 paras 2, 22, 24, 30, 56*].

In May 2003, R created an offshore settlement in which he retained the reversionary interest. It is accepted that *TCGA 1992, s 86* applies to the settlement such that any chargeable gains accruing to the trustees are chargeable on R as settlor. In July 2013, the

Losses   CGT 216.3

trustees realised a gain of £18,418 on a disposal of quoted securities which they had held since creation of the settlement. They made no other disposal in the year. R, meanwhile, made two disposals in 2013/14 on which he realised a chargeable gain of £4,000 and an allowable loss of £9,000. Neither the trustees nor R have any losses brought forward from earlier years. R pays income tax for 3/14 at the higher rate

R's CGT position for 2013/14 is as follows.

	£
Personal gains	4,000
Attributed gains	18,418
Deduct Personal losses	9,000
	13,418
Deduct Annual exempt amount	10,900
Taxable gains 2012/13	£2,518
CGT payable by R at 28% (recoverable from trustees)	£705.04
Personal losses carried forward	Nil

Note

(a)   Personal losses can be set against gains attributed to the taxpayer under *TCGA 1992, s 86* (charge on settlor of non-UK resident settlement in which he has an interest). Such losses cannot, however, be set off against gains treated under *TCGA 1992, s 87* or *s 89(2)* as accruing to a beneficiary of a non-UK resident settlement — see **201.2(B)** ANNUAL RATES AND EXEMPTIONS.

216.3 LOSSES ON SHARES IN UNLISTED TRADING COMPANIES

[*TCGA 1992, s 125A; ITA 2007, ss 131–151; FA 2008, Sch 2 paras 98–100*]

P subscribed for 3,000 £1 ordinary shares at par in W Ltd, a qualifying trading company, in June 1988. In September 1995, P acquired a further 2,200 shares at £3 per share from another shareholder. In December 2013, P sold 3,900 shares at 40p per share.

Procedure

Firstly, establish the '*section 104* holding' pool.

	Shares	Qualifying expenditure
		£
June 1988 subscription	3,000	3,000
September 1995 acquisition	2,200	6,600
	5,200	9,600
December 2013 disposal	(3,900)	(7,200)
Pool carried forward	1,300	£2,400

Step 1. Calculate the CGT loss in the normal way, as follows

216.3 CGT Losses

	£
Disposal consideration 3,900 × £0.40	1,560
Allowable cost	7,200
Allowable loss	£5,640

Step 2. Applying a LIFO basis, identify the qualifying shares (1,700) and the non-qualifying shares (2,200) comprised in the disposal.

Step 3. Calculate the proportion of the loss attributable to the qualifying shares.

$$\text{Loss referable to 1,700 qualifying shares } \frac{1,700}{3,900} \times £5,640 \qquad £2,458$$

Step 4. Compare the loss in Step 3 with the actual cost of the qualifying shares, *viz.*

$$\text{Cost of 1,700 qualifying shares } \frac{1,700}{3,000} \times £3,000 \qquad £1,700$$

The loss available against income is restricted to £1,700 (being lower than £2,458).

The loss not relieved against income remains an allowable loss for CGT purposes.

£5,640 − £1,700 = £3,940

Note

(a) For further examples on this topic, see **IT 13.5** LOSSES and **CT 117.4** LOSSES.

216.4 DEFERRED UNASCERTAINABLE CONSIDERATION: ELECTION TO TREAT LOSS AS ARISING IN EARLIER YEAR

[*TCGA 1992, ss 279A–279D; FA 2008, Sch 2 paras 43, 56(2)*]

Tanya owns 2,000 £1 ordinary shares in Be Good Ltd, for which she subscribed at par in January 1993. The shares qualify as business assets for taper relief purposes. On 31 March 2007, she and the other shareholders in Be Good Ltd sold their shares to another company for £20 per share plus a further unquantified cash amount calculated by means of a formula relating to the future profits of Be Good Ltd. The value in March 2007 of the deferred consideration was estimated at £5.10 per share. Tanya makes no other disposals of chargeable assets in 2006/07. On 30 April 2013, Tanya receives a further £3.60 per share under the sale agreement. The indexation factor for the period January 1993 to April 1998 is 0.179.

Losses CGT 216.4

Without an election under *TCGA 1992, s 279A*, Tanya's capital gains position is as follows.

2006/07

	£	£
Disposal proceeds	40,000	
Value of rights	10,200	50,200
Cost of acquisition		2,000
Unindexed gain		48,200
Indexation allowance £2,000 × 0.179		358
Pre-tapered gain		47,842
Taper relief £47,842 @ 75%		35,882
Chargeable gain 2006/07		£11,960

2013/14

Disposal of rights to deferred consideration

	£
Proceeds 2,000 × £3.60	7,200
Deemed cost of acquiring rights	10,200
Allowable loss 2013/14	£3,000

If Tanya makes an election under *TCGA 1992, s 279A* by 31 January 2016 the 2013/14 loss is treated as arising in 2006/07 and can be set off against the gain of that year as follows.

2006/7

	£
Pre-tapered gain as above	47,842
Less Allowable loss	3,000
	44,842
Taper relief £44,842 @ 75%	33,632
Chargeable gain 2006/07	£11,210

Notes

(a) Where a person within the charge to capital gains tax makes a disposal of a right to 'future unascertainable consideration' (as defined) acquired as consideration for the disposal of another asset, and a loss accrues, he may, subject to conditions, make an election for the loss to be treated as arising in the year in which that other asset was disposed of. Where the right was acquired as consideration for two or more disposals in different tax years (referred to as '*eligible years*'), the loss is utilised in the earliest year first. [*TCGA 1992, s 279A*].

(b) To the extent that the loss cannot be utilised in the earliest eligible year it may be carried forward for set-off against gains of later years. In the case of tax years falling between that year and the year of the loss, any remaining part of the loss can only be deducted if the year concerned is an eligible year. [*TCGA 1992, s 279C; FA 2008, Sch 2 paras 43, 56(2)*].

216.4 CGT   Losses

(c) The election is irrevocable and must be made by notice in writing to HMRC on or before the first anniversary of 31 January following the year of the loss. The notice must specify the amount of the relevant loss, the right disposed of, the tax year of the right's disposal, and, if different, the year of the loss, the tax year in which the right was acquired, the original asset or assets on disposal of which the right was acquired, the eligible year in which the loss is to be treated as accruing, and the amount to be deducted from gains of that year. [*TCGA 1992, s 279D*].

217 Married Persons and Civil Partners

217.1 TRANSFERS BETWEEN SPOUSES OR CIVIL PARTNERS
[*TCGA 1992, s 58*]

(A) **No transfer between spouses or civil partners**

Paul and Heidi are a married couple. For 2013/14 Heidi's taxable income (after personal allowance) is £50,000 and Paul's is £15,000. On 4 July 2013, Heidi sells two paintings which she had acquired in June 1994 at a cost of £5,000 each. Net sale proceeds amount to £16,000 and £25,000. Neither spouse disposed of any other chargeable assets during 2013/14.

Chargeable gains — Heidi

	£
Net proceeds of painting 1	16,000
Cost	5,000
Chargeable gain	£11,000
Net proceeds of painting 2	25,000
Cost	5,000
Chargeable gain	£20,000
Total chargeable gains (£11,000 + £20,000)	31,000
Annual exemption	10,900
Taxable gains 2013/14	£20,100
Tax payable £20,100 × 28%	£5,628.00

(B) **Transfer between spouses or civil partners**

The facts are as in (A) above except that in April 2013, Heidi gives painting 2 to Paul who then makes the sale on 4 July 2013.

Chargeable gains – Heidi

	£
Deemed consideration for painting 2 (April 2013) (note (a))	5,000
Cost	5,000
Chargeable gain	Nil
Net proceeds of painting 1	16,000

217.1 CGT Married Persons and Civil Partners

Cost	5,000
Chargeable gain	£11,000
Total chargeable gains	11,000
Annual exemption	10,900
Taxable gains 2013/14	£100
Capital gains tax £100 × 28%	£28.00

Chargeable gain — Paul

	£
Net proceeds (4.7.13)	25,000
Cost (April 2013)	5,000
Chargeable gain	20,000
Annual exemption	10,900
Taxable gain 2013/14	£9,100
Capital gains tax £9,100 × 18%	£1,638.00
Tax saving compared with (A) above (£5,628 − (£28 + £1,638))	£3,962

Notes

(a) The inter-spouse transfer is deemed to be for such consideration as to ensure that no gain or loss accrues. [*TCGA 1992, s 58*].

(b) The fact that transfers of assets between husband and wife or between civil partners are no gain/no loss transfers enables savings to be made by ensuring that disposals are made by a spouse or partner who has an unused annual exemption and/or pays CGT at a lower rate.

(c) A transfer between spouses or civil partners followed by a sale could be attacked by HMRC as an anti-avoidance device. To minimise the risk, there should be a clear time interval between the two transactions and no arrangements made to effect the ultimate sale until after the transfer. The gift should be outright with no strings attached and with no 'arrangement' for eventual proceeds to be passed to the transferor.

(C) **Transfer between spouses or civil partners before 6 April 2008**

The facts are as in (B) above except that Heidi gives painting 2 to Paul in January 2008. The indexation factor for the period June 1994 to April 1998 is 0.124.

Married Persons and Civil Partners   CGT 217.1

Chargeable gains — Heidi

2007/08

	£
Deemed consideration for painting 2 (January 2008) (note (a))	5,620
Cost	5,000
Unindexed gain	620
Indexation allowance (to April 1998) £5,000 × 0.124	620
Chargeable gain	Nil

2013/14

Net proceeds of painting 1	16,000
Cost	5,000
Chargeable gain	11,000
Annual exemption	10,900
Taxable gains 2012/13	£100
Capital gains tax £100 × 28%	£28.00

Chargeable gain — Paul

	£
Net proceeds (4.7.13)	25,000
Cost (January 2008)	5,620
Chargeable gain	19,380
Annual exemption	10,900
Taxable gain	£8,480
Capital gains tax £8,480 × 18%	£1,526.40
Tax saving compared with (A) above (£5,628 − (£28 + £1,526.40))	£4,073.60

Notes

(a) The consideration for the inter-spouse transfer is equal to cost plus indexation to April 1998. See **214.2** INDEXATION for further examples.

(b) The abolition of indexation allowance for capital gains tax purposes for disposals after 5 April 2008 does not affect the deemed consideration for which Paul is treated as acquiring painting 2.

217.2 CGT   Married Persons and Civil Partners

217.2 JOINTLY OWNED ASSETS

Derek and Raquel are a married couple. Derek had for many years owned an investment property which he purchased for £70,000 in May 1988. On 5 January 1996, he transferred to Raquel a 10% share in the property which was thereafter held in their joint names as tenants in common. At the time of the transfer, a 10% share of the property is worth £10,000 on the open market and a 90% share is worth £90,000. No declaration is made for income tax purposes under what is now *ITA 2007, s 837*, with the result that the rental income from the property is treated, by virtue of *ITA 2007, s 836* as arising in equal shares. On 29 June 2013, the property is sold for £140,000. The indexation factor for May 1988 to January 1996 is 0.414.

(i) **Inter-spouse transfer**

	£
Deemed consideration (January 1996)	9,898
Cost £70,000 × $\dfrac{10,000}{10,000 + 90,000}$ (see note(c))	7,000
Unindexed gain	2,898
Indexation allowance £7,000 × 0.414	2,898
Chargeable gain 1995/96	Nil

(ii) **2013/14 disposal**

	Derek	Raquel
	£	£
Disposal proceeds	126,000	14,000
Cost: Derek (£70,000 − £7,000)	63,000	
Raquel (see (i) above)	–	9,898
Chargeable gains 2013/14	£63,000	£4,102

Notes

(a) Where a joint declaration of unequal beneficial interests is made under *ITA 2007, s 837* it is presumed that the same split applies for capital gains tax purposes. In the absence of a declaration, and regardless of the income tax treatment of income derived from the asset, a gain on an asset held in the joint names of husband and wife is apportioned in accordance with their respective beneficial interests at the time of disposal. (Revenue Press Release 21 November 1990).

(b) See 217.1(C) above as to how the consideration for the inter-spouse transfer is arrived at.

(c) The allowable expenditure on the inter-spouse transfer is apportioned in accordance with the part disposal rules in *TCGA 1992, s 42* (see **208.2** COMPUTATION OF GAINS AND LOSSES).

218 Mineral Royalties

Cross-reference. See also **IT 15.1** MINERAL ROYALTIES.

218.1 GENERAL

[*ICTA 1988, s 122; TCGA 1992, ss 201–203; ITTOIA 2005, ss 157, 319, 340–343, Sch 1 para 106; CTA 2009, ss 274–276, Sch 1 paras 377, 378; FA 2012, Sch 39 paras 43–47*]

L Ltd, which prepares accounts to 31 December, is the holder of a lease of land acquired in 1998 for £66,000, when the lease had an unexpired term of 65 years. In January 2007, L Ltd grants a 10-year licence to a mining company to search for and exploit minerals beneath the land. The licence is granted for £60,000 plus a mineral royalty calculated on the basis of the value of any minerals won by the licensee. The market value of the retained land (exclusive of the mineral rights) is then £10,000. L Ltd receives mineral royalties as follows

Year ended		£
31 December 2007		12,000
31 December 2008		19,000
31 December 2009		29,000
31 December 2010		38,000
31 December 2011		17,000
31 December 2012		10,000

On 2 January 2013, L Ltd relinquishes its rights under the lease and receives no consideration from the lessor.

(i) **Chargeable gains 2007**

		£
(*a*) Disposal proceeds		60,000
Allowable cost $\dfrac{60,000}{60,000 + 10,000} \times £66,000$		56,571
Chargeable gain subject to indexation		£3,429
(*b*) $1/2 \times £12,000$		£6,000

218.1 CGT Mineral Royalties

(ii) **Chargeable gains 2008 to 2012**

		£
2008	½ × £19,000	9,500
2009	½ × £29,000	14,500
2010	½ × £38,000	19,000
2011	½ × £17,000	8,500
2012	½ × £10,000	5,000

(iii) **Loss 2013**

Proceeds of disposal of lease	Nil
Allowable cost £66,000 − £56,571	9,429
Allowable loss	£9,429

(iv) The loss may be set off against the chargeable gains arising on the mineral royalties as follows

	£
2012 (whole)	5,000
2011 (part)	4,429
	£9,429

Notes

(a) The rules illustrated in this example are repealed for royalties which a person becomes entitled to receive on or after 6 April 2013 (1 April 2013 for corporation tax purposes). [*FA 2012, Sch 39 paras 43–45*].

(b) Subject to (a) above, under *ITTOIA 2005, ss 157, 319, CTA 2009, ss 274–276* and *TCGA 1992, s 201*, one half of mineral royalties is taxed as income and one half as a chargeable gain. The gain is deemed to accrue in the tax year or company accounting period for which the royalties are receivable and is not capable of being reduced by any expenditure or by indexation allowance.

(c) A terminal allowable loss can be carried back to earlier years as illustrated in (iv) above only where the mineral lease concerned is entered into before 6 April 2013 (1 April 2013 for corporation tax purposes). [*FA 2012, Sch 39 para 46*].

219 Offshore Settlements

Cross-reference. See also **216.2** LOSSES.

219.1 CHARGE ON BENEFICIARY IN RECEIPT OF CAPITAL PAYMENTS

(A) **Charge under TCGA 1992, s 87**

C, resident and domiciled in the UK, is the sole beneficiary of a discretionary settlement created by his father in 2003 and administered in the Cayman Islands. The trustees are all individuals resident in the Cayman Islands. The trustees make no gains or capital payments in 2009/10 or any earlier year, but make the following capital payments to C in 2010/11 onwards.

	£
2010/11	50,000
2011/12	60,000
2012/13	50,000
2013/14	70,000

In 2013/14, the trustees sell two settlement assets realising a gain of £350,000 and a loss of £50,000. They make no other disposals in that year. C makes only one disposal in 2013/14, realising an allowable loss of £25,000. C pays income tax in 2012/13 at the higher rate.

The settlement's 'section 2(2) amount' for 2013/14 is:

	£
Gain	350,000
Less Loss	50,000
Section 2(2) amount for 2013/14	£300,000

The section 2(2) amount is matched with the capital payments made to C on a last in first out basis as follows.

	£
Section 2(2) amount	300,000
2013/14 capital payment	70,000
2012/13 capital payment	50,000
2011/12 capital payment	60,000
2010/11 capital payment	50,000
Unmatched amount carried forward	£70,000

C's liability to capital gains tax for 2013/14 is as follows.

£

219.1 CGT   Offshore Settlements

Matched section 2(2) amount (£70,000 + £50,000 + £60,000+ £50,000)	230,000
Less Annual exemption	10,900
Amount chargeable to capital gains tax 2012/13	£219,100
Capital gains tax (£219,100 × 28%)	£61,348

Notes

(a) For 2013/14 and subsequent years, *TCGA 1992, s 87* applies to a settlement for a tax year if there is no time in the year when the trustees are resident in the UK. For 2012/13 and earlier years, *TCGA 1992, s 87* applies to a settlement for a tax year if the trustees are neither resident not ordinarily resident in the UK during any part of the year. [*TCGA 1992, s 87(1)(6); FA 2013, Sch 46 paras 92, 112*].

(b) There are detailed rules for matching gains with capital payments. Broadly, capital payments are matched with section 2(2) amounts on a last in first out basis by applying the five step process in *TCGA 1992, s 87A*.

(c) The '*section 2(2) amount*' for a tax year for which the settlement is within *TCGA 1992, s 87* is the amount which would have been chargeable on the trustees under *TCGA 1992, s 2(2)* (i.e. chargeable gains less current year and brought forward losses) had they been resident (and, for 2012/13 and earlier years, ordinarily resident) in the UK in that year *less*, if *TCGA 1992, s 86* (offshore settlement where settlor has interest) applies to the settlement for the year, any chargeable gains for the year under that section. The section 2(2) amount for a tax year for which *section 87* does not apply is nil. [*TCGA 1992, s 87(4)(5); FA 2013, Sch 46 paras 92, 112*].

(d) C's personal loss of £25,000 for 2013/14 cannot be relieved against gains chargeable under *TCGA 1991, s 87*.

(e) Where gains are attributed to a beneficiary under *TCGA 1992, s 87* in 2010/11, they are treated as arising before 23 June 2010 (and therefore chargeable at the single rate of 18%) if they occur as a result of matching with capital payments received before that date. Otherwise such gains are treated as arising on or after 23 June 2010. [*F(No 2)A 2010, Sch 1 para 22*].

(B) **Surcharge on CGT under TCGA 1992, s 87**

[*TCGA 1992, s 91; FA 2008, Sch 7 paras 112, 115*]

D, resident and domiciled in the UK, is the sole beneficiary of a discretionary settlement created by his father in May 2009 and administered in the Cayman Islands. The trustees are all individuals resident in the Cayman Islands. In 2009/10, the trustees sell an asset realising a gain of £120,000, but otherwise make no disposals. In 2013/14, the trustees make a capital payment to D of £120,000, having made no previous capital payments. D makes no other disposals in 2013/14 but pays income tax for that year at the higher rate.

D's capital gains tax liability for 2013/14 is calculated as follows.

	£
CGT (subject to surcharge)	
(£120,000 − £10,900 annual exemption) × 28%	30,548
Surcharge £30,548 × 10% × 4 years (1.12.10–30.11.14)	12,219
Total tax payable 2013/14	£42,884

Notes

(a) The capital payment of £120,000 in 2013/14 is matched under *TCGA 1992, s 87A* with the section 2(2) amount for 2009/10 of £120,000. See (A) above.

(b) The surcharge is 10% per annum for a period beginning on 1 December following the end of the tax year the section 2(2) amount for which is matched with the capital payment and ending on 30 November in the tax year following that in which the capital payment is made but subject to a maximum period of six years. [*TCGA 1992, s 91(3)–(5)*].

220 Overseas Matters

220.1 COMPANY MIGRATION

[*TCGA 1992, ss 185, 187*]

Z Ltd is a company incorporated in Ruritania, but regarded as resident in the UK by virtue of its being managed and controlled in the UK. It is the 75% subsidiary of Y plc, a UK resident company. On 1 October 2013, the management and control of Z Ltd is transferred to Ruritania and it thus ceases to be UK resident, although it continues to trade in the UK, on a much reduced basis, via a UK permanent establishment.

Details of the company's chargeable assets immediately before 1 October 2013 were as follows.

	Market value	Capital gain after indexation (where applicable) if all assets sold
	£	£
Factory in UK	480,000	230,000
Warehouse in UK	300,000	180,000
Factory in Ruritania	350,000	200,000
Warehouse in Ruritania	190,000	100,000
UK quoted investments	110,000	80,000
Foreign trade investments	100,000	Loss (60,000)

The UK warehouse continues to be used in the UK trade. The UK factory does not, and is later sold. On 1 June 2014, the Ruritanian warehouse is sold for the equivalent of £210,000. On 1 October 2015, Y plc sells its shareholding in Z Ltd.

Prior to becoming non-UK resident, Z Ltd had unrelieved capital losses brought forward of £40,000.

The corporation tax consequences assuming no election under *TCGA 1992, s 187* are as follows

Chargeable gain accruing to Z Ltd on 1.10.13

	£
Factory (UK)	230,000
Factory (Ruritania)	200,000
Warehouse (Ruritania)	100,000
UK quoted investments	80,000
Foreign trade investments	(60,000)
	550,000
Losses brought forward	40,000
Net gain chargeable to corporation tax	£510,000

220.1 CGT   Overseas Matters

The later sale of the UK factory does not attract corporation tax as the company is nonresident and the factory has not, since the deemed reacquisition immediately before 1 October 2013, been used in a trade carried on in the UK through a permanent establishment. Similarly, the sale of the overseas warehouse, and of any other overseas assets, is outside the scope of corporation tax on chargeable gains. Any subsequent disposal of the UK warehouse *will* be within the charge to corporation tax, having been omitted from the deemed disposal on 1 October 2013, due to its being used in a trade carried on in the UK through a permanent establishment. On disposal, the gain will be computed by reference to original cost, or 31.3.82 value if appropriate, rather than to market value immediately before 1 October 2013 — see also note (d).

Y plc will realise a capital gain (or loss) on the sale of its shareholding in Z Ltd on 1 October 2014.

The corporation tax consequences if an election is made under *TCGA 1992, s 187* are as follows

Chargeable gain accruing to Z Ltd on 1.10.13

	£
Factory (UK)	230,000
UK quoted investments	80,000
	310,000
Losses brought forward	40,000
Net gain liable to corporation tax	£270,000

Postponed gain on foreign assets

	£
Factory (Ruritania)	200,000
Warehouse (Ruritania)	100,000
	300,000
Foreign trade investments	(60,000)
	£240,000

On 1 June 2014, a proportion of the postponed gain becomes chargeable as a result of the sale, within six years of Z Ltd's becoming non-resident, of one of the assets in respect of which the postponed gain accrued. The gain chargeable to corporation tax as at 1 June 2014 on Y plc is

$$\frac{100,000 \text{ (postponed gain on warehouse)}}{300,000 \text{ (aggregate of postponed gains)}} \times £240,000 = £80,000$$

On 1 October 2015, in addition to any gain or loss arising on the sale of the shares, Y plc will be chargeable to corporation tax on the remainder of the postponed gain, i.e. on £160,000 (£240,000 - £80,000), by virtue of Z Ltd having ceased to be its 75% subsidiary as a result of the sale of shares.

The position as regards the UK warehouse is the same as if no election had been made.

Overseas Matters   CGT 220.2

Notes

(a) The provisions of *TCGA 1992, s 185* apply where a company ceases to be resident in the UK. All companies incorporated in the UK are regarded as UK resident. As such a company cannot therefore cease to be resident, *section 185* can apply only to companies incorporated abroad which are UK resident. See also HMRC Statement of Practice SP 1/90 as regards company residence generally.

(b) If, with an election, Z Ltd's unrelieved capital losses had exceeded its chargeable gains arising on 1 October 2013, the excess could have been allowed against postponed gains at the time when they become chargeable on Y plc, subject to the two companies making a joint election to that effect under *TCGA 1992, s 187(5)*.

(c) *TMA 1970, ss 109B–109F* contain management provisions designed to secure payment of all outstanding tax liabilities on a company becoming non-UK resident. See also HMRC Statement of Practice SP 2/90.

(d) If the UK warehouse ceases to be a chargeable asset by virtue of Z Ltd's ceasing to carry on a trade in the UK through a permanent establishment, there will be a deemed disposal at market value at that time, under *TCGA 1992, s 25*. See **220.2** below.

(e) *FA 2013* introduced a facility for a company which becomes non-UK resident to enter into an exit charge payment plan, under which corporation arising under various exit charges, including *TCGA 1992, s 185* can be deferred. [*TMA 1970, s 59FA, Sch3ZB; FA 2013, s 229, Sch 49*].

220.2 NON-RESIDENTS CARRYING ON TRADE, ETC. THROUGH UK BRANCH OR AGENCY

[*TCGA 1992, ss 10, 25*]

X, who is not resident in the UK, practises abroad as a tax consultant and also practises in the UK through a London branch, preparing accounts to 5 April. The assets of the UK branch include premises bought in 1988 for £60,000 and a computer acquired in March 2009 for £20,000. On 31 January 2014, the computer ceases to be used in the UK branch and is immediately shipped abroad, and on 28 February 2014, X closes down the UK branch. He sells the premises in June 2014 for £118,000. Capital allowances claimed on the computer up to and including 2012/13 were £13,250 and short-life asset treatment had been claimed.

Relevant market values of the assets are as follows

		£
Computer,	at 31 January 2014	11,000
Premises,	at 14 March 1989	65,000
	at 28 February 2014	110,000

The UK capital gains tax consequences are as follows

	£	£
Computer		
Market value 31.1.14		11,000
Deduct		
Cost	20,000	

220.2 CGT Overseas Matters

Less capital allowances claimed	(note (f))	9,000	11,000
Chargeable gain			Nil

Premises	£
Market value 28.2.14	110,000
Deduct Market value 14.3.89	65,000
Chargeable gain	£45,000
Net chargeable gains 2013/14	£45,000

Notes

(a) X is within the charge to UK capital gains tax for disposals after 13 March 1989 by virtue of his carrying on a profession in the UK through a branch or agency. Previously, the charge applied only to non-residents carrying on a *trade* in this manner. X is deemed to have disposed of (with no capital gains tax consequences) and reacquired immediately before 14 March 1989 all chargeable assets used in the UK branch at market value, so that any subsequent CGT charge will be by reference only to post-13 March 1989 gains. [*FA 1989, s 126(3)–(5); TCGA 1992, s 10(5)*].

(b) There is a deemed disposal, at market value, of the computer on 31 January 2014 as a result of its ceasing to be a chargeable asset by virtue of its becoming situated outside the UK. [*TCGA 1992, s 25(1)*].

(c) There is a deemed disposal, at market value, of the premises on 28 February 2014 as a result of the asset ceasing to be a chargeable asset by virtue of X's ceasing to carry on a trade, profession or vocation in the UK through a branch or agency. [*TCGA 1992, s 25(3)(8)*]. See also note (g) below.

(d) There are no UK CGT consequences on the actual disposal of the premises in June 2014.

(e) X is entitled to the £10,900 annual exemption against UK gains, regardless of his residence status (unless he makes a claim under *ITA 2007, s 809B* for the remittance basis).

(f) Where a chargeable asset has qualified for capital allowances and a loss accrues on its disposal, the allowable expenditure is restricted, under *TCGA 1992, s 41*, by the net allowances given, which in this example amount to £9,000 (first-year and writing-down allowances £13,250 less balancing charge £4,250 arising on the asset's ceasing to be used in the trade).

(g) *TCGA 1992, s 25(3)* (see note (c) above) does not apply in relation to an asset where a non-UK resident company transfers its trade (carried on through a UK permanent establishment) to a UK resident company in the same group. The asset is deemed to be transferred at no gain/no loss. [*TCGA 1992, s 171*].

220.3 TRANSFER OF ASSETS TO NON-RESIDENT COMPANY

[*TCGA 1992, s 140; FA 2010, s 37(1)(3)*]

Q Ltd, a UK resident company, carries on business in a foreign country through a branch there. In September 2007, it is decreed that all enterprises in that country be carried on by locally resident companies. Q Ltd forms a wholly-owned non-UK resident subsidiary R and transfers all the assets of the branch to R wholly in consideration for the issue of shares. The assets transferred include the following

	Value £	Chargeable gains £
Goodwill	100,000	95,000
Freehold land	200,000	120,000
Plant (items worth more than £6,000)	50,000	20,000
Other assets	150,000	—
	£500,000	£235,000

In March 2009, there is a compulsory acquisition of 50% of the share capital of R for £300,000 (market value). The value of the whole shareholding immediately before disposal is £750,000. The value of Q Ltd's remaining 50% holding is £300,000.

In June 2013, R is forced to sell its freehold land to the government.

Q Ltd's capital gains position is as follows

2007

The gain of £235,000 is deferred. The allowable cost of the shares in R is £500,000.

2009

		£
Consideration on disposal		300,000
Add		
Proportion of deferred gain £235,000 × $\dfrac{300,000}{750,000}$		94,000
		394,000
Deduct		
Cost of shares sold £500,000 × $\dfrac{300,000}{300,000 + 300,000}$		250,000
Gain subject to indexation		£144,000

220.3 CGT   Overseas Matters

2013

		£
Proportion of deferred gain chargeable		
Gain arising $\frac{120,000}{235,000} \times £235,000$		£120,000
Balance of gain still held over		
(£235,000 − £94,000 − £120,000)		£21,000

Notes

(a) The 2013 gain arises under *section 140(5)*. If the sale of freehold land had taken place more than six years after the original transfer of assets, no part of the deferred gain would have become chargeable as a result.

(b) The 2009 gain arises under *section 140(4)*. In this case, there is no time limit as in (a) above. For disposals on or after 6 January 2010 the appropriate proportion of the deferred gain is treated as a separate chargeable gain rather than being added to the consideration received on the disposal as illustrated in this example for the 2009 gain.

(c) The 2009 gain is subject to indexation allowance on £250,000 from September 2007 to March 2009.

220.4 INDIVIDUAL TEMPORARILY NON-RESIDENT IN THE UK

[*TCGA 1992, ss 10A, 10AA; FA 2013, Sch 45 paras 109–115, 119, 153(3)*]

Mr Stephenson, who has lived in the UK all his life, leaves the UK on 1 May 2010 for a three year employment contract abroad, becoming resident and ordinarily resident outside the UK. On 16 May 2011 he sells his entire shareholding in Snow plc for £30,000. He had purchased the shares for £10,000 in April 2003. Mr Stephenson returns to the UK on 1 September 2013. He makes no other disposals in the period 1 May 2010 to 5 April 2013 inclusive.

No chargeable gain accrues on the disposal of the shares in 2011/12 as Mr Stephenson is not resident or ordinarily resident in the UK.

A chargeable gain is deemed to accrue in respect of the disposal of the shares in 2013/14, the year of Mr Stephenson's return to the UK, computed as follows.

	£
Proceeds	30,000
Acquisition cost	10,000
Chargeable gain	£20,000

Notes

(a) Subject to (d) below, *TCGA 1992, s 10A* applies where an individual leaves the UK for a period of temporary residence outside the UK and four out of the seven tax years immediately preceding the year of departure were years for which the individual satisfied 'the residence requirements', provided that there are fewer than five tax years between (and not including) the year of departure and the year of return. [*TCGA 1992, s 10A(1)*].

(b) An individual satisfies the '*residence requirements*' for a tax year if during any part of the year he is resident in the UK and not 'treaty non-resident' or if during the year he is ordinarily resident in the UK and not treaty non-resident. An individual is '*treaty non-resident*' at any time if he falls at that time to be regarded for the purposes of double tax relief arrangements as resident in a territory outside the UK. [*TCGA 1992, ss 10A(9), 288(7B)*].

(c) Where the year of return is 2010/11 gains chargeable under *TCGA 1992, s 10A* are treated as arising before 23 June 2010 (and are therefore chargeable at 18%). [*F(No 2)A 2010, Sch 1 para 19*].

(d) Following the introduction of the statutory residence test in *FA 2013*, the temporary non-residence rules have been amended with effect where the year of departure is 2013/14 or a later year. In particular, the revised rules apply if the period of temporary non-residence is five years or less and take account of split-year treatment where an individual is UK-resident for only part of a tax year. [*TCGA 1992, ss 10A, 10AA; FA 2013, Sch 45 paras 109–115, 119, 153(3)*].

221 Partnerships

221.1 ASSETS

[*TCGA 1992, s 59*]

G, H and I trade in partnership. They share capital in the ratio 5:4:3. Land occupied by the firm is sold on 15 April 2013 for £240,000, having been acquired for £60,000 in 1981. The agreed market value of the land at 31 March 1982 is £54,000. G has personal gains in 2013/14 of £2,500, H has losses of £1,000 and I made no disposals of personal assets. None of the partners has any capital losses brought forward from earlier years.

The gains of G, H and I in respect of the land are as follows

	G($5/12$) £	H($4/12$) £	I($3/12$) £
Disposal consideration	100,000	80,000	60,000
Market value 31.3.82	22,500	18,000	13,500
Chargeable gain	£77,500	£62,000	£46,500

Summary

	G £	H £	I £
Share of partnership gain	77,500	62,000	46,500
Personal gains/(losses)	2,500	(1,000)	—
Chargeable gain	80,000	61,000	46,500
Annual exemption	10,900	10,900	10,900
Taxable gain 2013/14	£69,100	£50,100	£35,600

Notes

(a) Each partner is regarded as owning a fractional share of each partnership asset, which is calculated by reference to his capital sharing ratio.

(b) For capital gains tax purposes (i.e. in relation to disposals by individuals, trustees and personal representatives), re-basing to 31 March 1982 applies to all disposals with no exceptions. Market value at 31 March 1982 is therefore substituted for the actual cost, even where, as in this example, the cost is higher than that value. See **205.1** ASSETS HELD ON 31 MARCH 1982.

221.2 CHANGES IN SHARING RATIOS

J and K have traded in partnership since 1990, sharing capital and income equally. The acquisition costs of the chargeable assets of the firm are as follows

221.2 CGT   Partnerships

	Cost £
Premises	60,000
Goodwill	10,000

The assets have not been revalued in the firm's balance sheet. On 1 June 2013, J and K admit L to the partnership, and the sharing ratio is J 35%, K 45% and L 20%.

J and K are regarded as disposing of part of their interest in the firm's assets to L as follows

£

J
Premises
Deemed consideration
£60,000 × (50% − 35%) …… 9,000
Allowable cost …… 9,000
Chargeable gain …… —

Goodwill
Deemed consideration
£10,000 × (50% − 35%) …… 1,500
Allowable cost …… 1,500
Chargeable gain …… —

£

K
Premises
Deemed consideration
£60,000 × (50% − 45%) …… 3,000
Allowable cost …… 3,000
Chargeable gain …… —

Goodwill
Deemed consideration
£10,000 × (50% − 45%) …… 500
Allowable cost …… 500
Chargeable gain …… —

The allowable costs of the three partners are now

	Freehold land £	Goodwill £
J	21,000	3,500

K	27,000	4,500
L	12,000	2,000

Notes

(a) The treatment illustrated above is taken from HMRC Statement of Practice SP D12 (17.1.75), para 4 as extended by SP 1/89. Each partner's disposal consideration is equal to his share of current balance sheet value of the asset concerned and each disposal treated as producing no gain and no loss.

(b) L's allowable costs comprise 20% of original cost.

221.3 ACCOUNTING ADJUSTMENTS

A, B and C trade in partnership. They share income and capital profits equally. The firm's only chargeable asset is its premises which cost £51,000 in 1989. C decides to retire. The remaining partners agree to share profits equally. Before C retires (in May 2013), the premises are written up to market value in the accounts, agreed at £180,000. C does not receive any payment directly from the other partners on his retirement.

The capital gains tax consequences are

On retiring, C is regarded as having disposed of his interest in the firm's premises for a consideration equal to his share of the then book value.

		£
Disposal consideration	$1/3 \times £180,000$	60,000
Acquisition cost	$1/3 \times £51,000$	17,000
Chargeable gain, subject to entrepreneurs' relief		£43,000

A and B will each be treated as acquiring a $1/6$ ($1/2 \times 1/3$) share in the premises, at a cost equal to one half of C's disposal consideration. Their acquisition costs are then

		A	B
		£	£
Cost of original share	$1/3 \times £51,000$	17,000	17,000
Cost of new share	$1/2 \times £60,000$	30,000	30,000
Total		£47,000	£47,000

221.4 CONSIDERATION OUTSIDE ACCOUNTS

D, E and F are partners in a firm of accountants who share all profits in the ratio 7:7:6. G is admitted as a partner in May 2013 and pays the other partners £10,000 for goodwill. The new partnership shares are D $3/10$, E $3/10$, F $1/4$ and G $3/20$. The book value of goodwill is £18,000, its cost on acquisition of the practice from the predecessor in 1990.

221.4 CGT Partnerships

The partners are treated as having disposed of shares in goodwill as follows

D

$^7/_{20} - {}^3/_{10} = {}^1/_{20}$

Disposal consideration

		£	£
Notional	$^1/_{20} \times £18,000$	900	
Actual	$^7/_{20} \times £10,000$	3,500	
			4,400
Allowable cost $^1/_{20} \times £18,000$			900
Chargeable gain			£3,500

E

$^7/_{20} - {}^3/_{10} = {}^1/_{20}$

	£
Disposal consideration (as for D)	4,400
Allowable cost (as for D)	900
Chargeable gain	£3,500

F

$^6/_{20} - {}^1/_{4} = {}^1/_{20}$

Disposal consideration

		£	£
Notional	$^1/_{20} \times £18,000$	900	
Actual	$^6/_{20} \times £10,000$	3,000	
			3,900
Allowable cost			900
Chargeable gain			£3,000

G's allowable cost of his share of goodwill is therefore

	£
Actual consideration paid	10,000
Notional consideration paid $^3/_{20} \times £18,000$	2,700
	£12,700

221.5 SHARES ACQUIRED IN STAGES

Q is a partner in a legal practice. The partnership's only chargeable asset is a freehold house used as an office. The cost of the house to the partnership was £3,600 in 1996 and it was revalued in the partnership accounts to £50,000 in 2012. Q was admitted to the partnership in June 1998 with a share of $^1/_6$ of all profits. As a result of partnership changes, Q's profit share altered as follows

2002	$^1/_5$
2010	$^1/_4$
2015	$^3/_{10}$

For capital gains tax, Q's allowable cost of his share of the freehold house is calculated as follows

		£
1998	$1/6 \times £3,600$	600
2002	$(1/5 - 1/6) \times £3,600$	120
2010	$(1/4 - 1/5) \times £3,600$	180
2015	$(3/10 - 1/4) \times £50,000$	2,500
		£3,400

Note

(a) On Q's acquisition of an increased share of the property in 2015 (subsequent to the revaluation in 2012), any partner with a reduced share will be treated as having made a disposal and thus a gain or loss.

221.6 PARTNERSHIP ASSETS DISTRIBUTED IN KIND

R, S and T are partners sharing all profits in the ratio 4:3:3. Farmland owned by the firm is transferred in November 2013 to T for future use by him as a market gardening enterprise separate from the partnership business. No payment is made by T to the other partners but a reduction is made in T's future share of income profits. The book value of the farmland is £50,000, its cost in 1993, but the present market value is £150,000.

R

		£
Deemed disposal consideration	$4/10 \times £150,000$	60,000
Allowable cost	$4/10 \times £50,000$	20,000
Gain		£40,000

S

Deemed disposal consideration	$3/10 \times £150,000$	45,000
Allowable cost	$3/10 \times £50,000$	15,000
Gain		£30,000

T

Partnership share	$3/10 \times £50,000$	15,000
Market value of R's share		60,000
Market value of S's share		45,000
Allowable cost of land for future disposal		£120,000

222 Payment of Tax

222.1 PAYMENT BY INSTALMENTS

(A) **Consideration payable by instalments**

[*TCGA 1992, ss 280, 281*]

Ian, a higher rate income tax payer, sells an asset on 31 March 2014 for £240,000. The consideration is to be paid by twelve annual instalments of £20,000 beginning on 31 March 2014. Ian originally purchased the asset for £15,000 in 1990 and his allowable costs of sale are £5,000. The gain does not qualify for entrepreneurs' relief and Ian has no other chargeable gains in 2013/14.

Ian's liability to capital gains tax for 2013/14 is as follows

	£
Consideration	240,000
Less costs of sale	5,000
Acquisition cost	15,000
Chargeable gain 2013/14	220,000
Annual exemption	10,900
Gain chargeable to tax	£209,100
Capital gains tax payable (£209,100 × 28%)	£58,548

If Ian opts under *TCGA 1992, s 280* to pay the tax by instalments, the following payments will be due.

31 January 2015	£10,000
31 March 2015	£10,000
31 March 2016	£10,000
31 March 2017	£10,000
31 March 20188	£10,000
31 March 2019	£8,548

Notes

(a) Where the whole or part of the consideration for a disposal is receivable by instalments over a period exceeding 18 months, beginning not earlier than the date of the disposal, the tax arising may at the option of the taxpayer by paid by such instalments as HMRC allows. The tax instalment period cannot exceed eight years and must end not later than the time at which the final instalment of the consideration is payable. [*TCGA 1992, s 280*].

222.1 CGT   Payment of Tax

    (b)   HMRC's practice is to ask for instalments of tax equal to half of each instalment of consideration until the total tax liability has been discharged. To the extent that instalments of consideration under the contract fall due on or before the normal due date for the payment of tax (31 January in the tax year following that in which the disposal occurred), the respective instalments of tax are payable on that normal due date. Where instalments of consideration fall due after that time, then the respective instalments of tax are payable on the dates when the taxpayer is contractually entitled to receive the consideration. (HMRC Capital Gains Manual CG 14912).

    (c)   Interest on unpaid tax is charged on each instalment only if it is paid late and will run from the date when the instalment was due until the date of payment. (HMRC Self-Assessment Manual SAM 80072).

    (d)   The above instalment provisions do not apply to deferred consideration which is unquantified and contingent. See **206.2** CAPITAL SUMS DERIVED FROM ASSETS.

(B)   **Gifts of land or shares**

On 1 June 2013, Sean gives a parcel of land to his daughter, Erica. The market value of the land on that date is £300,000. Sean purchased the land in 1990 for £99,100, and makes no other disposals in 2013/14. He is a higher rate income taxpayer. For the purposes of this example only, the rate of interest on unpaid capital gains tax is taken to be 4% throughout.

Sean's liability to capital gains tax for 2013/14 is as follows

	£
Consideration	300,000
Less acquisition cost	99,100
Chargeable gain 2013/14	200,900
Annual exemption	10,900
Gain chargeable to tax	£190,000
Capital gains tax payable (£190,000 × 28%)	£53,200

If Sean elects under *TCGA 1992, s 281*, before 31 January 2015 to pay the tax by instalments, the following payments will be due.

	£	£
1st instalment due 31.1.15		5,320
2nd instalment due 31.1.16	5,320	
Interest 4% × £47,880	1,915	7,235
3rd instalment due 31.1.17	5,320	
Interest 4% × £42,560	1,702	7,022
4th instalment due 31.1.18	5,320	

Payment of Tax CGT 222.1

	£	£
Interest 4% × £37,240	1,489	6,809
5th instalment due 31.1. 19	5,320	
Interest 4% × £31,920	1,276	6,596
6th instalment due 31.1.20	5,320	
Interest 4% × £26,600	1,064	6,384
7th instalment due 31.1.21	5,320	
Interest 4% × £21,280	851	6,171
8th instalment due 31.1.22	5,320	
Interest 4% × £15,960	638	5,958
9th instalment due 31.1.23	5,320	
Interest 4% × £10,640	425	5,745
10th instalment due 31.1.24	5,320	
Interest 4% × £5,320	212	5,532
Total tax and interest		£62,772

Notes

(a) Capital gains tax chargeable on a gift of land or certain shares or securities can, on election in writing, be paid by ten yearly instalments. The first instalment is due on the ordinary due date. The outstanding balance together with accrued interest may be paid at any time. Where the gift is to a connected person, the tax (and accrued interest) are payable immediately if any part of the subject-matter of the gift is subsequently disposed of for consideration. [*TCGA 1992, s 281(2)(4)(6)(7)*].

(b) Payment by instalments is also available in respect of a deemed disposal by trustees under *TCGA 1992, s 71(1)* (person becoming absolutely entitled to settled property) or *s 72(1)* (termination of life interest on death) and, in certain cases, to a chargeable gain accruing under *TCGA 1992, s 169C(7)* (clawback of hold-over relief under *TCGA 1992, s 165* or *s 260* if settlement becomes settlor-interested). [*TCGA 1992, s 281(1)(8)*].

(c) The disposal must *either* be one to which neither *TCGA 1992, s 165(4)* nor *s 260(3)* (see 213.2 and 213.1 HOLD-OVER RELIEFS) applies (or would apply if a claim was made) *or* one to which either of those *sections* does apply but on which the held-over gain only partly reduces the gain otherwise arising or is nil. [*TCGA 1992, s 281(1)*].

(d) The assets on a disposal of which an election can be made are: land or any interest or estate in land; any shares or securities of a company which, immediately before the disposal, gave control to the person making or deemed to be making the disposal; and any other shares or securities of a company not listed on a recognised stock exchange. [*TCGA 1992, s 281(3)*].

222.1 CGT   Payment of Tax

(e) Interest on unpaid tax is charged as if no election had been made. The interest on the unpaid portion of the tax is added to each instalment and must be paid accordingly. [*TCGA 1992, s 281(5)*].

223 Private Residences

223.1 PERIODS OF OWNERSHIP QUALIFYING FOR EXEMPTION AND LET PROPERTY EXEMPTION

[*TCGA 1992, ss 222, 223*]

(A)

P sold a house on 1 July 2013 realising an otherwise chargeable gain of £154,000. The house was purchased on 1 February 1980 and was occupied as a residence until 30 June 1989 when P moved to another residence, letting the house as residential accommodation. He did not re-occupy the house prior to its sale.

	£
Gain on sale	154,000
Deduct Exempt amount under main residence rules	
$\dfrac{7y\ 3m + 3y}{31y\ 3m} \times £154{,}000$	50,512
	103,488
Deduct Let property exemption	40,000
Net chargeable gain	£63,488

Notes

(a) The final three years of ownership are always included in the exempt period of ownership. [*TCGA 1992, s 223(1)*].

(b) The period of ownership for the exemption calculation does not include any period before 31 March 1982. [*TCGA 1992, s 223(7)*].

(c) The gain attributable to the letting (£103,488) is exempt to the extent that it does not exceed the lesser of £40,000 and the gain otherwise exempt (£50,512 in this example). [*TCGA 1992, s 223(4)*].

(B)

Q bought a house on 1 August 1981 for £40,000 and used it as his main residence. On 10 February 1982, he was sent by his employer to manage the Melbourne branch of the firm and continued to work in Australia until 4 August 1987, the whole of his duties being performed outside the UK. The house was let as residential accommodation during that period. Q took up residence in the house once again following his return to the UK, but on 30 September 2000 moved to Switzerland for health reasons. On this occasion, the property was not let. He returned to the UK in August 2003, but did not reside in the house at any time prior to its being sold on 31 December 2013 for £252,350. The house had a market value of £50,000 at 31 March 1982.

223.1 CGT Private Residences

Computation of gain before applying exemptions

	£
Disposal consideration	252,350
Market value 31.3.82	50,000
Gain before exemptions	202,350

The gain is reduced by the main residence exemptions as follows

Period of ownership (excluding period before 31.3.82)		31y 9m
Exempt periods since 31.3.82:		
31.3.82 – 30.9.00	18y 6m	
1.1.11– 31.12.13 (last three years)	3y 0m	21y 6m

	£
Gain as above	202,350

Deduct Exempt amount under main residence rules

$$\frac{21y\ 6m}{31y\ 9m} \times £202{,}350 \qquad 137{,}024$$

$$65{,}326$$

Deduct Let property exemption:

Period of letting 31.3.82 – 4.8.87   5y 4m

$$\text{Gain attributable to letting } \frac{5y\ 4m}{31y\ 9m} \times £202{,}350 = \quad £33{,}990$$

Exemption (note (e))		33,990
Net chargeable gain 2013/14		£31,336

Notes

(a) Periods of ownership before 31 March 1982 are excluded in applying the main residence exemptions. [*TCGA 1992, s 223(7)*].

(b) The period spent in Australia (regardless of its length but excluding that part of it before 31 March 1982) counts as a period of residence, as Q worked in an employment all the duties of which were performed outside the UK and used the house as his main residence at some time before and after this period of absence. [*TCGA 1992, s 223(3)(b)*].

(c) The period spent in Switzerland would have been exempt, having not exceeded three years, but the exemption is lost as Q did not occupy the property as a main residence at any time after this period. [*TCGA 1992, s 223(3)(a)*].

(d) The last three years of ownership are always exempt providing the property has been used as the owner's only or main residence at some time during the period of ownership, and for this purpose, 'period of ownership' is not restricted to the period after 30 March 1982. [*TCGA 1992, ss 222, 223(1)*].

(e) The let property exemption is the lesser of the gain attributable to the period of letting (£33,990), the gain otherwise exempt (£137,024) and £40,000. It cannot create a loss. It is available only if the property is let as residential accommodation. [*TCGA 1992, s 223(4)*].

223.2 ELECTION FOR MAIN RESIDENCE

[*TCGA 1992, s 222(5)*]

S purchased the long lease of a London flat on 1 June 2005. He occupied the flat as his sole residence until 31 July 2007 when he acquired a property in Shropshire. Both properties were thereafter occupied as residences by S until the lease of the London flat was sold on 28 February 2014, realising an otherwise chargeable gain of £75,000.

The possibilities open to S are

(i) Election for London flat to be treated as main residence throughout

Exempt gain £75,000

(ii) Election for Shropshire property to be treated as main residence from 31 July 2007 onwards

$$\text{Exempt gain } £75,000 \times \frac{2y\ 2m + 3y}{8y\ 9m} \qquad £44,286$$

(iii) Election for London flat to be treated as main residence up to 28 February 2011, with election for the Shropshire property to be so treated thereafter

$$\text{Exempt gain } £75,000 \times \frac{5y\ 9m + 3y}{8y\ 9m} \qquad £75,000$$

223.2 CGT   Private Residences

Note

(a) The elections in (iii) are the most favourable, provided they could have been made by 31 July 2009 in respect of the London flat, and by 28 February 2013 in respect of the Shropshire property. Note that the last three years' ownership of the London flat is an exempt period in any case. The advantage of (iii) over (i) is that the period of ownership 1 March 2011 to 28 February 2014 of the Shropshire property will be treated as a period of residence as regards any future disposal of that property. HMRC practice is that the *initial* election (which can be varied) must be made within two years of acquisition of the second property, and this was upheld in *Griffin v Craig-Harvey Ch D 1993*, 66 TC 396, [1994] STC 54.

223.3 HOLD-OVER RELIEF OBTAINED ON EARLIER DISPOSAL

[*TCGA 1992, ss 226A, 226B: FA 2004, s 117, Sch 22 paras 6–8*]

On 1 January 2003, Isobel gives a house which she has not occupied as a private residence to the trustees of a discretionary trust of which she is the settlor. She claims hold-over relief under *TCGA 1992, s 260* in respect of the disposal (see **212.1** HOLD-OVER RELIEFS) and the chargeable gain of £80,000 is held over. The trustees allow Isobel's daughter, Lyra, to occupy the house, under the terms of the settlement, as her main residence from 1 January 2003 to 31 December 2013. The house is then sold by the trustees on 20 January 2014 for £300,000. The market value of the house at 1 January 2003 is agreed to be £200,000. The trust is not a settlor-interested settlement for the purposes of *TCGA 1992, ss 169B–169G*.

The trustees' chargeable gain on disposal of the house is as follows.

	£	£
Disposal consideration		300,000
Cost	200,000	
Deduct held-over gain	80,000	120,000
Gain		180,000
Deduct Private residence exemption		
£180,000 × 343/4,038 (note (b))		15,290
Chargeable gain 2012/13		£164,710

Notes

(a) Subject to transitional rules (see (b) below), private residence relief under *TCGA 1992, s 223* is not available for disposals by individuals or trustees after 9 December 2003 where, in computing the chargeable gain which would (apart from that relief) accrue on that disposal, the allowable expenditure falls to be reduced to any extent in consequence, directly or indirectly, of a claim or claims under *TCGA 1992, s 260* (see **213.1** HOLD-OVER RELIEFS in respect of one or more earlier disposals (whether or not made to the person making the later disposal). [*TCGA 1992, s 226A: FA 2004, s 117, Sch 22 para 6*].

(b) Where the earlier disposal to which the *TCGA 1992, s 260* claim relates, or, if more than one, each of the earlier disposals, is made before 10 December 2003, total exemption (under *TCGA 1992, s 223(1)*) is excluded, but fractional exemption (under *TCGA 1992, s 223(2)*) can be obtained. In calculating the fractional exemption, the dwelling-house (or part thereof) in question is taken not to have been the individual's only or main residence at any time after 9 December 2003, and the period of ownership after that date is taken not to form part of the last 36 months of the period of ownership. In this case, the house was occupied as Lyra's main residence for 343 days before 10 December 2003 (i.e. 1 January 2003 to 9 December 2003, and the trustees' total period of ownership was 4,038 days (1 January 2003 to 20 January 2014).

224 Qualifying Corporate Bonds

[*TCGA 1992, ss 115–117*]

224.1 DEFINITION

[*TCGA 1992, s 117*]

B has the following transactions in 5% unsecured loan stock issued in 1983 by F Ltd.

			£
11.11.83	Purchase £2,000		1,800
10.7.89	Gift from wife £1,000 (original cost £800)		—
30.9.97	Purchase £2,000		2,100
5.6.13	Sale £4,000		(3,300)

Apart from the gift on 10.7.89, all acquisitions were arm's length purchases. B's wife acquired her £1,000 holding on 11.11.83. Indexation allowance of £266 arose on the transfer from wife to husband.

For the purposes of the accrued income scheme, the sale is without accrued interest and the rebate amount is £20. The stock is a corporate bond as defined by *TCGA 1992, s 117(1)* and therefore a 'relevant security' as defined by *TCGA 1992, s 108(1)*.

Under the rules for matching relevant securities in *TCGA 1992, s 106A*, the stock disposed of is identified with acquisitions as follows.

(i) Identify £2,000 with purchase on 30.9.97 (LIFO)

	£
Disposal consideration £3,300 × $\dfrac{2,000}{4,000}$	1,650
Add rebate amount £20 × $\dfrac{2,000}{4,000}$	10
	1,660
Allowable cost	2,100
Loss	£440

The loss is *not* allowable as the £2,000 stock purchased on 30.9.97 is a qualifying corporate bond (note (a)). [*TCGA 1992, s 115*].

224.1 CGT   Qualifying Corporate Bonds

(ii)   Identify £1,000 with acquisition on 10.7.89

	£
Disposal consideration £3,300 × $\dfrac{1,000}{4,000}$	825
Add rebate amount £20 × $\dfrac{1,000}{4,000}$	5
	830
Allowable cost (including indexation to 10.7.89)	1,066
Allowable loss	£236

The loss is allowable as the stock acquired on 10.7.89 is not a qualifying corporate bond (note (b)).

(iii) Identify £1,000 with purchase on 11.11.83

	£
Disposal consideration £3,300 × $\dfrac{1,000}{4,000}$	825
Add rebate amount £20 × $\dfrac{1,000}{4,000}$	5
	830
Allowable cost £1,800 × $\dfrac{1,000}{2,000}$	900
Allowable loss	£70

The loss is allowable as the stock acquired on 11.11.83 is not a qualifying corporate bond (note (c)).

Notes

(a)   The acquisition on 30.9.97 is a qualifying corporate bond as it was acquired after 13 March 1984 otherwise than as a result of an excluded disposal. [*TCGA 1992, s 117(7)(b)*].

(b)   The acquisition on 10.7.89 was the result of an excluded disposal, being a no gain/no loss transfer between spouses where the first spouse had acquired the stock before 14 March 1984. It is therefore not a qualifying corporate bond. [*TCGA 1992, s 117(7)(b)(8)*].

(c)   Securities acquired before 14 March 1984 cannot be qualifying corporate bonds in the hands of the person who so acquired them.

(d)   See **IT 2** ACCRUED INCOME SCHEME for the income tax effects of the accrued income scheme.

224.2 REORGANISATION OF SHARE CAPITAL

[*TCGA 1992, s 116*]

D holds 5,000 £1 ordinary shares in H Ltd. He acquired the shares in April 1999 by subscription at par. On 1 August 2006, he accepted an offer for the shares from J plc. The terms of the offer were one 25p ordinary share of J plc and £10 J plc 10% unsecured loan stock (a qualifying corporate bond) for each H Ltd ordinary share. Both the shares and the loan stock are listed on the Stock Exchange. In December 2013, D sells £20,000 loan stock at its quoted price of £105 per cent.

The value of J plc ordinary shares at 1 August 2006 was £3.52 per share and the loan stock was £99.20 per cent.

The cost of the H Ltd shares must be apportioned between the J plc ordinary shares and loan stock.

	£
Value of J plc shares	
5,000 × £3.52	17,600
Value of J plc loan stock	
£50,000 × 99.2%	49,600
	£67,200

Allowable cost of J plc shares

$$\frac{17,600}{67,200} \times £5,000 \qquad £1,310$$

Allowable cost of J plc loan stock

$$\frac{49,600}{67,200} \times £5,000 \qquad £3,690$$

Chargeable gain on H Ltd shares attributable to J plc loan stock to date of exchange

	£
Deemed disposal consideration	49,600
Allowable cost	3,690
Deferred chargeable gain	£45,910

Deferred chargeable gain accruing on disposal of loan stock in December 2013

Loan stock sold (nominal)	£20,000

224.2 CGT   Qualifying Corporate Bonds

Total holding of loan stock before disposal (nominal)	£50,000

Deferred chargeable gain accruing in 2013/14

$$\frac{20{,}000}{50{,}000} \times £45{,}910 \qquad £18{,}364$$

Notes

(a) The gain on the sale of J plc loan stock is exempt (as the stock is a qualifying corporate bond) except for that part which relates to the gain on the previous holding of H Ltd shares. [*TCGA 1992, s 115, s 116(10)*]. There will also be income tax consequences under the accrued income scheme (see **IT 2** ACCRUED INCOME SCHEME).

(b) The qualifying corporate bond is treated as acquired at the date of the reorganisation, so even if the original shares had been held at 31 March 1982, re-basing would *not* apply on the subsequent disposal of the loan stock.

(c) The exchange of J plc ordinary shares for H Ltd shares is dealt with under *TCGA 1992, ss 127–130*, and no gain or loss will arise until the J plc shares are disposed of. See **229.4** SHARES AND SECURITIES.

225 Remittance Basis

225.1 EFFECT OF ELECTION UNDER TCGA 1992, S 16ZA

[*TCGA 1992, ss 16ZA–16ZD; FA 2013, Sch 45 paras 98, 99*]

Kevin, who is domiciled in South Africa, comes to the UK on 6 April 2012 and is resident and ordinarily resident in the UK with effect from that date. He has substantial non-UK income and assets and makes claims under *ITA 2007, s 809B* for the remittance basis to apply for 2012/13 and 2013/14. Kevin disposes of two non-UK assets in 2012/13 realising a gain of £60,000 and a loss of £20,000. He also disposes of a UK asset on 1 May 2012, realising a gain of £10,000. He makes no disposals in 2013/14 but is treated as having remitted the £60,000 gain to the UK on 1 May 2013. Kevin is a higher rate income taxpayer for both years.

If Kevin makes an election under *TCGA 1992, s 16ZA* for 2012/13, his capital gains tax liabilities are as follows.

2012/13

	£
Gain on UK asset	10,000
Capital gains tax £10,000 × 28%	£2,800
Gain on non-UK asset	60,000
Deduct loss on non-UK asset	20,000
Net gain chargeable when remitted to UK	£40,000

2013/14

Net gain on non-UK asset remitted to UK	40,000
Capital gains tax £40,000 × 28%	£11,200

Notes

(a) Where an election has been made under *TCGA 1992, s 16ZA*, capital losses on non-UK assets arising in a tax year must be set against gains in the following order:

  (I) foreign chargeable gains arising and remitted to the UK in the year or, if the year is a split year, in the UK part of the year;

  (II) foreign chargeable gains arising in the year but not remitted to the UK in that year or, where the year is a split year, remitted to the UK in the overseas part of the year; and

  (III) all other chargeable gains arising in the year (other than gains treated as accruing on the remittance to the UK of foreign chargeable gains arising in a previous year).

[*TCGA 1992, s 16ZC; FA 2013, Sch 45 para 99*].

The 2012/13 loss cannot therefore be set against the UK gain arising in that year, as it must be set against the foreign gain within (II) above in priority.

225.1 CGT   Remittance Basis

(b) The election must be made within four years after the tax year to which it relates.

(c) If no election is made in respect of the first year for which a claim under *ITA 2007, s 809B* to the remittance basis is made, losses accruing in that year and any subsequent year (other than one in which the taxpayer is domiciled in the UK) on the disposal of assets situated outside the UK are not allowable losses. [*TCGA 1992, s 16ZA*]. In this case, therefore, if no election had been made, the whole of the remitted gain of £60,000 would have been chargeable in 2013/14.

(d) No annual exemption is available for a tax year in respect of which a claim for the remittance basis under *ITA 2007, s 809B* has been made. [*TCGA 1992, s 3(1A)*].

(e) An individual who claims the remittance basis for a tax year incurs an additional tax charge of £30,000 for that year if he is 18 years of age or over in that tax year and he has been UK resident in at least seven of the nine tax years immediately preceding that tax year. For 2012/13 onwards, the charge is increased to £50,000 where the individual has been UK resident in at least twelve of the fourteen tax years immediately preceding the tax year in question. [*ITA 2007, ss 809C(3)(4), 809H; FA 2009, Sch 27 para 5; FA 2012, Sch 12 para 2*].

226 Rollover Relief — Replacement of Business Assets

Cross-reference. See also 205.2 ASSETS HELD ON 31 MARCH 1982 for relief under *TCGA 1992, s 36, Sch 4* for certain gains accruing before 31 March 1982.

[*TCGA 1992, ss 152–158*]

226.1 NATURE OF RELIEF

[*TCGA 1992, s 152*]

(A)

N Ltd carries on a manufacturing business. It makes the following disposals and acquisitions of assets during the company's accounting periods ended 31 December 2011, 31 December 2012 and 31 December 2013.

	Asset	Bought/(sold) £	Chargeable gains £
1.10.11	Freehold depot	18,000	—
12.12.11	Leasehold warehouse	(50,000)	28,000
19.6.11	Business formerly carried on by another (unrelated) company:		
	Goodwill (note (c))	20,000	—
	Freehold factory unit	90,000	—
1.2.13	Land adjacent to main factory, now surplus to requirements	(40,000)	19,000
8.9.13	Industrial mincer (fixed plant)	(30,000)	5,000
1.11.13	Extension to new factory	35,000	—

(i) *The gain on the leasehold warehouse may be rolled over against the following*

	Cost £		Gain £
Freehold depot	18,000	$\dfrac{18,000}{50,000} \times £28,000$	10,080
Freehold factory (part)	32,000	$\dfrac{32,000}{50,000} \times £28,000$	17,920
	£50,000		£28,000

See note (b)

226.1 CGT   Rollover Relief — Replacement of Business Assets

(ii) *The gain on the surplus land may then be rolled over as follows*

    Freehold factory (part)   £40,000   Gain rolled over   £19,000

(iii) *The gain on the industrial mincer may be rolled over as follows*

    Extension to new factory (part)   £30,000   Gain rolled over   £5,000

The position at 31 December 2013 is then as follows

	£
Freehold depot	
Cost	18,000
Deduct gains rolled over	10,080
Allowable cost	£7,920
Freehold factory	
Cost	90,000
Deduct gains rolled over (£17,920 + £19,000)	36,920
Allowable cost	£53,080
Extension to new factory	
Cost	35,000
Deduct gains rolled over	5,000
Allowable cost	£30,000

Notes

(a) The expenditure still available to match against disposal proceeds is

    Extension to factory (£35,000 − £30,000)   £5,000

The expenditure is available only against disposals up to 31 October 2014.

(b) There is no statutory rule prescribing the way in which the gain on an asset must be rolled over against a number of different assets. The taxpayer's allocation of the rolled over gain against the cost of the new assets should be accepted by HMRC, providing specified amounts of consideration are positively earmarked and set against the cost of specified new assets (HMRC Capital Gains Manual, CG60770). In (i) the chargeable gain has been rolled over rateably to the costs of the items, but bringing in only part (i.e. the balance of proceeds) of the cost of the freehold factory.

(c) For corporation tax purposes, goodwill acquired from an unrelated party after 31 March 2002 falls within the intangible assets regime at *CTA 2009, ss 701–906* and is *not* a qualifying asset for chargeable gains rollover relief purposes. [*FA 2002, s 84, Sch 29 paras 132(5), 137*].

Rollover Relief — Replacement of Business Assets   CGT 226.1

(B)

L Ltd carries on a vehicle repair business. In December 2003 it sells a workshop for £90,000 net of costs. The workshop had cost £45,000 inclusive in April 1995. A new workshop is purchased for £144,000 (including incidental costs of acquisition) on 11 January 2005 and sold for £168,000 on 14 January 2014.

Indexation factors	April 1995 to December 2003	0.232
	January 2005 to January 2014 (estimated)	0.270

L Ltd claims rollover of the chargeable gain on the disposal of the workshop.

	£
Allowable cost of original workshop	45,000
Indexation allowance £45,000 × 0.232	10,440
	55,440
Actual disposal consideration	90,000
Chargeable gain rolled over	£34,560
Cost of new workshop	144,000
Deduct Amount rolled over	34,560
Deemed allowable cost	£109,440
Disposal consideration, replacement workshop	168,000
Allowable cost	109,440
Unindexed gain	58,560
Indexation allowance £109,440 × 0.270	29,549
Chargeable gain (January 2014)	£29,011

(C)

The facts are as in (B) above except that the business is carried on by M, an individual. The indexation factor for the period April 1995 to April 1998 is 0.091.

	£
Allowable cost of original workshop	45,000
Indexation allowance £45,000 × 0.091	4,095
	49,095
Actual disposal consideration	90,000
Chargeable gain rolled over (note (a))	£40,905
Cost of new workshop	144,000
Deduct Amount rolled over	40,905
Deemed allowable cost	£103,095
Disposal consideration, replacement workshop	168,000
Allowable cost	103,095
Chargeable gain 2013/14	£64,905

226.1 CGT   Rollover Relief — Replacement of Business Assets

226.2 PARTIAL RELIEF

(A) **Assets only partly replaced**

[*TCGA 1992, s 153*]

G carries on an accountancy practice. In March 2013, he agrees to acquire the practice of another sole practitioner, who is about to retire. As part of the acquisition, G pays £20,000 for goodwill. In January 2014, G moves to new premises, acquiring the remaining 70 years of a 99-year lease for £50,000. The sale of his former office on 25 February 2014 realises £80,000, and a chargeable gain of £59,000 arises.

	£	£
Amount of proceeds of disposal of old office		80,000
Costs against which gains can be rolled over		
Goodwill	20,000	
Lease	50,000	
		70,000
Chargeable gain not rolled over		£10,000
Chargeable gain rolled over (£59,000 − £10,000)		£49,000
Allowable cost of assets (see note (a))		
Goodwill		20,000
Gain rolled over $\dfrac{20{,}000}{70{,}000} \times £49{,}000$	14,000	
		£6,000
Lease		50,000
Gain rolled over $\dfrac{50{,}000}{70{,}000} \times £49{,}000$	35,000	
		£15,000

Notes

(a) There is no statutory rule prescribing the way in which a gain is to be rolled over against more than one acquisition. See note (b) to 226.1(A) above.

(b) It would not have been possible to roll over the gain only against the acquisition of the goodwill. The consideration not reinvested (£60,000) would be more than the gain (£59,000).

Rollover Relief — Replacement of Business Assets   CGT 226.3

(B) **Partial business use**

[*TCGA 1992, s 152(7)*]

N carries on a consultancy business from commercial premises formerly used as a shop. N has owned the property since 1 July 1981, but it was let until 1 March 1994 when N moved in, following the expiry of the lease held by the former tenant. On 1 February 2014, N sells the property for £100,000, moving to a new office with a long lease which he acquires for £70,000 and which is wholly used for his business. The value at 31 March 1982 of the property sold was £40,000.

For rollover relief purposes, N is treated as having disposed of two separate assets, one representing his occupation and professional use of the property, the other his ownership of it as an investment. In practice, the proceeds and chargeable gain may be allocated by a simple time apportionment.

Proceeds attributable to business use

$$\text{Proceeds } £100,000 \times \frac{19y11m}{31y10m} \text{(note }(c)\text{)} \qquad \underline{£62,565}$$

Chargeable gain attributable to business use

$$[£100,000 - £40,000] = £60,000 \times \frac{19y11m}{31y10m} \qquad \underline{£37,539}$$

Notes

(a) The proceeds attributable to business use are less than the cost of the new office, so that the whole of the chargeable gain attributable to business use can be rolled over. The allowable cost of the new office is then £32,461 (£70,000 − £37,539).

(b) The balance of the chargeable gain, £22,461 (£60,000 − £37,539) is not eligible for rollover.

(c) The time apportionment takes into account only the period of ownership after 30 March 1982. [*TCGA 1992, s 152(9)*].

226.3 WASTING ASSETS

[*TCGA 1992, s 154*]

(A) **Crystallisation of held-over gain**

In March 2009, a father and son partnership carrying on a car dealing trade sold a freehold showroom for £400,000 realising a chargeable gain (after indexation) of £190,000. On 30 June 2009, the firm purchased for £450,000 the remaining term of a lease due to expire on 30 June 2039 and used the premises as a new showroom. The whole of the gain on the old asset was held over under *TCGA 1992, s 154* on the acquisition of the new asset. In consequence of the father's decision to retire from the business and the resulting need to downsize the operation, the firm assigns the lease for £490,000 on 1 July 2013.

226.3 CGT   Rollover Relief — Replacement of Business Assets

The chargeable gains to be apportioned between the two partners for 2013/14 are as follows

	£	£
Proceeds of assignment		490,000
Cost (see note (a))	450,000	
Deduct Wasted $\dfrac{87.330 - 82.496}{87.330} \times £450,000$	24,909	425,091
Chargeable gain 2013/14 (see also note (b))		£64,909
Held-over gain becoming chargeable under *TCGA 1992, s 154(2)(a)*		£190,000

Notes

(a) The gain of £190,000 is deferred as opposed to being rolled over and does not reduce the cost of the new asset.

(b) See also 215.3(D)–(G) LAND for further examples on the assignment of short leases.

(B) Rollover of held-over gain

C Ltd, a manufacturing company, sells an item of fixed plant for £30,000 in February 2009. A chargeable gain of £7,200 arises. In 2011, the company buys storage facilities on a 20-year lease for £40,000. In 2013, an extension to the company's freehold factory is completed at a cost of £25,000.

The position is as follows

(i) The company may claim holdover of the £7,200 chargeable gain in 2009, against the cost of the lease.

(ii) In 2013, part of the chargeable gain can be rolled over against the cost of the factory extension, as follows

	£
Expenditure available for rollover	25,000
Maximum capable of rollover	
£7,200 − (£30,000 − £25,000)	2,200
Adjusted base cost of extension	£22,800

Notes

(a) The balance of the chargeable gain, £5,000 (£7,200 - £2,200) may continue to be held over against the cost of the lease, either until it crystallises or until further rollover is possible.

(b) Had the company not claimed holdover against the cost of the lease, a claim against the cost of the extension in 2013 would not have been possible, as the expenditure was incurred outside the normal three-year time limit.

227 Seed Enterprise Investment Scheme

227.1 DISPOSAL OF SEIS SHARES MORE THAN THREE YEARS AFTER ISSUE

[*TCGA 1992, s 150E(2)(4)(5); FA 2012, Sch 6 paras 3, 23(1)*]

On 8 November 2013 P subscribes £130,000 for 65,000 shares in the SEIS company, S Ltd, and obtains the maximum SEIS income tax relief of £50,000 (£100,000 × 50%) for 2013/14. On 3 April 2018 he sells the entire holding for £240,000.

The chargeable gain arising is calculated as follows

	£
Disposal proceeds	240,000
Cost	130,000
Gain	110,000
Less TCGA 1992, s 150E(2)(4)(5) exemption	
$£110,000 \times \dfrac{50,000}{65,000}$ (note(b))	84,615
Chargeable gain 2017/18	£25,384

Notes

(a) Gains arising on the sale more than three years after issue of shares qualifying for SEIS income tax relief are not chargeable gains unless the SEIS relief is fully withdrawn before disposal.

(b) Where the income tax relief is not given on the full SEIS subscription (otherwise than because of insufficient income), capital gains tax relief is given on a proportion of the gain on the disposal or part disposal.

The gain is reduced by the multiple R/T where

R = the actual income tax reduction and

T = the tax at the SEIS rate (50%) on the amount subscribed for the issue.

R = £100,000 × 50% = £50,000

T = £130,000 × 50% = £65,000

227.2 CGT   Seed Enterprise Investment Scheme

227.2 LOSS ON DISPOSAL OF SEIS SHARES

[TCGA 1992, s 150E(1)(3); FA 2012, Sch 6 paras 3, 23(1)]

(A) Disposal more than three years after issue

Assuming the facts otherwise remain the same as in 227.1 above but that the shares are sold for £50,000 on 3 April 2018.

The allowable loss arising is calculated as follows

	£	£
Disposal proceeds		50,000
Less Cost	130,000	
Less Income tax relief given (and not withdrawn)	50,000	80,000
Allowable loss 2017/18		£30,000

Note

(a) Any loss arising is reduced by deducting the amount of the SEIS relief (given and not withdrawn) from the acquisition cost. On the question of income tax withdrawal, see note (b) to (B) below.

(B) Disposal within three years of issue

The facts are otherwise as in (A) above except that the shares are sold in an arm's length bargain on 3 April 2015, i.e. within three years after their issue.

Income tax relief given for 2013/14 is withdrawn as follows

Relief attributable (£100,000 @ 50%) £50,000 (1)

Consideration

$$£50,000 \times \frac{50,000\ (£100,000\ @\ 50\%)}{65,000\ (£130,000\ @\ 50\%)} @ 50\% \qquad £19,230\ (2)$$

The amount at (1) is greater than that at (2), so income tax relief of £19,230 is withdrawn. [ITA 2007, ss 257FA, 257FB].

The relief not withdrawn is therefore £(50,000 − 19,230) = £30,770

The allowable loss arising is calculated as follows

	£	£
Disposal proceeds		50,000
Less Cost	130,000	
Less Income tax relief not withdrawn	30,770	99,230
Allowable loss 2013/14		£49,230

Notes

(a) For the purposes of computing an allowable loss, the consideration is reduced by the relief attributable to the shares. [*TCGA 1992, s 150E(1); FA 2012, Sch 6 para 3*]. The relief attributable is that remaining following any withdrawal of relief.

(b) A withdrawal of income tax relief arises on a disposal of SEIS shares within three years after their issue. [*ITA 2007, s 257FA; FA 2012, Sch 6 para 1*].

227.3 SEIS REINVESTMENT RELIEF

[*TCGA 1992, s 150G, Sch 5BB; FA 2012, Sch 6 paras 4, 5; FA 2013, s 57*]

On 1 June 2012, X sells an asset for £365,000. The asset had cost X £240,000 in 2005. X makes no other disposals in 2013/14. On 1 February 2014, X acquires by subscription 50,000 shares in ABC Ltd at a total price of £100,000. X claims SEIS income tax relief in respect of the acquisition.

If X makes a claim under *TCGA 1992, Sch 5BB* then his CGT position for 2013/14 is as follows

	£
Consideration	365,000
Less Acquisition cost	240,000
Gain	125,000
Less Reinvestment relief	50,000
Chargeable gain	75,000
Less annual exemption	10,900
Taxable gain 2013/14	£64,100

Notes

(a) SEIS reinvestment relief can be claimed where:

- an individual realises a chargeable gain on a disposal at any time in 2012/13 or 2013/14 (the 'relevant year'); and

- he is eligible for, and claims, SEIS income tax relief for the relevant year in respect of an amount subscribed for an 'issue of shares' in a company made to him (or treated as made to him) in that year.

227.3 CGT   Seed Enterprise Investment Scheme

Where SEIS shares issued in 2013/14 are treated as issued in 2012/13 as a result of a SEIS income tax relief carry-back claim under *ITA 2007, s 257AB(5)*, it would appear that they will thereby qualify to be used in a reinvestment relief claim for 2012/13. Similarly, where SEIS shares issued in 2014/15 are treated as issued in 2013/14, it would appear that they will thereby qualify to be used in a reinvestment relief claim for 2013/14. This does not, however, affect the time limit for making a claim.

(b) For 2013/14, the amount of relief is restricted to 50% of the amount on which SEIS income tax relief is claimed. For 2012/13, relief is available for 100% of that amount, subject to an overall limit of £100,000.

(c) A claim for SEIS reinvestment relief in respect of shares issued in 2013/14 must be made no later than 31 January 2020. [*TCGA 1992, Sch 5BB para 3; ITA 2007, s 257EA; FA 2012, Sch 6 paras 1, 5; FA 2013, s 57(2)*].

(d) If SEIS income tax relief attributable to shares is withdrawn, any SEIS reinvestment relief attributable to those shares is also withdrawn. If SEIS income tax relief attributable to shares is reduced, any SEIS reinvestment relief attributable to those shares is reduced in the same proportion. In either case, a chargeable gain is then deemed to accrue to the individual in 2012/13 or 2013/14 of an amount equal to the amount of reinvestment relief to be withdrawn or the amount by which reinvestment relief falls to be reduced. [*TCGA 1992, Sch 5BB para 5; FA 2012, Sch 6 para 5; FA 2013, s 57(4)*].

228 Settlements

Cross-reference. See **220.1** OFFSHORE SETTLEMENTS as regards capital gains of non-resident settlements.

228.1 ANNUAL EXEMPTIONS AND RATES OF TAX

[*TCGA 1992, ss 3, 4, Sch 1 paras A1, 2; FA 2008, s 8*]

The trustees of the E settlement, created in 1974, realise net chargeable gains and allowable losses as follows:

	Chargeable gain/ (allowable loss) £
2009/10	(2,250)
2010/11	3,100
2011/12	5,400
2012/13	3,200
2013/14	12,550

The trustees' capital gains tax liability is computed as follows

	£
2009/10	
Taxable amount	Nil
Losses carried forward	£2,250
2010/11	
Net chargeable gains	3,100
Losses brought forward	—
Taxable amount (covered by annual exemption of £5,050)	£3,100
CGT	Nil
Losses carried forward	£2,250
2011/12	
Net chargeable gains	5,400
Losses brought forward	100
Taxable amount (covered by annual exemption)	£5,300
CGT	Nil
Losses carried forward (£2,250 − £100)	£2,150
2012/13	
Net chargeable gains	3,200
Losses brought forward	—

228.1 CGT Settlements

Taxable amount (covered by annual exemption of £5,300)	£3,200
CGT	Nil
Losses carried forward	£2,150
2013/14	
Net chargeable gains	12,550
Losses brought forward	2,150
Chargeable gains	10,400
Deduct Annual exemption	5,450
Taxable gains	£4,950
CGT at 28% on £4,950	£1,386
Losses carried forward	Nil

Notes

(a) For 2011/12 onwards the rate of capital gains tax on gains accruing to the trustees of any settlement is 28%, or 10% where entrepreneurs' relief applies. For 2010/11 the rate is 18% for gains made before 23 June 2010 and, for gains made on or after that date, either 28% or 10% where entrepreneurs' relief applies. [*TCGA 1992, s 4(3); F(No 2)A 2010, Sch 1 paras 2, 12, 18*]. For 2009/10, the rate of tax is 18%. [*TCGA 1992, s 4; FA 2008, s 8*].

(b) See *TCGA 1992, Sch 1 para 2(4)–(6)* for the annual exemption available to two or more settlements made by the same settlor after 6 June 1978.

228.2 TRUSTS WITH VULNERABLE BENEFICIARY

[*FA 2005, ss 23–45, Schs 1, 1A; FA 2013, Sch 44 paras 14–19*]

Harry was born in 2001. In June 2008 both of his parents are killed in a road accident. Neither parent has made a will, so that a statutory trust is established for Harry under the intestacy rules of *Administration of Estates Act 1925, ss 46, 47(1)*. The trustees and Harry's guardian make a vulnerable person election (by 31 January 2012) to take effect on 6 April 2009. On 16 May 2013, the trustees sell an asset, realising a chargeable gain of £20,000. The trustees (who are resident in the UK throughout) make no other disposals in 2013/14. Harry is resident in the UK throughout the tax year and has no personal chargeable gains. His taxable income for 2013/14 is lower than the amount of the personal allowance.

If the trustees make a claim for special tax treatment under *FA 2005, s 24* for 2013/14, their capital gains tax liability is calculated as follows.

	£
Gain	20,000
Annual exemption	5,450

Taxable gain 2012/13	£14,550
CGT £14,550 × 28%	4,074.00
Less reduction under *FA 2005, s 31*	2,436.00
CGT payable by trustees	£1,638.00

The reduction under *FA 2005, s 31* is equal to:

TQTG − (TLVA − TLVB)

where

TQTG = the amount of capital gains tax to which the trustees would, apart from these provisions, be liable for the tax year in respect of qualifying trust gains;

TLVB = the total amount of capital gains tax to which the vulnerable person is liable for the tax year; and

TLVA = what TLVB would be if the qualifying trust gains accrued to the vulnerable person instead of the trustees, and no allowable losses were deducted from them.

In this case, TQTG = £4,074 (as above), TLVB is nil, and TLVA is calculated as follows.

	£
Gain	20,000
Annual exemption	10,900
Taxable gain	£9,100
CGT £9,100 × 18% (TLVA)	£1,638.00
The reduction is therefore £4,074 − (£1,638 − Nil) =	£2,436.00

Notes

(a) The trustees are effectively able to make use of the beneficiary's annual exemption and, where applicable, lower rate of tax.

(b) A claim for special tax treatment applies to both income tax and capital gains tax. No separate claim can be made in respect of each tax.

(c) Where the vulnerable beneficiary is not UK resident, see *FA 2005, ss 32, 33, Sch 1*.

228.3 CREATION OF A SETTLEMENT

[*TCGA 1992, s 70*]

(A)

In December 2013, C transfers to trustees of a settlement for the benefit of his disabled daughter 10,000 shares in W plc, a quoted company. The value of the gift is £85,000. C bought the shares in 1981 for £20,000 and their value at 31 March 1982 was £35,000.

228.3 CGT   Settlements

	£
Deemed disposal consideration	85,000
Market value 31.3.82	35,000
Chargeable gain	£50,000
Trustees' allowable cost	£85,000

Note

(a) If the transfer had been a chargeable lifetime transfer for inheritance tax purposes, or would be one but for the annual inheritance tax exemption and the settlement is not settlor-interested within *TCGA 1992, ss 169B–169G*, C could have elected under *TCGA 1992, s 260* to roll the gain over against the trustees' base cost of the shares. The trustees do not join in any such election.

(B)

In late April 2013 H settles farmland on trust for himself for life, with interests in reversion to his children. The land cost £20,000 in 1975 and its agreed values are £60,000 at 31 March 1982 and £125,000 at the date of settlement. H's interest in possession in the settled property is valued at £90,000.

The chargeable gain is computed as follows

	£
Deemed disposal proceeds	125,000
Market value 31.3.82	60,000
Chargeable gain 2013/14	£65,000

Notes

(a) The value of H's interest in the settled property is ignored and the transfer is not treated as a part disposal.

(b) As the settlement is settlor-interested, H cannot claim hold-over relief under *TCGA 1992, s 260* even though the transfer of the land into settlement is a chargeable lifetime transfer. See note (a) to (A) above.

228.4 PERSON BECOMING ABSOLUTELY ENTITLED TO SETTLED PROPERTY

[*TCGA 1992, s 71*]

(A)

M is a beneficiary entitled to an interest in possession in settled property, under a settlement made by her mother. The trustees exercise a power of appointment to advance capital to M, and, in September 2013, transfer to her a house valued at £80,000. The house was acquired by the trustees by gift from the settlor in 2003, when its value was £45,000.

Settlements   CGT 228.4

The trustees realise a gain of £35,000 (£80,000 - £45,000) on the advancement of capital to M.

Note

(a) If, while it was settled property, the house had been occupied by M as her private residence with the permission of the trustees, then all or part of the gain would qualify for the private residence exemption under *TCGA 1992, s 225*.

(B) **Transfer of settlement losses**

[*TCGA 1992, s 71(2)–(2D)*]

F is the sole remaining beneficiary of an accumulation and maintenance settlement established under his late uncle's will and in which he became entitled to an interest in possession upon reaching the age of 18 in 1996. On 18 September 2003, his 25th birthday, he becomes absolutely entitled as against the trustees to the capital of the trust. At that date, the trust capital consists of the following

- cash of £12,000,
- 10,000 shares in ABC Ltd (purchased for £6,000 in May 2002 and currently valued at £11,000), and
- 15,000 shares in DEF Ltd (transferred into the trust at a CGT value of £27,000 but now valued at only £13,000).

On 30 June 2003, the trustees had sold shares in GHK Ltd at a gain of £3,000 (after deducting indexation allowance to April 1998). On 7 July 2003, they sold shares in LMN Ltd at a loss of £500. None of the above-mentioned trust investments were business assets for taper relief purposes. At 6 April 2003, the trustees had allowable capital losses of £1,000 brought forward from earlier years.

In December 2003, F sells the ABC Ltd shares for £11,600. He also disposes of other assets in 2003/04 realising chargeable gains of £9,400 (with no taper relief due). In 2013/14, he sells the DEF Ltd shares for £15,700 and also disposes of other assets realising chargeable gains of £19,000 and allowable losses of £1,500.

F takes over entitlement to trust losses as follows

	£	£
Loss on DEF Ltd shares transferred to F £(27,000 − 13,000)		14,000
Deduct Trustees' 'pre-entitlement gains'[*]:		
(i) gain on ABC Ltd shares transferred to F	5,000	
(ii) other gains in period 6.4.03–18.9.03	3,000	8,000
Loss treated as accruing to F (note (a))		£6,000

[*] See *TCGA 1992, s 71(2A)*

228.4 CGT Settlements

F's CGT position for 2003/04 and 2013/14 is as follows

2003/04

	£
Gain on sale of ABC Ltd shares £(11,600 − 11,000)	600
Other gains	9,400
	10,000
Deduct Annual exemption	7,900
Gains chargeable to tax 2003/04	£2,100
Ex-trust losses carried forward	£6,000

2013/14

	£	£
Gain on sale of DEF Ltd shares £(15,700 − 13,000)	2,700	
Deduct Ex-trust losses brought forward and treated as a loss for the year	2,700	—
Other gains	19,000	
Deduct Losses for the year	1,500	17,500
		17,500
Deduct Annual exemption		10,900
Gains chargeable to tax		£6,600

	£
Ex-trust losses brought forward	6,000
Utilised in 2013/14	2,700
Unused balance (note (b))	£3,300

Notes

(a) Trust losses of £1,000 brought forward and £500 accruing in 2003/04 cannot be transferred to F and in this case are wasted. The 'pre-entitlement gains' cannot be reduced by those losses before being set against the loss on DEF Ltd shares.

(b) In F's hands, the loss can only be set against a gain on the DEF Ltd shares on which it arose. As all those shares are sold in 2013/14, the loss cannot be carried forward any further and the unused balance of £3,300 is written off.

228.5 TERMINATION OF INTEREST IN POSSESSION ON DEATH

[*TCGA 1992, s 72; FA 2006, Sch 12 para 30(2)*]

(A)

K is entitled to an interest in possession under a settlement. The settled property consists of shares and cash. On K's death, L is entitled to a life interest in succession to K. K dies on 1 December 2013, when the shares are valued at £200,000. The trustees' allowable cost in respect of the shares is £40,000.

Settlements CGT 228.5

On K's death, the trustees are deemed to have disposed of and immediately reacquired the shares for £200,000, thus uplifting the CGT base cost, but no chargeable gain then arises.

Note

(a) Where the deceased became entitled to the interest in possession on or after 22 March 2006, the above treatment applies only if

(i) the deceased died under the age of 18 and, immediately before his death, *IHTA 1984, s 71D* (age 18 to 25 trusts) applies to the property in which the interest subsists; or

(ii) immediately before his death,

(a) the interest in possession is an immediate post-death interest within *IHTA 1984, s 49A*;

(b) the interest is a transitional serial interest within *IHTA 1984, s 49C*;

(c) the interest is a disabled person's interest within *IHTA 1984, s 89B(1)(c)(d)*; or

(d) *IHTA 1984, s 71A* (trusts for bereaved minors) applies to the property in which the interest subsists.

[*TCGA 1992, s 72(1)–(1C)*].

(B)

In 1976, E created a settlement for the benefit of his children M and N and his grandchildren, transferring an investment property valued at £10,000 to the trustees. The terms of the settlement were that M and N each have a life interest in half of the trust income, with the remainder passing to E's grandchildren. In 1990, N assigned his interest to P, an unrelated party, for £35,000, its then market value. In 2013, N dies. The value of a half share of the trust property is then £65,000.

On N's death, his life interest terminates. There is no effect on the trustees as N was no longer the person entitled to the life interest within the meaning of *TCGA 1992, s 72*.

Notes

(a) No chargeable gain arises on the disposal by N of his interest. [*TCGA 1992, s 76*].

(b) P may claim an allowable loss on extinction of the interest. For an example of the computation if the interest is a wasting asset, see **231.3** WASTING ASSETS.

229 Shares and Securities

Cross-references. See also 204 ASSETS HELD ON 6 APRIL 1965, 205 ASSETS HELD ON 31 MARCH 1982, 214 INDEXATION, 224 QUALIFYING CORPORATE BONDS and 230 SHARES AND SECURITIES — IDENTIFICATION RULES.

229.1 REORGANISATION OF SHARE CAPITAL — VALUATION OF DIFFERENT CLASSES OF SHARE ON SUBSEQUENT DISPOSAL

[*TCGA 1992, ss 126–131*]

(A) **Unquoted shares**

V acquired 10,000 ordinary shares in X Ltd, an unquoted trading company, in April 1997 at a cost of £15,000. In April 2003, as part of a reorganisation of share capital, V was additionally allotted 3,000 new 9% preference shares in X Ltd for which he paid £3,900. In June 2013, V sold his ordinary shareholding, in an arm's length transaction, for £20,000, but retained his preference shares, then valued at £4,000.

The chargeable gain on the disposal of the ordinary shares is calculated as follows

	£
Disposal consideration	20,000
Cost (£15,000 + £3,900) × $\dfrac{20,000}{20,000 + 4,000}$	15,750
Chargeable gain 2013/14	£4,250
Allowable cost of 3,000 preference shares (£15,000 + £3,900 − £15,750)	£3,150

Note

(a) The ordinary shares and preference shares held after the reorganisation (the 'new holding') constitute a single asset. [*TCGA 1992, s 127*]. A disposal of part of the new holding is thus a part disposal. If neither class of shares comprising the new holding is quoted on a recognised stock exchange at any time not later than three months after the reorganisation, acquisition cost on a part disposal is apportioned by reference to market values at the date of disposal. [*TCGA 1992, s 129*].

(B) **Quoted shares**

Assume the facts to be as in (A) above except that both the ordinary and preference shares are quoted on a recognised stock exchange. On the first day of dealing after the reorganisation took effect, the ordinary shares were quoted at £1.85 and the preference shares at £1.35. V's holdings were therefore valued at £18,500 and £4,050 respectively.

229.1 CGT Shares and Securities

The chargeable gain on the disposal of the ordinary shares is calculated as follows

	£
Disposal consideration	20,000
Cost (£15,000 + £3,900) × $\dfrac{18,500}{18,500 + 4,050}$	15,506
Chargeable gain 2013/14	£4,494
Allowable cost of 3,000 preference shares (£15,000 + £3,900 − £15,506)	£3,394

Note

(a) Where one or more of the classes of shares or debentures comprising the new holding is quoted on a recognised stock exchange at any time not later than three months after the reorganisation, acquisition cost on a part disposal is apportioned by reference to market values on the first day of dealing on which the prices quoted reflect the reorganisation. [*TCGA 1992, s 130*].

(C) **Quoted shares — reorganisation after 31 March 1982, original holding acquired on or before that date**

In 1980, W subscribed for 5,000 £1 ordinary shares at par in L plc, a quoted company. The value of his holding at 31 March 1982 was £8,000. In November 1990, L plc offered ordinary shareholders two 7% preference shares at £1 per share in respect of each five ordinary shares held. W took up his entitlement of 2,000 preference shares. On the first day of dealing after the reorganisation, the ordinary shares were quoted at £3.00 (making W's holding worth £15,000) and the preference shares at £1.02 (valuing W's holding at £2,040). In June 2013, W sells his preference shares on the market at £1.40 (total proceeds £2,800). (For simplicity, costs of acquisition and disposal are ignored in this example.)

The gain on the disposal of the preference shares is computed as follows

	£
Disposal consideration	2,800
(31.3.82 value £8,000 + cost £2,000) × $\dfrac{2,040}{2,040 + 15,000}$	1,197
Chargeable gain 2013/14	£1,603

Note

(a) On a subsequent disposal of the ordinary shares, their cost would be £8,803 (£8,000 + £2,000 − £1,197).

Shares and Securities   CGT 229.2

229.2 BONUS ISSUES

[*TCGA 1992, ss 126–128, 130*]

(A) **Bonus of same class**

In October 5, Y plc made a scrip issue of one ordinary share for every 10 held. L held 5,000 ordinary shares, which he acquired in May 1997 for £5,500, and therefore received 500 shares in the bonus issue. In October 2013, L sells 3,000 of his shares for £10,000.

Section 104 holding	Shares	Qualifying expenditure
		£
May 1997 acquisition	5,000	5,500
October 2005 bonus issue	500	—
	5,500	5,500
October 2013 disposal	(3,000)	(3,000)
Pool carried forward	2,500	£2,500

Calculation of chargeable gain		£
Disposal consideration		10,000
Allowable cost $\dfrac{3,000}{5,500} \times £5,500$		3,000
Chargeable gain 2013/14		£7,000

(B) **Bonus of different class**

On 6 April 1985, R bought 2,000 'A' shares in T plc for £3,800. In June 1990, R bought a further 500 'A' shares for £800. In October 1994 T plc made a bonus issue of 2 'B' shares for each 5 'A' shares held, and R received 1,000 'B' shares, valued at £1.20 each (total value £1,200) on the first dealing day after the issue. On the same day, the 'A' shares were quoted at £2 each (total value £5,000). In December 2013 R sells his 1,000 'B' shares for £4,000.

Section 104 holding — 'A' shares	Shares	Qualifying expenditure
		£
April 1985 acquisition	2,000	3,800
June 1990 acquisition	500	800
	2,500	4,600
October 1994 bonus issue of 'B' shares: transfer proportion of expenditure to 'B' shares (see note (a))	—	(890)
Pool of 'A' shares carried forward	2,500	£3,710

229.2 CGT Shares and Securities

	Shares	Qualifying expenditure
Section 104 holding — 'A' shares		£
Section 104 holding — 'B' shares		
October 1994 bonus issue: proportion of pool transferred from 'A' shares holding	1,000	890
December 2013 disposal	1,000	890

Calculation of chargeable gain on disposal of 'B' shares	£
Disposal consideration	4,000
Allowable cost (as allocated)	890
Chargeable gain 2013/14	£3,110

Notes

(a) The cost of the 'A' shares is apportioned between 'A' and 'B' shares by reference to market values on the first day of dealing after the reorganisation.

$$\text{Proportion of qualifying expenditure } £4,600 \times \frac{1,200}{1,200 + 5,000} \quad £890$$

(HMRC Capital Gains Manual CG 51965 onwards.).

(b) A different basis of apportionment applies to unquoted shares (see HMRC Capital Gains Manual CG 51919 onwards.).

229.3 RIGHTS ISSUES

[*TCGA 1992, s 42, s 123(1), s 128(4)*]

Cross-reference.
See **229.8(B)** below as regards sale of rights.

(A) Rights issue of same class

W plc is a quoted company which in June 2003 made a rights issue of one £1 ordinary share for every eight £1 ordinary shares held, at £1.35 payable on allotment. V, who held 16,000 £1 ordinary shares purchased in May 1995 for £15,000, took up his entitlement in full, and was allotted 2,000 shares. In December 2013, he sells 6,000 of his shares for £30,000.

'Section 104' holding	Shares	Qualifying expenditure
		£
May 1995 acquisition	16,000	15,000

Shares and Securities   **CGT 229.3**

'Section 104' holding	Shares	Qualifying expenditure
		£
June 2003 rights issue	2,000	2,700
	18,000	17,700
December 2013 disposal	(6,000)	(5,900)
Pool carried forward	12,000	£11,800

Calculation of chargeable gain	£
Disposal consideration	30,000
Allowable cost $\dfrac{6,000}{18,000} \times £17,700$	5,900
Chargeable gain 2013/14	£24,100

(B) **Rights issue of different class**

On 1 March 1993, A acquired 6,000 quoted £1 ordinary shares in S plc at a cost of £7,800. In October 1996, S plc made a rights issue of one 50p 'B' share for every five £1 ordinary shares held, at 60p payable in full on application. A took up his entitlement in full, acquiring 1,200 'B' shares. On the first dealing day after issue, the 'B' shares were quoted at 65p and the £1 ordinary shares at £1.50. A sells his 'B' shares in December 2013 for £20,000.

'Section 104' holding — ordinary shares	Shares	Qualifying expenditure
		£
March 1993 acquisition	6,000	7,800
October 1996 rights issue of 'B' shares	—	720
	6,000	8,520
Transfer proportion of expenditure to 'B' shares (note (a))	—	(680)
Pool carried forward	6,000	7,840

'Section 104' holding — 'B' shares	Shares	Qualifying expenditure
		£
October 1996 rights issue: proportion of pool transferred from ordinary shares holding	1,200	680
December 2013 disposal	(1,200)	(680)
Pool carried forward	—	—

229.3 CGT   Shares and Securities

Calculation of chargeable gain on disposal of 'B' shares	£
Disposal consideration	20,000
Allowable cost (as allocated)	680
Chargeable gain 2013/14	£19,320

Notes

(a) The cost of the original shares is apportioned between the original shares and the 'B' shares by reference to market values on the first day of dealing after the reorganisation.

Proportion of qualifying expenditure

$$£8,520 \times \frac{1,200 \times 0.65}{(1,200 \times 0.65) + (6,000 \times 1.50)} \qquad £680$$

(HMRC Capital Gains Manual CG 51965 et seq.).

(b) A different basis of apportionment applies to unquoted shares (see HMRC Capital Gains Manual CG 51919 et seq.).

(C) **Rights issue of same class: disposal out of section 104 holding and 1982 holding**

G Ltd has purchased 100,000 25p ordinary shares in C plc as follows

Date	Number of shares acquired	Cost £
22.5.80	20,000	0.78
5.11.83	15,000	1.10
14.9.84	40,000	1.00
30.4.02	25,000	2.30

In May 1992, C made a rights issue of one ordinary share for every five held, at £1.50 payable in full on application. G took up its rights in full (15,000 ordinary shares). It sells 105,000 shares in August 2013 for £4.50 per share. The shares were quoted at 90p on 31 March 1982. Incidental costs of acquisition and disposal are disregarded for the purposes of this example.

Indexation factors		
	March 1982 to August 2013 (assumed)	2.051
	November 1983 to April 1985	0.094
	September 1984 to April 1985	0.052
	April 1985 to May 1992	0.470
	May 1992 to April 2002	0.261
	April 2002 to August 2013 (assumed)	0.248

Shares and Securities   CGT 229.3

Section 104 holding	Shares	Qualifying expenditure £	Indexed pool £
5.11.83 acquisition	15,000	16,500	16,500
Indexed rise: November 1983 to April 1985			
£16,500 × 0.094			1,551
14.9.84 acquisition	40,000	40,000	40,000
Indexed rise: September 1984 to April 1985			
£40,000 × 0.052	—	—	2,080
Pool at 6.4.85	55,000	56,500	60,131
Indexed rise: April 1985 to May 1992			
£60,131 × 0.470			28,262
May 1992 rights issue	11,000	16,500	16,500
	66,000	73,000	104,893
Indexed rise: May 1992 to April 2002			
£104,893 × 0.261			27,377
30.4.02 acquisition	25,000	57,500	57,500
	91,000	130,500	189,770
Indexed rise: April 2002 to August 2013			
£189,770 × 0.248	—	—	47,063
	91,000	130,500	236,833
August 2013 disposal	(91,000)	(130,500)	(236,833)

1982 holding	Shares	Cost £	Market value 31.3.82 £
22.5.80 acquisition	20,000	15,600	18,000
May 1992 rights issue (note (*a*))	4,000	6,000	6,000
	24,000	21,600	24,000
August 2013 disposal	(14,000)	(12,600)	(14,000)
Pool carried forward	10,000	£9,000	£10,000

Calculation of chargeable gain

	£
(i) Identify 91,000 shares sold with *section 104* holding	
Disposal consideration 91,000 × £4.50	409,500
Allowable cost	130,500
Unindexed gain	279,000
Indexation allowance £236,833 − £130,500	106,333

229.3 CGT Shares and Securities

	£
Chargeable gain	£172,667

(ii) Identify 14,000 shares with 1982 holding

Without re-basing to 1982

	£
Disposal consideration 14,000 × £4.50	63,000
Cost $\dfrac{14,000}{24,000} \times £21,600$	12,600
Unindexed gain	50,400
Indexation allowance (see below)	22,449
Gain after indexation	£27,951

With re-basing to 1982

	£
Disposal consideration	63,000
Allowable expenditure $\dfrac{14,000}{24,000} \times £24,000$	14,000
Unindexed gain	49,000

Indexation allowance

	£	
$£14,000 \times \dfrac{18,000}{24,000} \times 2.051$	21,535	
$£14,000 \times \dfrac{6,000}{24,000} \times 0.261$	914	
	22,449	
Gain after indexation		£26,551
Chargeable gain		£26,551
Total chargeable gain £172,667 + £26,551		£199,218

Notes

(a) The 1982 holding cannot be increased by an 'acquisition', but can be increased by a rights issue as this is not treated as involving an acquisition. [*TCGA 1992, s 109(2), ss 127, 128*].

(b) See **230 SHARES AND SECURITIES — IDENTIFICATION RULES** for further examples of the identification rules and the different rules applicable for capital gains tax purposes.

229.4 EXCHANGE OF SECURITIES FOR THOSE IN ANOTHER COMPANY

[*TCGA 1992, ss 135, 137, 138*]

(A) **Takeover by quoted company**

S was a shareholder in N Ltd, an unquoted company. He subscribed for his 20,000 50p ordinary shares at 60p per share in 1979 and the shares were valued at £3 each at 31 March 1982. In July 1987, the shareholders accepted an offer by a public company, M plc, for their shares. Each ordinary shareholder received one £1 ordinary M plc share plus 45p cash for every two N Ltd shares held. S acquired 10,000 M plc shares and received cash of £4,500. The M plc shares were valued at £7.50 each at the time of the acquisition. On 25 April 2013, S sells 4,000 of his 10,000 M plc shares for £54,000. The indexation factor for March 1982 to July 1987 is 0.281.

(i) *On the merger in 1987/88, S makes a disposal only to the extent that he receives cash*

	£
Disposal consideration	4,500
Allowable cost $\dfrac{4,500}{4,500 + (10,000 \times £7.50 = £75,000)} \times £12,000$	679
Unindexed gain	3,821
Indexation allowance £679 × 0.281	191
Chargeable gain 1987/88	£3,630

Note

(a) The fraction applied to allowable cost corresponds to 5.66%. If the percentage had not exceeded 5% the cash distribution of £4,500 would have been regarded as 'small' and could have been deducted from allowable cost (Revenue Tax Bulletin November 1992 p 46). [*TCGA 1992, s 122*]. No gain would then have arisen in 1987/88, but the allowable cost would have been reduced by £4,500. See also **229.8(B)** below. (A distribution made after 23 February 1997 can additionally be regarded as 'small' if it does not exceed £3,000 — Revenue Tax Bulletin February 1997 p 397.)

(ii) *The chargeable gain on disposal in 2013/14 is*

	£
Disposal consideration	54,000
Market value 31.3.82	
$£(20,000 \times £3) \times \dfrac{75,000}{75,000 + 4,500} \times \dfrac{4,000}{10,000}$ (note (b))	22,642
Chargeable gain 2013/14	£31,358

229.4 CGT   Shares and Securities

Notes

(a) The M plc shares are regarded as the same asset as the original N Ltd shares. [*TCGA 1992, ss 127, 135*]. Re-basing to 31 March 1982 thus applies, as the original shares were held on that date.

(b) Where there has been a part disposal after 31 March 1982 and before 6 April 1988 of an asset held on the earlier of those dates, and this is followed by a disposal after 5 April 1988 to which re-basing applies, the re-basing rules are deemed to have applied to the part disposal. [*TCGA 1992, Sch 3 para 4(1)*].

(B) **Takeover by unquoted company**

Y Ltd, a small unquoted company, is taken over in June 1998 by another unquoted company, C Ltd. The terms of the acquisition are that holders of £1 ordinary shares in Y Ltd receive two £1 ordinary shares and one £1 deferred share in C Ltd in exchange for every two ordinary shares held.

B acquired his holding of 500 Y Ltd shares on the death of his wife in May 1994, at probate value of £10,000. In May 2013, B sells his 250 C Ltd deferred shares for £4,500. The value of his 500 C Ltd ordinary shares is then £25,000.

There is no CGT disposal in 1998/99. The chargeable gain on the 2013/14 disposal is calculated as follows

	£
Disposal consideration	4,500
Allowable cost $\dfrac{4,500}{4,500 + 25,000} \times £10,000$	1,525
Chargeable gain 2013/14	£2,975
The allowable cost carried forward of the 500 C Ltd ordinary shares is (£10,000 − £1,525)	£8,475

(C) **Earn-outs**

K owns 10,000 ordinary shares in M Ltd, which he acquired for £12,000 in December 2005. In July 2012, the whole of the issued share capital of M Ltd was acquired by P plc. Under the terms of the takeover, K receives £2 per share plus the right to further consideration up to a maximum of £1.50 per share depending on future profit performance. The initial consideration is receivable in cash, but the deferred consideration is to be satisfied by the issue of shares in P plc. In December 2013, K duly receives 2,000 ordinary shares valued at £6 per share in full settlement of his entitlement. The right to future consideration is valued at £1.40 per share in July 2012.

Shares and Securities CGT 229.4

If K elects to disapply *TCGA 1992, s 138A* the position would be

2012/13

	£	£
Disposal proceeds 10,000 × £2	20,000	
Value of rights 10,000 × £1.40	14,000	34,000
Cost		12,000
Chargeable gain 2012/13		£22,000

2013/14

	£
Disposal of rights to deferred consideration:	
Proceeds — 2,000 P plc shares @ £6	12,000
Deemed cost of acquiring rights	14,000
Allowable loss 2013/14	£2,000
Cost for CGT purposes of 2,000 P plc shares	£12,000

Without an election, the position would be
2012/13

	£
Proceeds (cash) (as above)	20,000
Cost £12,000 × $\dfrac{20,000}{20,000 + 14,000}$	7,059
Chargeable gain 2012/13	£12,941
Cost of earn-out right for CGT purposes (£12,000 − £7,059)	£4,941

2013/14

The shares in P plc stand in the place of the right to deferred consideration and will be regarded as having been acquired in December 2005 for £4,941. No further gain or loss arises until a disposal of the shares takes place.

229.4 CGT   Shares and Securities

Notes

(a) Under *TCGA 1992, s 138A* the right to deferred consideration (the 'earn-out right') is treated as a security within *TCGA 1992, s 132*. The gain on the original shares (to the extent that it does not derive from cash consideration) can then be held over against the value of the new shares. This treatment is automatic where the conditions are satisfied, subject to the right to elect for such treatment not to apply.

(b) Various conditions must be satisfied for *section 138A* treatment to apply. In particular, the value or quantity of the securities to be received as deferred consideration must be 'unascertainable' (as defined). Any right to receive cash and/or an ascertainable amount of securities as part of the deferred consideration does not fall within these provisions and must be distinguished from the earn-out right, though this does not prevent these provisions from applying to the earn-out right.

(c) See 206.2 CAPITAL SUMS DERIVED FROM ASSETS above for deferred consideration generally.

229.5 SCHEMES OF RECONSTRUCTION

[*TCGA 1992, s 136; FA 2002, s 45, Sch 9 paras 2, 7*]

N Ltd carried on a manufacturing and wholesaling business. In 2006, it was decided that the wholesaling business should be carried on by a separate company. Revenue clearance under *TCGA 1992, s 138* was obtained, and a company, R Ltd, was formed which, in consideration for the transfer to it by N Ltd of the latter's wholesaling undertaking, issued shares to the shareholders of N Ltd. Each holder of ordinary shares in N Ltd additionally received one ordinary share in R Ltd for each N Ltd share he held. W, who purchased his 2,500 N shares for £10,000 in December 1993, received 2,500 R shares. None of the shares involved is quoted. In August 2013, W sells 1,500 of his N shares for £6 each, a total of £9,000, agreed to be their market value. The value of W's remaining 1,000 N shares is also £6 per share, and the value of his R shares is £4.50 per share.

	£
Disposal consideration	9,000
Allowable cost £10,000 × $\dfrac{9{,}000}{9{,}000 + (1{,}000 \times £6) + (2{,}500 \times £4.50)}$	3,429
Chargeable gain 2013/14	£5,571

229.6 CONVERSION OF SECURITIES

[*TCGA 1992, s 132*]

N bought £10,000 8% convertible loan stock in S plc, a quoted company, in June 2002. The cost was £9,800. In August 2009, N exercised his right to convert the loan stock into 'B' ordinary shares of the company, on the basis of 50 shares for £100 loan stock, and acquired 5,000 shares. In June 2013, N sells 3,000 of the shares for £5.00 each.

	£
Disposal consideration	15,000

$$\text{Cost } \frac{3{,}000}{5{,}000} \times £9{,}800 \qquad \underline{5{,}880}$$

Chargeable gain 2013/14 £9,120

Notes

(a) The shares acquired on the conversion in 2009 stand in the shoes of the original loan stock. [*TCGA 1992, s 132*].

(b) The loan stock cannot be a corporate bond (and thus cannot be a qualifying corporate bond) as it is convertible into securities other than corporate bonds, i.e. into ordinary shares. [*ICTA 1988, Sch 18 para 1(5); TCGA 1992, s 117(1)*].

229.7 SCRIP DIVIDENDS

[*TCGA 1992, ss 141, 142; ICTA 1988, ss 249, 251(2)–(4)*]

D holds ordinary 20p shares in PLC, a quoted company. The company operates a scrip dividend (also known as a stock dividend) policy whereby shareholders are given the option to take dividends in cash or in new fully-paid ordinary 20p shares, the option being exercisable separately in relation to each dividend. D purchased 2,000 shares for £1,500 in March 1980 and a further 3,000 shares for £8,100 in May 1992 and up until the end of 1997 he has always taken cash dividends. In July 1998, he opts for a scrip dividend and receives 25 shares instead of a cash dividend of £100. On 20 April 2000, he purchases a further 1,000 shares for £3,950. He opts for cash dividends until, in July 2008, he opts for a scrip dividend of 44 shares instead of a cash dividend of £180. He opts for cash dividends thereafter. In May 2013, he sells 2,069 shares for £8,550 (ex div), leaving himself with a holding of 4,000.

In the case of both scrip dividends taken by D, the market value of the new shares is equivalent to the cash dividend forgone. The 'appropriate amount in cash' (see *TCGA 1992, s 142*) is thus the amount of that dividend. [*ICTA 1988, s 251(2)*]. The market value at 31 March 1982 of 20p shares in PLC is 80p.

The gain on the disposal in May 2012 is calculated as follows

The 'section 104 holding' is as follows.

	Shares	Qualifying expenditure £
March 1980 acquisition	2,000	1,600
May 1992 acquisition	3,000	8,100
July 1998 scrip dividend	25	100
April 2000 acquisition	1,000	3,950
July 2008 scrip dividend	44	180
	6,069	13,930
May 2013 disposal	(2,069)	(4,749)
Pool carried forward	4,000	9,181

229.7 CGT   Shares and Securities

	Shares	Qualifying expenditure
		£
Proceeds		8,550
Costs £13,930 × 2,069/6,069		4,749
Chargeable gain 2013/14		£3,801

Notes

(a) Scrip dividends after 5 April 1998 are treated as free-standing acquisitions. Previously, a scrip dividend received by an individual was treated as a reorganisation within *TCGA 1992, s 128* so that the new shares equated with those already held.

(b) See also 230.1 and 230.2 SHARES AND SECURITIES — IDENTIFICATION RULES.

229.8 CAPITAL DISTRIBUTIONS

(A)

[*TCGA 1992, s 122*]

T holds 10,000 ordinary shares in a foreign company M SA. The shares were bought in April 1996 for £80,000. In February 2014, M SA has a capital reconstruction involving the cancellation of one-fifth of the existing ordinary shares in consideration of the repayment of £10 to each shareholder per share cancelled. T's holding is reduced to 8,000 shares, valued at £96,000.

	£
Disposal consideration (2,000 × £10)	20,000
Allowable cost $\dfrac{20,000}{20,000 + 96,000} \times £80,000$	13,793
Chargeable gain 2013/14	£6,207
The allowable cost of the remaining shares is £80,000 − £13,793	£66,207

(B) Sale of rights

[*TCGA 1992, ss 122, 123*]

X is a shareholder in K Ltd, owning 2,500 £1 ordinary shares which were purchased for £7,000 in October 1996. K Ltd makes a rights issue, but X sells his rights, without taking them up, for £700 in August 2013. The ex-rights value of X's 2,500 shares at the date of sale was £14,500.

	Shares	Qualifying expenditure
'Section 104 holding' of K £1 ordinary shares		
October 1996 acquisition	2,500	£7,000

HMRC cannot require the capital distribution to be treated as a disposal, as the £700 received for the rights does not exceed 5% of (£700 + £14,500) and in any case does not exceed £3,000 (see Revenue Tax Bulletin February 1997 p 397). [*TCGA 1992, s 122(2)*]. If the transaction is not treated as a disposal, the £700 is deducted from the acquisition cost of the shares, leaving a balance of £6,300. If the transaction is treated as a disposal (possibly because X wishes to utilise part of his annual exemption), the computation is as follows.

	£
Disposal proceeds	700
Allowable cost $\dfrac{700}{700 + 14,500} \times £7,000$	322
Chargeable gain 2013/14	£378

The allowable cost of the shares is then reduced to £6,678 (£7,000 − £322).

230 Shares and Securities — Identification Rules

Cross-reference. See 229 SHARES AND SECURITIES.

230.1 CAPITAL GAINS TAX IDENTIFICATION RULES

Z, who is resident and ordinarily resident in the UK throughout, has the following acquisitions/disposals of ordinary 25p shares in MIB plc. MIB ordinary 25p shares were worth 210p per share at 31 March 1982. In 2013/14, Z made no disposals of chargeable assets other than as shown below.

Date	No. of shares bought/(sold)	Cost/(proceeds) £
1 May 1980	1,000	2,000
1 October 1983	2,000	4,500
1 December 1996	500	1,800
1 May 2013	(1,000)	(3,900)
25 May 2013	2,000	7,600
2 January 2014	(3,000)	(18,000)
Remaining holding	1,500	

The disposal on 1 May 2013 is matched with 1,000 of the shares acquired on 25 May 2013 (under the 30-day rule — see note (a)). The resulting chargeable gain is as follows.

	£
Proceeds 1.5.13	3,900
Cost (£7,600 × 1,000/2,000)	3,800
Chargeable gain	£100

The disposal of 3,000 shares on 2 January 2014 is matched with 3,000 of the 4,500 forming the 'section 104 holding' as follows.

	No. of shares	Qualifying expenditure £
Shares acquired 1 May 1980 (note (b))	1,000	2,100
Additional shares 1 October 1983	2,000	4,500
Additional shares 1 December 1996	500	1,800
Additional shares 25 May 2013	1,000	3,800
	4,500	12,200
Disposal 1 January 2014	(3,000)	(8,133)
Pool carried forward	1,500	£4,067

The chargeable gain is as follows.

230.1 CGT   Shares and Securities — Identification Rules

	£
Proceeds 2.1.14	18,000
Cost (£12,200 × 3,000/4,500)	8,133
Chargeable gain	£9,867
Total chargeable gains 2013/14 £100 + £9,867	£9,967

Notes

(a) For capital gains tax purposes, disposals are identified (1) with shares acquired on the same day (with certain limited exceptions by election); (2) with acquisitions in the following 30 days; (3) with the 'section 104 holding'; (4) with shares acquired after the disposal (and after the expiry of the 30-day period in (2)) taken in the order in which such acquisitions occur. [*TCGA 1992, ss 104, 105, 106A, 288(7B); FA 2008, Sch 2 paras 85–87, 100*].

(b) Re-basing to market value at 31 March 1982 applies automatically for capital gains tax purposes. Accordingly, the qualifying expenditure included in the section 104 holding in respect of the shares acquired on 1 May 1980 is the market value of those shares on 31 March 1982.

230.2 SHARE IDENTIFICATION RULES FOR COMPANIES

[*TCGA 1992, ss 104, 105–110*]

B Ltd has the following transactions in 25p ordinary shares of H plc, a quoted company. At no time did B Ltd's holding amount to 2% of H plc's issued shares.

		Cost/(proceeds) £
6.6.78	Purchased 500 at £0.85	425
3.11.81	Purchased 1,300 at £0.80	1,040
15.5.82	Purchased 1,000 at £1.02	1,020
8.9.82	Purchased 400 at £1.08	432
1.2.86	Purchased 1,200 at £1.14	1,368
29.7.87	Sold 2,000 at £1.30	(2,600)
8.6.90	Purchased 1,500 at £1.26	1,890
21.12.93	Received 1,000 from group company (cost £1,250, indexation to date £250)	1,500
10.4.13	Sold 3,900 at £4.00	(15,600)

The shares stood at £1.00 at 31.3.82.

Indexation factors	March 1982 to April 2013	2.141
	May 1982 to April 1985	0.161
	September 1982 to April 1985	0.158
	April 1985 to February 1986	0.019
	February 1986 to July 1987	0.054

Shares and Securities — Identification Rules   CGT 230.2

July 1987 to June 1990	0.245
June 1990 to December 1993	0.120
December 1993 to April 2013	0.758

Disposal on 10 April 2013

The 'section 104 holding' pool immediately prior to the disposal should be as follows

	Shares	Qualifying expenditure £	Indexed pool £
15.5.82 acquisition	1,000	1,020	1,020
Indexation to April 1985			
£1,020 × 0.161			164
8.9.82 acquisition	400	432	432
Indexation to April 1985			
£432 × 0.158		—	68
Pool at 6.4.85	1,400	1,452	1,684
Indexed rise: April 1985 – Feb. 1986			
£1,684 × 0.019			32
1.2.86 acquisition	1,200	1,368	1,368
	2,600	2,820	3,084
Indexed rise: February 1986 – July 1987			
£3,084 × 0.054		—	167
	2,600	2,820	3,251
29.7.87 disposal	(2,000)	(2,169)	(2,501)
c/f	£600	£651	£750

	Shares	Qualifying expenditure £	Indexed pool £
b/f	600	651	750
Indexed rise: July 1987 – June 1990			
£750 × 0.245			184
8.6.90 acquisition	1,500	1,890	1,890
	2,100	2,541	2,824
Indexed rise: June 1990 – December 1993			
£2,824 × 0.120			339
21.12.93 acquisition	1,000	1,250	1,500
	3,100	3,791	4,663
Indexed rise: December 1993 – April 2013			

230.2 CGT   Shares and Securities — Identification Rules

	Shares	Qualifying expenditure £	Indexed pool £
£4,663 × 0.758		—	3,534
	3,100	3,791	8,197

The '1982 holding' is as follows

	Shares	Allowable expenditure £
6.6.78 acquisition	500	425
3.11.81 acquisition	1,300	1,040
	1,800	1,465

(i)   Identify 3,100 shares sold with '*section 104* holding'

	£
Disposal consideration 3,100 × £4.00	12,400
Allowable cost	3,791
Unindexed gain	8,609
Indexation allowance £8,197 − £3,791	4,406
Chargeable gain	£4,203

(ii)   Identify 800 shares sold with '1982 holding'

	£	£
Disposal consideration 800 × £4.00	3,200	3,200
Cost $\dfrac{800}{1,800} \times £1,465$	651	
Market value 31.3.82 $\dfrac{800}{1,800} \times £1,800$	—	800
Unindexed gain	2,549	2,400
Indexation allowance £800 × 2.141	1,712	1,712
Gain after indexation	£837	£688
Chargeable gain		£688

Shares and Securities — Identification Rules   CGT 230.2

Total chargeable gain 10 April 2013 (£4,203 + £688)   £4,891

Notes

(a) Share disposals by companies are identified firstly with the '*section 104* holding' and secondly with the '1982 holding', both of which are regarded as single assets.

(b) On share disposals identified with shares held at 31.3.82, the re-basing provisions have effect, and indexation is based on the higher of cost and 31.3.82 value. If an irrevocable election is made under *TCGA 1992, s 35(5)* for all assets to be treated as disposed of and re-acquired at their market value on 31.3.82, indexation must be based on the 31.3.82 value even if this is less than cost. [*TCGA 1992, s 55(1)(2)*].

231 Wasting Assets

Cross-references. See also **215.3** LAND, **226.3** ROLLOVER RELIEF — REPLACEMENT OF BUSINESS ASSETS.

231.1 GENERAL

[*TCGA 1992, ss 44–47*]

V bought an aircraft on 31 May 2008 at a cost of £90,000 for use in his air charter business. It has been agreed that V's non-business use of the aircraft amounts to one-tenth, on a flying hours basis, and capital allowances and running costs have accordingly been restricted for income tax purposes. On 1 February 2014, V sells the aircraft for £185,000. The aircraft is agreed as having a useful life of 20 years at the date it was acquired.

	£
Amount qualifying for capital allowances	
Relevant portion of disposal consideration $^9/_{10}$ × £185,000	166,500
Relevant portion of acquisition cost $^9/_{10}$ × £90,000	81,000
Chargeable gain 2013/14	£85,500

Amount not qualifying for capital allowances

Relevant portion of disposal consideration $^1/_{10}$ × £185,000		18,500
Relevant portion of acquisition cost		
$^1/_{10}$ × £90,000	9,000	
Deduct Wasted £9,000 × $\dfrac{5y\ 8m}{20y}$	2,550	6,450
Gain		£12,050
The whole of the £12,050 is exempt.		
The total chargeable gain is therefore		£85,500

Note

(a) Gains on tangible movable property which are wasting assets not qualifying for capital allowances are exempt (and any losses would not be allowable). [*TCGA 1992, s 45*].

231.2 OPTIONS

[*TCGA 1992, ss 44, 46, 146*]

Cross-reference.

See also **203.1** ASSETS.

231.2 CGT Wasting Assets

(A) Unquoted shares

On 1 July 2011, R grants C an option to purchase unquoted shares held by R. The cost of the option is £600 to purchase 10,000 shares at £5 per share, the option to be exercised by 31 December 2013. On 1 September 2013 C assigns the option to W for £500.

	£	£
Disposal consideration		500
Acquisition cost	600	
Deduct Wasted £6,000 × $^{26}/_{30}$	520	80
Chargeable gain		£420

(B) Traded options

On 1 December 2013, C purchases 6-month options on T plc shares for £1,000. Two weeks later, he sells the options, which are quoted on the Stock Exchange, for £1,200.

	£
Disposal consideration	1,200
Allowable cost	1,000
Chargeable gain	£200

Note

(a) The wasting asset rules do not apply to traded options. [*TCGA 1992, s 146*].

231.3 LIFE INTERESTS

[*TCGA 1992, s 44(1)(d)*]

(A)

N is a beneficiary under a settlement. On 30 June 1999, when her actuarially estimated life expectancy was 40 years, she sold her life interest to an unrelated individual, R, for £50,000. N dies on 31 December 2013, and the life interest is extinguished.

R will have an allowable loss for 2013/14 as follows

	£	£
Disposal consideration on death of N		Nil
Allowable cost	50,000	
Deduct wasted $\dfrac{14\text{y 6m}}{40\text{y}} \times £50,000$	18,125	
		31,875

		£	£
Allowable loss			£31,875

Note

(a) The amount of the cost wasted is computed by reference to the predictable life, not the actual life, of the wasting asset.

(B)

Assume the facts to be as in (A) above except that the sale of the life interest was on 30 June 1981 and N's life expectancy *at that date* was 40 years. The value of the life interest remained at £50,000 at 31 March 1982.

		£	£
Disposal consideration			Nil
Market value 31.3.82		50,000	
Deduct wasted			
$£50,000 \times \dfrac{31\text{y 9m } (31.3.82 - 31.12.13)}{39\text{y 3m (life expectancy at 31.3.82)}}$		39,937	
		10,063	
Allowable loss 2013/14			£10,063

Note

(a) Where, by virtue of the re-basing rules, an asset is deemed to have been disposed of and re-acquired at its market value on 31 March 1982, that market value must be reduced in accordance with the period of ownership *after* that date and the predictable life of the wasting asset *at* that date.

Inheritance Tax

301	Accumulation and Maintenance Trusts
302	Agricultural Property
303	Anti-Avoidance
304	Business Property
305	Calculation of Tax
306	Charities
307	Close Companies
308	Deeds of Variation and Disclaimers
309	Double Taxation Relief
310	Exempt Transfers
311	Gifts with Reservation
312	Interest on Tax
313	Liability for Tax
314	Life Assurance Policies
315	Mutual Transfers
316	National Heritage
317	Payment of Tax
318	Protective Trusts
319	Quick Succession Relief
320	Settlements with Interests in Possession
321	Settlements without Interests in Possession
322	Transfers on Death
323	Trusts for Bereaved Minors
324	Trusts for Disabled Persons
325	Trusts for Employees
326	Valuation
327	Woodlands

301 Accumulation and Maintenance Trusts

[*IHTA 1984, s 71; FA 2006, Sch 20 paras 2, 3*]

301.1 CHARGE ON FAILURE TO QUALIFY AS ACCUMULATION AND MAINTENANCE TRUST

On 1 January 1989 G settled £50,000 on trust equally for his great nephews and nieces born before 1 January 2009. The beneficiaries were to take absolute interests at age 18, income being accumulated for minor beneficiaries. By 2009 G had three great nephews and nieces, A (his brother's grandson) born in 1982 and B and C (his sister's grandsons) born in 1999 and 2002 respectively. The settlement was valued at £150,000 on 1 January 2014.

On 1 January 2014 the settlement fails to qualify as an accumulation and maintenance settlement as more than 25 years have elapsed since the date of settlement and the beneficiaries do not have a common grandparent. There will be a charge to IHT on the value of the settlement on 1 January 2014.

The rate of tax is the aggregate of

0.25% for each of the first	40	quarters	10%
0.20% for each of the next	40	quarters	8%
0.15% for each of the next	20	quarters	3%
	100		21%

The IHT charge is 21% × £150,000 = £31,500

Notes

(a) There was no charge to IHT on A becoming entitled to one-third on his eighteenth birthday in 1999.

(b) Settlements created on or after 22 March 2006 cannot qualify as accumulation and maintenance trusts. [*IHTA 1984, s 71(1A); FA 2006, Sch 20 para 2(3)*]. Accumulation and maintenance settlements created prior to that date continued to be treated under *IHTA 1984, s 71* until 6 April 2008 (unless they qualified as TRUSTS FOR BEREAVED MINORS (323)). From that date onwards any existing settlement must conform to revised rules to continue to receive *section 71* treatment: the beneficiary or beneficiaries must obtain a right to *capital* on or before the age of eighteen. No charge under *section 71* arose where as a consequence a settlement failed to qualify as an accumulation and maintenance trust on 6 April 2008. [*IHTA 1984, s 71(1)(a); FA 2006, Sch 20 para 3*].

(c) Settlements which failed to qualify as accumulation and maintenance trusts from 6 April 2008 as a result of the provisions in note (b) above are from that date either treated as 18-to-25 trusts (see 301.2 below) or taxed under the rules for SETTLEMENTS WITHOUT INTERESTS IN POSSESSION (321).

(d) See **323** TRUSTS FOR BEREAVED MINORS for certain settlements (including those created on or after 22 March 2006) which are taxed on a similar basis to accumulation and maintenance trusts.

301.2 IHT   Accumulation and Maintenance Trusts

301.2 PRE-22 MARCH 2006 SETTLEMENTS AFTER 5 APRIL 2008

(A) **18-to-25 Trusts**

[IHTA 1984, ss 71D–71G; FA 2006, Sch 20 para 1]

On 30 April 1983 George, who had made no chargeable transfers in the previous seven years, settled £100,000 on trust equally for his grandchildren. The beneficiaries were to take absolute entitlements at age 25, income being accumulated for minor beneficiaries. George has two grandchildren; Alex, who is 25 on 28 February 2008, and Stephanie, born 27 September 1994. On Stephanie's 25th birthday on 26 September 2019 the remaining settlement property is valued at £600,000. It is assumed for the purposes of this example that the IHT threshold is then £455,000.

An exit charge arises under *IHTA 1984, ss 71F* on Stephanie becoming absolutely entitled to the settlement property on reaching age 25 on 26 September 2019 as follows.

	£
Assumed chargeable transfer	600,000
Assumed cumulative total	—
Deduct Nil rate band	(455,000)
	£145,000
IHT at lifetime rates	£29,000

$$\text{Effective rate } \frac{29{,}000}{600{,}000} = 4.83\%$$

Relevant faction

The number of complete quarters that have elapsed between the time of Stephanie's 18th birthday and the day before her 25th birthday is 28. The relevant fraction is therefore 28/40.

The IHT is charged at the relevant fraction of the effective rate on the property to which Stephanie becomes absolutely entitled

28/40 × 4.83% = 3.381%

IHT payable: 3/10 × 3.381% × £600,000   £14,200

Notes

(a) There is no charge to IHT on Alex becoming absolutely entitled to one half of the settled property on 28 February 2008.

(b) On 6 April 2008, the settlement ceases to be an accumulation and maintenance trust because the remaining beneficiary does not become entitled absolutely to settled property on or before attaining age 18 as required from that date (see note (b) to 301.1 above). No charge to IHT arises.

Accumulation and Maintenance Trusts   IHT 301.2

(c) From 6 April 2008 the settlement qualifies as an 18-to-25 trust because it has failed to qualify as an accumulation and maintenance trust by reason only of the change in rules on that date and the settlement secures that the remaining beneficiary becomes absolutely entitled to the settled property, any income arising from it and any accumulated income on or before attaining the age of 25. [*IHTA 1984, s 71D(4)(6); FA 2006, Sch 20 para 1*].

(d) No charge to tax would arise on a beneficiary becoming absolutely entitled before the age of 18. [*IHTA 1984, s 71E(2); FA 2006, Sch 20 para 1*].

(B) **Failure of 18-to-25 trust**

On 31 December 2002 Gilbert, who had made no cumulative chargeable transfers within the previous 7 years, settled £150,000 on an accumulation and maintenance settlement for his son Charles born on that date. The trust is contingent on Charles attaining the age of 25 years at which time he will become absolutely entitled to the settled property. If Charles dies before reaching age 25, Gilbert's nephew James, born on 22 March 1988, becomes the beneficiary, becoming absolutely entitled on attaining the age of 26. Charles dies on 6 April 2011. The settlement is valued at £640,000 on 30 December 2012. The property in the settlement is valued at £700,000 at 21 March 2014, the day before James's 26th birthday, when the funds are released to him.

Charges to IHT arise in respect of the settlement as follows.

Ten-year anniversary charge 31 December 2012

	£
Value of relevant property on 31.12.12	640,000
Less nil rate band £325,000	325,000
IHT at lifetime rates on £315,000 @ 20%	£63,000

$$\text{Effective rate } \frac{63,000}{640,000} = 9.84375\%$$

Appropriate fraction

The number of complete quarters that have elapsed between the date of Charles's death on 6 April 2011 and the tenth anniversary of the date of the settlement is 6. The appropriate fraction is therefore 6/40.

The IHT is charged at 30% of the appropriate fraction of the effective rate on the relevant property

IHT payable = 30% × 6/40 × 9.84375% × £640,000 = £2,835

Exit charge on James becoming absolutely entitled at 22 March 2014

Effective rate (as above, assuming no increase in nil rate band) = 9.84375%

The number of complete successive quarters between 31 December 2011 and 22 March 2013 is 4.

The proportionate charge is therefore:

301.2 IHT   Accumulation and Maintenance Trusts

9.84375% × 30% × 4/40 × £700,000 = £2,067

Notes

(a) The settlement qualifies as an accumulation and maintainance settlement until 5 April 2008 after which date it failed to qualify because Charles does not become absolutely entitled until age 25 (see note (b) to **301.1** above). No charge to IHT arose at that date.

(b) From 6 April 2008 the settlement is an 18-to-25 trust (see note (c) to A above). It ceases to qualify as an 18-to-25 trust on Charles's death on 6 April 2011 because the requirement for the beneficiary to become absolutely entitled on or before reaching age 25 is no longer met (James becomes absolutely entitled only at age 26). No charge to IHT arises on Charles's death. [*IHTA 1984, s 71E(2)(b); FA 2006, Sch 20 para 1*].

(c) Following Charles's death the settlement comes within the relevant property charging regime for SETTLEMENTS WITHOUT INTERESTS IN POSSESSION **(321)** resulting in a 10-year anniversary charge on 31 December 2012 and an exit charge on 22 March 2014 when James reaches age 26.

302 Agricultural Property

[*IHTA 1984, ss 115–124B; FA 2009, s 122*]

302.1 RELIEF FOR TRANSFERS AND OTHER EVENTS

(A) **Relief given at 100%**

[*IHTA 1984, ss 116(1)(2)(7), 124A(1)(3)*]

X has owned since 1983 1,000 acres of land. In June 1992 he began to farm the land, utilising 800 acres for that purpose. The remaining 200 acres are not used for any business purposes. On 1 July 2013 X transfers all the land to his son, Y, at a time when its agricultural value was £1,000 per acre and its open market value £1,500 per acre. He had not used his annual exemptions for 2012/13 and 2013/14. X died on 6 September 2016. Y has continued to run the farm business since the date of the gift.

The value of the gift for inheritance tax purposes before relief is

		£	£
1,000 acres at £1,500 per acre			£1,500,000
The transfer subject to tax is			
(i)	Agricultural value of land		
	800 acres × £1,000	800,000	
	Less agricultural property relief at 100%	(800,000)	—
(ii)	Non-agricultural value of land		
	800 acres × £500		400,000
(iii)	Value of land not used in business		
	200 acres at £1,500 per acre		300,000
			700,000
Deduct Annual exemptions (2012/13 and 2013/14)			(6,000)
Value transferred by PET becoming chargeable on death			£694,000

Notes

(a) Relief is at 100% because

  (i) immediately before the transfer, X enjoyed the right to vacant possession;

302.1 IHT Agricultural Property

        (ii)   X had farmed the land for two years before the transfer;

        (iii)   X had acquired the land more than seven years before the transfer and it had been farmed throughout those seven years (by X or any other person); and

        (iv)   the land was farmed by Y between the date of gift and X's death.

        Note that although conditions (ii) and (iii) were both satisfied in this case, it is only necessary to satisfy one of them to qualify for 100% relief.

(b)   Annual exemptions are deducted *after* deducting the agricultural property relief.

(c)   Business property relief may be available in respect of the £400,000 excess of the open market value over the agricultural value.

(d)   IHT will be charged at 80% of full rates as X died more than 3 but not more than 4 years after the gift.

(B)   **Transfer where land is held tenanted under an agricultural lease entered into on or after 1 September 1995**

[IHTA 1984, s 116(1)(2)(7)]

A is the freehold owner of agricultural land which at current vacant possession value is estimated to be valued at £850,000. On 29 September 1992, he enters into an agricultural tenancy (with more than two years to run) with a farming partnership comprising his two sons and his grandson for a full market rental of £25,000 p.a. The tenanted value is estimated at £500,000.

In July 2012 his grandson is killed in a farming accident and a new letting agreement is made between the two sons and A for a full market rent of £35,000 p.a. on 15 September 2012.

A dies on 1 October 2013 when the tenanted value of the land has risen to £600,000.

	£
Transfer at death (tenanted valuation)	600,000
Deduct Agricultural property relief	600,000
IHT payable on	Nil

Notes

(a)   No IHT charge arises on the grant of the lease to the partnership on the basis that it is for full consideration. [*IHTA 1984, s 16*].

(b)   As A terminated the existing agricultural tenancy and entered into a new tenancy on or after 1 September 1995, agricultural property relief of 100% is available. Only 50% relief would have been available if the existing tenancy had continued, [*FA 1995, s 155; FA 1996, s 185*].

Agricultural Property IHT 302.2

(C) **Interaction with capital gains tax**

A discretionary settlement has 400 acres of tenanted agricultural land, the tenancy having commenced before 1 September 1995. On 31 October 2011, the trustees appoint the agricultural land to a beneficiary who then becomes absolutely entitled to the land. 50% agricultural property relief is available. The value of the 400 acres as tenanted is £450,000. The trustees fail to pay the capital gains tax due of, say, £60,000 by 31 January 2014 and the beneficiary is assessed and pays the liability.

	£
Value transferred	450,000
Agricultural property relief 50%	225,000
	225,000
Capital gains tax	60,000
Chargeable transfer (subject to grossing-up)	£165,000

Notes

(a) An election may be made for the CGT to be held over. [*TCGA 1992, s 260(1)–(5)*].

(b) If the trustees fail to pay all or part of the capital gains tax within twelve months of the due date, an assessment may be made on the beneficiary [*TCGA 1992, s 282*] and the amount of such tax borne by the donee is treated as reducing the value transferred. The beneficiary must become absolutely entitled to the property to obtain the relief. [*IHTA 1984, s 165*].

(c) If it were possible for the trustees to arrange for a new tenancy to begin after 31 August 1995 but before the transfer, the transfer would have attracted 100% agricultural property relief. [*FA 1995, s 155*]. This could possibly be achieved by terminating the existing lease and entering into a new lease with the same tenants, subject to the terms of the existing lease, the tenants' agreement and general legal requirements.

302.2 SHARES ETC. IN AGRICULTURAL COMPANIES

[*IHTA 1984, ss 122, 123*]

AC Ltd is an unquoted agricultural company of which A owns 60% of the shares.

The company owns	£
4,000 acres of — land agricultural value	4M
Other trading assets (net)	2M
Total value of company	£6M
A's shareholding is valued at	£4.5M

All necessary conditions for relief are satisfied.

302.2 IHT   Agricultural Property

If A were to die in, say, November 2013 the position as regards his shareholding would be as follows

	Total Value £	Land £	Other Assets £
Value of assets of company	6M	4M	2M
Value of shares, split in same proportions	4.5M	£3M	£1.5M
Agricultural property relief (100% of £3M)	(3.0M)		
Business property relief (100% of £1.5M)	(1.5M)		
Chargeable to IHT	Nil		

Notes

(a) Part of the value transferred is attributable to the agricultural value of agricultural property, so agricultural property relief is available. [*IHTA 1984, s 122*].

(b) The legislation appears to require that both agricultural property relief and business property relief be given, each against its appropriate part of the value. [*IHTA 1984, s 114*]. See also **304 BUSINESS PROPERTY**. When some of the land owned by the company is tenanted (agreement in force before 1 September 1995), attracting only 50% agricultural property relief, the total relief given will be less than would be the case if business property relief at 100% were given on the whole value.

303 Anti-Avoidance

303.1 ASSOCIATED OPERATIONS
[*IHTA 1984, s 268*]

(A)

H owns a set of four Chippendale chairs valued, as a set, at £6,000. Individually they would be valued at only £1,000, although a pair would be worth £2,500 and three £4,000.

He gives one chair to his son each year over four years, during which time all values increase at 10% p.a. (simple). In the fifth year H dies.

	£	£
Year 1		
Value of four chairs	6,000	
Deduct value of three	4,000	
Value transferred		2,000
Year 2		
Basic computation ignoring the associated operations rule		
Current value of three chairs	4,400	
Deduct value of two	2,750	
Value transferred	£1,650	
Revised to take account of associated operations rule		
Current value of four chairs	6,600	
Deduct value of two	2,750	
	3,850	
Deduct value transferred in Year 1	2,000	
		1,850
Year 3		
Current value of four chairs	7,200	
Deduct value of one	1,200	
	6,000	
Deduct value transferred in Years 1 and 2	3,850	
		2,150
Year 4		
Current value of four chairs	7,800	
Deduct value transferred in Years 1, 2 and 3	6,000	
Value transferred		1,800

303.1 IHT   Anti-Avoidance

	£	£
Total values transferred		£7,800

Note

(a)   The normal rule would be that the transfer of value is the loss to the donor's estate, as in Year 1. However, if a series of transfers are treated as associated operations, the transfer is treated as if made at the time of the latest transfer, reduced by the value transferred by the earlier transfers.

(B)

If in (A) above H had wished to give away the chairs over two years instead of four, he might first have given two chairs to his wife, so that each could give the son one chair each year.

		£	£
Year 1			
(i)	Value transferred by husband to son		
	Value of two chairs (as half of a set of four linked by the related property rule)	3,000	
	Deduct value of one chair (as half of a pair)	1,250	
			1,750
(ii)	Value transferred by wife		
	(similar calculation)		1,750
Year 2			
(i)	Value transferred by husband, applying the associated operations rule		
	Current value of four chairs	6,600	
	Deduct value transferred in Year 1 by H to son	3,500	
	Value transferred		3,100
	Total values transferred		£6,600

Notes

(a)   In this case, the total of the values transferred can exceed the value of the assets, although it must be doubtful whether HMRC would seek to apply the full rigours of the section unless the transfer by the wife in Year 1 had fallen within her annual exemptions, or she had survived seven years so that the gift was exempt.

(b)   See *IHTA 1984, s 161* for the related property rule, and see also **326.2** VALUATION.

(c)   The result above could have been achieved in another way. The first transfer by the husband to his spouse is quantified at £3,000 – the second to the son is quantified at £1,750 as in the example. If through *section 268* one looks at the position as if the transfer of value was made on the last of the operations, the calculation would be:

£

Anti-Avoidance IHT 303.1

Value in H's estate before any transfer	
(i.e. value of 4 chairs at the date of last transfer)	6,600
Value in husband's estate after all transfers	Nil
Value transferred	6,600
Deduct value of earlier operations:	
Transfer to wife disregarded *section 268(3)*	Nil
Transfer to son	1,750
Value transferred	£4,850

So the value transferred is £1,750 + £4,850 = £6,600. HMRC would not seek to raise a charge to tax on the actual transfers by the wife to the son.

HMRC may ask the District Valuer for the value effectively transferred by one transfer being the last of a series of associated operations. If any of the earlier operations were themselves transfers of value, other than transfers between spouses or civil partners [*IHTA 1984, s 18*], then the adjustment will be dealt with by HMRC.

304 Business Property

[*IHTA 1984, ss 103–114, 269*]

304.1 RELEVANT BUSINESS PROPERTY

(A) **Shares in a holding company with a non-qualifying subsidiary**

[*IHTA 1984, s 111*]

A owns 85% of the share capital of H Ltd, an unquoted company which has two wholly-owned subsidiary companies S Ltd and P Ltd. H Ltd and S Ltd are trading companies and P Ltd is a property investment company. The issued share capital of H Ltd is 100,000 ordinary shares of £1 each valued at £8 per share. The values of the issued shares in S Ltd and P Ltd are £250,000 and £300,000 respectively.

A gives 10,000 shares in H Ltd to his son in August 2011. He has already made chargeable transfers using up his basic exemptions. His son agrees to pay any IHT. A dies in January 2014, at which time his son still owns the shares. It is agreed that the fall in value in A's estate (reduction of a 85% holding to a 75% holding), by which the value of the gift for IHT purposes is measured, is equivalent to the actual value of the shares transferred.

	£	£
Value of gift		80,000
Deduct business property relief 100% × £80,000	80,000	
Less 100% × 80,000 × $\frac{300,000}{800,000}$	30,000	
		50,000
PET becoming chargeable transfer on death		£30,000

(B) **Land used by a business**

M has for many years owned a factory used in the business of Q Ltd, of which he has control. In September 2012, M gives the factory to his son S when its value is £740,000. He has made no previous chargeable transfer, but made a gift of £3,000 in 2012/13. M dies in October 2014, when the factory is being used for business purposes by S's partnership. S agreed to pay any IHT on the gift.

	£
Value of gift	740,000
Deduct business property relief (50%)	370,000
	370,000
Deduct annual exemption (2013/14)	(3,000)
PET becoming chargeable transfer on death	£367,000

304.1 IHT   Business Property

IHT payable at full rates
(death within 3 years)   £16,800

Notes

(a) If M wishes also to dispose of shares in Q Ltd by sale or gift after which he would no longer have control, he should give the factory to his son *before* disposing of the shares, or else the business property relief would not be available on the gift of the factory.

(b) If the factory had been used by Q Ltd at the date of M's death, no business property relief would be available on the gift since the factory would not be relevant business property in S's hands at the date of death.

(C) **Land and buildings owned by trustees**

X died in 1976 leaving a life interest in factory premises to his son A, with remainder to his grandsons B and C. A occupies the premises for the purposes of his trade, rent-free. In September 2012 A gives up his life interest when the value of the premises is £660,000. B and C agree to pay any IHT. A has already made chargeable transfers using up his annual exemptions. A dies in November 2013, when the factory is still being used in the trade which was then being carried on by B and C in partnership.

	£
Value of gift	660,000
Deduct business property relief (50%)	(330,000)
PET becoming chargeable transfer on death	£330,000

IHT payable at full rates
(death within 3 years)   £2,000

(D) **Further conditions for lifetime transfers**

X transfers the share of his 25% interest in Amalgam Ltd (an AIM company) to his son Y and also transfers land and buildings in his partnership to his other son Z on 16 June 2010. X has already used his annual exemptions for 2010/11 and 2009/10. The shares are valued at £640,000 and the land and buildings at £676,000. In February 2012 Amalgam Ltd is quoted on the London Stock Exchange and Y's share value increases to £1 million.

Z sells the land and property to one of the partners in May 2012 and invests the whole proceeds in an unquoted company receiving shares to the value of £800,000. X dies on 6 June 2013.

Theoretical computation on death if shares in Amalgam Ltd had remained unquoted

	£	Gross	Tax
Value of shares to Y	640,000		

Business Property IHT 304.1

	£	Gross	Tax
Deduct BPR 100%	640,000	Nil	Nil
Partnership assets to Z	676,000		
Deduct BPR 50%	338,000		
PET becoming chargeable transfer on death	338,000	£13,000	£5,200

Actual computation on death — tax payable on failed BPR and PETs that have become chargeable because of X's death within 7 years

	£	
Value of shares to Y	640,000	
Value of property to Z after BPR	338,000	
	978,000	
Less nil rate band	(325,000)	
	653,000	× 40% = £261,200

Apportionment of tax

Gift to Y $£261,200 \times \dfrac{£640,000}{£978,000} = £170,928$

Gift to Z $£261,200 \times \dfrac{£338,000}{£978,000} = £90,272$

Notes

(a) X's death within 3 years of the gift of the shares in Amalgam Ltd results in the loss of business property relief, because on a notional transfer by Y immediately before X's death, the shares, being a non-controlling shareholding in a quoted company, would not have qualified as relevant business property. [*IHTA 1984, s 113A(3)*]. In determining whether on the notional transfer an asset qualifies as relevant business property, the requirement for the asset to be held for two years by the transferor prior to the notional transfer is ignored.

(b) Z has sold the business assets in the partnership and reinvested the proceeds in other relevant business property which attracts 100% BPR (i.e. unquoted shares) as opposed to 50% for the original assets (i.e. land and buildings) in the partnership. Z's replacement of the partnership assets with unquoted shares qualifies for replacement property relief. [*IHTA 1984, s 113B*]. However, Z's position is affected by Y's loss of 100% BPR in respect of the transfer of shares to Y by X.

(c) Z could have taken the view that his position was vulnerable to Y's decision to accept quoted shares (with no control) and X's death within seven years of the gifts. Insurance on a reducing basis could have been taken out by Z to protect his position and cover the liability of £85,072 (i.e. £90,272 — £5,200).

305 Calculation of Tax

305.1 THE CUMULATION PRINCIPLE: POTENTIALLY EXEMPT TRANSFERS
[*IHTA 1984, ss 3, 3A, 7*]

On 1 May 2006 A gave £50,000 to his daughter, D, and on 1 May 2009 he gave £215,000 to his son, S. Both D and S agreed to pay any IHT due on the gifts.

On 7 March 2014 A died, leaving his estate, valued at £300,000, equally to D and S. The only other transfer made by A was an immediately chargeable transfer of £121,000 during 2004/05.

Gift on 1 May 2006

The gift is a PET, which becomes exempt since A does not die within seven years of the date of the gift. No IHT is payable.

Gift on 1 May 2009

This PET becomes chargeable since A dies between 4 and 5 years after the gift. IHT is payable by S following the death at 60% of full rates on the basis of the Table of rates in force in 2013/14.

As this PET has become chargeable, it must be cumulated with other chargeable transfers made in the seven years before the date of the gift. The PET made on 1 May 2006 has become exempt and is excluded from the computation but the immediately chargeable transfer of £121,000 made during 2004/05 must be cumulated with the 2009 gift. Note that a transfer made more than seven years before the death of the transferor and which is not itself aggregated with the estate on death is thus brought into the computation of the IHT payable on the 2009 gift.

		£	£
Gift			215,000
Deduct annual exemptions	2009/10	3,000	
	2008/09	3,000	
			6,000
			£209,000

IHT on £209,000 charged in band £121,000 to £330,000

121,001–325,000 at nil%	—	
325,001–330,000 at 40%	2,000	
	£2,000	
IHT payable at 60% of full rates — £2,000 at 60%		£1,200

Death 7 March 2014

The chargeable transfers in the seven years prior to death comprise only the gift on 1 May 2009 of £209,000.

305.1 IHT   Calculation of Tax

IHT on death on estate of £300,000 chargeable in band £209,001 to £509,000

	£
209,001–325,000 at nil%	—
325,001–509,000 at 40%	73,600
IHT payable	£73,600

Notes

(a) If A directs in his will that, despite the earlier agreement, any IHT due on the gift to S is to be borne by his estate, this amounts to a pecuniary legacy to S of the amount of the tax. The reduction in A's estate by the transfer is unchanged at £215,000 as is the tax of £1,200. The legacy is paid out of the death estate of £300,000 with previous chargeable transfers of £209,000. Since the whole of the estate is liable on death, the IHT remains at £73,600.

(b) If S has not by 1 April 2015 paid the IHT of £1,200 due on the gift from A, the personal representatives of A become liable for the tax as it has not been paid by S within 12 months after the end of the month in which A died. The IHT due remains £1,200 since the gross chargeable transfer is £209,000. A had no liability for the tax at the time the transfer was made and the reduction in value to his estate was, therefore, the amount of the gift to S, £215,000. The personal representatives have a right under general law to reimbursement for the tax from S. To the extent that reimbursement is probable, the tax is not a deduction from the estate. Since the personal representatives can claim reimbursement from the half estate due to S, no deduction will be given. Tax on the estate remains, therefore, at £73,600. [*IHTA 1984, ss 199, 204*]. If S had not benefited under A's will so that no assets were available to reimburse the personal representatives, the tax due of £1,200 might fall to be met from the estate.

305.2 THE CUMULATION PRINCIPLE: GROSSING UP A CHARGEABLE TRANSFER

[*IHTA 1984, ss 3, 3A, 5, 7*]

(A)

On 13 July 2006 B gave £324,000 to his nephew N, who agreed to pay any IHT on the gift. On 24 December 2007 B settled £295,000 on discretionary trusts for his great-nephews and nieces, paying the IHT himself.

On 9 July 2013 B died with an estate worth £78,000, having made no other gifts.

Gift 13 July 2006

The gift is a PET but becomes chargeable since B dies between 6 and 7 years after the gift. The annual exemption for 2006/07, and that brought forward from 2005/06 are, however, available, reducing the chargeable transfer to £331,000.

IHT is charged on the transfer at 20% of full rates, using the Table of rates in force in 2013/14.

Calculation of Tax   IHT 305.2

		£
IHT on gift		
1–325,000 at nil%		—
325,001–331,000 at 40%		2,400
		£2,400
IHT payable by N at 20% of full rates, i.e. 20% × £2,400		£480

Gift 24 December 2007

Initial liability

The gift to the discretionary trust is an immediately chargeable transfer on which the transferor, B, has agreed to pay the IHT. The annual exemption for 2007/08 is set against the chargeable transfer, reducing it to £292,000.

As B is paying the tax on the transfer, his estate is reduced by two amounts: the gross amount of the transfer itself (i.e. before deducting the annual exemptions) and by the tax due on the net transfer (i.e. after deducting the annual exemptions). The total tax will not merely comprise the tax due on the transfer, but the tax upon that tax, and so on. In order to determine the total tax due, where applicable the excess of the chargeable transfer above the nil rate band (or part thereof) is grossed up, using the following formula:

$$E \times \frac{100}{100 - T} \times T\% = G$$

E = excess over nil rate band

T = applicable rate of tax

G = tax due on gross chargeable transfer

In this example, as chargeable lifetime transfers are charged at 20%, being one half of the full death rates, T will be 20. The computation therefore proceeds as follows.

		£
Value of transfer		295,000
Deduct Annual exemption		(3,000)
		292,000
IHT payable on gift		
£(292,000 − 285,000) × $\frac{100}{100-20}$ × 20%		1,750
B's gross chargeable transfer		£293,750

Revision on death

B's death occurs between 5 and 6 years after the gift, so the tax on the chargeable transfer is revised to the IHT payable at 40% of full rates. The PET on 13 July 2006 becomes chargeable, so IHT is charged on the gross chargeable transfer of £293,750 in the bracket £331,001 to £624,750.

£

305.2 IHT   Calculation of Tax

331,001–624,750 at 40%	117,500
IHT at 40% of £117,500	47,000
Less paid on chargeable lifetime transfer	1,750
Additional IHT payable following death	£45,250

Death 9 July 2013

Chargeable transfers in the seven years prior to death amount to £624,750, so IHT is charged on the death estate of £78,000 in the bracket £624,750 to £702,750.

IHT payable	
624,750–702,750 at 40%	£31,200

(B)

Facts are as in (A) above except that B died on 9 July 2014. It is assumed that the nil rate band remains unchanged after 6 April 2009.

The PET on 13 July 2006 is exempt and thus not cumulated when reworking the IHT on the chargeable transfer on 24 December 2007 or on death.

Gift 24 December 2007

IHT on gift, as before	£1,750

Following B's death between 6 and 7 years after the gift, IHT is reworked at 20% of full rates. No additional IHT is payable as the cumulative transfers fall within the NIL rate band.

Death 9 July 2014

Chargeable transfers in the previous 7 years amount to £293,750 so IHT is charged on the death estate of £78,000 in the bracket £293,751 to £371,750.

IHT payable	
325,000–371,750 at 40%	£18,700

Note

(a)   No IHT is repayable in respect of the chargeable transfer on 24 December 2007, even though the IHT on death is less than the IHT originally paid on the gift.

Calculation of Tax IHT 305.3

305.3 PARTLY EXEMPT TRANSFERS

[IHTA 1984, ss 36–42]

(A) **Where the only chargeable part of a transfer is specific gifts which do not bear their own tax**

A, a widow, dies on 8 June 2013. Her estate is valued at £420,000 and her will provides for a tax-free legacy to her nephew of £348,000 and the residue of her estate to the National Trust. A had made no chargeable transfers during her lifetime.

Gross-up tax-free legacy at 'death' rates

	£
Tax-free legacy	348,000
Tax thereon	
$(348{,}000 - 325{,}000) \times \dfrac{100}{100-40} \times 40\%$	15,333
Gross chargeable transfer	£363,333

Calculation of net residuary estate	£
Value of estate	420,000
Deduct gross value of legacy	(363,333)
Residue	£56,667

Allocation of estate at death	
Nephew	348,000
National Trust	56,667
Tax	15,333
	£420,000

(B) **Where tax-free specific gifts are not the only chargeable gifts**

A dies on 1 January 2014 leaving a widow, son and nephew. His estate is valued at £560,000 before deduction of business property relief of £50,000 and his will provides for a tax-free legacy to his son of £360,000, a legacy to the nephew of £13,000 bearing its own tax, a bequest to charity of £26,000, with the residue shared three-quarters by his widow and one-quarter by the son. A had made no previous chargeable transfers.

Allocation of business property relief

[IHTA 1984, s 39A]

Since the will made no specific gifts of the business property, the business property relief is apportioned between each of the specific gifts and the residue, i.e. each is multiplied by

$$\dfrac{\text{Estate less business property relief}}{\text{Estate before business property relief}}$$

305.3 IHT Calculation of Tax

Son	£360,000 ×	$\dfrac{510{,}000}{560{,}000}$	=	£327,858
Nephew	£13,000 ×	$\dfrac{510{,}000}{560{,}000}$	=	£11,839
Charity	£26,000 ×	$\dfrac{510{,}000}{560{,}000}$	=	£23,678
Residue	£161,000 ×	$\dfrac{510{,}000}{560{,}000}$	=	£146,625
	£560,000			£510,000

Hypothetical chargeable estate £   £   £
Tax-free legacy to son   327,858
Tax thereon

$$£(327{,}858 - 325{,}000) \times \dfrac{100}{100-40} \times 40\% \qquad\qquad 1{,}905$$

		329,763
Legacy to nephew		11,839
		341,602
Chargeable residue:		
Gross estate	510,000	
Deduct gross legacies	341,602	
charity	23,678	
	(365,280)	
	£144,720	
Son's one-quarter share		36,180
Hypothetical chargeable estate		£377,782

Hypothetical chargeable estate — calculation of assumed tax rate

Tax on £377,782   £21,112

$$\text{Assumed rate } \dfrac{21{,}112}{377{,}782} \times 100 = 5.5884\%$$

Calculation of Tax IHT 305.3

Re-gross tax-free legacy to son using assumed rate

$$£327,858 \times \frac{100}{100 - 5.5884} \qquad £347,264$$

Calculate chargeable estate and tax thereon

	£	£	£
Grossed-up value of tax-free legacy			347,264
Legacy to nephew			11,839
			359,103
Chargeable residue			
Gross estate		510,000	
Deduct gross legacies	359,103		
charity	23,678		
		(382,781)	
		£127,219	
Son's one-quarter share			31,804
Chargeable estate			£390,907
Tax on estate			
0–325,000 at nil %		—	
325,001–390,907 at 40%		26,362	
		£26,362	

$$\text{Estate rate is } \frac{26,362}{390,907} \times 100 = 6.7438\%$$

Calculation of residue

		£	£
Gross estate			560,000
Specific legacies	— son	360,000	
	— nephew	13,000	
	— charity	26,000	
		399,000	
Tax on son's legacy			
£347,264 at 6.7438%		23,418	
Legacies plus tax thereon			422,418
Residue			£137,582

Distribution of estate

	£	£
Widow — three-quarters of residue		103,187
Son — specific legacy	360,000	

305.3 IHT   Calculation of Tax

Distribution of estate	£	£
— one quarter share of residue	34,395	
	394,395	
Deduct tax on share of residue		
£34,395 × 6.7438%	2,319	
		392,076
Nephew — specific legacy	13,000	
Deduct tax thereon		
£11,839 × 6.7438%	798	
		12,202
Charity		26,000
Tax payable £(23,418 + 2,319 + 798)		26,535
		£560,000

(C) As (B) above but with settled property

The facts are as in (B) above except that in addition to his free estate valued at £560,000, A has a life interest acquired before 22 March 2006, worth £100,000 at 1 January 2014, in his late father's estate, with remainder to his son.

The hypothetical chargeable estate is £377,782 as in (B) above and thus the assumed rate remains at 5.5884%. The settled property is ignored at this stage — see note (a).

Calculate chargeable estate and tax thereon	£
Chargeable free estate as in (B) above	390,907
Settled property	100,000
Chargeable estate	£490,907
Tax on estate	
0–325,000 at nil %	—
325,001–490,907 at 40%	66,362
	£66,362

$$\text{Estate rate is } \frac{66,362}{490,907} \times 100 = 13.51824\%$$

Calculation of residue	£	£
Gross estate		560,000
Specific legacies — son	360,000	
— nephew	13,000	
— charity	26,000	
	399,000	
Tax on son's legacy		
£347,264 at 13.51824%	46,943	

Calculation of Tax   IHT 305.3

Calculation of residue	£	£
Legacies plus tax thereon		445,943
Residue		£114,057

Distribution of estate

	£	£
Widow — three quarters of residue		85,543
Son — specific legacy	360,000	
— one quarter share of residue	28,514	
— settled property	100,000	
Deduct		
tax on share of residue		
£34,395 × 13.51824%	(4,649)	
tax on settled property		
£100,000 × 13.51824%	(13,518)	
		470,347
Nephew — specific legacy	13,000	
Deduct tax thereon		
£11,839 × 13.51824%	(1,600)	
		11,400
Charity		26,000
Tax payable (46,943 + 4,649 + 13,518 + 1,600)		66,710
		£660,000

Notes

(a) Where gifts take effect separately out of the deceased's free estate and out of a settled fund the provisions of *IHTA 1984, ss 36–39A* (partly exempt transfers) apply separately to each fund. [*IHTA 1984, s 40*]. HMRC take the view that the rate of tax to be used for grossing up, i.e. the 'assumed rate' in this example, should be found by looking at each fund separately and in isolation. Thus, the settled property is not taken into account above in the calculation of the assumed rate for gifts out of the free estate.

(b) The IHT on the settled property, payable by the trustees, is found by applying the estate rate of 13.51824% to the value of that property.

306 Charities

[*IHTA 1984, s 70*]

306.1 PROPERTY LEAVING TEMPORARY CHARITABLE TRUSTS

(A) **Gross payment to beneficiaries**

On 1 January 1974 A settled £100,000 on temporary charitable trusts. The income and capital were to be applied for charitable purposes only for a period of 25 years from the date of settlement, and thereafter could be applied for charitable purposes or to or for the settlor's grandchildren. On 1 January 2014 the trustees paid £50,000 to charity and the balance of the settlement, valued at £75,000, to the three grandchildren.

The relevant period is the period from settlement of the funds or, if later, 13 March 1975 to 1 January 2014, i.e. 155 complete quarters, and the amount on which tax is charged is £75,000 gross.

The rate of tax is

0.25% for 40 quarters	10.00%
0.20% for 40 quarters	8.00%
0.15% for 40 quarters	6.00%
0.10% for 35 quarters	3.50%
	27.50%

IHT payable is 27.50% × £75,000 = £20,625

(B) **Net payment to beneficiaries**

Assume the same facts as in (A) above except that the trustees apply £75,000 net for the settlor's three grandchildren, and the balance to charity.

The rate of tax is, as before, 27.10%.

$$\text{IHT payable is } \frac{27.50}{100 - 27.50} \times £75,000 = £28,448$$

The gross payment to the beneficiaries is £75,000 + £28,448 = £103,448

307 Close Companies

[*IHTA 1984, ss 94–98, 102*]

307.1 VALUE TRANSFERRED

The ordinary shares of companies A and B are held as follows (in January 2014)

		A	B
Individuals	X		80%
	Y		20%
	Z		10%
Company	A		90%

Company B is non-resident and Z is domiciled in the UK. Company A sells a property valued at £220,000 to a mutual friend of X and Y for £20,000. The following month, company B sells a foreign property worth £100,000 to X for £90,000.

Company A

		£
The transfer of value is £220,000 − £20,000		200,000
Apportioned to X 80% × £200,000		160,000
Y 20% × £200,000		40,000
		£200,000

Company B
The transfer of value of £10,000 is apportioned

To X	80% × 90% × £10,000	7,200
	Deduct increase in X's estate	10,000
		—
To Y	20% × 90% × £10,000	1,800
To Z	10% × £10,000 note (c)	1,000
		£2,800

Notes

(a) If the sale by company A were to X (or Y), there would be no apportionment because the undervalue would be treated as a net distribution, thus attracting income tax.

(b) On the sale by company B, X would not be liable to income tax.

(c) If Z were not domiciled in the UK, his share of the transfer of value would not be apportioned to him. [*IHTA 1984, s 94(2)(b)*].

307.2 IHT   Close Companies

307.2 CHARGE ON PARTICIPATORS

Assume the values transferred by X, Y and Z in 307.1 above and that X and Y have each made previous chargeable transfers in excess of £325,000 since January 2007 and have used up their annual exemptions for 2012/13.

Company A

	X £	Y £	Z £
Value transferred	160,000	40,000	
Annual exemptions 2013/14	(3,000)	(3,000)	
	157,000	37,000	
Tax (25% of net)	39,250	9,250	
Gross transfer	£196,250	£46,250	
IHT	£39,250	£9,250	

Company B

	X	Y	Z
Value transferred	7,200	1,800	1,000
Deduct increase in X's estate	(10,000)	—	—
		1,800	1,000
Deduct annual exemption		—	1,000
		1,800	—
Tax (25% of net)		450	
Gross transfer		£2,250	
IHT		£450	

Note

(a)   Although it is understood that HMRC would follow this method of calculation, there is an alternative view which follows the exact wording of *IHTA 1984, s 94(1)*. This view is that the grossing-up should take place before the increase in X's estate is deducted. In the above example, it makes no difference as the gross transfer would still be less than the increase in X's estate. But suppose that X held 90% of the ordinary shares in Company A. His value transferred would then be £8,100 (90% × 90% × £10,000) and this alternative method would proceed as follows.

	£
Value transferred	8,100
Tax (25% of net)	2,025
	10,125
Deduct increase in X's estate	(10,000)
	£125
IHT thereon at 20%	£25

307.3 ALTERATION OF SHARE CAPITAL

In January 2014 the share capital of company H, an investment company, is owned by P and Q as follows

P	600
Q	400
	1,000 ordinary £1 shares

The shares are valued at £10 per share for P's majority holding and £4 per share for Q's minority holding.

The company issues 2,000 shares at par to Q and the shares are then worth £3.50 per share for Q's majority holding and £1.50 per share for P's minority holding. P has previously made chargeable transfers in excess of £325,000 since January 2007 and has utilised his 2013/14 and 2012/13 annual exemptions.

The transfer of value for P is

	£
Value of holding previously	6,000
Value of holding now	900
Decrease in value	5,100
Tax (25% of net)	1,275
Gross transfer	£6,375
IHT thereon at 20%	£1,275

Notes

(a) P's transfer of value is *not* a potentially exempt transfer. [*IHTA 1984, s 98(3)*].

(b) An alternative charge may arise under *IHTA 1984, s 3(3)* (omission to exercise a right) but the transfer would then be potentially exempt and only chargeable if P died within seven years.

308 Deeds of Variation and Disclaimers

[*IHTA 1984, ss 17, 142, 218A; FA 2012, Sch 33 paras 9, 10*]

308.1 A died in December 2013 leaving his estate of £354,000 to his wife absolutely. His wife, having an index-linked widow's pension, agreed with her sons, B and C, that they could benefit from the estate to the extent of £325,000 in equal shares, i.e. £162,500 each. A deed of variation is duly executed, incorporating a statement that the variation is to have effect for inheritance tax purposes.

A had made no chargeable transfers before his death.

	£
Exempt transfer to widow	29,000
Transfer to B	162,500
Transfer to C	162,500
	£325,000
IHT payable	Nil

Notes

(a) If A's widow died 5 years later when her estate was valued at, say, £354,000, IHT payable would be £11,600 (assuming that the nil rate band was then £325,000). If no deed of family arrangement had been made, the personal representatives of the widow's estate would be entitled to claim A's unused nil rate band, (increased to the amount of the band at that time) and the total estate of the widow would potentially be covered by the two nil rate bands. The instrument has in this case potentially increased the IHT liability by £11,600 but has ensured that the sons received their £162,500 five years earlier than would have been the case if the widow had retained A's property until her death. [*IHTA 1984, s 8A; FA 2008, s 10, Sch 4 para 2*].

(b) The persons making an instrument of variation and (if additional tax results) the personal representatives, must include in the instrument a statement that the variation is to have effect for inheritance tax purposes. If additional tax results, the persons making the statement must deliver a copy of the instrument to HMRC and notify them of the additional tax payable. [*IHTA 1988, ss 142(2), 218A*]. For variations where the death of the deceased occurred on or after 6 April 2012, and where the variation is to any extent in favour of a charity or charitable trust, it is a requirement that the charity or charitable trustees must be notified of the existence of the variation. [*IHTA 1984, s 142(3A)(3B); FA 2012, Sch 33 paras 9, 10*].

309 Double Taxation Relief

[*IHTA 1984, s 159*]

309.1 UNILATERAL RELIEF

(A) **Where property is situated in an overseas territory only**

A, domiciled in the UK, owns a holiday home abroad valued at £396,000 which he gives to his son in July 2013. He is liable to local gifts tax of, say, £8,830. He has made no previous transfers and does not use the home again at any time before his death in February 2018. It is assumed for the purposes of this example that the nil rate band is then £325,000.

		£	£
Market value of holiday home			396,000
Annual exemption	2013/14	(3,000)	
	2012/13	(3,000)	
			(6,000)
Chargeable transfer			£390,000
IHT payable at 60% of full rates by son (death between 4 and 5 years after gift)			
£65,000 × 40% × 60%			15,600
Unilateral relief for foreign tax			(8,830)
IHT borne			£6,770

Note

(a) If the overseas tax suffered exceeded the UK liability before relief, there would be no IHT payable but the excess would not be repayable.

(B) **Where property is situated in both the UK and an overseas territory**

M, domiciled in the UK, owns company shares which are regarded as situated both in the UK and country X under the rules of the respective countries. On M's death in June 2013 the shares pass to M's son S. The UK IHT amounts to £5,000 before unilateral relief. The equivalent tax liability arising in country X amounts to £2,000.

$$\text{Applying the formula } \frac{A}{A+B} \times C$$

where

A = amount of IHT

B = amount of overseas tax

309.1 IHT   Double Taxation Relief

C = smaller of A and B

The unilateral relief available is

$$\frac{5{,}000}{5{,}000 + 2{,}000} \times £2{,}000 = £1{,}429$$

IHT payable = £5,000 − £1,429 = £3,571

(C) **Where tax is imposed in two or more overseas territories on property situated in the UK and each of those territories**

Assume the facts in (B) above except that a third country imposes a tax liability on the death as the shares are regarded as also situated in that country.

UK IHT before unilateral relief	£5,000
Tax in country X	£2,000
Tax in country Y	£400

$$\text{Applying the formula} \frac{A}{A+B} \times C$$

where

A = amount of IHT

B = aggregate of overseas tax

C = aggregate of all, except the largest, of A and the overseas tax imposed in each overseas territory

The unilateral relief available is

$$\frac{5{,}000}{5{,}000 + 2{,}000 + 400} \times (2{,}000 + 400) = £1{,}622$$

IHT payable £5,000 − £1,622 = £3,378

(D) **Where tax in one overseas territory is relieved against another overseas territory's tax**

Assume the same facts as in (C) above except that country X allows a credit for tax paid in country Y.

Unilateral relief for IHT

$$\frac{5{,}000}{5{,}000 + (2{,}000 - 400) + 400} \times £((2{,}000 - 400) + 400) = £1{,}429$$

IHT payable £5,000 − £1,429 = £3,571

310 Exempt Transfers

310.1 ANNUAL EXEMPTION

[*IHTA 1984, s 19*]

(A)

S, who has made no other transfers of value, made gifts to his sister of £5,000 on 1 June 2011 and £4,000 on 1 May 2012. S dies on 1 September 2013 with an estate valued at £325,000.

Annual exemptions are available as follows

2011/12	£	£
1 June 2011 Gift		5,000
Deduct 2011/12 annual exemption	3,000	
2010/11 annual exemption (part)	2,000	
		5,000
		Nil

2012/13	£
1 May 2012 Gift	4,000
Deduct 2012/13 annual exemption	3,000
PET becoming chargeable on death	£1,000

The PET, having become a chargeable transfer as a result of death within seven years, is covered by the nil rate band but is aggregated with the death estate in computing the IHT payable on death.

Note

(a) Although the annual exemption, to the extent that it is not fully utilised in the year, can be carried forward to the following year, the current year's exemption is treated as utilised before any exemption brought forward. [*IHTA 1984, s 19(1)(2)*]. If S had gifted £6,000 in 2011/12 and £3,000 in 2012/13, the total gifts would have been the same but they would have been fully covered by annual exemptions.

310.1 IHT   Exempt Transfers

(B)

T made a gift to his son of £2,000 on 1 June 2013. On 9 November 2013, he settled £20,000 on a discretionary trust for his children and grandchildren. T had made no other gifts since 6 April 2013, but had used his annual exemptions in each year up to and including 2012/13. T died on 13 February 2019.

The gift on 1 June 2013 is a potentially exempt transfer which becomes chargeable since T died within seven years of the gift. The gift on 9 November 2013 is a chargeable transfer.

	£
1 June 2013 Gift to son — PET becoming chargeable	2,000
Deduct annual exemption 2013/4 (part)	2,000
	Nil
9 November 2013 Gift to trust	20,000
Deduct annual exemption 2013/14 (balance)	1,000
Chargeable transfer	£19,000

Note

(a) The annual exemption is allocated to earlier rather than later transfers within the same tax year regardless of whether they are PETs or chargeable transfers when made. Although this approach seems to render *IHTA 1984, s 19(3A)* otiose, *this is HMRC's current interpretation* (HMRC Inheritance Tax Manual, IHTM 14143).

310.2 NORMAL EXPENDITURE OUT OF INCOME

[*IHTA 1984, s 21*]

A wife pays annual life assurance premiums on a policy in favour of her son. The income of her husband and herself for 2013/14 is

	£
Husband's salary	35,000
Wife's salary	6,600
	£41,600

Income levels are not expected to fluctuate wildly from year to year.

The wife's disposable income is

	£
Salary	6,600
Tax thereon (personal allowance £9,440)	Nil
Personal income	£6,600

Depending on her lifestyle, the wife is probably able to show that she has sufficient income to justify a 'normal expenditure' gift of, say, a £1,000 premium paid annually (and therefore habitual). In form P11 (Notes) HMRC state that, 'examples of usual expenditure are where the deceased was paying a regular premium on an insurance policy for the benefit of another person, or perhaps they were making a monthly or other regular payment.'

If the wife was also accustomed to pay personally for an annual holiday costing, say, £2,500, it might be difficult to show that the life assurance premium was paid out of income.

310.3 NIL RATE BAND — TRANSFER OF UNUSED AMOUNT TO SPOUSE OR CIVIL PARTNER

[*IHTA 1984*, ss 8A–8C; *FA 2008*, Sch 4 paras 2, 9, 10]

(A)

John dies on 25 August 2008 with an estate of £312,000 and he leaves by his will £50,000 to each of his two grandchildren on discretionary trusts and the balance is left to his widow, Jean. He has made no transfers in the seven years prior to his death. Jean dies in October 2013 when the nil rate band is £325,000.

If Jean's personal representatives make a claim under *IHTA 1984*, s 8A, the nil rate band maximum available at the time of her death is as follows.

	£
Unused nil rate band at time of death	12,000
Less non-exempt transfers on John's death	100,000
Nil rate band unused by John	£212,000

The percentage increase to be made to Jean's nil rate band is therefore

$$\frac{£212,000}{£312,000} \times 100 = 67.95\%$$

Jean's nil rate band is increased to

£325,000 + (£325,000 × 67.95%) = £545,838

Notes

(a) Where a person dies on or after 9 October 2007, his nil rate band maximum at the time of death is, on a claim, treated as increased by the amount of the unused nil rate band of a predeceased spouse or civil partner. The nil rate band maximum is increased by the percentage given by the formula:

$$\frac{E}{NRBMD} \times 100$$

where

E = M - VT;

M = the maximum amount that could be transferred by a chargeable transfer on the predeceased person's death if it were to be wholly chargeable at the nil rate;

310.3 IHT   Exempt Transfers

VT = value actually transferred by the chargeable transfer on the death of the predeceased person (or nil if applicable);

NRBMD = the nil rate band maximum applying at the time of the predeceased person's death.

[*IHTA 1984, s 8A(2)–(4); FA 2008, Sch 4 paras 2, 9*].

(b)   The increase in the surviving partner's nil rate band maximum is subject to a maximum of 100% of that band. This could apply where, for example, the person had more than one predeceased spouse or civil partner each of whom died with unused nil rate band. [*IHTA 1984, s 8A(5)*]. See (B) below for the maximum increase in the nil rate band maximum of the survivor.

(c)   A claim under *IHTA 1984, s 8A* must be made by the personal representatives of the surviving partner within two years from the end of the month of death or, if later, within three months beginning with the date the personal representatives first act as such, or within such longer period as HMRC allow. If no such claim is made, a claim can be made by any other person liable to tax on the surviving partner's death within such period as HMRC allow. [*IHTA 1984, s 8B; FA 2008, Sch 4 para 2*].

(B)

Betty has been married and widowed twice before. Her first husband, David, died in October 1974 when estate duty applied. He left all his assets in his will to Betty having made no previous transfers. His estate was wholly within the £15,000 spouse's exemption applying at that time so that none of his tax free band was utilised in 1974. Betty's second husband Jack died on 18 June 2005 and left his assets to Betty excepting a £165,000 gift he made to his daughter in 2003. Betty died in December 2013.

If the personal representatives make a claim under *IHTA 1984, s 8A*, Betty's nil rate band maximum is increased as follows.

Increase in respect of David's nil rate band.

David used none of his nil rate band, and the percentage increase to Betty's maximum is therefore 100%.

Increase in respect of Jack's nil rate band.

	£
Unused nil rate band at time of death	275,000
Less non-exempt transfers on John's death	165,000
Nil rate band unused by Jack	£110,000

The percentage increase to Betty's maximum is therefore

$$\frac{£110,000}{£275,000} \times 100 = 40\%$$

The total increase to Betty's nil rate band maximum would therefore be (100% + 40% =) 140%. This is, however, restricted to 100%, making Betty's nil rate band maximum on death £650,000 (£325,000 + £325,000).

Exempt Transfers IHT 310.3

Notes

(a) The increase in the surviving partner's nil rate band maximum is subject to a maximum of 100% of that band. This could apply where, as in this example, the person had more than one predeceased spouse or civil partner each of whom died with unused nil rate band. [*IHTA 1984, s 8A(5); FA 2008, Sch 4 para 2*].

(b) It is immaterial when the predeceased spouse or civil partner died. Unused nil rate bands can be transferred even if the death was before 25 July 1986 (i.e. when capital transfer tax or estate duty applied) and the provisions of *IHTA 1984, ss 8A–8C* apply as modified by *FA 2008, Sch 4 para 10* to enable this.

(C) **Charges subsequent to death of predeceased spouse or civil partner**

[*IHTA 1984, s 8C; FA 2008, Sch 4 para 2*]

C died in August 2002 having made a conditionally exempt gift of heritage property to his brother, B. C left a property worth £125,000 to B and left the balance of his estate to his wife, D. In October 2008, the heritage property conditional exemption is breached when the property is valued at £104,000. D dies in February 2014.

If the personal representatives make a claim under *IHTA 1984, s 8A*, D's nil rate band maximum is increased as follows.

	£
Unused nil rate band at time of C's death	250,000
Less non-exempt transfers on C's death	125,000
Nil rate band unused by C	£125,000

The percentage increase to be made to D's nil rate band is therefore

$$\left(\frac{£125,000}{£250,000} - \frac{£104,000}{£312,000}\right) \times 100 = 16.67\%$$

D's nil rate band is increased to

£325,000 + (£325,000 × 16.67%) = £379,178

Notes

(a) Where, after the death of the first spouse or partner and before the death of the survivor, tax is charged on an amount under *IHTA 1984, ss 32 or 32A* (see **316 NATIONAL HERITAGE**) or *s 126* (see **327 WOODLANDS**) by reference to the rate that would have been applicable if the amount had been included in the estate of the first spouse or partner, *IHTA 1984, s 8A* applies using the following formula to replace that at (A) above:

$$\left(\frac{E}{NRBMD} - \frac{TA}{NRBME}\right) \times 100$$

where

E = M − VT;

310.3 IHT Exempt Transfers

M = the maximum amount that could be transferred by a chargeable transfer on the predeceased person's death if it were to be wholly chargeable at the nil rate;

VT = value actually transferred by the chargeable transfer on the death of the predeceased person (or nil if applicable);

NRBMD = the nil rate band maximum applying at the time of the predeceased person's death;

TA = the amount on which tax is subsequently charged;

NRBME = the nil rate band maximum at the time of the event giving rise to that charge.

[*IHTA 1984, s 8C(1)(2); FA 2008, Sch 4 para 2*].

(b) If the tax is charged after the death of the survivor, it is charged as if the personal nil rate band maximum of the predeceased spouse or partner were reduced by the amount by which the survivor's nil rate band was increased under *IHTA 1984, s 8A*. [*IHTA 1984, s 8C(4)(5); FA 2008, Sch 4 para 2*].

310.2 ELECTION TO BE TREATED AS DOMICILED IN THE UK

[*IHTA 1984, ss 267ZA, 267ZB; FA 2013, s 177*]

George is UK domiciled and his only asset is a house in the UK worth £3 million. His wife Monique is not domiciled in the UK for inheritance tax purposes and has only foreign assets worth £2 million. George dies on 1 August 2013 leaving his estate to Monique.

If no election under *IHTA 1984, s 267ZA* is made, the IHT on the death of George is:

	£
Estate	3,000,000
Less spouse exemption	325,000
Nil rate band	325,000
	£2,350,000
Inheritance tax £2,350,000 @ 40%	£940,000

On death of Monique on 1 September 2018 when her domicile status for IHT remains unchanged, IHT will once again be due on the UK house. Assuming that its value has not changed, and that the IHT on George's death was paid from her overseas assets, the IHT on Monique's estate will be:

	£
Estate	3,000,000
Less nil rate band	325,000
	£2,675,000
Inheritance tax £2,675,000 @ 40%	£1,070,000
Total inheritance tax on George and Monique's deaths £940,000 + £1,070,000 =	£2,010,000

Exempt Transfers IHT 310.2

If Monique had elected, under *IHTA 1984, s 267ZA* and before 1 August 2015, to be treated as domiciled in the UK with effect from 1 August 2013, no IHT would be payable on George's death. On Monique's death, IHT would then be due on both her UK and foreign assets. If they remain unchanged from George's death and have the same values, and the nil rate band remains unchanged, the IHT liability would be:

	£
Estate	5,000,000
Less nil rate band	650,000
	£4,350,000
Inheritance tax £4,350,000 @ 40%	£1,740,000
Total inheritance tax on George and Monique's deaths	£1,740,000

Notes

(a) With effect from 6 April 2013 an individual who is not domiciled in the UK (disregarding the IHT deemed domicile provisions of *IHTA 1984 s 267*), but whose spouse or civil partner is so domiciled, may elect to be treated as UK domiciled. The election may be either:

- a 'lifetime election' made at any time when the person making the election is non-UK domiciled, or

- a 'death election' made within two years of the death on or after 6 April 2013 of the person's UK domiciled spouse or civil partner.

A death election may be made by the personal representatives of the non-UK domiciled spouse, in the event of that person's death.

An election has effect on the date specified in it, which must be on or after 6 April 2013. Subject to this, a lifetime election may specify a date which is within the period of seven years ending with the date on which it is made, and a death election may specify a date which is within the seven years ending with the date of the death of the UK domiciled spouse or civil partner. In both cases the parties must have been married or civil partners throughout the period covered by the election.

[*IHTA 1984, ss 267ZA, 267ZB; FA 2013, s 177*].

(b) Both elections are irrevocable, and apply only for IHT purposes. They have no application to the remittance basis rules for other tax purposes (see IT 23 and CGT 225 REMITTANCE BASIS).

(c) For transfers of value made on or after 6 April 2013, the exemption for transfers to a non-UK domiciled spouse or civil partner is equal to the nil rate band (currently £235,000). Previously the exemption was £55,000. [*IHTA 1984, s 18; FA 2013, s 178*].

311 Gifts with Reservation

[*FA 1986, ss 102–102C, Sch 20; FA 2006, Sch 20 para 33; SI 1987 No 1130*]

311.1 GIFTS WITH RESERVATION

(A) Reservation released within seven years before death

On 19 June 1995 D gave his house to his grandson G, but continued to live in it alone paying no rent. The house was valued at £130,000. On 5 May 2009 D remarried, and went to live with his new wife F. G immediately moved into the house, which was then valued at £333,000.

On 3 January 2014 D died, leaving his estate of £200,000 equally to his granddaughter H and his wife F.

Gift 19 June 1995

As the gift was made more than seven years before death, it is a PET which has become exempt.

5 May 2009 release of reservation

The release of D's reservation is a PET which becomes chargeable by reason of D's death between 4 and 5 years later. IHT is charged, at 60% of full rates on the basis of the Table of rates in force at the time of death, on the value of the house at the date of release of reservation.

		£	£
Gift			333,000
Deduct annual exemptions	2009/10	—	
	2008/09	—	
Chargeable transfer			£333,000
Tax thereon)			
0–325,000 at nil%		—	
325,001–333,000 at 40%		3,200	
		£3,200	
IHT payable at 60% of full rates, 60% × £3,200			£1,920

Death 3 January 2014

IHT is charged at full rates on the chargeable estate of £100,000 (£100,000 passing to the wife is exempt) in the bracket £333,000 to £433,000.

Tax thereon

333,001–433,000 at 40%	£40,000

IHT   Gifts with Reservation

Note

(a) HMRC consider that the annual exemption is not available against the deemed PET arising on the release of a reservation (HMRC Inheritance Tax Manual, IHTM 14343).

(B) **Reservation not released before death**

The facts are as in (A) above except that the gift was on 19 June 2008 when the house was valued at £239,000, that D remained in his house on remarriage, and that G did not move in until D's death. The house was valued at £251,000 at the date of D's death on 3 January 2013.

Gift 19 June 2008

This is a potentially exempt transfer which becomes chargeable by reason of D's death within seven years.

Death 3 January 2014

As the reservation had not been released at the date of D's death, D is treated as beneficially entitled to the house, which thus forms part of his chargeable estate on death.

A double charge would arise by virtue of the house being the subject of a PET and a part of the chargeable estate on death. *The Inheritance Tax (Double Charges Relief) Regulations 1987 [SI 1987 No 1130]* provide relief as follows.

First calculation under Reg 5(3)(a)

Charge the house in the death estate and ignore the PET.

		£
Chargeable estate		
Free estate passing to H		100,000
House		251,000
		£351,000

There are no chargeable transfers within the previous seven years.

	£
IHT payable	
0–325,000 at nil %	—
325,001–351,000 at 40%	10,400
	£10,400

572

Gifts with Reservation   IHT 311.1

Second calculation under Reg 5(3)(b)

Charge the PET and ignore the value of the house in the death estate.

		£	£
Gift 19 June 2008			239,000
Deduct annual exemptions	2008/09	3,000	
	2007/08	3,000	
			6,000
Chargeable transfer			£233,000
Tax thereon			
0–233,000		Nil	

	£
Chargeable estate on death (excluding house)	100,000
IHT payable in the bracket £325,001 to £333,000	
325,001–333,000 at 40%	£3,200
Total IHT payable	£3,200

The first calculation yields the higher amount of tax (£10,400), so tax is charged by reference to the value of the gift with reservation in the estate, ignoring the PET.

Note

(a)   The comparison between the two calculations is made *before* credit is given for tax already paid (should there be any) (see HMRC Inheritance Tax Manual, IHTM 14712).

312 Interest on Tax

[IHTA 1984, s 233; FA 1989, s 178; SI 1989 No 1297]

312.1 B died on 10 February 2013. The executors made a payment on account of IHT of £70,000 on 30 June 2013 on delivery of the account. The final notice of determination was raised by HMRC Inheritance Tax on 19 June 2014 in the sum of £102,500. The rate of interest is assumed to be 5%.

Date of chargeable event (death)	10 February 2013
Date on which interest starts to accrue	1 September 2013

	£
IHT payable	102,500
Payment made on account 30 June 2013	70,000
Balance due	£32,500

Assessment raised by HMRC 19 June 2014	
Interest payable (1.9.13 to 19.6.14)	
£32,500 at 5% for 292 days	£1,300

Note

(a) Further interest may be charged if payment of the balance is not made promptly.

312.2 F gave his holiday home in Cornwall to his granddaughter G on 7 August 2009. On 23 May 2013 F died. He had made no use of the property at any time after 7 August 2009. G made a payment of £15,000, on account of the IHT due, on 1 January 2014. The liability was agreed at £27,000, and the balance paid, on 17 February 2014. The rate of interest is assumed to be 5%.

Date of PET	7 August 2009
Date on which PET becomes chargeable	23 May 2013
Date on which IHT is due	1 December 2013

	£
IHT payable	27,000
Payment made on account 1 January 2014	15,000
Balance due	£12,000

Interest payable

On £27,000 from 1.12.13–1.1.14	
£27,000 at 5% for 31 days	115
On £12,000 from 1.1.14–17.2.14	
£12,000 at 5% for 47 days	77
Total interest payable	£192

IHT Interest on Tax

313 Liability for Tax

[IHTA 1984, ss 199(1), 204(2)(3)(5)(6)]

313.1 LIFETIME TRANSFERS

(A) **Transferor**

A settled £78,000 on discretionary trusts in December 2013, having previously made chargeable transfers on 31 March 2013 totalling £328,000.

A's liability is as follows	£
Gift	78,000
Deduct 2013/14 annual exemption	3,000
	£75,000
Grossed at 20%	£93,750
IHT thereon at 20%	£18,750

(B) **Transferee**

In example (A) above A pays only £10,000 of IHT and defaults on the balance of £8,750, so that the trustees become liable as transferee.

The trustees' liability is not however £8,750 but is as follows

	£
Original gross	93,750
Deduct IHT unpaid	8,750
Revised gross	£85,000
IHT thereon at 20%	17,000
Deduct Paid by A	10,000
Now due from trustees	£7,000

(C) **Person in whom property is vested**

In January 2014 C transferred to trustees of a discretionary trust shares in an unquoted property company worth, as a minority holding, £50,000. However, the transfer deprives C of control of the company with the result that the value of his estate is reduced by £210,000. He has already used his nil rate band and annual exemptions.

313.1 IHT   Liability for Tax

C's liability is as follows

Net loss to him	£210,000
Grossed at 20%	£262,500
IHT thereon at 20%	£52,500

C fails to pay so that the trustees become liable, as follows

	£
Original gross	262,500
Deduct unpaid IHT	52,500
	£210,000
IHT thereon at 20%	£42,000

Note

(a) The trustees' liability cannot exceed the value of the assets which they hold, namely the proceeds of sale of the shares, less any CGT and costs incurred since acquisition, plus any undistributed income in their hands.

313.2 TRANSFERS ON DEATH

[*IHTA 1984, ss 200(1)(3), 204(1)–(3)(5), 211*]

Personal representatives of E, who died on 30 September 2013, received the following assets

	£
Free personal property	155,265
Land bequeathed to F (which, under the terms of the Will, bears its own IHT)	29,735
Private residence, bequeathed to spouse	51,000

A trust in which E had a pre-April 2006 life interest was valued at £154,000. Under the will of E, legacies of £15,000, each free of IHT, were given to F and G and the residue was left to H. E had made no chargeable transfers during his lifetime.

	Persons liable	£	IHT £
IHT is borne as to			
Chargeable transfer			
Free personal property	PRs	155,265	2,565
Land bequeathed to F	F	29,735	491

Liability for Tax   IHT 313.3

	Persons liable	£	IHT £
Private residence to spouse	—	Exempt	Nil
Trust fund	Trustees	154,000	2,544
		£339,000	£5,600

The residue left to H is as follows		£	£
Free personal property			155,265
Deduct IHT		2,565	
Legacies to F and G		30,000	32,565
			£122,700

Note

(a) If the will had not directed that the IHT on the land bequeathed to F be borne by F, the IHT would be payable out of residue. [*IHTA 1984, s 211*].

313.3 LIFETIME TRANSFER WITH ADDITIONAL LIABILITY ON DEATH

[*IHTA 1984, ss 131, 199(2), 201(2)*]

(A)

On 31 December 2013, H, who had made no earlier chargeable transfers other than to utilise his annual exemptions for 2013/14 and earlier years, transferred £368,000 into a discretionary trust and, a month later, settled an asset worth £20,000 into the same trust. H paid the appropriate IHT. On 30 June 2016, H died. It is assumed that the nil rate band on 30 June 2016 is £350,000.

The trustees become liable to further IHT as follows

	£	£
Original net gift	£368,000	£20,000
Grossed-up at half of full rates	£378,750	£25,000
IHT (paid by H)	£10,750	£5,000
IHT at 80% of death rates applicable in June 2016 on original gross (death between 3 and 4 years after gifts)	5,040	8,000
Deduct paid originally by H	10,750	5,000
Now due from trustees	—	£3,000

313.3 IHT   Liability for Tax

Note

(a) The additional IHT on death is calculated using the rates in force at the date of death. Where the IHT at the new death rates, as tapered, is less than the IHT paid on the original chargeable transfer, there is no repayment.

(B)

The second gift in (A) above had fallen in value to £18,000 by the time of H's death.

The trustees may claim to reduce the IHT payable as follows

	£
Original gross gift	25,000
Deduct drop in value (£20,000 − £18,000)	2,000
Revised gross	£23,000
IHT thereon at 80% of death rate applicable in June 2016	7,360
Deduct paid by H	5,000
	£2,360

Note

(a) If the asset had fallen in value to £10,625 or less, so that the revised gross became £15,625 or less and the IHT at 80% of death rates £5,000 or less, the trustees would have no liability because H had already paid IHT of £5,000.

313.4 POTENTIALLY EXEMPT TRANSFER BECOMING CHARGEABLE ON DEATH

[*IHTA 1984, ss 199, 201, 204; FA 1986, Sch 19 paras 26–28*]

On 19 May 2010 M gave N £336,000. M died on 3 August 2013 having made no other gifts.

		£
Gift		336,000
Deduct annual exemptions	2010/11	(3,000)
	2009/10	(3,000)
		£330,000

The IHT at 80% of full rates on the gift to N is payable by N on 1 March 2014.

	£
0–325,000 at nil%	—
325,001–330,000 at 40%	2,000
	£2,000

580

Liability for Tax   IHT 313.4

IHT payable by N 80% × £2,000 = £1,600

Notes

(a) If N has not paid the IHT due of £1,600 by 1 March 2015 the personal representatives of M are liable, although their liability cannot exceed the death estate of M. The amount is a deductible liability from the estate only to the extent that reimbursement from N cannot be obtained.

(b) See also **305.1** CALCULATION OF TAX for liability to tax on potentially exempt transfers.

314 Life Assurance Policies

[*IHTA 1984, ss 21, 167*]

314.1 A has paid premiums of £2,000 p.a for 6 years on a policy on his own life. He gives the policy to his son B. The market value of the policy at the date of gift is £11,000. A also pays annual premiums of £2,000 on a policy on his life written in favour of his son.

Assignment of policy

The gift is valued either at

(i)   market value (£11,000), or

(ii) the accumulated gross premiums paid (£12,000) if greater.

Annual premiums

The payment of an annual premium is regarded as an annual gift, the amount of the transfer being the net premium after deduction of any tax relief at source or the gross premium where paid without deduction.

Notes

(a) The gifts are PETs. The assignment of the policy will only become chargeable if A dies within seven years, and only the annual premiums paid within seven years of A's death will be chargeable.

(b) Exemptions available for reduction of the chargeable transfer on assignment include the annual exemption and the marriage exemption.

(c) The normal expenditure exemption may be available to A for premiums paid and the annual exemption may also be claimed to exempt the gift in whole or in part. See also note (a) to **310.2 EXEMPT TRANSFERS**.

(d) Normal expenditure relief is not available when a policy and annuity have been effected on a back-to-back basis (with certain exceptions).

315 Mutual Transfers

[*FA 1986, s 104; SI 1987 No 1130*]

315.1 POTENTIALLY EXEMPT TRANSFERS AND DEATH

A, who has made no previous transfers of value other than to use his annual exemptions for 2009/10 and 2010/11, makes a gift of £330,000 to B on 1 July 2010. On 15 July 2011 and 20 January 2012, he makes gifts of £238,000 and £96,000 respectively into a discretionary trust and the trustees pay the IHT due of £1,200 on the later transfer. On 2 January 2013, B dies and the 2009 gift is returned to A by virtue of B's Will. On 4 April 2014, A dies. His taxable estate on death is valued at £410,000 which includes the 2010 gift returned to him in 2013 which is still valued at £330,000.

First calculation under Reg 4(4)(a)

The gift in 2010 is a PET and would normally become a chargeable transfer by virtue of A's death within seven years of making the gift. However, for the purpose of this calculation, it is ignored and the returned gift is charged as part of A's death estate.

Additional tax due on chargeable lifetime transfers

	£
Gift on 15 July 2011	238,000
Deduct 2011/12 annual exemption	3,000
	235,000
Gift on 20 January 2012	96,000
	£331,000
IHT at death rates on £331,000	2,400
IHT previously paid	1,200
Additional IHT payable by trustees	£1,200

Tax on death estate of £410,000 charged at 40%

IHT payable note (a)	£164,000

Total IHT payable as consequence of death (£1,200 + £164,000)	£165,200

Second calculation under Reg 4(4)(b)

The 2010 gift is charged as a PET but the returned gift is ignored in the death estate.

The tax due on PET of £330,000 at death rates

315.1 IHT   Mutual Transfers

	£
0–325,000 at nil%	Nil
325,001–330,000 at 40%	2,000
	£2,000

IHT payable at 80% of full rates (death between 3 and 4 years after gift)	£1,600

Tax due on chargeable lifetime transfers of £331,000 (after annual exemption) charged at 40%

	£
IHT payable	132,400
IHT paid	1,200
Additional IHT payable	£131,200

Tax on death estate of £80,000 charged at 40%	
IHT payable	£32,200

Total IHT payable as consequence of death (£1,600 + £131,200 + £32,000)	£164,800

The first calculation gives the higher amount of tax, so the PET is ignored and the returned gift included in the death estate, the tax liabilities being as in the first calculation above.

Note

(a) Quick succession relief under *IHTA 1984, s 141* (see **319.1** QUICK SUCCESSION RELIEF below) might be due in respect of the returned PET by reference to any tax charged on that PET in connection with B's death. If, as a result of such relief, the first calculation produces a lower tax charge than the second, then the second calculation will prevail, i.e. the PET will be charged and the returned gift ignored in the death estate.

315.2 CHARGEABLE TRANSFERS AND DEATH

C, who had made no other transfer of value, gifted £308,000 on 31 May 2006 into discretionary trust, on which IHT of £3,400 was paid. On 5 October 2006, he gave D a life interest in shares worth £85,000; IHT of £17,000 was paid. On 3 January 2012, C makes a PET of £36,000 to E. On 31 December 2012, D dies and the settled shares return to C, the settlor (no tax charge arises on D's death). On 10 August 2013, C dies; his death estate is valued at £300,000 which includes the shares returned from D, now worth £60,000.

First calculation under Reg 7(4)(a)

The gift in October 2006 is ignored and the returned shares included as part of the taxable estate on death.

No additional tax arises on the May 2006 lifetime transfer of £302,000 (after annual exemptions) as it was made more than seven years before death.

Tax due on PET of £30,000 (after annual exemptions) made in January 2012 charged in band £325,001–332,000.

£7,000 at 40% = £2,800.

Tax on death estate of £300,000 charged in band £30,001 to £330,000 (the gift to the discretionary trust having fallen out of cumulation)

	£
30,001–325,000 at nil%	
325,001–330,000 at 40%	2,000
Total IHT payable as consequence of death (£2,800 + £2,000) (but see note (a) below)	£4,800

Second calculation under Reg 7(4)(b)

The October 2006 gift is charged and the returned shares are excluded from the taxable estate on death.

Additional tax due on October 2006 transfer as a result of death — charged in band £325,001 to £387,000.

325,001–387,000 at 40%	£24,800
IHT payable at 20% of full rates (death between 6 and 7 years after gift)	4,960
IHT paid £17,000, but credit restricted to	4,960
Additional IHT	Nil

Tax due on PET of £30,000 (after annual exemptions) charged in band £387,001 to £417,000.

£30,000 at 40%	£12,000

Tax on death estate of £240,000 charged in band £115,001 to £355,000.

115,001–325,000 at nil %	
325,001–355,000 at 40%	£12,200
Total IHT payable as consequence of death (£12,000 + £12,200)	£24,400

The second calculation gives the higher amount of tax so the returned gift is excluded from the death estate, the tax liabilities being as in the second calculation above.

Note

(a) If the first calculation had given the higher amount, a credit for IHT would have been due, restricted to the lower of

315.2 IHT   Mutual Transfers

(i) the IHT paid on the lifetime transfer (i.e. £17,000); and

(ii) the IHT attributable to the returned shares on death, calculated as follows:

$$\text{Estate rate } \frac{2,000}{300,000} = 0.67\%$$

£60,000 × 0.67% = £400

The IHT actually payable as a consequence of death would have been £4,400 (£4,800 − £400).

316 National Heritage

[*IHTA 1984, ss 30–35, 57A, 77–79, 207, Sch 2 paras 5, 6, Sch 4, Sch 5; FA 2012, Sch 33 para 4*]

316.1 CONDITIONS FOR EXEMPTION

Lord A died in 1952 leaving Netherington Hall in Wiltshire to his son B together with all its contents. These contents included a painting by Whistler of Netherington Hall and also a rare painting of Mary Queen of Scots alongside Lord Bothwell her second husband. The pictures and other items in the Hall were all exempted from estate duty which, at the time Lord A died, was applied at a marginal rate of 80%.

Unfortunately the son Lord B dies in a hunting accident on Boxing Day 2013 and the Hall together with contents are left to his son, now Lord C. HMRC consider the painting by Whistler of the Hall to be pre-eminent for its artistic interest. The painting is accepted as pre-eminent and is re-exempted on the death of Lord B, subject to a contingent liability to IHT on any breach of undertaking or subsequent disposal by sale when the rate of IHT would be 40%.

HMRC do not consider the painting of Mary Queen of Scots, now valued at £5 million, to be pre-eminent.

As the Mary Queen of Scots painting fails the pre-eminence test IHT of £2 million (£5 million × 40%) is due and paid by the estate. Lord C sells the painting for £8 million (net of expenses and CGT) six months later in June 2014 thereby breaking the estate duty undertaking.

In view of HMRC's decision, there will be a tax charge calculated as follows:

	£
Estate duty at 80% on £8 million	6,400,000
Less credit for IHT paid on Lord B's death	2,000,000
Estate duty payable on sale	4,400,000

Note

(a) For claims made on or after 31 July 1998, any picture, print, book, work of art or scientific object, or any other thing not yielding income, or a collection or group of such objects, only qualifies (apart from by virtue of a historical connection with a building of outstanding historic or architectural interest) for conditional exemption, if it appears to HMRC to be *pre-eminent* for its national, scientific, historic or artistic interest [*IHTA 1984, s 31(1)(5)*]. Previously such objects simply had to appear to the Treasury to be of national, scientific, historic or artistic interest.

316.2 CONDITIONALLY EXEMPT TRANSFERS AFTER 6 APRIL 1976

(A) **Chargeable event during lifetime of relevant person**

C, who has made previous chargeable transfers during 2006 of £230,000, makes a conditionally exempt gift of property in February 2008. In October 2013, the property is sold for £500,000 and capital gains tax of £80,000 is payable.

316.2 IHT   National Heritage

	£
Cumulative total of previous chargeable transfers of relevant person	230,000
Net sale proceeds of conditionally exempt property	500,000
Deduct Capital gains tax payable	(80,000)
Chargeable transfer	420,000
Revised cumulative total for relevant person	£650,000
Inheritance tax payable (by reference to lifetime rates in October 2013) £325,000 at 20% =	£65,000

(B) **Chargeable event after relevant person is dead**

D died in April 1999 leaving a taxable estate of £350,000 together with conditionally exempt property valued at £600,000 at the breach in October 2013.

	£
Value of relevant person's estate at death	350,000
Value of conditionally exempt property at date of breach	600,000
	£950,000

Inheritance tax payable (by reference to full rates applicable in October 2013).

£600,000 at 40% = £240,000

Notes

(a) As the chargeable event occurs after tax is reduced by the substitution of a new Table of rates, the new rates are used.

(b) Where a chargeable event arises in respect of property which was allowed conditional exemption on an earlier death, the lower 36% rate of inheritance tax cannot be claimed on that event even if the remaining estate had satisfied the conditions for that rate. [*IHTA 1984, s 33(2ZA); FA 2012, Sch 33 para 4*]. See **322.2** TRANSFERS ON DEATH.

(C) **Multiple conditionally exempt transfers**

D died in December 1987 leaving a conditionally exempt property to his son E. D's taxable estate at death was £230,000. In 1996 E gave the property to his daughter F. F gave the necessary undertakings so this transfer was also conditionally exempt. In December 2013 F sold the property for its market value of £500,000 and paid capital gains tax of £50,000. During 1996 E had made chargeable transfers of £20,000 and he has made no other transfers.

	£	£
Value of relevant person's estate at death		230,000
Net sale proceeds of conditionally exempt property	500,000	
Deduct capital gains tax	50,000	
Chargeable transfer		450,000
		£680,000
Inheritance tax payable by F		
£355,000 at 40% =		£142,200
Previous cumulative total of E		20,000
Add chargeable transfer		450,000
E's revised cumulative total		£470,000

Notes

(a) There have been two conditionally exempt transfers within the period of 30 years ending with the chargeable event in December 2013. HMRC may select either D or E as the 'relevant person' for the purpose of calculating the tax due. The IHT liability will be higher if D is selected. [*IHTA 1984, ss 33(5), 78(3)*].

(b) As F receives the proceeds of sale, she is the person liable to pay the IHT. [*IHTA 1984, s 207(1)*].

(c) Although the IHT is calculated by reference to D's cumulative total, it is E whose cumulative total is adjusted as he made the last conditionally exempt transfer of the property. [*IHTA 1984, s 34(1)*].

(d) As the chargeable event occurs after a reduction in the rates of tax, the new rates are used to calculate the tax payable. [*IHTA 1984, Sch 2 para 5*].

316.3 CONDITIONALLY EXEMPT TRANSFERS ON DEATH BEFORE 7 APRIL 1976

(A) Chargeable event more than 3 years after death

B died on 31 December 1975 leaving a taxable estate of £100,000 together with a conditionally exempt painting valued at £50,000. In June 2013 the painting was sold for £110,000.

		£
Value of deceased's taxable estate		100,000
Value of exempt property at date of chargeable event	note (a)	110,000
		£210,000
Recalculated IHT liability	note (b)	£90,750

316.3 IHT   National Heritage

IHT payable on conditionally exempt property

$$£90,750 \times \frac{110,000}{210,000} \qquad £47,536$$

No further liability accrues to the estate of the deceased.

Notes

(a) The value of the exempt property will be reduced by any capital gains tax chargeable in respect of the sale. [*TCGA 1992, s 258(8)*].

(b) The IHT liability is calculated using rates in force at the date of death.

(B) Estate Duty

Lord A dies in 1952 (see example at 316.1 above) leaving Netherington Hall and its contents to his son now Lord B. The paintings were exempted from estate duty which was at an 80% marginal rate at the time.

On Boxing Day 2013 Lord B dies in an accident and the Hall and contents are left to his son Lord C. The Executors omit to make claim within the two years to exempt the chattels even though these would have been considered to be pre-eminent under *IHTA 1984, s 31*. The sum of £2,400,000 is paid as IHT on the death in relation to the paintings' value of £6,000,000.

Lord C sells the paintings in the year 2014 for a total sum of £8,000,000 and estate duty at 80% becomes payable on these proceeds (net of expenses), and a credit for the tax previously paid of £2,400,000 is given.

	£
Estate duty 80% × £8m	6,400,000
Less credit for IHT paid on Lord B's death	2,400,000
Estate duty payable on sale	4,000,000

Note

(a) If a new exemption claim in respect of the paintings had been made on B's death then the old estate duty liability would have fallen out of account on the chargeable event as only IHT would have been relevant. [*IHTA 1984, Sch 6 para 4(2)(3)*]. The IHT due would have been £8m × 40% = £3,200,000.

316.4 CHARGE TO TAX

Tax credit

[*IHTA 1984, s 33(7)*]

Property inherited in 1984 from A's estate by B, who gave the necessary undertakings so that the property is conditionally exempt, is given in December 2013 by B to C. C agrees to pay any inheritance tax arising from the transfer but does not wish to give the necessary undertakings, so a chargeable event arises. B dies in March 2014.

	£
A's estate at date of death in 1984	180,000
B's cumulative chargeable transfers at date of chargeable event in December 2013 (all in 2012/13)	86,000
Value of property at date of chargeable event	250,000

Inheritance tax on chargeable event (subject to tax credit)

		£
Value of A's estate at date of death		180,000
Value of property at date of chargeable event		250,000
		£430,000
Inheritance tax payable		
£105,000 at 40%		£42,000
Inheritance tax on B's gift		
Cumulative total of previous transfers		86,000
Value of property gifted	250,000	
Deduct Annual exemption 2013/14	3,000	247,000
		£333,000
Inheritance tax arising on gift of £247,000		£3,200
Tax credit		
IHT on B's gift		3,200
IHT on chargeable event	42,000	
Deduct tax credit	(3,200)	
		38,800
Total inheritance tax borne		£42,000

316.5 SETTLEMENTS — EVENTS AFTER 8 MARCH 1982

(A) **Chargeable events following conditionally exempt occasions**

A, who is still alive, settled property and investments on discretionary trusts in September 1988, conditional exemption being granted in respect of designated property. In April 2002, the designated property was appointed absolutely to beneficiary C who gave the necessary undertakings for exemption to continue. However, in February 2014, C sold the property for £135,000 net of costs, suffering a capital gains tax liability of £20,000. At the time of C's sale, A had cumulative chargeable transfers of £40,000.

316.5 IHT   National Heritage

		£
Cumulative total of previous chargeable transfers of relevant person		40,000
Net sale proceeds of conditionally exempt property		115,000
		£155,000

Inheritance tax payable by C			
£110,000 at nil%	—		
£5,000 at 20%	1,000		
£115,000	£1,000		£1,000

Notes

(a) A is the relevant person in relation to the chargeable event as he is the person to effect the only conditionally exempt transfer *and* the person who is settlor in relation to the settlement in respect of which the only conditionally exempt occasion arose. [*IHTA 1984, ss 33(5), 78(3)*].

(b) HMRC have discretion to select either the conditionally exempt transfer (by A to the trustees) in 1988 or the conditionally exempt occasion (from the trustees to C) in 2002 as the 'last transaction' for the purposes of determining who is the relevant person. A is the relevant person regardless of which is selected but HMRC are more likely to choose the earlier transfer as this will result in a greater amount of tax being collected. [*IHTA 1984, ss 33(5), 78(3)(4)*].

(c) The chargeable amount of £115,000 does not increase either A's cumulative total or that of the trustees for the purpose of calculating the IHT liability on any subsequent transfers. As the last conditionally exempt transaction before the chargeable event was a conditionally exempt occasion rather than a conditionally exempt transfer, the provisions of *IHTA 1984, s 34* (which allow for an increase in the cumulative total) do not apply. [*IHTA 1984, s 78(6)*].

(B) **Exemption from the ten-year anniversary charge**

[*IHTA 1984, s 79; FA 2006, Sch 20 para 34*]

Trustees own National Heritage property for which the necessary undertakings have been given and the property has been designated by the Treasury. The property was settled in July 1974 and is the sole asset of the trust. No appointments or advances of capital have been made. On 30 October 2013, there is a breach of the undertakings. At this date the property is valued at £150,000.

Ten-year anniversary charge

There is no liability in 1984, 1994 or 2004.

Breach in October 2013

Value of property at time of event	£150,000

The relevant period is the period from the date of settlement or, if later, 13 March 1975 to 29 October 2013, i.e. 154 complete quarters.

The rate of tax is

0.25% for 40 quarters	10.00%
0.20% for 40 quarters	8.00%
0.15% for 40 quarters	6.00%
0.10% for 34 quarters	3.40%
	27.40%

IHT payable is 27.40% × £150,000 = £41,100

316.6 MAINTENANCE FUNDS FOR HISTORIC BUILDINGS

[*IHTA 1984, Sch 2 para 6, Sch 4 paras 8, 12–14*]

On 1 January 1994 P settled £500,000 in an approved maintenance fund for his historic mansion during the lives of himself and his wife, W. P died in February 1998, his taxable estate and lifetime transfers chargeable on death amounting to £175,000. On 1 January 2014, the date of death of W, the fund, which has been depleted by extensive repairs to the mansion, is valued at £300,000. £80,000 is transferred to the National Trust, which also accepts the gift of the mansion, and the balance is paid to P's grandson G.

No IHT is payable on the £80,000 paid to the National Trust, but the balance passing to G is liable to IHT at the higher of a tapered scale rate (the 'first rate') and an effective rate calculated by reference to P's estate (the 'second rate'). [*IHTA 1984, Sch 4 paras 12–14*].

First rate

The property was comprised in the maintenance fund for 20 years, i.e. 80 quarters.

The scale rate is

0.25% for each of the first 40 quarters	10.0%
0.20% for each of the next 40 quarters	8.0%
	18.0%

Second rate

The effective rate is calculated, using half Table rates applying on 1 January 2014, as if the chargeable amount transferred (£220,000) had been added to the value transferred by P on his death (£175,000) and had formed the highest part of the total. Half Table rates are used because the fund was set up in P's lifetime.

		£
£150,000	at nil	—
£70,000	at 20%	14,000
£220,000		£14,000

316.6 IHT   National Heritage

$$\text{The effective rate is } \frac{14{,}000}{220{,}000} \times 100\% =$$

£

6.36%

As the second rate (6.36%) is lower than the first rate (18%) the first rate is used.

IHT payable is £220,000 at 18% =   £39,600

317 Payment of Tax

[*IHTA 1984, ss 227, 228, 234*]

317.1 PAYMENT BY INSTALMENTS ON TRANSFER OR DEATH

(A)

F died on 17 December 2013 leaving a free estate of £395,000, including £75,000 (after business property relief at 50%) in respect of plant and machinery in a partnership. An election is made to pay inheritance tax on the plant and machinery by 10 equal yearly instalments.

Inheritance tax on free estate		£
On first	£325,000	Nil
On next	£70,000 at 40%	28,000
	£395,000	£28,000

IHT applicable to plant and machinery

$$\frac{75,000}{395,000} \times 28,000 \qquad \text{£5,316}$$

1st instalment due 1.7.14	£531
2nd instalment due 1.7.14	£531
and so on.	

Notes

(a) Instalments continue to be due at yearly intervals for 10 years or until the business property is sold, at which time all unpaid IHT becomes payable.

(b) Interest is payable on each instalment from the day it falls due. If payments are made on time, no interest is payable.

(B)

On 1 December 2013 G gave his land in a partnership of which G was a partner to his son S who agreed to pay any IHT on the transfer. The land was valued at £600,000. G had made prior chargeable transfers of £140,000, had already used his 2012/13 and 2013/14 annual exemptions, and he died on 31 December 2017.

S elected to pay the IHT by 10 yearly instalments and paid the first on 1 August 2018, and the second on 1 September 2019. On 1 December 2019 he sold the land, and paid the balance of the IHT outstanding on 1 February 2020. It is assumed that the rate of interest on unpaid inheritance tax is 3% throughout.

317.1 IHT Payment of Tax

Inheritance tax on gift

		£
Value of land		600,000
Deduct business property relief at 50%		300,000
PET becoming chargeable on death		£300,000
IHT payable in the band £140,001–£440,000	£	
140,001–325,000 at nil%	Nil	
325,001–440,000 at 40%	46,000	
	£46,000	
Total IHT payable at 60% of full rates (death between 4 and 5 years after gift)		£27,600
1st instalment due 1.7.18	2,760	
Interest at 3% from 1.7.18 to 1.8.18		
$^{31}/_{366} \times £2,760 \times 3\%$	7	
		2,767
2nd instalment due 1.7.19	2,760	
Interest at 3% from 1.7.19 to 1.9.19		
$^{62}/_{366} \times £2,760 \times 3\%$	14	
		2,774
Balance due on sale on 1.12.19	22,080	
Interest at 3% from 1.12.19 to 1.2.20		
$^{62}/_{366} \times £22,080 \times 3\%$	112	
		22,192
Total IHT and interest		£27,733

Note

(a) Interest on unpaid tax is calculated using 366 days as the denominator rather than 365 days.

318 Protective Trusts

318.1 FORFEITURE BEFORE 12 APRIL 1978

[*IHTA 1984, s 73*]

In 1951 X left his estate on protective trusts for his son Z. On 1 January 1978 Z attempted to assign his interest and the protective trusts were accordingly determined. On 1 May 1983 the trustees advanced £25,000 to Z to enable him to purchase a flat. At the same time, they also advanced £10,000 (net) to his granddaughter D. On 1 May 2013 Z died and the trust fund, valued at £200,000, passed equally to his grandchildren absolutely.

1 May 1983

There is no charge to IHT on the payment to Z, but a charge arises on the payment to D. The relevant period is the period from the determination of the protective trusts (1 January 1978) to 1 May 1983 i.e. 21 complete quarters.

The rate of tax is 0.25% for each of 21 quarters 5.25%

$$\text{IHT payable is } \frac{5.25}{100 - 5.25} \times £10,000 = £554$$

The gross payment is £10,554

1 May 2013

There is a charge to IHT when the trust vests on the death of Z. 137 complete quarters have elapsed since the protective trusts determined.

The rate of tax is

0.25% for each of the first 40 quarters	10.0%
0.20% for each of the next 40 quarters	8.0%
0.15% for the next 40 quarters	6.0%
0.10% for the next 21 quarters	2.1%
	26.10%

IHT payable is 26.1% × £200,000 = £52,200

318.2 FORFEITURE AFTER 11 APRIL 1978

[*IHTA 1984, s 88*]

Assume the same facts as in 318.1 above but that Z attempted to assign his interest on 1 January 1980.

1 May 1983

There is no charge to IHT on the payment to Z who is treated as beneficially entitled to an interest in possession under the trust. The payment to D is a chargeable transfer. Tax is charged at Z's personal cumulative rate of tax so that if he had made no previous transfers, the payment would be covered by his nil rate tax band. If the payment had been made after 16 March 1987, it would have been a potentially exempt transfer.

318.2 IHT   Protective Trusts

1 May 2013

There is a charge to IHT when the trust vests on the death of Z, calculated by aggregating £200,000 with all other chargeable property passing on his death and applying the normal death rates.

Notes

(a)   For settlements created on or after 22 March 2006, *IHTA 1984, s 88* applies only if the interest of the principal beneficiary is an immediate post-death interest within *IHTA 1984, s 49A*, a disabled person's interest within *IHTA 1984, s 89B(1)(c)(d)* or a transitional serial interest within *IHTA 1984, ss 49B–49E*. [*IHTA 1988, s 88(4)–(6); FA 2006, Sch 20 para 24*].

(b)   For settlements created before 22 March 2006, where the protective trusts fail or are determined on or after that date, for inheritance tax purposes the principal beneficiary is treated as if he became beneficially entitled to an interest in possession in the settled property before that date. [*IHTA 1984, s 88(3); FA 2006, Sch 20 para 24*]. Therefore the changes to the SETTLEMENTS WITH INTERESTS IN POSSESSION **(320)** provisions made by *FA 2006* do not apply and the beneficiary continues to be treated under *IHTA 1984, s 49* as beneficially entitled to the settled property concerned whether or not his interest is an immediate post-death interest, a disabled person's interest or a transitional serial interest.

319 Quick Succession Relief

[*IHTA 1984, s 141*]

319.1 TRANSFERS AFTER 9 MARCH 1981

On 1 January 2014 A died with a net estate valued at £400,000. In December 2009 he had received a gift from B of £20,000. B died in November 2011 and A paid the IHT (amounting to £8,000) due as a result of B's potentially exempt transfer becoming chargeable.

A was also entitled to an interest in possession in the whole of his father's estate. His father had died in February 2011 with a net estate of £331,000 on which the IHT paid was £2,400. On A's death, the property passed to A's sister and was valued at £145,000. A had made no previous transfers and left his estate to his brother.

	£
Free estate	400,000
Settled property	145,000
Taxable estate	£545,000

IHT on an estate of £545,000 = £88,000

Quick succession relief

The gift from B was made more than four but not more than five years before A's death so quick succession relief at 20% is available.

$$\text{QSR} = 20\% \times £8,000 \times \frac{12,000}{20,000} \qquad £960$$

Interest in possession in father's will trust	£
Net estate before tax	331,000
Tax	2,400
Net estate after tax	£328,600

A's death was more than two but not more than three years after his father's so relief is given at 60%.

$$\text{QSR} = 60\% \times £2,400 \times \frac{328,600}{331,000} \qquad £1,429$$

Tax payable on death of A	£	£
IHT on an estate of £545,000		88,000

319.1 IHT   Quick Succession Relief

		£	£
Tax payable on death of A			
Deduct QSR			
On gift from B		960	
On father's estate		1,429	
			2,389
IHT payable			£85,611

$$\text{On free estate } \frac{400{,}000}{545{,}000} \times £85{,}611 \qquad £62{,}834$$

$$\text{On settled property } \frac{145{,}000}{545{,}000} \times £85{,}611 \qquad £22{,}778$$

Note

(a) The relief is given only by reference to the tax charged on the part of the value received by the donee. Therefore, the tax paid must be apportioned by applying the fraction 'net transfer received divided by gross transfer made'.

320 Settlements with Interests in Possession

[*IHTA 1984, ss 49–49E, 51(1)–(1B), 52(1)(2A), 54A, 54B, 57; FA 2006, Sch 20 paras 4, 5, 12, 13, 16; FA 2008, s 141; FA 2010, s 53*]

320.1 TERMINATION OF AN INTEREST IN POSSESSION

A had an interest in possession in a settlement valued at £222,000 with remainder to his son S for life. A's interest in possession commenced in 2002. On 1 July 2013, A released his life interest to S in consideration of S's marriage on 2 July 2013. A had made no gifts since 5 April 2013 but had used his annual exemptions prior to that date. His cumulative total of chargeable transfers at 5 April 2013 was £126,000, and these had all been made since 1 July 2006.

The release of A's life interest is an immediately chargeable transfer.

	£	£
Value of property		222,000
Exemptions		
Annual 2013/14	3,000	
In consideration of marriage	5,000	
		8,000
Chargeable transfer		£214,000

IHT on £214,000 is charged in the band £126,001 to £340,000.

	£
126,001–325,000 at nil%	Nil
325,001–340,000 at 20%	3,000
	£3,000
Tax payable by trustees as a consequence of A's death	£3,000

Notes

(a) The annual gifts exemption and the exemption of gifts in consideration of marriage apply if notice is given to the trustees by the donor within 6 months of the gift.

(b) The tax payable is computed by reference to the transferor's cumulative total of chargeable transfers within the previous seven years, and the chargeable transfer forms part of his cumulative total carried forward.

(c) The interest in possession provisions apply in respect of interests to which a person becomes beneficially entitled on or after 22 March 2006 only if the interest is an immediate post-death interest within *IHTA 1984, s 49A* (see 320.4 below), a disabled person's interest within *IHTA 1984, s 89B(1)(c)(d)* or a transitional serial interest within *IHTA 1984, ss 49B–49E* (see **320.3** below). The provisions also apply where a UK-domiciled person becomes beneficially entitled to an interest in possession on

320.1 IHT Settlements with Interests in Possession

or after 9 December 2009 by a disposition which is not a transfer of value as a result of *IHTA 1984, s 10* (dispositions not intended to confer gratuitous benefit). [*IHTA 1984, s 49(1A); FA 2010, s 53*]. Otherwise, an interest in possession to which a person becomes beneficially entitled on or after 22 March 2006 is treated as relevant property subject to the SETTLEMENTS WITHOUT INTERESTS IN POSSESSION (321) rules. [*IHTA 1984, s 59(1)(2); FA 2006, Sch 20 para 20*].

(d) As the release of A's life interest to S occurred after 5 October 2008, S's interest in possession is not a transitional serial interest and is subject to the SETTLEMENTS WITHOUT INTERESTS IN POSSESSION (321) rules.. The release is an immediately chargeable transfer. See also **320.2** below.

320.2 TRANSITIONAL SERIAL INTERESTS

[*IHTA 1984, ss 49B–49E; FA 2006, Sch 20 para 5; FA 2008, s 141*]

Rick had an interest in possession in a settlement to which he became beneficially entitled in 1998. The terms of the settlement are that remainder goes to his son Robbie for life. Rick released his life interest to Robbie. At the date of the release, the settlement was valued at £350,000, Rick's cumulative chargeable transfers in the last seven years amounted to £130,000 and he had not used his annual exemptions for any year.

On the assumption that the release takes place on (i) 31 August 2007 and (ii) 5 November 2013, the IHT consequences for Rick are as follows.

(i) **Release on 31 August 2007**

Robbie's interest in possession is a transitional serial interest within *IHTA 1984, s 49C*. The transfer is therefore a potentially exempt transfer and will become chargeable only in the event of Rick's death within seven years.

(ii) **Release on 5 November 2013**

As the release occurs after 5 October 2008 Robbie's interest cannot be a transitional serial interest within *IHTA 1984, s 49C*. As his interest is not a transitional serial interest within *IHTA 1984, s 49D*, the relevant property regime (see **321** SETTLEMENTS WITHOUT INTERESTS IN POSSESSION) applies to it. Rick's transfer is therefore a chargeable transfer and IHT is due as follows.

		£	£
Value transferred by Rick on 5 November 2013			350,000
Deduct annual exemptions 2013/14		3,000	
2012/13		3,000	6,000
			£344,000

IHT on £344,000 is charged in the band £130,001 to £474,000.

	£
£130,001–325,000	Nil

Settlements with Interests in Possession   IHT 320.3

£325,001–474,000 at 20%	29,800
IHT payable	£29,800

Notes

(a) The interest in possession provisions apply in respect of interests to which a person becomes beneficially entitled on or after 22 March 2006 only if the interest is a disabled person's interest within *IHTA 1984, s 89B(1)(c)(d)*, a transitional serial interest within *IHTA 1984, ss 49B–49E* or an immediate post-death interest within *IHTA 1984, s 49A* (see 320.4 below). The provisions also apply where a UK-domiciled person becomes beneficially entitled to an interest in possession on or after 9 December 2009 by a disposition which is not a transfer of value as a result of *IHTA 1984, s 10* (dispositions not intended to confer gratuitous benefit). [*IHTA 1984, s 49(1A); FA 2010, s 53*]. Otherwise, an interest in possession to which a person becomes beneficially entitled on or after 22 March 2006 is treated as relevant property subject to the SETTLEMENTS WITHOUT INTERESTS IN POSSESSION (321) rules. [*IHTA 1984, s 59(1)(2); FA 2006, Sch 20 para 20*].

(b) An interest in possession to which a person ('B') becomes beneficially entitled during the period 22 March 2006 to 5 October 2008 is a transitional serial interest if the settlement was created before 22 March 2006, immediately before that date a person was beneficially entitled to an interest in possession (the '*prior interest*'), and B became beneficially entitled to his interest on the prior interest coming to an end. B's interest must not be a disabled person's interest and the settlement must not be within the rules for TRUSTS FOR BEREAVED MINORS (323). [*IHTA 1984, s 49C; FA 2006, Sch 20 para 5; FA 2008, s 141*].

(c) Where a person ('C') becomes beneficially entitled to an interest in possession after 5 October 2008, that interest qualifies as a transitional serial interest only where the interest arises on coming to an end of a prior interest in possession on the death of C's spouse/civil partner. The prior interest must have been held by the spouse or civil partner immediately before 22 March 2006. C's interest must not be a disabled person's interest and the settlement must not be within the rules for TRUSTS FOR BEREAVED MINORS (323). [*IHTA 1984, s 49D; FA 2006, Sch 20 para 5; FA 2008, s 141*]. See also *IHTA 1984, s 49E* for treatment of an interest as a transitional serial interest where the settled property consists of rights under a life assurance contract.

320.3 IMMEDIATE POST-DEATH INTERESTS

[*IHTA 1984, s 49; FA 2006, Sch 20 para 5*]

Garth, who is married to Maud, dies on 12 January 2012 having already made potentially exempt gifts on 21 May 2009 of £331,000. By his will he leaves his assets to Maud in trust for life and then on her death on trusts to his adult son Richard for life. His estate is valued at £760,000. Garth had made no gifts prior to 5 April 2009 other than to use his annual exemptions prior to 2008/09.

Maud dies on 8 January 2014 when the trust assets are valued at £800,000. Her free estate is valued at £100,000 and she has made no transfers in the preceding seven years, other than to utilise her annual exemptions.

320.3 IHT   Settlements with Interests in Possession

IHT payable on death of Garth

		£	£
Value transferred on 21 May 2009			331,000
Deduct annual exemptions	2009/10	3,000	
	2008/09	3,000	6,000
			£325,000

IHT on chargeable gift of £325,000 is charged in the nil rate band up to £325,000. The balance of the estate left on trust for wife Maud is exempt under *IHTA 1984, s 18*. Garth has no unused nil rate band to transfer to Maud.

IHT payable on death of Maud

	£
Trust assets	800,000
Free estate	100,000
	900,000

	£
£0–325,000	Nil
£325,001–£900,000 at 40%	£230,000
IHT payable	£230,000

Notes

(a) The interest in possession provisions apply in respect of interests to which a person becomes beneficially entitled on or after 22 March 2006 only if the interest is a disabled person's interest within *IHTA 1984, s 89B(1)(c)(d)*, a transitional serial interest within *IHTA 1984, ss 49B–49E* (see 320.3 above) or an immediate post-death interest within *IHTA 1984, s 49A*. The provisions also apply where a UK-domiciled person becomes beneficially entitled to an interest in possession on or after 9 December 2009 by a disposition which is not a transfer of value as a result of *IHTA 1984, s 10* (dispositions not intended to confer gratuitous benefit). [*IHTA 1984, s 49(1A); FA 2010, s 53*]. Otherwise, an interest in possession to which a person becomes beneficially entitled on or after 22 March 2006 is treated as relevant property subject to the SETTLEMENTS WITHOUT INTERESTS IN POSSESSION (321) rules. [*IHTA 1984, s 59(1)(2); FA 2006, Sch 20 para 20*].

(b) An interest in possession in a settlement is an immediate post-death interest only if the settlement is effected by will or intestacy and the person holding the interest became beneficially entitled to it on the death of the testator or intestate. The interest in possession must not be a disabled person's interest and the settlement must not be within the rules for TRUSTS FOR BEREAVED MINORS (323). [*IHTA 1984, s 49A; FA 2006, Sch 20 para 5*].

Settlements with Interests in Possession   IHT 320.3

(c)   Richard's interest in possession is not an immediate post-death interest as he did not become entitled to his interest in possession on the death of Garth. It is not a transitional serial interest (see note (c) to **320.3** above) or a disabled person's interest. His interest is therefore relevant property subject to the SETTLEMENTS WITHOUT INTERESTS IN POSSESSION **(321)** rules.

321 Settlements without Interests in Possession

In all examples in this chapter, where the value of trust property is given, it is assumed that this does not include any undistributed and unaccumulated income. Such income is not treated as a taxable trust asset. (Revenue Statement of Practice SP 8/86).

321.1 RATE OF TEN-YEAR ANNIVERSARY CHARGE

(A) **Post-26 March 1974 settlements**

[*IHTA 1984, ss 64, 66*]

On 1 May 1993 S settled £150,000 net, £100,000 to be held on discretionary trusts and £50,000 in trust for his brother B for life. At the date of the transfer S had a cumulative total of chargeable transfers of £67,000. £20,000 (gross) was advanced from the discretionary trusts to C on 1 March 2001.

The property held on discretionary trusts was valued at £177,000 on 1 May 2003.

On 1 January 2013 B died, when the property subject to his interest in possession was valued at £95,000. The whole trust property was valued at £322,000 on 1 May 2013 of which £105,000 derived from B's fund. The trustees had made no advances other than that to C.

It is assumed that rates of tax remain at the level for transfers after 5 April 2013.

1 May 2003 Ten-year anniversary charge

	£
Assumed chargeable transfer	
(i) value of relevant property immediately before the ten-year anniversary	177,000
(ii) value, at date of settlement, of property which was not, and has not become, relevant property	50,000
(iii) value, at date of settlement, of property in related settlement	—
	£227,000
Assumed transferor's cumulative total	
(i) value of chargeable transfers made by settlor in seven-year period ending on date of settlement	67,000
(ii) amounts on which proportionate charges have been levied in ten years before the anniversary	20,000
	£87,000

	Gross	Tax
	£	£
Assumed cumulative total	87,000	—

321.1 IHT Settlements without Interests in Possession

	Gross £	Tax £
Assumed transfer	227,000	11,800
	£314,000	£11,800

$$\text{Effective rate of tax } \frac{11,800}{227,000} \times 100 = \underline{5.19823\%}$$

Ten-year anniversary charge

The IHT payable is at 30% of the effective rate on the relevant property

IHT payable = 30% × 5.19823% × £177,000 = £2,760

1 May 2013 Ten-year anniversary charge

	£
Assumed chargeable transfer	
(i) value of relevant property immediately prior to the ten-year anniversary	322,000
(ii) value at date of settlement of property which was not and has not become relevant property	—
(iii) value at date of settlement of property in related settlement	—
	£322,000
Assumed transferor's cumulative total	
(i) value of chargeable transfers made by settlor in seven-year period ending on date of settlement	67,000
(ii) amounts on which proportionate charges have been levied in ten years before the anniversary	—
	£67,000

	Gross £	Tax £
Assumed cumulative total	67,000	—
Assumed transfer	322,000	12,800
	£389,000	£12,800

$$\text{Effective rate of tax } \frac{12,800}{322,000} \times 100 = \underline{3.97515\%}$$

Ten-year anniversary charge

Of the relevant property, £105,000 had not been relevant property for the period 1 May 2003–1 January 2013, i.e. 38 complete quarters.

IHT payable

Settlements without Interests in Possession   IHT 321.1

			£
At 30% × 3.97515%	= 1.19% on £217,000		2,582

At 30% × 3.97515%	= 1.19%		
Less 38/40 × 30% × 3.97515%	= 1.13%		
	0.06% on £105,000		63
Total IHT payable			£2,645

(B) **Pre-27 March 1974 settlements**

[*IHTA 1984, ss 64, 66*]

On 1 June 1971 T settled property on discretionary trusts. The trustees made the following advances (gross) to beneficiaries

1.1.74	H	£10,000
1.1.77	B	£20,000
1.1.82	C	£60,000
1.1.88	D	£40,000
1.1.94	E	£80,000

On 1 June 1991 the settled property was valued at £175,000, on 1 June 2001 £180,000.

1 June 1991 Ten-year anniversary charge

Assumed chargeable transfer			
Value of relevant property		£	£175,000
Assumed transferor's cumulative total			
(i) Aggregate of distribution payments made between 1 June 1981 and 8 March 1982		60,000	
(ii) Aggregate of amounts on which proportionate charge arises between 9 March 1982 and 1 June 1991		40,000	£100,000

	Gross	Tax
	£	£
Assumed cumulative total	100,000	—
Assumed chargeable transfer	175,000	27,000
	£275,000	£27,000

$$\text{Effective rate of tax} = \frac{27,000}{175,000} \times 100 = \underline{15.429}\%$$

Ten-year anniversary charge

The IHT payable is at 30% of the effective rate on the relevant property.

IHT payable = 30% × 15.429% × £175,000 = £8,100

321.1 IHT Settlements without Interests in Possession

1 June 2001 Ten-year anniversary charge

Assumed chargeable transfer		
Value of relevant property		£180,000
Assumed transferor's cumulative total		
Aggregate of amount on which proportionate charge arises between 1 June 1991 and 1 June 2001		£80,000

	Gross £	Tax £
Assumed cumulative total	80,000	—
Assumed chargeable transfer	180,000	3,600
	£260,000	£3,600

$$\text{Effective rate of tax} = \frac{3,600}{180,000} \times 100 = 2\%$$

Ten-year anniversary charge

The IHT payable is at 30% of the effective rate on the relevant property.

IHT payable = 30% × 2% × £180,000 = £1,080

1 June 2011 Ten-year anniversary charge

Not illustrated.

321.2 RATE OF PROPORTIONATE CHARGE BEFORE THE FIRST TEN-YEAR ANNIVERSARY

(A) **Post-26 March 1974 settlements**

[*IHTA 1984, ss 65, 68*]

On 1 April 2005 M settled £60,000 (net) on discretionary trusts. His cumulative total of chargeable transfers (gross) prior to the settlement was £290,000. On 3 December 2013 he added £20,000 (net), having made no chargeable transfers since 1 April 2005.

On 11 October 2013 the trustees had advanced £40,000 to N, and on 1 March 2014 the trustees distributed the whole of the remaining funds equally to P and Q. The remaining funds were valued at £110,000, of which £88,000 derived from the original settlement, and £22,000 from the addition.

11 October 2013 proportionate charge

Assumed chargeable transfer		
(i) Value of property in the settlement at date of settlement		60,000

Settlements without Interests in Possession   IHT 321.2

(ii) Value at date of settlement of property in related settlement —
(iii) Value at date of addition of property added —

£60,000

Assumed transferor's cumulative total
 Value of chargeable transfers made by settlor in seven-year period ending on date of settlement   £290,000

	Gross £	Tax £
Assumed cumulative total	290,000	—
Assumed transfer	60,000	5,000
	£350,000	£5,000

$$\text{Effective rate of tax} = \frac{5{,}000}{60{,}000} \times 100 = \underline{8.33\%}$$

Appropriate fraction

The number of complete quarters that have elapsed between the date of settlement, 1 April 2005, and the advance on 11 October 2013 is 34.

IHT is charged at the appropriate fraction of the effective rate on the property advanced.

$$\text{IHT payable} = 30\% \times \frac{34}{40} \times 8.33\% \times £40{,}000$$

$$= 2.12\% \times £40{,}000$$

$$= \underline{£848}$$

Had the advance of £40,000 been net, the IHT payable would be

$$\frac{2.12}{100 - 2.12} \times £40{,}000 = \underline{£866}$$

and the gross advance would be £40,866

1 March 2014 proportionate charge

As property has been added to the settlement, the effective rate of tax is recalculated.

Assumed chargeable transfer	£
(i) Value of property in settlement at date of settlement	60,000
(ii) Value at date of settlement of property in related settlement	—
(iii) Value at date of addition of property added	20,000
	£80,000

Assumed transferor's cumulative total
 Value of chargeable transfers made by settlor in seven-year period ending on date of settlement   £290,000

321.2 IHT Settlements without Interests in Possession

	Gross	Tax
	£	£
Assumed cumulative total	290,000	—
Assumed transfer	80,000	9,000
	£370,000	£9,000

$$\text{Effective rate of tax} = \frac{9,000}{80,000} \times 100 = 11.25\%$$

Appropriate fraction

The number of complete quarters that have elapsed between the date of settlement, 1 April 2005, and the advance on 1 March 2014 is 35.

The number of complete quarters that elapsed between the date of settlement, 1 April 2005, and 3 December 2013, the date on which property was added, was 34.

The IHT is charged at the appropriate fraction of the effective rate on the property advanced

		£
$30\% \times \frac{35}{40} \times 11.25\%$ on £88,000 =		2,598
$30\% \times \frac{(35-34)}{40} \times 11.25\%$ on £22,000 =		18
	£110,000	
IHT payable on advance of £110,000		£2,616

(B) **Settlor dies within 7 years of settlement — post-26 March 1974 settlement**

On 1 July 2009 T settled £335,000 net on discretionary trusts. His only other transfer had been a gift of £70,000 to his brother B on 1 June 2008. On 7 March 2011 the trustees advanced £70,000 to B, who agreed to pay any IHT due. On 30 August 2013 T died.

Proportionate charge 7 March 2011

At the time of the advance, T had made no chargeable transfers in the seven years prior to the settlement (the gift to B being a PET).

Assumed chargeable transfer	
Value of property in the settlement at the date of settlement	£335,000
Assumed transferor's cumulative total	Nil

Settlements without Interests in Possession IHT 321.2

Tax on an assumed transfer of £335,000 = £2,000

$$\text{Effective rate of tax} = \frac{2,000}{335,000} \times 100 = 0.59\%$$

Appropriate fraction

The number of complete quarters that have elapsed between the date of the settlement, 1 July 2009, and the advance on 7 March 2011 is 6.

IHT is charged at the appropriate fraction of the effective rate on the property advanced.

$$\text{IHT} = 30\% \times \frac{6}{40} \times 0.59\% \times £70,000$$

$$= 0.06165\% \times £70,000$$

$$= £19$$

On the settlor's death within seven years, the PET on 1 June 2008 becomes a chargeable transfer. There will be additional IHT payable by the trustees on the creation of the settlement, and additional IHT payable by B on the advance to him from the settlement.

The gross gift to the settlement, after deducting the 2009/10 annual exemption, was

	Gross	Tax	Net
	£	£	£
	312,000	—	312,000
	24,000	4,000	20,000
	£336,000	£4,000	£332,000

Additional IHT is payable to increase the charge to 60% of full rates at the time of death (death between 4 and 5 years after gift), with a previous chargeable transfer to B of £67,000 (after deducting the 2008/09 annual exemption).

	Gross	Tax	Net
	£	£	£
Prior transfer	67,000	—	67,000
	336,000	31,200	304,800
	£403,000	£31,200	£371,800

	£
IHT at 60% of full rates 60% × £31,200	18,720
Deduct paid on lifetime chargeable transfer	4,000
Additional IHT payable	£14,720

The additional IHT is payable by the trustees, reducing the value of property settled to £335,000 − £14,720 = £320,280.

321.2 IHT   Settlements without Interests in Possession

The IHT on the advance to B is recalculated

Assumed chargeable transfer	£320,280

Assumed transferor's cumulative total
Chargeable transfers made by the settlor in 7 years prior to the settlement (gift 1 June 2008)   £67,000

	Gross	Tax
	£	£
Assumed cumulative total	67,000	—
Assumed transfer	320,280	12,456
	£387,280	£12,456

$$\text{Effective rate of tax} = \frac{12,456}{387,280} \times 100 = 3.22\%$$

The appropriate fraction is $^6/_{40}$ (unchanged).

$$\text{IHT borne} = 30\% \times \frac{6}{40} \times 3.22\% \times £70,000$$

$$= 0.1449\% \times £70,000$$

$$= £101$$

	£
IHT due	101
Deduct already paid	19
IHT payable	£82

321.3 RATE OF PROPORTIONATE CHARGE BETWEEN TEN-YEAR ANNIVERSARIES

[*IHTA 1984, ss 65, 69, Sch 2 para 3*]

On 1 January 1994 G settled £70,000 (net) on discretionary trusts. His cumulative total of chargeable transfers at that date was £150,000. On 1 January 2004 the funds were valued at £140,000, no advances having been made. On 1 February 2006 the trustees advanced £30,000 (gross) to H. On 1 January 2007 G added £80,000 to the settlement, having made cumulative chargeable transfers in the previous seven years of £30,000. On 1 May 2013 the trustees advanced £40,000 to F from the funds originally settled.

It is assumed that rates of tax remain unchanged following the change of rates on 6 April 2009.

1 February 2006 advance to H

8 complete quarters have elapsed since the ten-year anniversary charge so the appropriate fraction is 8/40ths. The rate of tax is therefore 8/40ths of the rate at which IHT would have been charged on the last ten-year anniversary if the Table of Rates in force at 1 February 2006 had been in force at the date of the ten-year anniversary, 1 January 2004.

Settlements without Interests in Possession   IHT 321.3

Tax would have been charged at the last ten-year anniversary as follows

	£
Assumed chargeable transfer	
(i) value of relevant property immediately before the ten-year anniversary	140,000
(ii) value, at date of settlement, of property which was not, and has not become, relevant property	—
(iii) value at date of settlement of property in related settlement	—
	£140,000

	£
Assumed transferor's cumulative total	
(i) value of chargeable transfers made by settlor in seven-year period ending on date of settlement	150,000
(ii) amounts on which proportionate charges have been levied in ten years before the anniversary	—
	£140,000

	Gross £	Tax £
Assumed cumulative total	150,000	—
Assumed transfer	140,000	3,000
	£290,000	£3,000

$$\text{Effective rate} = \frac{3{,}000}{140{,}000} \times 100 = 2.143\%$$

Rate of tax at ten-year anniversary = 30% × 2.143% = <u>0.643%</u>

Therefore rate of tax on advance to H

$$= 8/40 \times 0.643\%$$

IHT payable = 8/40 × 0.643% × £30,000 = £38

1 May 2013 advance to F

Since property has been added to the settlement, a hypothetical rate of tax at the previous ten-year anniversary must be recalculated as if the added property had been added prior to the anniversary.

	£	Gross £	Tax £
Assumed cumulative total		150,000	—
Assumed transfer			
property at anniversary	140,000		
added property	80,000	220,000	9,000

321.3 IHT   Settlements without Interests in Possession

	Gross	Tax
£	£	£
	£370,000	£9,000

$$\text{Effective rate} = \frac{9{,}000}{220{,}000} \times 100 = 4.09\%$$

Rate of tax that would have been charged at the ten-year anniversary
$$= 30\% \times 4.09\%$$
$$= 1.227\%$$

The advance to F took place 37 complete quarters after the ten-year anniversary. The rate of tax is 37/40 × 1.227% = <u>1.135%</u>

If the advance to F was £40,000 gross

$$\text{IHT payable} = £40{,}000 \times 1.135\% = \underline{£454}$$

If the advance to F was £40,000 net

$$\text{IHT payable} = \frac{1.135}{100 - 1.135} \times £40{,}000 = £459$$

The gross distribution would then be £40,459.

322 Transfers on Death

322.1 POTENTIALLY EXEMPT TRANSFER FOLLOWED BY LOAN FROM DONEE TO DONOR

[*FA 1986, ss 103, 104; SI 1987 No 1130, Reg 6*]

X gives cash of £330,000 to Y on 1 November 2008. On 20 December 2008, Y makes a loan of £330,000 to X. On 31 May 2009, X makes a gift of £20,000 into a discretionary trust. X dies on 15 April 2014, his death estate is worth £345,000 before deducting the liability of £330,000 to Y which remains outstanding. X has made no lifetime transfers other than those specified, except that he has used his annual exemptions for all relevant years. It is assumed that rates of tax remain unchanged following the change made on 6 April 2009.

First calculation under Reg 6(3)(a)

The transfer of £330,000 in November 2008 is a PET which becomes chargeable by virtue of X's death within seven years. However, for the purpose of this calculation the PET is ignored but no deduction is allowed against the death estate for the outstanding loan.

No IHT is due in respect of the chargeable transfer in May 2009 as it is covered by the Nil rate band.

The estate of £345,000 is charged in the band £20,001 to £365,000.

		£
20,001–325,000	at nil%	Nil
325,001–365,000	at 40%	16,000
IHT due		£16,000

Second calculation under Reg 6(3)(b)

The PET in November 2008 is charged on death in the normal way and the loan is deducted from the death estate.

The PET is charged in the band £0 to £330,000.

		£
0–325,000	at nil%	Nil
325,001–330,000	at 40%	2,000
		£2,000

IHT at 40% of full rates	
(death between 5 and 6 years after transfer)	£800

Additional tax is due on the chargeable transfer in May 2009, £20,000 is charged in the band £330,001 to £350,000.

20,000 at 40%	£8,000

322.1 IHT   Transfers on Death

IHT at 60% of full rates	
(death between 4 and 5 years after transfer)	£4,800

Tax is charged on the death estate of £15,000 (£345,000–330,000) in the band £350,001 to £365,000.

350,001–365,000 at 40%	£6,000
Total IHT due £(800 + 4,800 + 6,000)	£11,600

The first calculation gives the higher amount of tax, so the PET is ignored and no deduction is allowed for the outstanding loan against the death estate.

Notes

(a) If the PET had exceeded the loan, the excess would not be ignored for the purpose of the first calculation above.

(b) If X had made more than one PET to Y and the total PETs exceeded the amount of the loan, only PETs up to the amount of the loan are ignored for the purpose of the first calculation above, later PETs being disregarded in preference to earlier ones.

322.2 REDUCED RATE FOR ESTATES WITH 10% GIFTS TO CHARITIES

[*IHTA 1984, Sch 1A; FA 2012, s 209, Sch 33*]

(A)

The estate of Percival who died on 30 April 2013 is valued at £425,000, comprising quoted investments and cash. He leaves a legacy of £10,000 to the National Trust and the residue of £415,000 less inheritance tax passes to his children. Percival had made no chargeable transfers in the seven years before his death.

Percival's estate consists of only one component (see note (b)), the general component, and its baseline amount is calculated as follows.

	£
Step 1. Determine value transferred by chargeable transfer attributable to component	425,000
Estate	
Less gift to charity	10,000
	415,000
Step 2. Deduct available nil-rate band	325,000
	90,000
Step 3. Add back gift to charity	10,000
Baseline amount	£100,000

As the donated amount (£10,000) is at least 10% of the baseline amount for the general component, that component (and in this case the entire estate) qualifies for the 36% rate of inheritance tax.

Transfers on Death   IHT 322.2

The inheritance tax due on the chargeable estate (£425,000 – £10,000) is charged in the band £Nil to £415,000.

		£
Nil–325,000	at nil%	Nil
325,001–415,000	at 40%	32,400
IHT due		£32,400

Notes

(a) For deaths on or after 6 April 2012, inheritance tax is charged on the net chargeable value of any component (see note (b)) of an estate at a rate of 36% where 10% or more of the 'baseline amount' of that component has been left to charity. [*IHTA 1984, Sch 1A paras 1, 2; FA 2012, Sch 33 paras 1, 10*].

(b) An estate can consist of up to three components:

- the survivorship component, consisting of any joint or common property liable to pass on death by survivorship;
- the settled property component, consisting of settled property comprised in the estate by virtue of an interest in possession to which the deceased was beneficially entitled; and
- the general component, consisting of all other property comprised in the estate other than gifts with reservation.

[*IHTA 1984, Sch 1A para 3; FA 2012, Sch 33 para 1*].

(c) The steps taken in calculating the baseline amount are those set out in *IHTA 1984, Sch 1A para 5*. In this simple example the deduction of the gift to charity in step 1 followed by its adding back in step 3 appears redundant but where there is more than one component, this is necessary in apportioning the nil-rate band between components. See (B) below.

(d) The gift to charity reduces the residue by only £2,400 (£10,000 gift less IHT reduction (£40,000 – £32,400)).

(e) Where the conditions are satisfied, the reduced rate applies automatically. An election can, however, be made to disapply the reduced rate for all or any components of the estate. Such an election must be made within two years after the death by all the appropriate persons (as in note (b) to (B) below). [*IHTA 1984, Sch 1A paras 8, 9; FA 2012, Sch 33 para 1*].

(B) **Election to merge parts of the estate**

The facts are as in (A) above, except that Percival's legacy to the National Trust is £25,000 and he has also had an interest in possession since 2000 in a settlement valued at death at £100,000.

If no election is made under *IHTA 1984, Sch 1A para 7*, the inheritance tax position is as follows.

General component

322.2 IHT   Transfers on Death

	£
Step 1. Determine value transferred by chargeable transfer attributable to component	
Estate	425,000
Less gift to charity	25,000
	400,000
Step 2. Deduct appropriate proportion of available nil-rate band*	260,000
	140,000
Step 3. Add back gift to charity	25,000
Baseline amount	£165,000
*£325,000 × (£400,000/£500,000) = £260,000	

As the donated amount (£25,000) is at least 10% of the baseline amount for the general component (£16,500), that component qualifies for the 36% rate of inheritance tax. No gift to charity is made out of the settled property component, so that component does not qualify for the lower rate. Inheritance tax is chargeable as follows.

	£
Free estate	425,000
Interest in possession	100,000
	525,000
Less gift to charity	25,000
	500,000
Less nil-rate band	325,000
	175,000
£140,000 @ 36%	50,400
£35,000 @ 40%	14,000
	£64,400

If an election is made under *IHTA 1984, Sch 1A para 7*, the inheritance tax position is as follows.

Merged components

	£
Step 1. Determine value transferred by chargeable transfer attributable to merged components	
Free estate	425,000
Interest in possession	100,000
	525,000
Less gift to charity	25,000
	500,000
Step 2. Deduct available nil-rate band*	325,000
	175,000
Step 3. Add back gift to charity	25,000
Baseline amount	£200,000

As the donated amount (£25,000) is at least 10% of the baseline amount for the merged components (£20,000), those components qualify for the 36% rate of inheritance tax. Inheritance tax is chargeable as follows.

	£
Free estate	425,000
Interest in possession	100,000
	525,000
Less gift to charity	25,000
	500,000
Less nil-rate band	325,000
	175,000
£175,000 @ 36%	£63,000

Notes

(a) Where an estate includes more than one component and one of the components qualifies for the reduced rate, an election may be made to treat that component and one or more other eligible parts as one single component. If the 10% test is met for the merged component, then the reduced rate applies to the whole of the merged component. The parts that are eligible to be merged with the qualifying component are the other two components and all the property forming part of the estate by reason of the gifts with reservation provisions. [*IHTA 1984, Sch 1A para 7(1)–(5); FA 2012, Sch 33 para 1*].

(b) The election must be made within two years after the death by all those who are appropriate persons with respect to the qualifying component and each of the eligible parts to be included. The appropriate persons are:

- in relation to the survivorship component, all those to whom the property in the component passes;
- in relation to the settled property component, the trustees;
- in relation to the general component, all the personal representatives (or, if there are none, all those who are liable to inheritance tax attributable to the property in the component); and.
- in relation to property forming part of the estate under the gifts with reservation provisions, all those in whom the property concerned is vested when the election is to be made.

[*IHTA 1984, Sch 1A paras 7(6)(7), 9; FA 2012, Sch 33 para 1*].

(c) Where there is more than one component, the available nil-rate band is apportioned between the components for the purposes of step 2, in proportion to the amounts determined at step 1 for each component. [*IHTA 1984, Sch 1A para 5; FA 2012, Sch 33 para 1*].

323 Trusts for Bereaved Minors

[*IHTA 1984, ss 71A–71H; FA 2013, Sch 44 paras 2–6, 9*]

323.1 TRANSITIONAL PROVISIONS FOR PRE-22 MARCH 2006 TRUSTS

(A)

Jacob dies in 2000. Under the terms of his will he leaves his estate on accumulation and maintenance trusts for the benefit of his two children, Lisa and Luke, then aged six and four. The children are to become absolutely entitled to their share of the settled property at 18.

From its creation in 2000 until 21 March 2006 the trust is within the regime for ACCUMULATION AND MAINTENANCE TRUSTS (**301**).

On and after 22 March 2006 the trust is a trust for bereaved minors within *IHTA 1984, ss 71A–71C*. No IHT charges will arise on the children becoming absolutely entitled, on the death of either of the children, or on the settled property being paid or applied for their advancement or benefit.

Notes

(a) To qualify as a trust for a bereaved minor, the settlement (whether the settled property is settled before, on or after 22 March 2006), must be for the benefit of a bereaved minor and must be established under the will of a deceased parent (including a step-parent or other person with parental responsibility) of the minor, on the intestacy of a parent or under the Criminal Injuries Compensation Scheme. The minor must become absolutely entitled to the settled property and any income arising (including accumulated income) on or before attaining the age of 18. [*IHTA 1984, s 71A*].

(b) Existing accumulation and maintenance trusts which meet the above conditions are treated as trusts for bereaved minors from 22 March 2006. [*IHTA 1984, s 71(1B)*].

(B)

The facts are as in (A) above, except that the children become absolutely entitled only at 25.

From its creation in 2000 until 5 April 2008 the trust is within the regime for ACCUMULATION AND MAINTENANCE TRUSTS (**301**).

On and after 6 April 2008, the trust is an 18-to-25 trust within *IHTA 1984, ss 71D–71G*. See **301.2(A)** ACCUMULATION AND MAINTENANCE TRUSTS.

Notes

(a) The settlement does not qualify as a trust for bereaved minors as the beneficiaries do not become entitled absolutely to settled property on or before attaining age 18.

(b) On its failure as an accumulation and maintenance settlement, the trust qualifies as an 18-to-25 trust under both the transitional provisions of *IHTA 1984, s 71D(3)(4)* and the bereaved minors provisions of *IHTA 1984, s 71D(1)(2)*.

323.1 IHT   Trusts for Bereaved Minors

(c)   On 6 April 2008, the settlement ceases to be an accumulation and maintenance trust because the remaining beneficiaries do not become entitled absolutely to settled property on or before attaining age 18 as required from that date (see note (b) to **301.1** ACCUMULATION AND MAINTENANCE TRUSTS). No charge to IHT arises and the settlement becomes an 18-to-25 trust.

(C)

The facts are as in (A) above, except that the children become entitled only to an interest in possession on attaining the age of 18.

From its creation in 2000 until 5 April 2008 the trust is within the regime for ACCUMULATION AND MAINTENANCE TRUSTS **(301)**.

On and after 6 April 2008, the trust is a relevant property trust, subject to the rules for SETTLEMENTS WITHOUT INTERESTS IN POSSESSION **(321)**.

Note

(a)   After 5 April 2008, the settlement does not qualify as an accumulation and maintenance settlement, a trust for bereaved minors or an 18-to-25 trust as the beneficiaries take only an interest in possession at age 18.

324 Trusts for Disabled Persons

[*IHTA 1984, ss 74, 89, 89A; FA 2013, Sch 44 paras 6–10*]

324.1 PROPERTY SETTLED BEFORE 10 MARCH 1981

In 1972 Q settled £50,000 in trust mainly for his disabled son P, but with power to apply property to his daughter S. On 1 January 2013 the trustees advanced £5,000 gross to S on her marriage.

There will be a charge to IHT on the payment to S.

The relevant period is the period from settlement of the funds or, if later, 13 March 1975, to 1 January 2014, i.e. 155 complete quarters.

The rate of IHT is the aggregate of

0.25% for each of the first	40	quarters	10.00%
0.20% for each of the next	40	quarters	8.00%
0.15% for each of the next	40	quarters	6.00%
0.10% for each of the next	35	quarters	3.50%
	155		27.50%

IHT payable is £5,000 × 27.50% = £1,375

324.2 PROPERTY SETTLED AFTER 9 MARCH 1981 AND BEFORE 8 APRIL 2013

Assume the facts in 324.1 above except that the settlement was made on 1 July 1982.

If the trust secures that not less than half the settled property which is applied during P's life is applied for his benefit, then P is treated as beneficially entitled to an interest in possession in the settled property. The transfer to S is a potentially exempt transfer which may become chargeable in the event of P's death within seven years of the transfer. The gift in consideration of marriage exemption applies (£1,000 on a gift from brother to sister) subject to the required notice.

Otherwise, the trust is discretionary and the IHT liability, if any, would be calculated under the rules applying to SETTLEMENTS WITHOUT INTERESTS IN POSSESSION (321).

324.3 PROPERTY SETTLED AFTER 7 APRIL 2013

Assume the facts in 324.1 above except that the settlement was made on 1 July 2013, and the advance to S was made on 1 April 2014.

The trustees have the power to apply amounts otherwise than for the benefit of the disabled person in excess of the annual limit. The annual limit is the lower of £3,000 and 3% of the maximum value of the settled property in the period in question (in this case £1,500).

The trust is discretionary and falls within the rules applying to SETTLEMENTS WITHOUT INTERESTS IN POSSESSION (321).

324.4 IHT   Trusts for Disabled Persons

324.4 SELF-SETTLEMENT BY PERSON WITH CONDITION EXPECTED TO LEAD TO DISABILITY

[*IHTA 1984, s 89A; FA 2013, Sch 44 paras 7, 9*]

On 31 July 2013 X, who is in the early stages of Alzheimer's disease and currently resides in a care home, settles £300,000 into discretionary trust for his benefit in the future.

X is treated as beneficially entitled to an interest in possession in the settled property. The transfer into settlement of the property is a potentially exempt transfer which may become chargeable in the event of X's death within seven years of the transfer.

325 Trusts for Employees

[*IHTA 1984, s 72; FA 2006, Sch 20 para 21*]

325.1 POSITION OF THE TRUST

A qualifying trust for employees of a close company was created on 1 July 1984. On 4 May 1994, £15,000 is paid to a beneficiary who is a participator in the close company and holds 15% of the issued ordinary shares. On 4 August 2013, the whole of the remaining fund of £200,000 ceases to be held on qualifying trusts.

4 May 1994

There is a charge to IHT. The relevant period is the period from 1 July 1984 to 4 May 1994, i.e. 39 complete quarters.

The rate of tax is

0.25% for 39 quarters = 9.75%

$$\text{IHT payable is } \frac{9.75}{100 - 9.75} \times £15,000 = £1,620$$

1 July 1994 and 1 July 2004

There is no liability at the ten-year anniversaries.

4 August 2013

There is a charge to IHT. The relevant period is the period from 1 July 1984 to 4 August 2012, i.e. 116 complete quarters.

The rate of tax is

0.25% for 40 quarters =	10.00%
0.20% for 40 quarters =	8.00%
0.15% for 36 quarters =	5.40%
	23.40%

IHT payable is £200,000 × 23.4% = £46,800

326 Valuation

326.1 LAND SOLD WITHIN FOUR YEARS OF DEATH
[*IHTA 1984, ss 190–198*]

(A)

A (a bachelor) died on 1 May 2010 owning four areas of land, as follows.

(i) 10 acres valued at death £20,000

(ii) 15 acres valued at death £30,000

(iii) 20 acres valued at death £30,000

(iv) 30 acres valued at death £40,000

He also owned a freehold house valued at death at £50,000.

In the four years following A's death, his executors made the following sales.

(A) Freehold house sold 15.11.10, proceeds £53,000, expenses £2,000.

(B) Land area (iii) sold 1.6.12, proceeds £29,500, expenses £1,500.

(C) Land area (ii) sold 8.8.13, proceeds £27,000, expenses £1,000.

(D) Land area (iv) sold 19.9.13, proceeds £42,000, expenses £3,000.

The following revisions must be calculated on a claim under IHTA 1984, Pt VI, Chapter IV

	£	
Gross sale proceeds of house	53,000	
Deduct probate value	50,000	£3,000
Gross sale proceeds of land area (ii)	27,000	
Deduct probate value	30,000	£(3,000)
Gross sale proceeds of land area (iii)	29,500	
Deduct probate value	30,000	£(500)

Notes

(a) The sale of area (iii) is disregarded as the loss on sale (before allowing for expenses) is less than 5% of £30,000 (£1,500) and is also lower than £1,000. [*IHTA 1984, s 191*].

(b) The overall allowable reduction on all sales is therefore nil even though there is a loss after expenses.

(c) For deaths after 15 March 1990, a sale *for less than the value at death* which is made in the fourth year after death is treated as having been made in the three years after death. [*IHTA 1984, s 197A*].

326.1 IHT Valuation

(B) Further purchases of land

A died on 30 June 2013 owning a house and a seaside flat.

At death the valuations were

	£
House	50,000
Flat	30,000
	£80,000
Sales by the executors realised (gross)	
House proceeds 1.7.14	42,000
Flat proceeds 1.12.14	33,000
	£75,000

On 1 May 2014, the executors bought a town house for the daughter for £40,000 (excluding costs).

Initially relief is due of £(80,000 − 75,000) £5,000

Recomputation of relief

$$\text{Appropriate fraction} = \frac{\text{Purchase price}}{\text{Selling price}} = \frac{40,000}{75,000} = \frac{8}{15}$$

	£	House £	£	Seaside Flat £
Value on death		50,000		30,000
Sale price	42,000			
Add (£50,000 − £42,000) × 8/15	4,267			
Revised value for IHT		46,267		
Sale price			33,000	
Deduct (£33,000 − £30,000) × 8/15			1,600	
Revised value for IHT				31,400
Revised relief		£3,733		£(1,400)
Total			£2,333	

Note

(a) The purchase is taken into account because it is made within the period 30 June 2013 (date of death) and 1 April 2015 (four months after the last of the sales affected by the claim). [*IHTA 1984, s 192(1)*]. If a sale made in the fourth year after death was affected by the claim (under *IHTA 1984, s 197A*), it would *not* be taken into account in determining the above-mentioned period. [*IHTA 1984, s 197A(3)*].

Valuation IHT 326.3

326.2 RELATED PROPERTY

[IHTA 1984, s 161]

On the death of a husband on 31 October 2013, the share capital of a private company was held as follows

	Shares	
Issued capital	10,000	
Husband	4,000	40%
Wife	4,000	40%
Others (employees)	2,000	20%
	10,000	100%

The value of an 80% holding is £80,000, while the value of a 40% holding is £24,000. In his will, the husband left his 4,000 shares to his daughter.

The related property rules apply to aggregate the shares of

Husband	4,000	
Wife	4,000	
Related property	8,000	shares

Chargeable transfer on legacy to daughter

| IHT value of 8,000 shares (80%) | £80,000 |
| IHT value attributed to legacy of husband's shares (4,000) | £40,000 |

(Subject to 100% business property relief if conditions satisfied.)

326.3 SHARES AND SECURITIES

Quoted shares sold within twelve months after death

[IHTA 1984, ss 178–189]

An individual died on 30 June 2013 and included in his estate was a portfolio of quoted investments. The executors sold certain investments within twelve months of death. The realisations were as follows

	Probate Value £	Gross Sales £
Share A	7,700	7,200
Share B	400	600
Share C	2,800	2,900

326.3 IHT Valuation

	Probate Value £	Gross Sales £
Share D	13,600	11,600
Share E	2,300	2,300
Share F	5,700	5,100
Share G	19,400	17,450
Share H	8,500	8,600
	£60,400	55,750
Incidental costs of sale		2,750
Net proceeds of sale		£53,000

On 1 September 2013, share J, having a probate value of £200 and still held by the executors was cancelled.

On 1 December 2013, share K, having a probate value of £1,000 has its stock exchange quotation suspended. On 30 June 2014, the investment is still held by the executors, its estimated value is £49 and the quotation remains suspended.

On 30 April 2014, the executors purchased a new holding for £1,750.

The executors would initially be able to claim a reduction of = £5,800
(£60,400 − £55,750) + (£200 − £1) + (£1,000 − £49)

After the purchase, the reduction is restricted as follows

$$\text{Relevant proportion} = \frac{\text{Reinvestment}}{\text{Total sales}} = \frac{1,750}{£55,750 + £1 + £49} = \frac{1,750}{55,800}$$

Original relief restricted by

$$\frac{1,750}{55,800} \times £5,800 = £182$$

Total relief £5,800 less £182   £5,618

Notes

(a) No costs of selling investments may be deducted from the sale proceeds.

(b) The cancelled shares are treated as sold for £1 immediately before cancellation. The suspended shares are treated as sold on the first anniversary of death at their value at that time (provided that value is less than their value on death). [*IHTA 1984, ss 186A, 186B*].

(c) The purchase is taken into account as it is made during the period beginning on date of death and ending two months after the end of the last sale taken into account (including deemed sales as in (b) above).

(d) The probate value of each of the investments sold will be adjusted, both for CGT and IHT purposes, to the gross sale proceeds plus the relevant proportion of the fall in value. Thus the probate value of share A will be revised from £7,700 to

Valuation IHT 326.3

$$£7,200 + \left(\frac{1,750}{55,800} \times (7,700 - 7,200)\right) = £7,216$$

(e) Although excluded from computation of the loss on sale for inheritance tax purposes, incidental costs of sale are deductible from proceeds in calculating CGT.

327 Woodlands

[*IHTA 1984, ss 114(2), 125–130, 208, 226(4), Sch 2 para 4*]

327.1 TAX CHARGE

(A)

A died owning woodlands valued at £275,000 being land valued at £200,000 and trees growing on the land valued at £75,000. The woodlands passed to his son D. The marginal IHT rate applicable was 50% but the executors elected to exclude the value of the trees from the taxable estate on A's death. D died six years later leaving the woodlands to trustees for his grandchildren. They were then valued at £400,000 being land at £250,000 and trees at £150,000. The rate of tax which would have applied to the value of trees on D's death was 40%, but once again the executors elected to exclude the value of the trees from his estate.

The trustees sold the woodlands for £500,000, including trees valued at £180,000, four years later.

The IHT on the trees is payable when the trees are sold. The trustees of the settlement pay IHT at what would have been the marginal rate on D's death had the tax scale at the time of the sale applied on D's death, e.g. 40% on £180,000 (the proceeds of sale) = £72,000.

Note

(a) If D had gifted the land (with the trees) just before his death, the IHT would have become payable on the trees at what would have been the marginal rate on A's death had the scale at the time of the gift applied on A's death, on the value of the trees at the date of the gift. IHT would also have been payable on D's lifetime transfer (this being a PET but becoming chargeable by virtue of D's death shortly afterwards) but the value transferred by this transfer would have been reduced by the deferred IHT charge. See (B) below.

(B)

B died in 1984 leaving woodlands, including growing timber valued at £100,000, to his daughter C. The executors elected to exclude the value of the timber from the taxable estate on B's death. B had made prior transfers of £50,000 and his taxable estate (excluding the growing timber) was valued at £210,000.

On 1 February 2008 C gave the woodlands to her nephew N, when the land was valued at £355,000 and the growing timber at £125,000. N agreed to pay any IHT on the gift. C died in January 2014, and had made no prior transfers other than to use her annual exemptions each year. It is assumed that IHT rates remain at their current level.

IHT on B's death

No IHT is payable on the growing timber until C's disposal when tax is charged on the net value at that time. The rates are those which would have applied (using the death scale applying on 1 February 2008) if that value had formed the highest part of B's estate on death. The tax was payable on 1 September 2008.

327.1 IHT   Woodlands

Deferred IHT payable £125,000 at 40%   £50,000

IHT on C's lifetime transfer

IHT is payable on C's gift to N as C died within 7 years of the gift. The deferred IHT is deducted from the value transferred.

	£
Value of land and timber	480,000
Deduct deferred IHT	50,000
Chargeable transfer	£430,000
IHT at death rates	
On first £325,000	—
On next £105,000 at 40%	42,000
£430,000	£42,000
IHT payable at 20% of full rates (death between 6 and 7 years after gift)	£8,400
Total IHT payable	
Deferred IHT	50,000
Lifetime transfer	8,400
	£58,400

Note

(a) In the above calculations it has been assumed that the woodlands were not run as a business either at the time of B's death or at the time of C's gift. If B had been running the woodlands as a business, such that business property relief would have been available on his death, the amount chargeable on C's disposal would have been reduced by 50%, i.e. to £62,500, on which IHT payable would have been £25,000. [*IHTA 1984, s 127(2)*]. If C ran the woodlands as a business (whether or not B had done so), business property relief would be available on her gift to N provided N also ran the woodlands as a business, but would be given after the credit for the deferred IHT. (With business property relief now usually at 100%, the order of set-off is not so relevant.)

		£
Value of land and timber		480,000
Deduct deferred IHT	say	25,000
		455,000
Deduct business property relief at, say, 100%		455,000
Chargeable transfer		Nil

Value Added Tax

401	Bad Debt Relief
402	Capital Goods
403	Catering
404	Hotels and Holiday Accommodation
405	Input Tax
406	Motor Cars
407	Output Tax
408	Partial Exemption
409	Records
410	Reduced Rate Supplies
411	Retail Schemes
412	Second-Hand Goods

401 Bad Debt Relief

[*VATA 1994, s 36; SI 1995 No 2518, Regs 165–172E; VAT Notice 700/18/13*]

401.1 PART PAYMENTS AND MUTUAL SUPPLIES

W Ltd has supplied goods to A Ltd. The sales ledger reveals the following amounts due

Invoice	Gross £	Net £	VAT £
16159 dated 31.7.13	487.39	406.16	81.23
15874 dated 12.7.13	364.19	364.19	—
14218 dated 12.6.13	238.04	238.04	—
14104 dated 10.6.13	256.58	213.82	42.76
	1,346.20	£1,222.21	£123.99
Less paid on account on 14104	100.00		
Amount due from A Ltd	£1,246.20		

A Ltd was, however, used by W Ltd for delivery work and there is one unpaid invoice for £143.75.

The bad debt relief claimable is as follows

	£
Amount due from A Ltd	1,246.20
Less amount due to A Ltd	143.75
Debt due from A Ltd	£1,102.45

The debt is attributed to

	Gross £	VAT £
Invoice 16159	487.39	81.23
Invoice 15874	364.19	—
Invoice 14218	238.04	—
Invoice 14104 (part) *	12.83	2.14
	£1,102.45	£83.37

The amount of bad debt relief claimable is £83.37.

*12.83 / 256.58 × £42.76 = £2.14

Notes

(a) Relief can be claimed provided the debt has been written off as a bad debt in the supplier' accounts and provided six months have elapsed from the date of supply and from the time when the consideration became due and payable.

401.1 VAT   Bad Debt Relief

(b) Where payments on account are specifically allocated by the customer, this allocation must be followed. General payments on account must be allocated to earliest supplies first, supplies on the same day being aggregated. Where the claimant owes money to the purchaser which can be set off, the amount of the debt for bad debt relief purposes must be reduced by the amount so owed.

401.2 SECOND-HAND GOODS

B, a second-hand dealer, buys a table for £400 and sells it for £500 under the margin scheme, i.e. his profit margin is £100.

If the customer only pays £450, bad debt relief claimable is

1/6 × £50 = £8.33

If the customer only pays £350, bad debt relief claimable is

1/6 × £100 = £16.67

Note

(a) Where a bad debt arises on goods sold under the margin scheme,

    (i) if the debt is equal to or less than the profit margin, relief may be claimed on the VAT fraction of the debt; and

    (ii) if the debt is greater than the profit margin, relief is limited to the VAT fraction of the profit margin.

401.3 REPAYMENT OF REFUND

In July 2013 a business sells goods for £120 (£100 plus £20 VAT). It receives no payment by the relevant date and claims bad debt relief of £20. It subsequently receives £75.00 from the customer for the goods.

The business must repay to HMRC the VAT element of the £75 received, calculated as follows.

$$\frac{75}{120} \times £20 = £12.50$$

402 Capital Goods

402.1 THE CAPITAL GOODS SCHEME

[SI 1995 No 2518, Regs 112–116; VAT Notice 706/2/11]

On 1 July 2006, A Ltd, a partly exempt business, acquired the freehold of a five storey office block, incurring VAT of £112,500. The premises are used as the head office administration block for the whole company. On 1 October 2013 the building is sold at a profit for £1.5 million to a company which only makes exempt supplies. The option to tax is not exercised.

A Ltd's partial exemption year runs to 31 March. Its claimable percentage of non-attributable input tax is as follows.

Year ended			
31 March 2007	80%	31 March 2011	75%
31 March 2008	90%	31 March 2012	85%
31 March 2009	75%	31 March 2013	90%
31 March 20010	60%	31 March 2014	95%

The input tax position is as follows

Year ended 31 March 2007 (Interval 1)
Initial input tax claim £112,500 × 80% =   £90,000

Year ended 31 March 2008 (Interval 2)
Additional input tax claimed

$$\frac{112{,}500}{10} \times (90 - 80)\% =$$ £1,125

Year ended 31 March 2009 (Interval 3)
Input tax repayable

$$\frac{112{,}500}{10} \times (80 - 75)\% =$$ (£562.50)

Year ended 31 March 2010 (Interval 4)
Input tax repayable

$$\frac{112{,}500}{10} \times (80 - 60.00)\% =$$ (£2,250)

402.1 VAT   Capital Goods

Year ended 31 March 2011 (Interval 5)
Input tax repayable

$$\frac{112{,}500}{10} \times (80-75)\% =$$
(£562.50)

Year ended 31 March 2012 (Interval 6)
Additional input tax claimed

$$\frac{112{,}500}{10} \times (85-80)\% =$$
£562.50

Year ended 31 March 2013 (Interval 7)
Additional input tax claimed

$$\frac{112{,}500}{10} \times (90-80)\% =$$
£1,125.00

Year ended 31 March 2014 (Interval 8)
Additional input tax claimed

$$\frac{112{,}500}{10} \times (95-80)\% =$$
£1,687.50

Adjustment in respect of Intervals 9 and 10
Input tax repayable

$$2 \times \frac{112{,}500}{10} \times (80-0)\% =$$
£18,000.00

(£16,312.50)

Notes

(a) The adjustment period for buildings is normally ten years.

(b) For the interval in which the building is sold, the adjustment is calculated in the normal way as if it had been used for the whole of the interval. This applies whether it was sold on the first or last day of the interval. For the remaining intervals, the recovery percentage is nil as the option to tax has not been exercised and the supply of the building is therefore exempt.

(c) If the option to tax is exercised on the sale of the building in Interval 8, instead of input tax of £18,000 being repayable in respect of Intervals 9 and 10, further input tax is claimable of

Capital Goods   VAT 402.1

$$2 \times \frac{112{,}500}{10} \times (100 - 80)\% = \qquad \underline{£4{,}500}$$

On the other hand, VAT of £300,000 is chargeable on the sale which is not recoverable by the exempt company, increasing the effective price to £1,800,000 which might not be acceptable to the purchaser.

(d)   See IT 3.3 CAPITAL ALLOWANCES for the interaction between the VAT Capital Goods Scheme and capital allowances on assets within the scheme.

403 Catering

403.1 SPECIAL METHOD FOR CATERERS

[*SI 1995 No 2518, Reg 73; VAT Notice 727, paras 8.3–8.8*]

A fish bar sells both fried fish and chips and wet fish and seafoods. It also has a small restaurant. It is impractical for the owner to keep a record of each sale as it takes place. He can, however, note his zero-rated supplies over a representative period which are

	£
Receipts from wet fish rounds	724
Shops sales of wet fish and seafoods	285
Sundries (cold leftovers)	28
	£1,037
Overall gross takings	£7,580

At the end of a given quarterly tax period, gross takings total £24,016.28.

Standard-rated percentage is

$$\frac{(7{,}580 - 1{,}037)}{7{,}580} \times 100 = 86\%$$

Output tax for the VAT period is

£24,016.28 × 86% × $^1/_6$ £3,442.33

Notes

(a) If each sale can be recorded as it takes place, the normal method of accounting can be used. Otherwise either the Point of Sale scheme or, if the business can satisfy HMRC that it is unable to operate the Point of Sale Scheme, the above catering adaptation can be used.

(b) It is not necessary to include the cost of food used for free meals for family and staff but the full cost of any standard-rated items of food taken out of business stock for own or family use should be included.

(c) The representative period chosen depends on the nature of the business but HMRC must be satisfied that it takes account of hourly, daily and seasonal fluctuations. Details of the sample, including dates and times, must be retained and a new calculation must be carried out in each VAT period.

404 Hotels and Holiday Accommodation

404.1 STAYS OVER FOUR WEEKS.

[*VATA 1994, Sch 6 para 9; VAT Notice 709/3/13*]

In 2013 weekly terms for accommodation, facilities and meals in a hotel are £720.00 (£600.00 plus £120.00 VAT) of which £288.00 (£240.00 + £48.00 VAT) represents the charge for meals.

For the first four weeks, the VAT charge is the full £120.00 but thereafter a reduced VAT value may be calculated in one of the following ways. The proportion for meals has been taken to be 40% but this will not always be so.

(a) **If charges are expressed in VAT-exclusive terms**

	£	£
Total VAT-exclusive weekly charge	600.00	
VAT-exclusive charge for meals	240.00	48.00
	£360.00	
VAT-exclusive value of facilities (20% minimum)	72.00	14.40
VAT due		£62.40

Weekly terms are therefore £600 + £62.40 VAT.

(b) **If charges are expressed in VAT-inclusive terms and the total amount charged to the guest is reduced to take account of the reduced element of VAT**

VAT is as under (a) above but the calculation is

	£	£
Total VAT-inclusive charge	720.00	
VAT-inclusive charge for meals	288.00	48.00
VAT-inclusive charge for facilities and accommodation	432.00	
VAT included 1/6 × £432	72.00	
Balance (exclusive of VAT)	£360.00	
VAT-exclusive value of facilities (20% minimum)	72.00	14.40
VAT due		£62.40

The weekly terms are £600 + £62.40 VAT.

(c) **If charges are expressed in VAT-inclusive terms but the total amount charged to the guest is not reduced to take account of the reduced element of VAT**

404.1 VAT   Hotels and Holiday Accommodation

	£	£
Total VAT inclusive charge	720.00	
VAT-inclusive charge for meals	<u>288.00</u>	48.00
VAT-inclusive charge for facilities and accommodation	432.00	
VAT included *4/104 × £432	<u>16.62</u>	16.62
VAT-exclusive charge for facilities and accommodation	£415.38	
Total VAT		<u>£64.62</u>

The weekly terms are not reduced (i.e. £720.00 including £64.62 VAT).

Notes

(a)   *At least 20% of the VAT-exclusive charge, after deducting meals, must be treated as being for standard-rated facilities. In this example, the 20% minimum has been used, hence the fraction

$$\frac{20 \times \text{facilities element}\%}{100 + (20 \times \text{facilities element}\%)} = \frac{20 \times 20\%}{100 + (20 \times 20\%)} = \frac{4}{104}$$

If the true value of facilities is more than 20%, the higher value must be used. At a specialist hotel, such as a health farm, the charge for facilities could be as high as 40% and the VAT charge would then be correspondingly higher.

(b)   The taxable turnover of a hotel with many long stay guests is very different from its gross takings. It may not therefore need to apply for registration.

405 Input Tax

405.1 REPAYMENT OF INPUT TAX WHERE CONSIDERATION NOT PAID

[*VATA 1994, s 26A; SI 1995/2518, Regs 172F–172J; VAT Notice 700/18/13*].

(A)

In 2013 B purchases goods for £1,200 (£1,000.00 plus £200.00 VAT) and reclaims the full amount of VAT. By the relevant date (see note (a)), it has only paid £500.00 (leaving £700 unpaid).

It must make a repayment of input tax to HMRC of

$$200 \times \frac{700}{1,200} = £116.67$$

(B)

After making the repayment of £116.67 to HMRC, B subsequently makes a further payment of £300 for the goods.

B can now reclaim VAT from HMRC of

$$116.67 \times \frac{300}{700} = £50.00$$

Notes

(a) Where a customer claims VAT on a supply as input tax and all or part of the amount due for that supply is not paid to the supplier within six months of

   (i) the date of the supply, or

   (ii) if later, the date on which the consideration for the supply becomes payable

   the customer must make a refund to HMRC for the VAT period in which the end of the relevant six-month period falls. This does not apply where the cash accounting scheme is used (so that the date for the recovery of input tax is the date of payment).

(b) Where a customer is in dispute with the supplier, and the supplier agrees to extend the due date for payment of the amount in dispute, repayment is not required until six months after the agreed extended date for payment.

(c) Where, subsequent to making a refund to HMRC under (a) above, a customer pays the whole or part of the consideration for the supply in relation to which the input tax repayment was made, his entitlement to input tax on the supply is restored in proportion to the amount of consideration paid.

405.2 VAT   Input Tax

405.2 NON-BUSINESS ACTIVITIES

[*VATA 1994, s 24(5); VAT Notice 700, paras 32.1–32.7*]

A church receives income not only by way of donations, but also through the sale of books, cards and light refreshments in its bookcentre and coffee shop. For the first quarter its total income is £34,671.49 of which £15,246.22 is donations. VAT on purchases directly attributable to religious activities is £217.95, VAT on purchases related to the bookcentre and coffee shop is £738.95, VAT on general repairs, maintenance and overheads is £2,185.27.

	£
Input tax is calculated as follows	
VAT on purchases related to business activities	738.95
Add proportion of VAT on general repairs etc.	
$\dfrac{(34{,}671.49 - 15{,}246.22)}{34{,}671.49} \times £2{,}185.27$	1,224.33
	£1,963.28

Notes

(a)   VAT on purchases directly attributable to religious activities (non-business) is not input tax and cannot be recovered.

(b)   The calculation continues in the same way, quarter by quarter, until the VAT year end when an annual adjustment is made by applying the same calculation to the total figures for the year.

(c)   There is no UK legislation covering the apportionment of VAT to arrive at input tax. If computations based on times, attendance, floor areas, etc. produce a fairer result, they can be used. Prior approval of HMRC is, however, required.

(d)   If some element of business income arises from exempt supplies, input tax may have to be further apportioned to arrive at deductible input tax. See **408** PARTIAL EXEMPTION.

406 Motor Cars

[*VAT Notice 700/64/12*]

406.1 SCALE CHARGE FOR PRIVATE FUEL PRIOR TO 1 FEBRUARY 2014

[*VATA 1994, ss 56, 57*]

L Ltd provides its employees with cars and pays all day-to-day running expenses, including the cost of any petrol used for private motoring. Each employee submits a monthly return showing opening and closing mileage, together with fuel and servicing receipts for the period.

T, the sales director, has a car with CO_2 emission of 220g/km and puts in a monthly claim for July 2012 which includes petrol used for private motoring. He supports this with petrol bills totalling £176.49 and a service invoice for £288.00 (£240.00 plus VAT £48.00). The company prepares monthly VAT returns.

The company should code the expenses claim as follows

		£
Debit		
Servicing		240.00
Fuel £176.49 × 5/6	147.08	
Scale charge note (a)	31.5	
		178.58
Input VAT — on service	48.00	
— on petrol £176.49 × 1/6	29.42	
		77.42
		£496
Credit		
Expenses reimbursed to T		
£176.49 + £288.00		464.49
Output VAT		31.5
		£495.99

Note

(a) A fuel benefit scale is used to assess a VAT charge where any petrol or other motor fuel is provided by registered traders for private journeys made by employees, directors, partners or proprietors. The monthly scale charge for prescribed accounting periods beginning after 30 April 2012 for a car with CO2 emission of 220g/km is £189. The VAT charge is therefore £189 × 1/6 = £31.5.

407 Output Tax

[*VAT Notice 700, para 31.2*]

407.1 MIXED SUPPLIES

(A) **Apportionment based on cost of both supplies: VAT-inclusive price**

In July 2013 a VAT-inclusive price of £140 is charged for a supply of zero-rated goods which cost £23 and standard-rated goods which cost £40 (excluding VAT).

$$\text{Proportion of the total cost represented by standard-rated goods} = \frac{(40 + \text{VAT})}{(40 + \text{VAT}) + 23} = \frac{48}{71}$$

VAT-inclusive price of standard-rated goods = $^{48}/_{71}$ × £140 = £94.65

VAT included = £94.65 × 1/6 = £15.78

Tax value of zero-rated supply = £140 − £94.65 = £45.35

The total price is therefore apportioned

Value of standard-rated supply	78.87
VAT on standard-rated supply	15.78
Value of zero-rated supply	45.35
	£140

(B) **Apportionment based on cost of both supplies: VAT-exclusive price**

In July 2013 a VAT-exclusive price of £126 is charged for a supply of zero-rated goods which cost £23 and standard-rated goods which cost £40 (excluding VAT).

Proportion of the total cost represented by standard-rated goods = $^{40}/_{63}$

VAT-exclusive value of standard-rated goods = $^{40}/_{63}$ × £126 = £80

VAT on standard-rated goods = £80 × 20% = £16

Tax value of zero-rated supplies = £126 − £80 = £46

The total price is therefore apportioned

Value of standard-rated supply	80
Value of zero-rated supply	46
	126
VAT on £80 at 20%	16
	£142

407.1 VAT   Output Tax

(C) Apportionment based on the cost of one supply only

In July 2013 a VAT-inclusive price of £142 is charged for a supply of zero-rated goods which cost £26 and standard-rated services, the cost of which cannot be identified. A fair and reasonable uplift on the zero-rated goods, consistent with actual profit margins of the business, is 50%.

Value of zero-rated supplies = £26 + 50% = £39

VAT-inclusive price of the standard-rated goods = £142 − £39 = £103

VAT on standard-rated goods = £103 × $^1/_6$ = £17.17

The total price is therefore apportioned

Value of zero-rated supply	39.00
Value of standard-rated supply (103 − 17.17)	85.83
	124.83
VAT on £85.83 at 20%	17.17
	£142.00

(D) Apportionment based on the cost of one supply only: annual calculation (Method 1)

Assume that the figures in (C) above are representative of similar transactions and the total VAT-inclusive income from such transactions in the year is £25,000.

Zero-rated percentage = $^{39}/_{142}$ × 100 = 27.465%

Value of zero-rated supplies in year = £25,000 × 27.465% = £6,866

Consideration for standard-rated supplies in year = £25,000 − £6,866 = £18,134

Output tax due = £18,134 × $^1/_6$ = £3,022.33

(E) Apportionment based on the cost of one supply only: annual calculation (Method 2)

VAT-inclusive subscription income of £400,000 is received in a year in respect of supplies of zero-rated literature with direct costs of £42,000 and standard-rated services, the direct cost of which cannot be identified. The total costs of the business (excluding depreciation) amount to £250,000 in the year. A fair and reasonable uplift to the direct costs of the zero-rated goods to allow for indirect costs is 100%.

Direct cost of zero-rated supplies	42,000
Uplift of 100%	42,000
Full cost of providing zero-rated supplies	£84,000

$$\text{Proportion of costs attributable to zero-rated supplies} = \frac{84,000}{250,000} \times 100 = 33.6\%$$

Proportion of costs attributable to standard-rated supplies = 66.4%

Output Tax   VAT 407.1

Consideration for standard-rated supplies = £400,000 × 66.4% = £265,600

Output tax = £265,600 × 1/6 = £44,266.66

(F) **Apportionment based on normal selling prices: VAT-inclusive price**

A VAT-inclusive price of £200 is charged for a zero-rated supply (which would separately be charged at £50) and a standard-rated supply (which would separately be charged at £200 including VAT).

Proportion of the total normal price represented by standard-rated goods =

$$\frac{200}{200 + 50} = \frac{4}{5}$$

VAT-inclusive price of standard-rated goods = 4/5 × £200 = £160

VAT included = £160 × 1/6 = £26.67

Tax value of zero-rated supply = £200 − £160 = £40

The total price is therefore apportioned

Value of standard-rated supply (£160 − £26.67)	133.33
VAT on standard-rated supply	26.67
Value of zero-rated supply	40.00
	£200.00

408 Partial Exemption

408.1 STANDARD METHOD

[*SI 1995 No 2518, Regs 99–109; VAT Notice 706*]

In its tax year X Ltd makes the following supplies

	Total supplies (excl VAT)	Standard rated supplies (excl VAT)	Exempt supplies
	£	£	£
First quarter	442,004	392,286	49,718
Second quarter	310,929	266,712	44,217
Third quarter	505,867	493,614	12,253
Fourth quarter	897,135	876,387	20,748
	£2,155,935	£2,028,999	£126,936

Input tax for the year is analysed as follows

	Attributable to taxable supplies	Attributable to exempt supplies	Remaining input tax	Total input tax
	£	£	£	£
First quarter	36,409	4,847	11,751	53,007
Second quarter	20,245	311	5,212	25,768
Third quarter	34,698	1,195	10,963	46,856
Fourth quarter	69,707	5,975	9,357	85,039
	£161,059	£12,328	£37,283	£210,670

The proportion of residual input tax attributable to taxable supplies is calculated using the ratio of

$$\frac{\text{Value of taxable supplies}}{\text{Value of all supplies}}$$

expressed as a percentage and, if not a whole number, rounded *up* to the next whole number.

408.1 VAT   Partial Exemption

	£	£

First quarter

Input tax attributable to taxable supplies   36,409

Proportion of residual input tax deductible

$$\frac{392,286}{442,004} = 88.75\%$$

£11,751 × 89% =   10,458

                                                         46,867

Second quarter

Input tax attributable to taxable supplies   20,245

Proportion of residual input tax deductible

$$\frac{266,712}{310,929} = 85.78\%$$

£5,212 × 86% =   4,482
                                                  £24,727

The value of exempt input tax is £1,041 (311 + [5,212 − 4,482]). As this is not more than £625 per month on average and is less than 50% of all input tax in the quarter, all input tax in the quarter is recoverable.

Deductible input tax   25,768

Third quarter

Input tax attributable to taxable supplies   34,698

Proportion of residual input tax deductible

$$\frac{493,614}{505,867} = 97.58\%$$

£10,963 × 98% =   10,744
                                                  £45,442

Partial Exemption VAT 408.2

	£	£

The value of exempt income tax is £1,414 (1,195 + [10,963 − 10,744]). As this is not more than £625 per month on average and is less than 50% of all input tax in the quarter, all input tax in the quarter is recoverable.

Deductible input tax   46,856

Fourth quarter

Input tax attributable to taxable supplies   69,707

Proportion of residual input tax deductible

$$\frac{876,387}{897,135} = 97.69\%$$

£9,357 × 98% =   9,170

     78,877

     £198,368

Annual adjustment

At the end of the tax year the company carries out an annual adjustment.

     £

Input tax attributable to taxable supplies   161,059

Proportion of residual input tax deductible

$$\frac{2,028,999}{2,155,935} = 94.11\%$$

	£
£37,283 × 95% =	35,419
Deductible input tax for year	196,478
Deducted over the four quarters	198,368
Under declaration to be paid to HMRC	£1,890

408.2 SPECIAL METHOD

[*SI 1995 No 2518, Regs 99–109; VAT Notice 706*]

The facts are the same as in **408.1** above except that HMRC allow X Ltd to use a special method and calculate the proportion of remaining input tax attributable to taxable supplies by the formula

$$\text{Residual input tax} \times \frac{\text{Input tax attributable to taxable supplies}}{\text{Total input tax}}$$

408.2 VAT   Partial Exemption

	£	£

First quarter

Input tax attributable to taxable supplies   36,409

Proportion of residual input tax deductible

$$£11{,}751 \times \frac{36{,}409}{53{,}007} = \quad \underline{8{,}071}$$

44,480

Second quarter

Input tax attributable to taxable supplies   20,245

Proportion of residual input tax deductible

$$£5{,}212 \times \frac{20{,}245}{25{,}768} = \quad \underline{4{,}095}$$

£24,340

The value of exempt input tax is £1,428 (311 + [5,212 − 4,095]). As this is not more than £625 per month on average and is less than 50% of all input tax in the quarter, all input tax in the quarter is recoverable.

Deductible input tax $\underline{25{,}768}$

70,248

Third quarter

Input tax attributable to taxable supplies   34,698

Proportion of residual input tax deductible

$$£10{,}963 \times \frac{34{,}698}{46{,}856} = \quad \underline{8{,}118}$$

42,816

Fourth quarter

Input tax attributable to taxable supplies   69,707

Proportion of residual input tax deductible

Partial Exemption   **VAT 408.2**

	£	£
$£9{,}357 \times \dfrac{69{,}707}{85{,}039} =$	7,670	
		77,377
		£190,441

Annual adjustment

At the end of the tax year the company carries out an annual adjustment.

	£
Input tax attributable to taxable supplies	161,059

Proportion of residual input tax deductible

$$£37{,}283 \times \frac{161{,}059}{210{,}670} = \qquad 28{,}503$$

Deductible input tax for year	189,562
Deducted over the four quarters	190,441
Under declaration to be paid to HMRC	£879

Note

(a)   In fact, this special method leaves X Ltd worse off than in 408.1 above, but is included here for illustration purposes.

409 Records

409.1 ADJUSTMENTS OF ERRORS ON INVOICES

[*VAT Notice 700, para 19.10; VAT Notice 700/45/13, paras 3.1–3.3*]

F sells a vast range of foodstuffs. Due to a programming error some wholesale packs of citric acid are incorrectly invoiced as zero-rated 'lemon flavouring'. The company decides not to raise supplementary invoices.

The following adjustment is required

	£
Citric acid sales	1,725.00
VAT charged	64.70
	£1,789.70
£1,789.70 × $^1/_6$ =	298.28
Less VAT charged	(64.70)
Additional VAT payable	£233.58

Note

(a) With many computer systems it is difficult to raise invoices or credit notes for VAT only. It is essential to ensure that any VAT amount will appear in the correct position on the documentation and will be posted by the system to the VAT account.

410 Reduced Rate Supplies

410.1 GRANT-FUNDED INSTALLATION OF HEATING EQUIPMENT
[*VATA 1994, Sch A1, Sch 7A Group 2; VAT Notice 708/6/11*]

(A) **Full grant received covering all work**

A builder installs reduced rate heating equipment to a value of £300 and carries out other building work to a value of £700 (both excluding VAT) for C in his main residence. A grant is received to cover the full cost of the work.

	£	£
Value of reduced rate supplies	300	
VAT thereon (5%)	15	
		315
Value of other supplies	700	
VAT thereon (20%)	140	
		840
Total cost covered by grant		£1,155

(B) **Apportionment where partial grant received which the grant-awarding body allocates to the installation of reduced rate heating equipment**

The facts are as in (A) above except that C receives a grant of £200 towards the installation of the reduced rate supplies and pays for the rest of the work himself.

	£	£
Value of reduced rate supplies which are grant-funded	200	
VAT thereon (5%)	10	
		210
Value of other supplies	800	
VAT thereon (20%)	160	
		960
Total cost including VAT		1,170
Grant received		200
Contribution from C		£970

(C) **Apportionment where partial grant received which the grant-awarding body does not allocate**

The facts are as in (A) above except that C receives a grant of £200 towards the total cost and pays for the rest of the work himself.

410.1 VAT   Reduced Rate Supplies

Proportion of total grant allocated to reduced rate supplies

$$£200 \times \frac{300}{1000} = £60$$

	£	£
Value of reduced rate supplies which are grant-funded	60	
VAT thereon (5%)	3	
		63
Value of other supplies	940	
VAT thereon (20%)	188	
		1,128
Total cost including VAT		1,191
Grant received		200
Contribution from C		£991

411 Retail Schemes

[*VATA 1994, Sch 11 para 2(6); SI 1995 No 2518, Regs 66–75; VAT Notice 727*]

411.1 POINT OF SALE SCHEME

[*VAT Notice 727/3/13*]

N Ltd is a garden centre selling plants and gardening equipment. It also sells gardening books and magazines and barbecue supplies. Due to the product mix, the company splits takings at the time of sale using multi-button tills. At the end of its VAT period, standard-rated takings totalled £125,639.34, zero-rated sales of books, etc. totalled £1,549.28 and reduced rate sales of barbecue fuels totalled £194.32.

Output tax for the period is

(£125,639.34 × $^1/_6$) + (£194.32 × $^1/_{21}$) = £20,939.89 + £9.25 = £20,949.14

Notes

(a) The method of calculation is the same for all VAT periods.

(b) Taxable turnover must not exceed £100 million.

411.2 APPORTIONMENT SCHEME 1

[*VAT Notice 727/4/13*]

B Ltd has figures for the four quarterly periods in a VAT year as follows.

	Cost of standard-rated goods for resale (incl VAT) £	Cost of reduced rate goods for resale (incl VAT) £	Total cost of goods for resale (incl VAT) £	Gross takings £
First quarter	9,429	78	15,701	21,714.55
Second quarter	10,418	124	17,840	24,316.51
Third quarter	9,972	312	15,919	21,899.29
Fourth quarter	7,076	25	11,293	16,149.61
	£36,895	£539	£60,753	£84,079.96

First quarter

Standard-rated sales are

$$\frac{9{,}429}{15{,}701} \times £21{,}714.55 = £13{,}040.35$$

411.2 VAT Retail Schemes

Reduced rate sales are

$$\frac{78}{15{,}701} \times £21{,}714.55 = £107.87$$

Output tax $=(£13{,}040.35 \times {}^1/_6) + (£107.87 \times {}^1/_{21}) =$ £2,178.53

By similar calculations output tax in the remaining quarters is

Second quarter	2,374.73
Third quarter	2,306.80
Fourth quarter	1,688.21
	£8,548.27

Annual adjustment

Standard-rated sales for the year are

$$\frac{36{,}895}{60{,}753} \times £84{,}079.96 = £51{,}061.35$$

Reduced rate sales for the year are

$$\frac{539}{60{,}753} \times £84{,}079.96 = £745.96$$

Output tax $= (£51{,}061.35 \times {}^1/_6) + (£745.96 \times {}^1/_{21}) = £8{,}545.75$

£2.52 must be added to the amount of VAT deductible for the fourth quarter.

Notes

(a) VAT-exclusive retail sales must be less than £1 million.

(b) Any supplies of services, home-grown or self-made goods, or supplies of catering must be dealt with outside the scheme.

(c) The annual adjustment must be made on 31 March, 30 April or 31 May each year, depending upon the VAT return periods. The first adjustment may therefore cover less than a full year.

411.3 APPORTIONMENT SCHEME 2

[*VAT Notice 727/4/13*]

Z Ltd owns a store and can analyse all purchases of stock for resale. It decides to use Apportionment Scheme 2 and calculates that the expected selling price, including VAT, of stock for retail sale at the commencement of using the scheme is £818,703, of which £331,379 represents standard-rated lines. Trading figures for the first four quarters under the scheme are

Retail Schemes   VAT 411.3

	ESP of standard-rated goods received for resale (incl VAT)	Total ESP of goods received for resale (incl VAT)	Gross takings
	£	£	£
First quarter	393,741	1,009,199	835,265
Second quarter	400,829	891,685	829,524
Third quarter	314,227	905,859	1,018,784
Fourth quarter	493,207	1,235,087	1,486,381

Output tax is calculated as follows

First quarter

Opening stock	331,379	818,703
First quarter	393,741	1,009,199
	£725,120	£1,827,902

$$\text{Standard-rated sales} = \frac{725,120}{1,827,902} \times £835,265 = £331,345$$

Output tax = £331,345 × $^1/_6$ £55,224.16

Second quarter

Opening stock	331,379	818,703
First quarter	393,741	1,009,199
Second quarter	400,829	891,685
	£1,125,949	£2,719,587

$$\text{Standard-rated sales} = \frac{1,125,949}{2,719,587} \times £829,524 = £343,435$$

Output tax = £343,435 × $^1/_6$ £57,239.17

Third quarter

Opening stock	331,379	818,703
First quarter	393,741	1,009,199
Second quarter	400,829	891,685
Third quarter	314,227	905,859
	£1,440,176	£3,625,446

411.3 VAT   Retail Schemes

	ESP of standard-rated goods received for resale (incl VAT)	Total ESP of goods received for resale (incl VAT)	Gross takings
	£	£	£

$$\text{Standard-rated sales} = \frac{1{,}440{,}176}{3{,}625{,}446} \times £1{,}018{,}784 = £404{,}702$$

Output tax = £404,702 × 1/6   £67,450.33

Fourth quarter

First quarter	393,741	1,009.199
Second quarter	400,829	891,685
Third quarter	314,227	905,859
Fourth quarter	493,207	1,235,087
	£1,602,004	£4,041,830

$$\text{Standard-rated sales} = \frac{1{,}602{,}004}{4{,}041{,}830} \times £1{,}486{,}381 = £589{,}136$$

Output tax = £589,136 × 1/6   £98,189.33

Notes

(a) For the fifth quarter, the method of calculation continues as in the fourth quarter above, the first quarter's figures being dropped and the fifth quarter's added to produce a rolling average across the last year.

(b) VAT-exclusive retail sales must be less than £100 million.

(c) Any supplies of services or supplies of catering must be dealt with outside the scheme.

(d) If it is not possible to perform a physical stock-take on the date of starting to use the scheme, the ESP values of goods received for resale in the previous three months may be used.

411.4 DIRECT CALCULATION SCHEME 1

[*VAT Notice 727/5/13*]

K runs a newsagent's shop. In addition to sales of newspapers and magazines (zero-rated), he also sells confectionery and tobacco (standard-rated), a limited range of food items (zero-rated) and barbecue fuels (reduced rate supplies). At the end of a VAT period, gross takings are £18,714.55. The expected selling prices of purchases in the period are £11,236.19 for standard-rated goods, £8,154.27 for zero-rated goods and £157.93 for reduced rate goods.

The minority goods are zero-rated and reduced rate supplies (i.e. the main goods are standard-rated).

Output tax is calculated as follows.

	£	£
Gross takings		18,714.55
Expected selling prices of zero-rated goods	8,154.27	
Expected selling prices of reduced rate goods	157.93	
	8,312.20	
Standard-rated element of takings		£10,402.35
Output tax = (£10,402.35 × $^1/_6$) + (£157.93 × $^1/_{21}$) =		£1,741.25

Notes

(a) VAT-exclusive retail sales must be less than £1 million.

(b) Minority goods are those at the rate of VAT which forms the smallest proportion of retail supplies or, where goods are supplied at three rates of VAT, which forms the two smallest proportions.

(c) Supplies of services with the same liability as the minority goods must be dealt with outside the scheme, as must supplies of catering.

(d) If the minority goods are standard-rated and reduced rate supplies (i.e. the main goods are zero-rated) output tax is simply:

(ESP of standard-rated goods × $^1/_6$) + (ESP of reduced rate goods × 1/21)

411.5 DIRECT CALCULATION SCHEME 2

[*VAT Notice 727/5/13*]

K decides to use Direct Calculation Scheme 2. When he starts to use the scheme, his opening stock, valued at expected selling prices, is

	£
Standard-rated goods	3,145.91
Zero-rated goods	2,250.34
Reduced rate goods	142.51

For the first four quarters, his relevant details are

	ESP of standard-rated goods purchased	ESP of zero-rated goods purchased	ESP of reduced rate goods purchased	Gross takings
	£	£	£	£
First quarter	11,236.19	8,154.27	157.93	18,714.55
Second quarter	9,075.02	11,667.67	259.32	20,726.40
Third quarter	9,872.90	10,124.75	137.54	20,855.88
Fourth quarter	11,431.39	11,008.62	21.43	22,649.04

411.5 VAT Retail Schemes

	ESP of standard-rated goods purchased	ESP of zero-rated goods purchased	ESP of reduced rate goods purchased	Gross takings
	£	£	£	£
	£41,615.50	£40,955.31	£576.22	£82,945.87

At the end of the fourth quarter, his closing stock, valued at expected selling prices, is

	£
Standard-rated goods	4,217.22
Zero-rated goods	3,151.44
Reduced rate goods	119.19

First quarter

The minority goods are zero-rated and reduced rate supplies. Output tax is calculated as follows.

	£	£
Gross takings		18,714.55
ESP of zero-rated goods	8,154.27	
ESP of reduced rate goods	157.93	
	8,312.20	
Standard-rated element of takings		£10,402.35
Output tax = (£10,402.35 × $1/6$) + (£157.93 × $1/21$) =		£1,741.25

Second quarter

The minority goods are standard-rated and reduced rate supplies. Output tax is calculated as follows.

(£9,075.02 × $1/6$) + (£259.32 × $1/21$) = £1,524.85

Third quarter

The minority goods are standard-rated and reduced rate supplies. Output tax is calculated as follows.

(£9,872.90 × $1/6$) + (£137.54 × $1/21$) = £1,652.03

Fourth quarter

The minority goods are zero-rated and reduced rate supplies. Output tax is calculated as follows.

Retail Schemes   **VAT 411.5**

	£	£
Gross takings		22,649.04
ESP of zero-rated goods	11,008.62	
ESP of reduced rate goods	21.43	
		11,030.05
Standard-rated element of takings		£11,618.99
Output tax = (£11,618.99 × $^1/_6$) + (£21.43 × $^1/_{21}$) =		£1,937.52

The annual adjustment is as follows

The minority goods are zero-rated and reduced rate supplies. Output tax is calculated as follows.

	£	£
Gross takings		82,945.87
Less zero-rated goods		
opening stock	2,250.34	
ESP of goods purchased	40,955.31	
	43,205.65	
closing stock	3,151.44	
		40,054.21
		42,891.66
Less reduced rate goods		
opening stock	142.51	
ESP of goods purchased	576.22	
	718.73	
closing stock	119.19	
		599.54
Standard-rated element of takings		£42,292.12
Output tax = (£42,292.12 × $^1/_6$) + (£599.54 × $^1/_{21}$) =		7,077.24
Output tax already calculated		
£1,741.25 + £1,524.85 + £1,652.03 + £1,937.52		6,855.65
Additional VAT payable with return for fourth quarter		£221.59

Notes

(a)   VAT-exclusive retail sales must be less than £100 million.

(b)   Minority goods are those at the rate of VAT which forms the smallest proportion of retail supplies or, where goods are supplied at three rates of VAT, which forms the two smallest proportions.

(c)   Supplies of services with the same liability as the minority goods must be dealt with outside the scheme, as must supplies of catering.

412 Second-Hand Goods

412.1 PART EXCHANGE

[*VAT Notice 718, para 13.6*]

A car dealer sells a car for £2,000 cash plus a car for which £1,000 is allowed in part exchange.

Selling price. A selling price of £3,000 must be entered in the stock book.

Purchase price. As the car taken in exchange is eligible to be resold under the scheme, the amount allowed in part exchange (£1,000) is the purchase price. The purchase must also be recorded in the stock book.

412.2 GLOBAL ACCOUNTING SCHEME — NEGATIVE MARGIN

[*SI 1995/1268, Art 13; SI 1999/3120; VAT Notice 718, para 14.8*]

A dealer starts to use the global accounting scheme and values his opening stock on hand at £10,000. In the first VAT period, his total purchases from his purchase summary are £2,000 and his sales from his sales summary are £8,000. In his second VAT period purchases are £1,000 and sales are £7,000.

The margin for the first VAT period is

£8,000 − (£10,000 + £2,000) = (£4,000)

There is a negative margin and no VAT is due. The negative margin is carried forward to the next period.

The margin for the second VAT period is

£7,000 − (£4,000 + £1,000) = £2,000

VAT due = £2,000 × $^1/_6$ = £333.33

Notes

(a) If there is a negative margin (because total purchases exceed total sales), no VAT is due and the negative margin is carried forward to the following VAT period for inclusion in the calculation of the total purchases of that period.

(b) A negative margin cannot be set off against other VAT due in the same VAT period on transactions outside the global accounting scheme.

412.3 AUCTIONEERS' SCHEME

[*SI 1992/3122, Art 8(7); SI 1995/1268, Art 12(7); VAT Notice 718, paras 11.1–11.4*]

Goods are sold at auction for £1,000 (the hammer price). Commission is charged to the seller at 10% net of VAT and a buyer's premium is charged of 15% net of VAT.

412.3 VAT   Second-Hand Goods

Commission = (£1,000 × 10%) + 20% VAT =	£120
Purchase price = £1,000 − £120 =	£880
Buyer's premium = (£1,000 × 15%) + 20% VAT =	£180
Selling price = £1,000 + £180 =	£1,180
Margin = £1,180 − £880 =	£300
Output tax = £300 × $1/6$ =	£50

Note

(a)   The purchase price, selling price, margin and VAT due are calculated from the successful bid price (hammer price) and commission and other charges.

'*Purchase price*' is the hammer price less commission payable to the auctioneer under his contract with the seller for the sale of the goods.

'*Selling price*' is the hammer price plus the consideration for any supply of services by the auctioneer to the purchaser (e.g. buyer's premium) in connection with the sale of the goods.

The margin is the difference between the purchase price and the selling price. The margin is regarded as being VAT-inclusive i.e. the VAT included is VAT-inclusive margin × VAT fraction (currently $1/6$).

National Insurance Contributions

501   Age Exception

502   Aggregation of Earnings

503   Annual Maximum

504   Class 1 Contributions: Employed Earners

505   Class 1A Contributions: Benefits in Kind

506   Class 1B Contributions: PAYE Settlement Agreements

507   Class 4 Contributions: On Profits of a Trade etc.

508   Company Directors

509   Contracted-Out Employment

510   Deferment of Payment

511   Earnings from Self-Employment

512   Earnings Periods

513   Intermediaries

514   Partners

515   Repayment and Reallocation

501 Age Exception

501.1 PERSONS OVER PENSIONABLE AGE

[*SSCBA 1992, s 6(3); SI 2001 No 1004, Regs 7, 28, 29*]

(A)

Gail is approaching state pensionable age on 6 November 2013. She currently works full time earning £500 per week as a PA to the managing director. Although she will attain state pension age in November 2013 both she and the wages clerk are unsure what the position will be if she goes part time for three days of the week from that date earning £300 per week. The managing director is also keen to know whether he will have to pay more Class 1 secondary contributions by employing Jean for the other two days she is away on a wage of £200.

Gail must present her birth certificate to her employer so that the company has proof that age exception is warranted. If it is found that no proof has been obtained then the employer is entirely liable for any underpayment. As an alternative to providing her birth certificate Gail could supply her passport or a certificate of age exception (Form CA 4140 or CF 384) which is issued by HM Revenue and Customs NICO, Individuals Caseworker, Benton Park View, Newcastle upon Tyne NE98 1ZZ. The certificate will have a validity date on it from which time the wages clerk can stop deducting Class 1 primary contributions but must continue to deduct secondary contributions even though she is over pensionable age.

Weekly class 1 liabilities before job sharing arrangement in force

	£	Primary* %	£	Secondary† %	£
Gail	500.00	Nil/12	42.12	Nil/13.8	48.58

Weekly class 1 liabilities when job sharing arrangement in force

	£	%	£	%	£
Gail	300.00	Nil	Nil	Nil/13.8	20.98
Jean	200.00	Nil/12	6.12	Nil/13.8	7.18
	£500.00		£6.12		£28.16

(* Nil% × £149, 12% × remainder.) († Nil% × £148, 13.8% × remainder.)

The employer will save £20.42 (i.e. £48.58 − £28.16) each week in secondary contributions under the job sharing arrangement.

Notes

(a) An employed earner who attains pensionable age is excepted from liability for Class 1 primary contributions on any earnings paid to him or for his benefit after the date he attains pensionable age. The exception does not apply to earnings which would

501.1 NIC   Age Exception

normally have fallen to be paid to him or for his benefit before that date. Earnings which, though paid before he attains pensionable age, would normally fall to be paid to him in a subsequent tax year are within the exception. [*SSCBA 1992, s 6(3); SI 2001 No 1004, Regs 28, 29*].

(b)   See (B) below for the age at which a person attains state pensionable age.

(B)   **Pensionable age**

Imogen was born on 29 March 1954. Applying the table in *Pensions Act 1995, Sch 4 Part 1*, she attains pensionable age on 6 September 2019.

Note

(a)   Pensionable age is, in the case of a man born before 6 December 1953, 65, and in the case of a woman born before 6 April 1950, 60. For women born after 5 April 1950 and before 6 October 1954, and for men born after 5 December 1953 and before 6 October 1954, pensionable age rises on a sliding scale contained in *Pensions Act 1995, Sch 4, Part 1*. For men and women born after 5 October 1954 and before 6 April 1968 pensionable age is 66. A sliding scale under *Sch 4, Part 1* again applies to gradually increase the pensionable age for men and women born after 5 April 1968 and before 6 April 1969, so that for men and women born after 5 April 1969 pensionable age is 67. A further phased increase applies to those born on or after 6 April 1977 and before 6 April 1978, so that the pensionable age for those born after 5 April 1978 will be 68.

502 Aggregation of Earnings

502.1 EMPLOYMENT UNDER THE SAME EMPLOYER

[*SSCBA 1992, Sch 1 para 1(1)(a); SI 2001 No 1004, Reg 14*]

(A) **Earnings paid for different periods**

Arnold is employed by Bauble Bros as a sales representative. He receives a weekly salary, quarterly commission and an annual bonus. Under the earnings period rules, his earnings period is a week (unless HMRC has directed otherwise). In the week ended 20 July 2013, Arnold receives:

	£
Salary for the week ended 21 July 2013	100
Commission for the quarter ended 30 June 2013	387
Bonus for the year ended 31 December 2012	3,300
	£3,787

By virtue of *SSCBA 1992, Sch 1 para 1(1)(a)*, the contribution liabilities of Arnold and of Bauble Bros for that week will be assessed by reference to a single amount of earnings of £3,787.

Notes

(a) All earnings paid to an earner in a given earnings period in respect of one or more employed earner's employments under the same employer are aggregated and treated as a single payment of earnings in respect of one such employment. [*SSCBA 1992, Sch 1 para 1(1)(a); SI 2001 No 1004, Reg 14*]. See **512.1(A)(B) EARNINGS PERIODS** for the rules which determine the earnings period where there are multiple regular pay patterns.

(b) Aggregation does not take place if it is not reasonably practicable. [*SI 2001 No 1004, Reg 14*].

(c) See 502.5 below where an earner has been, but is no longer, a director of a company.

(B) **More than one contract**

Throughout 2013/14, Cyril is employed by the Dainty Dish Restaurant under two separate contracts of service. As barman, he is paid earnings of £70 per week and, as wine waiter, he is paid earnings of £185 per week.

502.1 NIC   Aggregation of Earnings

The total weekly Class 1 liability is as follows.

		£
Primary	£149 @ Nil	Nil
	£106 @ 12%	12.72
	£255	12.72
Secondary	£148 @ Nil	Nil
	£107 @ 13.8%	14.77
	£255	£14.77
		£27.49

Notes

(a) Because C's two employments are under the same employer, all his earnings in respect of those employments are aggregated and treated as a single weekly payment of £255 in respect of a single employment. [SSCBA 1992, Sch 1 para 1(1)(a)].

(b) See notes (b) and (c) to (A) above.

502.2 DIFFERENT EMPLOYMENTS, SECONDARY CONTRIBUTORS IN ASSOCIATION

[SSCBA 1992, Sch 1 para 1(b); SI 2001 No 1004, Reg 15(1)(a)]

Throughout 2013/14, Edward is paid earnings of £150 per week in respect of his employment with Fabrications Ltd; £160 per week in respect of his employment with Gudroofs; £85 per week in respect of his employment with Homemakers Ltd and £100 per week with Interiors Ltd. H is in voluntary liquidation under John, a liquidator, but is continuing to play its part in a joint project with F, G and I involving the development of a residential building site. Edward is employed by G, H and I in connection with that joint project but his employment with F is in connection with unassociated activities in which that company is involved.

There are four secondary contributors who pay earnings to Edward: F, G, J (as liquidator of H) and I, but of these only F, G and I are carrying on business in association (J, as liquidator, is not), and of these only G and I are doing so in respect of Edward's employments. Accordingly, only the earnings Edward receives from G and I fall to be aggregated, with Class 1 contribution liabilities arising as follows.

Aggregation of Earnings   NIC 502.4

	£	Primary* %	£	Secondary† %	£
F	150.00	Nil/12	0.12	Nil/13.8	0.28
G	160.00				
I	100.00				
	260.00	Nil/12	13.32	Nil/13.8	15.46
J	85.00	Nil	Nil	Nil	Nil

(* Nil% × £149, 12% × remainder.)

(† Nil% × £148, 13.8% × remainder.)

Notes

(a) All earnings paid to an earner in a given earnings period in respect of more than one employed earner's employments by different secondary contributors who, in respect of those employments, carry on business in association with each other, are aggregated and treated as a single payment of earnings in respect of one such employment. [*SSCBA 1992, Sch 1 para 1(1)(b); SI 2001 No 1004, Reg 15(1)(a)*].

(b) See notes (b) and (c) to 502.1(A) above.

502.3 DIFFERENT EMPLOYMENTS, DIFFERENT EMPLOYERS ONE OF WHOM IS SECONDARY CONTRIBUTOR

[*SSCBA 1992, Sch 1 para 1(1)(b); SI 2001 No 1004, Reg 15(1)(b)*]

From 6 April 2013, Keith is employed by the Lively Lazarites Central Fund as an accountant at a salary of £160 per week. He is also remunerated by that fund at the rate of £150 per week as minister of the LL Free Church in Lincoln.

Under the provisions of *SSCBA 1992, s 6(4)* (which require the earnings from each employment to be viewed in isolation from the other) Class 1 contribution liabilities of £1.32 primary and £1.66 secondary would arise on the earnings of £160 per week. On the earnings of £150 per week, Class 1 contribution liabilities of £0.12 primary and £0.28 secondary would arise. As the fund is not only Keith's employer, however, but also the secondary contributor as regards the earnings paid to him as a minister of religion, his earnings must, by virtue of *SI 2001/1004, Reg 15(1)(b)*, be aggregated and, in consequence, Class 1 contributions of £19.32 primary and £22.36 secondary will be payable on the combined earnings of £310.

502.4 DIFFERENT EMPLOYMENTS, SECONDARY CONTRIBUTOR OTHER THAN ONE OF THE EMPLOYERS

[*SSCBA 1992, Sch 1 para 1(1)(b); SI 2001 No 1004, Reg 15(1)(c)*]

In 2013/14, Marveltipe Agency obtains temporary employment for Norma, a secretary, with O Ltd, P Ltd and Q Ltd. Through Marveltipe, Norma is paid weekly earnings of £95 from O, £105 from P and £75 from Q. Marveltipe also obtains work for Jean with O, P and Q. Through Marveltipe, Jean is paid monthly earnings of £2,500, £1,900 and £1,100 respectively.

Although the earnings are in respect of different employments and are paid by different persons, Marveltipe (though not itself one of Norma or Jean's employers) is the secondary contributor as regards those earnings (see *SI 1978 No 1689, Sch 3 para 2(a)*). Both

502.4 NIC   Aggregation of Earnings

Norma's and Jean's earnings must therefore be aggregated. Class 1 contributions for Norma will therefore be payable on earnings of £275 per week as if it were a single payment in respect of one employment. Class 1 contributions for Jean will likewise be payable on earnings of £5,500 per month.

Notes

(a) All earnings paid by different persons to an earner in a given earnings period in respect of more than one employed earner's employments where some other person is, by regulation, treated as the secondary contributor in relation to those earnings, are aggregated and treated as a single payment of earnings in respect of one such employment. [*SSCBA 1992, Sch 1 para 1(1)(b); SI 2001 No 1004, Reg 15(1)(c)*].

(b) But for the requirement to aggregate Norma's earnings, they would have escaped liability as each amount falls below the 2013/14 weekly earnings thresholds of £148 and £149. In Jean's case, primary Class 1 contributions would have been 12% of the earnings (less £646 threshold) from each source – subject to the annual maximum. Aggregation results in a single calculation on the combined earnings so that only 2% is deducted on earnings of £2,046 (total earnings £5,500 less UEL £3,454).

502.5 EARNINGS RELATING TO PERIODS OF FORMER DIRECTORSHIP

[*SI 2001 No 1004, Reg 8(5)(a)*]

Throughout 2013/14, Richard is employed by Stiffs Ltd as an embalmer at a salary of £2,000 per month. Until 31 December 2012 he had been a director of the company but had, on that date, resigned because of worsening health. In September 2013, the board votes him a bonus of £7,000 in respect of his services as director during the year ended 31 December 2012 and a further £5,000 in respect of his services as embalmer during the same period.

Class 1 contributions are as follows.

		Primary		Secondary	
Salary		%	£	%	£
£646/£641		Nil		Nil	
£1,354/£1,359		12	162.48	13.8	187.54
£2,000	(less than *monthly* UEL for primary contribution purposes £3,454)				
Bonuses					
£7,755/£7,696		Nil		Nil	
£4,245/£4,304		12	509.40	13.8	593.95
£12,000	(less than *annual* UEL for primary contribution purposes £41,450)				
Total			£671.88		£781.49

Aggregation of Earnings   NIC 502.6

Notes

(a) Where an earner who was, but is no longer, a director of a company receives earnings in any tax year after that in which he ceased to be a director, those earnings, insofar as they are paid in respect of any period during which he was a director, are not to be aggregated with any other earnings with which they would otherwise fall to be aggregated. [*SI 2001 No 1004, Reg 8(5)(a)*].

(b) An annual earnings period applies to the earnings relating to the period when Richard was a director. [*SI 2001 No 1004, Reg 8(5)(b)*].

(c) Were it not for *Reg 8(5)(a)*, Richard's earnings in September 2013 would fall to be aggregated as the amounts are derived from different employments under the same employer (see 502.1(B) above).

502.6 AGGREGATION WITH GRATUITIES ETC. PAID SEPARATELY

Anthony runs a small hotel in which he employs Bonnie and Clyde as waiters. For the week ending 22 June 2013, Bonnie's earnings are £140 and Clyde's earnings are £160. On the face of it, no contribution liabilities arise as regards Bernie's earnings as they fall below the thresholds of £148 and £149, and liability for primary and secondary Class 1 contributions as regards Clyde's earnings are at only 12% primary and 13.8% secondary on the earnings over £148/£149. In the week concerned, however, guests have asked for tips of £50 to be added to their bills and Anthony has passed those tips to David, the hall porter, instructing him that Bonnie is to receive £25 and Clyde is to receive £25. In those circumstances, contribution liabilities for which Anthony is accountable are as follows:

		£		£
Bonnie	Class 1 primary:	149	@ Nil%	0.00
		16	@ 12%	1.92
		165		1.92
	Class 1 secondary:	148	@ Nil%	0.00
		17	@ 13.8%	2.35
		165		2.35
Clyde	Class 1 primary:	149	@ Nil%	0.00
		36	@ 12%	4.32
		185		4.32
	Class 1 secondary:	148	@ Nil%	0.00
		37	@ 13.8%	5.11
		185		5.11

Note

(a) Where tips, gratuities etc. are earnings for contributions purposes and their allocation is not carried out by the person who is the secondary contributor as regards the ordinary earnings of the employed earner to whom they are allocated, the secondary contributor must aggregate the tips etc. with the ordinary earnings and account for Class 1 contributions on the aggregate amount. (HMRC leaflet CWG2 (2013), page 27).

502.7 NIC   Aggregation of Earnings

502.7 AGGREGATION FOR CLASS 2 SMALL EARNINGS EXCEPTION PURPOSES

[*SSCBA 1992, s 11(4)*]

Esmerelda has been self-employed as a dressmaker and also as a hairdresser for many years. Her accounts reveal the following trading results

Year ended	Trade		£
31 December 2012	Dressmaker	Loss	(2,000)
31 December 2013	Dressmaker	Profit	6,000
30 September 2012	Hairdresser	Profit	5,000
30 September 2013	Hairdresser	Profit	7,000

Her 2012/13 earnings for Class 2 exception purposes are

	£
9/12 × £(2,000)	(1,500)
3/12 × £6,000	1,500
6/12 × £5,000	2,500
6/12 × £7,000	3,500
	£6,000

The exception is therefore not available to Esmerelda.

Notes

(a) A self-employed earner can be excepted from liability to pay Class 2 contributions in respect of any period in which his earnings from such employment are less than a specified amount (£5,725 for 2013/14). [*SSCBA 1992, s 11(4)*]. The net earnings from all self-employed activities in which a person is engaged must be aggregated and any net loss must be set against those aggregated profits.

(b) The earnings must be time apportioned to tax years. [*SI 2001 No 1004, Regs 1(2), 45(1)*].

502.8   AGGREGATION FOR CLASS 4 PURPOSES

[*SSCBA 1992, s 15*]

Francis is in business as an interior decorator and as a furniture renovator. He is also an equal partner in a firm that supplies fitted kitchens. His interior decorating business was established several years ago with a 31 October accounting date but the furniture renovating business commenced on 1 May 1999 with a 30 April accounting date. The fitted kitchen partnership is long-established (with a 31 December accounting date) and F's share of profits one-half. Trading results adjusted in accordance with the tax and Class 4 rules are as follows

Aggregation of Earnings   **NIC 502.8**

Year ended	Trade	
31 October 2010	Interior decorator	£10,000
31 October 2011	Interior decorator	£12,500
31 October 2012	Interior decorator	£13,500
31 October 2013	Interior decorator	£14,500
30 April 2010	Furniture renovator	£1,200
30 April 2011	Furniture renovator	£1,350
30 April 2012	Furniture renovator	£1,550
30 April 2013	Furniture renovator	£1,950
31 December 2010	Fitted kitchens	£28,500
31 December 2011	Fitted kitchens	£29,000
31 December 2012	Fitted kitchens	£32,000
31 December 2013	Fitted kitchens	£34,000

The amount of trading income chargeable to income tax, and in respect of which Class 4 contributions are calculated, for 2010/11 is as follows

	£
Interior decorator (current year basis)	10,000
Furniture renovator (current year basis)	1,200
Fitted kitchens (current year basis split according to profit share in 2010/11:1/2 × £28,500)	14,250
	£25,450

The amount of trading income chargeable to income tax, and in respect of which Class 4 contributions are calculated, for 2011/12 is as follows

	£
Interior decorator (current year basis)	12,500
Furniture renovator (current year basis)	1,350
Fitted kitchens (current year basis split according to profit share in 2011/12:1/2 × £29,000)	14,500
	£28,350

The amount of trading income chargeable to income tax, and in respect of which Class 4 contributions are calculated, for 2012/13 is as follows

	£
Interior decorator (current year basis)	13,500
Furniture renovator (current year basis)	1,550
Fitted kitchens (current year basis split according to profit share in 2012/13:1/2 × £32,000)	16,000
	£31,050

502.8 NIC   Aggregation of Earnings

The amount of trading income chargeable to income tax, and in respect of which Class 4 contributions are calculated, for 2013/14 is as follows

	£
Interior decorator (current year basis)	14,500
Furniture renovator (current year basis)	1,950
Fitted kitchens (current year basis split according to profit share in 2013/14:1/2 × £34,000)	17,000
	£33,450

Note

(a) Class 4 contributions are payable in respect of all profits which are immediately derived from the carrying on or exercise of one or more trade, professions or vocations and are profits chargeable to income tax under *ITTOIA 2005, Pt 2 Ch 2*. [*SSCBA 1992, s 15(1)*]. Profits must therefore be aggregated, but time apportionment to the tax year is not required. See also **514 PARTNERS**.

503 Annual Maximum

503.1 CLASS 1 AND CLASS 2 LIMITATION

[*SI 2001 No 1004, Reg 21*]

For the whole of 2013/14, Finch is employed by Grebe in a contracted-out employment at a salary of £3,330 per month. From 6 October 2013 to 5 April 2014, she is also employed by Heron in a not contracted-out employment at a salary of £1,450 per month; and from 1 January 2014, she is also self-employed. The Class 1 primary contributions paid on her earnings from her employed earner's employments are as follows

	£			£	£
Grebe	646.00	(monthly earnings threshold)	@ Nil%	0.00 × 12 =	0.00
	2,684.00		@ 10.6%	284.50 × 12 =	3,414.00
	3,330.00				3,414.00
Heron	646.00	(monthly earnings threshold)	@ Nil%	0.00 × 6 =	0.00
	804.00		@ 12%	96.48 × 6 =	578.88
	1,450.00				578.88
Total Class 1 paid:					3,992.88
Finch also pays:					
Class 2 contributions				£2.70 × 14 =	37.80
					£4,030.68

On the face of it, F will not have paid excessive contributions since the notional annual maximum for 2013/14 is £4,121.28. Such a judgement is premature, however. Before the question of any excess can be decided, the primary Class 1 contributions paid at less than standard rate (i.e. £3,414.00) must be converted to contributions at the appropriate standard rate (i.e. £3,414.00 × $^{12}/_{10}$ = £3,864.91) and a fresh total must be arrived at (i.e. £4,481.59). As this fresh total *exceeds* £4,121.28, excess contributions appear to have been paid. It is therefore necessary to consider Finch's personalised maximum using the following numbered steps.

Step			£	£
1.	Calculate 53 × (UEL – primary threshold), i.e. 53 × (£797 – £149)			34,344.00
2.	12% thereof			4,121.28
3.	Earnings from each employment that falls between primary threshold and UEL: £2,684 × 12 = £32,208 £804 × 6 = £4,824		37,032.00	
4.	Deduct figure in step 1. from 3. (£37,032 – £34,344)		2,688.00	
5.	As the line above gives a positive figure, multiply by 2%		53.76	
6.	Earnings from each employment which exceeds UEL		Nil	

503.1 NIC Annual Maximum

Step		£	£
7.	Multiply step 6 result by 2%		Nil
8.	Add steps 2, 5, 7 – this gives the personalised annual maximum		£4,175.04

The contributions paid do not exceed this personalised maximum.

Note

(a) Where an earner is employed in more than one employment (including self-employments), liability in any tax year for primary Class 1 contributions and, where payable, Class 2 contributions, cannot exceed an amount equal to 53 primary Class 1 contributions at the primary percentage payable on earnings at the upper earnings limit together with such other liabilities which arise at the additional 1% rate. [*SI 2001 No 1004, Reg 21*]. *Reg 21* sets out an eight step process for calculating an individual's personal maximum, as illustrated in this example.

503.2 CLASS 4 LIMITATION

[*SI 2001 No 1004, Reg 100*]

(A) **Case 1**

Kate is a self-employed artist with profits assessable to income tax under the self-assessment basis for 2013/14 (and requiring no further adjustment) of £15,000. Throughout the year she pays Class 2 contributions. Throughout 2013/14 she is also a director of Kate's Krafts Ltd. Her earnings from the company during the year were £13,000. Contributions are paid as follows:

		£
Class 1 primary	£7,755 × Nil%	0.00
	£5,245 (£13,000 − £7,755) × 12%	629.40
Class 2	£2.70 × 52 Note: As there are 52 Sundays in 2013/14 only fifty-two weeks of Class 2 is payable	140.40
		£769.80

Her Class 4 liability is not to exceed the amount determined using the following steps:

Step		£	£
1.	Subtract the Class 4 lower profits limit from upper profits limit i.e. £41,450 − £7,755		33,695.00
2.	9% thereof	3,032.55	
3.	Add 53 times the weekly rate of Class 2 i.e. 53 × £2.70	143.10	3,175.65
4.	Subtract from Step 3 the amount of Class 2 paid and Class 1 paid at the main percentage rate (i.e. other than 2%)		

Annual Maximum NIC 503.2

	£	£
Class 1	629.40	
Class 2 – £2.70 × 52	140.40	769.80
		(2,405.85)

This produces a positive result which must be compared with Class 1 and Class 4 – payable at the main rate – and Class 2:

Class 1		629.40
Class 2		140.40
Class 4 (£15,000 – £7,755) × 9%		652.05
		£1,421.85

As £2,405.85, is more than these potential liabilities, the figure of Class 4 payable at the main rate (i.e., 9%) is the figure calculated above (i.e. £652.05). This is a 'Case 1' situation and no further steps are necessary, because there is no liability at the additional rate of 2%.

Class 4 contributions ('Case 1', so equal to Step 4)	£652.05

Note

(a) Where for any year Class 4 contributions are payable in addition to primary Class 1 contributions and/or Class 2 contributions, the liability for Class 4 contributions is not to exceed the amount which, when added to the primary Class 1 and Class 2 contributions (after applying the limitation in 503.1 above) equals the sum of the amount of Class 4 contributions which would be payable on profits equal to the upper annual limit plus 53 times the amount of a Class 2 contribution, plus an amount in respect of the additional 2% rate. [*SI 2001 No 1004, Reg 100*]. *Reg 100* sets out a multi-step process for calculating each earner's personal maximum, with different further steps for each of three possible results at step four. See (B) and (C) below for cases 2 and 3.

(B) **Case 2**

Iris is a self-employed dressmaker with profits assessable to income tax under the self-assessment basis for 2013/14 (and requiring no further adjustment) of £19,000. Throughout the year she pays Class 2 contributions but, intermittently, when business is poor, she supplements her income by taking employment with Jeans Ltd. Her earnings from Jeans Ltd during the year were 32 weeks at £612. Contributions are paid as follows

		£
Class 1 primary	£149 × Nil% × 32	0.00
	£463 × 12% × 32	1,777.92
Class 2 Note: As there are 52 Sundays in 2013/14 only fifty-two weeks of Class 2 is payable	£2.70 × 52	140.40
		£1,918.32

503.2 NIC   Annual Maximum

In the absence of a relieving provision, Class 4 contributions of £1,012.05 (i.e. (£19,000 − £7,755) @ 9%) would also be payable. However, the Class 4 liability is not to exceed the amount determined following the numbered steps in the legislation as follows:

Step		£	£
1.	Subtract the Class 4 lower profits limit from upper profits limit i.e. £41,450 − £7,755		33,695.00
2.	9% thereof	3,032.55	
3.	Add 53 times the weekly rate of Class 2 i.e. 53 × £2.70	143.10	3,175.65
4.	Subtract from Step 3 the amount of Class 2 paid and Class 1 paid at the main percentage rate (i.e. other than 2%)		
	Class 1	1,777.92	
	Class 2 − £2.70 × 52	140.40	1,918.32
			1,257.33
	This produces a positive result which must be compared with Class 1 and Class 4 − payable at the main rate − and Class 2:		
	Class 1	1,777.92	
	Class 2	140.40	
	Class 4 (£19,000 − £7,755) × 9%	1,012.05	
		2,930.37	
	As £1,257.33 is less than these potential liabilities, this is the figure of Class 4 payable at the main rate (i.e. 9%) − a 'Case 2' situation.		
5.	Multiply the result of Step 4 (i.e. £1,257.33) by 100/9	13,970	
6.	Subtract the lower profits limit from the lesser of the upper profits limit and the amount of assessable profits	11,245	
7.	Subtract the answer in 5 from the answer in 6. (If negative, treat as nil.)	Nil	
8.	Multiply the above by 2%		Nil
9.	Multiply the profits less the upper profits limit by 2%		Nil
	Class 4 contributions ('Case 2', so add 4, 8 and 9)		£1,257.33

In consequence, Iris's liability is limited to that of someone deriving equivalent total earnings exclusively from self-employment.

(C) **Case 3**

Jan is a self-employed printer with profits assessable to income tax under the self-assessment basis for 2013/14 (and requiring no further adjustment) of £45,000. Throughout the year she pays Class 2 contributions. Throughout the year she is also a director of Jan's Jeans Ltd. Her earnings from the company during the year were £44,135. Contributions are paid as follows:

Annual Maximum   NIC 503.2

		£
Class 1 primary	£7,755 × Nil%	0.00
	£34,870 (£41,450 − £7,755) × 12%	4,043.40
	£1,660 (£44,135 − £41,450) × 2%	53.70
Class 2	£2.70 × 52 Note: As there are 52 Sundays in 2013/14 only fifty-two weeks of Class 2 is payable	140.40
		£4,237.50

Her Class 4 liability is not to exceed the amount determined using the following numbered steps:

Step		£	£
1.	Subtract the Class 4 lower profits limit from upper profits limit i.e. £41,450 − £7,755		33,695.00
2.	9% thereof	3,032.55	
3.	Add 53 times the weekly rate of Class 2 i.e. 53 × £2.70	143.10	3,175.65
4.	Subtract from Step 3 the amount of Class 2 paid and Class 1 paid at the main percentage rate (i.e. other than 2%)		
	Class 1	4,043.40	
	Class 2 − £2.70 × 52	140.40	4,183.80
			(1,008.15)
	This produces a negative result, called 'Case 3' in the legislation − see Step 9 also. No Class 4 contributions are payable at the main (9%) rate.		
	The consequence is that the result of this Step 4 is treated as nil.		Nil
5.	Multiply the result of Step 4 by 100/9	Nil	
6.	Subtract the lower profits limit from the lesser of the upper profits limit and the amount of assessable profits	33,695	
7.	Subtract the answer in 5 from the answer in 6. (If negative, treat as nil.)	33,695	
8.	Multiply the above by 2%		673.90
9.	Multiply the profits less the upper profits limit by 2%		
	i.e. £45,000 − £41,450 × 2%		71.00
Class 4 contributions ('Case 3', so add 4, 8 and 9)			£744.90

695

504 Class 1 Contributions: Employed Earners

Cross-reference. See also 502 aggregation of earnings.

504.1 RATES

[*SSCBA 1992, ss 8, 9*]

Kevin employed Glenn at a rate of £900 per week from 26 March to 7 April 2013, making payment on Saturday each week.

Primary contributions due are:

Week ended 31 March 2013	146 × Nil%	Nil
	671 × 12%	80.52
	83 × 2%	1.66
		£82.18
Week ended 7 April 2013	148 × Nil%	Nil
	649 × 12%	77.88
	103 × 2%	2.06
		£79.94

Kevin's secondary contributions in respect of Glenn's employment are as follows:

Week ended 31 March 2013	144 × Nil%	Nil
	756 × 13.8%	104.33
		£104.33
Week ended 7 April 2013	148 × Nil%	Nil
	752 × 13.8%	103.77
		£103.77

504.2 CALCULATION METHODS

[*SI 2001 No 1004, Reg 12*]

Alistair is in a contracted-out (COSR) employment. His earnings for the quarter ended 30 June 2013 are £11,257 and, in accordance with the normal procedures of the company by which he is employed are paid to him on 3 July 2013. Class 1 contributions can be calculated by either the exact percentage method or the tables method, as follows.

Exact percentage method
Employee's Earnings Threshold = £7,755 ÷ 12 × 3 = £1,939.00*
Employer's Earnings Threshold = £7,696 ÷ 12 × 3 = £1,924.00*
Employee's Upper Accrual Point= £3,337 × 3 = £10,011.00

504.2 NIC   Class 1 Contributions: Employed Earners

Employee's Upper Earnings Limit = £41,450 ÷ 12 × 3 = £10,363.00 *rounded up to next whole pound

	£		£
Primary:	1,939.00 × Nil% =		0.00
	8,072.00 × 10.6% =		855.63
	352.00 × 12% =		42.24
	894.00 × 2% =		17.88
	£11,257.00		£915.75
Secondary:	1,924.00 × Nil% =		0.00
	8,087.00 × 10.4% =		841.04
	352.00 × 13.8% =		48.57
	894.00 × 13.8% =		123.37
	£11,257.00		£1,012.98

Tables method
Tables CA 39, either:
Weekly Table D
£11,257.00/13 = £865.92
Table entry £797.00
Primary: £68.51 × 13 =   £890.63
(per calculator at end of Table – on £68) £1.36 × 13 =   £17.68
                                                                     £908.31

Secondary: £67.08 × 13 =   £872.04
(per calculator at end of Table – on £68) £9.38 × 13 =   121.94
                                                                     £993.98

Or:
Monthly Table D
£11,257.00/3 = £3,752.33
Table entry £3,454.00
Primary: £296.87× 3 =   £890.61
(per calculator at end of Tables – on £298) £5.96 × 3 =   £17.88
                                                                     £908.49

Secondary: £290.82 × 3 =   £872.46
(per calculator at end of Tables – on £298) £41.12 × 3 =   123.36
                                                                     £995.82

Notes

(a)   For the tables to be used in the tables method see HMRC Employer's Help Book E13 (2013).

(b)   From the total contributions calculated on the exact percentage method would also be deducted the employee's and employer's contracted-out rebate on earnings falling between the respective lower earnings limits and the earnings thresholds. See **509** CONTRACTED-OUT EMPLOYMENT.

505 Class 1A Contributions: Benefits in Kind

505.1 THE PERSON LIABLE

[*SSCBA 1992, ss 10–10ZB*]

(A) **Benefits provided by third party**

Avant is a sales representative. Throughout 2013/14, his contract of service is with Ballade and they pay Avant his salary and commission, he is provided with a car and private medical insurance; but the car he uses is owned and made available to him by Cavalier, Ballade's parent company and they also pay the medical insurance premium. Because Avant has been provided with benefits and private use of the car, he is chargeable to income tax on an amount arrived at under *ITEPA 2003, ss 201–203*, and, in consequence, a Class 1A contribution is payable for 2013/14 in respect of Avant and the benefits provided to him. But, because the secondary Class 1 contribution on the last payment of earnings made to Avant in 2013/14 is paid by Ballade, Ballade must pay the Class 1A contribution even though Cavalier, not Ballade, is the person who owns the car and paid for the medical insurance.

(B) **Two or more employers in tax year**

Herald works for Integra until 5 January 2014 when he changes jobs and takes up employment with Jetta. He is provided with a car (which is available for his private use) in each job. A tax charge will arise in respect of each car for 2013/14 so a Class 1A contribution will be payable in respect of each car for that year. Integra will pay secondary Class 1 contributions in relation to Herald's last earnings in his employment with Integra so Integra will be liable to pay a Class 1A contribution in respect of the car provided in that job, while Jetta will pay secondary Class 1 contributions in relation to Herald's last earnings in the tax year so Jetta will be liable to pay a Class 1A contribution in respect of the car provided in the second job.

(C) **Person succeeding to a business**

Orion works for Panda by whom he is provided with a car which is available for his private use. In October 2013, Panda sells his business to Quinta and Quinta continues to employ Orion and to allow him the private use of the car. As Quinta will pay a secondary Class 1 contribution in relation to Orion's last payment of earnings in 2013/14 in respect of the employment by reason of which the car is made available, he (to the exclusion of Panda) will be liable to pay the entire Class 1A contribution for the year in respect of the car – and any other benefits in kind – provided throughout the year.

If, of course, Orion had left Panda's employment before the change took place, the Class 1A liability in respect of the car provided to Orion from 6 April 2013 to the date of his leaving would rest with Panda.

505.2 NIC   Class 1A Contributions: Benefits in Kind

505.2 CARS PROVIDED FOR THE PRIVATE USE OF THE EMPLOYEE

(A) **Reduction for periods when car not available for use**

[*ITEPA 2003, s 143*]

Kadette takes up employment by Legend on 2 June 2013 and a new petrol driven, 1,800 cc car, with carbon dioxide emissions of 165 g/km costing £15,000 is made available for his business and private use. Petrol is also provided. On 15 June, Kadette is involved in an accident and the car is off the road until 8 July. On 21 September, Kadette is involved in another accident and this time the car is off the road until 29 October. On 2 November, Kadette is moved into a clerical post within the company where he no longer has the use of a company car.

The cash equivalent of the car and fuel benefits for 2013/14 are £3,750 (£15,000 × 25%) and £5,275 (£21,100 × 25%) respectively, but the car is unavailable for 57 days at the start of the tax year, for 37 days in September/October, and for 155 days at the end of the tax year. The period of repair in June/July does not count as unavailability because it lasted for only 22 consecutive days. The cash equivalents of £3,750 and £5,275 are, therefore, reduced by $^{249}/_{365}$ to £1,191 and £1,676.

(B) **Car made available by reason of more than one employment**

[*SI 2001 No 1004, Reg 36*]

Robin works for Senator, Trevi and Uno and, by reason of those three employments, is provided with a petrol driven car costing £11,000 and with carbon dioxide emissions of 119 g/km. This is available for his private use but fuel is not provided. In 2013/14 the car benefit of £1,650 (15% × £11,000) is reduced by deducting from it

$$£1,650 \times \frac{3-1}{3} = £1,100$$

In other words, each employer will be liable for a Class 1A contribution on £550 and the aggregate of those reduced scale amounts (3 × £550) is £1,650, i.e. the scale amount on which a single employer of Robin would have been liable for a Class 1A contribution.

(C) **Shared cars**

[*SI 2001 No 1004, Reg 36*]

Accord, Bacara and Clio work for Dedra and, by reason of their employments, are concurrently provided with one car for private use costing £10,000 and with CO2 emissions of 119 g/km. This is available for private use but fuel is not provided. The scale charge in each case is £1,500 (£10,000 × 15%) but these three amounts are then each reduced by deducting

$$£1,500 \times \frac{3-1}{3} = £1,000$$

In other words, Dedra will be liable for three Class 1A contributions on £500 and the aggregate of those reduced scale amounts (3 × £500) is £1,500, i.e. the car benefit on which he would have been liable for a Class 1A contribution if he had made the car available to just one employee.

506 Class 1B Contributions: PAYE Settlement Agreements

506.1 CALCULATION OF CONTRIBUTIONS

[*SSCBA 1992, s 10A*]

Benevolent Ltd has 500 employees who are all provided with late night taxis each year prior to Christmas when a large, regular and anticipated order is placed by an overseas customer that is time sensitive. The taxi fares amount to an average of £50 per employee during the year ended 5 April 2014. Of the employees affected, 400 are basic rate taxpayers and the other 100 are higher rate (but not additional rate) taxpayers. Also, 100 employees receive expenses amounting to £2,000 in total relating to home to work travel (all higher rate taxpayers). Benevolent Ltd seeks a PSA. The PSA negotiation might be as follows:

	£	£
Tax due under PSA.		
Value of benefits provided to basic rate taxpayers (400 × £50)	20,000.00	
Tax thereon @ 20%	4,000.00	
Gross up tax $£4,000 \times \dfrac{100}{100-20}$		5,000.00
Value of benefits provided to higher rate taxpayers (100 × £50)	5,000.00	
Value of expenses provided to higher rate taxpayers	2,000.00	
	7,000.00	
Tax thereon @ 40%	2,800.00	
Gross up tax £2,800 × 100 / 100 − 40		£4,666.67
Total tax		£9,666.67
NICs due under PSA.		
Value of expenses otherwise liable for Class 1 NICs	2,000.00	
Class 1B NICs due @ 13.8% on £2,000		276.00
Value of benefits otherwise liable to Class 1A NICs	25,000.00	
Class 1B NICs due @ 13.8% on £25,000		3,450.00
Tax paid by employer liable to Class 1B charge	9,666.67	
Class 1B NICs due re tax paid by employer @ 13.8%		1,334.00
Total NICs and tax payable by Benevolent Ltd		£14,276.67

The tax and Class 1B is payable to HMRC on or before 19 October 2014 (22 October 2014 if paid electronically and value is received by this date).

507 Class 4 Contributions: On Profits of a Trade etc.

Cross-reference. See also 502.10 AGGREGATION OF EARNINGS; 511 EARNINGS FROM SELF-EMPLOYMENT.

507.1 EXCEPTION OF CLASS 1 CONTRIBUTORS FOR EARNINGS CHARGEABLE TO TAX AS TRADING INCOME

[*SI 2001 No 1004, Reg 94*]

Ariadne is a practising solicitor and also the company secretary of Web Ltd. Her accounting year ends on 30 June and her 2013/14 assessable profits for Class 4 purposes (based on her accounts to 30 June 2013 under *ITTOIA 2005, ss 198(1), 200(3), 201(1)*) are £33,000. During 2013/14 she is paid secretarial fees (under deduction of standard rate primary Class 1 contributions, as appropriate) on a quarterly basis as follows.

	Gross fees £	Class 1 £	
June 2013	500.00	—	(below earnings threshold)
September 2013	500.00	—	(below earnings threshold)
December 2013	2,000.00	Nil	(Nil% on [£646 × 3 = £1,938])
		7.44	(12% on remainder [£2,000 − £1,938 = £62])
March 2014	14,000.00	Nil	(Nil% on [£646 × 3 = £1,938])
		1,010.88	(12% on remainder up to the UEL [3 × £2,808 = £8,424])
		72.76	(2% on the remainder up to £14,000 = £3,638).
	£17,000.00	£1,124.32	

As these fees are included gross in Ariadne's accounts (the Class 1 contributions being correctly debited to drawings), the amount of £17,000 is deducted from the profits on which Class 4 contributions would be payable. The position for 2013/14 will be:

	£
Profits as stated	33,000
Less: Class 4 exception	17,000
	16,000
Less: lower annual limit	7,755
	£8,245
Total Class 4 liability	
£8,245 × 9% =	£742.05

508 Company Directors

Cross-reference. See also 502 AGGREGATION OF EARNINGS; 512 EARNINGS PERIODS.

508.1 EARNINGS

[*SI 2001 No 1004, Reg 22(2)*]

(A)

Gary Newsmith is a director of Lesstain Ltd, which has an accounting date of 5 July. Gary has no balance standing to his credit with the company at 6 July 2012 and fees already voted and paid have exactly equalled his drawings up to that date. G has substantial earnings from other sources and takes only one payment annually from L in respect of his services. A meeting is held on 2 April 2013 at which Gary's fees for the year ending 5 July 2013 are determined at £10,000, but this amount is neither credited to his current account nor made available to him. Due to cash flow problems and the desire to tie Gary to the company, it is agreed that Gary will only become entitled to his emoluments on 4 October 2013.

Gary is taxable on these earnings in 2013/14, since that is the year in which the end of the accounting period falls, and Lesstain Ltd has to apply PAYE to the general earnings on 5 July 2013, despite the fact that Gary may not draw the general earnings before 2 October 2013. When that date arrives, the company must deduct and account for National Insurance contributions, since it is only then that the money is put unreservedly at Gary's disposal.

Note

(a) Fees voted to a director in advance become earnings for contribution purposes on the date the director has an unreserved right to draw on them. (*Garforth v Newsmith Stainless Ltd* [1979] 2 All ER 73).

(B) **Fees voted in advance**

Dawn is a director of East Ltd. On 31 March 2013 E votes fees to D of £800 payable on the last Friday in each month for the next twelve months. D will have earnings for contribution purposes thus:

	£
26 April 2013	800
31 May 2013	800
28 June 2013	800
Etc.	

508.1 NIC   Company Directors

(C) **Fees credited to overdrawn account**

Sherlock is a director of Homes Ltd. On 16 July 2013, his current account with the company is overdrawn by £2,800, of which £2,000 has been treated as earnings for contribution purposes. On 19 July 2013 fees of £30,000 are voted to him and credited to the account. £28,000 of those fees are earnings for contribution purposes.

Note

(a) To the extent that items creating an overdrawn account have already been treated as earnings for contribution purposes, the fees etc. credited will not be earnings for contribution purposes, but any other part of the amount credited will be. [*SI 2001 No 1004, Sch 3 Part X para 2*].

508.2 CALCULATION OF CONTRIBUTIONS

[*SI 2001 No 1004, Regs 8, 22(2)*]

Frederick is appointed a director of Great Ltd on 1 November 2013. Not contracted-out earnings are paid to Frederick as follows:

Date	Payment £	Cumulative £
30 November	700	700
31 December	800	1,500
31 January	5,000	6,500
28 February	900	7,400
31 March	12,600	20,000

There are 23 whole or part contribution weeks left in 2013/14, not counting for this purpose the one day which constitutes week 53 (Leaflet CA 44, Para 25 and page 35). His earnings period as a director is therefore 23 weeks. As the weekly primary earnings threshold, secondary earnings threshold, upper accrual point and the upper earnings limit for 2013/14 are £149.00, £148.00, £770.00 and £797.00 respectively, Frederick's primary earnings threshold, secondary earnings threshold, upper accrual point and upper earnings limit are £3,427.00 (i.e. £149 × 23), £3,404.00 (i.e. £148 × 23), £17,710.00 (i.e. £770.00 × 23) and £18,331.00 (i.e. £797.00 × 23). (The calculation of these limits and thresholds is necessary only if contributions in respect of earnings are to be calculated by use of the modified exact percentage method.)

Contributions can be calculated by use of either the *modified exact percentage method* or the *modified tables method*.

The *modified exact percentage procedure* would operate as follows:

Cum. Pay £		Cum. Primary £	Primary payable £	Cum. secondary £	Secondary payable £
700	Nil% × £700	—	—	—	—
1,500	Nil% × £1,500	—	—	—	—
6,500	Nil% × £3,427				

Company Directors NIC 508.3

Cum. Pay £			Cum. Primary £	Primary payable £	Cum. secondary £	Secondary payable £
	12%	× £3,073	368.76	368.76		
	Nil%	× £3,404				
	13.8%	× £3,096			427.25	427.25
7,400	Nil%	× £3,427				
	12%	× £3,973	476.76	108.00		
	Nil%	× £3,404				
	13.8%	× £3,996			551.45	124.20
20,000	Nil%	× £3,427				
	12%	× £14,904				
	2%	× £1,669	1,821.86	1,345.10		
	Nil%	× £3,404				
	13.8%	× £16,596			2,290.25	1,738.80
				£1,821.86		£2,290.25

Alternatively, the *modified tables procedure* could have operated, thus:

Cum.Pay ÷ 23 £	Weekly table band £	Primary per table × 23 £	Primary payable £	Secondary per table × 23 £	Secondary payable £
30.43	—	—	—	—	—
65.22	—	—	—	—	—
282.61	282.00	368.46	368.46	426.88	426.88
321.74	321.00	476.10	107.64	550.62	123.74
869.57	797+72	1,821.60	1,345.50	2,288.50	1,737.88
			£1,821.60		£2,288.50

Note

(a) The above procedures are set out in HMRC booklet CA 44, Paras 42 to 45 and Employer's Help Book E13 (2013), pages 11 and 12. It will be noted that there are only minor discrepancies between the two results.

508.3 CHANGES DURING THE EARNINGS PERIOD

(A) **Employment becoming not contracted-out**

Greenfinch, a director of Starling Ltd, leaves S's occupational pension scheme on 16 April 2013. His earnings were £1,000 before the change and £13,000 after the change. As G's earnings from his contracted-out employment do not exceed the annual earnings thresholds (£7,755 or £7,696), Class 1 liabilities arise as follows:

508.3 NIC   Company Directors

Primary:

£7,755 × Nil% =	£0.00
£6,245 × 12% =	£749.40
£14,000	£749.40

Secondary:

£7,696 × Nil% =	£0.00
£6,304 × 13.8% =	£869.95
£14,000	£869.95

Notes

(a) Where, during the course of a tax year, a director's employment changes from contracted-out employment to not contracted-out employment or vice versa and total earnings reach or exceed the earnings threshold, but contracted out earnings do not reach or exceed that amount, the primary Class 1 liability for the year is arrived at by applying the not contracted-out rate to the chargeable earnings up to and including the upper earnings limit and 2% on the excess. The secondary liability is arrived at by applying the not contracted-out rate to the earnings in excess of the secondary earnings threshold. (CA 44, Para 63).

(b) This example disregards the employer's contracted-out rebate for earnings between the lower earnings limit and the earnings threshold. See **509 CONTRACTED-OUT EMPLOYMENT**.

(B) **Employment becoming contracted-out**

Redwing is appointed a director of Starling Ltd on 7 May 2013 so his pro-rata primary earnings threshold, secondary earnings threshold, upper accrual point and upper annual earnings limit are £7,152 (i.e. £149 × 48), £7,104 (£148 × 48), £36,960 (i.e. £770 × 48) and £38,256 (£797 × 48) respectively. He was not an employee of S at all prior to that date. He joins S's salary-related occupational pension scheme on 2 August 2013. His earnings were £11,550 before the change and £40,000 after the change. As R's earnings from his contracted-out employment exceed the pro-rata earnings thresholds, Class 1 liabilities arise as follows:

Primary:

£7,152 × Nil% =	£0.00
£29,808 × 10.6% =	£3,159.65
£1,296 × 12%	£155.52
£13,294 × 2% =	£265.88
£51,550	£3,581.05

Secondary:

£7,104 × Nil% =	£0.00
£29,856 × 10.4%	£3,105.02
£14,540 × 13.8%	£2,006.52
£51,550	£5,111.54

Notes

(a) Where, during the course of a tax year, a director's employment changes from not contracted-out employment to contracted-out employment or vice versa and contracted out earnings reach or exceed the earnings threshold, the primary Class 1 liability for the year is arrived at by treating the earnings threshold as comprising wholly contracted-out earnings, then applying the contracted-out rate to the remaining contracted-out earnings (up to a maximum of the upper earnings limit). To the extent that the upper earnings limit has not already been exceeded, the not contracted-out rate is then applied to the not contracted-out earnings, up to and including the upper earnings limit. 2% contributions are charged on the excess. The secondary liability is arrived at by applying the contracted-out rate to the contracted-out earnings in excess of the earnings threshold, and the not contracted-out rate to all the other earnings. (CA 44, Para 63).

(b) This example disregards the employer's contracted-out rebate for earnings between the lower earnings limit and the earnings threshold. See **509** CONTRACTED-OUT EMPLOYMENT.

509 Contracted-Out Employment

509.1 REDUCTION IN CONTRIBUTIONS — SALARY RELATED SCHEME EMPLOYMENT

[*Pension Schemes Act 1993, s 41; SI 2006 No 1009*]

Aphid, Bollweevil, Chafer and Dungbeetle are all employed in *contracted-out salary related scheme* employment with Earwig Ltd. During June 2013, their weekly earnings are £112, £151, £161 and £780 respectively. In January 2014 Dungbeetle's weekly earnings are increased to £850 per week. Their contribution rates and those of Earwig Ltd for 2013/14 are determined as follows.

Aphid

£112 falls above the lower earnings limit but below the earnings thresholds of £148 for the employer and £149 for the employee, so no contributions are due.

However, the employer's contracted-out rebate is due on any earnings in the band from £109 to £112 i.e. £3 at 3.4% (10p), notwithstanding that there are no employer's contributions due and there is an employee's contracted-out rebate due of £3 × 1.4%, i.e. 4p. As no employee's contributions are due at this level of earnings the employee's rebate is given to the employer, in addition to the employer's own rebate.

Bollweevil

£151 falls above the earnings thresholds. Therefore,

on £109 (LEL)	Nil
on £40 (LEL to primary ET)/£39 (LEL to secondary ET)	Nil
on £2 (balance) for employee/£3 for employer	the primary contracted-out rate is (12 − 1.4)% = 10.6% and the secondary contracted-out rate is (13.8 − 3.4) = 10.4%.

However, the employer's contracted-out rebate is due on the earnings from £109 to £148 i.e. £39 at 3.4% (= £1.32), and there is an employee's contracted-out rebate due of £40 × 1.4%. This amounts to 56p. As the employee's contribution is only 21p (£2 × 10.6%), 21p of the rebate goes to the employee so that nothing is deducted from the employee's gross pay in respect of NIC. The balance of the employee's rebate (35p) benefits the employer.

Chafer

£161 falls above the earnings thresholds. Therefore,

on £109 (LEL)	Nil
on £40 (LEL to primary ET)/£39 (LEL to secondary ET)	Nil
on £12 (balance for employee)/ £13 (employer))	the primary contracted-out rate is (12 − 1.4)% = 10.6% and the secondary contracted-out rate is (13.8 − 3.4)% = 10.4%.

In addition, the employer's contracted-out rebate is due on the earnings from £109 to £148 i.e. £39 at 3.4% (= £1.32) and there is an employee's contracted-out rebate due of £40 × 1.4%, i.e. 56p. As this is exceeded by the employee's contributions due at 10.6% on £(161 − 149) = £12, i.e. £1.27, all of it may be used to reduce to £0.71 the deduction made from gross pay in respect of NIC. The employer benefits only to the extent of the employer's own contracted-out rebate (£1.32).

509.1 NIC   Contracted-Out Employment

Dungbeetle

£780 falls above the upper accrual point of £770 so the primary contacted-out rate is due up to the UAP, the main primary rate is due beyond the UAP up to the UEL and additional primary contributions are due beyond the UEL; secondary contributions are due on all earnings above the secondary earnings threshold as follows.

on £109 (LEL)	Nil
on £40 (LEL to primary ET)/£39 (LEL to secondary ET)	Nil
on £621 (balance to UAP for employee)/£622 (employer))	the primary contracted-out rate is (12 − 1.4)% = 10.6% and the secondary contracted-out rate is (13.8 − 3.4)% = 10.4%.
on £10 (remainder)	The primary not contracted-out rate is 12% and the secondary not contracted-out rate is 13.8%.

In addition, the employer's contracted-out rebate is due on the earnings from £109 to £148 i.e. £39 at 3.4% (= £1.32) and there is an employee's contracted-out rebate due of £40 × 1.4%, i.e. 56p. As this is exceeded by the employee's contributions due, all of it benefits the employee by reducing by 56p the NIC calculated for deduction from gross pay. The employer benefits only to the extent of the employer's own contracted-out rebate (£1.32).

And in January 2014, the liability on D's earnings is as follows.

on £109 (LEL)	Nil
on £40 (LEL to primary ET)/£39 (LEL to secondary ET)	Nil
on £621 (balance to UAP for employee)/£622 (employer))	the primary contracted-out rate is (12 − 1.4)% = 10.6% and the secondary contracted-out rate is (13.8 − 3.4)% = 10.4%.
on £27 (UAP to UEL)	the primary not contracted-out rate is 12% and the secondary not contracted-out rate is 13.8%.
on £53 (remainder)	the additional primary contribution rate is 2% and the secondary contribution rate is 13.8%.

In addition, the employer's contracted-out rebate is due on the earnings from £109 to £148 i.e. £39 at 3.4% (= £1.32) and there is an employee's contracted-out rebate due of £40 × 1.4%, i.e. 56p. As this is exceeded by the employee's contributions due, all of it benefits the employee by reducing by 56p the NIC calculated for deduction from gross pay. The employer benefits only to the extent of the employer's own contracted-out rebate (£1.32).

510 Deferment of Payment

510.1 CLASS 1 DEFERMENT

[*SSCBA 1992, s 19(1)(2); SI 2001 No 1004, Regs 68, 84*]

(A) **Contracted-out and not contracted-out employments**

Afghan is employed by Beagle Ltd (contracted-out, salary £480 per week); Collie Ltd (contracted-out, salary £540 per week); and Doberman Ltd (not contracted-out, salary £450 per week). He seeks Class 1 deferment for 2013/14.

There are two possibilities: either liability on earnings from Beagle Ltd may be deferred (leaving contributions payable on earnings from Collie Ltd and Doberman Ltd which, together, will exceed the required amount for 2013/14 (i.e. weekly upper earnings limit of £797 plus £149 per additional employment), or liability on earnings from Doberman Ltd may be deferred (leaving contributions payable on earnings from Beagle Ltd and Collie Ltd which, together, will also exceed the required amount). As Afghan's employment with Doberman Ltd is a not contracted-out employment, however, whereas his employment with Beagle Ltd is not, deferment will be granted in relation to Afghan's employment with Doberman Ltd.

Note

(a) An earner has no choice as to which of his employments are to be included in a deferment arrangement. That decision lies with HMRC. Where, however, an earner is employed both in contracted-out employment and in not contracted-out employment, HMRC will generally defer *not contracted-out contribution liability rather than contracted-out liability*, whenever this is possible.

(B) **Post-deferment assessment**

Eel is employed by Flounder Ltd, Grunion Ltd and Hake Ltd. In March 2013, when his earnings from the three companies were £630, £300 and £490 per week respectively, he applied for Class 1 deferment for 2013/14.

As his anticipated earnings from Flounder Ltd and Hake Ltd together (£1,120) exceeded the required amount for 2013/14 (£797, plus £149 per additional employment) deferment was granted in respect of the primary Class 1 contribution liability which would otherwise have arisen on his earnings from Grunion Ltd.

If, when the year ends, it is found that earnings from Flounder Ltd and Hake Ltd, contrary to expectations, have not together reached the upper earnings limit throughout the year, HMRC will issue a demand for the balance of contributions due (relating those contributions to Eel's earnings from Grunion Ltd but calculating the amount by reference to his actual total earnings in the year). If (as is more likely), however, the earnings from Flounder Ltd and Hake Ltd have together exceeded the upper earnings limit throughout the year, any excess contributions paid on those earnings will be refunded and the earnings from Grunion Ltd will be automatically excepted from the liability at the main rate which, until its exception, had been merely deferred.

510.1 NIC   Deferment of Payment

Note

(a) In making application for deferment, a contributor has to agree to pay any amount by which contributions fall short of the total liability within 28 days of demand (see from CA 72A).

510.2 CLASS 2 AND/OR CLASS 4

[*SSCBA 1992, s 19(1)(2); SI 2001 No 1004, Regs 90, 95*]

Inigo is a self-employed architect whose 2013/14 assessable Class 4 profits are £37,000. He is, however, also retained by Jones Ltd at an amount of £300 per week and expects the retainer to continue throughout 2013/14, but at an increased rate. His anticipated contribution liability for 2013/14 is, therefore,

	£
Class 1: £300: Nil% on £149 × 52 weeks	0.00
+ 12% on £151 (balance) × 52 weeks	942.24
Class 2: 52 × £2.70	140.40
	1,082.64
Class 4: £37,000 – £7,755 (lower limit) × 9%	2,632.05
	£3,714.69

As the estimated Class 1 and Class 2 total (£1,082.64) falls short of the 2013/14 Class 4 limiting amount (£3,175.65), Class 4 contributions at the main rate will be reduced from £2,632.05 to whatever the shortfall (estimated at £3,175.65 – £1,082.64 = £2,093.01) is ultimately found to be. Class 4 income so displaced (i.e. £2,632.05 – £2,093.01 = £539.04 × 100/9 = £5,989.33 will then be liable at 2% (i.e. £119.78). However, because the amount may not be determined with accuracy until 6 April 2014 or later, he may apply for deferment of Class 4 liability at the main rate and pay only 2% in the meantime on all profits above the lower annual limit.

Note

(a) Were Inigo's anticipated earnings from his employed earner's employment to be in excess of £797 per week, Class 2 liabilities could be deferred also as, in that case, his Class 1 contributions alone would approximate to his overall, personalised annual maximum.

511 Earnings from Self-Employment

Cross-reference. See also 507 CLASS 4 CONTRIBUTIONS: ON PROFITS OF A TRADE ETC.

511.1 EARNINGS FOR CLASS 2 PURPOSES

[*SI 2001 No 1004, Reg 45*]

Jerry is an unsuccessful builder. His accounting year ends on 30 June and his accounts for the last two years show results as follows

Year to		£
30.6.2012	Profit	18,000
30.6.2013	Loss	(1,500)

For the purpose of an application for Class 2 exception, his profits for 2012/13 are

	£
3/12 × £18,000	4,500
9/12 × £(1,500)	(1,125)
	£3,375

Note

(a) In ascertaining whether Class 2 exception can be obtained, the exception limit (£5,725 for 2013/14, £5,595 for 2012/13) is compared with the earnings in respect of that year. [*SI 2001 No 1004, Reg 45(1)*]. It is therefore necessary to time-apportion profits where a person's accounting period overlaps 5 April.

511.2 EARNINGS FOR CLASS 4 PURPOSES — LOSS RELIEF

[*SSCBA 1992, Sch 2 para 3(1)(4)*]

Kit has a sportswear business. His trading results (adjusted for tax purposes) are

Year to		£
5 July 2010	Profit	12,000
5 July 2011	Loss	(17,200)
5 July 2012	Profit	4,000
5 July 2013	Profit	19,400

K's assessable amounts of profit and other income are

	Tax and Class 4	Investment Income
	£	£
2010/11	12,000	1,500

511.2 NIC Earnings from Self-Employment

	Tax and Class 4	Investment Income
	£	£
2011/12	Nil	1,700
2012/13	4,000	1,800
2013/14	19,400	2,200

If K claims relief for his 2011/12 loss of £17,200 under *ITA 2007, s 64*, it will be apportioned against 2010/11 earned income i.e. £12,000 profits, then against 2010/11 investment income i.e. £1,500 and then against 2011/12 investment income i.e. £1,700. The balance of the loss (£2,000) is then carried forward against profits of the same trade only. This will result in revised assessable amounts of profit and income, thus

	Tax and Class 4	Investment Income
	£	£
2010/11	Nil	Nil
2011/12	Nil	Nil
2012/13	2,000	1,800
2013/14	19,400	2,200

For Class 4 purposes, however, only £14,000 of the loss has been relieved (£12,000 in 2010/11 and £2,000 in 2012/13) and the remaining £3,200 must, therefore, also be carried forward to 2013/14 (and subsequent years, if necessary, as in the example), giving revised Class 4 profits as follows

	Class 4
	£
2010/11	Nil
2011/12	Nil
2012/13	Nil
2013/14	18,200

Notes

(a) Loss relief available for income tax purposes under *ITA 2007, s 83* (carry-forward against subsequent profits) and *s 89* (carry-back of terminal loss) is also available for Class 4 purposes. Relief under *ITA 2007, ss 64, 72* (set-off against general income) is also so available provided that the loss arises from activities of which any profits would have been earnings for Class 4 purposes (and see note (b) below). [*SSCBA 1992, Sch 2 para 3(1)*]. See also **IT 13** LOSSES.

(b) Where a loss deducted for income tax purposes is deducted from income other than trading profits, the loss is, to that extent, carried forward for Class 4 purposes and set off against the first available trading profit for subsequent years. [*SSCBA 1992, Sch 2 para 3(4)*].

Earnings Periods   NIC 512.1

512 Earnings Periods

512.1 PAY PATTERNS

[*SI 2001 No 1004, Regs 2–9*]

(A) **Multiple regular pay pattern**

Clive is a salesman for Dubbleglays Ltd. He is paid a monthly salary, a quarterly commission and an annual bonus and has, therefore, three regular pay intervals: a month, a quarter and a year.

As the shortest of these is a month, Clive's earnings period is a month and all the earnings paid to him in a year will be related to one or other of the twelve such periods it contains. If, therefore, he is paid £830 commission on 8 May for the quarter ended 31 March, £500 salary on 15 May for the month of May and £2,500 bonus on 29 May for the year ended 31 December of the preceding year, his earnings for the earnings period from 6 May to 5 June (PAYE month 2) will be £3,830, irrespective of the fact that only £500 of the total is earned within the month and the remainder relates to previous tax years and was earned over a period of between three and twelve months.

Notes

(a) Where two or more regular pay patterns run concurrently, the earnings period is normally the length of the shorter or shortest interval at which any part of the earnings is paid. [*SI 2001 No 1004, Reg 3(1)(2)*].

(b) See (B) below for the power for HMRC to direct that the longer or longest interval should be the earnings period.

(c) See **502.1(A)** AGGREGATION OF EARNINGS for the aggregation of earnings where two or more regular pay patterns run concurrently. See also **502.6**, **502.7** AGGREGATION OF EARNINGS for circumstances in which a common earnings period must be determined for related employments.

(B) **Multiple regular pay pattern — HMRC direction**

For the tax year, Everard (one of Clive's colleagues—see (A) above) had total earnings of £15,200 comprising:

	£	Pay interval
Salary	7,200	month
Commission	4,000	quarter
Bonus	4,000	year

A similar pattern had subsisted during the preceding two tax years.

If HMRC direct on, say, 5 June that, from the date of the direction onwards, and for all future years, E is to have an annual earnings period, E's earnings periods for the tax year would be:

512.1 NIC   Earnings Periods

month to	5 May
1 month to	5 June
44-week period to	5 April

and his earnings period for the next and all future tax years would be the tax year concerned.

Note

(a) Where two or more regular pay patterns run concurrently and it appears to HMRC that the greater part of earnings is normally paid at intervals of greater length than the shorter or shortest, HMRC may, by notifying the earner and secondary contributor, specify the longer or longest pay interval as the earnings period. [*SI 2001 No 1004, Reg 3(2A)–(3)*].

(C) **Irregular payments**

On 15 July, Jack is employed by Kwest Films Ltd as a researcher but, because of his age, is not entitled to the adult minimum wage. He is to be paid £5 per hour and to work in his own time and at his own convenience. He has, however, to meet the following deadlines

'Health Service' material	31 August
'Aids' material	28 October
'Disarmament' material	31 October

Jack works 106 hours on the first project, 151 hours on the second and 12 hours on the third. Earnings periods and earnings will be as follows

	£
48 days from 15 July to 31 August	530
58 days from 1 September to 28 October	755
Week ended 1 November (though only a four-day fixed period)	60

Note

(a) Where earnings are paid at irregular intervals and neither follow nor can be treated as following a regular pay pattern, the earnings period is the length of that part of the employment for which the earnings are paid or a week, whichever is the longer. [*SI 2001 No 1004, Reg 4(a)*].

512.2 CHANGE OF REGULAR PAY INTERVAL

[*SI 2001 No 1004, Reg 18*]

(A) **Change to longer interval**

Nuthatch and Osprey are both employed by Partridge Ltd. N is paid £400 per week and O is paid £150 per week. In June 2013, they become salaried employees and begin to be paid monthly at £1,800 and £650 per month, respectively. The last weekly wage is paid to each of them on 8 June and their first monthly salaries are paid on 29 June.

Earnings Periods   NIC 512.2

The first new earnings period is the month from 6 June to 5 July and their last payments of weekly wage fall within this period. Contributions have already been calculated on that wage as follows.

		Primary*		Secondary*	
		%	£	%	£
N	£400	Nil/12	30.12	Nil/13.8	34.78
O	£150	Nil/12	0.12	Nil/13.8	0.28

If contributions on the payment of salary on 5 July are calculated without regard to that wage payment, those contributions will be

		Primary*		Secondary*	
		%	£	%	£
N	£1,800	Nil/12	138.48	Nil/13.8	159.94
O	£650	Nil/12	0.48	Nil/13.8	1.24

If, however, contributions are calculated on the total payments in the earnings period, contributions will be

		Primary*		Secondary*	
		%	£	%	£
N	£2,200	Nil/12	186.48	Nil/13.8	215.14
O	£791	Nil/12	18.48	Nil/13.8	21.94

**First £646 (monthly) or £149 (weekly) at Nil% for primary contributions and £641 and £148 for secondary.

Under *SI 2001/1004, Reg 18(3)*, the contributions due on the two separate parts of earnings are not to exceed the contributions due on the total and they do not.

However, HMRC guidance requires the calculation on the total payments in the earnings period to be performed regardless of any comparison and thus, N's separate contributions (primary, £30.12 + £138.48 = £168.60 and secondary, £34.78 + £159.94 = £194.72) become primary, £186.48 and secondary £215.14, and O's separate contributions (primary £0.12 + £0.48 = £0.60 and secondary, £0.28 + £1.24 = £1.52) are to be uplifted to £18.48 primary and £21.94 secondary. Thus, according to HMRC, primary contributions of £156.36 (£186.36 – £30.12) and secondary contributions of £180.36 (£215.14 – £34.783) are to be paid on the first payment of monthly salary to N, while primary contributions of £18.36 (£18.48 – £0.12) and secondary contributions of £21.666 (£21.94 – £0.28) are to be paid on the first payment of monthly salary to O. The legal validity of this HMRC's instruction in these circumstances is questionable.

Notes

(a) An earner's earnings period may be changed as a result of a change in the regular pay interval. If the new earnings period is longer than the old, then where a payment of earnings at the old interval falls within the first new earnings period, contributions on all payments made during the new earnings period are not to exceed the contributions which would have been payable had all those payments been made at the new interval. [*SI 2001 No 1004, Reg 18(3)*].

512.2 NIC   Earnings Periods

(b) In such circumstances HMRC instruct employers to calculate contribution liabilities on the total of all payments of earnings made in the new earnings period and then to deduct from those amounts the contribution liabilities already calculated on payments of earnings made at the old interval within the new earnings period. (HMRC Leaflet CWG2 (2013), page 9).

(B) **Change to shorter interval**

Snipe is employed by Teal Ltd at a salary of £800 per month. He receives £800 on 1 August 2013 but then, from 1 September 2013, his pay arrangement is changed to one under which he receives a weekly wage of £200. His first weekly wage under the new arrangement is paid on 1 September 2013. It follows that, in the contribution month ended 5 September, S has received two payments of earnings.

The payments are not aggregated so that liabilities are as follows:

Primary	(on a monthly earnings period basis)	£800 @ Nil%/12% =	£18.48
	(on a weekly earnings period basis)	£200 @ Nil%/12% =	£6.12
			£24.60
Secondary	(on a monthly earnings period basis)	£800 @ Nil%/13.8% =	£21.94
	(on a weekly earnings period basis)	£200 @ Nil%/13.8% =	£7.18
			£29.12

Note

(a) Where an employed earner's regular pay interval is changed so that the new interval is shorter than the old interval and, as a result, the first of the new earnings periods is contained within the last of the old earnings periods, the two payments are treated separately. (HMRC Leaflet CWG2 (2013), page 9).

512.3 HOLIDAY PAY

[*SI 2001 No 1004, Reg 19*]

Utrillo and Vermeer are both employed by Whistler Ltd. Each is paid a wage of £260 and holiday pay (for the following two weeks) of £250 each per week on 24 June 2013. U works during his holiday period and earns £180 paid to him on 1 July and £220 paid to him on 8 July. His wage on 15 July is £260. V takes his holiday but £40 in overtime pay becomes due for payment to him on 1 July. This is paid (along with a wage of £250) on 15 July after his return to work.

If W adopts *method A*, final calculations will be as follows.

U	£	*Primary*	£	*Secondary*	£
24 June 2013	260	Nil%/12%	13.32	Nil%/13.8%	15.46
1 July 2013	430	Nil%/12%	33.72	Nil%/13.8%	38.92
8 July 2013	470	Nil%/12%	38.52	Nil%/13.8%	44.44
15 July 2013	260	Nil%/12%	13.32	Nil%/13.8%	15.46
	£1,420		£98.88		£114.28

Earnings Periods NIC 512.4

V	£	Primary	£	Secondary	£
24 June 2013	260	Nil%/12%	13.32	Nil%/13.8%	15.46
1 July 2013	390	Nil%/12%	28.92	Nil%/13.8%	33.40
8 July 2013	250	Nil%/12%	12.12	Nil%/13.8%	14.08
15 July 2013	260	Nil%/12%	13.32	Nil%/13.8%	15.46
	£1,160		£67.68		£78.40

If W adopts *method B*, final calculations will be as follows.

U	£	Primary	£	Secondary	£
24 June 2013	760 ÷ 3 = 253	Nil%/12%	12.48 × 3 = 37.44	Nil%/13.8%	14.49 × 3 = 43.47
1 July 2013	180	Nil%/12%	3.72	Nil%/13.8%	4.42
8 July 2013	220	Nil%/12%	8.52	Nil%/13.8%	9.94
15 July 2013	260	Nil%/12%	13.32	Nil%/13.8%	15.46
	£1,420		£63.00		£73.29

V	£	Primary	£	Secondary	£
24 June 2013	760 ÷ 3 = 253	Nil%/12%	12.48 × 3 = 37.44	Nil%/13.8%	14.49 × 3 = 43.47
1 July 2013	—	—	—	—	—
8 July 2013	—	—	—	—	—
18 July 2013	400	Nil%/12%	30.12	Nil%/13.8%	34.77
	£1,160		£67.56		£78.24

Note

(a) Where a payment of earnings includes a payment in respect of one or more week's holiday, the earnings period may be the length of the interval in respect of which the payment is made ('*method B*'). Alternatively, the holiday pay may simply be treated for contribution purposes as pay in the weeks in which earnings would normally have been paid ('*method A*'). Method B cannot be used in respect of a payment on termination of employment which includes a payment in respect of such holiday. [*SI 2001/1004, Reg 19*]. If method B is used and the length of the interval in respect of which the payment is made includes a fraction of a week, that fraction is treated as a whole week.

512.4 PAYMENTS TO DIRECTORS AND EX-DIRECTORS

[*SI 2001 No 1004, Reg 8*]

Anchovy is a director of Barracuda Ltd. His drawings (treated as earnings) are £3,600 per month. On 30 June 2013 he resigns his office and begins to work as an ordinary employee of Carp Ltd (a completely unconnected company) who pay him a weekly wage. In May 2014 Anchovy is paid a bonus of £10,000 by B in respect of the year ended 31 March 2014.

512.4 NIC   Earnings Periods

An earnings period of one year is to apply to his earnings for the months April, May and June 2013 of £10,800 from B. A weekly earnings period will then apply in respect of his earnings from C. The £10,000 bonus will attract an annual earnings period.

Notes

(a) Where a person is a company director at the beginning of a tax year, the earnings period in respect of his earnings is that tax year. If a person is appointed as a company director during a tax year, the earnings period is the number of weeks remaining in the tax year. [*SI 2001 No 1004, Reg 8(2)(3)*].

(b) Where any payments are made to an ex-director in any year *after* that in which his directorship ceased the earnings period is the tax year in which they are paid if they are in respect of any period during which he was a company director. [*SI 2001 No 1004, Reg 8(5)*].

(c) See also **508 Company directors**.

513 Intermediaries

Cross-reference. See also **IT 19** PERSONAL SERVICE COMPANIES ETC.

513.1 CALCULATION OF DEEMED PAYMENT

[*SI 2000 No 727*]

Graham is an IT consultant working through his own service company and has secured a job with Benevolent Ltd through an agency to work on the computerised accounts system for seven months from October 2012 to April 2013 inclusive. In accounts, a team leader (another IT contractor) tells Graham what work he is to carry out but he is left to his own experience to determine 'how' the work is carried out. Graham is expected to be in attendance at Benevolent Ltd a regular 40 hours per week. Graham's company is paid an hourly rate for his services at 1.5 times the normal hourly rate. Billed monthly, Benevolent Ltd pays the agency who in turn are invoiced by Graham's company. The total invoices for the seven months will amount to £35,000. Graham draws a salary of £10,000 from his company over the period. Allowable expenses up to 5 April 2013 amount to £750 and there are pension contributions of £2,000. The main indications that self-employment arises here is the minimal financial risk from invoicing, the ability to work for others and the existence of Graham's company. In contrast, the engagement is relatively long and he must carry out the services personally. Also Benevolent Ltd provides the equipment and working accommodation and he works the usual working hours of the client. The engagement with Benevolent Ltd would appears to have been an employment had it been between Graham and the client direct rather than through the service company. The intermediary rules therefore apply for 2013/14 as follows:

Relevant income received (October, November, December, January, February; March not paid as at 5 April 2013; April 2013 not yet invoiced)		£25,000
Deduct		
Pension contributions paid	£2,000	
Expenses paid (allowable)	£750	
Flat rate allowance (5% of £25,000)	£1,250	
Salary paid in year to 5 April 2013	£10,000	
Class 1 NICs paid and due on salary paid in year (on £10,000)	£584	(£14,584)
Net deemed payments before NICs		£10,416
Employer's NICs (£10,416 × 13.8/113.8)		(£1,263)
Deemed payment		£9,153

Note

(a) The post-expense figure before NICs (i.e. £10,416) is multiplied by 100/113.8 to reach the deemed payment figure since the earnings threshold has already been taken into account on the £10,000 salary. Clearly, an adjustment will be necessary if none or only part of the earnings threshold has not been set against salary payments

513.1 NIC Intermediaries

already made in the tax year in question. In any year, other fractions will be applicable if the employment is, perhaps unusually, contracted-out or if the married woman's reduced rate applies.

514 Partners

Cross-reference. See also IT **17** PARTNERSHIPS.

514.1 CLASS 4 CONTRIBUTIONS

[*SSCBA 1992, Sch 2 para 4*]

(A)

Alder, Birch and Cypress are in partnership as arboriculturists. Their profit for the year ended 30 June 2013 is £34,000 and during that year C is a salaried partner while A and B share the remaining profit in equal shares. The tax assessment for 2013/14 is £34,000. Although A and B continue to share profits on the same basis, however, C's salary for the year ended 30 June 2013 is £12,000 and for the year ended 30 June 2013 is £14,000. For Class 4 purposes the 2013/14 assessment is to be

			£
C		=	12,000
A	1/2 × (£34,000 − £12,000)	=	11,000
B	1/2 × (£34,000 − £12,000)	=	11,000
			£34,000

Note

(a) Where a trade or profession is carried on in partnership, the liability of any partner in respect of Class 4 contributions arises in respect of his share of the profits of that trade or profession. [*SSCBA 1992, Sch 2 para 4(1)*]. The share of profits is determined on the basis of the profit sharing arrangements in the basis period for the year concerned. See also IT **17** PARTNERSHIPS.

(B)

Diamond and Emerald are in partnership as jewellers sharing profits in the ratio of 1:1 until 30 September 2011 and in the ratio of 1:2 after that date. Diamond also runs a nightclub. The partnership profits for the years to 30 September 2011, 30 September 2012 and 30 September 2013 are £36,000, £38,000 and £34,000. D's profits from his nightclub are £28,000 for 2011/12, £24,000 for 2012/13 and £32,000 for 2013/14.

D and E will each separately self-assess their income tax and Class 4 National Insurance liabilities. In the case of D, this will be based on the total income from both sources of self-employment income.

D's Class 4 liability for 2011/12 is

	£
£36,000 × 1/2	18,000
Nightclub	28,000
	46,000

514.1 NIC   Partners

		£
Less: Excess over upper annual limit (£42,475)		3,525
		42,475
Less: Lower annual limit		7,225
		£35,250

Class 4
contributions
due:

£35,250 @ 9% =	£3,172.50
£3,525 @ 2%	70.50
	£3,243.00

E's Class 4 liability for 2011/12 is

		£
£36,000 × 1/2		18,000
Less: Lower annual limit		7,225
Class 4 contributions due:		£10,775
£10,775 @ 9% =	£969.75	

D's Class 4 liability for 2012/13 is

		£
£38,000 × 1/3		12,666
Nightclub		24,000
		36,666
Less: Lower annual limit		7,605
Class 4 contributions due:		£29,061
£29,061 @ 9% =	£2,615.50	

E's Class 4 liability for 2012/13 is

	£
£38,000 × 2/3	25,333
Less: Lower annual limit	7,605
Class 4 contributions due:	£17,728
£17,728 @ 9% =	£1,595.52

D's Class 4 liability for 2013/14 is

	£
£34,000 × 1/3	11,333
Nightclub	32,000
	43,333
Less: Excess over upper limit (£41,450)	1,883
	41,450
Less: Lower annual limit	7,755
Class 4 contributions due:	£33,695
£33,695 @ 9% =	3,032.55
£1,883 @ 2% =	37.66
	£3,070.21

E's Class 4 liability for 2013/14 is

	£
£34,000 × 2/3	22,666
Less: Lower annual limit	7,755
Class 4 contributions due:	£14,911
£14,911 @ 9% =	£1,341.99

D and E's Class 4 liabilities for 2011/12 were payable in two equal interim instalments on 31 January 2012 and 31 July 2012 based on the 2010/11 self-assessments, with the balance payable on 31 January 2013. Similarly, their Class 4 liability for 2012/13 is payable in two equal instalments on 31 January 2013 and 31 July 2013 based on the 2011/12 self-assessment, with the balance payable on 31 January 2014 and so on.

The self-assessment payments will, therefore, include the following amounts in relation to Class 4 contributions.

	D	E
	£	£
31 January 2013 (2012/13 POA)	1,621.50	484.87
31 July 2013 (2012/13 POA)	1,621.50	484.87
31 January 2014 (2012/13 repayment/balance)	(627.50)	625.77
31 January 2014 (2013/14 POA)	1,307.75	797.76

514.1 NIC   Partners

	D	E
	£	£
31 July 2014 (2013/14 POA)	1,307.75	797.76
31 January 2015 (2013/14 repayment/balance)	454.71	(253.53)
31 January 2015 (2014/15 POA)	1,535.10	670.99
31 July 2015 (2014/15 POA)	1,535.10	670.99

Notes

(a)　See note (a) to (A) above.

(b)　Where a trade or profession is carried on in partnership, the liability of any partner in respect of Class 4 contributions is calculated by aggregating his share of the profits with his share of the profits of any other trade or profession. [*SSCBA 1992, Sch 2 para 4(1)*].

515 Repayment and Reallocation

515.1 REPAYMENT OF EXCESS CONTRIBUTIONS

[*SI 2001 No 1004, Reg 52*]

Throughout 2013/14 Auk is employed by Bunting Ltd, Curlew Ltd and Dipper Ltd. Until 5 October 2013 he was also self-employed. His employments with C and D were contracted-out. His assessable profits for 2013/14 are £10,000 and earnings from B, C and D are £10,000, £16,500 and £41,000 respectively. Each employer pays weekly and there is no appropriate personal pension. He paid contributions as follows

	Class 2	Class 4	Class 1 Not contracted-out employment (n-c-o)	Contracted-out employment (c-o)
	£	£	£	£
Trade	70.20	202.05		
B (n-c-o)			269.40	
C (c-o)				926.97
D (c-o)				3,422.21
D (c-o above UAP)			115.20	
	£70.20	£202.05	£384.60	£4,349.18

The basic annual maximum for 2013/14 is £4,121.28 (see Step 2 below) but this has to be adjusted to a personalised maximum to allow for the 2% charge. The calculation of the personalised annual maximum is as follows

Step		£	£
1.	Calculate 53 × (UEL – PT), ie 53 × (£797 – 149)		34,344.00
2.	12% thereof		4,121.28
3.	Earnings from each employment that falls between PT and Upper Earnings Limit: 10,000 – 7,755 = 2,245 16,500 – 7,755 = 8,745 41,000 – 7,755 = 33,245	44,235	
4.	Deduct figure in step 1 (34,344)	9,122	
5.	As the line above gives a positive figure, multiply by 2%		197.82
6.	Earnings from each employment which exceeds UEL –	Nil	

515.1 NIC   Repayment and Reallocation

Step		£	£
7.	Multiply step 6 result by 2%		Nil
8.	Add steps 2, 5, 7 – this gives the personalised annual maximum		£4,319.10

It is clear that the personalised annual maximum has been exceeded, but in order to ascertain by how much it has been exceeded it is necessary to convert to standard rate any Class 1 contributions paid at other rates.

	£
Class 1 (Not contracted-out rate)	384.60
Class 1 (Contracted-out rate £4,298.32 × 12/10.6)	4,923.60
Class 2	70.20
Class 4	202.05
	5,580.45
Personalised annual maximum	4,319.10
Excessive notional contributions	£1,261.35

It is on this *notional* figure of £1,261.35 that the repayment calculation is based.

	£	Repayment due £
Excessive notional contributions	1,261.35	
Repay: Class 4	202.05	202.05
	1,059.30	
Repay: Class 2	70.20	70.20
	989.10	
Repay: Class 1 (not contracted-out)	384.60	384.60
	604.50	
	604.50 × 10.6/12	533.97
Total repayment due		£1,190.82

Note

(a) Written application must be made for repayment of excess contributions. [*SI 2001 No 1004, Reg 52(2)*].

Index

This index is referenced to chapter and paragraph number within the six main sections of the book. The entries in bold capitals are chapter headings in the text.

A

Accounting date, change of IT 29.2
ACCOUNTING PERIODS CT 101
  See also Periods of Account
  different lengths, of (loss relief) CT 114.3(B)
  exceeding twelve months CT 101.2
  liquidation, effect of CT 112.1
  overlapping two financial years CT 101.1
ACCRUED INCOME SCHEME IT 2
  CGT effect CGT 213.3; 224.1
ACCUMULATION AND MAINTENANCE TRUSTS IHT 301
  18-to-25 trusts IHT 301.2
  —failure of IHT 301.2(B)
  after 5 April 2008 IHT 301.2
  charge on failure to qualify IHT 301.1
  income tax IT 26.2; 26.3(B)
AGE EXCEPTION NIC 501.1
  pensionable age, persons over IT 1.2(C); 14.1
Age-related allowances IT 1.3
  married couples IT 1.3(C); 15.1(A)
AGGREGATION OF EARNINGS NIC 502
  Class 2 small earnings exemption NIC 502.7
  Class 4 contributions NIC 502.8
  different employers NIC 502.3
  different employments NIC 502.2; 502.3; 502.4
  former directorships NIC 502.5
  gratuities paid separately NIC 502.6
  same employer NIC 502.1
  secondary contributors in association NIC 502.2
AGRICULTURAL PROPERTY IHT 302
  interaction of CGT and IHT IHT 302.1(C)
  land with vacant possession IHT 302.1(A)
  shares etc. in agricultural companies IHT 302.2
  tenanted land, transfers of IHT 302.1(B)(C)
Allowable and non-allowable expenditure CGT 208.1
Allowable deductions IT 29.4; 29.7; CT 116.1
  employment income IT 8.2
ALLOWANCES AND TAX RATES IT 1
  age-related allowances IT 1.3
  dividend additional rate IT 1.1(E)
  life assurance relief IT 13.3
  maintenance payments IT 15.2
  married couple's allowance IT 1.3(C)(D); 15.1
  married persons IT 15
  rates of tax

ALLOWANCES AND TAX RATES – *cont.*
  —IT IT 1.1
  —CGT CGT 201.1
  —small profits (CT) CT 119
  restriction of personal allowance IT 1.2
Annual allowance IT 18.3
  carry-forward of IT 18.3(A)(B)
  transitional period, for IT 18.3(C)
Annual exemption (IHT) IHT 310.1; 320.1
ANNUAL MAXIMUM NIC 503
  Class 1 and Class 2 limitation NIC 503.1
  Class 4 limitation NIC 503.2
ANNUAL RATES AND EXEMPTIONS CGT 201
  losses, interaction with CGT 201.2
  —attributed settlement gains CGT 201.2(B)
  married persons CGT 217.1
  rates of tax CGT 201.1
  settlements CGT 228.1
ANTI-AVOIDANCE CGT 202; IHT 303
  associated operations IHT 303.1
  disposal to connected person CGT 202.3
  gains of offshore settlements CGT 219.1
  groups of companies
  —depreciatory transactions CGT 202.4
  value-shifting CGT 202.1; 202.2
Approved share option schemes IT 27.3
Assessable profits IT 29.4; 29.7; CT 116.1
ASSETS CGT 203
  negligible value CGT 216.2(B)
  options CGT 203.1; 231.2
Assets disposed of in series of transactions CGT 202.3; IHT 303.1
ASSETS HELD ON 6 APRIL 1965 CGT 204
  buildings CGT 204.3(B)
  chattels CGT 204.3(A)
  land and buildings CGT 204.3(B)
  land reflecting development value CGT 204.2
  part disposals after 5 April 1965 CGT 204.3(F)
  quoted shares and securities CGT 204.1
  time apportionment CGT 204.3
  unquoted shares CGT 204.3(C)(D)(E)
ASSETS HELD ON 31 MARCH 1982 CGT 205
  assets transferred at undervalue CT 103.2(B)
  capital gains tax CGT 205.1
  corporation tax CGT 205.2
  deferred gains, relief for CGT 205.3

Index

ASSETS HELD ON 31 MARCH 1982 – *cont.*
no gain/no loss disposals CGT 214.2(A)(C)
part disposals before 6 April 1988 CGT 208.2(B)
partnerships, held by CGT 220.1
private residences CGT 223.1(A)(B)
short leases CGT 215.3(E)
wasting assets CGT 231.3(B)
Associated operations IHT 303.1
Averaging, creative artists IT 29.5
Averaging of farming profits IT 29.6

B

BAD DEBT RELIEF VAT 401
income tax IT 27.4
mutual supplies VAT 401.1
part payments VAT 401.1
repayment of refund VAT 401.3
second-hand goods VAT 401.2
Basis periods
trading profits IT 17.1; 29.1–29.3
Benefits code
close company participators CT 104.3
directors and employees (other than lower-paid employees) IT 8.3
—assets given and leased IT 8.3(C)
—cars IT 8.3(A)
—loans IT 8.3(D); 8.5
—petrol IT 8.3(A)
—vans IT 8.3(B)
living accommodation IT 8.4
medical insurance IT 8.6
overnight incidental expenses IT 8.6
relocation expenses IT 8.5
removal expenses IT 8.5
vouchers IT 8.6
Bereaved minors, trusts for IHT 323
Bondwashing IT 2
CGT effect CGT 224.1
Buildings in enterprise zones IT 3.3
Business assets
deferment of chargeable gain on replacement of assets CGT 226
gift of CGT 213.2
transfer to a company CGT 213.3
Business premises renovation allowances IT 3.1
BUSINESS PROPERTY IHT 304
allocation of relief IHT 305.4(B)
further conditions for lifetime transfer IHT 304.1(D)

BUSINESS PROPERTY – *cont.*
land and buildings used by business IHT 304.1(B)(C)
—owned by trustees IHT 304.1(C)
shares or securities IHT 304.1(A)
—non-qualifying subsidiary IHT 304.1(A)

C

CALCULATION OF TAX (Inheritance tax) IHT 305
cumulation principle IHT 305.1; 305.2
lifetime chargeable transfers IHT 305.2
partly exempt transfers IHT 305.3
potentially exempt transfers IHT 305.1
CAPITAL ALLOWANCES IT 3; CT 102
See also Capital Allowances on Plant and Machinery
accounting periods
—given by reference to CT 102.1
annual investment allowance, periods spanning 6.4.12 IT 4.6
annual investment allowance, periods spanning 1.1.13 IT 4.7
business premises renovation IT 3.1
capital gains, effect on CGT 208.1(B); 219.2; 229.1
capital goods scheme IT 4.6
dredging IT 3.2
enterprise zone buildings IT 3.3
flat conversion IT 14.6
FYAs
—reduced claim for CT 102.2
long-life assets IT 4.5
mineral extraction IT 3.4
mines IT 3.4
patent rights IT 3.5
periods of account
—given by reference to IT 4.1
plant and machinery IT 4; CT 102.1; 102.2
qualifying expenditure IT 4.3
research and development IT 3.6
short-life assets IT 4.4
successions IT 4.2
transfer of trade CT 102.1
VAT capital goods scheme IT 4.8
WDAs
—reduced claim for CT 102.2
CAPITAL ALLOWANCES ON PLANT AND MACHINERY IT 4
See also Capital Allowances
FYAs
—reduced claim for CT 102.2

732

Index

CAPITAL ALLOWANCES ON PLANT AND MACHINERY – *cont.*
long-life assets IT 4.5
periods of account
—given by reference to IT 4.1
qualifying expenditure IT 4.3
short-life assets IT 4.4
successions IT 4.2
WDAs
—reduced claim for CT 102.2
CAPITAL GAINS (Companies) CT 103
capital losses CT 103.1
close company transferring asset at undervalue CT 103.2
groups of companies
—degrouping charge CT 103.3(E)
—intra-group transfers of assets CT 103.3(B)(C)
—notional transfer of assets CT 103.3(A)
—pre-entry losses CT 103.3(F)
—rollover relief on replacement of business assets CT 103.3(D)
migration of companies CGT 220.1
substantial shareholdings exemption CT 103.4
CAPITAL GOODS (VAT) VAT 402
capital allowances, interaction with IT 4.8
Capital losses
See Losses
CAPITAL SUMS DERIVED FROM ASSETS CGT 206
deferred consideration CGT 206.2; 216.4; 229.4(C)
receipt of compensation CGT 206.3; 215.2
—capital sum exceeding allowable expenditure CGT 206.3(D)
—compulsory acquisition CGT 215.2
—part application of capital sum received CGT 206.3(C)
—restoration using insurance moneys CGT 206.3(B)
Car hire CT 116.1
Cars
See also Motor cars
assessable benefit IT 8.3(A); NIC 505.2
mileage allowances IT 8.2(A)
Cash basis for small businesses IT 30
cash basis IT 30.1
CATERING VAT 403
special method for caterers VAT 403.1
Cemeteries, allowances for IT 29.10
Charitable donations IT 5.1; CT 106.5; 111.1; 114.1; 116.1; 116.2
CHARITIES IT 5; IHT 306
gift aid IT 5.1; CT 116.1

CHARITIES – *cont.*
property leaving temporary charitable trusts IHT 306.1
reduced rate (IHT) for estates with 10% gifts to charity IHT 322.2
Chattels CGT 212.1
held on 6.4.65 CGT 204.3(A)
Cheap loan arrangements IT 8.3(D); 8.5
Child benefit, high income charge IT 28.1
CIVIL PARTNERS
See also Married Persons and Civil Partners
transfers between CGT 214.1(D); 214.2(A); 217.1; 217.2
Claims
involving more than one year IT 25.2
CLASS 1 CONTRIBUTIONS: EMPLOYED EARNERS NIC 504
annual maximum NIC 503.1
calculation methods NIC 504.2
deferment NIC 510.1
rates NIC 504.1
CLASS 1A CONTRIBUTIONS: BENEFITS IN KIND NIC 505
cars for private use NIC 505.2
person liable NIC 505.1
—person succeeding to business NIC 505.1(C)
—third party benefits NIC 505.1(A)
—two or more employers NIC 505.1(B)
CLASS 1B CONTRIBUTIONS: PAYE SETTLEMENT AGREEMENTS NIC 506
calculation of contributions NIC 506.1
CLASS 4 CONTRIBUTIONS: PROFITS OF A TRADE ETC. NIC 507
aggregation of earnings NIC 502.8
annual maximum NIC 503.1
deferment NIC 510.2
earnings NIC 511.2
exception of Class 1 contributors for trading income NIC 507.1
loss relief NIC 511.2
partners NIC 514.1
CLOSE COMPANIES CT 104; IHT 307
alteration of share capital to transfer value IHT 307.3
benefits in kind for participators CT 104.3
charge on participators IHT 307.2
definition CT 104.1
loans to participators CT 104.2
transfer of asset at undervalue CT 103.2
value transferred IHT 307.1
COMPANIES (Capital gains of) CGT 207
See also Capital Gains
capital losses CT 103.1; CGT 207.1
exchange of securities CGT 229.4
reconstruction schemes CGT 229.5

Index

COMPANIES (Capital gains of) – *cont.*
  transfer of assets to non-resident company CGT 220.3
Companies (migration of) CGT 220.1
COMPANY DIRECTORS NIC 508
  calculation of contributions NIC 508.2
  changes during earnings period NIC 508.3
  —employment becoming contracted out NIC 508.3(B)
  —employment becoming not contracted out NIC 508.3(A)
  earnings NIC 508.1
  —fees credited to overdrawn account NIC 508.1(C)
  —fees voted in advance NIC 508.1(B)
Compensation
  CGT on receipt of CGT 206.3; 215.2
Compulsory acquisition of land CGT 215.2
COMPUTATION OF GAINS AND LOSSES CGT 208
  allowable expenditure CGT 208.1
  —effect of capital allowances CGT 208.1(B)
  —enhancement expenditure CGT 208.1(C)
  compulsory acquisition of land CGT 215.2
  connected persons CGT 202.3
  part disposal CGT 206.1(A); 208.2; 206.3(A); 215.2; 217.2
  —assets held on 6.4.65 CGT 204.3(E)
  —small part disposals of land CGT 215.1
  premiums payable under leases IT 21.4; CGT 215.3
  sets, assets forming CGT 202.3
  value passing out of shares CGT 202.1; 202.2
Conditional exemption from IHT
  See National Heritage
Consortium relief CT 106.6
CONTRACTED-OUT EMPLOYMENT NIC 509
  reduction in contributions NIC 509.1
Convertible shares IT 27.3
Corporate bonds, qualifying CGT 224; 229.6
Creative artists, averaging of profits IT 29.5
Crematoria, allowances for IT 29.10
Cumulation principle (IHT) IHT 305.1; 305.2
Current year basis of assessment
  capital allowances IT 4.1
  losses IT 14.1; 14.3(B)
  partnerships IT 17.1
  trading income IT 29.1; 29.2(B)

Debenture interest CT 116.1
DECEASED ESTATES IT 6
  absolute interest IT 6.1
  limited interest IT 6.2
DEEDS OF VARIATION AND DISCLAIMERS IHT 308
Deeply discounted securities IT 23.1
Deferment of chargeable gain
  See Hold-over reliefs and Rollover relief
DEFERMENT OF PAYMENT NIC 510
  Class 1 deferment NIC 510.1
  —contracted-out employments NIC 510.1(A)
  —not contracted-out employments NIC 510.1(A)
  —post-deferment assessment NIC 510.1(B)
  Class 2 NIC 510.2
  Class 4 NIC 510.2
Deferred consideration CGT 206.1(B); 215.4; 229.4(C)
Depreciatory transactions CGT 202.4
Directors' remuneration (unpaid) CT 116.1
Disabled persons, trusts for IHT 324
Disincorporation relief CGT 213.4
Discretionary trusts IT 26.2; 26.3(B)
  See also Settlements without interests in possession
Dividend income
  See also Franked Investment Income
  accumulation trusts, received by IT 26.2
  deceased estates, received by IT 6.1; 6.2
  discretionary trusts, received by IT 26.2
  individuals, received by IT 1.1(A)–(E)
  losses set against IT 1.1(B)
  overseas companies, from IT 7.1; CT 105
  restriction on set-off of tax credits IT 1.1(D)
  trusts, received by IT 26.1; 26.3(A)
Domicile
  See Residence and Domicile
Double charges relief IHT 311.1(B); 315; 322.1
DOUBLE TAX RELIEF IT 7; CT 105; CGT 209; IHT 309
  exemption for profits of foreign permanent establishments CT 105.2
  limits on IT 1.3(B); 7.1(B)
  measure of relief IT 7.1; CT 105.1; CGT 209.1
  unilateral relief IT 7.1; CT 105.1; IHT 309.1
Dredging, allowance for IT 3.2
Dwelling house, gains on CGT 223

D

Death, capital losses on CGT 216.1(C)

E

Earn-outs CGT 216.4; 229.4(C)

Index

EARNINGS FROM SELF-EMPLOYMENT NIC 511
  earnings for Class 2 purposes NIC 511.1
  earnings for Class 4 purposes NIC 511.2
  —loss relief NIC 511.2
EARNINGS PERIODS NIC 512
  change of regular pay interval NIC 512.2
  —longer interval NIC 512.2(A)
  —shorter interval NIC 512.2(B)
  directors NIC 512.4
  holiday pay NIC 512.3
  pay patterns NIC 512.1
  —irregular payments NIC 512.1(C)
  —multiple regular NIC 512.1(A)(B)
  —HMRC direction NIC 512.1(B)
Emoluments
  See Employment Income
Employee share schemes IT 27
Employees, trusts for IHT 325
EMPLOYMENT INCOME IT 8
  benefits IT 8.3–8.6
  —assets given and leased IT 8.3(C)
  —cars IT 8.3(A)
  —employees earning £8,500 per annum or more and directors IT 8.3
  —living accommodation IT 8.4
  —loans IT 8.3(D); 8.5
  —medical insurance IT 8.6
  —overnight incidental expenses IT 8.6
  —relocation expenses IT 8.5
  —removal expenses IT 8.5
  —travelling expenses IT 8.2(B)
  —vans IT 8.3(B)
  —vouchers IT 8.6
  cars IT 8.2; 8.3(A)
  mileage allowances IT 8.2(A)
  personal service companies etc. IT 19
  work done abroad
  —travelling expenses IT 8.1
ENTERPRISE INVESTMENT SCHEME IT 9; CGT 210
  capital gains and losses IT 9.2
  —disposal more than three years after acquisition CGT 210.1; 210.2
  carry-back of relief IT 9.1(B)
  conditions for relief IT 9.1
  deferral relief CGT 210.3
  form of relief IT 9.1
  restrictions on relief IT 9.1
  withdrawal of relief IT 9.2
Enterprise management incentives IT 27.5
Enterprise zone buildings IT 3.3

Entertainers and sportsmen, non-resident IT 16.2
ENTREPRENEURS' RELIEF CGT 211
  associated disposals CGT 211.3
  computation CGT 211.1
  deferred gains CGT 211.5
  lifetime limit CGT 211.1(B)–(D)
  partnerships CGT 211.2
  reorganisations CGT 211.4
  transitional provisions CGT 211.5
Errors on invoices VAT 409.1
Estate income IT 6
Exempt supplies (VAT)
  See Partial exemption
EXEMPT TRANSFERS IHT 310
  annual exemption IHT 310.1; 320.1
  election to be treated as UK domiciled IHT 310.4
  —termination of an interest in possession IHT 320.1
  gifts in consideration of marriage IHT 320.1; 324.2
  Nil-rate band, transfer of unused amount IHT 308.1; 310.3
  normal expenditure out of income IHT 310.2
Exemption for profits of foreign permanent establishments CT 105.2
EXEMPTIONS AND RELIEFS CGT 212
  chattels CGT 212.1
  dwelling house CGT 223
  qualifying corporate bonds CGT 224
  tangible movable asset CGT 212.1

F

Farming and market gardening
  averaging profits IT 29.6
  herd basis IT 10
  transfer of agricultural property IHT 302
Finance leases IT 29.7
First-year allowances
  reduced claim for CT 102.2
Flat conversion allowances IT 14.6
Foreign income
  See Double Tax Relief
Foreign permanent establishments, exemption for profits of CT 105.2
Foster care IT 29.9
Franked investment income
  small profits rate, effect on CT 119.1(A)(C); 119.2(A)

Index

Furnished holiday accommodation IT 21.2

G

Gifts CGT 213
  assets held on 31 March 1982 CGT 206.2
  business assets CGT 213.2
  charities IT 5.1; CT 116.1
  deduction from trading income CT 116.1
  deferment of gain CGT 213.1; 213.2; 226.3
  exempt transfers IHT 310; 320.1
  land CGT 222.1(B)
  marriage, in consideration of IHT 320.1; 324.2
  shares CGT 222.1(B)
GIFTS WITH RESERVATION IHT 311
  reservation not released before death IHT 311.1(B)
  reservation released before death IHT 311.1(A)
Grossing up (IHT) IHT 305.2
GROUP RELIEF CT 106
  calculation CT 106.1
  companies joining or leaving group CT 106.4
  consortium relief CT 106.6
  overlapping periods CT 106.3
  relationship to other reliefs CT 106.5
Groups of companies
  consortium relief CT 106.6
  degrouping charge CT 103.3(E)(F)
  depreciatory transactions CGT 202.4
  distribution followed by disposal of shares CGT 202.3
  group relief CT 106
  —companies joining or leaving group CT 106.4
  —overlapping periods CT 106.3
  —relationship to other reliefs CT 106.5
  intra-group transfers of assets CT 103.3(A)(B)(C); CGT 214.2(C)(D)
  pre-entry losses CT 103.3(F)
  rollover relief on replacement of business assets CT 103.3(D)
  surrender of tax refunds CT 110.1(D)

H

HERD BASIS IT 10
Heritage property IHT 316
High income child benefit charge IT 28.1
HOLD-OVER RELIEFS CGT 213
  See also Rollover Relief
  assets held on 31 March 1982 CGT 205.2
  chargeable lifetime transfers CGT 213.1(A)

HOLD-OVER RELIEFS – *cont.*
  disincorporation relief CGT 213.4
  disposal consideration CGT 213.1(B)
  gifts
  —business assets CGT 213.2
  —chargeable lifetime transfers CGT 213.1
  IHT relief CGT 213.1(C)
  private residences and CGT 222.4
  transfer of business to company CGT 213.3
  —election to disapply relief CGT 213.3(B)
  —incorporation relief CGT 213.3(A)
HOTELS AND HOLIDAY ACCOMMODATION VAT 404
  furnished holiday accommodation IT 21.2
  stays over four weeks VAT 404.1
Husband and wife
  See Married Persons

I

Immediate post-death interests IHT 320.3
INCOME TAX IN RELATION TO A COMPANY CT 107
  accounting for income tax on receipts and payments CT 107.1
Incorporation relief CGT 213.3; 213.3(A)
  election to disapply CGT 213.3(B)
INDEXATION CGT 214
  allowance on receipt of compensation CGT 206.3(E)
  assets held on 31.3.82 CGT 214.1(B)
  general rules CGT 214.1
  indexation factor, calculation of
  —companies CGT 214.1(A)
  no gain/no loss disposals CGT 214.2(A)–(C)
  —intra-group transfers CT 103.3(B); CGT 214.2(C)(D)
  —transfers between spouses or civil partners CGT 214.2(A)(B)
  restriction CGT 214.1(C)
  shares and securities, identification rules CGT 230.2
INPUT TAX VAT 405
  non-business activities VAT 405.2
  repayment where consideration not paid VAT 405.1
Installation of heating equipment VAT 410.1
Instalments, payment by IHT 317.1
  interest
  —on overpaid tax CT 109.1(C)
  —on unpaid tax CT 110.2(B)
  large companies CT 115.1
INTANGIBLE ASSETS CT 108

Index

INTANGIBLE ASSETS – *cont.*
  debits and credits CT 108.1
  non-trading losses CT 108.2
  rollover relief CT 108.3
INTELLECTUAL PROPERTY IT 11
  patent royalties IT 11.1
Inter-spouse transfers CGT 214.1(C); 214.2(A); 217.1; 217.2
Interest in possession
  immediate post-death IHT 320.3
  settlements with IHT 320
  settlements without IHT 321
  termination of CGT 228.4; 228.5; IHT 320.1
  transitional serial IHT 320.2
INTEREST ON OVERPAID TAX CT 109; 110.1
INTEREST ON TAX (IHT) IHT 312
  payment by instalments IHT 317.1(B)
INTEREST ON UNPAID TAX IT 12; CT 110; IHT 312; 317.1(B)
Interest received IT 2.1
INTERMEDIARIES NIC 513
  calculation of deemed payment NIC 513.1
INVESTMENT COMPANIES AND INVESTMENT BUSINESS CT 111
  management expenses CT 111.1
Invoices, errors on VAT 409.1

L

LAND CGT 215
  compulsory purchase CGT 215.2
  development value, reflecting CGT 204.2
  gifts of CGT 222.1(B)
  held on 6.4.65 CGT 204.2; 204.3(B)
  leases CGT 215.3
  —assignment of short lease CGT 215.3(D)–(G)
  —grant of long lease CGT 215.3(B)
  —grant of short lease CGT 215.3(C)
  —premiums on short leases IT 21.4; CT 116.1; CGT 215.3(C)(G)(H)(J)
  —short leases which are not wasting assets CGT 215.3(A)
  —sub-lease granted out of short lease CGT 215.3(H)(J)
  small part disposals CGT 215.1
  valuation IHT 326.1
LATE PAYMENT INTEREST AND PENALTIES IT 12
Leases
  See Land *and* Finance leases
Letting of property IT 21
LIABILITY FOR TAX IHT 313

LIABILITY FOR TAX – *cont.*
  lifetime transfers IHT 313.1
  —with additional liability on death IHT 313.3
  potentially exempt transfers becoming chargeable IHT 313.4
  transfers on death IHT 313.2
LIFE ASSURANCE POLICIES IT 13; IHT 314
  adjustments for non-UK residence IT 13.3
  gains and non-qualifying policies IT 13.1
  partial surrender of IT 13.2
  relief IT 13.4
  top-slicing relief IT 13.1
  transfer of IHT 314
Lifetime allowance IT 18.2
Lifetime transfers IHT 305.1; 305.2
  liability for tax IHT 313.1
Limited liability partnerships IT 17.4
Limited partner's losses IT 17.3
LIQUIDATION CT 112
  accounting periods CT 112.1
LOAN RELATIONSHIPS CT 113
  non-trading CT 113.2
  non-trading deposits CT 113.3
  trading CT 113.1
Loans, from donee to donor IHT 322.1
Loans to employees IT 8.4(D)(E); 8.6
Loans to participators CT 104.2
Loans to settlor of settlement IT 26.5
LOSSES IT 14; CT 114; CGT 216
  accounting periods of different length CT 114.3(B)
  asset of negligible value CGT 216.1(B)
  capital gains, individual's trading losses set-off against IT 14.2
  capital losses CT 103.1; CGT 207.1
  —election to treat as arising in earlier year CGT 216.4
  —indexation losses CGT 214.1(D)
  —pre-entry losses CT 103.3(F)
  —set-off against settlement gains CGT 216.2
  —tangible movable assets CGT 212.1(B)
  carry-back of CT 114.3
  —death, from year of CGT 216.1(C)
  —early losses IT 14.3(A)
  —terminal losses IT 14.4; CT 114.3(A)
  carry-forward of IT 13.4(B); CT 103.2; 114.2
  cessation of trade IT 14.4; CT 114.3(A)
  chattels CGT 212.1(B)
  consortium relief CT 106.6
  death, year of CGT 216.1(C)
  early losses in new business IT 14.3
  groups of companies CT 102.2; 106
  intangible assets CT 108.2
  interest on overpaid tax CT 109.1(A); 109.2
  partnership IT 17.2; 17.3; 17.4

Index

LOSSES – cont.
property business IT 14.6; CT 114.6
reconstruction
—restriction of trading losses CT 114.5
rights to unascertainable consideration CGT 216.4
set-off of trading losses
—against capital gains (individuals) IT 14.2
—against other income or profits IT 1.1(B); 14.1; 14.3(A); CT 114.1
terminal IT 14.4; CT 114.3(A)
unlisted companies CGT 216.3
unquoted shares, capital losses available for set-off against income IT 14.5; CT 114.4; CGT 216.3

M

Maintenance funds for historic buildings IHT 316.6
Maintenance payments IT 15.2
Management expenses CT 106.2; 111.1
Marginal relief (small profits) CT 119.1; 119.2
Married couple's allowance
transfer of IT 1.3(C)(D); 15.1(A)
transfer of surplus IT 15.1(B)
MARRIED PERSONS AND CIVIL PARTNERS IT 15; CGT 217
age-related allowances IT 1.3(C); 15.1(A)
end of marriage IT 15.2
jointly owned assets CGT 217.2
maintenance payments IT 15.2
married couple's allowance
—transfer of IT 1.3(C)(D); 15.1(A)
—transfer of surplus IT 15.1(B)
no gain/no loss transfers CGT 214.2(A)(B); 217.1; 217.2
transfer of personal reliefs IT 15.1
Medical insurance (benefits) IT 8.6
Migration of companies CGT 220.1
Mileage allowances IT 8.2(A)
Mineral extraction IT 3.4
MINERAL ROYALTIES CGT 218
Mines, allowances for IT 3.4
Mixed supplies VAT 407.1
MOTOR CARS VAT 406
See also Cars
scale charge for private fuel VAT 406.1
Mutual supplies, bad debt relief where VAT 401.1
MUTUAL TRANSFERS IHT 315
Chargeable transfers and death IHT 315.2

MUTUAL TRANSFERS – cont.
Potentially exempt transfers and death IHT 315.1

N

NATIONAL HERITAGE IHT 316
charge to tax IHT 316.4
conditionally exempt occasions IHT 316.5
conditionally exempt transfers IHT 316.2; 316.3; 316.4
—after 6.4.76 IHT 316.2(A)(B)
—multiple IHT 316.2(C)
—on death before 7.4.76 IHT 316.3
—tax credit on subsequent transfer IHT 316.4
conditions for exemption IHT 316.1
estate duty IHT 316.3(B)
maintenance funds for historic buildings IHT 316.6
settlements IHT 316.5
—conditionally exempt occasions IHT 316.5(A)
—ten-year anniversary charge exemption IHT 316.5(B)
Negligible value, asset of CGT 216.1(B)
Non-business activities VAT 405.2
Non-resident, company becoming CGT 220.1
Non-resident company, transfer of assets to CGT 220.3
Non-resident entertainers and sportsmen IT 16.2
NON-RESIDENTS IT 16
life assurance plicies IT 13.3
limit on liability to income tax IT 16.1
non-resident entertainers and sportsmen IT 16.2
Non-residents trading through UK permanent establishment CGT 220.2

O

OFFSHORE SETTLEMENTS CGT 219
gains attributed to UK beneficiary CGT 219.1
Options CGT 203.1; 231.2
See also Share Incentives and Options
OUTPUT TAX VAT 407
mixed supplies VAT 407.1
Overdue tax
See Interest on Tax *and* Interest on Unpaid Tax
Overnight incidental expenses IT 8.6
OVERSEAS MATTERS CGT 220
See also Double Tax Relief, Offshore Settlements and Residence and Domicile
company migration CGT 220.1

Index

OVERSEAS MATTERS – *cont.*
  earnings abroad
  —travelling expenses IT 8.1
  individual temporarily non-resident CGT 220.4
  non-resident entertainers and sportsmen IT 16.2
  non-residents trading through UK branch or agency CGT 220.2
  overseas resident settlements CGT 219
  transfer of assets to non-resident company CGT 220.3
  UK beneficiary of an overseas resident settlement CGT 219.1

P

Part disposals
  See Disposal
Part exchange
  second-hand goods VAT 412.1
Part payments, bad debt relief where VAT 401.1
PARTIAL EXEMPTION VAT 408
  capital goods scheme VAT 402.1
  self supply
  —stationery VAT 412.1
  special method VAT 408.2
  standard method VAT 408.1
Participators
  See Close Companies
Partly exempt transfers IHT 305.3
PARTNERS NIC 514
  Class 4 contributions NIC 514.1
PARTNERSHIPS IT 17; CGT 221
  accounting adjustments CGT 221.3
  allocation of profits/losses IT 17.2
  assessments IT 17.1
  assets CGT 221.1
  —distribution in kind CGT 221.6
  capital allowances on successions IT 4.2
  changes in partners IT 17.1; CGT 221.2–221.4
  changes in sharing ratios IT 17.1; CGT 221.2–221.5
  consideration outside accounts CGT 221.4
  current year basis IT 17.1
  disposal of partnership asset to partner CGT 221.6
  indexation CGT 214.2(A)(C); 221.2
  investment income IT 17.1(B)
  losses IT 17.2; 17.3
  —limited liability partnerships IT 17.4
  —limited partner IT 17.3
  revaluation of assets CGT 221.3; 221.5
  savings income IT 18.1(B)

PARTNERSHIPS – *cont.*
  shares acquired in stages CGT 221.5
Patents IT 11
  allowances for IT 3.5
  royalties, spreading of IT 11.1
PAYMENT OF TAX (CGT) CGT 222
  consideration payable by instalments CGT 222.1(A)
  gifts of land or shares CGT 222.1(B)
PAYMENT OF TAX (CT) CT 115
  instalment payments CT 109.1(B); 110.1(C); 115.1(B)
  interest on overpaid CT CT 109.1(A)(B)
  large companies CT 115.1(A)
PAYMENT OF TAX (IHT) IHT 317
  by instalments IHT 317.1
  —with interest IHT 317.1(B)
PENSION PROVISION IT 18
  annual allowance IT 18.3
  contributions by individuals, relief for IT 18.1
  lifetime allowance IT 18.2
Pension schemes
  See Pension Provision
Pensionable age NIC 501.1
Periods of account
  See also Accounting periods
  capital allowances IT 4.1
  exceeding twelve months (CT) CT 101.2
Permanent establishment CGT 220.2
  foreign, exemption for profits of CT 105.2
Personal reliefs
  See Allowances and Tax Rates
PERSONAL SERVICE COMPANIES ETC. IT 19
  calculation of deemed employment payment IT 19.1
Persons liable to IHT
  See Liability for Tax
Petrol, private
  assessable benefit IT 8.3(A)
  VAT scale charge VAT 407.1
Plant and machinery, allowances for IT 4; CT 102.1; 102.2
POST-CESSATION EXPENDITURE IT 20; 20.2
POST-CESSATION RECEIPTS IT 20; 20.1
Potentially exempt transfers IHT 305.1
  annual exemption, allocation of IHT 310.1(B)
  followed by loan from donee to donor IHT 322.1
  liability for tax on death IHT 313.4
Pre-entry losses CT 103.3(F)
Premiums on short leases IT 21.4; CT 116.1; CGT 215.3(C)(G)(H)

Index

Private medical insurance
  benefit IT 8.6
PRIVATE RESIDENCES CGT 223
  capital gains tax exemption CGT 223
  —hold-over relief obtained on earlier disposal CGT 223.3
PROFIT COMPUTATIONS CT 116
  allowable deductions CT 116.1
  assessable profits CT 116.1
PROPERTY INCOME IT 21
  expenses deductible IT 21.1
  furnished holiday accommodation IT 21.2
  general IT 21.1
  lodgers IT 21.3
  losses IT 14.6; CT 114.6
  premiums on leases IT 21.4
  rent-a-room relief IT 21.3
PROTECTIVE TRUSTS IHT 318
  forfeiture IHT 318.1; 318.2
  —after 11.4.78 IHT 318.2
  —before 12.4.78 IHT 318.1

Q

QUALIFYING CORPORATE BONDS CGT 224
  conversion of securities CGT 229.6
  definition CGT 224.1
  reorganisation of share capital CGT 224.2
QUICK SUCCESSION RELIEF IHT 319
  mutual transfers IHT 315.1

R

RECORDS VAT 409
  errors on invoices VAT 409.1
REDUCED RATE SUPPLIES VAT 410
  installation of energy-saving materials VAT 410.1
Reinvestment relief, SEIS CGT 227.3
Related property, valuation of IHT 303.1(B); 327.2
Relocation expenses IT 8.5
REMITTANCE BASIS IT 22; CGT 225
  effect of election CGT 225.1
  mixed funds, remittances from IT 22.1
Removal expenses IT 8.5
Rent-a-room relief IT 21.3
REPAYMENT AND REALLOCATION NIC 515
  excess contributions NIC 515.1

Repayments of tax, interest on CT 109; 109.1(A)(B)
RESEARCH AND DEVELOPMENT CT 117
  above the line expenditure credits CT 117.2
  allowances for IT 3.6
  tax credits CT 117.1
Reservation, gifts with IHT 311
  reservation not released before death IHT 311.1(B)
  reservation released before death IHT 311.1(A)
Residence
  See Private Residences
Residence and domicile
  election to be treated as UK domiciledt IHT 310.4
  individual temporarily non-resident CGT 220.4
  life assurance policies and IT 13.3
  non-resident company, transfer of assets to CGT 220.2
  non-resident entertainers and sportsmen IT 16.1
  offshore settlements CGT 219.1
Restricted shares IT 27.2
RETAIL SCHEMES VAT 411
RETURNS (CT) CT 118
  filing dates CT 118.2
  return periods CT 118.1
ROLLOVER RELIEF CGT 226
  compulsory acquisition of and CGT 215.2
  gifts CGT 205.3; 213.1; 213.2; 228.3
  receipt of compensation not treated as disposal CGT 206.3(B)–(D); 215.2
  replacement of business assets CGT 226
  —groups of companies CT 103.3(D)
  —nature of relief CGT 226.1
  —partial relief CGT 226.2
  —taper relief CGT 226.1(C)
  —wasting assets CGT 226.3
  transfer of business to a company CGT 213.3
Royalties and licences
  mineral royalties CGT 218
  patent rights IT 3.6; 16

S

Salaries
  See also Employment Income
  deductible against profits IT 30.4; CT 116.1
SAVINGS AND INVESTMENT INCOME IT 23
  deeply discounted securities IT 23.1
  partnerships IT 17.1(B)
SECOND-HAND GOODS VAT 412
  auctioneer's scheme VAT 412.3

Index

SECOND-HAND GOODS – *cont.*
  bad debt relief on VAT 401.2
  global accounting scheme VAT 412.2
  part exchange VAT 412.1
Securities
  See Shares and Securities
SEED ENTERPRISE INVESTMENT SCHEME IT 24; CGT 227
  capital gains and losses IT 24.2(B); CGT 227.1; 227.2
  income tax investment relief IT 24.1
  reinvestment relief CGT 227.3
  withdrawal of income tax relief IT 24.2(A)
SELF-ASSESSMENT IT 25
  calculation of Interim Payments IT 25.1
  claims involving more than one year IT 25.2
  interest arising on insufficient interim payment IT 12.1(B)
  interest on unpaid tax IT 12.1; CT 110.1
SETTLEMENTS IT 26; CGT 228
  accumulation and maintenance trusts IT 26.2; 26.3(B); IHT 301
  annual exemptions CGT 228.1
  beneficiaries, income of IT 26.3
  creation of CGT 228.3
  death of life tenant CGT 228.5; 231.3
  disabled persons, trusts for IHT 324
  discretionary trusts IT 26.2; 26.3(B)
  —basic rate band IT 26.2(A)
  dividends received by IT 26.1; 26.2; 26.3(A)
  employees, trusts for IHT 325
  interest in possession CGT 228.5
  loan to settlor IT 26.5
  National Heritage IHT 316.5; 316.6
  offshore CGT 219.1
  parent's settlement in favour of child IT 26.4
  person becoming absolutely entitled to settled property CGT 228.4
  proportionate charge IHT 321.2; 321.3
  protective trusts IHT 318
  rates of tax (CGT) CGT 228.1
  tax payable by trustees IT 26.1
  temporary charitable trusts IHT 306.1
  ten-year anniversary charge IHT 321.1
  termination of an interest in possession CGT 228.4; 228.5; 231.3; IHT 320.1
  vulnerable beneficiary, with CGT 225.3
Settlements—Accumulation and Maintenance IHT 301
  assessments on trust income IT 26.2
  beneficiaries, income of IT 26.2(B)
SETTLEMENTS WITH INTERESTS IN POSSESSION CGT 228.5; IHT 320
  assessments on trust income IT 26.1
  beneficiaries, income of IT 26.3(A)

SETTLEMENTS WITH INTERESTS IN POSSESSION – *cont.*
  immediate post-death interests IHT 320.3
  termination of an interest in possession CGT 228.4; 229.6; IHT 320.1
  —losses (CGT) CGT 228.5(C)
  transitional serial interests IHT 320.2
SETTLEMENTS WITHOUT INTERESTS IN POSSESSION IHT 321
  post 26.3.74 settlements IHT 321.1(A); 321.2(A)(B)
  pre 27.3.74 settlements IHT 321.1(B)
  proportionate charge
  —before the first ten-year anniversary IHT 321.2
  —between ten-year anniversaries IHT 321.3
  ten-year anniversary charge IHT 321.1
SHARES AND SECURITIES CGT 229
  agricultural property relief IHT 302.2
  bonus issues CGT 229.2
  business property relief IHT 304.1(A)
  capital distributions CGT 229.8
  conversion of securities CGT 229.6
  corporate bonds, qualifying CGT 224
  deeply discounted securities IT 21.1
  deferred consideration CGT 206.2; 216.4; 229.4(C)
  earn-outs CGT 216.4; 229.4(C)
  exchange of securities CGT 229.4
  gifts CGT 222.1(B)
  holdings at 6.4.65
  —quoted CGT 206.1
  —unquoted CGT 206.3(C)(D)
  options and incentives IT 27
  qualifying corporate bonds CGT 224
  reconstruction schemes CGT 229.5
  reorganisation of share capital CGT 224.2; 229.1
  rights issues CGT 229.1; 229.3
  —sale of rights CGT 229.8(B)
  scrip dividends CGT 229.7
  sold within 12 months after death IHT 326.3
  time apportionment
  —unquoted shares CGT 204.3(D)
  transfer of business to a company for shares CGT 212.3
  unquoted shares
  —losses relieved against income IT 14.5; CT 114.4; CGT 216.3
  —time apportionment CGT 204.3(D)
  valuation IHT 326.3
  value passing out of CGT 202.1; 202.2
SHARES AND SECURITIES—IDENTIFICATION RULES CGT 230
  after 5 April 2008 CGT 230.1

Index

SHARES AND SECURITIES— IDENTIFICATION RULES – *cont.*
companies CGT 230.2
qualifying corporate bonds CGT 224.1
SHARE-RELATED EMPLOYMENT INCOME AND EXEMPTIONS IT 27
convertible shares IT 27.3
employee share ownership plans IT 27.4
enterprise management incentives IT 27.5
restricted shares IT 27.3
share incentive plans IT 27.5
share options
—charge to tax IT 27.1
Short-life assets IT 4.4
SMALL PROFITS — REDUCED RATES CT 119
company with an associated company CT 119.2
marginal relief CT 119.1; 119.2
SOCIAL SECURITY INCOME IT 28
high income child benefit charge IT 28.1
Special schemes for retailers
See Retail Schemes
Sportsmen and entertainers, non-resident IT 16.2
Substantial shareholdings exemption CT 103.4
Successions to trade
capital allowances IT 4.2

T

Tangible movable property CGT 212.1
Tax credits
research and development CT 117.1
restriction on set-off of dividend IT 1.1(C)
Temporary non-residence CGT 220.4
Thin capitalisation CT 120.1(B)
Timber, growing IHT 327
Time apportionment CGT 204.3
Top-slicing relief IT 13.1
TRADING INCOME IT 29
See also Current year basis of assessment
barristers, adjustment on change of basis IT 29.8
cash basis for small businesses IT 30.1
cemeteries IT 29.10
change of accounting date IT 29.2
closing year of assessment IT 29.3
creative artists IT 29.5
crematoria IT 29.10
farming and market gardening IT 29.6
finance leases IT 29.7
foster care IT 29.9

TRADING INCOME – *cont.*
opening years of assessment IT 29.1
profit computations IT 29.4
TRADING INCOME — CASH BASIS FOR SMALL BUSINESSES IT 30
cash basis IT 30.1
Transfer of business to a company CGT 213.3
Transfer of unused nil-rate band IHT 308.1; 310.3
TRANSFER PRICING CT 120
thin capitalisation and CT 120.1(B)
TRANSFERS ON DEATH IHT 322
liability for tax IHT 313.2
reduced rate for estates with 10% gifts to charities IHT 322.2
Transitional serial interests IHT 320.2
Trusts
See Settlements
TRUSTS FOR BEREAVED MINORS IHT 323
Transitional provisions IHT 323.1
TRUSTS FOR DISABLED PERSONS IHT 324
property settled
—after 9.3.1981 and before 8.4.2013 IHT 324.2
—after 7.4.2013 IHT 324.3
—before 10.3.1981 IHT 324.1
self-settlement where condition expected to lead to disability IHT 324.4
TRUSTS FOR EMPLOYEES IHT 325

V

VALUATION IHT 326
land sold within four years after death IHT 326.1
related property IHT 303.1(B); 326.2
shares and securities sold within 12 months after death IHT 326.3
stock and work in progress IT 29.7
Value-shifting
anti-avoidance CGT 202.1; 202.2
Vans, assessable benefit IT 7.3(B)
Variation, Deeds of IHT 308
VENTURE CAPITAL TRUSTS IT 31
capital gains tax
—relief on disposal IT 31.3
distribution relief IT 31.2
investment relief IT 31.1
—withdrawal IT 31.1(B)
Vouchers IT 29.6
Vulnerable beneficiary
trusts with CGT 228.2

Index

W

WASTING ASSETS CGT 231
eligible for capital allowances CGT 231.1
leases IT 21.4; CGT 215.3
—assignment of short lease CGT 215.3(D)–(G)
—grant of long lease CGT 215.3(B)
—grant of short lease CGT 215.3(C)
—short leases which are not wasting assets CGT 215.3(A)
—sub-lease granted out of short lease CGT 215.3(H)(J)

WASTING ASSETS – *cont.*
life interests CGT 231.3
options CGT 203.1; 231.2
rollover relief CGT 228.3

WOODLANDS IHT 327
deferred IHT charge IHT 327.1
—credit for, on subsequent transfer IHT 327.1(B)

Writing-down allowances
reduced claim for CT 102.2